Old Houses of the Antient Town of Norwich, 1660-1800

Mary E. Perkins

Alpha Editions

This edition published in 2020

ISBN : 9789354013249

Design and Setting By
Alpha Editions
email - alphaedis@gmail.com

As per information held with us this book is in Public Domain.
This book is a reproduction of an important historical work. Alpha Editions uses the best technology to reproduce historical work in the same manner it was first published to preserve its original nature. Any marks or number seen are left intentionally to preserve its true form.

OLD HOUSES

OF

THE ANTIENT TOWN

OF

NORWICH

1660 – 1800

WITH MAPS, ILLUSTRATIONS,

PORTRAITS and GENEALOGIES

By

MARY E. PERKINS

NORWICH, CONN.
1895

PREFACE.

THIS book is one of a projected series of volumes, which will aim to give an account of the old houses of Norwich, their owners and occupants, from the settlement of the town to the year 1800.

This first volume includes all the buildings on the main roads, from the corner of Mill Lane, or (Lafayette Street), to the Bean Hill road, at the west end of the Meeting-house Green.

In the genealogical part will be found the first three generations of the earliest settlers, but beyond this point, in order not to add to the bulk of the book, the only lines carried out, are of those descendants who resided in the district covered by this volume, and these, only so long as they continued to reside in this locality. An effort has been made to follow back the direct line of each resident to his first American progenitor, but this has not been feasible in every case, owing to the great expense of such a search, in both time and money. In these difficult cases, a possible ancestry is sometimes given, marked by a line across the page, in the hope that some descendant, through family papers or personal search, may furnish the missing links, or prove another line of descent.

The records of the early land grants of Norwich are very imperfect, and various attempts were made from the year 1672 to the beginning of the eighteenth century " to find the names of the first purchasers and what estate each of them put in" to the town. The first book of records give the bounds of estates, but not the measurements, and the second and third registers vary, as other lands have been added to or sold from the original grants. Then some of the proprietors failed to record their home-lots, and the measurements and situation of these can only be ascertained from the deeds of sale, so, in the map of 1705, it was found impossible to accurately define the home-lots, or to give more than their approximate measurements or outlines.

In many cases, houses have probably, for a longer or shorter period, been occupied by other tenants than those mentioned, but unless they were actual purchasers of the property, there is often no trace of this occupancy, as leases were seldom recorded, and even in case of an actual purchase, the grantee does not necessarily become an occupant, so mistakes are easily made. It has been endeavored, when possible, by reference to deeds and other records, to distinguish between owners and occupants, but if any persons, through documents in their possession, can rectify any errors in this respect, or in any dates of births, deaths, or marriages, or in lines of descent, and will address P. O. Box 63, Norwich, Conn., such information will be gratefully received.

In the long period of 140 years (1660-1800), many generations come and go, and new residents are continually appearing, so space will not permit any very extended account of each individual, still the author hopes that the meagre details she has given of these lives of the early inhabitants, may be of some interest to their descendants of the present day.

To mention all the genealogical and historical works consulted, and all the persons who have furnished copies of pictures, dates, and many items of interest, would be impossible, so the author must confine her acknowledgments to those who have made more substantial contributions to the work: as to DONALD G. MITCHELL, who has generously given the colored map, the frontispiece, which will recall to his contemporaries many old landmarks which have long since passed away; to the Hon. JOHN T. WAIT, who has supplied most of the anecdotes and reminiscences of the past which help to enliven these otherwise dry pages; to H. W. KENT of the Slater Museum, who has furnished the map of 1705, and the Church plans of 1756; to FREDERIC P. GULLIVER, who has drawn the map of 1795; to CHARLES E. BRIGGS, who has contributed photographs of the old Indian sites, and the relics of the last "Church on the Hill;" to HENRY MCNELLY and EDWIN S. BARROWS, who have given the author much information about the old localities; to J. MILLAR WILSON, by whose aid the material for the book-cover was procured; to RUTH H. BOND of New London, who supplied the cover design; to the Town Clerk of Norwich, SAMUEL H. FREEMAN, whose courtesy and helpfulness have been unfailing, and under whose careful supervision, the old town books have been copied, fully indexed, and attractively bound, and are now a pleasure to the eye, and accessible for reference; to the Rev. RICHARD H. NELSON, Rev. CHARLES A. NORTHROP, HERBERT L. YERRINGTON and WILLIAM H. ALLEN, for access to the records and pamphlets of Christ Church and the First and Second Churches; to Mrs. DANIEL F. GULLIVER, for the sketches of the lives of her father and grandfather, Henry Strong and the Rev. Joseph Strong; and last but not least to ELLEN D. LARNED, author of the History of Windham County; Mrs. GEORGE B. RIPLEY, MARIA P. GILMAN, Mrs. FREDERIC L. OSGOOD, EMILY N. PERKINS, SARAH H. PERKINS, Mrs. HENRY REYNOLDS, and Mrs. HENRY L. BUTTS of Norwich; Mrs. CLARENCE DEMING and LOUISE TRACY of New Haven; JULIA CHESTER WELLS and ELIZABETH N. PERKINS of New York; JOHN BLISS of Brooklyn, L. I.; Gen. EDWARD HARLAND of Norwich; HENRY R. BOND of New London; WARREN F. KELLOGG of Boston, Mass., publisher of the New England Magazine; WILLIAM READ HOWE of Orange, N. J.; WILLIAM H. SHIELDS of Norwich; Rev. CHRISTOPHER LEFFINGWELL of Bar Harbor, Me.; and JOSEPH H. CARPENTER of Norwich, who by information furnished, and the loan of valuable books, newspapers, manuscripts, letters, &c., have greatly facilitated the author's labors.

M. E. P.

Norwich, Conn., Nov. 26, 1895.

CONTENTS.

Chapter I.

Projected Settlement at Mohegan. — Deed of Land from Uncas, Owaneco and Attawanhood. — Arrival of the Settlers. — Naming of the Town. — List of Settlers. — Indian Attack. — Poem on Norwich by McDonald Clarke. — Description of Norwich by Mrs. Sigourney.

Chapter II.

Home-lots and Fences. — Houses and Furniture. — Modes of Heating. — Vehicles and Roads. — First Turnpike-road and Toll-rates.

Chapter III.

Dress of the Early Settlers. — Law of 1676. — Fashions preceding and during the Revolution. — Fashions of 1793. — Letter of Rachel Huntington. — Fashions of the 19th Century. — Entertainments. — Guy Fawkes' Day. — Barrel-bonfires on Thanksgiving Day.

Chapter IV.

Classes, Trades, and Occupations. — Business Enterprises.

Chapter V.

John Reynolds' Home-lot. — Old Reynolds Homestead. — Journal of Abigail Reynolds. — Visit to Lyme. — Small-pox. — Epidemics of 1702-3-4-5. — Drought of 1792. — Influenza of 1793.

Chapter VI.

Home-lot of Thomas Bliss. — Samuel Bliss, as a Merchant. — Inventory of Elizabeth (Bliss) White. — Geometry Bridge. — Mills of Christopher and Elisha Leffingwell. — Old Stocking Shop. — Louis Barrel and William Cox. — Jackson Browne House.

Chapter VII.

Lt. Thomas Leffingwell's Home-lot. — Samuel Leffingwell, 2nd. — Col. Hezekiah Huntington. — Capt. William Hubbard. — Love Letter of Daniel Hubbard to Martha Coit. — Boston Citizens take refuge in Norwich at the beginning of the Revolution. — Hezekiah Williams. — Joseph Strong. — Meteorological Disturbances of 1806-8.

Chapter VIII.

Lt. Thomas Leffingwell's Home-lot, (continued). — House built by Thomas Leffingwell, 4th. — Peabody Clement. — Capt. Samuel Leffingwell's House. — Judge John Hyde. — Samuel Leffingwell's Stocking Factory. — Rufus Darby. — Capt. Philemon Winship's House.

CONTENTS.

Chapter IX.

Jonathan Pierce's Home-lot. — Col. Hezekiah Huntington. — John Hutchins. — Dr. Jonathan Marsh, 1st. — Dr. Jonathan Marsh, 2nd. — Anecdotes of Dr. Samuel Lee, and Dr. Benjamin Dyer. — Jacob Ladd. — Family of Joseph Marsh.

Chapter X.

Thomas Leffingwell, 2nd's, First Grant. — Joseph Bushnell's Home-lot. — Bushnell House. — James Lincoln's House.

Chapter XI.

Home-lot of Thomas Leffingwell, 2nd, (later Ensign T. L.) — Old Garrison House on Sentry Hill. — Thomas Leffingwell, 3rd. — House of Thomas Leffingwell, 4th, (now known as Edgerton House).

Chapter XII.

Home-lot of William Backus, Sen. — Stephen Backus, 1st. — Stephen Backus, 2nd. — Leffingwell Inn. — Ensign Thomas Leffingwell. — Benajah Leffingwell. — Col. Christopher Leffingwell. — Leffingwell Row. — Stocking Factory, Mills and other Business Enterprises of Col. Leffingwell. — War Correspondence. — Visit of Gen. Washington. — Ruth Leffingwell, (widow).

Chapter XIII.

William Backus' Home-lot (continued). — Footpath. — Opening of Lower Road or Cross Highway. — Leffingwell Shop (later Strong Shop). — Shop in rear of Leffingwell Shop. — David Greenleaf's House. — Jesse Williams. — (Widow) Mary Billings. — Timothy Lester. — House of Capt. William Billings. — John Huntington, Jun. — Joseph Coit. — Charles Lathrop. — Goodell Family. — Miss Sally Goodell's School. — Cary Throop's shop. — First Fire Engine House. — Judah Paddock Spooner. — Thomas Hubbard and Ebenezer Bushnell. — William Leffingwell. — Visit of Dr. Mason Cogswell. — John Huntington, Jun. — Epaphras Porter. — House owned by Thomas Williams. — Rufus Sturtevant. — Ira Tossett. — Col. Leffingwell's Stoneware Kiln (later Charles Lathrop's). — Christopher Potts & Son. — Cary Throop's Shop.

Chapter XIV.

Home-lot of Ebenezer Carew. — Old Carew Homestead and Shop. — Carew Lineage and Family. — Changes in the Lower Road.

Chapter XV.

Rev. James Fitch's Home-lot. — Zebadiah Lathrop House. — Asa Lathrop. — Jabez Avery House. — Rev. John Sterry. — Luther Case. — Capt. Joseph Winship's House. — Thomas Tilden. — Hon. John T. Wait. — Rockwell Manning House. — William Baldwin. — Samuel Manning House. — Diah Manning. — Revolutionary Services of Diah and Roger Manning. — Asa Manning's Service in the War of 1812. — Jean Pierre Boyer, afterward President of the Republic of Hayti. — William Clegg.

Chapter XVI.

Rev. James Fitch's Home-lot (continued). — Fitch Homestead. — Life and Family of Rev. James Fitch. — Inscription on the Rev. James Fitch's Grave-stone. — Love Letter of Rev. Edward Taylor to Elizabeth Fitch. — Theological Students. — John Waterman. — Eleazer Lord's Tavern. — Winthrop Saltonstall and Judge Marvin Wait. — Asa Lathrop. — William Lathrop. — Bridge Across the Yantic.

Chapter XVII.

Common Lands on Town Street. — Early Home-lots. — Highway Survey of 1705. — Old Highway Over Sentry Hill. — Common Lands laid out in 1737-8.

Chapter XVIII.

Shop of Tracy & Coit. — Charles P. Huntington. — Epaphras Porter. — Jesse Huntington. — Law Office of Henry Strong.

Chapter XIX.

Shop of Huntington & Carew. — David Nevins' Shop. — James Lincoln. — William Cox. — House of Thomas Harland. — Watch and Clock Trade. — Fire Engine.

Chapter XX.

Thomas Williams' House and Shop. — William Beard. — Naming of the Town Streets. — Cary Throop.

Chapter XXI.

Brick School House. — Mrs. Sigourney's Early School Experiences. — Consider Sterry. — Hon. John T. Wait's Early Teachers, Dyar Harris and Samuel Griswold. — Asher Smith. — George Bliss.

Chapter XXII.

Col. Simon Lathrop's Shop. — Rufus Lathrop's Shop. — Old Primus and Flora. — Fire Engine House. — Oldest Fire Engine of Norwich. — Subscription List of 1769. — Bills for Work on Engine.

Chapter XXIII.

Slavery in Early Times. — Slave Advertisements and Bills of Sale. — Runaway Slaves. — Aaron Cleveland's Articles Against Slavery. — Grave-stones of Bristo Zibbero and Boston Trow-Trow. — Laws Against Slavery. — Anti-Slavery Society. — Records of Slave Births. — Abolition of Slavery.

Chapter XXIV.

John Olmstead's Home-lot. — John and Elizabeth Olmstead. — Samuel Lathrop, 2nd. — Division of Lathrop Property. — Col. Simon Lathrop's House. — Mason Controversy. — Campaign Song. — Obituary Notice of Col. Lathrop. — Rufus Lathrop. — Jonathan Bellamy. — Aaron Burr. — Lucretia and Rufus Huntington.

Chapter XXV.

John Olmstead's Home-lot (continued). — Thomas Lathrop. — Dr. Daniel Lathrop. — Madam Jerusha Lathrop. — Mrs. Sigourney's Reminiscences of the Lathrop House and Family. — Daniel Lathrop. — Stephen Fitch. — Mrs. Elizabeth (Coit) Gilman.

Chapter XXVI.

Simeon's Case's House. — Dr. Joshua Lathrop. — Mrs. Sigourney's Recollections of Dr. Lathrop and His Wife. — Gardner Thurston.

CONTENTS.

Chapter XXVII.

Lathrop Drug Shop. — Drs. Daniel and Joshua Lathrop. — Benedict Arnold. — Solomon Smith. — Dr. Joseph Coit. — Coit & Lathrop. — Daniel Lathrop Coit. — Ebenezer Carew.

Chapter XXVIII.

Thomas Lathrop's House. — Thomas Lathrop's Family. — Letter of Rev. David Austin. — Mrs. Thomas Lathrop.

Chapter XXIX.

Josiah Read's Home-lot. — Josiah Read. — Capt. Richard Bushnell. — Great Snow-storm of 1717-18. — Capt. Benajah Bushnell. — Gift of Christ Church Lot to the Episcopal Society. — Church Lot given by Phinehas Holden. — Capt. Joseph Coit. — Early Voyages. — Daniel Lathrop Coit. — Thomas Coit. — Dr. Joseph Coit. — Journey to Europe of Daniel Lathrop Coit. — Daniel Wadsworth Coit. — Old Elm Trees.

Chapter XXX.

Noah Mandell's Shop. — Jabez Perkins. — Old Elm Trees of Norwich. — Nathan Cobb. — Nathaniel Parish House. — Ebenezer Case. — Calvin Case. — Adgate Shop. — Samuel Case. — James Norman's Home-lot. — Ebenezer Case House. — Asahel Case. — Joshua Prior House. — Gideon Birchard. — Jeremiah Griffing. — Joshua Norman. — Elisha Birchard. — Mrs. Mary Lathrop. — Hannah Dawson. — Joseph Smith. — Abial Marshall Lot. — Aaron Chapman's House. — Matthew Adgate, 2nd. — John Huntington's House and Shop.

Chapter XXXI.

Home-lot of Dea. Thomas Adgate. — Dea. Thomas Adgate, 2nd. — Adgate Shop. — Matthew Adgate. — William Adgate's House. — Lathrop Cotton Factory. — Joseph Lord's Shoemaker's Shop. — Daniel Lathrop's Shop. — Henry Cobb.

Chapter XXXII.

Christopher Huntington's Home-lot. — Christopher Huntington, 1st. — Christopher Huntington, 2nd. — Jeremiah Huntington. — Samuel Avery. — Caleb Huntington. — John Huntington. — Ezra Huntington. — Malt House. — Old Huntington Homestead. — John Huntington, 1st. — Capt. René Grignon. — Isaac Huntington. — Isaac Huntington's Day-Book. — Benjamin Huntington. — Poem by Benjamin Huntington. — Philip Huntington. — Joseph Griffin.

Chapter XXXIII.

Land Owned by Josiah Read. — Jonathan Crane House. — Israel Lathrop. — William Lathrop. — Reasons Given by William Lathrop and Wife for Joining the Separatists. — Capt. Ebenezer Lathrop. — Jedediah Lathrop. — Felix Huntington, 1st. — Augustus Converse, Sen. — House Built by Felix Huntington. — Daniel Lathrop. — James Stedman. — George C. Raymond. — Daniel Tracy's House. — Stephen Backus. — Capt. Elisha Leffingwell. — Charles Bliss. — George Rudd.

CHAPTER XXXIV.

Home-lot and House of Thomas Sluman. — Thomas Huntington. — Barn-lot of Jonathan Crane. — Blacksmith Shop. — Shop of Avery & Tracy. — Samuel Avery & Son — Roger Huntington & Co. — House of William Lathrop, Jun. — Ezekiel Huntley. — Early Home Life of Mrs. Lydia (Huntley) Sigourney. — First Experiences as a School-teacher. — Marriage to Charles Sigourney of Hartford.

CHAPTER XXXV.

Thomas Danforth's House. — John Danforth's House. — Lineage of Thomas Danforth. — Danforth Shop.

CHAPTER XXXVI.

Land granted to John Elderkin. — Home-lot of Samuel Lathrop, 1st. — Rev. John Lothropp (or Lathrop). — Removal of Samuel Lathrop from New London to Norwich. — Abigail (Doane) Lathrop. — Israel Lathrop. — Jabez Lathrop.

CHAPTER XXXVII.

Samuel Lathrop's Home-lot (continued). — Capt. Joshua Huntington. — Hannah (Perkins) (Huntington) Lynde. — Zachariah Huntington. — Judge Andrew Huntington. — Death of Lucy (Coit) Huntington. — Hannah (Phelps) Huntington. — Bill of Wedding Dress. — Dr. Charles Phelps of Stonington. — Lathrop Lots. — Felix Huntington Shop. — Samuel Danforth's Shop. — Roger Huntington & Co.

CHAPTER XXXVIII.

Samuel Lathrop's Home-lot (continued). — House of Samuel Lathrop, 2nd. — Joseph Lathrop, 1st. — Joseph Lathrop, 2nd. — Thomas Grist. — Early Meeting of the Episcopal Society at the house of Thomas Grist. — Shop of John Grist. — Zephaniah Huntington.

CHAPTER XXXIX.

Samuel Lathrop's Home-lot (continued). — House of Col. Joshua Huntington. — Capt. Charles Whiting's House. — Mundator Tracy.

CHAPTER XL.

Samuel Lathrop's Home-lot (concluded). — Zachariah Huntington's Shop. — Gen. Jedediah Huntington. — Samuel Loudon. — House of Gen. Jedediah Huntington. — Faith (Trumbull) Huntington. — Ann (Moore) Huntington. — Entertainment for French Officers. — Duke de Lauzun. — Gen. Lafayette. — His Last Visit to Norwich in 1824. — Gen. Ebenezer Huntington.

CHAPTER XLI.

Home-lot of Lt. Thomas Tracy. — Tracy Ancestry. — Division of Property. — Sale of the Tracy Homestead to Israel Lathrop. — Daniel Tracy. — Accident at Lathrop's Bridge. — Purchase by Daniel Tracy, 2nd, of part of the Tracy Home-lot from Israel Lathrop. — Samuel Tracy. — Maj. Thomas Tracy. — Ann Thomas (Tracy) Richards. — Shop of Capt. Charles Whiting. — Charles Beaman. — Roswell Huntington. — Mundator Tracy.

CONTENTS.

Chapter XLII.

Home-lot of Lt. Thomas Tracy (continued). — Dr. Solomon Tracy's Home-lot. — Simon Tracy, 1st. — Simon Tracy, 2nd. — Shop of Simeon and Jabez Perkins. — Nathaniel Townsend. — Talleyrand.

Chapter XLIII.

Home-lot of Lt. Thomas Tracy (concluded). — Gov. Samuel Huntington. — Nathaniel Huntington, Jun. — Betsey Devotion. — Mrs. Gov. Huntington. — Public Life of Gov. Huntington. — Death and Funeral. — Visit of Dr. Mason Fitch Cogswell. — Gov. Samuel Huntington of Ohio. — Frances (Huntington) Griffin. — Rev. Edward Dorr Griffin. — Asa Spalding. — Luther Spalding.

Chapter XLIV.

Home-lot of Simon Huntington. — Simon Huntington, 1st. — Inventory of his Library. — James Huntington. — Peter Huntington. — Col. Samuel Abbot. — Capt. Simeon Huntington. — Francis Green of Boston and the Sons of Liberty. — Cemetery Lane.

Chapter XLV.

Home-lot of Simon Huntington (continued). — Philip Turner. — John Manly. — Thomas Danforth. — Richard Charlton. — Charlton Family. — Jesse Charlton. — Samuel Charlton. — Capt. Jacob Perkins. — Mrs. Martha Greene. — Capt. Russell Hubbard. — David Nevins. — Drowning of David Nevins, 1st. — Revolutionary Services of Capt. David Nevins.

Chapter XLVI.

Home-lot of Simon Huntington (continued). — Simeon Carew. — Joseph Carew. — Com. Gen. Joseph Trumbull. — Business Life. — Visits to Norwich of Gov. Trumbull and his Wife. — Mrs. Trumbull's Scarlet Cloak. — Com. Gen. Joseph Trumbull's Public Services and Death. — Epitaph. — Amelia (Dyer) Trumbull's Costly Dress. — Newcomb Kinney. — Asa Lathrop. — Alice Baldwin.

Chapter XLVII.

Home-lot of Simon Huntington (continued). — Grant to Simon Huntington, 2nd. — Samuel Abbot's Shop. — Thomas Carey. — Daniel Abbot. — Capt. Joseph Carew. — Family of Capt. Joseph Carew. — Joseph Huntington. — Hon. Jabez Huntington. — Obituary Notice.

Chapter XLVIII.

Simon Huntington's Home-lot (continued). — John Arnold. — Samuel Huntington. — Home-lot of John Bradford. — Thomas Bradford. — Sale to Simon Huntington, 2nd. — Division of Simon Huntington, 2nd's, Property. — David Rogers. — Cyrus and Lucy (Huntington) Miner. — Lyman Roath's Shop. — Boy's Lending Library.

Chapter XLIX.

Simon Huntington's Home-lot (continued). — André Richard. — Daniel Needham. — Benjamin Butler. — Anecdote of Benjamin Butler. — Dr. Benjamin Butler. — Gardner Carpenter. — Rev. Hiram P. Arms.

CONTENTS.

CHAPTER L.

Home-lot of Simon Huntington (continued). — Gen. Jabez Huntington's Distillery and Cooper's Shop. — Andrew Huntington. — William Bradford Whiting. — Emigrates to New York. — Anecdote of Amy, wife of William Bradford Whiting. — Zenas Whiton (or Whiting). — His Skill as a Bridge-builder. — Dr. Rufus Spalding.

CHAPTER LI.

Home-lot of Simon Huntington (concluded) and part of John Bradford's Home-lot. — Joseph Carew's Shop. — Asa Lathrop's Shop. — Shop of Charles Gildon. — Isabella Gildon's School. — Shop of Capt. Jacob Perkins. — Capt. Russell Hubbard. — David Nevins' Hat Factory. — Samuel Gaine. — Simon Carew. — Jeremiah Leach's Shop. — Simeon Huntington's Store and Blacksmith Shop. — John Hughes. — Nathaniel Townsend. — Jabez Perkins. — Capt. Joseph Gale. — Azor Gale. — Shop of Gen. Jabez Huntington. — Andrew Huntington. — Shop of Zachariah Huntington.

CHAPTER LII.

Home-lot of John Bradford (continued). — Gen. Jabez Huntington. — Revolutionary Services. — Illness and Death. — Elizabeth (Tracy) Backus. — Hannah (Williams) Huntington. — Col. John Chester and His Wife, Elizabeth Huntington. — Gen. Zachariah Huntington. — Leader of the Choir. — Family of Gen. Zachariah Huntington.

CHAPTER LIII.

Peter Morgan's Home-lot. — Rev. Joseph Strong's House. — Rev. Joseph Strong. — Henry Strong. — Mary (Huntington) Strong. — Robert Lancaster's House and Shop. — John Lancaster.

CHAPTER LIV.

Home-lot of the Rev. James Fitch. — Maj. James Fitch's House. — Public Career of Maj. James Fitch. — Alice (Bradford) (Adams) Fitch. — Family of Alice (Bradford) Adams. — Rev. Samuel Whiting.

CHAPTER LV.

Home-lot of the Rev. James Fitch (continued). — Illness of the Rev. James Fitch. — Efforts of the Church to Procure a Settled Pastor. — Rev. Jabez Fitch. — Rev. Henry Flint. — Rev. Joseph Coit. — Settlement of the Rev. John Woodward. — Disagreement about the Saybrook Platform. — Dismissal of the Rev. John Woodward.

CHAPTER LVI.

Home-lot of the Rev. James Fitch (continued). — Sale of the Parsonage to Madam Sarah Knight. — Lineage of Madam Knight. — Her Journal. — Removal to New London. — Edmund Gookin.

CHAPTER LVII.

Home-lot of the Rev. James Fitch (continued). — Curtis Cleveland's House. — His Lineage. — Joseph Peck. — Elizabeth (Lathrop) (Carpenter) Peck. — Gardner Carpenter. — André Richard. — Sylvanus Jones. — William Darby. — Capt. William Fountain. — Huguenot Ancestry of Elizabeth (Ramé) Fountain. — Capt. Philip Turner. — Joseph Peck. — Peck Tavern. — Entertainments at the Tavern. — John Wheatley. — Service in the Revolution. — Deodat Little. — Jonathan Trott. — Peace Celebrations. — Trott Lineage and Family.

xii   CONTENTS.

CHAPTER LVIII.

Home-lot of Rev. James Fitch (continued). — Sylvanus Jones' House. — Ebenezer Jones. — Sale of Lots. — George Wickwire's House. — Asa Lathrop's Shoe-shop. — Eliphaz Hart's Dwelling House. — Sketch of the Wickwire Family. — John Manly's Shop. — Thomas Danforth's Shop. — William Morgan. — William Morgan's House. — James Noyes Brown. — Lineage of James Noyes Brown. — Nathan Stedman. — Dr. Gurdon Lathrop. — Gerard Lathrop. — Peter Lanman.

CHAPTER LIX.

Home-lot of Rev. James Fitch (concluded). — Jonathan Wickwire's House. — Jonathan Goodhue. — Samuel Waterman's Shop. — Sketch of Goodhue Family. — John Perit. — Rev. Peter Perit. — Inscription on Grave-stone. — Family of Rev. Peter Perit. — John Perit's Services in French War and in the Revolution. — His Family. — Perit Shop. — Asa Spalding. — County House and Jail. — Store of George D. Fuller. — Alexander McDonald. — Gurdon Lathrop. — Removal of Gurdon Lathrop to a New Shop. — Burying-ground Lane. — Old Burying-ground. — Death and Burial of French Prisoners. — Burial of a Pequot and a Mohegan Indian.

CHAPTER LX.

Home-lot of Maj. Mason. — Sketch of the Life of Maj. Mason. — Pequot War. — Death of Maj. Mason. — Anne (Peck) Mason. — Sermon by Rev. James Fitch on the Death of Mrs. Anne Mason. — Sketch of Maj. Mason's Family. — Capt. John Mason, 2nd. — Capt. John Mason, 3rd. — Mason Controversy About Indian Lands.

CHAPTER LXI.

Home-lot of Maj. Mason (continued). — Call Extended by the First Church to Rev. Benjamin Lord. — Sketch of the Rev. Benjamin Lord. — Ann (Taylor) Lord. — Inscription of Tombstone of Rev. Benjamin Lord. — Anecdotes of the Rev. Dr. Lord. — Inventory of Abigail (Hooker) Lord. — Division of the Lord Property. — Ebenezer and Benjamin Lord. — Lucy (Lord) (Avery) Perkins. — William Cleveland. — Cleveland Shop. — Rev. Joseph Howe.

CHAPTER LXII.

Home-lot of Maj. Mason (continued). — Nathaniel Lathrop. — Lathrop Tavern. — First Stage Line to Providence. — Azariah Lathrop. — Anecdote by Hon. John T. Wait. — Augustus Lathrop. — Burning of the Tavern. — "Sans Souci" Assemblies. — Poem by William Pitt Turner. — Jabez Smith, Singing Teacher. — Theatricals and Wax Works.

CHAPTER LXIII.

Maj. Mason's Home-lot (continued). — First Courts in Norwich. — Building of First Court House. — Second Court House. — Powder House. — Blowing Up of Powder House. — Boston Circular. — Tea Drinking Parties Prohibited. — Committee of Correspondence. — City Hall Built at New London. — Removal of Court House. — Whipping Posts, Stocks and Pillory. — Early Sentences of the Court. — Theatrical Entertainments. — Singing School. — Dancing Classes. — Removal of Courts to the Landing. — Court House Used as a School House. — Destruction of the Old Court House.

CHAPTER LXIV.

First Meeting House of Norwich. — New Church Building Erected on the Rocks in 1673. — Seating of People According to Rank. — Repairing the Meeting House in 1708. — Bell Presented by Capt. Réne Grignon in 1708. — New Meeting House Built in 1713. — A Fourth Church Building Begun in 1753. — Church Singing as Described by Mrs. Sigourney. — Church Burned by an Incendiary in 1801. — New Church Erected Partly by Subscription and Partly by Lottery. — Laying of Corner Stone for the New Church in 1801. — Lombardy Poplars. — Names of Pastors of the Church.

CHAPTER LXV.

Home-lot of Stephen Gifford. — Family of Stephen Gifford. — Sale of Gifford Lot to the Town. — Land granted as "Parsonage Land" to Rev. John Woodward. — Granted to Rev. Benj. Lord. — Building of Court House on this Land in 1735. — Land Ceded by the Lords to the Church Society. — Ebenezer Lord's House and Shop on Common Land. — Ebenezer Lord. — Dudley Woodbridge. — Lineage and Family of Dudley Woodbridge. — Gurdon Lathrop Occupies Woodbridge Shop. — Joseph Huntington. — Carew & Huntington. — Jos. & Chas. P. Huntington. — Roger Griswold. — Family of Roger Griswold. — Public Life of Gov. Roger Griswold. — Inscription on Tomb-stone — Incendiarism. — Huntington Shop and Griswold House and Church Burnt in 1801. — Joseph & Chas. P. Huntington Build a Brick Store. — Brick Store sold to Capt. Bela Peck, and later presented for a Chapel to the Norwich Town Church by Mrs. Harriet (Peck) Williams. — Lot No. 1 of Parsonage Lands, leased to Dudley Woodbridge and Roger Griswold.

CHAPTER LXVI.

Parsonage Lands. — Lease of Lot No. 2 to Jesse Brown. — Brown Tavern. — Jesse Brown's Marriages. — Revolutionary Services. — Visit of Pres. John Adams and Wife to Norwich. — Stage Lines to Hartford, Boston, Providence, and New York. — John and Ann (Brown) Vernet. — Dr. I. Greenwood, Dentist. — Capt. Bela Peck. — Peck Library. — "The Rock Nook Home."

CHAPTER LXVII.

Parsonage Lands. — Lots No. 3 and No. 4 Leased to Joseph Carpenter. — Carpenter Family. — Building of Joseph Carpenter's Shop. — Joseph Carpenter as a Goldsmith. — Gerard Carpenter. — Seth Miner's House on Parsonage Land. — Sketch of Asher Miner and the Hon. Charles Miner. — "The Judges' Chamber." — Judge William Noyes. — Judge Benjamin Coit. — Judge William Hillhouse. — Judge Noyes in Family Prayer. — The Hon. Charles Miner's Last Visit to Norwich.

CHAPTER LXVIII

Early Schools and Schoolmasters of Norwich. — John Birchard. — Daniel Mason. — John Arnold. — Richard Bushnell. — Thomas Eyre. — Jared Bostwick. — Old Brick School House on the Plain. — Mr. Goodrich. — School Exhibitions. — Dr. Daniel Lathrop's Endowment. — Ebenezer Punderson. — Sketch of the Punderson Family. — Tea Drinking Episode. — School Reminiscences of the Hon. Charles Miner. — Mr. White. — Newcomb Kinney. — His Skill in Penmanship, and Advertisement as a School Teacher. — Alexander McDonald. — As Author, School Teacher and Bookseller. — William Baldwin. — Mrs. Sigourney's Recollections of William Baldwin.

CHAPTER LXIX.

School Reminiscences of Mrs. Sigourney (continued). — Pelatiah Perit. — Rev. Daniel Haskell.

CHAPTER LXX.

Parsonage Lands (continued). — Gardner Carpenter's Store. — Nathaniel Townsend's Barber Shop. Store and Baker House. — John Wheatley's Shoe Shop. — Nathaniel Patten's Book Store. — Gideon Denison.

CHAPTER LXXI.

Parsonage Lands (continued). — Earliest Jail. — Second Jail (Burnt in 1786). — Jailers. — Sims Edgerton. — Dr. Benjamin Church. — John Barney, Jun. (Jailer). — Darius Peck. — Seth Miner. — Ebenezer Punderson. — Escape of Prisoners. — New Jail Built on Opposite Side of Green in 1815. — Office of Norwich Packet. — William Lax. — Darius Peck. — Joseph Carpenter. — Beginning of "The Norwich Packet." — Alexander and James Robertson.

CHAPTER LXXII.

Parsonage Lands (continued). — Darius Peck House. — Gideon Denison. — Dr. Philemon Tracy. — Mrs. Sigourney's Recollections of Dr. Tracy. — Medical Practice and Family of Dr. Tracy. — Houses of Samuel and John Charlton. — Parmenas Jones House. — William Osborne House. —

CHAPTER LXXIII.

Norwich Town Green. — Early Trainings. — Nathaniel Lathrop's Shop. — Liberty Pole. — Field Reviews. — The British and American Flags. — Scenes on the Green During the Revolution and on the Yearly Training Days. — Military Uniforms. — Election of the Colored Governor. — Games of Norwich Town Boys. — Anecdote by the Hon. John T. Wait.

ILLUSTRATIONS.

LIST OF MAPS AND HALF-TONE PRINTS.

		Photographer	Page
1.	Colored Map of Norwich,	*By Donald G. Mitchell*	Frontispiece
2.	The William W. Backus Hospital,	*M. E. Jensen*	6
3.	Thanksgiving Barrel-burning on Jail Hill,	*Clarence E. Spalding*	14
4.	Reynolds House,	*M. E. Jensen*	23
5.	Silhouette of Abigail Reynolds,	" "	26
6.	Bliss House,	" "	31
7.	Old Stocking Shop,	" "	34
8.	Jackson Browne House,	" "	37
9.	Lt. Thomas Leffingwell's House,	" "	38
10.	Site of Shantok Fort and Mohegan Burying-ground,	*Charles E. Briggs*	40
11.	House Built by Thomas Leffingwell, 4th,	*M. E. Jensen*	47
12.	Capt. Samuel Leffingwell's House,	" "	49
13.	Rufus Darby's House,	" "	51
14.	Probable Site of Joseph Bushnell's House,	" "	57
15.	Old Bushnell Apple Tree,	" "	59
16.	James Lincoln's House,	" "	60
17.	Home-lot of Ensign Thos. Leffingwell and Sentry Hill,	" "	63
18.	House of Thomas Leffingwell, 4th,	" "	64
19.	View Looking Down the Street from House of T. L., 4th,	*Wm. S. Laighton*	65
20.	East Side of Leffingwell Inn,	" "	66
21.	North Side of Leffingwell Inn,	" "	68
22.	Silhouette of Col. Christopher Leffingwell,		72
23.	Fork of Roads, Site of Christopher Leffingwell's Store,	*Francis Gilman*	74
24.	David Greenleaf's House,	*M. E. Jensen*	77
25.	Capt. William Billing's House,	" "	78
26.	House Occupied by Judah Paddock Spooner,	*N. A. Gibbs*	80
27.	Zebadiah Lathrop's House,	" "	85
28.	Jabez Avery's House,	" "	88
29.	Capt. Joseph Winship's House,	" "	91
30.	Rockwell Manning's House,	*M. E. Jensen*	92
31.	Old Miniature of Diah Manning,		93
32.	Samuel Manning's House,	" "	93
33.	Eleazer Lord's Tavern,	" "	95
34.	View of Yantic Looking South from the Bridge Back of the Lord Tavern,		102
35.	Map of Norwich as in 1705,	*Drawn by H. W. Kent*	104
36.	Thomas Harland's House,	*Ansel E. Beckwith*	112
37.	View of Old Clock, Made by Thomas Harland, in the Hall of His House,	*M. E. Jensen*	113

ILLUSTRATIONS.

		Photographer	Page
38.	Clockface, by Thomas Harland,	*M. E. Jensen*	114
39.	Thomas Williams' House and Shop,	" "	117
40.	School House,	" "	119
41.	Old Fire Engine, Formerly Used at Norwich Town,	*Clarence E. Spalding*	124
42.	Old Fire Buckets, Formerly Belonging to Levi Huntington,	*C. E. Briggs*	126
43.	House of Dr. Daniel Lathrop,	*Norris S. Lippitt*	137
44.	Dining Room of Lathrop House (now owned by the Misses Gilman),	*M. E. Jensen*	138
45.	Corner Dining Room Closet,	" "	139
46.	Simeon Case's House,	" "	146
47.	Dr. Joshua Lathrop's House,		147
48.	Old Lathrop Drug Shop,	*W. Hamilton Burnett*	150
49.	Thomas Lathrop's House,	*M. E. Jensen*	152
50.	Garden Walk,		153
51.	View from the Lathrop Terrace,	*Norris S. Lippitt*	154
52.	Approach to House of Daniel Lathrop Coit,	*M. E. Jensen*	155
53.	Daniel L. Coit's House,		161
54.	Old Elm Trees in front of Coit House,	*Frederic L. Osgood*	165
55.	Nathan Cobb's House,	*M. E. Jensen*	167
56.	Plan of Norwich as in 1795,	Drawn by *Frederic P. Gulliver*	168
57.	Joshua Prior's House,	*M. E. Jensen*	170
58.	Old Norman House,	" "	171
59.	William Adgate's House,	" "	176
60.	Old Homestead of Christopher Huntington,	*Elisha Ayer*	178
61.	Jeremiah Huntington's House,		180
62.	Ezra Huntington's House,	*M. E. Jensen*	182
63.	Daniel Tracy House and House Built by Capt. Reynolds on Site of Jonathan Crane House,	" "	188
64.	House Built by Felix Huntington,	" "	191
65.	Avery & Tracy Shop and House of Wm. Lathrop, Jun., (Early home of Mrs. Sigourney.)		193
66.	Thomas Danforth's House,	" "	202
67.	Capt. Joshua Huntington's House (possibly built by Samuel Lathrop, 1st),		209
68.	View from Capt. Joshua Huntington's Grounds,	" "	213
69.	Col. Joshua Huntington's House,	" "	218
70.	Capt. Charles Whiting's House,	" "	219
71.	Gen. Jedediah and Gen. Ebenezer Huntington's House,	" "	221
72.	Samuel Tracy House,		229
73.	Gov. Samuel Huntington's House,	" "	238
74.	Portrait of Martha Lathrop Devotion (Wife of Rev. Ebenezer Devotion),	*Wm. S. Laighton*	240
75.	Cemetery Gate, Erected by "The Rural Society," near or on Site of the Early Homestead of Simon Huntington, 1st,	*Frederic P. Gulliver*	249
76.	Capt. Jacob Perkins' House, (later Nevins house),	*M. E. Jensen*	253
77.	Com. Gen. Joseph Trumbull's House and Col. Samuel Abbot's Shop,	" "	256

ILLUSTRATIONS. xvii

		Photographer	Page
78.	Capt. Joseph Carew's House,	Frederic P. Gulliver	260
79.	Gardner Carpenter's House,	M. E. Jensen	271
80.	Wm. Bradford Whiting's House,	" "	272
81.	Silhouettes of Whiting Family,		272
82.	Jabez Perkins' House (the fourth white house to the left of picture is the Col. Samuel Abbot house, which formerly stood on opposite side of the street),	" "	279
83.	Corner of Huntington Lane, with a View Down the Town Street to the Gardner Carpenter House,	" "	281
84.	Gen. Jabez Huntington's House,	N. A. Gibbs	282
85.	Rev. Joseph Strong's House,	M. E. Jensen	287
86.	Silhouette of Rev. Joseph Strong,	" "	288
87.	Curtis Cleveland's House and Peck Tavern,	" "	306
88.	Sylvanus Jones' House,	" "	314
89.	Gerard Lathrop's House,	" "	317
90.	John Perit's House,	" "	319
91.	John Perit's Store,	" "	321
92.	Burying-Ground Lane,	" "	324
93.	Court House,	Frederic P. Gulliver	343
94.	View from Meeting House Rocks (Site of the Second and Third Churches),	N. A. Gibbs	350
95.	Plan of Pews in Church about 1756,	Drawn by H. W. Kent	352
96.	Church,		357
97.	Chapel,	Frederic P. Gulliver	363
98.	Jesse Brown Tavern,	M. E. Jensen	365
99.	Mourning Piece by Charlotte and Harriet Peck,	" "	367
100.	Joseph Carpenter's House and Store,	" "	368
101.	Old Brick School House,	" "	374
102.	Dr. Philemon Tracy House,	" "	381
103.	Parmenas Jones' House,	" "	394
104.	Pencil Sketch of Norwich Town Plain about 1840,	" "	395
105.	View of the Plain in 1895,	" "	402

ILLUSTRATIONS.

LIST OF PORTRAITS AND MINIATURES.

		Page
1.	Joseph Reynolds,	26
	Copied by permission of the owner, Mrs. Henry L. Reynolds.	
2.	Enoch and Sally (Canfield) Reynolds,	28
	Copied by permission of the owner, Miss Mary Reynolds, Washington, D. C.	
3.	William and Sally (Beers) Leffingwell,	82
	Copied by permission of the New Haven Art School.	
4.	Rufus and Hannah (Choate) Lathrop,	134
	Copied by permission of the former owner, Miss Lucretia H. Grace.	
5.	Dr. Joshua and Mercy (Eels) Lathrop,	148
	Copied by permission of the owner, Mrs. George B. Ripley.	
6.	Hannah Bill Lathrop,	154
	Copied by permission of the owner, Mrs. George B. Ripley.	
7.	Daniel L. and Elizabeth (Bill) Coit,	164
	Copied by permission of the owners, the Misses Gilman.	
8.	Lydia (Huntley) Sigourney,	200
	Copied by permission of the owner, Rev. Francis T. Russell of Waterbury, Ct.	
9.	Gen. Jedediah Huntington,	222
	Copied by permission of the owner, Miss Sarah L. Huntington.	
10.	Gen Ebenezer Huntington,	228
	Copied by permission of the owner, Miss Sarah H. Perkins.	
11.	Col. Simeon Perkins,	236
	Copied by permission of the owner, Rev. Newton Perkins, of East 52nd Street, N. Y.	
12.	Gov. Samuel Huntington of Connecticut,	238
	Copied by permission of E. Huntington of Painesville, O.	
13.	Gov. Samuel Huntington of Ohio,	242
	Copied by permission of E. Huntington of Painesville, O.	
14.	Com. Gen. Joseph Trumbull,	256
	Copied by permission of the owner, Mrs. L. R. Cheney of Hartford, Ct.	
15.	Joseph and Eunice (Carew) Huntington,	262
	Copied by permission of the owner, Mrs. Daniel F. Gulliver.	
16.	Amy (Lathrop) Whiting,	274
	Copied by permission of the owner, Thomas C. Brainerd, of Montreal, Canada.	
17.	Gen. Jabez Huntington,	282
	Copied by permission of the owner, Mrs. Mary H. Childs of Florence, Italy.	
18.	Elizabeth (Huntington) Chester, in Youth and Old Age,	284
	Copied by permission of the owner, Miss Julia Chester Wells, of West 31st Street, N. Y.	
19.	Col. John Chester,	286
	Copied by permission of the owner, Miss Julia Chester Wells, of West 31st Street, N. Y.	
20.	Mary (Huntington) Strong,	290
	Copied by permission of the owner, Mrs. Daniel F. Gulliver.	
21.	Ruth (Webster) (Perit) Leffingwell,	322
	Copied by permission of the owners, the Misses Huntington.	
22.	John Perit,	324
	Copied by permission of the owner, P. Webster Huntington of Columbus, Ohio.	
23.	Dr. Benjamin Lord,	336
	Copied by permission of the owner, John Bliss of Brooklyn, L. I.	
24.	Jesse Brown,	
25.	William Brown,	364
	Copied by permission of the owners, the Misses Ingham of Wilkesbarre, Penn.	
26.	Ann (Brown) Vernet,	
27.	John Vernet,	368
	Copied by permission of the owners, the Misses Ingham of Wilkesbarre, Penn.	

PART I.

OLD HOUSES OF NORWICH.

ERRATA.

Page 16, Line 1, Read "Rachel" for "Rebecca" Huntington.
" 32, " 15, " Richard "Carder" for Richard "Caider."
" 101, " 25, " "Winthrop" Saltonstall for "Gilbert" Saltonstall.
" 102, " 3, " "second" election (1793) for "first" election of Gen. Washington.
" 239, " 6, " "Frances" Huntington for "Hannah."
" 242, " 1, " " " " "
" 392, " 2, " "Diadema" for "Jerusha" (Hyde) Butler.

CHAPTER I.

IN May, 1659, a large number of the inhabitants of Saybrook applied to the General Court at Hartford for permission to make a settlement at Norwich, or, (as it was then called), Mohegan. The Court "considered," "approved," and "consented to" the desire of "ye petitioners respecting Mohegin, provided y' within ye space of three yeares they doe effect a plantation in ye place propounded."

The settlers evidently lost no time in arranging for removal, for in June, 1659, the three sachems of Mohegan, Onkos (Uncas), Owaneco, and Attawanhood deeded to "the Towne and Inhabitants of Norwich" a tract of land, beginning on the southern line "at the brooke falling into the head of Trading Cove," and extending from thence east, west and north, on both sides of the river over a territory nine miles square.

The town was first known as Mohegan.* The first reference to it as Norwich is in March, 1661, when the constable at "Seabrook" is required to levy a certain sum "upon ye estates of such at Norridge, as are defective in their rates." In 1662 it is "enrolled as a legal township."† This is all that is actually known of the settlement of the town. The records, both of Saybrook and of Norwich, are silent as to the reasons for removal, the naming of the new township, and the arrival of the settlers ; so on these matters we may speculate at will.

Some may believe the tradition recorded in President Stiles' diary, that our ancestors were driven from Saybrook by the immense flocks of crows and black-birds, which infested the fields in May and June, and others that Maj. Mason, in one

---

*The original deed has not been found, but a copy was recorded at Hartford in 1663, and later at Norwich and New London. These all vary somewhat in wording, but the fact that the first entry was made after the town received its name may account for this phrase "Towne and Inhabitants of Norwich."

† Miss Caulkins' History of Norwich, p. 71.

of his numerous expeditions, perceiving the great natural advantages which this Mohegan country offered for a settlement, persuaded some of his friends to leave their level coast-lands for this more attractive region of wooded hills, and sheltered vales, and rushing streams. We may suppose that any project of Maj. Mason's would naturally meet with approval, and that, when it was seconded by the pastor, Rev. Mr. Fitch, most of the settlers would be ready to follow, wherever their military and religious leaders should show the way.

As the adventurers sailed up the river, the Indian stone fort, towering up on Weequaw, or Waweequaw Hill, later called Fort Hill (now Jail Hill), may have suggested the castle-crowned Norwich, on the other side of the water, perhaps to the brothers Huntington, who are supposed to have emigrated from Norwich, England, or perchance to William Backus, for whom the historian of the Backus' family claims the honor of having named the town; but the silence of the records on this point, gives us all liberty to decide the matter for ourselves, and the erratic spelling of the earliest manuscripts will allow us to christen the town Norwitch, Norwhich, Norwig, Norige, or Norridge, as we prefer.

The number of first settlers is usually given as thirty-five, and this is based upon a manuscript of Dr. Lord's, which says: "The town of Norwich was settled in the spring of 1660: the Purchase of sd Town was made in ye month of June, 1659, by 35 men." We learn from Miss Caulkins, that the number is altered in the manuscript from thirty-four, and the name of John Elderkin is interlined, as if there was some doubt of his right to be named among the first settlers.

In 1694, the inhabitants of Norwich, "being sensible of their neglect in not recording at first settling, what was laid out in the first, second, and third divisions, as also the names of the first purchasers," appoint Lt. Leffingwell, John Post, Lt. Backus, Thomas Adgate, John Birchard, Simon Huntington, Sr., and Jonathan Tracy "to search out and do the best they can," to find the names of the original settlers, what estate each one "put into the town and make return;" but this effort, only thirty-four years after the settlement, to obtain a perfect registry of the first proprietors, and their lands, seems to have been as unsuccessful as several former ones in 1673, 1681, and 1684, and neither on these, nor on a later record, prepared by Capt. James Fitch, can we entirely rely.

Miss Caulkins gives in her history of Norwich the names of twenty-eight men, whom she believes to have indisputable claims to rank as first proprietors, and an additional list of ten doubtful ones, bringing the number up to thirty-eight. Two of these, Hendy and Wallis, though possibly among the first purchasers of land, cannot be numbered among the first settlers, as Wallis did not come to Norwich to reside until about 1670, and Hendy was probably never an actual resident of the town. The Rev. E. B. Huntington, of Stamford, Ct., names thirty-six men, whom he supposes to have been original proprietors; but one of these was Richard Wallis, and another was Caleb Abel, who in 1660 was only about fourteen years of age.

Now when Dr. Lord was ordained in 1717, many were living, who were in their boyhood, when the town was settled, and who must have often heard discussed by their fathers these questions of proprietary rights, and the incidents of the settlement, and from their testimony, this list of Dr. Lord's was probably prepared.

We have been unable to discover any trace of Dr. Lord's manuscript, but have found a list naming thirty-five original settlers, in which John Elderkin's name appears, and this, rather than make one of our own, we will adopt, believing that it may possibly be a copy of the list of Dr. Lord. Among these names are several which figure in Miss Caulkins' doubtful list, but the entries of their home lots bear, as do the others, the date 1659, and though the youngest* was at the time of the settlement, only sixteen years of age, it is possible that he was considered old enough to receive an allotment of land.

The following is the list, from which we shall exclude the name of John Elderkin, as his earliest land grant was dated 1667, and we will assume that he did not become an inhabitant until that year. This reduces the number to thirty-four. With the wives and children, whose births are found on record, the whole number of earliest inhabitants would amount to 143, but as it is probable that some of these children did not survive until 1660, and very uncertain whether the wives of Thomas Tracy, Robert Allyn, and William Hyde, were then living, we may conclude that the correct number lies between 130 and 140.

---

*Thomas Waterman.

First Settlers.	Wives.	Children.	
Maj. John Mason,	Anne,	Priscilla, Samuel, John, Rachel, Anne, Daniel, Elizabeth,	9
Rev. James Fitch,		James, Abigail, Elizabeth, Hannah, Samuel, Dorothy,	7
Thomas Leffingwell,	Mary,	Rachel, Thomas, Jonathan, Joseph, Mary, Nathaniel,	8
Thomas Adgate,	Mary,	Elizabeth, Hannah, *Bushnell Children.* Richard, Joseph, Mary, Mercy.	8
William Backus, Sr.,	Ann,	Stephen,	3
Thomas Bingham, (Stepson of W. Backus, Sr.)			1
William Backus, Jun., (Son of W. B., Sr.)	Elizabeth,	William,	3
Christopher Huntington,	Ruth,	Ruth,	3
Simon Huntington,	Sarah,	Sarah, Mary, Simon,	5
Thomas Tracy,	— (?),	Thomas, Jonathan, Miriam, Solomon, Daniel, Samuel,	8
John Tracy, (Son of T. T.)			1
Thomas Waterman,			1
John Bradford,	Martha,		2
John Olmstead,	Elizabeth,		2
William Hyde,	— (?),		2
Samuel Hyde, (Son of W. H.)	Jane,		2
John Reynolds,	Sarah,	John, Sarah, Susanna, Joseph,	6
Thomas Bliss,	Elizabeth,	Elizabeth, Sarah, Mary, Thomas, Dolinda, Samuel,	8
Thomas Post,	Mary,	Sarah,	3
John Post,	Hester,	Margaret, Elizabeth, John, Sarah,	6
John Gager,	Elizabeth,	John, Elizabeth, Sarah, Hannah, Samuel, Bethiah,	8
John Birchard,	Christian,	John,	3
Morgan Bowers,	Judah (?),		2
Nehemiah Smith,	Ann,	Sarah, Mary, Hannah, Mercy, Nehemiah, Lydia, Ann, Mehitable,	10
Richard Edgerton,	Mary,	Mary, Elizabeth, Hannah,	5
Robert Allyn,	— (?),	John, Mary, Deborah, Hannah,	6
Jonathan Royce,	Deborah (?),		2
John Baldwin,	Hannah,	John, Hannah, Sarah,	5

First Settlers.	Wives.	Children.	
Francis Griswold,	——,	Sarah, Mary, Hannah,	
Hugh Calkins,	Ann,		2
John Calkins, (Son of H. C.)	Sarah,	Hugh,	3
Robert Wade,	Susanna (?),		2
Thomas Howard,			1
John Pease,			1
			143

The lands of the new township were surveyed, and home lots assigned by November, 1659, but it seems hardly probable that the settlers would bring their wives and children, so late in the season, to face the discomforts of the winter in Norwich. A rude building may have been hastily put together for shelter, and some of the men may have braved the cold and storms, constructing houses for the families, who were to arrive in the spring. One building was certainly standing in the spring of 1660, as a document of the General Court, dated June 9, 1660, thus reads:

"Not many weeks now past, we are by sufficient information certified, that one night at ye New Plantation at Monheage, some Indians, as will appear, of the Narragansetts shot 11 bullets into a house of our English there, in hopes, as they boasted, to have slain him whome we have cause to honor, whose safety we cannot but take ourselves bound to promote, our Deputy Gov' Major Mason."

Another account says that 8 bullets were fired into an English house, "wherein 5 Englishmen were asleep." Miss Caulkins thinks this may have been the house of Maj. Mason, which is said to have stood on the site of the Norwich Town school-house at the south-east corner of the Green, but there is nothing in the record to confirm this supposition.

We shall probably never know whether the families who were to settle in Norwich, all arrived at the same time, or came one by one, as fast as homes were ready to receive them. It is not probable that the family of Joseph Reynolds, whose son Joseph was born in March, 1660, at Saybrook, or that of William Backus, Jun., whose eldest son William was born in the following May, arrived before the late spring, or early summer of that year. But we know that Samuel Hyde and his wife were domiciled here by August, as their daughter Elizabeth, who came into the world in that month, was the first child born in Norwich.

But whether all together, or in separate parties, the settlers no doubt came by water from Saybrook, disembarked at the old Indian landing-place at the Falls, and following the Indian trail, later know as Mill Lane (now Lafayette Street), through No-man's Acre, along the banks of the Yantic, arrived at the corner, near the spot where now stands the new William W. Backus Hospital. Here, sheltered by the

hills on one side, the meadows and lowlands spreading out to the west and south along the river, formed the attractive spot chosen for the new settlement.

The highway had probably been roughly staked out, and the lands covered with rocks, trees and underbrush, must have revealed more of "the Caledonian wildness," which Mrs. Lydia Huntley Sigourney mentions as a feature of Norwich scenery, and less of "the tender softness of the vale of Tempe," than characterizes its present aspect.

Mrs. Sigourney, who was born in Norwich, always writes in glowing terms of her early home. In a book published in 1824, entitled "Connecticut Forty Years Since," and in other of her works, she gives many pictures of the town, and its inhabitants. These carry us back about one hundred years, but farther into the past we shall have to travel in imagination, for we know of no earlier description of the town and people than this.

One writer, who flourished in the beginning of this century, Macdonald Clarke (b. 1798, d. 1842), called by his contemporaries the "Mad Poet," though not a native of the place, has written a little poem about Norwich, two verses of which we will quote, as they voice the prevailing sentiment of many a lover of the old town.

> "'Tis the village town, and many a voice,
>   And many a gladden'd gaze,
> Have said 'twould be their dearest choice
>   Here to spend their fading days.
> For this little white town,
>   Half-naveled among the rocky hills,
> In summer's smile, or winter's frown,
>   The sweetest spot of memory fills."
>
> "The wild villages among the Alps
>   Are far less lovely to the sight,
> With a green coronet on their scalps,
>   Their brows bound with a band of light,
> When sun-down sheds its golden glare
>   Across the silent air."

Mrs. Sigourney describes Norwich* "as viewed from the eastern acclivity," seeming "like a citadel, guarded by parapets of rock, and embosomed in an amphitheatre of hills, whose summits mark the horizon with a waving line of forest green." "Its habitations bear few marks of splendour, but many of them retiring behind the shelter of lofty elms, exhibit the appearance of comfort and respectability." "In the northern division of Norwich" (the seat of the first settlement), may be found "a society remarkable for the preservation of primitive habits." "A more moral state of society can scarcely be imagined, than that which existed within the bosom of these rocks. Almost it might seem as if their rude summits, pointing in every direction, had been commissioned to repel the intrusion of vice."

Into this moral region, we are now about to enter. But before we walk through the town, it would be well to know something of the customs, dress, style of houses, and general surroundings of the people, whose acquaintance we are about to make.

---

* "Connecticut Forty Years Since."

CHAPTER II.

THE home-lots of the first settlers were surrounded by high fences, the early law requiring that those in front should be "a five rayle or equivalent to it, and the general fence a three rayle." Later "a good three rail fence, four feet high, or a good hedge or pole fence well staked, four and a half feet high" was allowed. These were quite necessary, on account of the free range that the cattle, sheep and swine enjoyed, the latter proving a great nuisance, so much so, that many laws were passed, requiring that they be "yoked" or "ringed," even as late as 1757. Two pounds were established at the ends of the town, but later, owing to the numerous "strays," the number was greatly increased. Every man's cattle had a special ear mark—one or more slits, variously shaped crosses, holes, &c., to distinguish them as they fed in common, or wandered off to distant pastures. After a time, goat-raising became a source of profit, and though no laws had then been made for their restraint, who can blame Joseph Tracy for impounding the fifty-four belonging to Joseph Backus, which like a devastating army invaded his lands in 1722.

It is probable that, as in all new settlements, many of the earliest houses of Norwich were log-houses; but the nearness of the New London saw-mill, and the fact that the services of experienced carpenters could be procured from there, would lead one to believe that those of the "well-to-do" settlers were possibly of better finish and construction. The smaller houses of this period were usually of one story, or one story and a half, with two rooms, a kitchen, and a large "best" room (often utilized as a bed room), upon the first floor, and rude sleeping places in the attic above.

The larger houses were of two stories, generally square, with a huge central chimney, and a long roof, which, extending at the back of the house almost to the ground, formed a one story projection called the lean-to in the rear. On the first floor were generally four rooms—the "Great Room" or "Company Room," or "Keeping Room" (as it was sometimes called), a large chamber, a kitchen, and a pantry or milk-room. On the second floor were chambers, and very often a porch chamber, which, according to the early deeds, seems to have been quite a feature of the first Norwich houses. Heavy beams crossed the ceiling overhead, ran along the sides of the wall, and down the corners, and these in the oldest buildings are rough-hewn, often showing the mark of the axe. The doors and window shutters were fastened with huge bars of wood, a feature still to be seen in some houses of ancient date.

The kitchen was the principal room, and made a cheerful gathering place for the family circle, with its rows of burnished pewter dishes on the dresser, the log seats and high settle in the chimney corner, the deep cavernous fire-place, with its imposing array of cranes, kettles, jacks, spits, pot-hooks or trammels, and the fire-dogs, on which the burning logs piled up against the huge back-log blazed far up into the chimney. Into one side of the chimney was built the oven, and over the fire-place was a high shelf, and there were recesses for books, and closets in most unexpected places. Hanging from the ceiling were the family stores of flitches of bacon, venison, skins of wild animals, and strings of dried apples, ears of corn and pumpkins. The floors were sanded, and before the introduction of glass the small windows were of oiled paper. After glass came into use, the panes were at first diamond-shaped with lead casings.

High chests of drawers, huge carved chests, stiff old-fashioned chairs, and stools, and high-post bedsteads with hangings, formed the furniture of the other rooms. The food was plain. Samp, pounded maize, hasty puddings (or mush), succotash and yokéng, baked beans, bean-porridge and Indian pudding, were staple articles of diet. Norwich puddings were of huge size, and as famous among the local wits as New London dumplings.

The open wood-fire was for a long time the only mode of heating. There was no way of warming the churches, so that the women carried little foot stoves and the men sat with their feet incased in large leather overshoes called "boxes." The Franklin stove was not invented until 1741. Though the English cannel coal was occasionally used in the early part of this century, the hard anthracite did not come into general use until after 1820. The daughters of Daniel Lathrop Coit used to tell how their hope and faith in this new fuel were shaken, when their father brought from the West a lump of anthracite, placed it upon the burning logs in the open fire-place, and the assembled household waited long and in vain for the flame to appear. The draft not being strong enough, it obstinately refused to kindle. As wealth increased toward the middle of the eighteenth century, the style of building changed, the gambrel and other roofs replaced the lean-to, the beams and stairways were often carved, wide halls extended through the house, the rooms were heavily wainscoted, carpets were introduced, and deep window seats, and larger windows with square panes of glass took the place of the small high windows and diamond-shaped panes of the early days. Tall clocks, and more elaborately carved chairs, sofas and lounges appeared. Oil portraits, paintings on glass, and colored prints adorned the walls. China superseded the earthen and wooden ware, and silver began to take the place of pewter.

Paint came into use on houses toward the middle of the eighteenth century, and a cheerful coloring, principally red, but often yellow, blue and white prevailed. One inventory mentions a green house. Two colors were often used, one as a trimming. The almost universal use of white paint did not appear until toward the middle of the nineteenth century. Macdonald Clarke, in alluding to the changes in the style of building of this latter period, writes:—

> "Houses in clusters hang around
>   These pleasant hills, like nestling grapes,
> And ripening Taste I've lately found
>   Are giving them classic shapes.
> The Corinthian and the Doric styles
>   Mix'd with the old hum-drum,
> And some of our Grannies often smile
>   And say, 'What next'll come?'"

For a long time the only way of getting from place to place was by horseback, on saddle or pillion, and rude carts were used for the conveyance of goods. In 1768, the first stage-coach line was established between Norwich and Providence, running weekly, and leaving Lathrop's tavern every Wednesday morning.

Miss Caulkins relates that Samuel Brown set up the first chaise in Norwich, and was fined for riding in it to meeting. She also says that "Col. Simon Lathrop's effeminacy in this respect was excused on account of the feeble health of his wife." Only six chaises, or gigs (as they are now called), were owned in Norwich, at the time of the Revolution. "The owners of these six were: 1st, Gen. Jabez Huntington; this gig was large, low, square-bodied, and studded with brass nails, that had square and flat heads; it was the first in town that had a top which could be thrown back. 2nd, Col. Hezekiah Huntington. 3rd, Dr. Daniel Lathrop; this was regarded as a splendid vehicle; it had a yellow body, with a red morocco top, and a window upon one side. 4th, Dr. Theophilus Rogers. 5th, Elijah Backus, Esq. 6th, Nathaniel Backus, Esq., of Chelsea; this afterwards belonged to Capt. Seth Harding." *

Mrs. Sigourney, in her "Connecticut Forty Years Since," describes this chaise of Dr. Daniel Lathrop, when long past its prime: "This equipage (Madame Lathrop's), which moved rather slowly, was a chaise whose form displayed none of the light and graceful elegance of modern times. Its heavy body was painted a dun yellow, and studded thick at the sides and edges with brass nails. This supported a top, whose wide and low dimensions jutted over in so portentous a manner, that had a person of the height of six feet essayed to be benefited by its shelter, he must have persisted in maintaining that altitude which Dr. Franklin recommended to those who would enter his study. Its clumsy footstep, and uncurved shaft was so near the ground as greatly to facilitate the exploit of ascending, and likewise to diminish the danger of a fall in case of accident. This vehicle, which was of venerable antiquity, was the first of its kind which had been seen in the streets of Norwich. In those early days, it was viewed as a lamentable proof of aristocratic pride, particularly as on the back might be traced the semblance of a coat of arms. It was drawn by a heavy black steed, who some fifteen years before had been in his prime, and who had as much the habit of stopping at the abodes of poverty as Peveril's Black Hastings had of turning towards the window of mourning. In summer he was carefully guarded from the depredations of flies by a net made of twine, while one of bleached cotton with tassels and balls, exquisitely white, overshadowed his huge frame, when he bore his load on Sundays to the house of God."

* Miss Caulkins' History of Norwich.

The early roads were rough cart-paths, or foot paths, and until about the middle of the eighteenth century, there was little attempt to keep them in order. In 1794, Dr. Joshua Lathrop, having observed "that Norwich Town Street has many sloughs and bad places in it, which I don't see are like to be effectually mended in the common mode of highway work," gives $300 to be laid out on the improvement of the road, "beginning at the bridge below the widow Reynolds, and so round the old street by Benjamin Huntington, Jun., Esq., to the Bridge at the upper end of the Town Street."

The first road to New London was laid out about 1670, under the direction of Joshua Raymond, who for his services was granted a large farm on the route, which his descendants have recently sold. In 1789, an effort was made to improve this road; money was raised by a lottery granted for the purpose, and in 1792, it was made the first turnpike road in the United States. The toll-rate was as follows:—

Four-wheel carriages,	9 d.
Two-wheel carriages,	4½ d.
Loaded team,	3 d.
Empty team,	2 d.
Horse-cart, loaded,	2 d.
Horse-cart, empty,	1 d.
Neat cattle, etc., each,	1 d.
Pleasure sleigh,	3 d.
Loaded sled or sleigh,	2 d.
Empty sled or sleigh,	1 d.
Man and horse,	1 d.

CHAPTER III.

AMONG the early settlers, long cloaks, hats with broad brims and steeple-crowns, and square-toed shoes with enormous buckles were worn by both sexes. The men often wore boots with short, broad tops. The doublet was also used by both men and women, the former wearing it over a sleeved waistcoat, the sleeves often slashed and embroidered. Stiffly starched ruffs, falling bands and deep linen collars, gloves with heavily embroidered and fringed gauntlets, and large breeches tied with ribbons above the knee, later coming below the knee and fastened with buckles, completed the prevailing costume for men. Swords were suspended from elaborately embroidered belts. Long hair, though much inveighed against, remained in fashion until superseded by the wig. Laborers wore knit caps often ornamented with a tassel, and leather clothing, though the latter was frequently worn by the better sort.

Under the pointed stomacher and gown with elbow sleeves, the women wore petticoats of woolen, but sometimes of silk or brocade, and fine, stiffly starched aprons. The matrons wore caps, and silk and velvet hoods were much in vogue, as well as the riding-hood—a short cape with hood attached.

In 1676 a law was passed in Connecticut forbidding anyone with an estate of less than £150, to indulge in gold or silver lace, gold buttons, ribbons, bone-lace, &c., except the families of public officials, military officers, and those who had been reduced from a state of affluence; but these laws were little regarded, and the style of dress became much more costly and elaborate in the eighteenth century.

In the early part of this latter period wigs were worn, but later the long hair was combed back, powdered, and tied into a queue, which was bound with black ribbon. The men also wore three-cornered hats, deep, broad-skirted coats, sometimes black, but often gay in color, generally of broadcloth, but for full dress, of silk or brocade and trimmed with gold or silver lace; large, deep-pocketed under-waistcoats of holland, dimity, grogram, silk or velvet, often richly embroidered; neck bands, and ruffled or lace-trimmed shirts, with a trimming of the same at the wrist; small clothes ornamented at the knee with buckles; long stockings often of silk, and buckled shoes. Long cloaks, sometimes scarlet in color (Hopestill Tyler, of Preston, has in his inventory, 1733, an orange-colored cloak), and "roquelaures" (long, buttoned surtouts), were also worn.

The high-heeled, pointed slipper of kid, silk or satin replaced for women the square-toed shoe. For out-door wear, clogs, goloshes, and pattens* kept the fair wearers out of the mud. Hoops appeared, and over the rich silk or satin under-petticoat long trains were worn, which in the street were carried on the arm. Ruffles of lace adorned the neck and elbow sleeves. The hair was powdered, and brushed high over an under-cushion stuffed with wool, which necessitated for street-wear the calash, an immense silken structure ribbed with whalebone, which could be pulled and stretched at will over the mountain of hair, and which bobbed and swayed with every motion of the wearer.

Miss Caulkins quotes from a Norwich paper of 1780, a poem ridiculing this fashion:

> "Hail, great Calash! o'erwhelming veil,
> By all-indulgent heaven,
> To sallow nymphs and maidens stale,
> In sportive kindness given."

> "Safe hid beneath thy circling sphere,
> Unseen by mortal eyes,
> The mingled heap of oil and hair
> And wool and powder lies."

This high head structure, according to the Norwich Packet, made the female figure so

> "Heavy above and light below
> She sure must Tops-a-Turvey go,
> Unless she's in proportion."

---

*Pattens were formed of iron rings raised on upright supports and holding wooden soles fastened to the foot by leather straps. One of these curious specimens of foot-wear, belonging to a Huntington ancestress, is still preserved by a New London resident.

So hoops were introduced, as the poet goes on to say:—

> "Invention to complete the whole
> Produced a thing just like a bowl
> And placed it on the hip, sir,
> Which kept them all in equipoise,
> No longer now the sport of boys,
> Nor prone to make a slip, sir."

Just before the Revolution, turbans of gauze or muslin, adorned with feathers and ribbons, were worn, and a poem taken from a London paper, and printed in the Packet, alludes to this Gallic fashion of "martialized" and "cockatooned" heads. At this time great extravagance in dress prevailed. The daughters of Gen. Jabez Huntington, Elizabeth, who afterward married Col. John Chester, of Wethersfield, and Mary, who became the wife of the Rev. Joseph Strong, were sent to a boarding school in Boston, and an outfit of twelve silk gowns was deemed sufficient for the needs of one of the daughters, but the instructress wrote to the parents, that another gown of a rich stuff, recently imported, was absolutely necessary to complete her wardrobe.

At the beginning of the Revolution all these rich goods of foreign manufacture were discarded, and long home-made gray woolen stockings, top-boots, and garments of home-spun were adopted by the men, and simple gowns of domestic manufacture by the women. But this period of simple attire did not last long. After the struggle for liberty was over, the silks and satins again appeared, and costumes were as costly as ever. The Norwich Packet of 1784 deplores "the extravagance of the present day," inveighs against "the broadcloth coats, the silk gowns, the powder and feathers, the ruffles and cardinals, the silk stockings, and feet trappings, the feasts, the dancing parties, &c.," and asks "where is that simplicity of dress and manners, temperance in meats and drinks, which formed the virtuous character of our illustrious ancestors? O the degeneracy of the times!"

In 1793, according to the Norwich Weekly Register, to be in the fashion, one must have "a head, bonnet and all, as big as the head of a great pin, little tiny straw hats, a waist as large as the aforesaid pin, and bent forward in the middle at an angle of 135°, petticoats," &c., as usual, "the whole supported on the tips of the toes, and a little stick about three inches long at each heel."

A young Norwich girl, ~~Rebecca~~ Rachel Huntington (b. 1779), daughter of the Hon. Benjamin Huntington, and later the wife of William Gedney Tracy, of Whitestown, N. Y., writes from New York, in 1797, to her sister Lucy:—

"I have bought two bands, which are the most fashionable trimmings for beaver hats, a white one for the blue hat, and a yellow one for the black one, they should be put twice round the crown, & fastened forward in the form of a beau knot. Brother has got each of you a pink silk shawl which are very fashionable, also many ladies wear them for turbans, made in the manner that you used to make muslin ones last summer. George has given me one like them. The fine lace cost 10 shillings a yard, & I think it very handsome, there is enough for two handkerchiefs and two double tuckers, the way to make handkerchiefs is to set lace or a ruffle on a strait piece of muslin (only pieced in the back to make it set to your neck), & put it on so as to show only the ruffle, & make it look as if it was set on the neck of your gown, many Ladies trim the neck of their gowns with lace, & go without handkerchiefs, but I think it is a neater way to wear them with fashionable gowns, it will not be necessary to have much more than half a yard in the width of your tuckers."*

It was customary at this time, in the larger cities, to exhibit the fashions on dolls imported for this purpose from Europe, so this young girl dresses a doll in the latest style, to send to her sisters in the country. She writes:—

"I send a doll by Brother George, which I intended to have dressed in a neater manner but really could not find time. It however has rather a fashionable appearance, the cap is made in good form, but you would make one much handsomer than I could, the beau knot to Miss Dolly's poultice neck-cloth is rather large but the thickness is very moderate. I think a cap, crown and turban would become you. I have got a braid of hair which cost four dollars, it should be fastened up with a comb (without platting), under your turban if it has a crown, & over it if without a crown. Brother has got some very beautifull sattin muslin & also some handsome tartan plad gingham for your gowns, there is a large pattern for two train gowns of the muslin, which should be made three breadths wide, two

---

*Copied from the original letter, by permission of the writer's granddaughter, Julia Chester Wells, of West 31st Street, N. Y.

breadths to reach to the shoulder straps forward, and one breadth to be cut part of the way down before to go over the shoulder, and part of it to be pleated on to the shoulder straps meeting the back breadths, and some of it to go around the neck like the dolls—the pleats should be made pretty small, and not stitched to the lining, but you should wear binders over your shoulders, an inch and a half should be the width of your binders. (I must have done writing this pretty soon, the last sentence if you observe is quite poetical—but let me stick to my text Fashion). It is the fashion to have draw strings fastened on the corners of the shoulder straps, by the sleeves on the back, and have a tuck large enough for them to run in, made to cross on the back, run under the arms an inch below the sleeves & tie before. I should advise you to have your gingham ones made in that way with draw'd sleeves for sister Hannah, & I have seen as large ladies as you with them, & I think they would look very well for you. Sleeves should be made half a yard wide, and not draw'd less than seven or eight times. I think they look best to have two or three drawings close together, and a plain spot alternately. Some of the ladies have their sleeves covered with drawing tucks, and have their elbows uncovered. If you dont like short sleeves, you should have long ones, with short ones to come down allmost to your elbows drawed four or five by the bottom—if you want to walk with long gowns you must draw the train up thro' one of the pocket holes. I have bought some callico for chintz trimmings for old gowns, if you have any that you wish to wear short they are very fashionable at present & yours that are trimmed with them should be made only to touch the ground, there is enough of the dark stripe for one gown, & enough of the light for one, there should be enough white left on the dark stripe to turn down to prevent its ravelling. I gave 10 shillings for the callico & have been laughed at for my foolish bargain but I am not convinced that it is foolish. The Williams Street merchants ask three shillings a yard for trimmings like the wide stripe, & two for the narrow. The kid shoes are of the most fashionable kind, and the others of the best quality."

She writes again to her sister: "I am now engaged in making a gown for myself which (I rejoice to tell you) Fashion (that tyraness) will permit to swing above the dirty puddles and filthy seinque drains."

The fashions of the early part of the nineteenth century were comparatively simple. Mrs. Sigourney says that frocks low in the neck, and with short sleeves were worn for both winter and summer. A plain white frock, a broad blue or pink sash usually passed over the shoulder, and shoes of the same color was the usual costume on gala occasions of the young girl of that period. The hair was worn "full-mane or half-mane" (as Mrs. Sigourney's friend Nancy Maria Hyde had christened their style of hair-dressing), the one meaning "the whole mass of tresses pendent," the other "a portion confined by the comb, and falling gracefully over it." The dress for winter and summer varied very little; open-work stockings, kid slippers, a leghorn hat tied down with ribbon, a blue satin pelisse lined with yellow, and a white muslin gown being considered ample protection against the Boston east winds by a Norwich belle, who was going to that city for a winter's visit. Petticoats were few and scant. No wonder that Rev. Joseph Strong, in one of his anniversary sermons, alludes to "the pulmonary complaints," which, in the early years of his ministry, formed "an awful besom of destruction." Even the huge muffs, now seen occasionally unearthed from ancient attics, and which, in 1786, were of such huge size, that the Norwich Packet says "a Hermit's beard bears nothing in comparison," might at this period of light attire have proved some protection against the keen and piercing winter cold, but even these were frowned upon by English fashion writers, as rather "gross and bourgeois."

Men's coat tails became narrower at this period, powder was no longer used, and the hair was combed over the forehead very much in the style of the "dude" of later days. Ruffled shirts were still worn and high and full cravats. Blue coats with brass buttons were fashionable, and tall beavers appeared.

Sleighing parties to some half-way tavern, tripe suppers, turtle entertainments, afternoon tea parties, and dances which began early, and ended usually at nine o'clock, (on very festive occasions at one), and where the simple refreshment consisted of fruit, nuts, cake, and wine or cider, were the principal gaieties. Ordinations were a mild form of dissipation, and the clergy showed their skill in mixing the punch, which was a great feature of such occasions.

Thanksgiving day, Fast day, Election and Training days were the great holidays of the year. The Weekly Register of November, 1792, hopes that "the savage practice of making bonfires on the evening of Thanksgiving may be exchanged for some other mode of rejoicing, more consistent with the genuine spirit of christianity." Mrs. Daniel Lathrop Coit (b. 1767, d. 1848), used to tell her grandchildren of the Guy Fawkes day, observed in Norwich in her childhood. An effigy of straw was carried through the streets, and afterward burned, and she remembered snatches of the doggerel sung:—

> The fifth of November
> You must always remember;
> The Gunpowder Plot
> Must never be forgot.
> Ding! Dong!
> The Pope's come to town.

It is said that in Portsmouth, N. H., November 5th is still observed by the boys with bonfires. Miss Caulkins mentions that Washington, in one of his

army orders, prohibited the soldiers from any demonstrations on Guy Fawkes or Pope-day out of deference to our French allies, and that the New London boys, for the same reason, were persuaded during the war to give up their usual celebration.

After the Revolution was over, Pope-day revived again, and the New London authorities then prevailed upon the populace to substitute Sept. 6th, the day that Arnold burnt the town, and to burn the traitor in effigy instead of the Pope. Patriotic motives may have also influenced the Norwich boys to transfer their annual barrel burning to our New England festal day, and long may they keep up this custom, peculiar to the town.

CHAPTER IV.

CLASS distinctions were very marked in the early days of the country. The title of Esq. (or "Squire") was only used by officials and persons of distinction. Mr. was applied to clergymen, and deputies, and those known to be of good English descent. Only a very few were allowed to write after their names "gentleman," or "gent" (as it was often written). "Goodman" was the common term for yeomen and farmers, and "goodwife" or "goody" for their wives. The office of deacon was highly esteemed, and also the positions of captain, lieutenant, ensign, and sergeant in the train-bands. The term mistress designated usually a young unmarried woman. Miss was not used until about the middle of the eighteenth century.

Though some of the settlers of Norwich were probably of humble origin, the greater part evidently belonged to the respectable middle classes of England, and some could trace descent from the landed gentry. The civil war and religious troubles had probably either diminished or made away with their property in many cases. They could bring but few household goods with them, as the difficulties of transportation were so great. Money was scarce, even in England, whence they came, so we find the great body of settlers, using all ways and means to make a fortune.

The lands must first be cleared, and the houses built. As laborers and servants were scarce, everyone must lend a hand. Each village must have its blacksmith, its cooper, weaver, shoemaker, carpenter and wheelwright, so in the new settlements the skilful mechanic always finds a warm welcome and a prosperous livelihood awaiting him. Those, who have not already learned a trade, find it for their interest to do so. Young men were obliged to serve an apprenticeship, usually of seven years, ere they were considered capable of starting in business for themselves.

The early laws of Connecticut allowed "no person or householder" to "spend his time idlely or unprofittably," for the constables were instructed to "use speciall care and dilligence to take knowledge of offenders in this kind," and to bring them before the courts; so if we could have looked in upon our forefathers in the early days of Norwich, we should have found them laboring to fulfil the scriptural injunction of doing with all their might whatever their hands found to do.

Farming operations were often combined with a trade, and those who were fortunate enough to possess capital became merchants, and as money was scarce, and country produce must often be taken in payment, cargoes of this were shipped to foreign lands; and by these "ventures," as they were called, fortunes were gradually accumulated. Almost all the prosperous merchants began life as captains of merchant ships, and so acquired a knowledge of the needs and resources of foreign markets. The hat, shoe, and carriage trades were especially prosperous, as great numbers of these articles were shipped to the West Indies; so shoe-shops, hat and carriage factories and tanneries abounded. The blacksmiths carried on a thriving trade in farming tools, and, during the war, in furnishing muskets and cannon for the army. A former inhabitant, writing of the business activity of Norwich, as he remembered it one hundred years ago, compared the place to a "beehive." The innkeeper was always an important member of the community. In early times only well-to-do citizens were licensed to keep an inn.

By the waters of the rapid Yantic and Shetucket, which at first were only utilized for the town saw-mill and grist-mill, were soon located, in the eighteenth century, fulling-mills, woolen-mills, foundries, oil-mills, paper mills, &c., followed in the nineteenth century by other industries, gradually increasing in number and size until the present day.

Now, with this short preamble, let us be prepared not to expect too much of our plain, quiet forefathers, as we start to wander through the town which they founded two hundred and thirty-five years ago.

CHAPTER V.

STARTING from Mill Lane (now Lafayette Street), the first home lot on the left, as we enter the main highway, is that of John Reynolds,* of whose antecedents we only know, that he came from that part of Saybrook, which is now Lyme, where he had married shortly before the emigration, Sarah, daughter of William Backus, and brought with him to Norwich his wife and four children— John, Sarah, Susanna, and Joseph. Four more children were born after his settlement in Norwich—Mary, Elizabeth, Stephen, and Lydia. He was by trade a wheelwright, and in his will he calls himself a kinsman of Ensign Thomas Leffingwell.

The two following entries of his home-lot will show how the early records vary. In the first book, it is described as of four and a quarter acres, abutting east

---

*It is possible that John Reynolds may be a descendant of either Robert or John Reynolds, early settlers of Watertown, who moved from there to Wethersfield. John Reynolds moved to Stamford, and Robert is believed to have returned to Massachusetts. The same names occurring in succeeding generations of the Norwich and Stamford Reynolds families may be an indication of kinship.

on the highway to the Landing Place, abutting north on the highway to the Great Plain, west on land of Lt. Thomas Leffingwell, south-east on the way to the Mill, with an addition on the south of six acres adjacent to it, abutting south on the land of William Hyde, and south-east on the highway to the Mill.

The second book gives the following record:—Six acres and ten acres of first division land, in all sixteen acres of meadow and upland, more or less, abutting on the Town Street, and the way to the Mill 68 rods, "being a crooked line," abutting south on land of Samuel Hyde 52 rods, abutting west on land of Thomas Leffingwell 31 rods,* "and the nor-west a crooked line being in length 10 rods," then abutting north on the highway 36 rods. The home lot was laid out in November, 1659, the first division land in April, 1661.

The highway to the Great Plain is the little lane between the Reynolds and Bliss properties, which, crossing the river at "the fording place," joins "the Great Plain path" near the residence of the late Hezekiah Rudd. This was ordered, in 1663, to be a pent highway, and so remained as late as 1793.

The house, and the land on which it stands, is still in possession of descendants of the first John Reynolds, but the greater part of the land has recently been sold by the family of Charles Reynolds (great-great-great-grandson of John Reynolds, the first propietor), to the founders of the hospital. The house, the framework of which, it is claimed, is the same that was erected by John Reynolds, the first proprietor, still retains its huge central chimney, and many old-fashioned features, though it has been greatly modernized. When first built, the entrance door was on the south, and by this door still stands the old well. The present street door opens into a hall, which was formerly a room, where the pillions and saddles were kept. This was always known as "the pillion room."

John, the first-born son of the proprietor, was killed by the Indians, while spreading flax "over Showtuckett River" in 1676. The account says that "Josiah Rockwell and John Renolls, Jun., were found dead, and thrown down ye River bank, theire scalps cutt off." The son of Josiah Rockwell, about thirteen years of age, was carried off by the Indians, but soon afterward restored to his friends.

To his only remaining son, Joseph, John, according to the early custom, deeds

* This is the "Point" lot now belonging to the W. W. Backus Hospital.

in 1690, the west "halfe" of the house and home-lot, and the other half in reversion on the death of himself and wife. In this deed he mentions the pond south of the house. This was probably the one recently drained and filled up in the laying out of the hospital grounds.

Joseph Reynolds marries Sarah, daughter of Richard Edgerton. In 1711-12 he was allowed liberty "to sett the shop, he hath already sett up the frame of, to sett the one halfe of sd shop in the street, and so to continue during the towne's pleasure." This may have been the old house which formerly stood facing the south close to the street, near the present entrance to the hospital grounds. In the early years of the century, this was occupied as a dwelling, and about the middle of the century, was moved down the lane to a site back of the Reynolds house, where it now remains. It is said to have been used formerly as a shop, but no one remembers the date of its erection, and no record of it has been discovered.

In 1714, Joseph Reynolds was licensed to keep a house of entertainment, and in 1717-18 (his wife having died in 1714), he deeds to his son John, his house and home lot, "except reserving" to himself "ye West Room," "ye Lodging Room, with ye Porch chamber" &c., "during my natural life," and then makes the wise, (but in this case) unnecessary provision "if I do marry again, and it shall please God to remove me by death, and leave my wife surviving that she shall have ye free use and benifet of ye west rooms and ye Lodging Room," &c., "during ye time of her living in sd house a widow."

This son John married in 1720, Lydia Lord, daughter of Captain Richard Lord of Lyme, and his wife, Elizabeth Hyde, who was the first child born in Norwich. This Lydia, Miss Caulkins says, "was an admirable Christian woman, surviving her husband more than forty years, and dying in 1786, aged 92." On her gravestone is inscribed, "Here lies a lover of Truth."

John and Lydia Reynolds had eight children, who married prominent inhabitants of Norwich, Middletown, and Lyme. Their eldest son, John, while visiting friends on Long Island in 1752, was killed by a riding accident, his horse running against a tree. His brother Joseph inherited the home-lot after the death of his mother. He had married in 1755, Phoebe Lee, daughter of Elisha and Hephzibah Lee of Lyme, and had eleven children. He died after a very short illness in 1792, and the house and home-lot came into the possession of the widow and son Elisha, who was second mate on the ship Gen. Lincoln. Elisha was lost overboard in a gale in 1799, while only three days out of New London. After the widow Phoebe's death in 1818, the daughters, Phoebe and Sarah, reside with Capt. Giles and Abigail L'Hommedieu, their sister and brother-in-law, who then owned the homestead.

Many years ago an old manuscript record of the Reynolds family was found in a Norwich Town attic, which says: "This family name is likely to become extinct in this town as there is not any of this name that will probably keep it up. It may truly be said of the most of those that descended from the first John, that they have been smart, active, sensible men and women for a period of 148 years; the few relatives which now remain will in a short time be off the stage, and the name will be forgotten, as there is not at this time, 1808, a man of the name living here." This melancholy prophecy is not yet fulfilled, as after the death of Capt. Giles L'Hommedieu, the nephews, Henry and Charles Reynolds, entered into possession of the property, and the heirs of Henry Reynolds still retain the old homestead.

An old journal exists, written by Abigail Reynolds (Mrs. Giles L'Hommedieu), which gives such a vivid and interesting picture of a young girl's mind and life one hundred years ago, that we venture to give a few extracts from it. The spelling is ingenious and characteristic of those days.

Abigail Reynolds.

"I have seated myself down to contemplate on the vanity of all human enjoyments, to read the book of Nature, and beholde the misteries of Divine Providence. Nature has put on its lovelyest charmes, and smiles in all its gayest attire, the virder of spring breaths forth ambrosial sweets, whence are these flowers but to please our sight, to captivate our senses, and to teach us admiration for the power who formed them, and to teach us our own frailty, our own dissolution."

At the age of sixteen, she goes to Lyme to visit her relatives, the Elys and the Griswolds. Here, she says, "a youth of brilliant appearance paid his addresses to me, and this was the first time in my life, that ever I was accosted

with the language of love. I heard the sound, but felt not its immotions—my young and bashful heart was quite confused at such an interview—words wanted utterance, nor could I answer him, only with a blush."

She writes, that she found him of "a caracter not pleasing to me," but, by the advice of friends gave him "admittiance" to visit her after her return home. "The indifferance with which I treated him, prompted him to retalliate, and his visit was delayed after the time appointed. I considered him as beneath my attention, and resolved to treat him with no more than common civillity. My heart, I was sure, was safe from his intrusion. I consider^d him void of that true dignity which constitutes a man of honnor. Very unexpectedly he came to visit me. I pretended not to know him during the whole evening. I treated him as one who had taken lodgings for the knight,—poor youth was obleaged to make himself known,—requested my forgiveness, which I granted, after pointing out the impoliteness he had treated me with, and forbad him to visit me more. He rose in the morning before the sun, and left us while we war yit in silant repose, this manieuvier put our family upon inquiry."

Another admirer soon appears, "a young lawyer of distinguished beauty," whom her brother Joseph met at the South. She is soon displeased that he should attempt to make a conquest of her heart "of the affect of flattery." She writes "he could not persuade me to think I was more than mortal," and she soon convinced him that "he carried his compliments to far." After this "he put on airs of respect, which I doughted he in reality felt, and took care to believe as much as I thought proper." The admirer soon "retired to his father's seat in the country," and shortly after this her two sisters "ware anockolated for the small pox," and were absent from home for four weeks. "Overjoyed at their returne" she "inconsiderately flew to meet them." "But," she writes, "how just was our imprudence rewarded."

In four days after their arrival, she went to Saybrook to visit her relatives, and was there "taken sick." "My secret conjectors ware, that I had the small-pox, but I dare not make it known, and was willing to put that dismal idea from me, as it afflicted my mind, and added greatly to my bodily distress,—the third night after my illness,—My good Mrs. Wood came into my room with a countinance which expressed a great tenderness and conscearn. She informed me my disorder terminate in the small-pox—she was sure I had every symtom—altho my fears ware great, yet theas words struck me like thunder.—The next day, I was conveyed to a hospital—everyone in the hous ware intire strangers to me, and it resembled the abode of savages more than that of sivilized people. I was taken like an infant from the shays, and laid in a low bunck, instead of an ornamental dress I was covered with rags. My friend Mary who accompany^d me to this dreary place left me to the company of a noisy gang who felt not my distress."

She had the disease very badly, and writes, "This affliction was subsurviant to my good. While it disfigured my extarnal form, it was a lesson of virtue to my soul." She returned to her parents "more a child of pity than of pleasure." "My appearance shocked every beholder." I had not been home more than a fortnait, when Alfaret (this is the name she gives to her last admirer), "came to visit me." She says she felt "quite disconscearted at his appearance." He stayed three days, gave her "the offer of his hand" and assured her she "had his heart" but she considered "his love but momentary" and "refused to encourage him."

She then continues: "When he left us, I was blest with an indulgent father, but now that loved voice is no more, but a fortnat after his diparture Heaven was pleased to bereave us of that tender parent. But that God of infinite goodness, who bestows our blessings and preserves our lives has an undoughted right to us, and we must acquiesce in all his dealings. I can never forget with what composure he bad adieu to everything mortal. O what an awful scean! Death how frightful is thy appearance. I have seen but felt its terrors,—his illness was from Saturday til Monday noon, when (I trust) all his pains ware ended, the 10th of December, 1794, it is now two years since this bereaveing stroke of Providence, and every sircomstance is still fresh in my memory."

Then follows a poem on her father's death, and many melancholy reflections, which ended with another visit to Saybrook at the Lay's, and also at Gov. Matthew Griswold's. On her return home she became engaged to Giles L'Hommedieu. She writes: "In the twenty-second year of my age, on the 10th day of May, 1795, did

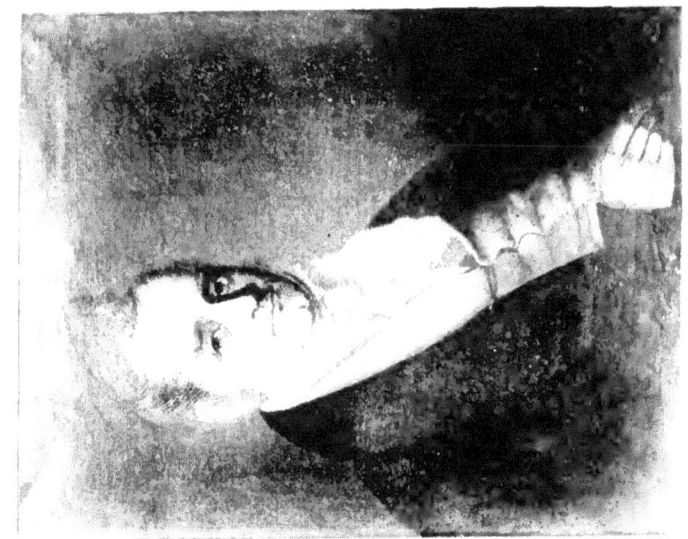

I binde myself with the indisolviable tie of marriage to a man of my choice, happy hour, never to be forgotten, and I hope never to be repented of."

After her marriage, she gives the account of two "voiges" taken with her husband, who was a sea captain, in 1808-9, to Virginia, which are extremely interesting. In one part of her journal, she says: "I have retired to my chamber to reflect on the maloncholy situation of the times" and then proceeds to tell of the small pox epidemic in Boston, in 1792, which raged for two or three months, "when all business was stopped, and a great part of the people left the town, and great numbers ware swept away by this shocking disease," of the "pestilence" which appeared in Philadelphia the summer following, "to which 'tis supposed one third of the inhabitants fell a sacrafice." "Hundreds ware buried in a day. Some ware well and dead in the course of a few hours." "Parents denyed children, and children denyed parents thair assistance—when once they fell they had none to help, the markets ware stopped, and those that ware left almost perished for want of food." "Thair was no remedy for some time—almost everything was tryed but inaffectnas, till they applyed cold water and fresh air, which proved very beneficial and releaved many."

"The next year after this disease broak out in New Haven, but proved not so mortal as before,—to prevent its proving so fatal, when they first began to feel this disorder, which took them with a violent pain in the head, and continual puking, the phisions bled them almost to death, to take away the putrifaition which made the disease more favourable."

"For the three last years the ajasient towns have been visited with distressing sickness called the canker rash." She also speaks of New York, as afflicted, in 1795, with "the same voilent disease which raged first in Philadelphia." In this same year she writes: "Connecticut has been afflicted with a severe dearth" (the word "drouth" has been commenced, but the spelling uncertain, has been partly erased and dearth substituted). "Our feailds, trees and wells have suffered from its effects,—from May to February we have been blest with but few small showers,—but none sufficiant to reach the springs." All these afflictions we may suppose, like the small-pox, were also "subsurviant to good," and so perhaps was the influenza which the Norwich Weekly Register alludes to as having "again made its appearance" in Norwich in 1793, "more than half the people being now under the operation of it." Abigail L'Hommedieu died in 1851, and her husband, Capt. Giles, in 1859, in the ninety-fourth year of his age, just six days after the celebration of the Norwich Bi-Centennial.

CHAPTER VI.

JUST beyond the little lane or "highway to Great Plain" lies the home-lot of Thomas Bliss, of five and a quarter acres, abutting east on the Town street 20 rods, south on the highway to Great Plain 58 rods, west on the river 16 rods, and north on the land of Stephen Backus 36 rods. This extends from the lane to the land of the late Benjamin Huntington.

Thomas Bliss was the son of Thomas Bliss, who was born in Okehampton, in the parish of Belstone, County Devonshire, England, came to Braintree (now Quincy), Mass., in 1635, and from thence went to Hartford, where he died in 1650. His widow, Margaret, an enterprising, capable woman, went with her other children to Springfield, Mass., where her descendants still remain. But the son, Thomas, though a home-lot had been assigned to him at Hartford, moved to Saybrook. He married, in 1644, Elizabeth ———, and came with the first settlers to Norwich in 1660.

His eldest son, Thomas, died in 1681-2, and the father in 1688, leaving to his only surviving son, Samuel, the house and home lot. This Samuel Bliss married, in 1681, Ann, daughter of John Elderkin. He was a merchant, and among the many valuable family papers owned by his great-great-great-grandson, Mr. John Bliss, of Brooklyn, L. I., are an account of Samuel Bliss with Daniel Johonnot, "the wine merchant of Boston," from 1704-6, for Rum, leather gloves, "hogs fatt," pork, &c., for which Samuel gives country pay, in pork, beeswax, "Baiberry wax," beaver skins, otter, mink, and "Deare" skins; another account with a Mr. Leaske from 1703-6 in which Samuel Bliss is credited with 14 "bare" skins, pork, "rackoon," mink, fox, and beaver skins &c.; the New London custom house clearance of the sloop Ann, in April, 1697, with a cargo of wooden ware, earthen ware and powder; the bill of sale from John Richards and Thomas Avery to Samuel Bliss, in 1705, of 1/8 part of the sloop Love and Ann for £46, 9s., 1d.; and another bill of sale dated 1700 from John Chandler of 1/8 part of the "brigantoon" Success, "about 54 tons burthen" for £37. In Aug., 1705, Samuel Bliss ships to Barbadoes in the sloop Love and Ann, Richard Calder, master, a new water hogshead, 1049 staves, and a horse, "paying frait for said horse ten pounds if he lives, and nothing if he dies."

In 1718, and again in 1722-3, he is accused of selling liquor to the Indians. The fine for this offense was 20s., one-half to go to the complainant; and as the Indian, Apeannchsuck, when brought before the justice, and sentenced to pay a fine of 10s., or to be "whipt 10 lashes on ye naked body," accused Samuel Bliss "yt he sold him two pots of cider," he obtained the money necessary to pay the fine, and doubtless went off rejoicing. Ann, the wife of Samuel Bliss, was disciplined by the church in 1724 for "neglecting the ordinances of religion," but was "restored" to all the privileges of membership in 1736. Her brother, John Elderkin, who had also been "under discipline" was "restored" in 1735.

In 1729, Samuel Bliss deeds to his second son, Samuel Bliss, Jun., his house and home lot, and dies in 1731. Samuel Bliss, Jun., had married, in 1715, Sarah Packer, probably daughter of John Packer, of Groton, and died in 1763.

The inventory of the sister of Samuel Bliss, 2nd, Elizabeth, widow of Capt. Daniel White, of Middletown, who came back to the homestead after the death of her husband in 1726, and died in 1757, is rather interesting as illustrative of the dress of that period.

To quote from Miss Caulkins, she had "gowns of brown duroy, striped stuff, plaid stuff, black silk crape, calico, and blue camlet, a scarlet cloak, a blue cloak, satin-flowered mantle, and furbelow scarf, a woolen petticoat with a calico border, a camlet riding hood, a long silk hood, velvet hood, white hoods trimmed with lace, a silk bonnet, 19 caps, a cambrick laced handkerchief, silk do., linen do., 16 handkerchiefs in all; a muslin laced apron, flowered laced apron, green taffety apron, 14 aprons in all; a silver ribband, silver girdle and blue girdle, 4 pieces of flowered satin, a parcel of crewel, a woman's fan, Turkey worked chairs, a gold necklace, a death's head gold ring, a plain gold ring, sett of gold sleeve buttons, gold locket silver hair peg, silver cloak clasps, a stone button set in silver, a large silver tankard, a silver cup with two handles, do. with one handle, and a large silver spoon."

Samuel Bliss, 2nd, leaves to his son John (b. 1717), the house and home-lot. From this son John, who died in 1809, the property passes to his son John (b. 1748-9), who dies unmarried in 1815. John Bliss, 2nd, wills it to his brothers Elias and Zephaniah. Elias was a bachelor, but Zephaniah had married in 1794, Temperance, daughter of Ebenezer Lord, and grandaughter of the Rev. Benjamin Lord. John Bliss, 1st, (b. 1717), was distinguished as a bridge builder. A model still remains in the possession of his great-grandson and namesake, John Bliss, of Brooklyn, L. I., of a bridge built by him, and known as "Geometry Bridge." It is thus described in a newspaper article of June 20, 1764:

"Leffingwell's Bridge over Shetucket River at Norwich Landing is completed. It is 124 ft. in length, and 28 ft. above the water. Nothing is placed between the abutments, but the bridge is supported by Geometry work above, and calculated to bear a weight of 500 tons. The work is by Mr. John Bliss, one of the most curious mechanics of the age. The bridge was raised in two days, and no one hurt. The former bridge was 28 days in raising."

This bridge is supposed to have stood on the site of the present Laurel Hill bridge. It is said that John Bliss, in early life, desiring to learn the art of paper manufacture, journeyed on horseback to Germantown, there sold his horse, and travelled on foot to Philadelphia, where was located a large paper factory, in which he applied for employment as a common operative; and long after, he was able to put the knowledge so gained to practical use in building for Col. Christopher

Leffingwell the first paper mill in Connecticut, in 1766. He also built a chocolate mill, and a grist mill for Christopher and Elisha Leffingwell.

From Elias and Zephaniah, the property passed to George, Sarah, and Lydia, children of Zephaniah. After the death of George Bliss, the two sisters occupied the homestead for many years, and dying, left it to a nephew, Charles Bliss, who sold it, in 1885, to its present owner, Angell Stead. The house has always been kept in good repair and though the chimney was rebuilt, has probably been otherwise little altered since first erected, and still retains its old lean-to.

The small, old, gambrel-roofed house, which formerly stood near the lane, and which was torn down in 1894, was at one time a stocking factory, and the traces of red paint, its original color, and the faint outline of a stocking could still be seen upon the door, just before its destruction. The first deed of the building, in which it is called "the red shop," is dated 1809, but it is known to have been in existence long before that date.

Now the shops in Norwich were many, and were constantly changing occupants, and the advertisements of those in this neighborhood, always locate them indefinitely, "just below the shop of Christopher Leffingwell," or "a few rods south of the store of Tracy & Coit." As this "red shop," and another between the Sheltering Arms and the house of Mr. William Bliss on the corner, are the only ones we know of, to which this description would apply, we assume that this is the shop, in which Louis Barral or (Barrel) carried on his business of stocking weaving in 1792, "a few rods south of Tracy & Coit's store."

In 1784, Louis "Barrel" advertises that he has just moved into the shop lately occupied by Samuel Leffingwell, and as no advertisement has been found between 1784 and 1792 to indicate a removal on the part of Barrel, we may suppose that Samuel Leffingwell had also been an occupant of this building. Where Louis Barrel (or Barral or Bariel) came from, we have not ascertained, but he married in 1780, Mary Beckwith, and the births of two children are recorded in Norwich, Mary (b. 1782), and Louis (b. 1784). The entries of baptism of Henry (1781), and Lucretia (1787), children of Louis and Mary "Baral," are to be found in the Christ Church records. In 1785, Louis "Baral" buys land on Mill Lane of Joseph Reynolds, and builds the house, at present occupied by Hunt, the florist, and owned by Mrs. Goldsworthy. In the latter part of 1792, intending to leave Norwich, he offers his house and shop for sale or to rent, and in 1795, he is living in Northampton, Mass. Philip Hyde purchases the house in 1800, and after his death it is sold to David Yeomans in 1826, and in 1846 to Daniel Tree, the father of Mrs. Goldsworthy. It is said that Mill Lane was later christened Lafayette Street, to commemorate a call that Lafayette made at this house upon Louis Barrel, who was a Frenchman. This was possibly in 1785, when the General was in America for a short time.

There is no record of the lease of the shop, but in 1793, William Cox, another stocking weaver, moves into Barrel's shop from his former stand "opposite Col. Leffingwell's Long Row." Miss Caulkins says that both Barrel and Cox were foreigners. William and Anna Cox, children of William and Sarah Cox, were baptized, in 1780, in Christ Church, Norwich. The marriage probably of William Cox, 2nd, to Polly Averill, of Preston, in 1809, is to be found in the town records, and the births of two children, Olive (1811), and Mary Abby (1813). The William Cox who in 1837 marries Elizabeth Thompson, John Cox who in 1829 marries Mary M. Baker, and George who marries Maria Merryfield in 1854, may also belong to this family.

This shop is said to have been at one time used as a turning shop by Elias

Bliss, and also by the firm of John and Consider Sterry, and Epaphras Porter, as the printing office for their paper, "The True Republican." This must have been between 1804-7. At the death of John Bliss in 1809, "the red shop" and garden became the property of his son William (b. 1766), and the shop was converted into a house (dimensions 40 x 13 ft.), which was sold by William to Elias Bliss in 1826. George Bliss taught school here in the winter of that year. This old building was for many years occupied by the Lowrey family, and at the time of its destruction was owned by Angell Stead.

The north part of the Bliss lot, with a frontage of 5 rods, 17 links, was deeded by John Bliss, in 1784, to his son Zephaniah. Shortly before 1783, Zephaniah had built a house upon the lot, which, according to a deed in the possession of Mr. John Bliss, of Brooklyn, resembled in "modle and dimensions 38 x 29 ft.," the house now standing on the west side of North Washington Street, just below the corner of Lafayette Street, and now occupied by Thomas Moran, except that the Zephaniah Bliss house had a lean-to in the rear. Zephaniah Bliss was not married until 1794, so probably did not occupy the house, but Jackson Browne, an Englishman, was living here in 1801, when it was burnt to the ground, and his little daughter, Sophia, about seven years of age, perished in the flames. The Browne family moved to the Teel House on the Parade (now the Park Church parsonage, but formerly well known as the residence of Gen. William Williams). Mr. Browne went later to Barbadoes, where he died in 1804. Mr. Charles Miner thus alludes to the Brownes* in his recollections of Norwich. "Note that dashing gentleman and lady on the fine pair of blacks. They have a foreign air. It is Jackson Browne, supposed to be an agent of the British Commissary Department. They do not stop to have a gate opened, but bound over it as if in pursuit of a fox."

In 1828, the Bliss heirs sold this land to Mrs. Hannah Lathrop, widow of Thomas Lathrop, who built the house now standing on the lot. The Bliss family

---

*Children of Jackson and Eliza Browne:

Louisa,
Emily,
Jackson,
Thomas Sanford,   } Bapt., 1801, in Christ Church.

Sophia—Perished in the burning of the house in 1801, aged 7.

made many acquisitions of land, and perhaps the spirit which animated Samuel Bliss, 2nd, to retard the building of the Second Church, in 1760, by his determination "not to sell an inch" of his adjoining land, has descended from generation to generation, for the heirs still retain a large portion of their early grants.

CHAPTER VII.

JUST across the street from the Bliss home-lot, was that of Lieut. Thomas Leffingwell, with a frontage of 61 rods on the main road, and of 25 rods on the highway leading into the woods (now the road by the Sheltering Arms). It was first recorded as six acres, more or less, abutting west on the highway to the Landing Place, north on the highway into the woods, east "on the top of the ledge of rocks," with an addition of 18 acres of "plow" and rocky land adjacent, abutting south and west on the land of Christopher Huntington, and south-east on the brook.

In the second record, the points of the compass have changed, the ledge has moved to the north, and with the Christopher Huntington land on the south, has become the property of Joseph Bushnell. This record gives the property as "12 acres,—abutting north on the land of Joseph Bushnell 17 rods, abutting west on the highway 86 rods, abutting south-east on the land of Joseph Bushnell 20 rods, abutting east on his own pasture land, with 10 acres of pasture land, abutting west on his home-lot, and land of Joseph Bushnell, east on the Rocks, and northerly to a point." These measurements bring the north line of the lot beyond the old Samuel Leffingwell barn, which stood, until within a few months, north of the house of Thomas Gilroy.

This is the Thomas Leffingwell, who, about the year 1645, when Uncas was besieged by the Narragansetts at his fort on Shantok Point, nearly opposite Poquetanock, and reduced to a starving condition, "loaded a canoe with beef, corn, and pease, and under cover of the night paddled from Saybrook into the Thames, and had the address to get the whole into the fort." At the dawn of day, Miss Caulkins says, "the Mohegans elevated a large piece of beef on a pole," to show their enemies the relief they had obtained. When the Narragansetts learned that the English had come to the assistance of Uncas, they abandoned the siege. Trumbull says, "For this service, Uncas gave said Leffingwell a deed of great part, if not the whole town of Norwich."

There is, however, no record of such a deed, but in 1667, Leffingwell, petitioning the General Court to confirm to him some land offered by Uncas in return for this great service, received 200 acres on the east side of the Shetucket river.

At the time of Thomas Leffingwell's arrival in Norwich, he was in the prime of life, about 37 or 38 years of age. According to a family tradition, cited by Miss Caulkins, he came to America from Croxhall, County Yorkshire, England, when 14 years old, but returned to England at the age of 21, and married Mary White. He then came back to America, bringing with him a younger brother, Stephen, 15 years of age. The births of four sons, Thomas, Jonathan, Joseph and Nathaniel, and of two daughters, Rachel and Mary, are recorded at Saybrook. Another son, Samuel, was probably born in Norwich, though his birth was not registered. It is possible that Jonathan and Joseph died before the family moved to Norwich, as there is no further trace of them. Rachel married Robert Parke, and Mary became the wife of Joseph Bushnell.

Lt. Leffingwell took a leading part in the new settlement, was frequently chosen townsman, and was one of the first deputies to the General Court, which office he held for many years. He also served in the Courts of Commission, was chosen ensign of the train-band in 1672, rendered important service in the Indian wars, and in 1680 received his commission as lieutenant. He had many grants, and made many purchases of land, and became a wealthy man for those days; but all these lands he divided among his heirs before his death. Miss Caulkins thinks this occurred about 1710, but in September, 1714,* Thomas Leffingwell "(yeoman)" "in ye consideration of my comfortable maintainence Dureing my naturall life, . . . by my grandson Samuel Leffingwell" deeds him "all my home-lot that is not disposed of before ye date hereof, with ye Buildings upon it," &c., &c.; and Richard Bushnell testifies that "ye subscriber, Thomas Leffingwell personally appeared, and acknowledged the above written instrument to be his own voluntary act and deed before me." At this time, Lt. Leffingwell must have been about 92 years of age.

The grandson Samuel (b. 1691) was the son of Lt. Leffingwell's son Samuel, who had married in 1687, Ann Dickinson. The mother and father both died in 1691, probably leaving the child to the care of the grandparents, and he grew up to be the support and comfort of their old age. He married in 1725, Judith, daughter of Christopher Huntington, 2nd, and lived in the old homestead until 1731-2, when he bought two farms on Plain Hills, of Thomas Bingham and Samuel Griswold, and sold his house and home-lot to his brother-in-law, Hezekiah Huntington. The deed reads, "bounded, beginning at the west corner by the Town Street, from thence running east as the fence stands (abutting north on the street or highway), to the slaughter-house." A later deed of this same property gives this highway frontage as 3½ rods, which would locate the slaughter-house just below the Sheltering Arms, and unpleasantly near the Leffingwell mansion.

Col. Hezekiah Huntington, son of Christopher Huntington, 2nd, was the third proprietor of this house. He was born in Norwich, 1696, and married (1) 1719, Hannah Frink, whom we believe to be a daughter of Samuel and Hannah (Miner) Frink of Stonington, Ct. She died in 1746, and he married (2) 1748-9, Dorothy (Paine) Williams, daughter of Nathaniel and Dorothy (Ransford) Paine and widow of John Williams of Bristol, R. I.

In 1737, Hezekiah Huntington was appointed deacon of the First Church,

---

*Lt. Leffingwell must have died shortly after, as in Jan., 1714-15, Thomas Leffingwell, 2nd, signs his name without the Junior.

OLD INDIAN BURYING-GROUND AT MOHEGAN.

SITE OF UNCAS'S FORT.

[These photographs are contributed by Governor L. Buckley, of Norwich, Conn., who, after many explorations of the river shore in search of Indian relics, has decided that this is the only spot, which, in its natural features, its steep, easily defended sides, the spring by the bank, and the remains of stone-work, answers to the description of the old fort of Uncas. It lies near the Mohegan Station, north of the old burying-ground, and nearly opposite Poquetanock.]

and in 1746, he had a slight "difference" with his pastor, which was happily "accomodated." This "difference" was not explained, but it may have had some connection with the later accusation brought against him by Dr. Benjamin Wheat, of sympathizing with the seceding Separatists, and allowing them to hold a meeting at his house. This accusation was afterward retracted by Dr. Wheat, who confessed that it was instigated "by a lack of brotherly love."

In 1761, Col. Huntington was connected with John Ledyard of Hartford, William Williams, Col. Eleazer Fitch, and Jonathan Trumbull of Lebanon, in a contract to furnish supplies to the colonial army. He was prominent in all town affairs, and the early Revolutionary movements; was a deputy to the General Court for many years; and in 1739 was appointed lieut.-colonel of the Third Regiment. He was also a Judge of Probate and of the County Court; and, while engaged in his official duties, died suddenly at New London in 1773, and was buried in the Norwich Town burying-ground, where, on his grave-stone may be read, "His piety, affability, prayers and example, wisdom, and experience endeared him to his friends and the State;" and to this is added,—

> "And all Judah and ye Inhabitants of Jerusalem
> Did him Honour at his Death."

His widow Dorothy died in 1774 in her sixty-seventh year, after a short illness, "having labored under bodily infirmities for many years."

Eight daughters and four sons were born to Hezekiah, but one by one the children, and many of his grandchildren passed away; and at his death in 1773, his grandson, Hezekiah Williams, son of his daughter Eunice, inherited the house. This grandson (b. 1762), died in 1790, leaving a widow Dorothy and a young son, Hezekiah, who died in 1815 aged 25, and Hinman mentions this coincidence, related to him by Nathaniel Shipman, that Col. Samuel Coit and Col. Hezekiah Huntington were both colonels of militia, and Judges of the County Court at the same time. Nine children of each family arrived at maturity. In 1835, all that remained of the blood of Col. Hezekiah Huntington was contained in the veins of five children of the Hon. Frederick Wolcott of Litchfield, while Col. Coit's descendants numbered over five hundred.

During the minority of Hezekiah Williams, the house was rented, and Miss Caulkins says that Capt. William Hubbard occupied it for many years.

William Hubbard (b. 1740), was the son of Daniel Hubbard of New London, and Martha Coit, daughter of John and Mehetabel (Chandler) Coit. Daniel Hubbard (b. 1706), was the son of Rev. John and Mabel (Russell) Hubbard of Jamaica, L. I., and descended from a long line of distinguished ancestors. His great-grandfather, Rev. William Hubbard of Ipswich, was the historian of the Indian wars. Daniel Hubbard graduated at Yale in 1727, was for a while a tutor of the college, then settled at New London as a lawyer, and became High Sheriff of New London county. He celebrated his appointment to this office, by opening his house for the reception of guests at an evening entertainment, July 28, 1735. He was "of upright and honored life, religious and poetic."

The following letter addressed to

Mr Jhon Coit

att

N—London.

will show how his wooing was conducted 164 years ago:

"Honoured Sir & Mad^m, J blush & tremble on my knees while J study how to approach your Presence, to ask of you a Blessing for which J have long address'd ye Skies. From my first Acquaintance at your House I have wish'd my Happiness thence; nor have I yet found it in my Power to seek it from an Other. My careful Thoughts with ceaseless Ardors commend ye Affair to that Being, who alone inspires a pure & refined Love. The Eye-Lids of ye Morning discover me in my secret Places, with my first Devotions solliciting ye dear important Cause; and ye Evening-Shades are conscious to ye Vows J make for ye f^r Creature, who next to Heaven holds the Empire of my Heart. And now while I write J pray ye great Master of Souls to incline yours to favour my Address. By ye Love of God J beseech you—Ye happy Parents of my Partner Soul—but J forbare till J may be honoured with ye Oppertunity of a personal Application. In ye mean time

I consecrate my best wishes To y' Interest of y' Family—& with y' highest Respect subscribe my Self, Sir and Madam, y' most devoted most humble Serv'nt
D. HUBBARD

Stonington, Decem'br 1730."*

"The partner soul" and her parents were not unmoved by these ardent protestations of love, and Daniel and Martha were married in August, 1731. After the death of Daniel, the widow married in 1744, Thomas Greene, son of Nathaniel and Ann (Gould) Greene of Boston, Mass., whose first wife was Elizabeth, daughter of John Gardiner of Gardiner's Island. A portrait of the fair Martha, and one of her second husband, Thomas Greene, painted by Copley, are in the possession of their great-grandson, Rev. David Greene Haskins, D. D., of Cambridge, Mass.

Capt. William Hubbard married in 1764 his first cousin, Lydia, daughter of Capt. Joseph and Lydia (Lathrop) Coit, then of New London, but later residents of Norwich. In 1773, he was established in business in Norwich as a member of the firm of Hubbards & Greene. Their store was in that part of Norwich, then known as Chelsea or the Landing. In the early part of his residence in Norwich, Capt. Hubbard occupied the Benedict Arnold house, but in 1776, he had moved to the Hezekiah Huntington house, and advertises in February of that year to sell at this house a variety of articles, window glass, nail rods, coffee, sugar, brandy, &c. In September of that year, he advertises again at his Landing Store. In 1777, he calls upon "the humane and benevolent farmers" to furnish him with "a part of that bounty Heaven has blessed them with," "that he may have it in his power to sell to those who stand in greatest need."

In November, 1778, Lydia, his wife, died of consumption, having, as her father, Joseph Coit, writes in his diary, "been in a decline 5 months and a half. Most remarkable was her faith, patience and Resignation, even from the first to the last—a day or two before her death, I asked her if she had no scruples that she was deceived, and after a short pause, she answered, not the least, for, said she,—I know whom I have believed I have the witness in myself and ye spirit of God witnesseth with my spirit that I am a child of God."

The Norwich Packet says: "Few of her sex were more esteemed or

*From N. E. Historical and Genealogical Register of October, 1894.

engaging. An enemy to all forbidding moroseness, both of temper and conduct; she in life exemplified the fact that cheerfulness and piety are not incompatible."

William Hubbard married (2) about 1779, Joanna Perkins, daughter of James and Joanna (Mascarene) Perkins of Boston, Mass. Joanna was of Huguenot descent. Her great-grandfather, Jean Mascarene, a councilor of France, and of a distinguished Languedoc family, imprisoned and finally exiled from France for his devotion to the Protestant faith, wrote, while in prison: "Although my religion passes for a crime, and I well know that but for my religion I should not be in my present position, I make bold to justify this so-called crime, and choose rather to be the criminal I am, than to recover all I have lost." He lived for ten years in exile, and died in 1698, aged thirty-eight years. His son, Jean Paul Mascarene, the grandfather of Joanna Hubbard, fled from France to England, there entered the army, rose to high rank, and was appointed governor and commander-in-chief of the province of Nova Scotia, which office he held from 1740 to 1749. He then retired to Boston, where he died in 1760, aged seventy-five.

In 1784, the firm of Hubbards and Greene dissolved partnership, and shortly after William Hubbard moved to Boston. In 1788, his wife Joanna died, and in 1789, his eldest son William, and another son aged nine years, the child of his second wife; and in 1790 he was again afflicted in the death of his daughter Lydia, wife of Thomas Lathrop, and of another son, Joseph, aged twenty years. The marble slab inserted in the tomb-stone of the Hubbard family in the Norwich Town burying-ground, having been within the last year removed, and destroyed, we will give the inscription entire:

"Tomb of Lydia Hubbard, daughter of Joseph & Lydia Coit, & wife of William Hubbard, who died Nov. 2, 1778, aged 37 years, also the remains of four children of William & Lydia Hubbard, Lydia Lathrop, wife of Thomas Lathrop, who died Dec. 26, 1790, aged 25, William who died Sept. 10, 1789, aged 22, Joseph who died May 25, 1790, aged 20, Lucretia who died Oct. 14, 1775, aged 5.

> "Each humane virtue their mild eyes exprest,
> And a young heaven was opened in their breasts;
> In the last hour their triumph shone complete,
> And death disarm'd sat smiling at their feet.
> And now, thou faithful stone, proclaim aloud,
> A Christian is the noblest work of God."

William Hubbard died in Colchester, Ct., in 1801, aged 61 years. During his residence in Norwich, he was most active in all benevolent enterprises, and gave largely to public improvements, notably the widening and beautifying of Crescent Street, and the old cross highway.

At the beginning of the Revolution many Boston citizens sought a quiet refuge in Norwich, among others, Dea. William Phillips, who, it is said, arrived in a coach with outriders, and lived for a while in the Benedict Arnold house. Rev. Joseph Howe of the New South Church, the family of Josiah Quincy, and some of the Greenes also came to Norwich, the latter residing with Capt. William Hubbard during their stay in town. It is said that when the Greenes returned to Boston, that Zachary, an Indian runner, carried their little daughter in a basket, fastened by a leather strap bound around his head.

Two of the daughters of Hezekiah Huntington, Eunice and Lucy, married, the former John Williams in 1757, the latter Samuel Williams in 1741, possibly relatives or sons of the widow Dorothy Williams, Col. Hezekiah's second wife. John Williams, the husband of Eunice, was lost at sea in 1764, and his wife, Eunice, died in 1766, leaving two children, John (b. 1760), and Hezekiah (b. 1762). To Hezekiah, his namesake, Col. Hezekiah wills the house, and the two young men possibly live here while in business together in 1786. The shop, which they advertise as a few rods south of Col. Christopher Leffingwell's, may possibly be the one between their grandfather's house, and the house now known as the "Sheltering Arms," for one formerly stood there, though we have not yet given its history. Hezekiah later moved to the Landing.

John Williams, 2nd, died in 1787. In his will, he leaves a bequest to his cousin, Dorothy Leonard (b. 1764), daughter of the Rev. Abiel and Dorothy (Huntington) Leonard, to whom he seems to have been attached. Very shortly after his death, in 1789, Dorothy marries his brother Hezekiah.

In 1790, Daniel Lathrop moves for a time into the shop formerly occupied by Hezekiah Williams. It may be, that into the former Hezekiah Huntington house John Sterry moved his book shop from the Landing in 1793, and possibly he remained here until he purchased the Jabez Avery house in 1806. In 1797, he seems to have been associated in business with Nathaniel Patten. In 1806, the widow Dorothy Williams, as guardian to her young son Hezekiah, sells this house to Joseph Strong, son of the Rev. Joseph and Mary (Huntington) Strong, who lived here for many years, and it is still called by old residents, "the Strong house." Since the death of Joseph Strong, it has been bought and sold many times, and is now owned by William H. Bliss.

About 1738, Hezekiah Huntington set out two elm trees in front of the house, which flourished for seventy years, then met with a melancholy fate, according to the journal of Abigail Reynolds, from which we will quote a little, for the benefit of those who are interested in meteorological matters.

"28. June, 1808, we experienced a violent tornado in Connecticut, it came up on a sudden about three in the afternoon, & Blew for several minutes very violent, attended with thunder, lightning, & rain in torrents, in New London one boy killed while at school, 1 man in Lyme, one Girl in Stoonningtown with lightning —the wind was much more severe in Norwich, Preston, & Lisbon. 2 large elm trees which had stood seventy years ware blown up by the roots in front of Mr. Joseph Strongs house, many fruit trees ware blown down, but in Lisbon whole forrests ware laid flat, some of 100 acres, some of less, whole orchards ware blown down, with many barnes, in Preston 19 barnes of 1 mile & half distance ware blown down, but I do not hear of much dammage among the shipping."

"2 weeks previous to the tornado 15 June we experienced a severe hail storm which cut down whole fields of grain, gardens, & swept everything before it. Several days after the hails measured three inches in circumference."

"In the year 1806, June 6, at 11 in the Morn, the sun was eclipsed in some places total which made it dark to lite a candle for a few moments to say half an hour."

The question naturally arises, as to whether any part of the framework of the original Leffingwell house still exits in the present structure standing on the lot. Mrs. Henry Butts, who occupied the house about twenty-five years ago, relates that when alterations were made in the interior, an old beam was uncovered, bearing a date, which unfortunately she failed to write down, but figured at the time that the house must then have been 175 years old, which would bring its present age to 200 years, and this would carry it back to the lifetime of Lt. Thomas Leffingwell.

CHAPTER VIII.

IN the first survey of town highways, this road on the north of the Leffingwell lot, is described as "a highway turning out toward Wequanock by Thomas Leffingwell's the younger, att his house two rodds wide, att the house of Joseph Bushnell 5 rodds wide, between the lotts of sd Bushnell & the lott of Ensign Thomas Leffingwell in the narrowest place 4 rodds wide, from thence to the norwest corner of sd Leffingwells lot, from sd corner to Capt Bushnells lott 6 rodds 6 foot wide, from thence to the house that formerly belonged to Samuel Rood, and there to be 3 rodds wide, from thence to the common that is between the pastures to be 3 rodds wide." This is later known as the Centre Hill road, and more recently as the old Canterbury road.

In 1728, Samuel Leffingwell, 2nd, sells to Thomas Leffingwell, 3rd, "one and a half acres of my home-lot, with part of hill adjoining at the east end, beginning at the north-west corner of my home-lot, and abutting on the highway and Benajah Leffingwell's slaughter house and yard 9 rods, 6 ft, to the south-east corner of the slaughter house, then abutting south on Samuel Leffingwell's land

36 rods," &c., &c. Thomas Leffingwell, 3rd, gives this land, both by deed and will, to his son Thomas Leffingwell, 4th, in 1733, and the latter buys in 1737-8 "the slaughter house," and land on which it stands, of Benajah Leffingwell, who had inherited it from his father, Ensign Thomas. Some time after 1733, but at what date we cannot tell, Thomas Leffingwell, 4th, built the house, (now the "Sheltering Arms"), and a shop, which stood on the south part of the lot, on the probable site of the old slaughter house. It is impossible to tell all the occupants of this house from the time of its erection, as there is no deed referring to it until 1783, when it is given to Thomas Leffingwell, 5th, by his father, and then passes by inheritance successively, to Lydia, (wife of Rev. Levi Hart), in 1814; in 1820 to Elizabeth, widow of Peabody Clement, and in 1834, the Bliss heirs (Elizabeth Clement, daughter of Peabody C., has married Charles Bliss) quit-claim to Mary Ann Clement (the sister of Elizabeth Bliss), who in 1836 marries Gilbert Huntington. Mrs. Gilbert Huntington sells the house in 1865 to Miss Eliza P. Perkins, who sells it in 1878 to the Society of United Workers. Since that time the house has well fulfilled for the sick and the suffering, the mission that its name, the "Sheltering Arms," implies.

Miss Caulkins says in her history, that Jabez Perkins at one time occupied a house on this road. It may have been that this was the house, as his wife was a niece of Thomas Leffingwell, 4th. If Miss Caulkins' statement is correct, he must have lived here prior to 1758, but no record of his occupancy has been found. We have reason to believe that Capt. Joseph Coit, on his arrival from New London in 1775, lived here for a time. His payments of rent were made to Martin Leffingwell, son of Thomas, and it is possible that the house was considered as Martin's property, though not formally deeded to him by his father. Martin died in 1781, and Andrew in 1782. In 1783, Thomas Leffingwell, 4th, deeds the property, consisting of house and shop, to his only remaining son, Thomas Leffingwell, 5th. The house was then occupied by a Mrs. Cary. Peabody Clement came here to live shortly before his death, which occurred in 1820. To Peabody Clement, the town is indebted for the beautiful enclosed elm at the foot of Washington Street, which he planted in his twenty-first year. He was born in 1746, which would make the age of the elm at this date, about 128 years.

The shop, which stood quite near the house of William Bliss, may be the one which was tenanted in 1786 by Hezekiah and John Williams, and on their removal, by Daniel Lathrop, for a short time in 1790. In April, 1791, Lester & Hazen, cabinet makers, may have established their business here, a "few rods below the store of Tracy & Coit." The partnership is dissolved in 1792, and Timothy Lester carries on the business alone until 1796, when he moves to the Greenleaf house. This shop was moved from here about 1865.

Next above the "Sheltering Arms," lies the land, given by Lt. Thomas Leffingwell to his son Ensign Thomas, and by the Ensign to his son Thomas, and at the death of the latter in 1733, it passes to his son Samuel.

This Samuel Leffingwell (b. 1722), probably lived for a time with his widowed mother, in the homestead across the street. In the will of Lydia Leffingwell, widow of Deacon Thomas, made in 1737-8, though not probated until 1763, she leaves to Samuel, "nails, boards &c preparatory for building." It is possible that these materials were designed for the new house, which was built upon this lot, just north of the "Sheltering Arms," either shortly

after the making of this will, or perhaps about the time of Samuel's marriage in 1744. We know certainly, that the old house, across the way, had disappeared, and this new one was built, before 1759.

The first wife of Samuel Leffingwell was Hannah, daughter of Daniel and Elizabeth (Perkins) Buck of Southington, Ct. She died in 1761, and he married (2) Sarah, daughter of Joseph and Sarah (Paine) Russell of Bristol, R. I., and (3) Abigail, daughter of Jonathan and Mary (Chester) Burnham of Glastonbury,

Ct. He had eleven children, who all died young, except Daniel (b. 1752), who married in 1772, Elizabeth, daughter of Col John Whiting, and died in 1776.

Daniel Leffingwell left three daughters, Hannah, who married Peleg Tracy, Betsey, who became the wife of Joseph Chapman, and Sarah Russell Leffingwell, who married in 1798 Judge John Hyde, son of Ezekiel and Rachel (Tracy) Hyde. Judge Hyde was for many years a citizen of prominence at Norwich Town, as a lawyer, justice of the peace, postmaster, and judge of probate. Miss Caulkins says of him "he is remembered also as a school teacher—a friend of the young, and an enemy to all oppression." He died in 1848, aged seventy-four. Samuel Leffingwell died in 1797. The house has become so identified with the Hyde family, who occupied it for many years, that it is always mentioned even at this late day as "the Hyde house." Abigail Hyde (b. 1800), a daughter of Judge John and Sarah (Leffingwell) Hyde, married, 1822, Henry Harland, and her heirs still own their great-grandfather's house, which, little altered since its first erection, is now occupied by the House family.

On Wednesday, Oct. 12, 1774, the family of Capt. Samuel Leffingwell were greatly excited over the advent of a burglar to their quiet household. A tankard marked M. C., a silver can marked S. $_H$. R. and several spoons were missing. A rather suspicious looking individual, dressed in a blue coat and yellow breeches, with thick, bushy, light brown hair, appeared at the house the day before, and when it was learned, that the same person had delivered a watch to a Norwich jeweller, from which the maker's name had been erased, and wished the name of Joseph Greenhill substituted, and also attempted to sell some melted bullion, efforts were made to arrest him. A reward was offered and on Oct. 20th, he was found at Pawtucket, and committed to "goal;" but alas! the old silver heirlooms were already melted into bars. It was discovered that he was an old offender, and bore the mark of amputation on his ears, which may have accounted for the bushy nature of his hair. He was sentenced to Newgate prison, Simsbury, for ten years. Capt. Samuel Leffingwell was one of the committee appointed in 1786 to arrange for the division of the town. He received his captain's commission in 1758, was first selectman in 1774, and was one of the committee appointed by the town to see to the enforcement of the non-importation agreement.

The small house, now occupied by Thomas Gilroy, just beyond the Samuel Leffingwell house, is said to have been an old building, which was moved here long ago, but its early history is unknown. It was standing here in the year 1800. It is said to have been used as an office at one time by Judge Hyde. Rufus Darby occupied it as a dwelling in the early part of this century. It is

possible that this may have been the building which Daniel Leffingwell used as a stocking manufactory in 1776. After Daniel's death, his father carried on the business. The advertisement reads:—

"At Samuel Leffingwell's Esq: Stocking Manufactory are
now taken in,
Silk, Thread, Cotton and Worsted, to make into Stockings, Breeches-Patterns, and all Fashions of Mitts, and Gloves, by the celebrated workman William Cox, heretofore so well known and approved of, as an excellent workman at Christopher Leffingwell's, Esq; Stocking Shop. The said noted William Cox is now engaged as a Foreman to Samuel Leffingwell's, Esq; Stocking Manufactory, at his house in Norwich," &c., &c.

"Norwich, Dec. 28, 1775."

We have reason to think that Samuel Leffingwell may have afterward moved to the shop on the main road (known recently as the Lowrey house), where Louis Barrel was later located.

After passing the site of the Samuel Leffingwell barn, which has recently been torn down, we come to a highway, turning off from the main road, toward the woods. This is the continuation of the old Indian trail, leading over the hill to the ford at the Shetucket. It is described in the old highway survey, as "a highway turning up into the woods by Joseph Bushnells, between sd Bushnells lot and Ensign Thomas Leffingwells lot fourteen rodds to the brook, and from thence to be four rodds in width till it be past all the pastures." On the right hand side of this road stands a small, old house, lately occupied by the Abner family, and known for many years as the Mead house. This was built by Capt. Philemon Winship, on land purchased of Samuel Leffingwell in 1772. In 1826, it passes out of Winship possession, and in 1830 is purchased by John Mead, a colored man, son of Samson Mead of Norwich, and here the old man and his wife lived for many years, the former dying about 1871, and the latter in 1869, both aged 88. The property passed then into the possession of the Abner family, and in June of this year (1895), was purchased by Gilbert Pierce. The father of John Mead was a slave, in the days before slavery was abolished at the North.

Capt. Philemon Winship (b. 1735), was the son of Joseph Winship of Charlestown, Mass. He came to Norwich with his brother Joseph. They were both sea captains. He married in 1762, Mary, daughter of Nathan Stedman, a prominent attorney of Norwich, and had four children.

Just beyond the Winship house stood the tan-yard of Jesse Williams, on land purchased of Samuel Leffingwell in 1770. This is sold in 1801 to John Hyde. Beyond this was the Wigwam pasture, where long after the law had been made, forbidding any Indians to linger in the town, or any of the inhabitants to harbor them under penalty of 20 s. fine, there still stood for many years an old wigwam, the last vestige of Indian occupation. In the woods near by, were several of the mortars, in which they ground their corn, but only one, we believe, is now remaining.

CHAPTER IX.

ON the opposite side of the lane, stood formerly a large, square, gray house, known as the Marsh house. This was torn down about twenty-three years ago, but the remains of the cellar are still visible. It is one of the most beautiful sites in town, the high ground back of the house, commanding an extensive view in almost every direction. The lower part of the present lot was the land, which, in 1705, the town sets apart "above the Cold Spring between the highwayes, adjoining to Ensign Leffingwell's land by Joseph Bushnell's house" "for the encouragement of a blacksmith to come and settle in the Town and do the Town's work." This is granted in 1711-12 to Jonathan Pierce, who, with Ebenezer Pierce, is voted in as an inhabitant in 1714. It is difficult to say with any certainty, who were the parents of Jonathan and Ebenezer Pierce. If they were brothers, we have found no record of their birth. If only relatives, it is possible that Ebenezer was the son of Thomas and Rachel (Bacon) Pierce, who came from Woburn, Mass., to settle at Plainfield, Ct., at the end of the seventeenth century, and Jonathan may have been the Jonathan (b. 1693), son of Jonathan and Hannah (Wilson) Pierce, of Woburn. To be sure, it is recorded that he died in 1694, but the father is also said to have died in the same year, and there may have been an error in the record, and Jonathan may have been one of the many children, who are reported to have died in infancy, and who yet return to life again in a most wonderful manner. Jonathan married, 1715, Hannah Mix, and had four children :

1. JONATHAN, b. 1715-6. d. ——. m. 1744 Mary Gates.
2. ANN, b. 1717-18. d. ——.
3. (Capt.) MOSES, b. 1720. Drowned at sea 1751. m. Thankful ——. b. 1728-9. d. 1821.
4. CYPRIAN, b. 1724. d. ——.

In 1719, Jonathan Pierce sells this land with all the buildings, orchard, &c., to Hezekiah Huntington, and moves to Preston. Hezekiah Huntington resides here until the spring of 1732, when he moves to the Samuel Leffingwell house on the "Town Street," and sells this house and land to John Hutchins, "beginning at the north-west corner at a rock in Mr. Leffingwell's fence, thence abutting north on Leffingwell land a bowing line inward 16 rods, thence abutting east on Commons 4 rods 5 ft., then abutting south on the highway 11½ rods, then abutting west some° south on the highway 8 rods, thence abutting west some° north on the highway 2 rods, 6 ft. to the first corner" &c., &c., "except reserving to myself the shop that adjoins the house, and the malt house and works." In 1746, John Hutchins straightens the "bowing inward" line on the north of the property by purchasing additional land of Benajah Leffingwell, and in the same year sells the house and land to Dr. Jonathan Marsh.

John Hutchins, whom we believe to be a descendant of the Haverhill, Mass., family of that name, married, 1715, Jerusha, daughter of Joseph and Mary (Leffingwell) Bushnell. He was a tailor by trade, with evidently some veterinary knowledge as well, for in the settlement of Samuel Bliss's estate in 1730-1, £1, 5s., is paid to John Hutchins for "medicons for a sick horse," and 8s. for "curing another of Ghistile." We believe that his first home was near the house of his father-in-law, Joseph Bushnell, but where, we have not discovered. In 1726, he purchases of his father-in-law, a lot of land, south of the Samuel Leffingwell home-lot. On this he builds a house, which he sells in 1730 to Absalom King, formerly of Southold, L. I., which property passes later into the possession of Benedict Arnold, who marries the widow King. John Hutchins fills the office of constable in 1726, and 1727. In 1746-7, he sells to Dr. Jonathan Marsh the house and home-lot, purchased of Hezekiah Huntington in 1732, and moves to another part of the town.

Dr. Jonathan Marsh was the son of Ebenezer and Mary (Parsons) Marsh, of Hadley, Mass., and great-grandson of John and Ann (Webster) Marsh, first of Hartford, later of Hadley and Northampton, Mass. He is said to have studied medicine with his brother-in-law, Dr. Ezekiel Porter of Wethersfield, Ct., and married in 1747 Sarah Hart of Farmington. He was a surgeon in the army at

Crown's Point in 1755-6. Dr. Ashbel Woodward writes: "Dr. Marsh was chiefly distinguished for skill in bone setting. His death in 1766 was caused by the absorption of virus, in treating a wound accidentally inflicted at a celebration of the repeal of the stamp act in Hartford." He left four daughters and two sons. His daughter Sarah married in 1769, Dr. Samuel Lee, the inventor of Lee's pills, which sustain their reputation to the present day. Dr. Lee was not only a skilled physician but a great social favorite. He was also famous for his great strength.* It is said that he once lifted a cart, in which were nine of the strongest men in Windham, by placing himself under the axle. He could hop forty feet at three bounds. He served also as an army surgeon. Dr. Marsh's second daughter, Abigail, married John Ripley of Windham; his third daughter, Hannah, married Dr. Joshua Sumner, first of Windham, and later we believe of Middletown. The youngest daughter, Mary, married in 1783, Dr. Benjamin Dyer, (son of the Hon. Eliphalet Dyer of Windham), who first opened a drug store in Norwich, but later moved to Windham. Dr. Dyer was remarkable, as the late William Weaver narrates, "for his short, pithy sayings, and terse laconic expressions." As a specimen of his business correspondence, Mr. Weaver tells of a Providence merchant, who after inspecting some of Dr. Dyer's dairy products wrote to him that he would like to buy one half of a cheese. The doctor's letter was short and to the point:

"Dear Sir.

Whole or none.

B. Dyer."

Jonathan Marsh, Jun., was only twelve years old, when his father died, but under the tuition of his mother, who claimed skill in the art of bone setting, he became famous in that special department. It seems to have been a custom in this family for the husbands to impart their medical knowledge to their wives. Dr. Jonathan Marsh, Sen., may have seen the practical benefit of this in his sister Mary's case, who, instructed by her husband, Dr. Porter, was enabled, after his death, to carry on his practice for many years.

Dr. Jonathan Marsh, 2nd (b. 1754), married, 1776, Alice Fitch, daughter of John Fitch, 3rd, of Windham. His death in 1798 was considered "a great public

* Lee Family Memoir.

calamity." It was said of him, "that he was ever ready to exercise his skill for the relief of the distressed and the destitute." His widow at once advertises "that she herself understands bone setting, and with the assistance of a partner will carry on the business." Dr. Marsh left three daughters. One of these, Mary Marsh, was teaching school in 1803. She marries in 1811 Bela B. Hyde of Rome, N. Y., son of Benjamin Hyde, at one time of Franklin, later of Taberg, N. Y.

In 1811, William Leffingwell sells to Jacob Ladd the land north of the Marsh house, extending to the stone wall on the north of the present lot. This had been the Leffingwell pasture, since the days of the old Ensign, passing from him to his son Benajah, and then to Col. Christopher Leffingwell. In 1816, the widow, Alice Marsh, sells her house and land to Jacob Ladd. In 1824, Russell Ladd sells to Ephraim Kittle. In 1830, the property is sold to Phinehas Marsh (b. 1801), the son of Joseph (brother of the second Dr. Jonathan Marsh), and remains in the possession of this branch of the family until 1871, when it is sold to Monroe Huntington. The old house was then destroyed.

CHAPTER X.

WE will not wander farther up this road, but crossing the street, and leaving out the upper part of the Thomas property, (which, in the early days of the settlement, belonged to Josiah Read), we will take the land which, fronting on the road, begins about the middle of the Thomas garden, and extends to the Edgerton property on the corner of the main highway.

At a "towne" meeting, on Dec. 26, 1679, "one acker where he hath built his house," is granted to Thomas Leffingwell, Jun. (later known as Ensign Thomas Leffingwell), "and a small pees the quantity being about an acker more or less, joyning to his father's home lot a lying betweene the cold spring and the brooke." This small "pees," "being measured by the appoyntement of the towne, appears to be but ¾ of an acker, and is bounded upon the south upon the home-lot of Leiftenant Leffingwell, upon the East bounded upon a small brooke, upon the North and the West upon the highwayes, leaving out the spring called the Cold Spring, leaving about 2 rodds between the spring and his fence for cattels coming to the water."

This three-quarters of an "acker" is the north part of the lot on the opposite side of the street, just above where the old barn stood, which has recently been torn down. The cold spring is still there to refresh the weary traveller, and passing "cattels" can still come "to the water." Other land was also added to the home-lot grant, for in Feb., 1688, Thomas Leffingwell, Jun., sells to Joseph Bushnell, "two acres of land more or less, which land ye sd Joseph hath built on, and is bounded southward upon land of Thomas Leffingwell Jun., and westward upon the commons, and northward on ye land of Josiah Read, and eastward on the highway, (a highway for carting to lye open between the house of Joseph Bushnell and his barne excepted.)" The small "pees" on the opposite side of the highway is also included in this sale. The town also grants additional land to Joseph Bushnell, and he now records his home-lot as of "two and a half acres—beginning at a stone at the south-east corner"—from thence, it abuts east on the highway 33½ rods "a compassing line,"—abuts north on Josiah Read's land 22 rods,—then abuts west on the street, and south-west on Commons 18½ rods to a rock, thence south on land of Thomas Leffingwell, Jr., 7 rods to the first bound," "(part grant and part purchase, only highway excepted)." This extends from about the middle of the Thomas garden to the south line of the house-lot recently occupied by Gilbert Pierce.

Joseph Bushnell, aged nine years, came with his step-father, Dea. Thomas Adgate, and his mother, Mary, widow of Richard Bushnell, to Norwich in 1660. In 1672, Thomas Leffingwell, Jr, married Mary Bushnell, and in 1673, Joseph married Thomas Leffingwell's sister Mary, and the brothers-in-law settled side by side upon this road. They all lived to a good old age, Joseph Bushnell, dying in 1746 at ninety-five years of age, and Mary, his wife, and his sister Mary, both dying in 1745 at the age of ninety-one. On Mary Bushnell's grave-stone is inscribed this testimony:—

"A virtuous woman, a loveing wife,
It was the habit of her life."

In 1708, Joseph Bushnell of Norwich (probably this Joseph, as his son would certainly have been entitled Junior), "complained against himself" to

Richard Bushnell, "Justice of the Peace," "for y' he had killed a Buck contrary to law." He was sentenced to pay a fine of 10 s., "one half to y'' county treasury and one half to complainant." One is puzzled to know whether to admire Joseph most for his conscientiousness or his shrewdness, as by his self-accusation, in the abatement of the fine, and the value of the buck, he must have made a little money. He was by trade a weaver.

After the death of Joseph in 1746, Jonathan Bushnell, whose house was in the Wequonnock region, became the owner of the house and home-lot, and at his death in 1758, "the old house in ye town near Dr. Marsh's," is set out to his widow, Hannah, and in 1761, the land where Joseph Bushnell "last dwelt and died," (with no mention of a house, though it was possibly still standing), is sold to Dr. Jonathan Marsh. In 1789, the north part of the lot (now included in the Thomas garden), is sold by Joshua and Hannah (Marsh) Sumner to Dr. Joshua

Lathrop, and is given by the latter to his son Thomas. The middle of the lot, extending down to the part recently occupied by Gilbert Pierce, was sold in 1780 by John and Abigail (Marsh) Ripley to Thomas Harland, and is still retained by his heirs. "The small pees" on the opposite side of the road, passed, in the distribution of Joseph Bushnell's estate, to Job and Rebecca (Bushnell) Barstow, and was sold by them in 1748 to Samuel Leffingwell. In the deed, it is called "the little orchard," and the old apple tree, with its huge propped limb, which stands near the spring, may be one of the trees planted by Joseph Bushnell more than 150 years ago.

When the old Bushnell house disappeared, we do not know, nor who occupied it after the death of Joseph. There are remains of the foundation of a house, and of an old well near the bars on the Harland property. The line of the wall at the rear of this home-lot can still be traced above the rocks, at the back of the former Pierce house. We should judge from the wording of the old highway survey, that the barn must have stood north of the house. We have found no traces of the highway between the house and the barn. In the latter part of the eighteenth, and early part of the nineteenth century, a small one-story and a half cottage stood on that part of the Bushnell lot, which is now the Thomas garden, and was then owned by Thomas Lathrop. This cottage was occupied by an old servant of his, named Ownie Douglass, and has long since disappeared.

In 1716, Joseph Bushnell deeds to his son-in-law, John Hutchins, who has married his daughter Jerusha, the south part of the home-lot (site of the Pierce house). This is sold in 1747-8 to Dr. Jonathan Marsh, and is called the Hutchins' "Calf or Close pasture," and in 1757, it is purchased by Thomas Leffingwell, 4th.

In 1784, Thomas Leffingwell, 4th, sells a part of this land, with a frontage of 3 rods, 12½ feet, to James Lincoln, who builds the house lately occupied by Gilbert Pierce, where he lives until 1793, when he moves across the river to a house formerly occupied by Hezekiah Leffingwell, near the paper mill. He still owns this house, which is tenanted by various persons, and at his death in 1807, it passes to his daughter Hannah, who has married in 1801 James Day. The house was at one time occupied by Thomas Lathrop's coachman, Anthony Church. In 1833, it was sold by Capt. James L. Day, son of James and Hannah (Lincoln) Day, to Henry Harland, and is still in the possession of the Harland family.

CHAPTER XI.

AFTER the sale by Thomas Leffingwell, Jun., of a part of his grant to Joseph Bushnell, the record reads "he hath reserved 16 rods of ground about his house upon the side of the hill to himself." A second grant is also given him by the town of "a small parcel of land to build on, beginning at a rock between Joseph Bushnell's house and his running southerly and abutting east on the highway 12 rods, then running west up hill and abutting on Commons 7 rods, then running North-westerly and Northerly and North-east by the rocks to Joseph Bushnell's line, thence runs East and abuts North 7 rods to the highway on Joseph Bushnell's land." This is the rocky lot of land between the Lincoln lot and the wall at the back of the Edgerton property, and here stood the house, "founded upon a rock, and sheltered by the hill,"* which Miss Caulkins wrongly believed to have been the house of Lieut. Thomas Leffingwell.

---

* Miss Caulkins. See History of Norwich, 1866, p. 65.

In 1681, the town grants to "Thomas lepingwell, Jun , (later Ensign Leffingwell), a small pece of land above his house to sett a barn upon." In 1710, "Sargt." Thomas Leffingwell, Jun., (Thomas Leffingwell, 3rd), is allowed to set up an end to his new barn, not to exceed 11 foots into Common lands." In 1720, the same "Sargt." Thomas is granted "liberty to fence in a yard on ye Commons at ye north end of his barn, and to improve ye same for his use, so long as he shall leave open to ye Commons for ye Town's use, so much of ye south part of his own land there adjoining." Where this house and barn stood, we can only conjecture. From the wording of a deed of 1759, we should judge the house stood within the first six rods of frontage above the Edgerton wall, and from another land record, that the barn stood on the site of the Harland garden. In 1759, the house had disappeared, whether burnt or torn down, we know not.

In 1700, Thomas Leffingwell, Jun., (afterward Ensign Leffingwell), buys and moves into the house on the "Town Street" (later known as the Christopher Leffingwell house), and he probably gives the house on the side hill to his son Thomas (b. 1674), who has married, 1698, Lydia, daughter of Dr. Solomon Tracy, though there is no formal deed of the property until 1719, when Thomas Leffingwell, 3rd, is living in the house.

In describing this lot, Miss Caulkins says "Sergt. Leffingwell was peculiarly the soldier and guardsman of the new town,* and Sentry Hill was the lookout post, commanding the customary Indian route from Narragansett to Mohegan. A sentry box was built on the summit, and in times of danger and excitement, a constant watch was kept from the height. Here too, in the war with Philip, a small guard-house was built, sufficient for some ten or twelve soldiers to be housed. It has of late been called Center Hill, an unconscious change from Sentry."

In December, 1675, during King Philip's war, the inhabitants of Norwich requested that a guard should be sent to protect them, "they bordering upon the enemie and haveing so many in the field." The General Council sent ten men from Hartford County, eight from New Haven, and eight from Fairfield, "to lye in garrison" at Norwich. This may have been the time when the garrison-house

---

*This description refers to Thomas Leffingwell, 1st.

was built, though we have found no mention of it on the records, and no allusions to Sentry Hill, though at a later date, the name of Center Hill often appears. If a guard-house had been built at this time, it would be natural that such an important matter should appear on the town books; but is it not possible that the guard-house had been already built long before, at the time of the settlement, and perhaps this was the very building into which the bullets had been fired in 1660. How much more natural, that the first guard-house should be erected here, on high ground, overlooking the Indian trail for a long distance, than on the enclosed plain. As we can find no record to set us right, let us suppose, that here, from the earliest years of the town, it stood, used as a shelter and watch-tower for the first settlers, and as a garrison-house during King Philip's war. By 1705 it may have disappeared, as in the highway survey, there is no mention of it.

Thomas Leffingwell, 3rd, (who is better known by his title of Deacon), probably occupied his father's house, from the time of the latter's removal to the main road, though he did not receive a deed of the property until 1719. The deed gives to him "the house and tan-yard, and home-lot on both sids of ye highway, and ye Rock pasture above ye sd home-lot," &c. Thomas was by trade a "tanner" and "cordwainer." He died in 1733, and in his will he bequeaths to his "dearly beloved" wife, Lydia, "the halef of my now dwelling house for hur one youse during her natural life," &c., and as he has already given a house and barn, and "sum" land to his son Thomas, he gives to Samuel, "my well-beloved sun, the now dweling houes I live in, and hom lot one both sids of the hieway, with the barn, with the heither end of the pastor at hom, and the pastor up the hill, lying between the two heyways with the woodland adjoyning tharto," &c. Samuel, and his mother, Lydia, occupy for a time the old homestead, but before 1759 it has disappeared, and they are living in the house across the street, later known as the Hyde house, and now occupied by the House family. We do not know when the Leffingwell barn disappeared. The land between the Leffingwell lot and the commencement of the high board fence on the Edgerton property, was early common land, in part used as a branch of the highway which led down over the hill. It came later into the possession of Thomas Leffingwell, 4th.

Coming down to the corner, we pass an old, square, gray house (still retaining, in spots, some traces of its original red color), which has been known for many years as the "Edgerton house." This stands on land, granted by the town to Stephen Backus, and sold by him in 1704 to Dr. Caleb Bushnell. In 1718, Caleb sells to Thomas Leffingwell my "40 rods of land lying in ye crotch of ye highwayes near Ensign Thomas Leffingwell's now dwelling house, on ye northeast side of ye common street, near ye southeast end of the Norwich Town

plot," &c., "being encompassed with highwayes, which land hath an allowance for a way through it to a shop." This land has a frontage on the street of 10 rods, and abuts south on the highway 5 rods. Here Thomas Leffingwell (cordwainer), builds a house, which he gives to his son Thomas, possibly on the latter's marriage to Elizabeth, sister of Rev. Benjamin Lord, in 1728-9, but there is no record of this transfer until 1732-3, the year of Dea. Thomas Leffingwell's death, when both by deed and will, it is given to his son Thomas Leffingwell, 4th. In 1783, ten years before his death, the latter deeds to his son Thomas Leffingwell, 5th, this house, and also the house opposite (now the "Sheltering Arms"), and adjoining shop. Thomas Leffingwell, 5th, was a bachelor. He died in 1814, and wills these houses to his sister, Lydia Hart, wife of Rev. Levi Hart of Preston. In 1820, Rev. Thomas L. Shipman inherits from his aunt Lydia this house, which he sells in 1833 to George

H. Edgerton. Both Thomas Leffingwell, 4th, and his son Thomas, 5th, were strong tories, and remained to the end of the war, though threatened with prosecution and imprisonment, staunch in their allegiance to the king. Thomas Leffingwell, 5th, insisted, to the last days of his life, that "the rebellion was all wrong."

CHAPTER XII.

ON the opposite side of the street, next to the Bliss property, began the home-lot of the first William Backus, which, including the triangle of land at the intersection of the highways, extended from the Bliss line to the lane south of Gager's store. It consisted of six acres, "more or less," abutting east on the highway 33 rods, north on the land of John Olmstead 36 rods, west on the river 34½ rods, and south on the land of Thomas Bliss 37½ rods.

William Backus is supposed to have been an inhabitant of Saybrook as early as 1637. He was a smith, or cutler by trade, and his first wife, Sarah, was the daughter of John Charles of Branford, Ct. She died in Saybrook, and just before removing to Norwich, he married Ann, widow of Thomas Bingham. On his arrival at Norwich, his household probably consisted of his wife, his son Stephen, and his step-son Thomas Bingham. Three daughters had married in Saybrook, one only, coming to Norwich, Sarah, the wife of John Reynolds. To his eldest son, William, had been assigned a home-lot near Bean Hill. William

Backus, Sr., died soon after the settlement of Norwich, probably between 1661 and 1664, so the land is recorded as the home-lot of his son Stephen.

Stephen Backus married in 1666 Sarah Spencer (possibly a daughter of Jared Spencer of Haddam, Ct.), and had two sons and six daughters. Miss Caulkins says that he removed to Canterbury in 1692, and died there in 1695. We have not found the date of his death, but know that it occurred before 1700, so the latter part of her assertion may be correct, but we doubt the removal to Canterbury.

In April, 1700, Stephen Backus, 2nd, of Norwich, in exchange for "150 acres of land lying on Rowland's Brook at Peagscosnuck (Canterbury), a house to be built on the land, and a yoke of oxen," sells the Backus home-lot to Sergeant (later Ensign) Thomas Leffingwell (yeoman), and this may have been the date of the family removal to Canterbury. Sergeant Thomas Leffingwell, leaving perhaps his son Thomas, who had recently married, to occupy the house on the "Sentry Hill" road, moved to the Backus homestead, and in May, 1701, is appointed Ensign of the train-band (a title, by which he is later designated), and in July of the same year, he is granted liberty by the town "to keep a publique house of entertainement of strangers." This house was probably then enlarged to suit the requirements of a tavern, and was known for many years, far and wide, as the "Leffingwell Inn."

The house is large and rambling, and many parts of it bear the marks of great age. Some of the rooms are on a much lower level than others, and these may indicate where additions were made to the original Backus homestead, for this is one of the houses which claims to date from the settlement of the town. The windows still retain their wooden shutters, the door its bar-fastening, and the rooms are heavily wainscoted, the large north parlor panelled throughout. The entrance door was formerly on the north of the house, and faced the old highway coming down over the hill. Either the course of this highway, or the desire to have the house stand due north and south, may perhaps account for its singular position at the present day. It is said that in early times, slave auctions were held at this north door.

Ensign Thomas was also a merchant, and we should judge from the word-

ing of some of the deeds of neighboring property, that his "warehouse" stood just beyond the inn, possibly where later stood the "Leffingwell Row." The shop and the inn must have prospered, and the Ensign's revenues yearly increased until his death in 1724, when he left the large estate, for those days, of £9,793, 9 s., 11 d. His wearing apparel was valued at £27, his wig at 20 s., his silver watch at £5. The walking staff with the silver head, said to have been brought by Lt. Thomas Leffingwell from England, descends from father to son, until, from the fifth Thomas, it passed to his nephew, Rev. Thomas Leffingwell Shipman. His "rapier, with silver hilt and belt," and his "French gun" must have seen constant service in the Indian wars, and his "three tankards," "two dram cups," and "four silver cups with handles," form quite an array of silver for those days. Ensign Thomas died intestate, so by agreement among the heirs, the widow Mary received "the use of the south part of the house, with back lean-to and bedrooms in sd lean-to," &c. P. Webster Huntington of Columbus, Ohio, remembers seeing some initials and the date 1715, which were cut in a clapboard at this end of the house, but later alterations necessitated their removal. In these rooms Mary lived, surviving her husband many years, and the inscription on her grave-stone reads:—

IN
MEMORY
of an aged nursing
Mother of GOD'S New-
english Israel, viz. Mrs.
Mary Leffingwell, wife
to Ensign Thomas Lef-
fingwell Gent" who died
Sept. ye 2^d A.D.
1745. Aged 91 years.

Of the sons of the Ensign, John lived near Bean Hill, and Thomas in his father's old homestead on the "Sentry Hill" road. Ensign Thomas had given to Benajah in 1717-18, the deed of the north part of the home-lot, and in the division of the property, Benajah received the rest of the land and house. The inn and the store continued to thrive under his management, and his inventory shows the tavern well provided to accommodate many more guests than in his father's day. There are large stores of bedding, sheets, table-linen and kitchen utensils. One is inclined to wonder in which of the chambers stood the bed with its "yaller" bed-curtains and hangings, which was adorned with the "sute of plaid curtains," or "the streaked linen" or the "blew lintiwooley," and where we should find "the bed that was Madam Livingston's," which, in the division of property, was given to the widow Joanna. We should much prefer the silk quilt as a bed-covering to the "black frog coverlid," which, if adorned with very life-like representations of that animal, must have been a grewsome sight to the waking eyes of some guest, who had partaken too largely of the landlord's tempting potations.

We would like to have looked into the kitchen, with its rows of pewter dishes, brass kettles, and chafing-dish, shining on the dresser, and its copper vessels and utensils of every description. In the "Great Room" or "Keeping" room, we might find possibly the "Great Black Chair," the "turke work" chairs, and some of the "straight-backed," standing stiffly against the walls, and in the guest-room, which we may fancy to be the north front room, commanding all the approaches to the Landing, we might get a glimpse of some of the prominent citizens, who had perhaps strolled in to chat with the landlord and the guests of the house, and get the latest news.

This room, which is panelled throughout, has cupboards in every possible cranny, in which were stored perhaps the "blew and white china," the "decanters," the "silver tankards and flagons," the "large flowered beekers," and the "blew and red beekers." In the evening, when the guests would gather round the tables, to drink from the "double flint drinking glasses," their daily potions of rum and Geneva brandy, cider or metheglin, undoubtedly, at times, the "two beekers with handles," filled with flip, stirred with a red hot poker, were passed from lip to lip, and jokes and stories were interchanged, until the curfew rang the signal to retire.

Benajah had married in 1726, Joanna, daughter of Judge Richard Christophers, a wealthy citizen of New London, and had a large family of sons and daughters. His son, Benajah, settled early at the Landing. Hezekiah lived for a time near the paper mill. Elisha also lived at the Falls, and Richard was a prosperous sea-captain, and died in the Mole of Hispaniola, while on a voyage in 1768. At one time, in 1767, he carried 240 Acadians back to Nova Scotia, from which they had been exiled in 1755. At Benajah's death in 1756, the property was divided among his numerous children. Christopher received the house and home-lot, and the widow Joanna, "the use of the Great South Room," and the same "lean-to" rooms, which her mother-in-law, Mary, had formerly occupied, but these she did not long enjoy, as she married in 1759 Col. John Dyer of Canterbury. It is said that she took her chaise with her to Canterbury, which caused such a sensation in that small town at its first appearance on the Sabbath day, that she was obliged to postpone her church-going, until the congregation had assembled.

Christopher Leffingwell, at his father's death, was only twenty-two years of age. He married (1) 1760 Elizabeth Harris, daughter of John Harris of New London; (2) in 1764 Elizabeth, daughter of Capt. Joseph Coit, then of New London, but later a resident of Norwich; and (3) in 1799 Ruth, widow of John Perit, and daughter of Pelatiah Webster of Philadelphia. By purchase and inheritance, he regained all the home-lot, except the land on which stood the Greenleaf and Billings houses, and he also purchased a small piece of land adjoining on the north, belonging to the Lathrop lot.

Many were the business enterprises of Col. Christopher Leffingwell, who is still well remembered as one of the most prominent and public-spirited of citizens. Miss Caulkins says that he was one of the first to begin the business of stocking weaving in 1766, with an English superintendent, William Russell. In 1791, he had 9 looms in operation, producing annually from 1200 to 1500 pair of hose, also gloves and purses. Miss Caulkins also says that the long, low building, known as "Leffingwell Row," formerly standing north of the house, was built by Col. Leffingwell "after 1780, to accommodate his looms and other utilitarian projects." This possibly stood on the site of the old Leffingwell "ware-house," occupied by the Ensign in 1705. The north shops of "Leffingwell Row" consisted of one story and a basement, the south part was of two stories. In this south upper story, a school was kept, in which, at one time, Judge John Hyde, and we believe also at another period, Judge Henry Strong, were teachers. It is possible that until "Leffingwell Row" was built, the old ware-house may have remained standing, and here Col. Leffingwell may have started the stocking factory under the superintendence of William Russell, who was later succeeded by William Cox.

In 1784, Daniel Williams, "Taylor," occupied No. 2, Leffingwell Row. In October, 1788, Alexander McDonald (book-binder), moves from the Landing into the same No. 2. In 1787, Thomas Hubbard and Christopher Leffingwell carry on in partnership in this building, the manufacture of Breeches, Waistcoat pieces, Stockings, Mitts, Gloves, &c. In 1791, Thomas Hubbard moves to his father's former shop near the Green. For some time before 1787, David Nevins occupies one of the shops in this Row, No. 5, as a hat shop, but in 1787, moves to a shop near Gov. Huntington's, formerly occupied by Capt. Russell Hubbard, and shop No. 5 is advertised as "having proper bow-room and other accomodations for a hatter." In 1788, Roswell Gaylord takes possession, and advertises to sells hats, and buy shipping furs at "No. 5 Leffingwell Row," where he continues for several years. In 1813, Henry Strong has his law office in this building, but in the same year moves to the opposite side of the street. There was also a cooper shop, and in the basement a potash shop. In 1814, the south two-storied part was sold to Charles P. Huntington, who either pulls it down, or moves it away, and builds a new store, which he occupies for many years, and in which was later located the tin-smith, Jacob Miller, and at one time Henry McNelly, and later, Cady & Gorman. In 1836, Leffingwell Row was sold by the Leffingwell heirs to William C. Gilman, who sells it in 1838 to Henry Harland. About fifteen or more years ago, as the "Holly Tree Inn," it offered a resting-place and refreshments at a very moderate rate to weary teamsters and pedestrians. It was burnt to the ground in 1882, with the adjoining store of Cady & Gorman, and the land now forms a part of the Huntington grounds.

Col. Christopher Leffingwell built the first paper-mill in Connecticut in 1766, the Connecticut Gazette being printed on paper from his factory, in December of that year. In 1770, with his brother Elisha, he started a fulling-mill and dye-house, a grist-mill, and a chocolate-mill. A pottery was also among the enterprises of Col. Leffingwell. He was an ardent patriot, and as one of the committee of correspondence, appointed in 1775, "the chief labor" (as President Daniel Gilman, of John Hopkins' University, says, in his historical discourse delivered at the Norwich Bi-Centennial Celebration in 1859),* "of that arduous post, seems to have fallen upon him."

"Five days before the battle of Lexington, we find John Hancock, president of the provincial congress just adjourned, thanking Mr. Leffingwell for the important intelligence he had communicated; which appears to have been a full private letter from England, giving an account of the action of the ministry."

"The first announcement of the battles of Lexington and Concord was addressed to him. . . . Col. Jedidiah Huntington writes to him a little later from the camp at Roxbury, and Col. Trumbull from the camp at Cambridge, asking for supplies. Whenever New London was threatened by the enemy's fleet, a message was sent to Norwich, and more than once, Capt. Leffingwell and his light infantry, went down to the defense of their friends at the river's mouth." It was said that none of all the companies, who marched to the relief of New London, equaled in order and equipments the light infantry under Capt. Leffingwell.

*Pres. Daniel Gilman's Historical Discourse in "The Norwich Jubilee."

Col. Christopher Leffingwell
1734—1810.

"In May, 1776, Nicholas Brown of Providence, sends him muskets to be forwarded to Gen. Washington—relying on 'his well-known lead in the common cause, to send them as soon as possible.' At a later day, load after load of tents are brought him to be forwarded with all expedition to the commander-in-chief." At the beginning of the war, " he was one of those sagacious citizens of Connecticut, who saw the importance, of promptly securing the forts upon Lake Champlain, and who quietly united in sending a committee to Vermont, supplied with the necessary funds, to engage the services of Col. Ethan Allen, and the Green mountain boys, for that hazardous undertaking."

"Gen. Washington, in one of his visits, partakes of the hospitalities of the Leffingwell home, and Gov. Trumbull sends his respectful apology that he is unable to meet, at Mr. Leffingwell's, the commander-in-chief." *

Col. Leffingwell was the first naval officer of the port appointed under the U. S. Government, in 1784. In that year, he contributed land toward the opening of Broadway, and planted some of the fine elms, which are such an ornament to the town. He died in 1810, and the house became the property of his widow, Ruth Leffingwell, who lived to the good old age of 85, dying in 1840, and leaving the house to the children of her granddaughter, Mrs. Benjamin Huntington, who still retain possession.

* Gilman's Historical Discourse.

CHAPTER XIII.

THE road on the left, after we pass the Leffingwell Inn, was, in 1661, "a footway 6 foote broad through the home lots of Steven Backus, John Holmsted, and Mr. Fitch," coming out near the church and parson's domicile, whither all paths led in olden times. This remained for nearly one hundred years a pentway with gates and turnstiles at each end, and between the lands of the several proprietors. In 1739-40, an attempt made to open a highway through these lands, was voted down by a large majority, but in 1752, at the motion of William Hyde, and sundry of the inhabitants of Norwich, and neighboring towns, showing the great necessity of this measure, land was purchased of Benajah Leffingwell, the Watermans, and Col. Simon Lathrop, and a road 2 rods, 6 ft. wide was laid out through this district; the part through the Leffingwell land, "beginning at the Town Street between the Leffingwell shop and the little gate, and running through sd home lot to Col. Simon Lathrop's home lot, touching sd Lathrop's home lot a little southerly from ye style."

The road was soon completed, in spite of remonstrances from Col. Simon Lathrop. According to Miss Caulkins, much was done to beautify and improve it, at a later date, by Capt. William Hubbard. It was early known as "the road through the grove," but after 1752, as the "cross road" or "cross highway." "Tradition depicts it," Miss Caulkins says, "as a beautiful winding cart-path along the river bank, over-arched with lofty trees, and crossing a rapid stream, where the teamsters paused on a hot summer's day to refresh themselves and their cattle in the shade." But though beautiful and romantic by day, adventurous indeed were those, who dared to pass through it in the night-time. It is said that in the early years of the town, a young man named Waterman, going to visit his lady-love, who lived below the Plain, was hissed at by a rattlesnake, and snapped at by a wolf, as he passed through the turn stile at the corner.*

About the middle of the nineteenth century, the road was filled out and straightened, which process resulted probably in the destruction of many beautiful trees, for long after, it was a sunny, dusty road, until the present time, when the trees set out during the highway alterations by Wolcott Huntington, and in later years by the Norwich Town Rural Association, are beginning to afford a protection from the noontide glare.

On the triangle of land, at the fork of the roads, stood the shop of Col. Christopher Leffingwell, built possibly, shortly after his father's death. Here he sold goods of his own manufacture, and everything else that could satisfy the needs of those days, and here he was later succeeded by his two sons, William and Christopher.

William Leffingwell served as post-master from 1789 (when the office was transferred from the Woodbridge shop on the Green to this shop on the corner), till 1793. He advertises in 1790, that the eastern mail will close on Mondays and Thursdays, and the western mail on Tuesdays and Fridays, at seven o'clock P. M. This gave plenty of time to get the mails ready for the morning coach.

In 1793, William Leffingwell left Norwich, and entered into a business partnership in New York with Hezekiah Beers Pierpont, as the firm of Leffingwell & Pierpont. Christopher Leffingwell, Jun., carried on the post-office and the store for a while, then went to Albany, and later we believe to Ohio. In 1801, the shop is occupied by the firm of Baldwin & Strong.

---
*Miss Caulkins' Hist. of Norwich.

In 1808, Joseph Strong purchased the store, which was of two stories, painted yellow, with a gable roof, the gable end facing down the street. In front of the shop was a level plot of land, which necessitated a high wall and basement, and an approach by steps from the lower road. Behind the store was a lane, leading from the upper to the lower road, and on this side of the store was a high door, where the carts loaded and unloaded their goods. Standing on the other side of the lane, just behind the Leffingwell store, its site marked by the beginning of the present picket-fence, stood another two-storied shop, with doors opening on the lane and street. When this shop was built, and by whom, we are unable to say, but as early as 1773, there was a shop standing "near the store of Christopher Leffingwell," in which Thomas Harland began his watch-making business in 1773, where Thomas Leffingwell, 4th, was located in 1776, in which John Richards, in 1778, give swool-cards in exchange for well-tanned sheepskins, and James Lincoln sells wool-cards in 1785, and Thomas Morrow advertises as a weaver in 1786. All these announce themselves as "near the store of Christopher Leffingwell," so we shall have to assume that they occupied this shop, or possibly another on the same site. This building was later used as a store-house by Joseph Strong. These two shops stood close to the walk on the upper road, and the walk passed outside of the large elm tree on the corner, so the present sidewalk passes over the site of Christopher Leffingwell's store. Both buildings were removed in 1866.

In the boughs of the many-branched elm tree, in front of the Christopher Leffingwell shop, some years before the middle of this century, the boys of Norwich Town built an arbor, to which they could ascend by means of a rope, and which, when the rope was also drawn up, formed as delightful and inaccessible a retreat, as a boy's heart could desire. It is said that under this tree the troops assembled, the day they marched to Lexington.

Opposite the store of Christopher Leffingwell, and just beyond the "Leffingwell Row," stood a house, which was built by David Greenleaf, on land purchased of Hezekiah, son of Benajah Leffingwell, in 1761. It was built possibly about 1763, the date of David's marriage to Mary Johnson.

David Greenleaf was a goldsmith. He was born possibly in Bolton, Mass., in 1737, where his father, Dr. Daniel Greenleaf, was a practicing physician. His grandfather, Rev. Daniel Greenleaf, was a physician in Cambridge, Mass., for some years, then, in 1706, became a preacher, was ordained pastor of a church in Yarmouth, Mass., where he remained for twenty years, then removed to

Boston, and opened a drug store on Washington Street. David's uncles were wealthy and influential citizens of Boston. One of them, Hon. Stephen Greenleaf, was the noted Tory High Sheriff of Suffolk County. Another brother, Gen. William Greenleaf, married Sally Quincy, sister of the famous Dorothy Quincy, wife of Gov. Hancock. David Greenleaf sold his house to Jesse Williams in 1769, and removed to Boston. He is later said to have resided in Coventry, Ct. From 1769 to about 1772, the house was owned and occupied by Jesse Williams.

We believe that this is the Jesse Williams, who married in 1768 Sarah Williams of Stonington, but whether he is the Jesse Williams (b. 1741-2), son of Samuel and Mary Williams of Stonington, or the Jesse (b. 1735-6), son of Jedediah and Hannah (Dawson) Williams of Preston, or some other Jesse Williams, we know not. Besides this house, he owned a tan-yard just beyond the Philemon Winship (now Abner) house. After 1772, we find no further trace of him, and think that he probably died between 1772 and 1775, and that his widow, Sarah, married in the latter year Charles Charlton of Norwich.

In 1774, this house passes into the possession of Capt. William Billings. In 1796, the widow Mary Billings is living in it, having rented her other house across the way. In this year it was sold to Timothy Lester, the cabinet maker, whom we suppose to have occupied at that time a shop near the house now known as the

Sheltering Arms. He moves his place of business to his new home, where he resides until his death. His heirs sell the property in 1854 to the family of its present owner.

Beyond the store of Christopher Leffingwell, on the same side of the street, stood a house built probably about 1758 by Capt. William Billings, who in 1757 had married Mary, widow of Nathaniel Richards, and daughter of Benajah Lef-

fingwell. Nathaniel Richards was the son of Capt. George Richards of New London. The date of his marriage to Mary Leffingwell has not been found, but he probably died shortly after. Capt. William Billings was the son of Capt. Roger Billings, and grandson of William Billings, both prominent citizens of Preston. His mother, Abigail Denison, was a great-granddaughter of the renowned Capt. George Denison of Stonington, and his wife, Lady Ann Borrodell, Boradil, or Borrowdale, as it is variously written. William Billings was a sea captain, and died "universally lamented," of a fever, in Dominica, while on a voyage to the West Indies in 1774. At the time of his death, he owned not only this house, but also the Greenleaf house on the other side of the street. In 1796, "the widow Billings," (whose only remaining son, Richard Leffingwell Billings (hatter), had died in 1795), was living in the Greenleaf house, and this house, known as "the widow Billings red house" was occupied by other tenants, perhaps by the family of John Huntington, Jun., who was living here in 1806, when it was sold by the Billings' heirs (Mary Billings having died in 1805), to Joseph Coit, of the firm of Tracy & Coit. In 1807, Joseph Coit died, and the house was, we believe, owned and occupied for a time by his mother, Mrs. Sarah Prentice. From 1820 to 1824, Charles Lathrop lived here. He had married in 1793, Joanna, daughter of Col. Christopher Leffingwell. In 1824, the house was sold to William, Sally and Lucretia Goodell, the son and daughters of Capt. Silas Goodell of Norwich. The lane on the north is mentioned for the first time in this deed.

In the old Rufus Lathrop house, later in a little building in her own grounds, and again, in the old brick school-house opposite Gager's store, and in several other locations, Miss Sally Goodell taught the rising generation of Norwich Town. Raps on the head with a thimble, suspensions from the wall in bags, the tying of bashful boys to the apron strings of pretty girls, to whom they had presumed to whisper during school hours, were punishments that linger yet in the memories of some of her pupils; but though painful at the time, these were the severest penalties which her gentle nature could inflict, and her scholars seem to cherish none but tender recollections of their former teacher.

Across the street, nearly on the site of the small house, which stands quite back from the street, stood after 1811, the blacksmith shop of Cary Throop, and also near by, it is said, the first fire-engine house.

Nearly opposite the foot of the lane, which leads by Gager's store, stands an old brown house, which, in the first deed that mentions it, seems to be the property of Col. Christopher Leffingwell, and to have been built between 1768 and 1774. It was at this latter date occupied by Judah Paddock Spooner, who, born in 1748, was the son of Thomas Spooner (a carpenter), who had moved from New Bedford to New London. Thomas Spooner's daughter, Rebecca, married in 1763 Timothy Green, printer and editor of the New London Gazette, and Judah married in 1770 Deborah, daughter of Nathan Douglass of New London. Judah was for a time a carrier of the New London Gazette, and not only wrote the New Year's address, but satires and other articles for the paper. In 1773, he came to Norwich to establish a printing office, in partnership with his brother-in-law,

Timothy Green. At this same time, the Robertsons and John Trumbull began to publish the Norwich Packet.

Judah Paddock Spooner remained in Norwich for five years, and in that time brought out an edition of Watts' Psalms in 1773, and of the Manual Exercise as ordered by his Majesty in 1774, various school books and almanacs, Dr. Hopkins' dialogue concerning African Slavery in 1776, and Paine's Common Sense.

At the time of the Revolution, leaving his family in Norwich, he marched to Boston, and took part in the battle of Bunker Hill, where, having delayed to fire a last shot, as his comrades were retreating, he was slightly wounded in the side. He was afterward in the privateer service, and was captured and imprisoned in the old prison ship, "Jersey," at Brooklyn, N. Y. From here he returned with a broken constitution.

He then went to Hanover, N. H., then belonging to Vermont, and here published a newspaper, but when New Hampshire claimed the east side of the river, he removed to Westminster, Vt., and in 1781, commenced the "Vermont Gazette," or "Green Mountain Post-Boy." In 1783, he sold out and returned to New London, but a few years later went back to Vermont to join his brother, who was editing the "Vermont Journal" at Windsor. Here, he was at that time persuaded by a man named Matthew Lyon, to start a paper called "The Freeman's Library" at Franklin, Vt. Lyon was indicted for too radical and seditious writings, and Spooner again relinquished his business, and soon after, discouraged and disheartened, died at the home of one of his daughters. His wife, it is said, taught school for many years at New London and Saybrook, and was distinguished "for her piety, prudence, talent and culture."

In 1790, Col. Christopher Leffingwell gives this house to his son William. At that time it was occupied by the brothers-in-law Thomas Hubbard, and Ebenezer Bushnell, who then moved to the house just beyond the church, where they published, for several years, "The Weekly Register."

William Leffingwell was born in 1765, and married in 1786 Sally Beers, daughter of Isaac Beers, the well-known bookseller of New Haven. They were married by the Rev. Achilles Mansfield, uncle of the bride, the evening before the commencement, which was to make the bridegroom a bachelor of arts. We do not know for a certainty, whether William Leffingwell occupied this house for the few years longer that he remained in Norwich, but we think it possible that he did. Where he lived from 1786 (the year of his marriage), to 1790, we also do not know, but think it must have been in one of the houses in this neighborhood, possibly the Billings house. We would like to know in which house he entertained Dr. Mason Cogswell in 1788, who writes in his diary, that "turkey and pompion pie" and "everything in nice order" graced the board. Samuel Huntington, Jun., and Daniel Lathrop were among the guests, and the late Rev. Dr. Leonard Bacon of New Haven, in his review of the Cogswell journal,* says:—"It could not but be a pleasant party,—six at the table, all young, four gentlemen, as well as the hostess, overflowing with memories of Yale and New Haven," and "that smart girl," Joanna Leffingwell, "with her pleasing countenance, expressive eye, and good manners." Dr. Bacon also says that "those who knew Mrs. William Leffingwell long afterward, when she had become a grandmother, and especially those who were acquainted with her housekeeping, cannot but understand that this dinner was not only well got up, everything in nice order, but well enlivened and brightened by her sprightly

---

*The New Englander of January, 1882.

talk." Dr. Cogswell was again entertained at the Leffingwells', in a circle of "no less than sixteen ladies besides many supernumeraries."

In 1793, William Leffingwell removes to New York. In 1809, he retires from active business, and moves to New Haven, where, as Dr. Bacon says, he resided till his death in 1834, in a stately but old fashioned mansion on Chapel Street, at the corner of Temple Street, with a terraced garden, which extended half way up to College Street. He was considered the richest citizen of New Haven. One of his daughters, Caroline Mary, married Augustus Russell Street, and her daughter Caroline, married Admiral Foote. Mrs. Street built and endowed the School of Fine Arts in New Haven.

This old mansion of William Leffingwell was built by Jared Ingersoll before the Revolution; was purchased by Pelatiah Webster of Philadelphia in 1782, as a wedding present for his daughter Sophia, wife of Thaddeus Perit; was sold in 1809 to William Leffingwell, and after his death became the residence of Mrs. Street, and later of her son-in-law, Admiral Foote.

In 1811, William Leffingwell sells his house in Norwich to Epaphras Porter. At that time it was occupied by John Huntington, Jun., father-in-law of Epaphras Porter. He had moved here probably about 1806, from the widow Billings house across the way. Epaphras Porter lived here until his death, and the house is still called by old residents "the Porter house." He married in 1806, Lucretia, daughter of John Huntington, was a bookseller and bookbinder, and in connection with the Sterrys, carried on a marble paper manufactory, and edited a paper called "The True Republican."

John Huntington (b. 1745), was the son of James and Elizabeth (Darby) Huntington. He married in 1773, Abigail, daughter of Capt. Joshua and Anne (Backus) Abel. He was a saddler, and in 1774 was in partnership with Daniel Carew in a shop formerly standing just north of the Harland house. In 1777, he enlisted in Capt. William Richards' company of the First Regiment for three years. He was at Reading in 1779, and on the first of January, 1780, he was on the muster roll of Col. Comfort Sagis' regiment as sergeant. His wife died in 1814, and he died in 1815.

Back of the Porter house stood a small house, which was built by Thomas

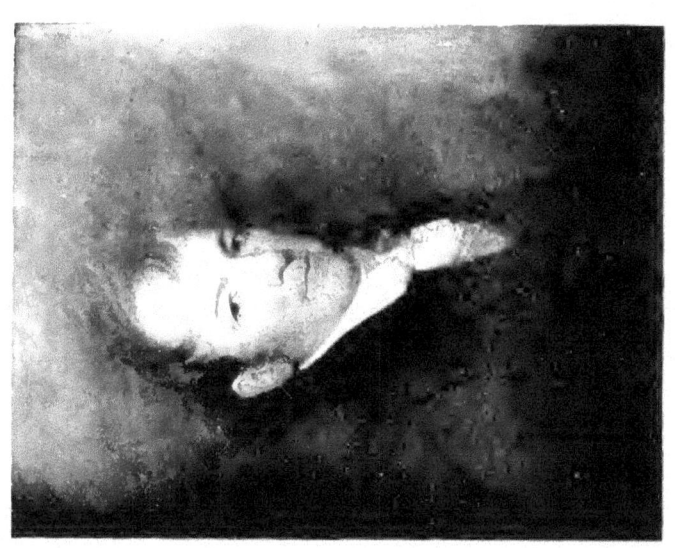
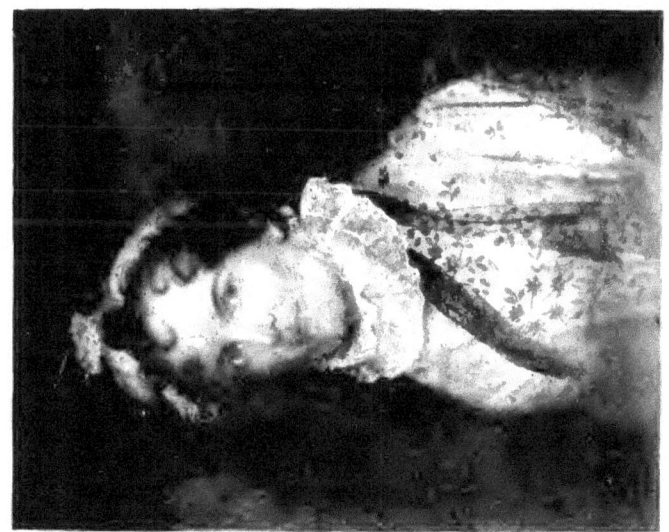

Williams, possibly the one who resided on the upper road. He bought the land of Col. Christopher Leffingwell in 1774. This house is purchased in 1797 by Rufus Sturtevant, a former paper-maker of Milton, Mass., who had married in 1794, Polly Manning. In 1797, it passed into the possession of Asa Spalding, and in 1816, it was sold to Epaphras Porter. It was torn down about 1850. It is not known who were its various occupants, during all the years of its existence.

At one time in 1811, and for some years after, a rather entertaining old colored man lived here, named Ira Tosset, who was famous for his hearty laughing powers, and a benevolent lady who resided in the neighborhood used to make him frequent presents, only asking in return that he should laugh for her, which he did to order, with a will which made the neighborhood resound. This Ira was the last of the old African Governors.

A path twenty feet wide led from this house to the lot on the north, on which stood Col. Leffingwell's (later Charles Lathrop's) stone-ware kiln and shop. This was one of the numerous enterprises of Col. Leffingwell, started about the time of the Revolution, in which he was succeeded by his son-in-law, Charles Lathrop, in 1793. It is possibly the one mentioned in Prime's "Pottery and Porcelain" as advertised in a newspaper of 1796, in which Christopher Potts & Son are named as successors of Charles Lathrop. In 1811, it was the shop of Cary Throop, "subject to removal on notice to that effect," and before 1816 it seems to have disappeared.

CHAPTER XIV.

THE land beyond the pottery kiln, extending to the brook, was the garden and barn lot of Ebenezer Carew, part of which was inherited from his wife's grandfather, Col. Simon Lathrop, and part purchased in 1776 of Rufus Lathrop. The land on the north side of the street, now a precipitous sandy bank, much cut away in places, was formerly a sloping grassy incline where, after the marriage of Ebenezer Carew and Eunice Huntington in 1771, the bride's grandfather, Col. Simon Lathrop, presented them with a house-lot (frontage 6 rods). Here Ebenezer, who was a carpenter, built his house and shop. In 1776, he purchased the adjoining land on the south (frontage 3 rods), of Rufus Lathrop. The shop, which in the early part of this century was occupied as a house by Lydia and Thankful Jones, daughters of Benjamin and Thankful (Vergason) Jones, has long since disappeared. About the middle of this century, the house was moved across the street, and is now owned by Mrs. Moore, and occupied by several families. All that remains to indicate the former situation of the old homestead, is a clump of lilac bushes, standing up on the bank, almost directly opposite its present site.

In the early part of the eighteenth century, three brothers, Palmer, Joseph and Thomas Carew came to Norwich. Palmer married in 1730, Hannah Hill of New London. Thomas married in 1724, Abigail, daughter of Daniel Huntington, and Joseph in 1730, Mary, the sister of Abigail.

A Thomas* Carew came in 1679 to Boston, in the ship Benjamin from Barbadoes, and it is possible that he was the ancestor of the Carews who came to Norwich. A Thomas Carew, possibly this Thomas, or perhaps his son,

---

*Possibly son or brother of Richard Carew, who at that time owned a plantation in Barbadoes.

married, sometime before 1700, Anna Tompson (b. 1676), daughter of Benjamin Tompson, the famous schoolmaster and town clerk of Braintree, Mass., who, according to the record of his successor in the last named office, was "a Practitioner of Physick for about 30 years, during which time he kept a Grammar School in Boston, Charlestown, & Braintry & having left behind him a weary world, 8 children, & 28 grand-children, he died Apr. 13, 1714, & lieth buried in Roxbury, Atatis sue 72." On his tombstone, he is called "the Renowned Poet of New England." Benjamin's father was the Rev. William Tompson, the first pastor of Braintree, and also one of the earliest missionaries sent to evangelize Virginia, whom Cotton Mather describes in his Magnalia as of

"Tall comely presence, life unsoiled with stain."

The births of John and Thomas Carew are recorded in Boston, and a daughter Anne is soon after born in Braintree. The records of birth of Palmer and Joseph have not yet been found. Benjamin Tompson had a daughter Elinor who married (1) Rev. Eleazer Moody, and (2) Rev. Thomas Symmes of Boxford, and we must acknowledge that the mention of "my aunt Elinor Symmes" in the will of Joseph Carew, forms the very slender clue, by which this lineage was traced, but we think, as far as it goes, it is probably correct.

Ebenezer Carew (b. 1745), was the son of Joseph and Mary (Huntington) Carew, and married in 1771, his cousin Eunice (b. 1747), daughter of Jonathan and Eunice (Lathrop) Huntington. According to the Norwich Packet, Eunice Carew died in 1785, in the thirty-eighth year of her age, "after languishing five years under a hectick disorder," and Ebenezer married in 1786, Mehetabel Gardiner (b. 1753), daughter of Samuel and Abigail Gardiner of New London. Her parents were cousins, and both were grandchildren of John, the third "Lord of Gardiner's Isle."

In 1779, Charles Staebehen from Berlin, proposes to teach the French language, and asks those desirous to learn, to call upon him at Ebenezer Carew's. Ebenezer Carew died in 1801, and his son Ebenezer (b. 1778), lived for a time in the homestead, and married in 1815, Sally, daughter of Edward and Mercy (Denison) Eels of Stonington. In 1801, he took the drug business of Daniel

Lathrop Coit, in the shop on the side-hill next to Dr. Joshua Lathrop's house, as Mr. Coit was intending to move to New York.

The road between the Carew house and the one next above, described in former days, a long, winding curve, crossing the brook by a bridge, but about the middle of this century, under the superintendence of Wolcott Huntington, the present road was filled in, and made to lead in almost a straight line to the church. It was possibly about this time, that the Carew house was moved across the street.

CHAPTER XV.

THE brook, which we are now approaching, formed the eastern bound of the Rev. James Fitch's home-lot, which, beginning at the river, and following for part of the way the line of the brook, and beyond this, the eastern bound of the oldest part of the cemetery, came out on the street leading by the Green, just north of the house of Miss Grace McClellan, and from here the street frontage extended to the river. The record gives the home-lot as 11 acres, "more or less," of meadow and upland, abutting south on the river 41 rods, east on land of John Olmstead 20 rods, south on land of John Olmstead 8 rods, east on Thomas Adgate 14½ rods, north on Lt. Thomas Tracy 15 rods, east on Lt. Thomas Tracy 8 rods, 4 ft., north on land of Simon Huntington 18 rods, east on land of Simon Huntington 29½ rods (changed in the record from 19 rods, 12 ft.), the line then runs 2 rods east over the brook, then north 2 rods, 4 ft., then north-west 4 rods, then abuts north on the land of Simon Huntington 8½ rods (changed from 14 rods), to the street, then the line runs south, south-west and south to the river 69½ rods, abutting north-west and west on "the Town Green," and west on the highway. Three acres of this land is given by the Rev. James Fitch to his eldest son James, which includes the old part of the cemetery, and all that part of the home lot, north of the cemetery lane. In 1702, the rest of the Fitch home lot is sold to John Waterman, and the Waterman heirs later dispose of the land on the north side of the street to various purchasers.

The small house just beyond the brook, was built by Zebadiah Lathrop shortly before 1790, on a part of the Fitch home-lot (frontage 6 rods, 10 l.), purchased of Dr. Joshua Lathrop, to whom it had been conveyed in 1768. In 1792, Zebadiah deeds it to his son Asa. In 1800, Asa sells it to Moses Cole or Cowles, and since that time, it has had many owners. In 1824, it is purchased

88 OLD HOUSES OF NORWICH.

by the widow Mary Clegg; in 1836, it is sold to Charles Robinson; in 1858, Nancy Chapman becomes the owner. It is now owned by Thomas McGarrity.

Zebadiah Lathrop (b. 1725), was the son of Nathaniel Lathrop, who kept the tavern on the Green. He married Clorinda Backus (b. 1730), daughter of the Rev. Simon Backus, and his wife, Eunice Edwards, a sister of the celebrated Rev. Jonathan Edwards of Stockbridge, Mass., and daughter of Rev. Timothy Edwards of East Windsor, Ct. One may infer that Clorinda Lathrop was a superior woman, as her mother and grandmother were highly educated for those days; the former, after receiving from her father a collegiate education, spending some time at a finishing school in Boston. Zebadiah and Clorinda had four sons and one daughter. The son Asa, who inherited the home, was a shoemaker. He married in 1793, Rachel, daughter of Ebenezer Jones. He occupied for a time a shoemaker's shop on the Green near the residence of his father-in-law.

The house, standing on high ground next to Zebadiah Lathrop's, is also on Fitch land, which was sold in 1760, by Nathaniel Backus (to whom it had been conveyed by the Waterman heirs), to John Avery, and by John Avery in 1762, to Jabez Avery, who builds the house. The frontage of the lot was 13½ rods.

Jabez Avery (b. 1733), was the son of John and Lydia (Smith) Avery of Preston. He is said to have married (1) Lydia ——— (though the record of his first marriage we have not found), and (2) in 1761 Lucy, daughter of Richard and Lucy (Perkins) Bushnell. He was a coachmaker, and died in 1779 of the small pox, leaving a widow and seven small children, five sons and two daughters. His widow, Lucy, died in 1788. In 1776, John Saltmarsh, a leather breeches-maker from London, "just arrived from Lyme," advertises "to make all sorts of of doe and buckskin breeches at Jabez Avery's near the Court House." A blacksmith shop formerly stood between this house and the Zebadiah Lathrop house, but this had disappeared before 1790. In 1806, the Jabez Avery heirs sell this house to John Sterry.

John Sterry (b. 1766), was the son of Roger and Abigail (Holms) Sterry of Preston. He married in 1792, Rebecca Bromley, daughter of Bethuel and Arabella (Herrick) Bromley of Preston. After serving an apprenticeship, John, and his brother, Consider, began business as booksellers and bookbinders at Norwich Landing. They were self-taught, and in many ways, remarkable men, with a special genius for mathematics. They wrote and published "The American Youth," a new and complete course of arithmetic and mathematics, the first volume of which appeared in 1788. In 1793, they removed to Norwich Town, and John occupied for some years, we believe, the Strong house, and there for a time established his book store. In 1795, he was associated in business with Nathaniel Patten, as the firm of Sterry & Patten. In 1806, he moved to this house on the "cross highway." Without previous instruction in the art, he undertook, and carried on successfully the manufacture of marble paper, in company with Epaphras Porter, and with the latter, and his brother Consider, issued from 1804 to 1807, a newspaper called "The True Republican." About 1816, he operated also a silk-spinning factory. In 1800, he assisted in organizing the First Baptist Church of Norwich, of which he was ordained Elder, an office which he held till his death in 1823. Miss Caulkins says:—"He was a fluent and forcible speaker, and large demands were made upon him in the way of preaching and exhortation." His salary was "a mere pittance." As one of his sons remarked:—"He preached for nothing, and furnished his own meeting-house."

He was a devoted Free Mason, and the following account of his funeral was taken from the journal of a thirteen-year old school girl:

Thursday, Nov. 6th. "This morning, I heard the bell toll for Mr. Sterry, pastor of the Baptist Church in Chelsea, who died after a lingering illness, which he bore with Christian fortitude."

Friday, Nov. 7th, 1823. "This afternoon the Rev. Mr. Sterry was buried with masonic honors—the procession attended the mourners from the house of the deceased to the Court House, where a sermon was preached by Elder Wilcox —the procession was then formed again, and proceeded to the burying-yard— first came a man with a drawn sword—then stewards with white rods—after these a long procession of masons with white aprons which is their badge of mourning —then the Holy Scriptures on a black velvet cushion borne by the oldest member of the lodge—then stewards with black rods—then the hearse with four clergymen for pall-bearers—followed by the mourners and other citizens. When they arrived at the grave the masons formed a circle around it, and the service was read by Dr. Eaton—then they threw into the grave a white apron as the emblem of innocence, and a right-hand glove then they walked round the grave, and each one cast in a sprig of evergreen."

In 1829, the property was sold to Luther Case.

In 1753 and 1756, Capt. Joseph Winship buys that part of the Fitch land, which is now the property of the Hon. John T. Wait, and Mrs. Cynthia Backus. He purchased the part nearest the Green (frontage 5 r., 12 ft.), in 1753, the land adjoining the Avery lot (frontage 8 r., 12 ft.), in 1756. Before 1761, he resides with his brother-in-law, Samuel Manning, who has married his sister Anna. About 1761 he builds the house now occupied by the Hon. John T. Wait.

Capt. Joseph Winship (b. 1727), was a descendant of Edward Winship of Charlestown, Mass. He, and his brother Philemon, with whom he came to Norwich, were both sea captains. Joseph married in 1750, Elizabeth, daughter of Jabez Lathrop, and had four sons and four daughters. We read in the town records, that "Capt. Joseph Winship sailed from New London, the 11th of October, 1765, and was spoke with on the coast the 18th of December following in a storm, and hath not since been heard of, but 'tis supposed was lost in sd storm, his son Joseph being on board with him." His daughter Elizabeth, at the age of fourteen, was summoned to appear before Justice Richard Hyde in 1770, and

answer to the heinous charge of walking "in the street" with another young girl, and some young boys of the town on the Sabbath Day, "upon no religious occasion." In 1805, the Winship heirs sell the house and land, to Asahel Case, who moves here from the upper road. In 1831, the property is sold to Thomas Tilden, and in 1842, is purchased by the Hon. John T. Wait. A drive, or "gangway," as it was called, branched off from the old highway near the house now owned by Mrs. Backus, and passing in front of the Winship house, led up to the Avery homestead. This was purchased by Mr. Wait in 1842, and is now a part of the main highway.

In 1783, and 1785, Frederick and Rockwell Manning purchase in two parcels, the land on which now stands the house of Mrs. Backus. In the 1783 purchase, a hatter's shop was included. In 1786, Rockwell Manning purchases the share of his brother Frederick, and builds the house, which stood for many years on the lot, and a few years ago was purchased by Fitch Allen, and moved down the street next to the Porter house, where it is still standing. Rockwell Manning advertises, in the Norwich Packet of 1785, that he "carries on the stone-cutting and engraving

business at his house in the City of Norwich, or at the house of Mr. William Bingham's in Canterbury. Any that are desirous of having the American marble which makes elegant Tables may be furnished by sd Manning."
In 1793, he deeds his house and land in Norwich to his son, Mansur, and daughter, Sally, who sell in 1806 and 1809 to Luther Spalding. In 1811, the property is purchased by William Baldwin, who, we believe, resides here till his death. In 1820, his widow, Alice Baldwin, in exchange for a house on "Pork Street,"

sells this house to Nabby (Lord) Tracy, wife of Mundator Tracy. Nabby Tracy died in 1821, and Eleazer Lathrop afterward occupied the house for many years. When the old house was moved from the lot a few years ago, the present house of Mrs. Backus was erected. We have not been able to find the record of birth or parentage of Rockwell Manning, but he married in 1783 Sarah Answorth of Canterbury, and had two children, Mansur (b. 1783), and Sally (b. 1788).

In 1750, David and Elizabeth Waterman sell 40 rods of land, "lying near our small dwelling house bounded by the highway to the Burying Place, at the north-east end of our lot," to Samuel Manning. This lot extended 12 rods, 3 ft., on the highway to the Burying Place, then south 17° w 6½ rods, then north-west 13 rods, 3 ft., to a point to the first corner. Here Samuel Manning builds a house. In 1753, he sells one-half of this house to his brother-in-law, Joseph Winship, and the two families reside together until 1761, when Joseph deeds his share of the house to Samuel.

Samuel Manning (b. 1723), was the son of Capt. John and Abigail (Winship) Manning of Windham, Ct., and a descendant of William Manning, a prominent and wealthy citizen of Cambridge, Mass. He married in 1746, his own cousin Anne, daughter of Joseph Winship of Charlestown, Mass., and came to Norwich

Diah Manning.

1760—1815

Drum-Major of Washington's body-guard, who carried to Maj. André his last breakfast on the morning of his execution.

[Copied from one of those old miniatures, in which the face alone is painted, the coat is of cloth, and fitted to the figure, and the hair is made of wool or flax, and tied into a queue.]

to reside. He died in 1783, and the widow Anne, daughter Eunice, and son Diah inherited the house, and the garden and shop were left to the son Roger, who died shortly after, and this part of the property passed later into the posses-

sion of the Winships, and a part of it was sold to Eliphalet Carew, who in 1816, sells it to William Clegg. The shop, which stood on Roger Manning's land, may have been the hatter's shop, which was later sold to Frederick and Rockwell Manning, but of this we are not certain.

Diah Manning (b. 1760), married in 1784, Anna Gifford, daughter of James and Susanna (Hubbard) Gifford. He was for many years the bell-ringer of Norwich Town and a famous drummer as well. Both he and his brother, Roger, served as drummers during the Revolutionary war. In 1775, Roger was in Col. Israel Putnam's regiment, and Diah in the Eighth regiment under Col. Jedediah Huntington. At Valley Forge, in 1778, both the brothers were among the picked men chosen to serve in Washington's body-guard.

Diah Manning's son, Asa (b. 1795), was also a drummer in the war of 1812, and from the history of Norwich, we quote his own account of the battle of Lundy's Lane. "There were some 45 of us Norwich boys, who fought at Lundy's

Lane, some of whom laid down their lives on that bloody field, and all fought with courageous gallantry. We brought off our flag, though it was shot from the staff, and riddled with 30 or 40 bullet holes."

The family of Diah Manning were extremely kind in their attentions to a young Haytien mulatto, who had been taken prisoner in 1800, by an American ship, during the Haytien war, and brought with several others of his countrymen to Norwich. This young mulatto, Jean Pierre Boyer, afterward became the President of the Republic of Hayti, and nearly twenty years afterward, sent a present of $400 each to the widows of Consider Sterry and Diah Manning, in return for their kindness to him in his captivity. The family of Diah Manning continued to reside here until 1813, when the house is sold to William Clegg, a recently naturalized Englishman, whose occupation was that of a blacksmith.

CHAPTER XVI.

JUST across the street from the Manning house, stood the house of the Rev. James Fitch. At the time of his occupancy, there was no road through the property, only a narrow foot-path, and the house stood, probably, facing the Green, about on the site of the one now occupied by William Lathrop. Rev. James Fitch was born in 1622, in the town of Bocking, Essex Co., England. His father was a clothier, and evidently a man of means. In his will, probated in 1632, he leaves £100 to his son James, "to be paid him when he shal be a batchelor of art of two yeares standinge in the univ'sity of Cambridge," and also "£30 a year from the tyme of his admission to be a scholler in Cambridge until he be or have tyme then to be a master of arts." In his will, he remembers his loving friends, Mr. Hooker and Mr. Nathaniel Rogers, who were possibly the two distinguished divines, who afterward came to New England. The widow Anne and three of the sons, Thomas, Samuel, and Joseph, came to America in 1638.

At the time of James's arrival in this country he was only sixteen years of age. He finished his theological studies under the direction of the Rev. Thomas Hooker of Hartford. In 1646, he was ordained pastor of the church at

Saybrook, and here he remained until 1660, when, though urgently desired to stay in Saybrook, he finally decided, after much meditation and prayer, or as Dr. Strong, in his anniversary sermon, says, "under the influence of imperious circumstances," to go with the majority of his church members to found the town of Norwich.

Shortly after his arrival at the new settlement, the Hartford church extended to him a flattering call to be their pastor, but though this offered him a wider field and greater influence, his only reply was, "With whom then, shall I leave these few poor sheep in the wilderness?" He was devoted to his people, and they retained to the last a deep affection for him.

Mr. Fitch was considered a man of great learning, and was called by Cotton Mather, "the holy, acute and learned Mr. Fitch." A few of his writings remain: —A sermon preached on the death of Mrs. Anne Mason, wife of Major Mason, and a small volume containing a treatise on the reformation of those evils, which have been the procuring cause of the late judgments upon New England; the Norwich Covenant, which was solemnly renewed by the church, March 22, 1675, and a brief discourse proving that the first day of the week is the Christian Sabbath. He preached in 1674, the oldest election sermon on record in Connecticut, from the text, "For I, saith the Lord, will be unto her a wall of fire round about, and will be the glory in the midst of her." Mr. Fitch took a deep interest in the Indians, learned their language, preached to them, and befriended especially those who were rendered homeless by King Philip's war. He obtained a grant of land for them to settle upon, on Waweekus Hill, near Bozrah, but for some reason, the settlement was never made. But in 1678 a small Indian village was formed between the Shetucket and Quinebaug rivers. These Indians were called "the Showtucketts." They lingered here for a while, but gradually became extinct.

In 1676, during a great drought, the Indians, having exhausted all their incantations, applied to Mr. Fitch, who promised to pray for rain, if Uncas would acknowledge, before all his people, that the Indian powwows had been in vain; and that if rain should come in answer to Mr. Fitch's prayer, he should know that God had sent it. As Mr. Fitch says, "the next day there was such plenty of rain that our river rose more than two feet in height."

The Indians were warmly attached to Mr. Fitch, and gave him several grants of land, one of 120 acres near what is now the town of Lebanon, and another of a tract five miles in length, and one in breadth, called "Mr. Fitch's Mile." These lands now form part of the town of Lebanon, the name of which was suggested to Mr. Fitch, by the height of the land, and a large cedar forest, lying within the limits of the Mile.

In 1694, Mr. Fitch was rendered unable to preach by a stroke of palsy, but though his people were obliged to seek another pastor, they paid yearly to Mr. Fitch from £30 to £70 until his death. In 1695, a settlement was made in Lebanon, to which removed four of Mr. Fitch's sons, Jeremiah, Nathaniel, Joseph, and Eleazer; and in 1701, Mr. Fitch retired there to end his days. He died in 1702, in the eightieth year of his age, and lies buried there in the old cemetery. On his gravestone is a long Latin inscription, said to have been written by his son, Rev. Jabez Fitch, which, translated, reads:—

"In this tomb are deposited the remains of the truly Reverend Mr. James Fitch; born at Bocking, in the county of Essex, England, Dec. 24, 1622:—who after he had been well instructed in the learned languages, came to New England at the age of 16, and passed seven years under the instruction of those eminent divines, Mr. Hooker and Mr. Stone. Afterward he discharged the pastoral office at Saybrook for 14 years, from whence, with the greater part of his church, he removed to Norwich, and there spent the succeeding years of his life, engaged in the work of the Gospel, till age and infirmity obliged him to withdraw from public labor. At length he retired to his children at Lebanon, when scarcely half a year had passed, when he fell asleep in Jesus, Nov. 18, 1702, in the 80th year of his age. He was a man for penetration of mind, solidity of judgment, devotion to the sacred duties of his office, and entire holiness of life, as also for skill and energy in preaching, inferior to none."

Mr. Fitch married (1), in 1648, Abigail, daughter of the Rev. Henry Whitfield of Guilford, who, as his successor in the ministry, Rev. Thomas Ruggles, writes, was "a well-bred gentleman, a good scholar, a great divine, and an excellent preacher." He was the son of an eminent English lawyer, and was settled at one time over a parish at Ockham, Co. Surry. Censured by Bishop Laud for not reading the royal proclamation for sports on the Sabbath, he resigned his living and came to America in 1637. Later, he went to found the town of Guilford, Ct., where he officiated as minister for 12 years. He built as a house for himself, and also as a fort for the protection of the settlers, the stone house, which is still standing in Guilford. In 1650, he returned to England, and died at Winchester, where it is said that he was settled as a minister. His daughter, Abigail Fitch, died in 1659, and in 1664, the Rev. James Fitch married Priscilla, daughter of Major John Mason. He had a large family of sons and daughters. James, the eldest son, resided for a while in Norwich, then went to found the town of Canterbury; Samuel settled in Preston, Daniel at Montville, John in Windham; Jabez lived in Ipswich, Mass., and Portsmouth, N. H., and Jeremiah, Eleazer, Joseph, and Nathaniel, made their homes in Lebanon. The daughters are said to have been very handsome and attractive. Abigail, the eldest, married Capt. John Mason, 2nd; Hannah, Thomas Mix or Meeks; Dorothy became the wife of Nathaniel Bissell; Anna of Joseph Bradford; and Elizabeth married the Rev. Edward Taylor, who had been one of her father's theological students. A quaint and curious love-letter from the Rev. Edward to his lady-love, is still extant. On the letter, is drawn a carrier dove with an olive branch in its mouth, and this inscription on its back, "this Dove and olive branch to you is both a post and emblem too."

The address reads:—

"For my friend and only beloved
Miss Elizabeth Fitch
at her father's house in Norwich."

"Westfield, Mass, 8th day of the 7th Month, 1674.

"My Dove

"I send you not my heart, for that I hope is sent to Heaven long since, and unless it has awfully deceived me it has not taken up its lodgings in any one's bosom on this side the royal city of the Great King; but yet the most of it that is allowed to be layed out upon any creature doth safely and singly fall to your share.

"So much my post pigeon presents you with here in these lines. Look not (I entreat you) on it as one of love's hyperboles. If I borrow the beams of some sparkling metaphor to illustrate my respects unto thyself by, for you having my breast the cabinet of your affections as I yours mine, I know not how to offer a fitter comparison to set out my love by, than to compare it unto a golden ball of pure fire rolling up and down my breast, from which there flies now and then a spark like a glorious beam from the body of the flaming sun. But alas! striving to catch these sparks into a love letter unto yourself, and to gild it with them as with a sunbeam, find that by what time they have fallen through my pen upon my paper, they have lost their shine, and fall only like a little smoke thereon instead of gilding them. Wherefore finding myself so much deceived, I am ready to begrudge my instruments, for though my love within my breast is so large that my heart is not sufficient to contain it, yet they can make it no more room to ride into than to squeeze it up betwixt my black ink and white paper. But know that it is the coarsest part that is couchant there, for the finest is too fine to clothe in any linguist and huswifry, or to be expressed in words, and though this letter bears but the coarsest part to you, yet the purest is improved for you. But now, my dear love, lest my letter should be judged the lavish language of a lover's pen, I shall endeavor to show that conjugal love ought to exceed all other love.

"1st. appears from that which it represents, viz: The respect there is betwixt Christ and his church. Eph. 5th, 25th, although it differs from that in kind; for that is spiritual, and this human, and in degree, that is boundless and transcendant, this limited and subordinate; yet it holds out that this should be cordial and with respect to all other transcendant.

"2nd. Because conjugal love is the ground of conjugal union, or conjugal sharing the effects of this love, is also a ground of this union.

"3rd. From those Christian duties which are incumbent on persons in this State as not only serving God together, a praying together, a joining in the ruling and instructing their family together, which could not be carried on as it should be without a great degree of true love, and also a mutual giving each other to each other, a mutual succoring each other, in all states, ails, grievances: and how can this be when there is not a love exceeding all other love to any creature?

And hereby if persons in this state have not love exceeding all love, it's with them for the most part as with the strings of an instrument not tuned up, when struck upon makes but a jarring harsh sound. But when we get the wires of an instrument equally drawn up, and rightly struck upon, sound together, make sweet music whose harmony doth ravish the ear; so when the golden strings of true affection are strung up into a right conjugal love, thus sweetly doth this state then harmonize to the comfort of each other and to the glory of God when sanctified. But yet, the conjugal love must exceed all other, yet it must be kept within bounds, for it must be subordinate to God's glory, the which that mine may be so, it having got you in its heart, doth offer my heart with you in it as a more rich sacrifice unto God through Christ, and so it subscribeth me yr true love till death.

EDWARD TAYLOR."

Several other young men studied for the ministry with the Rev. Mr. Fitch. Rev. Eliphalet Adams of New London was under his instruction, also the Rev. Samuel Whiting of Windham, who married, in 1696, Elizabeth Adams, the half-sister of Eliphalet, and step-daughter of Maj. James Fitch.

The date of the death of Priscilla, wife of Rev. James Fitch, is unknown.

In Feb., 1702, the Rev. James Fitch and his son Daniel, to whom he has deeded part of the house, sell the property to John Waterman (husbandman), in all, 9½ acres, with the buildings—bounded south on the river 41 rods, west on the highway leading to the river 31 rods, bounded north on Maj. James Fitch 64 rods, abutting east 20 rods on land formerly John Olmstead's, south 8 rods on Olmstead land, east 14½ rods on land of Thomas Adgate, and bounded north 15 rods on land of Thomas Tracy.

John Waterman (b. 1672), was the son of Lt. Thomas and Miriam (Tracy) Waterman, whose home-lot was on the road to Bean Hill. He married (1) 1701, Elizabeth, daughter of Samuel and Hannah (Adgate) Lathrop, who died in 1708. He married (2) 1709, Judith Woodward, daughter of Peter Woodward of Dedham, and sister of the Rev. John Woodward, second minister of the Norwich church. He married for the third time, in 1721, Elizabeth Basset, possibly daughter of David Basset of Boston, Mass., and if so, of Huguenot descent. He had eleven children. One of his daughters, Hannah, married (1) Absalom King and (2) Benedict Arnold, and was the mother of the traitor. After the death of John Waterman, the widow and her son, David Basset Waterman, lived in the homestead until 1755, when they transfer the property to Nathaniel Backus, Jr., husband of Elizabeth Waterman, and he sells it to Eleazer Lord, who at that time is residing on a farm in the Wequonnock region. In 1760, Eleazer Lord, Sen., deeds to Eleazer Lord, Jun., one acre of this lot (which is the corner where the house of William Lathrop now stands), abutting 4 rods on the cross-lot highway, and 30 rods on the highway to the river. There is no mention of a house on the property, and it is probably about this time that Eleazer Lord, Jun., builds the one now standing on the lot, which, according to family tradition, was built in forty days. Eleazer Lord, Sr., was the son of Benjamin and Elizabeth (Pratt) Lord of Saybrook, Ct. He married (1) Zerviah, daughter of Dea. Thomas Leffingwell, and again in 1754, Abigail, widow of Thomas Mumford of Groton, Ct.

Eleazer Lord, Jun., married, in 1753, his cousin Elizabeth, daughter of the Rev. Benjamin Lord, and had two daughters, Nabby (b. 1754), and Elizabeth, (b. 1757). The former married (as second wife), Mundator Tracy in 1786, and Elizabeth married, in 1780, Asa Lathrop (b. 1755), son of Nathaniel Lathrop, 2nd. Eleazer Lord, Jun., must have built his house sometime between 1760, when the land is deeded to him by his father, and 1773, the year his father's will is made, in which the house is mentioned. Here he keeps an inn for many years, which was much frequented by the lawyers, who came to attend the sessions of the court at Norwich. Among the constant patrons of the Lord tavern were two New London lawyers, Winthrop Saltonstall (son of Gen. Gurdon Saltonstall), and Judge Marvin Wait.

Judge Marvin Wait was born at Lyme in 1746. He was the son of Richard, and Elizabeth (Marvin) Wait of Lyme, and married for his first wife, in 1779, Martha (or Patty) Jones of New London, and (2), in 1805, Harriet (Babcock) Saltonstall, widow of Gilbert Saltonstall, and (3), in 1810, Nancy Turner, daughter of Dr. Philip and Lucy (Tracy) Turner of Norwich. He was a successful lawyer in New London, and for a time a partner of Gen. Samuel Holden Parsons of

Revolutionary fame. He retired from practice in 1800, was frequently a member of the State legislature, was a judge of the county court, a presidential elector at the first election of Gen. Washington, and was one of the council appointed to dispose of the lands belonging to the State, and to establish a school fund. He died at New London in 1815. His wife returned to Norwich to reside, and died here in 1851. He had seven children by his first wife, one of whom, Harriet, married Francis Richards of New London, and another, Eliza, married Jedediah Huntington of Norwich, who as a memorial of his wife, established and endowed

the Eliza Huntington Memorial Home for aged ladies. By his second wife, he had one son, Marvin (b. 1806), who resided for a time in Norwich, and died in Pensacola, Fla., in 1832, aged 26. Judge Wait's last wife was the mother of the Hon. John T. Wait, one of the most prominent lawyers of Norwich, and a member of Congress from 1876 to 1887, who, though eighty-four years old, still attends to an extensive law business, and is as hearty and vigorous, with a memory as clear, and a mind as keen, as in his younger days.

Eleazer Lord died in 1809, leaving his property to his two daughters and his grandchildren.

In 1810, Asa Lathrop moves to the inn to reside. His wife, Elizabeth, had died in 1805. Asa dies in 1835. The property descends through Asa's son, Eleazer, and the daughters, to William Baldwin Lathrop, son of Eleazer and Jerusha (Thomas) Lathrop, who still owns and occupies his great-grandfather's house.

Shortly after the town was settled, a horse-bridge was built across the Yantic at the west of the Fitch lot, which, owing to frequent and disastrous freshets, was being constantly rebuilt. The more substantial wooden bridges later erected met the same fate. The present structure is of iron.

CHAPTER XVII.

TO understand the division of lands on the east side of the main highway, from the Edgerton house to "Peck's corner," it will be necessary to first locate the lands allotted before 1705, the date of the earliest highway survey. At the settlement of the town, all the land on the east side of the street, except perhaps the home-lot of Josiah Read, was the town "commons," that is, land left open for general use, where the cattle could range at will.

The records of the Read lands vary so much, and are so confused with purchases from, and sales to Jonathan Crane, who came to Norwich about 1679, that, though it is easy to fix the probable site of the house, it will be impossible to entirely settle the question of bounds. The Read barn was on the lot now occupied by the dwelling of Miss C. L. Thomas. The house stood probably near, or on the site of the present residence of Gardiner Greene. The property was owned in 1705 by Richard Bushnell.

Just north of the Read house (leaving the Read home-lot a frontage of about 12 rods), began the orchard or barn-lot of Dea. Thomas Adgate, having a frontage of about 18 rods on the Read (later Bushnell) cartway, leading over the hill. The houses, standing at this time on the opposite side of the street, were that of Samuel Lathrop, 2nd, where the Misses Gilman now reside, and the Adgate homestead on the upper part of the meadow below the house of Jabez Lathrop. This house of Mr. Lathrop was possibly the former home of Deacon Christopher Huntington, 2nd, and north of this, on the lot now occupied by the Rogers and Yerrington houses, stood the dwelling of the first Christopher Huntington, which, in 1705, was in the possession of his son John.

The Jonathan Crane house (owned in 1705 by Israel Lathrop), stood on the

I. John Reynolds Home Lot, 1659 First division of land, 1661
   Occupied by Jos Reynolds, 1705
II. "Point" Lot owned by Lt. Thomas Leffingwell
III. Thomas Bliss Home Lot, 1659 House occ by Samuel Bliss, 1705.
IV. Lt. Thomas Leffingwell's Home Lot, 1659. Living here, 1705.
V. Land granted to Stephen Backus Sold to Dr Caleb Bushnell by Stephen Backus, Jr 1704
VI. Ensign Thomas Leffingwell's first Home Lot, 1679 Occupied by Thos. Leffingwell 3rd, 1705
VII. Joseph Bushnell's Home Lot. Purchase & Grant, 1688. Living here, 1705.
VIII. Josiah Read's barn lot. Purchased of Jonathan Crane. Owned by Richard Bushnell, 1705
IX. Josiah Read's Home Lot, 1659(?) Owned by Richard Bushnell, 1705
X. Dea Thomas Adgate's orchard and barn lot.
XI. Jonathan Crane's Home Lot, 1686 Owned by Israel Lathrop, 1705.
XII. Christopher Huntington 1st's Home Lot, 1659 Owned & probably occ by John Huntington, 1705.
XIII. Christopher Huntington 2nd Part of his father's Home Lot, 1659. Living here, 1705.
XIV. Dea Thomas Adgate, 1659. Living here, 1705.
XV. John Olmstead's Home Lot, 1659. Occupied by Samuel Lathrop, 2d, 1705.
XVI. William Backus 1st's Home Lot, 1659. Occupied by Ensign Thos Leffingwell, 1705.
XVII. Rev James Fitch (Part of his Home Lot) 1659. Occupied by John Waterman, 1705.
XVIII. Maj John Mason's Home Lot, 1659. Granted by Church to Mr. Woodward, 1700.
XIX. Part of Rev. Mr Fitch's Home Lot, 1659. Set off for burying ground, 1699
XX. Maj James Fitch's Home Lot. Part of Rev. Jas Fitch's Home Lot, 1659.
   Occupied by Rev. John Woodward, 1705.
XXI. "Meeting House" Plain Old Meeting House still standing, 1705
XXII. Stephen Gifford's Home Lot. House probably disappeared "Parsonage" land 1705.
XXIII. Simon Huntington's Home Lot, 1659 (North side of street.) House built by John Arnold
   Owned by Simon Huntington, Jr, 1705.
XXIV. Simon Huntington Jr's Home Lot Part of his father's Home Lot Given to him in 1688-9
   Living here, 1705.

XXV Simon Huntington Sr's Home Lot, 1659.   Living here in 1705.
XXVI. Lt. Thos Tracy's Home Lot, 1659. East house occ 1705, by Daniel Tracy Cross denotes former site of Lt. T. Tracy's house, probably disappeared before 1705 West house occupied by Dr Solomon Tracy, 1705.
XXVII John Bradford's Home Lot, 1659   Owned by Simon Huntington, Jr. 1705.
XXVIII Samuel Lathrop 1st's Home Lot Purchased, 1668 North house occ by Jos Lathrop, 1705
    South house occ by Israel Lathrop, 1705
XXIX Thomas Slumans Home Lot, 1663.   House probably disappeared before, 1705.

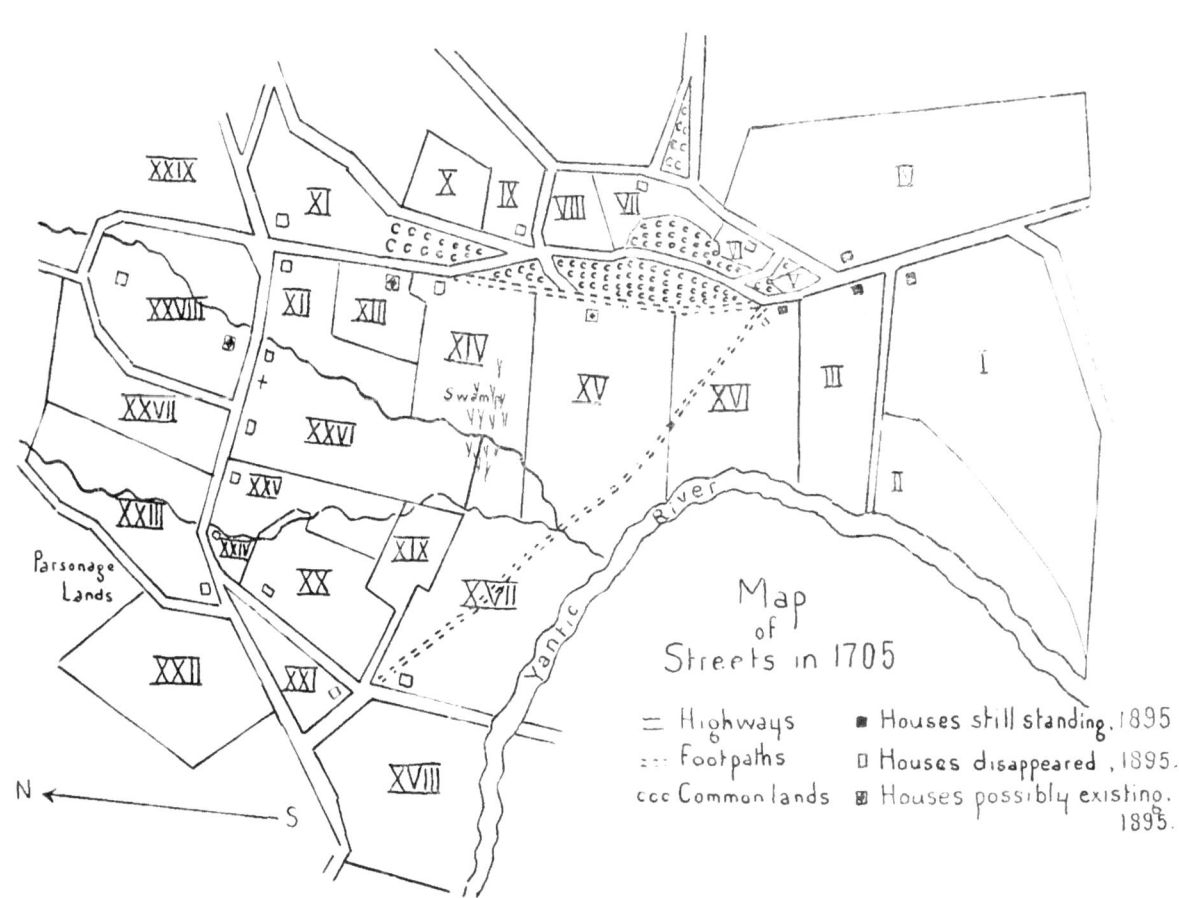

Map of Streets in 1705

= Highways   ■ Houses still standing, 1895
::: Footpaths   □ Houses disappeared, 1895.
ccc Commonlands   ▣ Houses possibly existing, 1895.

Lovett lot at the junction of the cross-roads, and the grounds extended below the Rudd house. The south part of the Rudd property, and the land on which now stands the house and barn of George Raymond, was owned formerly by Josiah Read, but, in 1705, was the orchard of Israel Lathrop.

We will now give the 1705 survey of the old highway, leading from the bridge over the Yantic, near the Norwich Town depot, to Mill Lane (now Lafayette street), but the part we shall especially consider, extends from Peck's corner to the Edgerton house.

HIGHWAY SURVEY OF 1705.

"The highway between Mr. John Woodwards[1] lot and the lot of John Waterman[2] from the river to the Meetinghouse green to be four rodds wide, and from sd Woodwards lot to the southeast corner of the Parsonage[3] lott to be seven rodds & eleven foot, and from the Parsonage lott square cross the Green, att the north end of the Meeting-house[4] to Mr. Woodwards[5] fence to be twenty-three rodds and nine foot, and from the northwest corner of sd Woodwards lott, cross the Green to the northeast corner of the Parsonage Lott, where it joynes to Simon Huntingtons[6] orchard, is ten rodds, and att the house of sd Simon Huntington[7] four rodds wide, and from thence to the brook att Israel Lothrop's[8] four rodds wide and of the same widdth five or six rodds beyond the brook and then the highwaye widens gradually to the southeast corner of sd Israels[9] house lot, and from thence to the northeast corner of the lot belonging to the heirs of Christopher Huntington, Senior,[10] the way to be nine rodds and ten foot from sd Huntingtons corner to Lothrops[11] orchard four rodds wide, and from the southwest corner of sd Lothrops orchard to the fence of Christopher Huntington[12] five rodds wide, and from sd

---

[1] Mr. John Woodward's lot is that now occupied by the school-house, Sterry and Hale houses, and extended from the Green to the river.

[2] John Waterman's lot is where the William Lathrop house now stands.

[3] The Parsonage lot extended from the chapel to Mediterranean lane.

[4] Probably the first old Meeting house, no longer in use.

[5] This is the home-lot of Mr. Woodward, and extended from the Burying-ground lane to the present house-lot of Rev. Wm. S. Palmer.

[6] Simon Huntington's orchard was on the site of the house now owned by Rev. William Clark.

[7] This is either the house of Simon Huntington, Jun., which stood on the site of the house recently occupied by Rev. C. A. Northrop, or the house of the first Simon Huntington, which stood between the Young and Dickey houses.

[8] This is the brook at the residence of Mrs. John White.

[9] The corner by the house of Ira Peck.

[10] The corner by the house of H. Yerrington.

[11] Lot where the Lovett, Rudd, and Raymond houses stand.

[12] The Jabez Lathrop and Potter houses stand on the former home-lot of Christopher Huntington, 2nd.

Huntingtons fence up hill eastward to the north corner of Thomas Adgates[13] lot seventeen rodds and six foot, att the house of sd Adgate[14] from his fence up the hill to his barn nine rodds two foot, from the southwest corner of Capt. Bushnells[15] lott formerly belonging to Josiah Read westward to Thomas Adgates fence nine rodds from the northwest corner of sd Bushnells[16] lott which lott joins to Joseph Bushnells[17] lott from sd corner to Sargt. Samuel Lothrops[18] fence westward ten rodds and thirteen foot, from the southwest corner of Joseph Bushnell's barn lott to sd Lothrops fence westward nine rodds, and from sd lothrops fence up the hill eastward to the fence of Joseph Bushnell on the west side of his house[19] twenty-five rodds ten foot, from Ensign Thomas Leffingwells ware-house[20] up the hill to his lot by his barn[21] nine rodds wide, the street between Lt. Thomas Leffingwells[22] and Samuel Blisses[23] home lotts and so to to the mill path to be four rodds wide," &c.

A great width of open land or "Common" is included in the general term "highway" from Christopher Huntington, 2nd's, house to Lt. Thomas Leffingwell's, but the traveled road for carts and horses, turning up the hill just beyond the Adgate house, led back of where now stands the Thurston and Donahue houses, and branched near the Harland house; one branch coming into the main road nearly opposite the Leffingwell Inn, and the other passing back of the Edgerton house into the Sentry Hill road. Another highway turned "out of the Town street by Samuel Lothrops between the lots of Capt. Richard Bushnell att the narrowest place three rodds wide." This is the present highway between the houses of Miss C. L. Thomas and Gardiner Greene.

Beyond the Adgate house, was the ravine mentioned by Miss Caulkins,

---

[13] The orchard and barn lot of Thomas Adgate are now a part of the property occupied by Gardiner Greene.

[14] The Adgate house stood in the upper part of the meadow just below the Jabez Lathrop house.

[15] Lower corner of the property now occupied by Gardiner Greene.

[16] The northwest corner of Miss Carrie Thomas' house-lot.

[17] The Joseph Bushnell lot began half way across the garden of Miss Carrie Thomas and the house faced on the upper road.

[18] The Samuel Lathrop lot extended from Gager's lane to the north garden wall of the Gilman grounds.

[19] The site of the Bushnell house was possibly near the bars in the lot above the Pierce house on the Sentry Hill road.

[20] The ware-house stood possibly on the later site of Leffingwell row.

[21] The barn stood possibly where now is the Harland garden.

[22] Now the residence of William Bliss.

[23] Now the residence of Angel Stead.

"with a pitch of several feet, through which, in times of abundant rain, a gurgling stream, formed by rivulets trickling down Sentry Hill passed into the dense alder swamp below." This was "the dark and dolorous swamp,* antecedently the haunt of wolves and venomous serpents, from whence it is said, often at nightfall low howlings issued, and phosphorescent lights were seen, very fearful and appalling to the early planters."

Mr. Henry McNelly remembers being told in his youth by an old resident, of his having heard an old lady narrate, that she once saw a bear shot in this swamp, now a fair and open meadow. For wild animals abounded in those early days, wolves, foxes, wild cats, deer and bears, and rattlesnakes were so numerous that large premiums were offered for their destruction.

On Feb. 4, 1737-8, the proprietors order in meeting that some common lands shall be sold, and appoint Messrs. Hezekiah Huntington, Simon Tracy and Richard Hyde "a commete" to sell "some of ye sd Common land lying in the Town platt between Ebenezer Lothrop's orchard and ye end of ye hill by Thomas Leffingwell's house and to attend ye following method, (viz.) to convey and lay out Lotts of sd Land and number the same, No Lott to be more than 4 Rods wide fronting on the street Westward, and so to run up ye Hill Eastward, leaving a highway on the hill at ye Rere of ye Lotts one rod and a halfe wide, and leaving the Street or highway at the west end of ye Lotts 3 rods wide," and also "to sell of sd Lotts at publick Vandue to the highest bidder for money till they have sold to ye value of 80£ or 90£ money, the Vandue to begin at one of ye Clock on ye first day of March next at ye house of Mr. Thomas Lothrop leaving needful highways up ye hill."

The auction was held, and enough lots, five in number, were sold to raise the required sum, and the rest of the land was then laid out in small lots, and distributed to various inhabitants of the town. One might infer from the great elevation of the Harland property, that where the road now passes below the house, there was formerly a steep bank, crossed perhaps by a foot-path. No record has been found of the time when this part of the main road was laid out, nor when the ravine was filled up in front of the Beach house, unless the clause in

*Miss Caulkins' History of Norwich.

this act of 1737-8 "leaving the street at the west end of ye lots 3 rods wide," has reference to these changes in the highway. It is plain, however, from the evidence of deeds, that the road over the hill ceased about this time, or shortly before, to be the traveled highway.

CHAPTER XVIII.

NOW, returning to the north bound of the Edgerton lot, the land between this point and the early south line of the Harland property came, in 1741 and 1747, into the possession of Thomas Leffingwell, 4th, who lived in the "Edgerton" house; that nearest to his house by grant, the land beyond by purchase. The purchased part was a piece of land, which had been granted to Isaac Cleveland in 1714, but not laid out to his heirs until 1734-5. This was opposite the Leffingwell ware-house, and, beginning about where the injured elm stands, abutted south-west on the street 5 rods, north-west 4 rods, north-east 4 rods, then south-east on a highway 5 rods, 1 ft. It was sold by the Cleveland heirs to Joshua Huntington, and by him, in 1741, to Thomas Leffingwell.

About 1780, Thomas Leffingwell leases land, beginning 4 rods, 9 ft. north of his house, where the remains of a cellar are still visible, to the firm of Tracy & Coit, and they possibly then build the shop, 50 ft. long and 32 ft. broad, in which they carry on for many years an extensive business. This shop was a long gambrel-roofed one story and a half structure, and is well remembered by many, as it was burnt down only about fourteen years ago.

Uriah Tracy and Joseph Coit were associated together as the firm of Tracy & Coit. The latter was the son of Joseph and Sarah (Mosier) Coit of New London. He was born in 1748, and died unmarried in 1807. Uriah Tracy (b. 1753), was the son of Joseph and Anna (Hinckley) Tracy. He married in 1794, Lydia Hallam of New London, who was said to have been engaged to Capt. Nathan Hale, "the martyr spy." Uriah Tracy buys in 1790 the Benedict Arnold house, where he afterward resided, and died in 1832. For a short time, his son, George William Tracy, carried on the store in partnership with Edward Tracy. At the death of George William Tracy, which occurred in 1834, this line became extinct.

At the time this store was established, in 1780, Norwich Town was the great centre of trade, as the "the Landing" is at the present day, and the shops were patronized by people from far and wide. The firm of Tracy & Coit was one of the representative stores of Norwich, so perhaps it would be well to look at their stock of goods, that we may get a general idea of "the trading shop" of those times. Their advertisements are of great length, and include every article under the sun—paints, dyes, pewter, brass kettles, warming-pans, frying-pans; looking-glasses, window-glass, saddlers' wares, Webster's Spelling-books, paper-hangings, New England, Jamaica, and "Demerary" rum, Geneva and "coniac" brandy, port, claret, Madeira, Lisbon, and Malaga wines; sugar, spices, Hyson, Bohea, and Souchong tea, "chocolet" coffee, codfish, raisins, &c.; mosaic and fancy chintzes, copper-plate and furniture calicoes, Queen's ware, rose blankets, baizes, jeans, fustians, birds-eye, bolting-cloths, denim, corduroy; London smoke, bottle-green, blue, drab, black and scarlet broadcloths, cassimeres, "furr" trimmings, laces, edgings, black silk mitts and gloves, and white fancy kid, and lamb gloves, men's and women's beaver gloves, serges, poplins, muslins, Irish linens, "cambricks," lawns, "sattins"; gauze, bandana, romal, pullicat and china silk handkerchiefs; "chain, souflee, cypress, nett and crape gauzes," stuff shoes, fans, ribbons, twilled velvet, plain and spotted black gauzes, "sattin" stripes and cords, shawls, lastings, wildbores, "dimothies," humhums, lutestrings, "taffeties," modes, pelongs, durants, shalloons, feathers; chip, beaver, castor, willow, Blenheim and Leghorn hats; moreens, taboreens, bombareens, velverets, sattinetts, camblets, corduretts, russeletts, sarsnetts, rattinetts, jennetts, muslinets, thick setts and toilinetts, &c., &c. Difficult indeed to please must be the feminine mind, which could find nothing to suit her taste and needs in all this attractive array. The firm did a lively shipping business as well, advertising for horses, oxen, live shoats, turkeys, oats, corn, barrel-staves, clover seed, pork, bees-wax, &c., &c., which they sent to foreign ports, and brought back foreign goods in exchange.

Charles P. Huntington at one time occupied this store before 1814. In 1825, it was sold to Epaphras Porter. At that date, the house below is occupied by

Mrs. Nancy Wait, the mother of the Hon. John T. Wait, who returned to Norwich, after the death of her husband, Judge Marvin Wait of New London, which occurred in 1815.

Epaphras Porter occupied this shop for some years, and Jesse Huntington (his brother-in-law), son of John and Abigail (Abel) Huntington, was also for a time established here as a saddler.

In 1813, Thomas Leffingwell, 5th, leases a lot of land (frontage 46 ft.) between the large elm tree and the Tracy & Coit store, to Henry Strong, who builds here a law office, which about 1835 or 1836 was moved to a site near the residence of his daughter, Mrs. Daniel Gulliver, where it still stands.

In 1833, Thomas Shipman sells to Henry Harland all the land between the Edgerton and Harland properties, extending back to the "Sentry Hill" road, subject to two unexpired leases, to Henry Strong and Epaphras Porter. This land still remains in the possession of the Harland family.

CHAPTER XIX.

NORTH of the Isaac Cleveland grant, 124 rods of land (frontage 10½ rods), were laid out in 1740, of which Col. Simon Lathrop becomes the owner, and in 1770, sells a small piece (frontage 2 rods), "beginning 14 links of a chain from the south-west corner of Thomas Williams Taylor's shop" to John Huntington, Jun., and Daniel Carew. On this they build a shop, in which they carry on the saddlery business. Col. Simon Lathrop also allows his grandson, David Nevins, to build a shop on the south part of the land, where David makes and sells hats, advertising frequently for musquash skins. This shop stands on land, having a frontage of 2 rods 20½ links, beginning 3 rods 4 links south of the middle of the Harland house. At Col. Simon Lathrop's death in 1774, both land and shop become the property of David, and in 1778, he sells to Thomas Harland. We are inclined to believe that in this year Thomas Harland moves into the shop formerly occupied by Carew & Huntington, and that John Richards takes the shop, where Harland was formerly located "near Christopher Leffingwell's." James Lincoln, a button-maker from Boston, also advertises in 1778, as located "opposite the store of Christopher Leffingwell, where he makes silver-plated, copper, brass, and white metal buttons," and we think that he is probably then occupying the former Nevins shop.

In 1779, the year of his marriage, Thomas Harland probably built the house, now occupied by his descendants. In 1787, he buys the land north of his  house of the firm of Carew & Huntington, and though no shop is mentioned in the deed, it may nevertheless have been included in the sale. We believe that this former shop of Carew & Huntington, or perhaps another built on the same site, was the "valuable clock & watch manufactory," which was burnt to the ground in December, 1795, "between the hours of eleven and twelve at night. The loss was computed at $1,500! through the spirited exertions of the citizens, the flames were prevented from communicating to any of the adjoining buildings."* After the fire, Thomas Harland must have moved into the Nevins shop, which he was occupying at the time of his death in 1807.

Between 1778 and 1795, this Nevins shop had probably various occupants. In February, 1791, William Cox informs his old customers, and the public in general, that he has "begun to work a compleat New Stocking Loom in a small shop opposite Col. Leffingwell's Long Row, where he will be glad to receive their stuff, and directions for Pattern Pieces, Stockings, Gloves, Mitts," &c. "With regard to pay, tho he does not mean to refuse cash, yet as he has heretofore found the pernicious qualities of that root of evil, he must beg his customers would not ungenerously crowd him with that article, but grain, pork, butter, cheese, and most other kinds of produce will be thankfully received, and a generous price allowed."

---
*The Norwich Packet of Dec. 17, 1795.

In this same shop James Lincoln sells woolcards in 1792, and Jeremiah Griffing works his stocking loom for a short time in 1793.

Thomas Harland came from England to America in one of the ships, which brought the tea to Boston in 1773. His intention had been to settle in Boston, but finding the town in an excited and unsettled state, he decided to go at once to some more remote place in the country, and so came to Norwich. He was an experienced goldsmith, and had served a long apprenticeship in England, and as was the custom in those days, after his apprenticeship was over, he journeyed from place to place, wandering as far east as Warsaw, possibly exercising his craft, and learning foreign ways of working. He was evidently a man of education, for the inventory of his library, which was a large one for those days, shows in the variety and selection of the books, a familiarity with the best historical and philosophical writers and poets of that period, and the large number of French books would imply a thorough knowledge of that language, which was then not common.

In his first advertisement, he calls himself "a watch and clock maker from London," and "begs leave to acquaint the public, that he has opened a shop near the store of Christopher Leffingwell, Esq.," "where he makes in the neatest manner, and on the most improved principles, horizontal, repeating, and plain watches, in gold, silver, metal or covered cases, spring, musical, and plain clocks, church clocks, regulators," &c. He also engraves and finishes clock faces for the trade, and cuts and finishes "watch-wheels and fuzees of all sorts and dimensions."

In November, 1774, not quite a year after his arrival in Norwich, he "returns thanks to his friends for their kind encouragement, and begs leave to inform them, and the public in general, that he has now compleated an Assortment of Warranted Watches, viz :—Horizontal, Shewing Seconds from the Centre,

Day of Month, Skeleton and Eight-Day Watches, in gilt, Tortoiseshell and plain Silver Cases; Eight-Day Clocks, in Mahogany and Cherry-Tree Cases. He also keeps Workmen in the Jewelry Business, and has for sale Brilliant, Garnet and plain Gold Rings, Gold Necklaces, Garnet and Brilliant Broaches, and Hair-Sprigs in Gold and Silver; Variety of Pearl, Brilliant, and Cypher Ear-Jewels; Cypher and Brilliant Buttons and Studds; a large Silver Tea-Pot, Sugar-Basket, Cream-ieure, Tea-Tongs, Spoons, &c., Chrystal, Silver, Plated and Pinchbeck Buckles of the neatest Patterns, Silver, Gilt and Steel Watch Chains; Variety of Seals, Keys, &c. The above Goods will be sold cheap for Cash or Country Produce."

In 1790, according to Miss Caulkins, he had twelve hands in constant employ, and it was stated, that he made annually two hundred watches and forty clocks. His price for silver watches varied from £4 10 s. to £7 10 s. Two of his numerous appprentices were Nathaniel Shipman and William Cleveland, the grandfather of the President. The row of elm trees, standing directly in front of the Harland house, were set out by Nathaniel Shipman, Sept. 6, 1781, the day that New London was burnt by the British.

In 1788, the citizens of Norwich Landing, disturbed by the many fires which were constantly occurring, resolved to have a fire-engine, and at the desire of some of his friends, Thomas Harland sent in proposals which were accepted, and he made, not as has been supposed the first fire-engine of Norwich, but one which was evidently of superior construction to the one then used at Norwich Town. To the assertion of a Litchfield correspondent of the Norwich Packet, that a "Mr. Samuel Thomas, coach and chaise-maker, was entitled to the credit given to Mr. Harland for this piece of curious workmanship," Mr. Harland makes such a fair and honest answer, that, quoting from the Norwich Packet, we will let him tell the story in his own words.

"The gentlemen of Norwich Landing having determined to purchase a Fire Engine" "expressed a wish that I would inspect some of the latest made and most approved machines of that kind, that if there were any new improvements I might adopt them."—"Having found one that appeared to me superior to any I had seen, I took the exact plan and dimensions of it, and as I did not see anything I could make any improvements upon, I adhered to said plan with very little intentional variation. Mr. Samuel Thomas assisted in making said engine; he did all the woodwork, and also assisted in some other parts of the machinery. The valves, the pistons, the large screws for the several joints, I made myself; two of my apprentices, with a smith, and a founder were also employed occasionally, till the whole was compleated."—"As Mr. Thomas seemed to wish to continue in this business," Thomas Harland gave him letters of recommendation, and offered him the use of a shop and tools, but as he himself happened "to have business enough in another line," he did not care for engine work, and never "assumed or arrogated" to himself "any merit as an inventor or improver of said machines" and he adds—"I never entertained an idea that it could be considered as a proof of mechanical genius to construct a machine so simple, so frequently and accurately delineated, so common, and so open to inspection as the Fire Engine."

Thomas Harland married in 1779, Hannah, daughter of Elisha and Hannah (Leffingwell) Clark, and had three sons and four daughters. At his death in 1807, the widow and daughters, Mary and Fanny, inherited the property, which finally passed into the possession of the only remaining son, Henry Harland, who married in 1822, Abigail, daughter of Judge John Hyde and Sarah Russell Leffingwell. The family of Henry Harland still retain possession of the homestead, which they have recently much altered and modernized. The shop has long since disappeared.

CHAPTER XX.

IN the division of common lands after 1638, 64 rods (beginning at the southwest corner of Simon Lathrop's shop, and with a frontage on the highway of 8 rods), were laid out to Joshua Huntington, and sold by him in 1741 to Thomas Leffingwell, who, in 1759, sells the south part (frontage 6 rods), "southerd" of "Rufus Lathrop's" shop, to Thomas Williams, who builds a house and shop. We are unable to determine which of the many Thomas Williamses of Stonington, Montville, Windham County, or Massachusetts, this may be. We are inclined to think that he may have been a Thomas Williams of Montville (b. 1735), son of Ebenezer and Hannah (Bacon) Williams, who is said to have married, in 1767, Jerusha Abel, and had one son, Elisha, (b. 1770). If this is the case, he probably sold all his possessions in Norwich, in the last years of the eighteenth century, and perhaps moved out of town. He was a tailor by trade, and built south of the house his shop, which we believe to be the building raised on a high foundation, now enclosed within the Harland grounds. He was also at one time engaged in manufacturing "flour of mustard."

In 1798, he sells his land and buildings "south of Rufus Lathrop's shop" to William Beard of Preston, whom, as we have found no record of marriage or births of children, we have been unable to locate. He may possibly have been a relative of Nathaniel Beard, "clothier from London," who lived at one time at Bozrah, and later at Poquetannock, or perhaps a descendant of the Milford Beards. He resided here until about 1811, when he sold his land and buildings on "Pickle" Street, "south of where Rufus Lathrop's shop formerly stood," to Daniel Mason of Lebanon.

It is said that many years ago, the wags of Norwich went about one night-time christening the streets, and the morning light revealed their titles in conspicuous places, "Pickle" Street, to designate this end of the present North Washington Street, and "Pork" Street, the one running at right angles. This must have occurred in the early part of this century, as from about this date, these names occasionally appear in deeds of property. It may have been at this time that the road, leading from the Green by the house of Dr. Tracy, received the name of Mediterranean Lane. Many years later, this christening feat was again attempted, and at that time the road leading by the Sheltering Arms received the name of "Maiden Lane."

Shortly after the purchase of this property by Daniel Mason, Cary Throop became the occupant of the house, which he purchased with the shop in 1823. This Cary Throop, was possibly a descendant of William Scrope, the regicide, who, on his arrival in this country, changed his name to Throop, and he may have inherited some of the puritanical spirit of this ancestor, for the Hon. John T. Wait tells us, in his inimitable way, how in the days of his boyhood, he once met Mr. Throop, returning on Sunday morning from a visit to his pasture on the hill, beyond the Mead house. Mr. Wait inquired eagerly if Mr. Throop had seen a swarm of bees, in which the boys had been much interested the night before, in the neighborhood of the pasture. Mr. Throop regarded him sternly, and in the severest manner replied: "Young man! aren't you ashamed to speak to me of bumble bees on Sunday morning." In 1831, the house and shop were sold to Henry Harland, whose family still retain possession.

CHAPTER XXI.

IN December, 1789, Thomas Leffingwell, 4th, "for £6 received of my son Thomas Leffingwell, Jun.," sells to the "Inhabitants of the East School District" the land north of the Williams' house (frontage 2 rods), "for the purpose of sd Inhabitants building a school thereon, and improving the same forever." Shortly after the purchase, the little brick school-house was built, which Mrs. Sigourney describes as similar to the one on the Green, having unpainted desks and benches on three sides, and on the other a recess for the teacher's desk, a closet for books, a water-pitcher, and a capacious fire-place.

The actual date of the building of this school-house, and the names of the first teachers have not been ascertained, but about the year 1795, Lydia Huntley (Mrs. Sigourney), then four years old, was a pupil here, and describes her first teacher, as a woman "above the medium height," with sharp black eyes, large hands, a manly voice, a capacious mouth, and a step that made the school-room tremble." She wore an immense black silk calash, and when Lydia saw it "bobbing up and down over the garden wall," she "hid like Eve in the garden." She does not give the name of this instructress, but it was possibly "Miss Molly" (?) (or Sally) Grover, whom Miss Caulkins mentions as a noted teacher in the "town plot."

Under her sway, the chief accomplishment seemed to be spelling, where the scholars "went above," according to their "skill" or "the mistakes of others." "The position being held but one night, the chieftain going to the bottom of the class, and rising again, pacified the discomfited, while at the same time it nourished an unslumbering ambition in the bosom of the aspirant."*

The next teacher,† to Mrs. Sigourney's horror, was a man, and his scholars spent most of their time "covering large sheets of paper with fine chirography of different sizes, they having been previously ruled and ornamented with devices in bright red, blue, and green ink." Mrs. Sigourney remembers them, as "having somewhat the effect of the old illuminated missals." She found her services in great demand in devising decorations and selecting poetry for these works of art, and soon became a great favorite with teachers and pupils. A graduate‡ of Trinity College, Dublin, was the next teacher, "grave, silver-haired and erudite," under whom she gained a thorough knowledge of mathematics.

In 1798, Consider Sterry opens an evening school "in the Brick school-house, a few rods north of Mr. Harland's, for instruction in Writing, Book-Keeping, in the Italian, American, and English systems." He teaches "Mathematics in their various branches both in theory and practice, particularly the modern, and most accurate practice of surveying without ploting, laying out of lands, &c. He would particularly notice those Gentlemen, *who go down to the sea in ships, and occupy their business on the great waters*, that he will teach them to find their Longitude at sea, by Lunar observations, also how to find their Latitude, by observations of the sun's altitude, either before or after his arrival to the meridian, &c." The price of tuition "for Writing and Common Arithmetic" was 1s. 3d. head per week, "for Book keeping and the higher branches of the Mathematics," 1s. 6d. per week, "for finding the Latitude as above, $1 for the complete

---

* Mrs. Sigourney's "Letters of Life."
† 1796.
‡ Possibly 1797.

knowledge." If sufficient encouragement is given, he offers to open a day school, at $3 per quarter. "None admitted but such as can at least read in class."

Consider Sterry (b. 1761), was a brother of the Rev. John Sterry. He married, in 1780, Sabra Park (b. 1763), daughter of Silas and Sarah (Ayer) Park of Preston, and had a large family of sons and daughters. Miss Caulkins writes, "Few men are gifted by nature with such an aptitude for scientific research as Consider Sterry. His attainments were all self-acquired under great disadvantages. Besides a work on lunar observations, he and his brother prepared an arithmetic for schools, and in company with Nathan Daboll, another self-taught scientific genius, he arranged and edited a system of practical navigation, entitled "The Seaman's Universal Daily Assistant," a work of nearly three hundred pages. He also published several small treatises, wrote political articles for the papers, and took a profound interest in free-masonry.

The Hon. John T. Wait, who came to Norwich from New London after 1815, attended school in this building for a while. He remembers vividly his first teacher, Dyar Harris, good-natured, addicted to naps in school-time and to taking snuff. He used to call his ruler "Old Goldings," and now and then, he would call out in school-hours, "Anyone who wants to go out can do so, by coming up to the desk, and taking two licks from 'Old Goldings,'" and the boys, ready enough to take the "licks" for the outing, would at once present themselves. He would then give one blow with the ruler, and refuse to give the other. At times, he would adjourn the whole school to the hill behind the school-house to try a new gun which he had recently purchased. These practices did not meet with the approval of the parents, so his stay was short, and his successor, Samuel Griswold, was much more severe in discipline. Mr. Wait relates how he used to sit with his feet on the table, and call the boys up to walk around it, hitting them in turn with his ruler as they made the round. Asher Smith also taught here, about 1822, and George Bliss, the latter teaching the public school at $22 per month in winter, and a private school in summer from 1823 to 1824, during a part of 1825 and 1826, and again in 1827. In 1828, he moved to the school-house on the Green, but returned to "the school-house near Mr. Throop's" in 1829. Many years later, Miss Goodell taught here for several years.

CHAPTER XXII.

IN 1733, a lot of land, on the side-hill opposite his house, with a frontage of 30 ft. and beginning 41 ft. from his land, is granted to Simon Lathrop, and on this, in 1734, he erects "a ware-house 30 foot one way and 20 ye other." Before 1759, this building has possibly disappeared, and his son Rufus builds another, for from this date, the shop standing on the lot is always called Rufus Lathrop's shop, and in the pile of stones now standing in the middle of the lot, the foundation-stone may still be seen with the initials R. L. and the date 1759.

After Rufus Lathrop, whom we believe to have been a goldsmith by trade, had relinquished the building as a shop, it became the home of an old colored man named Primus, who was formerly a slave.* Mrs. Sigourney describes "old Primus" as "venerable at once for years and virtue," and "respected alike by young and old." "The mild eye beaming love to mankind made the beholder forget the jutting forehead, and depressed nostrils." "A gentle yet dignified deportment, a politeness which seemed natural to him, and the white blossoms of the grave, curling closely around his temples, suffered not materially in their effect, from the complexion which an African sun had burnt upon him. It was remarked by children in the streets, that no one bowed so low or turned out their toes so well as Primus."

"Early instructed in reading, and the principles of religion, he had imbibed an ardent love for the Scriptures, and stored his memory with a surprising number of their passages." He might have been styled "a living concordance." It was the custom in private religious meetings, when the place of any text was doubtful to appeal to the venerable African. He had been for more than half a century a member of the Congregational church. "Though four-score

---
*See "Slaves" in Index.

years had passed over him," he still worked occasionally in the gardens of his neighbors. The school children would often pay him a visit, and he would explain to them the only picture which hung in his house " the tearing of the forty and two children who mocked at the bald-headed prophet," or tell the story of how he was brought in a slave ship from Africa, torn from the bedside of his sick mother, and when he arrived at the ship, among a crowd of other captives, he found his father ; of their sufferings on the voyage " between two low decks, where the grown people could not stand upright ;" how they were brought on deck to jump for exercise, or to sing, and punished with the cat-of-nine-tails, or put in irons, if they failed to comply ; how a fatal illness began among them, and his father was one of the first to die ; how at last he found a kind master, who taught him to read the Bible, and through him, he found his Saviour.

This old African had a daughter, who resembled her father neither "in person or mind." She was "a spy, and a gossip," and "the time-keeper" for all the single ladies of her acquaintance, " who approached the frontier of desperation." They could "never curtail a year from the fearful calendar " within her hearing, but they were brought back at once to the correct date. Cats were her favorites of every color. "At her meals, she was the centre of a circle," who, " with lynx eyes " and "discordant growls" "grudged every morsel which was not bestowed upon them."

" Frequently she was seen issuing from her habitation, her tall gaunt form clad in a sky-blue tammy petticoat, partially concealed from view by a short, faded, scarlet cloak, bearing a basket of kittens" to some "rat-infested" household. She used to mount guard over a barberry-bush, which grew on the rocks above her house, and drive away the children who essayed to pick the valued fruit. Her principal amusement was watching the sky to find signs of a coming storm. "No mariner, whose life balances upon the cloud, transcended her in this species of discernment." After old Primus' death the old house was torn down, or moved away. It disappeared sometime between 1798 and 1811.

In 1828, Charles P. Huntington purchased the lot, and erected a small building in which was housed for many years the town fire-engine. This engine was removed, presented as an old-time relic to the Thamesville fire-company, and the building was torn down not many years ago.

124 OLD HOUSES OF NORWICH.

Shortly before 1770, John Bliss collected subscriptions, and superintended the construction of what was probably the first fire-engine of Norwich. The old sub-

scription list is now in possession of his great-grandson and namesake, John Bliss of Brooklyn, L. I. The amount which was to have been raised was £60. The following is the list, from which unfortunately a fragment is missing, that would give the date, and a few of the subscribers names :

	£.	s.	d.		£.	s.	d.
Thomas Lathrop,		40	0	Hugh Ledlie,	1	0	0
Christopher Leffingwell,	3	0	0	Thomas Fanning,	1	0	0
Simeon Huntington,		15	0	William Hubbard,	1	0	0
Samuel Abbot,	1	10	0	Azariah Lathrop,	2	10	0
Ebenezer Whiting,		10	0	John Perit,	1	0	0
Jedediah Huntington,		30	0	Benj. Huntington, Jun.,	1	0	0
Andrew Huntington,		25	0	Benj. Butler,	1	0	0
Jabez Huntington,		40	0	Jacob Perkins, Jun.,		10	0
Samuel Tracy,		20	0	Elisha Tracy,		12	0
Ebenezer Lathrop,		20	0	Gideon Birchard,		10	0
Thomas Danforth,	1	0	0	Jedediah Hyde,		5	0
Samuel Wheat,		20	0	Simon Tracy, Jun.,		10	0
Samuel Huntington,	1	10	0	Hezekiah Huntington,		20	0
Ebenezer Thomas, Jun.,		12	0	John Bliss,		20	0

	£	s.	d.		£	s.	d.
Daniel Lathrop,	6	0	0	Simon Lothrop,		20	0
Samuel Leffingwell,	2	0	0	George Dennis,		15	0
Joseph Carew,	1	0	0	John Huntington,		10	0
Joseph Peck,	1	10	0	John Huntington, Jun.,			4
Thomas Leffingwell,	1	10	0	Benjamin Lord,		10	0
Thomas Leffingwell, Jun.,	1	0	0	Eleazer Lord, Jun.,		10	0
Thomas Williams,	1	0	0	Joseph Reynolds,		10	0
Rufus Lothrop,	1	0	0	Martin Leffingwell,		10	0
Nathan Cobb,		15	0	William Billings,		10	0
Daniel Hyde, Jun.,		3	0	Jabez Avery (to be paid in work),		10	0
Asa Waterman, Jun.,		10	0	John Lancaster,		10	0
Joshua Prior, Jun.,		10	0	Eliphalet Carew,		6	0
William Lathrop,		10	0	Jesse Williams,		4	0

Mr. Bliss has also bills from Nathan Cobb, Richard Collier, and others, which we will give, as a partial estimate of the cost of the work, for those who are interested in the old machine, and its construction.

Nathan Cobb sends in a bill for "work done on the enjoin" in 1769:

	£	s.	d.
To 8 hoops for the wheels,	0	5	0
" sharing (?) the wheels,	0	17	0
" makeing 2 axletrees & gaging,	1	4	9
" 24 Large brads,	0	2	0
" 3 bolts & keys,	0	2	6
" 4 screws & nuts,	0	5	0
" 2 staples,	0	0	5
" 2 hooks,	0	2	4
" 2 screws & nuts,	0	1	6

The following is a memorandum of "weight of work of Injine":

The pumps for the Engine,	35 $Lb.$
The plates and Crooks,	24 $Lb.$
The elbows,	8 $Lb.\frac{1}{2}$
The chamber,	32 $Lb.\frac{1}{2}$
The spout,	5 $Lb.\frac{1}{4}$

1770.	Mr. John Bliss.		Dr.	
		£	s.	d.
To Bras and copper & soudre of the arteels worked in to the enjine,		11	15	6
To working the above,		12	00	0
		23	15	6
Pd. George Denniss.				

In 1789, shortly after Thomas Harland had made an engine for the residents of Chelsea, or the Landing, this old machine is repaired, and Nathan Cobb's bill amounts to 9 s. 8 d. and Richard Collier charges for "Repairing Copper Air Vessell for Engine 12 s. 6 d." We are unable to say whether this old fire-engine is the one now so carefully preserved by the Thamesville fire-company, or whether the latter was built at a later date.

CHAPTER XXIII.

THERE are many old people now living, who remember the days when slavery was an institution in this town, for, until 1848, it was not entirely abolished. The first slaves in New England were the Indian prisoners captured in war. The males were sent to the West Indies, the women and children distributed in the various towns. Until about 1680, there were very few negro slaves, but after that date, they became more common. In the eighteenth century, there was hardly a Norwich household which did not own one or more slaves. This advertisement sounds curiously to us at the present day:—

TO BE SOLD VERY CHEAP.

A Likely, healthy good Natured, strait Limbed, honest NEGRO BOY, that can do any kind of Kitchen Work, and attend on a Gentleman's Table—he has no Fault.— For Particulars enquire of the Printers. oct. 30, 1775.

Or this, which appears in 1776:—

"To be sold—A likely Negro wench, Has no fault but want of employment."

The following bill of sale has been preserved in the family of a grandson of Capt. William Coit of Norwich:—

"To all People to whom these presents shall come Greeting:

Know ye that I Andrew Perkins of Norwich in y⁰ County of New London do Bargain Sell and Convey unto Mr. William Coit of s⁰ Norwich a certain Negro Man Named Pharaoh of the age of about thirty two years as a slave for life for & in consideration of forty Pounds Lawful money Received of Sd Coit. And I Assert that I have good right to Sell Sd Negro man as above said. And that he by virtue of these Presents shall & may have, hold & enjoy him ye Said Pharaoh as Such free from all Other rights & claims from any other Person whatsoever in witness whereof I have hereunto Sett my Hand this 14th March, 1774.*

In presents off   ANDREW PERKINS.
  ELISHA LATHROP.
  JOSEPH WILLIAMS.

In 1774, an act was passed, forbidding the importation of Indian, negro, or mulatto slaves into the State, under penalty of a £100 fine. In this same year, Samuel Gager frees, for faithful services, two of his slaves, Fortune and his wife Time, and grants them a farm on favorable terms, and also frees another slave, Peter. The slaves were as a rule, treated with kindness and consideration, were often educated, and taught a trade, through which they became frequently a source of revenue to their masters.

Fugitive slaves were often advertised. John, Hannah, and Joshua Perkins offer $20 reward in 1774, for the recovery of three runaway slaves, Jeam, Cudge and Bristol. The first of these was a shoemaker, and could read; the third could read, write, cypher, sing, and fiddle. John Perkins was the son of Capt. John Perkins of Hanover, who died in 1761, in whose inventory, fifteen slaves are mentioned. Hannah was the widow, and Joshua the son of Capt. Matthew Perkins, who died in 1773, of lockjaw, caused by a bite on the thumb, which he received from a young negro slave, whom he was chastising. Matthew's house is still standing in Hanover, and over the old-fashioned kitchen are the small chambers, where the slaves are said to have slept.

Capt. Joseph Coit brought with him from New London, two slaves, whose services were in constant demand, and on their master's account book appears frequently a charge against a neighbor for a day's work by Pero or Bristol. Bristol Barney (as the latter was called), was freed by his master in 1785, but two female slaves, Violet and Eunice, remained long in the service of the family.

Just before the Revolution, the question was constantly discussed, whether it was right to fight for liberty, and yet to hold others in bondage. Frequent com-

---
*Copied by permission of Miss Hannah Ripley, a great-granddaughter of William Coit.

munications appear in the Packet, inveighing against slavery, many of which are supposed to have been written by Rev. Aaron Cleveland (the great-grandfather of President Grover Cleveland), who, in 1775, published a poem against slavery, and in 1779, while a representative in the Legislature, "introduced a bill for its abolition." During the Revolution, many of the slaves enlisted, and fought for the country which held them in captivity. One such slave, Leb Quy, served during three years of the war as a faithful soldier.

The slaves had a special corner set apart for them in the meeting-house, and in the grave-yard. At one end of the old burying-ground may be seen a stone, erected "to the memory of Mr. Bristo Zibbero of Norwich, a captive from ye land of Affrica," who died Jan. 26, 1783, aged 66. Nearby, lies Boston Trow-Trow, "Govener of ye Affrican Trib," who died May 28, 1772, aged 66.

In 1784, a law was passed, that no negro, or mulatto, born after March, 1784, should be held as a slave, after reaching the age of 25, and in 1797, it was decreed that all slaves, born after Aug. 1797, should receive their freedom at the age of 21. In 1790, the Connecticut Anti-Slavery Society was formed, with Ezra Stiles for President, and a secretary of Norwich descent, Simeon Baldwin. At this time appear on record the births of slaves; Azariah Lothrop recording "Vilet" (b. 1784), Jack (b. 1788), Bristow, son of Nancy (b. 1793), Rose, daughter of Nancy (b. 1796). Rev. Joseph Strong records the birth of Jenny (b. 1792), daughter of Zylpha. Desire Dennis enters the birth of Martin (b. 1787), son of Chloe, and Joseph Williams, that of Jude (b. 1786), daughter of Phillis. Thomas Coit enters the births of Anthony (b. 1788), Robert (b. 1791), and James (b. 1796). Jabez Huntington emancipates a negro named Guy in 1780, and Col. Joshua Huntington, his negro servant Bena, in 1781. Dinah, wife of Scipio, both slaves of the Rev. Benjamin Lord, gives birth to twenty children who were all duly baptized by her master. According to Miss Caulkins, only forty-seven slaves remained in the State in 1800, and by an act of the Legislature, slavery was entirely abolished in 1848.

CHAPTER XXIV.

ACROSS the road, opposite the school-house, begins the Olmstead home-lot, recorded as 8 acres, more or less, abutting east on the Town street 30 rods, abutting south on the land of Stephen Backus 37 rods, north-west, and north on the land of Rev. James Fitch, and Deacon Thomas Adgate 73½ rods, and west on the river (with a foot-path through it). Miss Caulkins errs in her map of the early home lots of Norwich, in placing the Olmstead property west of the lower road, whereas it fronted on the present North Washington Street, extending from the Gilmans' north garden wall to the lower fence line of the lane leading by Gager's store, and was bounded on the west by the river.

Dr. John Olmstead (or Holmstead), is said to have come to New England with his uncle James, who was one of the first settlers of Hartford. Dr. John went from Hartford to Saybrook, and from thence, in 1659-60, to Norwich. On the Saybrook records of 1661, he is called John Olmstead of "Mohegan (shoemaker)," but with this trade, he probably combined the calling of a surgeon, as he served in that capacity in King Philip's war, and is known as the earliest physician of Norwich. Dr. Ashbel Woodward of Franklin, writes of Dr. John Olmstead: "He is said to have had considerable skill in the treatment of wounds, particularly, those caused by the bite of a rattlesnake. He was fond of frontier life, and enjoyed in a high degree the sports of the chase."

Dr. Olmstead married Elizabeth, daughter of Matthew Marvin of Hartford, later of Norwalk, Ct. He died in 1686. Even at this early date, several slaves are mentioned in his will, who are to have their freedom at the death of his wife. The widow, Elizabeth Olmstead, died in 1689, leaving in her will £50 to the poor of Norwich, £10 to the Rev. Mr. Fitch, legacies to Sergt. Richard Bushnell, to "brother Adgate's four children," and to the children of her husband's sister, Newell, but the greater part of her real estate, including house and home-lot, to her "friend, and kinsman, Samuel Lothrop." Samuel Lathrop had married Hannah Adgate, the step-daughter of Mrs. Olmstead's sister, Mrs. Mary Adgate. This is the only relationship which has been traced between them.

Miss Caulkins surmises that the original lot, assigned to John Elderkin, and sold to Samuel Lathrop, was in this neighborhood, which was not the case. We shall come to the Elderkin lot later. This land was Olmstead land, and Samuel Lathrop received it only by inheritance from Elizabeth Olmstead.

This Samuel Lathrop* (b. 1650), was the son of the first Samuel Lathrop, who came to Norwich about 1668. Samuel, 2nd, married in 1675, Hannah, daughter of Deacon Thomas Adgate. She died in 1695, and he married (2), in 1697, Mary (Reynolds) Edgerton, daughter of John Reynolds, and widow of John Edgerton. He had three daughters and four sons, and in a deed of 1714, gives the house lot to his sons, Thomas and Simon, the former receiving the north part with the house, and the latter the larger division of land on the south. In 1717, Samuel, 2nd, reserving only £30 per year, "for the maintenance of myself, and now wife Mary," and as much land as he "sees cause to improve," gives his remaining property to his four sons, Thomas, Samuel, Simon, and Nathaniel. He dies in 1732, and in 1731 Thomas and Simon execute a deed, making a more formal division of the home-lot, giving each an equal street frontage of 15 rods, 11 ft.; "then the dividing line runs west from sd street through the old part of the barn flower by the middle of the door and runs through the mowing land to the stone at the foot of the hill 21½ rods, thence west and by south ye nearest cross of ye hill to ye footway where the hill comes nearest ye river, then runs north, northwest on ye side of ye hill above sd footway to ye brook by ye bridge at ye west end of sd lot to a stone 21 rods," Simon receiving the southwest part, or "what lieth on ye south side of ye bounds and line," and Thomas the north part, and the house. This gives to Simon the land between the lane, and the south bound of the present Gilman property, and all the land facing on

---

*As it is difficult to mark the line when the various Lathrop families of Norwich made the change from the "o" to the "a" in the first syllable of this name, we use almost invariably the latter form, except when quoting from the town records.

the river, as far as the little brook, including the hill in the rear, now owned by the Misses Gilman.

On this south part of the Olmstead home-lot, and partly on the site of Gager's store, Simon Lathrop (b. 1689) builds a house, probably about 1714, the date of his father's deed, and of his own marriage to Martha Lathrop, twin-sister of his first wife, Mary, both daughters of Israel Lathrop.

Col. Simon Lathrop was a prominent character in the history of the town, commander of one of the Connecticut regiments in the expedition against Annapolis and Louisburg, and at one time in the chief command of the fortress at Cape Breton. At the time of the famous Mason controversy about the Indian lands, the second Court of Commissioners met at his house for two days in 1743. This must have been an exciting time for the neighborhood, when all the distinguished men of the colony assembled here, crowds of people whose lands were involved in the dispute driving in from the neighboring towns, and the whole tribe of Mohegan Indians hovering about, for whom the sympathizing Lathrops, Huntingtons, Leffingwells, Tracys, and other leading citizens kept open house during the proceedings. On the third day all this excitement proved too much for the household of Col. Simon Lathrop, and the sessions, which lasted for seven weeks, were adjourned to the meeting house on the Green. Col. Lathrop, by his skill in "traiding" in the shop "across the way," his real estate transactions, and probably also by old-fashioned frugality in household management, accumulated a large fortune for those days. The following campaign-song, sung by his soldiers, alludes to his faculty for money-making:

> "Col. Lotrop he came on
>   As bold as Alexander;
> He wa'n't afraid, nor yet ashamed,
>   To be the chief commander.
>
> "Col. Lotrop was the man,
>   His soldiers loved him dearly;
> And with his sword and cannon great,
>   He helped them late and early.
>
> "Col. Lotrop, staunch and true,
>   Was never known to baulk it;
> And when he was engag'd in trade,
>   He always filled his pocket."

In the first edition of Miss Caulkins' history of Norwich, she gives this anecdote of Col. Simon. "Some laborers were one evening sitting under a tree, and conversing about the moon. One said there was land there, as well as upon earth; others doubted it. At length Col. Lathrop's negro man, who was near, exclaimed—'Poh! Poh! no such thing—no land, there, I'm sure. If there was, Massa have a farm there before now!'"

At Col. Lathrop's death in 1774, at the venerable age of eighty-six, he left five slaves, Primus, Beulah and her child, Black Bess (then quite old, from the value attached to her), and Leah. The obituary notice, in the Norwich Packet, gives such a pleasant picture of the good old man, and tells so well the story of his life, that we will give it entire.

"On the 25th of January (1774), departed this life, Col. Simon Lathrop of this Town, in the 86th year of his Age. He was an Honour to the Respectable Family from which he desended, and to which he stood Related. He was naturally active and Industrious, and enjoyed a long series of Prosperity, by the Blessing of God. As his Genius was turned to military Exercises, he was long a Captain of Foot, in this Town. Present at, and engaged in two important Expeditions, one against Annapolis, and the other the memorable Seige of Louisburg, 1745, in which he was Col. of a Regiment. He was respected and beloved by his numerous Acquaintance, To whom he was very Benevolent, sociable and Friendly. He continued in the Marriage Relation about 60 years—thro all which Time, he shewed every Instance of the Dearest truest Friendship and Kindness to his Consort, who deeply mourns his Loss. He was a parent of Tenderness—a gentle Master, provident for, and Kind to all his Family, who sensibly feel his Loss.

"His Conduct from early Life was irreproachable; —and he was long a professor of the Holy Religion of Christ, and an Ornament to that profession, a Zealous Adherent to the perculiar Doctrines of the Gospel; Canded, Charitable, a Lover of Good Men; Faithful and Exemplary in the Instruction of his Family, with whom he took much pains to Train them up for God. A Man fervent and Instant in Prayer, and who delighted, and was very profitable, in Christian Conversation. In his last Months, which were peculiarly distressing, his Patience and Resignation were remarkable:—He shewed a quick sensibility and thankfulness to his Friends, for even the smallest Kindnesses, expressed a steadfast and persevering Trust in God, only thro the Merits of a Saviour to whom he expressed an ardent Love: full of Desire after Christ and Spiritual Things, he gently fell asleep without a struggle. He has left a sorrowful widow,—6 children, 34 Grand Children and 14 great Grand Children.

The Memory of the just is blessed."

To his wife, Martha, and his son, Rufus, Col. Simon leaves the house and home-lot. His wife Martha had joined the Separatists, and far from interfering with her religious convictions, he carried her every Sunday in his chaise up to the Separatist meeting at Bean Hill, while he went to his own church, and after the service, called to take her home again. Martha did not long survive him, dying in 1776.

Some of the articles of her inventory will give us a picture of her costume on state occasions: a velvet cloak, a crimson cloth cloak, a gauze hood, a velvet hood, a scarlet petticoat, a purple and white gown, a Persian apron, blue and red silver girdles, &c.

Rufus Lathrop (b. 1731), married (1) Hannah, daughter of Francis Choate of Ipswich, Mass. She died in 1785, and he married (2) his cousin Zerviah, daughter of Capt. Ebenezer Lathrop. The Norwich Packet, referring to the latter's death, and that of Martha, first wife of Dr. Dwight Ripley, in 1795, says, "Panegyricks on the dead are so common, and many times so undeserving that they become fulsome. But from the sweetness of disposition of the former (Mrs. Ripley), and the amiable deportment of the latter (Mrs. Lathrop), few we trust lived more esteemed, or died more lamented." By his first marriage, Rufus Lathrop became the great-uncle of the celebrated lawyer, Rufus L. Choate, who was his namesake. Rufus Lathrop was possibly a goldsmith, as, in the shop across the street, David Greenleaf (who was later a goldsmith), served as his apprentice, and "so faithfully" according to the testimony of Rufus, that he remembers him in his will with a bequest of £50. He leaves also to the First Church of Christ £30, for the poor and needy members, to the selectmen for the benefit of the poor of the town £30, to Hannah Teel,* who seems to have been placed in his

* Hezekiah Thatcher married, 1809, Hannah Teel.

care, and for whom he has a "particular affection," £20, desiring, that if his life "should be taken away, while sd Hannah is in her nonage, that his executors" see to it without fail, to place her in a family of known piety, and who are at least respecters of the religion of the blessed Jesus."

The house became the property of his niece, Lucretia, daughter of Jonathan and Eunice (Lathrop) Huntington. Lucretia Huntington (b 1749), became engaged to Jonathan, son of the Rev. Joseph Bellamy, probably about 1775–6. Jonathan or John Bellamy (b. 1752), graduated at Yale College in 1772, studied law with Gov. Samuel Huntington, and became a practicing attorney at Norwich. During the Revolution he entered the army, and just as he was returning to visit his friends in 1777, he was taken ill with the small pox, and died at Oxford, N. J., at the age of twenty-four.

Miss Lucretia Grace of Norwich Town, is the possessor of the mourning ring of Lucretia Huntington, which is of gold, with the name John Bellamy and the date 1777 in black enamel; the stone, a small crystal, in the shape of a coffin, in the centre of which is visible the miniature image of a skeleton.

In Davis' life of Aaron Burr are several letters from Jonathan Bellamy, and one from Burr to Matthias Ogden (later Col. Ogden) of New Jersey, dated 1775, in which he says: "I have struck up a correspondence with Jonathan Bellamy (son to the famous divine of that name). He has very lately settled in the practice of law at Norwich. He is one of the cleverest fellows I have to deal with, sensible, a person of real humor, and is an excellent judge of mankind, though he has not had opportunity of seeing much of the world."

In a letter to Aaron Burr, dated 1776, Jonathan Bellamy writes: "Curse on this vile distance between us. I am restless to tell you everything, but uncertainty, whether you would ever hear it, bids me be silent, till in some future happy meeting I may hold you to my bosom, and impart every emotion of my heart." Whether this confidence is his recent engagement or not, there is no further correspondence to explain.

Lucretia never married, and after her death in 1826, her brother, Rufus Huntington, and her sister, Abigail Pierce, inherit the house, and after the death of Rufus in 1837, the property passes into the possession of Ebenezer Carew.

Between this date and 1851, the house was torn down, and the land sold to several purchasers. Shortly after, according to Miss Caulkins, the tall old pine tree, which was standing for some time after the house was destroyed, also disappears.

CHAPTER XXV.

THE old homestead of John Olmstead and Samuel Lathrop, 2nd, passed, in the division of the property to Thomas Lathrop (b. 1681), the brother of Simon, who married in 1708-9, Lydia, daughter of Joshua and Bethiah (Gager) Abell. After a long and useful life, he died in 1774, in the 95th year of his age. His obituary says: "He was a Gentleman of a benevolent disposition, made the precepts of the Gospel the rule of his Conduct, and in the important stations of Husband, Father, and Master, acquitted himself well. His children, numerous Relatives, and Friends console themselves with the Hope, that the Creator, whom he fervently adored, has assigned him a Portion with the Just."

Mrs. Sigourney says that his death took place, "while his frame still possessed vigour, and his unimpaired mind expatiated freely upon the past, and looked undaunted toward the future." "Religion had been his anchor from his youth, sure and steadfast; and, with the dignity of a patriarch, he descended to the tomb, illustrious at once, by the good name he bequeathed to his offspring, and by the lustre which their virtues in turn, reflected upon him." He died intestate in 1774,

138   OLD HOUSES OF NORWICH.

and the heirs quit-claim to Dr Daniel Lathrop, "the house, in which he dwells."

This is the house which Miss Caulkins believes to have been "the house of Samuel Lathrop, Esq.," mentioned in a Boston paper, as having been "burnt at night," in February, 1745, and "almost all its contents destroyed, The loss estimated at £2000 Old Tenor." Miss Caulkins also says that the house (now occupied by the Misses Gilman), was built by Dr. Daniel Lathrop in this same year. At that date, 1745, Samuel Lathrop, 2nd, had been dead twelve years, and the house

mentioned, was probably that of his son Samuel (b. 1685), who as justice of peace in that year, would be naturally entitled Esq. This third Samuel died at Newent, then a part of Norwich, in 1754. This house on the Olmstead lot is continually referred to as "the house of Thomas Lathrop," and probably, as there is no deed on record, conveying it to his son Daniel, continued to belong to Thomas until his death in 1774. One part of the house is evidently very old, the ceilings low, and the beams showing in places the mark of the axe. The workmanship of this part does not resemble that of houses built in the middle of the eighteenth century, and we believe, that though Dr. Daniel Lathrop may have thoroughly repaired, added to, and remodeled the house, a portion of it, at least may possibly date from the time of the settlement.

Mrs. Sigourney, who, as a child, was brought up in the family of Mrs. Daniel Lathrop (her father being a valued retainer of Mrs. Lathrop), both in her "Letters of Life," and "Connecticut Forty Years Since," describes the old house and grounds, as she remembered them in her chilhood; with "the white rose, and the sweet-brier" climbing over its walls almost to the roof, and "its court of shorn turf, like the richest velvet, intersected by two paved avenues to the principal

entrances, and enclosed by a white fence, resting upon a foundation of hewn stone." "Two spruce trees, in their livery of dark green, stood as sentinels at the gate." "The house was environed by three large gardens." In the southern one, which "lay beneath the windows of the parlor," beds of mould were thrown up, and regularly arranged "in quadrangles, triangles and parallelograms," "according to what the florists of that age denominated "a knot." In a diamond shaped bed in the centre "a rich crimson peony" "reared its head like a queen upon her throne; surrounded by a guard of tulips, arrayed as courtiers in every hue, deep-crimson, buff streaked with vermilion, and pure white mantled with a blush of carmine."

"In the borders the purple clusters of the lilac, mingled with the feathery orb of the snowball, and the pure petals of the graceful lily." Here flourished also "the amaryllis family, white and orange-coloured, the queenly damask rose," "the protean sweet-william, the aspiring larkspur, the proud crown imperial, the snow-drop, the narcissus, and the hyacinth so prompt to waken at Spring's first call, side by side with the cheerful marigold, braving the frost-kiss;" "pinks in profusion, and a host of personified flowers, peeped out of their tufted homes, like nested birds,"—"the beauty by night," "the tawdry ragged lady," "the variegated bachelor," "the sad mourning bride," "the monk in his sombre hood," and "the mottled guinea-hen." "The dahlias had not then appeared with their countless varieties, but the asters instituted a secondary order of nobility ; coxcombs and soldiers in green rejoiced in their gay uniform ; the borders were enriched with shrubbery, tastefully disposed, at whose feet ran the happy blue-bell, and the bright eyed hearts ease intent with a few other lowly friends on turning every crevice to account and making the waste places beautiful." "A broad walk divided this garden into nearly equal compartments." The western part was "an expanse of fair even-shorn turf," "at whose termination was a pleasant arbor, with its lattice-work interwoven and overshadowed by an ancient thickly clustering grape-vine. Grouped around it was a copse of peach trees, the rich golden-fruited, the large crimson and white cling, the colorless autumn varieties, and the more diminutive ones, whose pulp blood-tinted throughout, were favorites for the preserving pan."

"Near the same region was a small nursery of medicinal plants ; for the mind which had grouped so many pleasures for the eye and the taste of man, had not put out of sight his infirmities, or forgotten where it was written, "in the garden was a sepulchre." "There arose the rough-leaved sage with its spiry efflorescence," or, as she describes it in another place, "the sapient sage, which seemed complacently satisfied with its own excellencies, or bearing on its roughened lip the classic question, *Cur moriatur homo, dum salis crescit in horto?*"* "The aromatic tansy" also grew here, the spearmint, "the pungent peppermint for distillation," "the healing balm," "the hoar-hound, foe of consumption," "the worm-wood and the rue, a spoonful of whose expressed juice, given either as a tonic or vermifuge, was never forgotten by the mouth that received it ;" "the spikenard and the lovage," and "the elecampane," "the aperient cumphrey," "the pennyroyal," "the bitter boneset, famed for subduing colds ;" and "the aromatic thyme that fought fevers." "Large poppies scattered here and there, perfected their latest anodyne, and hop-vines, clasping the accustomed arches, disclosed from their aromatic clusters some portion of their sedative powers."

"Yet the garden at the opposite extremity of the house was emphatically

* "Why need a man die, who has sage in his garden?"

the fruit region. It was longitudinally divided by a grassy terrace, and with the exception of a few esculents, rows of graceful peas, and beans, decking their rough props with blossoms, was directed to the varieties of fruit that a New England climate matures ; currants reached forth their rich and pendulent strings, large gooseberries rejoiced amid their thorny armor ; over a broad domain ran the red and white strawberry, hand in hand, like a buxom brother giving confidence to his pale exquisite sister. Through the apple boughs, peered the small orb of the deep-colored pearmain, and the full cheek of the golden sweeting, while many lofty pear trees aristocratically bore their varied honor thick upon them. There were the minute harvest pear, the coveted of childhood for its bland taste and early ripeness, the spreading bell, notching a century on its trunk, with unbowed strength, the delicious vergaloo, the high-flavored bennet with its deep blush, and multitudes of the rough-coated later pears, destined, with culinary preparation, to give variety to the wintry tea-table."

"Another extensive and highly cultured spot, called the lower garden, as it was approached from the rear of the establishment, by descending a long flight of wooden stairs, exulted in all manner of vegetable wealth to enrich the domestic board ; " "while a large turfy mound, rounded and entered like a tomb, the celery and the savoy cabbage claimed as their own exclusive winter palace."

"Beyond stretched an extensive meadow, refreshed at its extremity by a crystal streamlet, flowing on with a pleasant murmur to the neighboring river. The domain comprised also a hill, whose trees were sparsely scattered and which gently sloping toward the house, had at its foot a large barn." "Its yard communicated by a large gate with an area in the rear of the mansion, which was surrounded by a little village of offices. Among them were the carriage-house, the wood-house where ranges of sawed hickory were disposed with geometrical precision ; the gardener's tool-house, the distillery, where the richer herbs from the dispensary, and the fragrant petals of the damask-rose yielded their essence for health or luxury ; and the poultry house, with its glass windows and varied compartments, where the brooding mothers and their hopeful offspring found systematic lodgment and a large prosperity." Mrs. Sigourney describes as her "playhouse," "the spacious garret, covering the whole upper story of the mansion," in one corner of which, was "a heavy old-fashioned carved beaufet, upon whose curving shelves," she displayed her toys "so as to make the best appearance." In one of the garret chimneys was a closet, "where the ropes and pulleys of the great roasting-jack hissed and sputtered when put in motion by the fires below."

She speaks of the parlor "that low-browed apartment, with "its highly polished wainscot," its "crisom moreen curtains, the large brass andirons, with their silvery brightness, the clean hearth, on which not even the white ashes of the consuming hickory were suffered to rest, the rich dark shade of the furniture, unpolluted by dust," "the two stately candlesticks," "the antique candelabra;" "the closet, whose open door revealed its wealth of silver, cans, tankards, and flagons, the massy plate of an ancient family;" the "ancient clock, whose tall ebony case, was covered with gilded figures, of strikingly varied and fanciful character." She also mentions the storied tiles of the fire place, and pictures the kitchen with "the dressers unpainted, but as white as the nature of the wood permitted them to be," with "rows of pewter emulous of silver in its beautiful lustre," the "long oaken table" and "heavy oaken cupboard," the five or six tall chairs with rush bottoms, and the wooden settle "not far from the ample expanse of the fire-place." "Over the mantle-piece was a high and narrow shelf, which, at its western extremity, was multiplied into a triple row of shorter ones; forming a repository for a servant's library," which was "composed principally of pamphlet sermons, or what was considered Sunday reading." Near this servant's library hung the "roasting-jack, which, when put in motion, with its complicated machinery, extending from garret to cellar, alarmed the unlearned by its discordant sounds, and awoke in the minds of the superstitious some indefinite suspicion of the agency of evil spirits." The old housekeeper, Lucy Calkins, was quite a character in the household, and there were two colored servants, Beulah and Cuffee, children of former slaves.

Dr. Daniel Lathrop, the fourth proprietor of this mansion, was born 1712, graduated from Yale College in 1733, and went afterward to England to study "chirurgery" in St. Thomas's Hospital. He was there in 1737. While in Europe he purchased a large quantity of drugs and general merchandise, and on his return, started the first drug shop in Connecticut.

According to Mrs. Sigourney, "he possessed such acute sensibilities," and "was rendered so unhappy by the necessity of performing any surgical operation, that he commuted active practice for the business of an apothecary. This allowed him frequent opportunities of giving salutary advice especially to the poor, which gratified his benevolence, and kept his scientific knowledge from oblivion. To a competent patrimony, he added a very large fortune, gathered in his mercantile department, which he expended with great liberality. He was held in high honor and numbered among the benefactors of his native city, being the first to found a school where the common people might be instructed gratuitously in Latin and Greek, as well as in the more essential branches of a solid education."

Dr. Daniel Lathrop died in 1782, and in his funeral sermon, Dr. Strong testifies that "he attended well unto that charge to the rich, viz.: to do good, to be rich in good works, to be ready to distribute," that he was "kind and generous to the widow and the fatherless," "liberal in his contributions to the church, that he at one time offered a tenth part of the sum sufficient to support the ministry, and schools, free of public charge, though the offer was not at this time accepted." In his will he left £500 to Yale College, £500 for the support of the ministry, and £500 to found a Grammar School.

Dr. Lathrop married in 1744, Jerusha, daughter of Gov. Joseph Talcott of Hartford. Finding, on a visit to Europe, that the family, from which he was descended, wrote the name Lathrop, rather than Lothrop, he adopted that form on his return to America, and it is now universally used by the families of this name in Connecticut, though in other States the "o" is still retained.

Mrs. Jerusha Lathrop was born in 1717. Mrs. Sigourney describes her, as she appeared in old age when "her alert step and animated aspect would scarcely permit the beholder to believe that the weight of almost seventy years oppressed her." "A tall and graceful person, whose symmetry age had respected;" "the fair open forehead, clear, expressive, blue eye, and finely shaped countenance," "circled with thin folds of the purest cambrick, whose whiteness was contrasted with the broad, black ribband which compressed them, and the kerchief of the same colour, pinned in quaint and quaker-like neatness over her bosom," give us a mental picture of the charming old lady, as she appeared, pruning and training the flowers in her garden, or entertaining the little children of the neighborhood, whom she often gathered about her in the afternoons, by cutting with her scissors from white paper, groups of dancing girls, tall trees with little squirrels springing from bough to bough, or producing from her children's library those delightful books: "The Bag of Nuts ready-cracked," the renowned "History of Goody Margery Two-Shoes," or the wonderful exploits of the "Giant Grumbolumbo." In a poem dedicated to Mrs. Daniel Lathrop, Mrs. Sigourney depicts:—

> "The dext'rous scissors ready to produce
> The flying squirrel, or the long-neck'd goose;
> Or dancing girls with hands together join'd;
> Or tall spruce trees, with wreaths of roses twin'd;
> The well dress'd dolls whose taper forms display'd
> Thy pen knife's labour, and thy pencil's shade."

At these childrens fêtes, Madame Lathrop would sing songs at their request. "The Distracted Lady" and the "Address of the Ghost of Pompey to his wife Cornelia," were great favorites, also "Indulgent Parents Dear," in which the hero "loved a maid of low degree," and when he discovered that his proud mother had taken the life of the kneeling fair one, reproached her for the deed,

> "—— his rapier drew,
> And pierc'd his bosom through,
> And bade this world adieu,
> Forever more."

The song, "While shepherds watched their flocks by night," and an early supper usually closed the entertainment. Mrs. Sigourney was never tired of dilating on the virtues and charms of Madame Lathrop, of her liberality to the poor, of her piety, "which was not a strife about doctrines," "for she looked upon the varying sects of Christians, as travellers, pursuing different roads to the same eternal city," a liberality of sentiment not always found in later days. Three sons were born to Madam Lathrop, who all died within a few days of each other of some malignant disease. Then followed the death of her husband, and finally, her own mental powers failing, she died in 1805, at the age of eighty-eight (to quote from her funeral sermon), a loss "to the city," and "to the church of God, which she honored. The sick and the sorrowful mourn a benefactor; for she stretched forth her hands to the poor and needy; she comforted the widow and the fatherless. She opened her mouth with wisdom; on her tongue was the law of kindness; Give her of the fruits of her hands; let her own works praise her in the gates."

In 1806, after the death of Madam Lathrop, the property passed into the possession of her nephew, Daniel Lathrop (son of Dr. Joshua Lathrop), who was then living in the house now occupied by George C. Raymond. He was born in 1769, graduated at Yale College in 1787, and married in 1793, Elizabeth, daughter of Dr. Philip Turner. Mrs. Sigourney describes Daniel Lathrop as "a gentleman of portly form, whose movements were as leisurely as those of his elder brother were mercurial. He almost always smiled when he spoke, and ever had a kind word or benevolent deed for the lowly and poor. He and his fair wife were patterns of amiable temperament and domestic happiness." One of his daughters married Jonathan G. W. Trumbull, son of Gov. David Trumbull. His only son, Frank Turner Lathrop, married Elizabeth Macalester of Philadelphia, and died in 1832, *s. p.* Another daughter, Cornelia, married George Willis of Hartford, and, when left a widow, resided in this house for many years. In 1852, the house was sold to Stephen Fitch of Bozrah, and, in 1862, when purchased by Mrs. Elizabeth (Coit) Gilman, grand-niece of Dr. Daniel Lathrop, came again into the possession of the Lathrop family, to whom it for so many years belonged.

CHAPTER XXVI.

IN 1740, 21½ rods of land, "on the side hill near Capt. Simon Lothrop's shop," were laid out to John Reynolds. The southern line of this lot began "at the highway, four rods north from the north-west corner" of the Lathrop shop. The heirs of John Reynolds sell this land in 1755 and 1756, to Simeon Case, who builds the house now standing on the lot. The north part of the land (frontage 6 ft.), between the Reynolds lot and the Lathrop shop, became the property of Daniel Tracy, and was sold by him in 1760, to Simeon Case.

Simeon Case was the son of John Case, who came to West Farms (now Franklin), before 1727, and married in 1727, Hannah, probably daughter of John and Susanna Ormsby. We think he was possibly a son of John and Desire (Manton) Case, who came to Windham, Ct., from Martha's Vineyard, shortly before this time. Two of their sons, Barnard and Benjamin, settled in Windham. A Moses Case, possibly another son, appeared in Lebanon, married in 1717-18, Mary Haskins, and moved to Norwich between 1721 and 1727. A Mrs. Case is said to have died in Norwich, in 1764, aged 104, who perhaps was the aged mother of John and Moses Case. Six children were born to John and Hannah (Ormsby) Case, of whom Simeon was the third. He was born in 1733, married in 1759, Mehitable Allen of Pomfret, Ct., and died in 1785. He had nine children. Simeon, his second son (b. 1761), became the next owner of the house, and died in 1816. After his death, Susanna, widow of his brother Samuel, occupies the house, and buys, in 1822, the Isaac Tracy land on the south. In 1833, this house is occupied by Curtis Bliss. Susanna Case dies in 1848, and her son, Samuel, sells the property in 1855, to Amos Cobb; and in 1857, it is sold to Mrs. Lucy Blake. It is now the property of Thomas Donahue.

Three separate lots of land, with a combined frontage of 11 rods (the first beginning 8 rods north of Col. Simon Lathrop's shop), were laid out to various persons, but all sold between 1745 and 1752, to Dr. Joshua Lathrop, who built the house now owned by Mrs. Gardner Thurston. Dr. Joshua Lathrop (b. 1723), graduated at Yale College in 1743, and married in 1748, Hannah Gardiner, daughter of David Gardiner, "Lord of Gardiner's Isle." She died in 1760, and in 1761 he married Mercy, daughter of the Rev. Nathaniel Eels of Stonington, for whom the chapter of the Daughters of the Revolution in that town has recently been named. Mrs. Sigourney cherished a vivid recollection of Dr. Joshua Lathrop, of "his small, well-knit, perfectly erect form, his mild benevolent brow, surmounted by the large round white wig, with its depth of curls, the three-cornered smartly cocked hat, the nicely plaited stock, the rich silver buckles at knee and shoe, the long waistcoat, and fair ruffles over hand and bosom, which marked the gentleman of the old school."

"He was a man of the most regular and temperate habits, fond of relieving the poor in secret, and faithful in all the requisitions of piety. He was persevering to very advanced age in taking exercise in the open air, and especially in daily equestrian excursions, withheld only by very inclement weather. At eighty-four, he might be seen, mounted upon his noble, lustrous black horse, readily urged to an easy canter, his servant a little in the rear. Continual rides in that varied and romantic region were so full of suggestive thought to his religious mind, that he was led to construct a nice juvenile book on the works of nature, and of nature's God. Being in dialogue form, it was entitled 'The Father and the Son.'" "It was stitched in coarse flowered-paper, and sometimes presented as a Thanksgiving gift to the children of his acquaintance, or any whom he might chance to meet in the streets. How well I recollect his elastic step in walking, his agility in mounting or dismounting his steed, and that calm, happy temperament, which, after he was an octogenarian, made him a model for men in their prime."*

A large oil portrait of him, "with one of his beautiful wife, courteously presenting him a plentiful dish of yellow peaches, adorned their best parlor, covered with green moreen curtains." On these, Mrs. Sigourney says, she gazed, when a child, "with eyes dilated, as on the wonders of the Vatican." These portraits are now in the possession of Mrs. George B. Ripley, the grand-daughter of Dr. Joshua Lathrop. The Rev. Dr. Strong also adds this tribute to the good old doctor in his funeral sermon: "His enemies, if he had any, were silenced into respect by his virtues, and his friends were numerous and sincere. It was during his college life he commenced that race of godliness, in which he steadily persevered." "Though he was in his eighty-fifth year, he by no means outlived himself.

* Mrs. Sigourney's "Letters of Life."

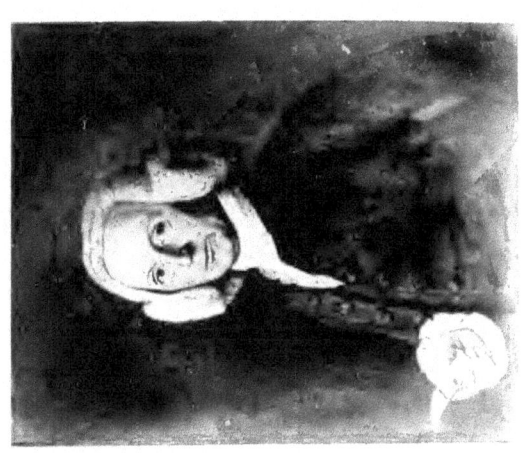

Neither debility of body, or mind, prevented his bringing forth much fruit, even at that very advanced period." "Though he had lived many years it was not long enough to satisfy the wishes of either his friends, or of the unfortunate."

Mercy (Eels) Lathrop (b. 1742), the second wife of Dr. Joshua, was the daughter of Rev. Nathaniel and Mercy (Cushing) Eels of Stonington, and granddaughter of the Rev. Nathaniel Eels of Scituate, Mass., and his wife, Hannah North, who was said to be the aunt of Lord North, Prime Minister of England. "This consort of Dr. Joshua Lathrop," according to Mrs. Sigourney,* "was a lady of fine personal appearance, and great energy. In an age when domestic science was in universal practice and respect, she maintained the first rank as a pattern housekeeper. The young girls brought up by her were uncommon workers, and thoroughly indoctrinated in moral and religious obligations. They often married well, and in thrift and industry were a fortune to their husbands. She was a sagacious observer of human nature, and not unfrequently a profitable adviser to her lord, whose unsuspicious charity made him occasionally the prey of imposture. One morning a man presented himself with a written paper, purporting that he was deaf and dumb." "This stranger enforced his claims by signs, and answered in pantomime such queries as were made palpable to the eye. The pity of the good old gentleman was warmly awakened." "The antique dark mahogany desk was opened, which never turned upon its hinges in vain. Still a pair of keen black eyes, occasionally raised from the needle, critically regarded the mute applicant. Suddenly a sharp report, like a pistol, issued from a chestnut stick that had intruded itself among the hickory on the great blazing fire, and he involuntarily started. 'My dear,' said the lady, 'this person can hear.' Horrorstruck, and enraged at thus losing the large bounty almost within his grasp, he discourteously, and it is to be hoped, unconsciously exclaimed, 'You lie!' And the illusion was dissolved."

"Mrs Joshua Lathrop survived her husband many years, and until past the age of ninety, retained her active habits, and mental capacity unimpaired."† She died in 1833, and the house was sold in that year to Gardner Thurston, whose widow still retains possession.

*† Mrs. Sigourney's "Letters of Life."

CHAPTER XXVII.

IN 1709, a Thomas Lathrop receives a grant of four rods of land, opposite his father's house. This is not "laid out" until 1714, when it is divided into two lots, each having a frontage of 2 rods. A ware-house, built by Benajah Bushnell before 1712, encroached on the north of this land, so Benajah buys the lot adjoining his own property in 1814. On the south lot stands for a while Thomas Lathrop's "bark house." Later, Dr. Daniel Lathrop established here the first drug shop in Connecticut, probably shortly after 1737. His brother Joshua, after graduating from Yale in 1743, became a member of the firm.

Miss Caulkins says that they imported not only medicines, but fruits, wines, European goods, &c., &c. The invoice of drugs, imported by them in one vessel, was valued at £8,000. A curious, old earthen drug-jar used formerly in the Lathrop shop may be seen at the store of C. P. Capron at Norwich Town.

It is said that this was the first drug-shop between Boston and New York, and Miss Caulkins relates an anecdote, which helps to confirm this statement. In 1749, a malignant epidemic prevailed in some of the western towns of the colony, and the Rev. Mark Leavenworth of Waterbury, came to Norwich on horseback to obtain medicines for his suffering people, making the journey hither and back, in three days. He would certainly have gone to New Haven or Hartford if there had been a drug shop in either town.

Benedict Arnold and Solomon Smith were among the apprentices of the Doctors Lathrop. Arnold settled as a druggist in New Haven, and Solomon Smith was assisted by the Drs. Lathrop in establishing the first drug-store in Hartford in 1757. Dr. Joseph Coit became later a member of the Hartford firm.

Mrs. Sigourney writes of the conscientious and kindly care which Dr. Daniel Lathrop and his wife bestowed upon their apprentices, receiving them into their own family, and constantly striving to bring them up to be good and useful members of society. But their efforts were wasted upon Benedict Arnold. He abused the cats, the dogs, and the horses, dismembered the birds, and stole and crushed their eggs. When dispatched to the mill for Indian corn, he would frighten the miller by clinging to the spokes of the revolving wheel, at one time submerged, then again flying through the air, while the miller called him "an imp of the Evil One."

In 1774, the firm of Drs. Daniel and Joshua Lathrop was dissolved, and Dr. Joshua formed a partnership with his nephews, and later with his son.

In 1785, the firm of Coit & Lathrop was established, the partners being Daniel L. Coit, and Thomas Lathrop, son of Dr. Joshua. In 1796, this partnership ceased, and Daniel L. Coit carried on the business until 1801, when he was succeeded by Ebenezer Carew, who soon moved to the Landing. The shop was destroyed within the last few years.

CHAPTER XXVIII.

ON the hill, above the Lathrop drug-shop, and approached by a succession of terraces, was the house of Thomas Lathrop, son of Dr. Joshua Lathrop. He was born 1762, and married in 1783, his cousin, Lydia, daughter of Capt. William and Lydia (Coit) Hubbard, who died in 1790, and he married (2) 1791, Hannah, daughter of Capt. Ephraim and Lydia (Huntington) Bill. The north part of his lot, where his house stood, was formerly the barn-lot of Josiah Read, and, when purchased by the latter from Jonathan Crane, to whom it was first granted, was recorded as "one acre of upland on the hill, abutting east on the highway 8 rods, south on land of Joseph Bushnell 22 rods, west on the street 16 rods, and north on a highway 16 rods." Josiah Read sells it with the rest of his property to Richard Bushnell in 1698. It then descends to Benajah Bushnell, and is sold by his heirs, Phinehas and Zerviah Holden, to Joshua Lathrop, in 1764. Joshua gives it, with an addition of part of the Joseph Bushnell lot, to his son Thomas, who, about the time of his marriage, builds the house at present occupied by Miss C. L. Thomas.

Mrs. Sigourney speaks of this "elegant mansion," which, to her, seemed "like that of Peveril of the Peak." She describes Thomas Lathrop as inheriting the energy and ambition of his mother. "No equipage was so conspicuous as his, no horses so fine, no harnesses so lustrous, no carriages of such immaculate neatness and taste." The Hon. Charles Miner also alludes to "the spanking bays," and "the plain, yet neat, double-carriage" of Mr. Thomas Lathrop. The same perfection which seemed to characterize all his belongings, appeared also in the attributes of his eldest daughter, Jerusha (later the wife of Pelatiah Perit). She was continually extolled as a model of goodness by mothers to their daughters, and teachers to their pupils, until one imperfect little mortal, goaded to desperation, was heard to say, "I wish there wa'n't no Rush' Lathrop. I'm tired out of the sound."

A long gravel-path, extending through the garden at the south of the house, commands a most extensive view over the river, the meadows and distant hills. A very beautiful letter from the Rev. David Austin to one of his nieces, the young daughter of Thomas Lathrop, pictures her walking with her mother, friend, and sister in this garden, "down the broad, cleanly, well-swept aisle, adorned

 with plants, flowers, shrubs, and vines." "We walk," he says, "we chatt, we admire, and catch from the lofty heighth and descending slope, and fertile valley, and rising, ragged, and verdant rocks, and meandering stream, the inspiration of the place," and he hopes that "the vines, and the plants, the rocks, and the plains, and the soul-inviting and heart-bending language of the skies," may "lead the thoughts" of his little niece, until "her eye is extended, her spirit ravished, in the multiplied and variegated beauties and glories of the Great Supreme;" and as she now walks in "this garden of the earth," so, he wishes, she may some day walk "in the garden of the Heavens."

Thomas Lathrop died in 1817, and his widow lived for a while in the house on the hill, but after her children married, she found her home too large and lonely, so, buying the lot on which formerly stood the Jackson Browne house, she built herself in 1828 a new house, in which she resided till her death in 1862, aged ninety-two. Mrs. Sigourney describes her, as exhibiting at the age of ninety, a rare example of comely appearance, active habitudes, and serene piety, and "with unbowed frame, directing the daily operations of a systematic household, and delighting in the skilful use of the needle." She classes her with "those, with whom, as Cicero says, wisdom is progressive to their latest breath."

Mrs. Lathrop (b. 1769), was one of the daughters of Capt. Ephraim Bill, all of whom (as their portraits testify), were handsome and attractive. Lydia Bill married Joseph Howland of Norwich, later of New York, and the other daughter, Elizabeth, married Daniel Lathrop Coit, who occupied the house just north of Thomas Lathrop's.

In 1828, the former home of Thomas Lathrop is sold to Henry Thomas, a New York merchant, of Norwich lineage, who returns to reside in his native place, and for 67 years his family have owned and occupied the house.

CHAPTER XXIX.

TWO approaches, from northerly and southerly directions, lead from the main highway, and unite in another road, separating the house of Thomas Lathrop from the one on the north, in which resided his cousin, and also brother-in-law, Daniel Lathrop Coit. The land on which this house stands, was the southern extremity of the Josiah Read home-lot, a partial description of which was given in the account of the old highway.

The first record of this home-lot gives it as 7½ acres, abutting south on the highway into the woods, east on Commons, north on land of Goodman Adgate and Commons, and west on the "Town Street." The second record is of 8 acres home-lot, and pasture land, with an addition granted by the town, abutting west on the Town Street 12 rods, south-east on a highway 92 rods, east on Commons 9 rods, north on a highway 21 rods, and west on Commons 15 rods to a stone "above the head of the spring."* This home-lot record was dated 1659. The

---

*Though the home-lot of Josiah Read bears the date 1659, his name appears in Miss Caulkins' list, of those whose claims to first proprietorship are doubtful, and not at all on the list of Dr. Lord.

pasture, which is registered as dating from 1663, abuts north on Commons, and land of Richard Bushnell 33 rods to a corner, abuts north-east on land of Bushnell 4 rods, and north-west and west on land of Richard Bushnell and Thomas Adgate 27 rods.

From these measurements it is not easy to exactly define the limits of this home-lot, but, if we leave a west frontage on the street of about 12 rods, then allow for the adjoining Adgate lot a depth of 12 rods, and a frontage on the cart-path over the hill of about 17 rods, then call the north-west corner beyond the Adgate lot the Bushnell grant, we may perhaps safely venture to include all the rest of this land bounded north, east, and south by highways, in the Josiah Read home-lot.

Of the parentage of Josiah Read we know very little. We quote from Miss Caulkins, that "the marriage of Josiah Read to Grace, the daughter of William Holloway, took place at Marshfield, in November, 1666." "It is probable that Josiah and John Read married sisters. The farm of William Holloway in Marshfield fell to his two daughters. It was sold, one half in 1670, by 'Josiah Read of Norridge, in the Colony of Connecticut,' as the inheritance of his wife Grace, and the other half in 1673, by 'Hannah Read, formerly Holloway,' whom we suppose to have been the wife of John. The only proof, however, is the coincidence of name. A third brother, Hezekiah Read, was considerably younger than the others. "The father, whose Christian name has not been recovered, died in 1679, leaving Hezekiah a minor, who, in accordance with his own request, was committed by the court to the guardianship of his brothers, Josiah and John, 'for his good education in the fear of God, good literature, and some particular calling.'* The mother of Hezekiah Read in 1680, was Ruth Percy." This Read home-lot was probably first granted to the father of Josiah, who, dying early, as in the case of William Backus, Sen., the home-lot was entered in the name of his son. A John Read received a grant of land in New London in 1651, which he afterward forfeited. A Robert Persey (Percy) bought a house in New London in 1678, and sold it in 1679. It is possible that these may have had some connection with the Reads of Norwich. Miss Caulkins also mentions a Joseph Read of New London, who may have been the father of the family. A Josiah Read, who

* Miss Caulkins' History of Norwich.

owns land at New London in 1662, may be the same who later came to Norwich, perhaps after the death of his father. Josiah Read was by trade a tailor. Miss Caulkins says that he removed to Newent, then known as "over Showtucket," to a farm he had purchased, in 1687, but the deed of the homestead to Richard Bushnell is dated 1698. He had eight children, four of whom were sons, Josiah, Jun., William, John and Joseph, who became "farmers in ye crotch of ye Rivers." Josiah, Sr., died in 1717, his wife Grace in 1727.

In purchasing this home-lot of Josiah Read, Richard Bushnell may have realized a youthful ambition to own the land, with whose streams and broad meadows he had been familiar from boyhood, when he lived with his step-father, Dea. Thomas Adgate, on the opposite side of the way. Here he now settles to a long life of usefulness and honor, in a neighborhood of relatives, his mother and step-father, and his two brothers-in-law, Samuel Lathrop and Christopher Huntington, 2nd, across the street, and his brother Joseph, and brother-in-law, Thomas Leffingwell, just below him on the "Sentry Hill" Road. Richard Bushnell was born in 1652, and was the son of Richard Bushnell of Norwalk, Ct., who married Mary, daughter of Matthew Marvin, and later moved to Saybrook, where he died about 1658. The widow, Mary, married just before coming to Norwich, Deacon Thomas Adgate, and when Richard arrived here with his mother and step-father he was about eight years of age. In 1672, he married his step-sister, Elizabeth Adgate, and had two sons and two daughters. Anne Bushnell was married in 1695 to William Hyde, and Elizabeth in 1709 to Jabez Hyde, sons of Samuel and Jane (Lee) Hyde. Caleb (b. 1679), married in 1699-1700 Anne Leffingwell, and Benajah (b. 1681), married in 1709 Zerviah Leffingwell, daughters of Ensign Thomas Leffingwell.

According to Miss Caulkins, in the early part of the eighteenth century, Richard Bushnell was one of the most noted and active men of Norwich, and very popular also, we should judge, from his being chosen to fill the important offices of townsman, constable, school-master, sergeant, lieutenant and captain of the train band, town agent, and justice of the peace. He was repeatedly chosen deputy to the General Court, in all thirty-eight times; and he officiated also as clerk, and speaker of the house for many years.

In 1683, he was appointed to take care of the town's stock of ammunition. In 1693, he was appointed ensign of the train band. In 1697, he was chosen school-master for two months in the year, the terms 4 d. per week for each scholar, the rest of the salary to be paid by the town, who empowered Lt. Leffingwell and Ensign Waterman "to satisfie" him in land "for his teaching school, to say what the schoolers doe not doe." At this same date, he was also called "shoemaker," and it is possible that he hammered nails into the shoes and ideas into the heads of the children at the same time. In 1698, he was commissioned lieutenant, and in 1701 captain of the train band.

He served as town clerk from 1691 to 1698, and again from 1702 to 1726, and his books show a great improvement on the work of his predecessor, John Birchard. The following specimen of his poetical powers was written by him, as a begging petition for Owaneco, Sachem of the Mohegans, who spent the last years of his life, wandering about the country, soliciting alms of the English :—

> "Oneco King, his queen doth bring,
>   To beg a little food ;
> As they go along, their friends among,
>   To try how kind, how good."
>
> "Some pork, some beef, for their relief,
>   And if you can't spare bread,
> She'll thank you for pudding, as they go a-gooding,
>   And carry it on her head." *

At the time of the great snow storm, in the winter of 1717-18, the meeting of Commissioners, in the Mason and Indian controversy, was appointed to take place at the house of Richard Bushnell, but on the 17th of February it began to snow, and continued for two nights and a day, with a furious wind, which piled the snow up into huge drifts ten or twelve feet high. For days, the Commissioners were hardly able to get together.

Richard Bushnell died in 1727. His son, Dr. Caleb Bushnell, who, as physician, captain of the train-band, and a prosperous merchant, was "almost as conspicuous

---

* "The last line alludes to the Indian custom of bearing burdens in a sack upon the shoulders, supported by a bark strap called a *metomp* passing across the forehead."—Miss Caulkins' History of Norwich.

in town affairs as his father," had died in 1724. In his will, Richard states that he never intended to give a double portion to his oldest son (as was the custom), but to give his children equal portions of his property. To his son, Benajah, he gives his double-barreled gun, silver-hilted sword, and belts, ivory-headed cane, and silver whistle; to his son, Richard, his small rapier, and two pistols. The gun, silver-hilted sword, and pistols may have been those left to him by Capt. Réné Grignon. The inscription on his grave-stone reads:

<pre>
        HERE LIES ye BODY
         OF CAPT. RICHARD
        BVSHNELL ESQUIRE
         WHO DIED AVGVST
        ye 27.. 1727.. & in ye
      75th YEAR OF HIS AGE
            AS YOU ARE
             SO WAS WE
           BUT AS WE ARE
           YOU SHALL BE.
</pre>

After the death of Richard, his son Benajah (b. 1681), occupied the house and home-lot. He had four children. One daughter (named for her mother), Zerviah, married in 1750-1 Phinehas Holden. Another daughter, Elizabeth, married in 1730 Isaac Tracy, son of John and Elizabeth (Leffingwell) Tracy, and the son Benajah (b. 1714-5), married (1) in 1740 Hannah Griswold, daughter of John and Hannah (Lee) Griswold of Lyme, and later in 1774, Betsey Webster of Lebanon. This son settles on a farm which was given to him by his father.

Benajah Bushnell, 1st, was chosen lieutenant of the first company, or train-band, in 1714. In 1720, he was elected deputy, an office which he filled eight times in different years. In 1721, he was appointed captain of the train-band, and in 1723, he took a prominent part in settling the boundary line between Norwich and Preston. He was an influential member of the Episcopal Church, was senior-warden and treasurer of that organization, and gave, in 1746-7, a lot of land "at the north-east end of Waweequaw's hill, near the old Landing Place," on which to build a church. This is the land on which Christ Church now stands. He also contributed £40 to forward the erection of the first Episcopal Church, which, built at that time, was later, in 1789, moved to another lot, given by his son-in-law, Phinehas Holden, a little east of the present Trinity Church, and again, in 1830, to the village of Salem, where it still stands, now serving as the Salem Town House.

During the latter part of Benajah Bushnell's life, he resided at the Landing. He died in 1762, and his wife in 1770. After their death, the old house at Norwich Town, and the land around it, passed to Elizabeth and Isaac Tracy, and the north part of the lot to Phinehas and Zerviah Holden. In 1775, Isaac Tracy, Sen., then living at the Landing, deeds this old house and land to his son Isaac, Jun., who is residing on Plain Hills. Isaac Tracy, Jun., sells the house and land to Joseph Coit in 1783, and in the course of several years the Coit family acquire nearly the whole of the former Bushnell property.

Capt. Joseph Coit was the son of John and Mehetabel (Chandler) Coit of New London. He was born in 1698, and married (1) 1732, Mary Hunting, daughter of the Rev. Nathaniel Hunting of East Hampton, L. I. His wife died in 1733, and he married (2) in 1739-40, Lydia, daughter of Thomas and Lydia (Abel) Lathrop of Norwich. In early life he went to Boston "to learn to be a boat-builder," but "likt it not" and returned home, and "learned of his father to be a ship carpenter." An injury to his foot, while at work at Gardiner's Island, in 1718, led to his adopting a seafaring life. From Jan. 12, 1719, to April 30, 1731, he made, to use his own words, "3 voyages before the mast, as mate 5, and as master 11, 19 in all, in which time, by the nearest calculation, I was 1100 days on the high seas, which is 3 years & 5 days, and what is very remarkable that in all these voyages, never lost but one white man, who dyed on ye Island of Barbadoes, viz., Andrew Denison, and an Indian boy before we left England, and out of 363 horses carryed out, lost only 3, one of which in good weather by the botts, one killed by carrying away of boom, and one by bad weather." After 1731, he became a merchant, and was active in all New London town affairs, until April 26, 1775, when, either influenced by the danger of invasion, which threatened New London, or the fact that most of his children were living in Norwich, he moved to the latter place, and went "to lodge" at Thomas Leffingwell's. We have reason to think, that for a time, he occupied the house (now the "Sheltering Arms"), which belonged to Thomas Leffingwell. In 1781, he lost two houses and two stores, in the burning of New London. In 1783, he bought the old homestead of the Bushnells. In 1785, his son, Daniel Lathrop Coit, built the house which is now occupied by Gardiner Greene, Sen., and the old Bushnell house was probably torn down or moved away. Capt.

Joseph Coit and his wife, Lydia, lived with their son, Daniel, until the father's death in 1787, the mother's in 1794. In his latter years, Capt. Joseph Coit lost his eyesight, but his mind remained bright and active till the last. Three of his daughters married Norwich citizens, Christopher Leffingwell, Andrew Huntington and William Hubbard, and three of his sons, Thomas, Joseph and Daniel also moved to Norwich.

Thomas Coit (b. 1752), was apprenticed at the age of twelve to his brother-in-law, Christopher Leffingwell, and afterward started in business at the Landing. He built the house on Broadway now occupied by ex-Mayor Hugh H. Osgood, and about 1795 moved to Pomfret, then to Canterbury where he died in 1832. Joseph and Daniel served as apprentices to their uncles, Drs. Daniel and Joshua Lathrop. Joseph married in 1775, Elizabeth Palmes of New London, daughter of Dr. Guy and Lucy (Christophers) (Douglas) Palmes, and in 1776, his uncles established him in the drug business at Hartford, in partnership with one of their former apprentices, Solomon Smith. On a visit to Norwich in 1779, Joseph died after a short illness, and on his grave-stone in the Norwich Town burying-ground may be read:—

> "Stop here, kind friend,
> and drop a tear
> Upon ye youthfull dust,
> that slumbers here.
> And while you read,
> the fate of me,
> Think of the glass,
> that runs for thee."

He is said to have possessed "a cheerful disposition, a fund of ready wit and humor, and the talent of easy versification." The widow, who, it is said, made in her youth a solemn vow that she would "never marry a Coit," again exercised a woman's privilege of changing her mind, and married in 1780, Capt. William Coit of Norwich, and after a long life, died in 1803, "leaving a reputation for intelligence, energy, and piety." The Hon. Joshua Coit was the only one of the children of Capt. Joseph Coit, who remained in New London.

Daniel Lathrop Coit was born in 1754, served with his brother Joseph, as an apprentice in the drug-shop, living at the time in the household of his uncle, Dr. Daniel Lathrop. In 1783, he left Norwich for a trip to Europe, and his journal shall tell us of the difficulties he encountered, in starting from "the head of navigation" on the Thames:—

"Thursday Morning, May 29, 1783.

Sailed from Norwich—11 o'clock A. M. Anchored about 5 miles down the River—lodged on Board. We got aground only 14 times. Braddick-Boatman. 4 Passengers. Went on shore & staid the night, next morning went on shore, & walked to New London.

30th. Arrived at N. L. about 2 o'clock friday.

31st. Sailed from N. L. for N. York in Sloop Polly Braddick & had a fine run—this day arrived within about 14 miles of N. York, when we anchored for the night.

June 1st. Arrived in N. York about 11 o'clock with 14 sail which passed Hell Gate with us. Weather Lowry & unpleasant. Passengers, W. Coit, Jun., Benjamin Coit, Capt. T. Fanning, L. McCurdy, Andrew Wattles.

June 7th. Went on board the Brig Iris about 3 o'clock. Fell down to Staten Island. Anchored for the night being Friday.

8th. Weighed anchor in the morning—ran down to the Hook where we waited for Mr. Cruden until about 12 o'clock when we sat sail."

On Saturday, July 6th, he landed at Portsmouth. He visited England, Holland, and France, and passed the winter of 1784 in Paris, to acquire a familiarity with the language. Here he enjoyed the acquaintance of Dr. Franklin, then our minister to France, and of the Marquis de La Fayette. He saw the first successful balloon-ascension, made by Messrs. Robert and Charles, in December, 1783, in the gardens of the Tuileries, and his letter, describing this event, was printed in the Norwich Packet. He writes: "The two men ascended to about 500 yards in the air, and then sailed on the wings of the wind about 9 leagues. The wind was small, and they sailed along very prettily; they were about 2 hours and a half in going 9 leagues. The novelty of the thing is so great that it ingrosses half the talk and attention of the city."

After his return from Europe he resided until his marriage in 1786, with Madam Jerusha Lathrop, the widow of his uncle Daniel. Mrs. Sigourney says: "His aged relative, whom he revered as a parent, and by whom his attachment was reciprocated, used familiarly to style him her 'philosophical nephew.'" "By casual observers, he was deemed reserved or haughty; but those who were able to comprehend him discovered a heart true to the impulses of friendship and affection, and a mind capable of balancing the most delicate points of patriotic and moral principle." "He was fond of the science of Natural History, and of exploring those labyrinths where nature loves to hide." After his return from Europe, he entered into partnership with Thomas Lathrop, succeeding Dr. Joshua in the drug business, and after the retirement of Thomas Lathrop about 1796, he continued it alone for some years. In 1801, he went to New York, where he was for two or three years in partnership with his brother-in-law, Joseph Howland. He then retired from active business, and returned to Norwich. He had invested largely in the lands of the Western Reserve, or New Connecticut (as it was called), in the State of Ohio, and experimented in silk-making, in order to ascertain if this industry could be made productive in the new region.

"Unassuming, and punctilious in rendering to everyone the dues and courtesies of life, nothing could surpass his forbearance and indulgence for the failings and weaknesses of others, while his sincerity, and freedom from prejudice, united with a judgment, ripened by a wide intercourse with mankind, gave a weight and sanction to his counsels, that were often sought, and were unobtrusively rendered." He married in 1786, Elizabeth Bill, daughter of Capt. Ephraim and Lydia (Huntington) Bill, "a woman of great benevolence, unpretending piety, and undeviating sweetness of disposition," who died in 1846. The portraits of Daniel and Elizabeth (Bill) Coit, painted by Fisher, are now owned by their granddaughters, the Misses Gilman.

Their daughter, Lydia, married Prof. James L. Kingsley of New Haven. Maria became the second wife of Peletiah Perit of New York, later of New Haven. Eliza Coit married William C. Gilman. Of their sons, Henry married Mary, daughter of Shubael Breed; Joshua graduated at Yale in 1819, practiced law in New York for many years, traveled in Europe, and then retired to New Haven, where he died a short time ago.

Daniel Wadsworth Coit, the eldest son (b. 1787), married in 1834 his cousin, Harriet Frances Coit, daughter of Levi and Lydia (Howland) Coit, and after many years spent in travel, settled down in the former home of his father, and died in 1876. The house has never passed out of the family, as, when sold by the heirs of Daniel Wadsworth Coit, it was purchased by the Misses Gilman, grand-daughters of the Daniel Lathrop Coit who first built it in 1784.

In front of the house, stand the immense elms, of which Mrs. Sigourney wrote:—

> "I do remember me
> Of two old elm trees' shade;
> With mosses sprinkled at their feet,
> Where my young childhood played."

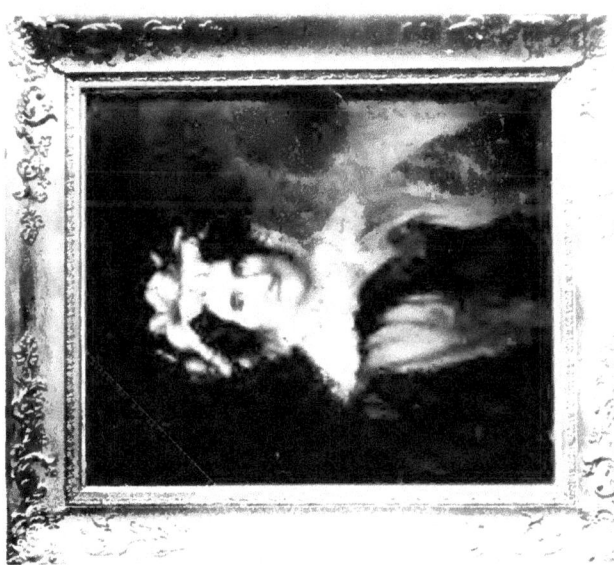

CHAPTER XXX.

IN 1740, a piece of land, containing 15 rods, was laid out near Capt. Bushnell's house on the south side of the brook, abutting west on the Town Street 6 rods. This came into the possession of Noah Mandell, who also purchased in 1748, 8 rods of adjoining land, which had been granted to Isaac Huntington, abutting west on the Town Street 4 rods, 4 ft. "to a heap of stones on a flat rock," then bounded south on a highway 1 rod, 11 ft., then bounded east on a highway 4 rods, then abutting north on Mandell's land 2½ rods to the first corner. Here Noah Mandell builds a blacksmith shop and coal house, which he sells in 1749 to Jabez Perkins, 3rd. We only know of Noah Mandell that he married in 1746, Sarah Corner, and had two children, John (b. 1748), and Mary (b. 1750). The name is probably Mendhall or Mendall.

Miss Caulkins relates of Jabez Perkins that he lived on the Sentry Hill road, and that one day in 1754, he brought from the woods two young elms of a size that he could conveniently bear upon his shoulder, and set them out in such positions that, when grown, they would throw their shade over the shop in which he worked. These she believes to be the great elms which stand in front of the former Coit house, now occupied by Gardiner Greene, Sr. This story may be true, but it seems to us that one of these elms may possibly antedate the other. Of course allowance must be made for habitat, injuries, and many other circumstances, which naturally retard or promote the growth of a tree, but in order that all may have an opportunity to judge for themselves, we will give a few statistics.

To begin with the famous elm on Boston Common, which was blown down in 1876, we find that in a map of Boston of 1722, this tree appears quite fully grown; in 1792 it is called an ancient tree; in 1854–5 its girth, measured four feet above the ground, was 17 feet; the average spread of its branches, diameter 101 feet.

Now the following are the Norwich trees for which the dates are given:—

	Supposed date.	*Girth 5 ft. above the ground.*
Coit Elms. (Set out by Jabez Perkins.)	1754.	17 feet, 11 inches. / 13 feet, 9½ inches
Elms in front of Mrs. John White's house. (Set out by Zachariah Huntington.)	1751–61.	13 feet, 3½ inches. / 13 feet, 1 inch.
Washington Street Elm.* (Set out by Peabody Clement.)	1767.	13 feet, 1 inch.
Harland Elms. (Set out by Nathaniel Shipman.)	1751.	7 feet, 10 inches. / 8 feet, 1 inch.

Now if this Boston elm, after all its reputed years of growth, could only boast of 17 feet of girth, 4 feet above the ground, is it not possible, that the larger Coit elm may have existed nearer the time of the town's settlement, than 1754? Yet, proud as we well may be of this beautiful elm, it is only a second class tree after all, for, according to the standard of Dr. Oliver Wendell Holmes, a first-class elm must have over twenty feet of girth, five feet above the ground, and a spread of branches a hundred feet across. In this last requirement, at least, our elms come up to his standard, for the Doctor tells, in his "Autocrat of the Breakfast

* When this tree was planted it was said to have been about "the size of a bean pole."

Table," of a "very pretty" letter he has received from Norwich, giving an account of these elms, and the spread of their branches, "one hundred and twenty-seven feet from bough-end to bough-end." The Doctor writes: "What do you say to that? and gentle ladies beneath it, that love it, and celebrate its praises! and that in a town of such supreme, audacious, Alpine loveliness as Norwich!* Only the dear people there must learn to call it Norridge, and not to be misled by the mere accident of spelling.

Nor*wich*.

Por*ch*mouth.

Cincinnat*ah*.

What a picture of our civilization!"

Jabez Perkins sells the blacksmith's shop in 1761 to Nathan Cobb, who builds the house, lately occupied by Thomas Donahue, near the brook, and resides here with his family till his death in 1807.

Nathan Cobb (b. 1734), was the son of Henry Cobb of Stonington, and a great-grandson of Elder Henry Cobb of Barnstable, Mass., who was a member

---

*Dr. Holmes is of Norwich descent through his grandmother, Temperance Bishop, (wife of Dr. David Holmes), who was a granddaughter of Joseph Lathrop.

of the Rev. John Lathrop's church in London, and, escaping imprisonment, when the pastor and many of the congregation were arrested, came to Plymouth in New England. From here he went to join his former pastor at Scituate, and also followed him to Barnstable. He was senior deacon of the church at Scituate, and in 1670 was chosen ruling elder of the church at Barnstable, which office he held till his death. His son, Henry, moved in 1705 to Stonington, Ct., and the latter's grandson, Nathan, came to Norwich about 1761. Nathan Cobb was a blacksmith (or rather gunsmith), by trade. He married in 1757 in Stonington, Katherine, daughter of Jonathan and Margaret (Stanton) Copp. After his death in 1807, his family continued to occupy the house until 1830, when they sell it to Ebenezer Lord, and the land, where the shop formerly stood, to Daniel Coit. In 1838, the house also comes into Coit possession. It is now owned by the Misses Gilman.

North of the brook, a small lot (frontage 3 rods), is laid out to Richard Charlton in 1741, and sold in 1771 to Nathaniel Parish who builds a house which, in 1791, is purchased by Asahel Case for his father, Ebenezer Case.

We think this was Nathaniel Parish (b. 1748), son of Nathaniel and Kesiah (Armstrong) Parish.

Ebenezer Case (b. 1730-1), was the son of John and Hannah (Ormsby) Case and the brother of Simeon, who lived a short distance down the street. Ebenezer married in 1762, Prudence Cooley of Windham, and had a family of eight children. He lived for a time in another house a few rods above the Parish house, which he relinquished in 1791 to his son Asahel. He resided in the former Parish house until his death. It was then occupied by his son Calvin (b. 1779), who married in 1799 Mary Killgrove—and later by Calvin's daughter Nancy, who had married John G. Smith, and in 1871 it was sold to Daniel W. Coit, and the house was soon after destroyed.

North of the Parish house was a narrow road, called in old times "the Adgate cartway," leading to the barn on the hill; and north of this was a small lot of land (with a frontage of 3½ rods on the Bushnell cartway leading over the hill, and a frontage of 6 rods, 6 feet on the main street, and Adgate cartway), which was laid out to Matthew Adgate between 1738 and 1740. A shop was

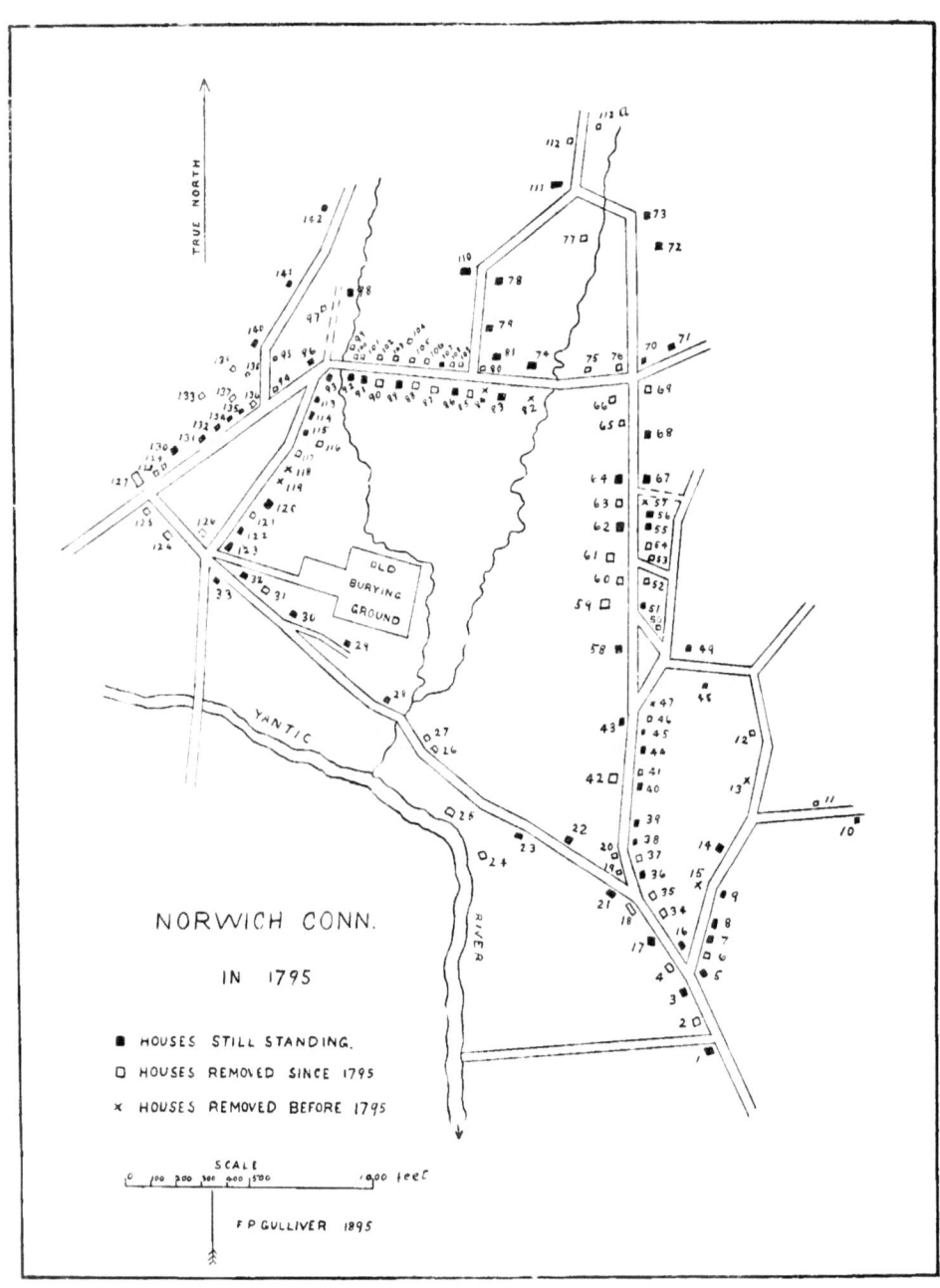

MAP OF 1795

1 Phoebe Reynolds (widow).
2 Stocking shop.
3 John Bliss.
4 Jackson Browne.
5 Hezekiah Williams' heirs (owner).
6 Timothy Lester (?) shop.
7 Thomas Leffingwell, 5th, (owner).
8 Samuel Leffingwell.
9 Samuel Leffingwell (owner).
10 Capt. Philemon Winship.
11 Dr. Jonathan Marsh, 2nd.
12 Thomas Lathrop (owner).
13 Former site Joseph Bushnell house.
14 James Lincoln.
15 Former site Ensign Leffingwell house.
16 Thomas Leffingwell, 5th.
17 Col. Chris. Leffingwell.
18 Leffingwell row.
19 Wm. Leffingwell's shop.
20 Shop back of Leffingwell's shop.
21 Widow Mary Billings.
22 Widow Mary Billings (owner).
23 Wm. Leffingwell (owner).
24 Thomas Williams (owner).
25 Pottery kiln and shop.
26 Carew shop.
27 Ebenezer Carew.
28 Asa Lathrop, 3rd.
29 Jabez Avery's heirs.
30 Family of Capt. Joseph Winthrop.
31 Rockwell Manning.
32 Diah Manning.
33 Eleazer Lord's tavern.
34 Tracy & Coit's store.
35 Shop.
36 Thomas Harland.
37 Thomas Harland's watch factory.
38 Thomas Williams' shop.
39 Thomas Williams.
40 School-house.
41 Old Primus.
42 Rufus Lathrop.
43 Jerusha Lathrop (widow).
44 Simeon Case.
45 Dr. Joshua Lathrop.
46 Lathrop drug shop.
47 Former site of Bushnell warehouse.
48 Thomas Lathrop.
49 Daniel L. Coit.
50 Cobb shop.
51 Nathan Cobb.
52 Ebenezer Case.
53 Case shop.
54 Asahel Case.
55 Jeremiah Griffing.
56 Tracy & Coit (owners). [house.
57 Former site of Aaron Chapman's
58 Eunice Adgate (widow).
59 Lathrop factory.
60 Daniel Lathrop's shop.
61 Henry Cobb.
62 Caleb Huntington.
63 Malt shop.
64 Ezra Huntington.
65 Town clerk's office.
66 Benjamin Huntington.
67 Daniel Lathrop.
68 Daniel Tracy (owner).
69 Ebenezer Carew (owner).
70 Avery & Tracy shop.
71 Dorcas Lathrop (widow).
72 Samuel Danforth (owner).
73 Samuel Danforth.
74 Andrew Huntington.
75 Samuel Danforth's shop.
76 Felix Huntington's shop.
77 Heirs of Thomas Grist.
78 Col. Joshua Huntington.
79 Mundator Tracy (owner).
80 Shop Ebenezer Huntington (owner).
81 Gen. Ebenezer Huntington.
82 Former site of Daniel Tracy's house.
83 Samuel Tracy.
84 Site of Charles Whiting's shop.
85 Mundator Tracy (owner).
86 Gov. Samuel Huntington.
87 Gov. Samuel Huntington (owner).
88 Capt. Simeon Huntington.
89 Capt. David Nevins.
90 Charles Charlton.
91 Asa Lathrop, 2nd.
92 Daniel Abbot.
93 Capt. Joseph Carew.
94 Simon Huntington (owner).
95 Benjamin Butler, 2nd, (owner), shop.
96 Gardner Carpenter.
97 Distillery.
98 Azariah Lathrop (owner).
99 Shop Joseph Carew (owner).
100 Asa Lathrop's shop.
101 Charles Gildon.
102 Nevins' hat factory.
103 Shop (Simeon Huntington, owner).
104 Jeremiah Leach's shop. [shop.
105 Simeon Huntington's blacksmith
106 Nathaniel Townsend.
107 Capt. Joseph Gale.
108 Andrew Huntington's shop.
109 Zachariah Huntington's shop.
110 Zachariah Huntington.
111 Rev. Joseph Strong.
112 John Lancaster.
112 John Lancaster's shop.
113 Widow Elizabeth Peck.
114 Capt. Bela Peck.
115 Ebenezer Jones.
116 Ebenezer Jones' shop.
117 Asa Lathrop's shop.
118 Former site of Manly shop.
119 Former site of Morgan shop.
120 Gurdon Lathrop.
121 Gurdon Lathrop's shop.
122 Asa Spalding.
123 Simon Carew's shop.
124 Ebenezer Lord.
125 Lathrop tavern.
126 Court House.
127 Church.
128 Carew & Huntington's shop.
129 Hon. Roger Griswold (owner).
130 Brown tavern.
131 Joseph Carpenter.
132 Joseph Carpenter's shop.
133 Seth Miner.
134 School-house.
135 Gardner Carpenter's shop.
136 N. Townsend's shop.
137 Jail.
138 Shop.
139 Shop.
140 Dr. Philemon Tracy.
141 Parmenas Jones.
142 William Osborn.

built on this land, which, in the division of the Adgate property in 1787, was given to Daniel Adgate (b. 1768), son of William. He sold it in 1789 to Samuel Case, who was a carpenter by trade. Samuel Case died in 1791. We have found no other deed of the property, but the land is sold by Asahel Case in 1802 to Jeremiah Griffing, and is now part of the present Jones' grounds.

In 1714, the town grants to Isaac Huntington 4 rods of land (frontage 2 rods), "on ye side of ye hill to be taken up between Sergt. Israel Lathrop's orchard and Sergt. Thomas Adgate's cartway," and here he builds a shop, and in 1717 he receives a grant of land south of this "to build a house on," but he evidently prefers to buy his grandfather's homestead, when the opportunity offers, and the land and shop (frontage 6½ rods) are sold in 1722 by Christopher Huntington, who has become the owner, to James Norman. James Norman either alters the shop into a dwelling, or builds a new house, which seems to stand on the former site of the shop.

At the auction sale of lands at Thomas Lathrop's in 1737-8, lot No. 2, of 29 rods of land (frontage 4 rods), north of James Norman's dwelling house, is sold to John Williams, who sells it in 1740 to Joshua Huntington, and it is purchased by James Norman in 1742-3. Lot No. 3, back of the Norman property, and No. 4, (with a frontage on the street of 3 rods), south of and adjoining No. 3 and the Norman lot, are sold to James Norman at the auction sale. Lot No. 5 (frontage 3 rods) is sold to Benjamin Durkee, and by the latter to Joshua Prior in February, 1739, and by Prior to James Norman in November of that year. These additions give the Norman lot a frontage of 16½ rods.

Miss Caulkins mentions a James Norman, who, in 1715 was captain of a vessel engaged in the Barbadoes trade, and in 1717 was licensed to keep a tavern. This James Norman may be the one whose house we have just located, or possibly the latter was the son of the sea captain. He was in 1723 a "cloathiar." No record has been found of his marriage, or of the birth of children, but we know that a James Norman married after 1730 Mary (Rudd) Leffingwell, widow of Nathaniel Leffingwell, of whose estate he was the administrator. Mary (Leffingwell) Norman died in 1734. James Norman died in 1743, leaving a widow, Elizabeth, and three children, Caleb, Mary, and Joshua, the two latter choosing their brother Caleb for guardian. The heirs divide the property in 1753-4. Mary Norman marries Eleazer Burnham, and sells her share, the south part of the lot (4 rods frontage), to John Hughes in 1753. In 1758, John Hughes sells the land to Ebenezer Case, who builds a house, in which he lives until about 1791. Ebenezer's son, Asahel, then occupies the house until October, 1801, when it catches fire from the snuff of a candle, thrown into a pile of shavings, and is burnt to the ground. In 1802, Asahel Case sells the land to Jeremiah Griffing. The rest of the Norman home-lot, with house and barn, passed into Joshua Norman's possession in 1759. In that year, the latter sells to Joshua Prior, Jun., a piece of land (frontage 4 rods) north of the Ebenezer Case house. Here Joshua Prior

builds a house, perhaps about 1766, the time of his marriage to Sarah Hutchins of Killingly, and resides here for a time, but in 1789 he is living on the road near Elderkin's bridge, and in 1790 he sells this house and land to Gideon Birchard, who also buys in 1795 a small piece of adjoining land (1½ rods frontage) of his son Elisha, who has purchased the property on the north.

Gideon Birchard (b. 1735), was the son of John and Jane (Hyde) Birchard and great-grandson of John Birchard, the first town clerk of Norwich. He married in 1757, Eunice Abel, daughter of Capt. Joshua and Jerusha (Frink) Abel, and had eight children. He was a carpenter by trade, and before 1799 moves to Whitestown, New York, and sells, in 1799, his house and land to Jeremiah Griffing. The house is still often called by old residents the Griffing house. In 1858, it is sold by the Griffing heirs to Daniel W. Coit, who sells it in 1871 to William Alfred Jones, who still resides here.

Jeremiah Griffing (b. 1773), was the son of James Griffing of New London, and a descendant of Sergt. Ebenezer Griffing, who came to New London about 1698, and married Mary (Harris) Hubbell, widow of Ebenezer Hubbell. Jeremiah married in 1793, Betsey Spinck, and had eight children. He was a stocking weaver, and also a Methodist lay-preacher.

Joshua Norman married in 1760, Content Fanning, and had seven children. He lived in the old Norman house for a while, but moved away before 1768, in which year he sold his house to Col. Simon Lathrop, whose heirs conveyed the property in 1791 to Elisha Birchard, son of Gideon. No house is mentioned as standing on this property at the time. The former Norman house faced the south, and stood on the site of the present house, now owned by Joseph Smith, and it is  possible that this, though not mentioned in this deed of 1791, may be the old Norman house. North of the house stood a barn. In 1801, Elisha Birchard sells this property to Samuel Avery and Thomas Tracy. In 1830, it is sold to Mrs. Mary Lathrop, widow of Augustus, and in 1846 to Hannah Dawson. In 1870, it comes into the possession of Joseph Smith, its present owner.

The 44 rods of land (frontage 4 rods), "south of Ebenezer Lathrop's orchard, beginning at the northwest corner near John Huntington's shop," was lot No. 1, sold to Abial Marshall, the highest bidder, at the "Public Vandue" at the house of Thomas Lathrop in 1737-8. Abial Marshall sells this lot to Aaron Chapman in 1742, and the latter builds a house, in which he may have resided for a time, but in 1757, he is living on a farm near the Shetucket river. In 1760, he sells the house to Matthew Adgate, who before 1767 moves to New Canaan, N. Y., and in the latter year sells the property to John Huntington, who resides here until about 1791, when Samuel Avery becomes the owner. In 1792, the land and house are sold to Joshua Lathrop, and presented by him to his son Daniel. It is probable that, about this time or shortly after the house disappears.

Aaron Chapman (b. 1718), was the son of Joseph and Mercy (Taylor) Chapman of Norwich, and a grandson of William Chapman of New London. He married in 1739, Kesiah Rood, possibly daughter of George and Hannah (Bush) Rood, and had nine children.

Matthew Adgate (b. 1737), was the son of Matthew and Hannah (Hyde) Adgate. He married in 1762, Lucy Waterman, daughter of Asa and Lucy (Hyde) Waterman, who died the same year. Matthew Adgate moved to Canaan, N. Y., where he married Eunice, daughter of Samuel Baldwin, and again for the third time in 1795, Mrs. Jane Williams, a widow, who died of the yellow fever in 1796. He soon after moved to a place called from him, Adgate's Falls, in Chesterfield, N. Y., and there married in 1815, the widow of Col. Rufus Norton of Chesterfield.

"In consequence of lameness, he was precluded from entering the army, but as a civilian he took an active part in the struggle. He was a member of the convention that formed the Constitution of New York in 1777."* He was afterward a judge of the County Court, and was, for several years in succession a member of the State legislature. He was a farmer and a mill-owner, and died in 1818, at Chesterfield. His last wife survived him, and died at Guilford, Ct. Asa Adgate (son of Matthew), was a member of Congress from Essex County, N. Y., from 1815 to 1817.

Dividing this property from the next was a lane, called in the deeds "Stonney" or Stony lane, and leading probably up to the Bushnell cartway, and

* Walworth's "Hyde Genealogy."

near this stood the shop of John Huntington, which the town granted him liberty in 1734, "to improve and maintain," where he had already built it, "over the highway against his father's house," "during the town's pleasure." In 1770, the town desires him to remove it, and for conveying the shop to another site, he pays John Bliss 4 s. in November of that year.

CHAPTER XXXI.

OPPOSITE the Josiah Read home-lot, and adjoining the Olmstead property, was the home-lot of Deacon Thomas Adgate. Miss Caulkins represents this lot as extending to the corner opposite the Harland house, whereas, its confines were the north wall of the Gilman grounds, and the south wall of the Jabez Lathrop property. The good old deacon had evidently such confidence in his neighbors, that he never thought it necessary to record the actual measurements of his home-lot, but gives it as six acres, abutting east on the highway, west on the lands of Rev. Mr. Fitch and Thomas Tracy, north on the home-lot of Christopher Huntington, and south on that of John Olmstead. He also buys before 1678, 25 rods of the home-lot of his neighbor, Christopher Huntington, and, though this sale is mentioned in the town book, no deed has been found on record. This is probably the 24 rods, sold afterward in 1788, by the Adgate heirs to Samuel Avery, and when Caleb Huntington purchases the Avery property, it comes again into the possession of a descendant of the first Christopher. It is now included in the Jabez Lathrop property.

Nothing is known of Thomas Adgate previous to his arrival at Saybrook. The name of his first wife, and the date of her death, are unknown. The births of two daughters are recorded at Saybrook, Elizabeth (b. 1651), and Hannah (b. 1653). Between 1658 and 1660, Thomas Adgate married Mary (Marvin) Bushnell, widow of Richard Bushnell, and daughter of Matthew Marvin of Norwalk. On their arrival at Norwich, the household consisted of Deacon Thomas and his wife, his two daughters, Elizabeth and Hannah, and the four Bushnell children, Joseph, Richard, Mary and Mercy. Three other daughters were born in Norwich, and one son. The family must have been not only a very united one, but uncommonly attractive as well, for Richard Bushnell married his step-sister, Elizabeth Adgate, and one by one, the neighbors' sons succumbed to the charms of the remaining daughters.

Thomas Adgate held many important offices, was frequently chosen townsman, and was one of the first deacons of Mr. Fitch's church, officiating for nearly half a century. He died in 1707, in the eighty-seventh year of his age. His wife, Mary, died in 1713. Two small, rough slabs of granite, with rudely-lettered inscriptions, still mark their resting places in the old burying-ground near the Green. Deacon Thomas deeded in 1702, one-half of the house and home-lot, also land and a barn on the opposite side of the street, to his son Thomas. This latter barn-lot adjoined the Read, or Bushnell lot, and is mentioned in the account of the old highway.

Thomas Adgate, 2nd (b. 1669-70), married (1) in 1692, Ruth, daughter of Benjamin and Anna (Dart) Brewster. His wife died in 1734, and he married (2) in 1749, Elizabeth (Morgan) Starr, widow of Capt. Jonathan Starr of Groton, and daughter of Capt. James Morgan. After his father's death, Thomas occupied the house and home-lot, and also succeeded his father as deacon, holding the office until his death in 1760, aged 91. His widow died in 1763.

In 1749-50, Deacon Thomas Adgate, 2nd, deeds the house and home-lot to his only remaining son, Matthew. The house stood a little south of the Jabez Lathrop grounds, and below this, in 1787, stood a shoe-maker's shop.

Matthew Adgate (b. 1706), married (1) 1727, Hannah, (daughter of William and Anne (Bushnell) Hyde, who died in 1766. In 1773, he married (2) Abigail (Culverhouse) Waterman, widow of John Waterman, who was born in 1719, and died in 1777. He had a large family of sons and daughters, of whom only two were living at the time of their father's death: Lucy, widow of Joseph Lord, and Matthew, who had moved to New York state.

The south end of the Adgate lot (frontage 4 rods), was deeded by Matthew in 1768 to his son William, who probably, about this time, built the house, now owned by the Misses Gilman, and occupied by the Rev. Nathaniel Beach.

William Adgate (b. 1744), was a goldsmith by trade, and married in 1767 his step-sister, Eunice, daughter of John and Abigail Waterman. He died in 1779. His widow resided here until her death in 1813. In 1818, the house and land is sold by the heirs of Dr. Joshua Lathrop, who had purchased it, to Daniel Lathrop, who occupied at that time the house on the south, now owned by the Misses Gilman.

Dr. Joshua Lathrop purchased in 1789, that part of the Adgate lot which adjoins the present garden-wall of Jabez Lathrop (frontage 14½ rods, 6 links), with house and shop, and on the lower part of the land he builds a cotton factory. Miss Caulkins says that he began with "five jennys, one carding machine, and six looms. This machinery was afterward increased, and a great variety of goods manufactured, probably to the amount of two thousand yards per year." The firm in 1793 was Lathrop & Eels (Joshua Lathrop and Cushing Eels), and in that year they advertise a great variety of cotton goods, consisting of "Royal Ribs, Ribdelures, Ribdurants, Ribdenims, Ribbets, Zebrays, Satinetts, Satin-Stripes, Satin Cords, Thicksetts, Corduroys, Stockinetts, Dimotys, Feathered Stripes, Birdseye, Denims, Jeans, Jeanetts, Fustians, and Bed Tickings that will hold feathers." This business was not found profitable and after eight or ten years was discontinued. North of the factory stood the shoe-maker's shop, which in 1787, was occupied by Joseph Lord. He advertises to sell Ladies' Everlasting

Shoes, Pumps and Slippers. When, and by whom this shop was built, we do not know.

Joseph Lord (b. 1762), was the son of Joseph and Lucy (Adgate) Lord. He married in 1784, Lucy Abel, daughter of Joshua and Lucy (Edgerton) Abel. About 1790, they removed from Norwich to Canaan, N. Y., "where he was a justice of the peace, and member of the state legislature." "He was brigade major of the militia for about thirty years, and was the author of two publications upon military tactics: 'Lord's Military Catechism,' and 'The Militiaman's Pocket Companion.' For one of these publications, the state of New York paid him $1600. He died 1844 at Canaan."*

Either in this shop, after the departure of Joseph Lord, or possibly in a new building on the same site, Daniel Lathrop, 2nd, established his drug and general merchandise business, which he carried on for many years. Both these buildings, the factory and the shop, had projecting roofs and were painted blue with white trimmings.

The upper part of his 1789 purchase (frontage 4 rods), adjoining the Lathrop wall, with the old Adgate house, were sold in 1794 by Joshua Lathrop to Nathan and Henry Cobb. The latter probably resided here until about 1803, when he removed to Stonington, and in 1813, the land and the house were sold by the heirs of Nathan Cobb to Elisha Leffingwell, who in 1814 sold the land with no mention of the house to Daniel Lathrop. We do not know the date of the disappearance of the shop, factory, and house, but it was probably very early in this century. Henry Stanton Cobb (b. 1761), married 1791, Mary Cobb of Stonington. He was the son of Nathan and Katharine (Copp) Cobb, who lived on the opposite side of the street.

*Chancellor Walworth's "Hyde Family Genealogy."

CHAPTER XXXII.

NEXT to Deacon Thomas Adgate's lot, and beginning at the south wall of the Jabez Lathrop property, was the home-lot of the first Christopher Huntington, of six acres, abutting north on the Town Street 21 rods, abutting west on the land of Thomas Tracy 42 rods, 4 feet, abutting south on Thomas Adgate's lot 34 rods, abutting east on the Town Street 42 rods.

Simon Huntington, the father of Christopher, was born in England, where he married Margaret Baret, who is supposed to have been a native of Norwich, England, and possibly a relative of Christopher Baret, who was mayor of Norwich in 1634. Simon Huntington died of small pox, while on the voyage to America in 1633, and was buried at sea. His widow, Margaret, who, with her four children, came to Roxbury, Mass., married soon after, Thomas Stoughton, a prominent citizen of Dorchester, Mass., who later removed to Windsor, Conn. The children probably went with their mother to Windsor, but in, or before 1649, Christopher Huntington was in Saybrook. He evidently returned to Windsor in 1652, and married Ruth Rockwell, daughter of William Rockwell, "a prominent and highly respected member of the community." He then went back to Saybrook, and later joined the band of settlers, who in 1660, came to found the town of Norwich. His house, situated on an exposed and conspicuous corner, commanding approaches from various directions, is said to have been one of the dwellings, which were fortified during King Philip's war. In 1678, he was appointed town clerk, which office was held by this family for one hundred and seventeen years. Christopher's term of service lasted thirteen years. He is said to have died in 1691, and was probably buried in the old grave-yard near Bean Hill. Before 1678, he sold twenty-five rods of land, the south-east corner of his home-lot, to Deacon Thomas Adgate, but no record has been found to establish the measurements of this piece, only a brief mention of the sale. The lower part of the Jabez Lathrop lot is probably the one in question.

Before the death of Christopher Huntington, 1st, he gave to his son, Christopher, Jun., a part of the home-lot (frontage 17 rods, 10 feet), north of the piece sold to Thomas Adgate. He had given the Sluman lot and house to his son Thomas, and the rest of the home-lot and the homestead passes to John, his youngest son.

The part of the home-lot given to Christopher Huntington, Jun., is recorded as 2 acres, 54 rods, beginning at the north-east corner, from thence it runs in a straight line west 16 rods, 9 feet, and from thence in a straight line south 24 rods, 9 feet, abutting north and west upon the remaining part of the sd home-lot, then runs east 17 rods, 4 feet, and from thence north 6 rods, 1½ feet, then east 4 rods, 3 feet to the street, abutting south and east on the land of Thomas Adgate, then abuts east on the street 17 rods, 10 feet, to the first corner. Christopher Huntington, 2nd, or Deacon Christopher (as he is usually called), (b. Nov. 1, 1660), was the first male child born in Norwich. He married (1) in 1681, Sarah, daughter of Dea. Thomas Adgate. She died in 1705-6, and he married (2) Mrs. Judith (Stevens) Brewster, widow of Jonathan Brewster.

Christopher Huntington was frequently chosen townsman, and also deputy. He succeeded Richard Bushnell as town-clerk, which office he held from 1698 to 1702. He was appointed deacon in 1695-6. He was an expert surveyor, and was frequently called upon to settle the question of bounds. He had four daughters, and seven sons. Christopher, his oldest son, settled in Franklin, Jabez in Windham, and Matthew in Preston; Hezekiah and Isaac were living in houses they had purchased; so to John and Jeremiah was given the home-lot, at the death of Christopher, in 1735. The brothers perhaps lived together until 1744-5, when Jeremiah marries Sarah, daughter of John Reynolds, and in 1745, the home-lot is divided, Jeremiah receiving the south part (frontage 6½ rods), and a house, which may be the paternal homestead, though it is not so called in the deed. John

receives the north part with a frontage of 10 rods, 13 feet, and a barn. Sarah, the wife of Jeremiah, dies in 1747, and he marries (2) 1748, Hannah Watrous, daughter of Ensign Isaac and Elizabeth (Brewster) Watrous of Lyme, Conn., who was born in 1725. Jeremiah resides in Norwich, until after the Revolution, then removes to Lebanon, N. H., where he dies in 1794. In 1786, after his departure from Norwich, he sells "my home-lot and buildings" to Samuel Avery, who also buys 24 rods of land on the south from the Adgate heirs in 1788, which is probably the piece of land alienated to Deacon Adgate shortly after the settlement of the town. In 1791, Samuel Avery sells this house and land to Caleb Huntington, son of John, and grandson of the Dea. Christopher who formerly owned it.

Samuel Avery (b. 1752?), son of John and Prudence (Miner) Avery of Montville, Ct., married in 1781 Candace Charlton, daughter of Richard and Sarah (Grist) Charlton of Norwich. He settled in Norwich as a tailor, and occupied a shop on the Tracy property, and was later associated in the mercantile business with Major Thomas Tracy, who married his daughter Elizabeth. He died in 1844, aged 92, and his wife died in 1816, aged 68.

Caleb Huntington was born in 1748-9, and married in 1795 Anna Huntington, daughter of Oliver Huntington of Lebanon, a descendant of the first Simon. He united with the first church in 1788, and was chosen deacon in 1808. He was at one time a brewer, and in 1777, the Council of Safety grant him a license "to distill from rye, the spirit called Geneva, and sell the same at a reasonable price, not to exceed 15 s. per gallon." In 1789, in partnership with Mundator Tracy, he sells tobacco of all kinds, "Plugtail, Pigtail, Carrot, and Smoaking tobacco at their shop near the Town Clerk's office." Yet, in spite of his dealing in these "roots of all evil," he is remembered as a most devout Christian. Whether this shop was the building standing near the house of Ezra Huntington, or the store on the opposite side of the street, we are unable to decide.

In the latter part of his life, he was a stone-cutter, and his shop stood south of his house. He lived to the advanced age of ninety-five, in full possession of his faculties. His children all died in infancy. Two nieces, daughters of Rev. Lynde Huntington of Branford, Ct., resided with him. He died in 1842 and his wife in 1851. At the division of his father's estate in 1794, he received land north of his house, with a frontage of 3 rods, 16½ links. After his death, the house and land were sold in 1857 to Jabez Lathrop, who still retains possession.

Now in the division of the home lot between John and Jeremiah, no house is mentioned as standing on John's share of the property. The only deed, which mentions a house, is in the sale to Samuel Avery in 1801. But John must have resided somewhere between 1746 and 1767, at which latter date he buys and moves into a house on the opposite side of the street, and it seems safe to assume that he built, probably about the time of the division, a house in which he resided until the date of this latter purchase. It may be that his house was burnt, or that he bought the neighboring house intending to resign the home lot to Ezra, who married in 1767. In 1771, he deeds to Ezra the north part of the home lot, with a frontage of 86 links, on which Ezra's barn stands. It may be that Ezra built the house, at present owned by Henry Potter, but of this we have found no record, so will leave the matter to be solved by John's descendants. In the division of John's property in 1794, Ezra receives land (frontage 4 rods, 9 links), and the malt house. This is, we believe, the land now occupied as a garden by Joseph Smith.

John Huntington (b. 1709), married in 1735, Civil, daughter of Simon and Mary (Leffingwell) Tracy. She died in 1748-9, and he married in 1749, her sister, Mary, who died in 1786. John's occupation was that of a brewer. He had a shop at one time across the street. His death occurred in 1794. His oldest son, John (b. 1736), was ordained minister of the Third Congregational church in Salem, Mass., and "gave much promise of future usefulness and eminence," but died unmarried in 1766 of a quick consumption, to the great grief of his people and friends. Solomon, the second son, settled as a saddler at Hebron, Ct. Andrew was a deacon of the church in Griswold, Ct., for fifty-one years. Thomas (b. 1744-5),

was a doctor, first in Ashford, and afterward in Canaan, Ct. He was a most genial man, and very fond of young people, and interested in their instruction, devoting great attention to the improvement of the common schools of that region. William lived in Hampton, Conn. Caleb probably lived with his father, until after his marriage in 1795, when he moved into the Jeremiah Huntington house. Ezra (b. 1742), to whom John gave the north part of the home-lot, married (1) in 1767, Elizabeth, daughter of James Huntington, 2nd. His wife died in 1796, and he married (2) 1797, the widow, Mary (Rudd) Dean of Franklin, who died at Franklin in 1804. In 1805, Ezra married (3) Elizabeth (Hyde) Lathrop, widow of Azel Lathrop and daughter of Phinehas and Ann (Rogers) Hyde of Franklin, who was born in 1755, and died at Ashford, Ct., in 1835. Ezra, like all the members of this family, was a very religious man, and believed in keeping strictly the Sabbath day, for he was the grand juror, who brought before Richard Hyde the three young boys (one of them his own apprentice, Asa Fuller), and two young girls, for profanely walking together on that day. He advertises as a maltster in 1776 and later as a "slaymaker." He sold his house and land to Samuel Avery in 1801, and moved to Franklin, where he died in 1820. Samuel Avery sells the property to Capt. Daniel Havens, late of Chatham, Mass., in 1812. In 1867, the Havens family sell to Henry F. Potter, who still owns and occupies the house.

North of this house, on the site of the house of Herbert Yerrington, stood the original Christopher Huntington homestead. After the death of the first Christopher, this was inherited by his son John (b. 1666), who married in 1686, Abigail, daughter of Samuel Lathrop. John Huntington had three daughters and two sons. One of the daughters, Martha, through her marriage with Noah Grant of Tolland, became the ancestress of Gen. U. S. Grant. In 1691, John Huntington was chosen constable. We have reason to believe that he left Norwich, and moved perhaps to Windsor. He died about 1714. In 1719, his son John, who inherits the home lot, sells to Isaac Huntington the house and land, about 4¼ acres, "beginning at the northwesterly corner by the brook, then running south, south-west, abutting west and northwest on Daniel Tracy's land 42 rods, 4 feet—abutting south on Thomas Adgate 16 rods, 9 feet, then east on Deacon Christopher Huntington's land 24 rods, 9 feet, then running east to the street 16 rods, 11 feet,—thence abutting east on the street 15 rods, 3 feet—thence north on the street 21 rods, 5 feet, to the first corner by the brook." John (the son of John Huntington), became a resident of Tolland, Ct., where he died in 1737. He married Thankful Warner of Windham, who died in 1739.

We learn from a deed of neighboring property, that in 1712, this house was occupied by Capt. Réné Grignon, a French Huguenot, who came to this country in the latter part of the seventeenth century, and joined the French settlement at East Greenwich, R. I.

Driven from thence with the rest of the settlers by persecution, in 1691, he went to Oxford, Mass., and when that French settlement was abandoned, after the Indian massacre of 1696, he moved to Boston, where he was at one time an "Ancien" or elder of the French church. In 1699, an attempt was made to re-establish the French settlement at Oxford, and many of the former inhabitants returned. René Grignon and Jean Papineau were associated with Gabriel Bernon in setting up "a 'chamoiserie,' or wash-leather manufactory on the mill-stream, that flowed through the plantation." This gave employment to the younger men of the community, in shooting and trapping game, and wagon loads of dressed skins were sent to Bernon in Providence, for the supply of the French hatters in Newport and Boston, but in 1704, occurred the Deerfield massacre, and the French at Oxford, thoroughly alarmed, and disheartened, again abandoned the settlement, and it was probably shortly after this date that Capt. Grignon came to Norwich, where he was admitted an inhabitant in 1710. Miss Caulkins says that when he came to Norwich he was master of a trading vessel, but settled here as a goldsmith. He died in 1715. His wife had died shortly before. He made Capt. Bushnell his executor and gave him in his will, his silver-hilted sword, double-barreled gun and pistols. He gives small legacies to Daniel Deshon and Jane Jearson, alias Normandy, and the greater part of his estate to his dear and well-beloved friend, Mary Urenne. To James Barret, an apprentice, he gives the remainder of his time.

Daniel Deshon, also of French descent, to whom Capt. Grignon gave his goldsmith's tools, and £10 when he should come of age, was afterward a prominent citizen of New London. It is possible that Capt. Grignon intended leaving, or had already left the Huntington house before his death, as he purchased in 1714-15 two valuable farms with a saw-mill and grist-mill on the outskirts of the town, and these are included in his inventory. This inventory is interesting from the values attached to the various articles of his stock in trade:—

Rare Jewels of Gold,	£2
316 Precious Stones,	£10
Pearls and Precious Stones,	£10
Bags of Bloodstones and others,	£5
Gold,	£9
Gold dust,	7 s. 6 d.
Plate and Bullion,	£41 3 s. 6 d.
Bullion,	19 s.

These are only a few of a long list, in which was included also a negro woman and child.

Isaac Huntington (b. 1688), who purchased in 1719, the old Christopher

Huntington homestead, was a son of Christopher Huntington, 2nd. He married, 1715-16, Rebecca, daughter of Israel Lathrop. He was by occupation a weaver. He was active in all good works, prominent in the civil affairs of the town, and was repeatedly chosen representative to the legislature. With Daniel Huntington and Philip Turner, he was appointed "to labor for the conviction and recovery of the Separates." He held the office of town clerk from 1726, till his death in 1764. The following items from his day-book, between 1752 and 1756, show the charges for recording, &c., at that time :—

For writing Benajah Leffingwell's will,	10 s.
" recording Jonathan Avery's marriage,	2 s.
" " Ruth Post's death,	1 s. 4 d.
" " deed,	5 s.
" mortgage deed to Dr. Lothrop from Oliver Arnold,	1 s. 3 d.
" license to Ebenezer Backus,	1 s. 6 d.
" three writs,	12 s.
" indorsing bounds of land,	4 s.
" probate of inventory,	£1 16 s.
" fees on will,	£1 6 s.
" writing and acknowledging deed,	10 s.

Isaac left a large property in lands, &c., which he divided among his many children, thirteen in all, of whom ten were living at his death. Three of his sons, Isaac, Nehemiah, and Elijah settled in Bozrah. Five of the daughters married prominent citizens and the two remaining sons, Joseph and Benjamin, inherited the homestead. Joseph (b. 1732), died unmarried in 1813. Benjamin (b. 1736), married in 1767, Mary (Carew) Brown, daughter of Joseph Carew and widow of James Noyes Brown. She died of small pox in 1777. In 1764, Benjamin was chosen to succeed his father as town-clerk, and held the office, with the exception of one year, 1778, when Samuel Tracy was appointed, until his death in 1801.

"He was one of the selectmen with Barnabas Huntington, Samuel Tracy, and Elijah Brewster, who called together the first revolutionary meeting held in Norwich, June 6, 1774. He was evidently a man of humor, and a rhymester, for about 1782 or 1783, he wrote the following :—

This day completes the eighteenth year,
That I have served in office here,
As clerk of this, a wealthy town.
And yet, I'm poor as any clown.
I have not spent my fees for grog,
Nor wasted time with gun and dog ;
Nor yet at cards a wager lost,
Nor on my back laid out much cost.
My house with painting never shone,
But tatter'd clapboards hear me groan,
For want of dry rooms in wet weather ;
And pork and beans to grace the platter.
I've bought no lands to drain my purse,
Nor haunted taverns which were worse ;
Nor jockey'd horses I but once,
For which I own I was a dunce.
Yet in one point, I've acted wrong ;
I own it freely to the throng ;
But as my crime from spite was free,
Some mercy yet, I hope to see.
'Tis this ; if you'll attend I'll tell.
I've used my customers too well.
I've not insisted on my pay,
When 'twas my due from day to day ;
Nay longer much from year to year,
Till they are dead or disappear ;
And so my due forever lost
And I with disappointment crost.
I did not ask for my reward,
When they required me to record
Their numerous deeds and bills of sale,
Their births and deaths, a long detail.
Thus I confess I was to blame,
And for my fault now suffer shame.
But I resolve to mend my ways,
Conduct more just, deserves more praise.
Now, gentlemen, observe ye well,
And I my new-made law will tell.
No more expect that I'll record,
Till fees are paid, my due reward.
And as at first, for lawfull fee,
A faithful clerk, I swore to be,
So now again, if swearing's just,
My fees I'll have, but never trust."

Benjamin was succeeded in the office of town-clerk by his son, Philip, (b. 1770), who married in 1796, Theophila Grist, daughter of John and Delight (Lathrop) Grist. She died in 1806, aged thirty-eight. Philip Huntington continued to hold this office till his death in 1825. His son Benjamin (b. 1798), became also town-clerk at the death of his father in 1825, and continued in the office with the exception of one year from 1828 to October, 1830. He married in 1830, Margaretta Perit, daughter of John and Margaretta (Dunlap) Perit of Philadelphia, and after a long and honorable life, died in 1881. In 1842, the old Huntington homestead was sold to Joseph Griffin. The land was purchased in 1884 by Lewis Hyde, the old house torn down, and two houses have since been erected on the lot.

The town clerk's office was a small gambrel-roofed building, painted red, standing close to the street, with the addition of an ell on one side, which latter was used at times as a shop.

CHAPTER XXXIII.

THE land between "Stony" Lane and the corner was owned, in the early years of the town, by Josiah Read, who sells the north part (frontage thirteeen rods), "on the side of the hill by Christopher Huntington's," to Jonathan Crane in 1686. The lower part, next to Stony Lane, is entered among his records of land, as "one acre, beginning at the northwest corner, abutting west on the street 10 rods, south on commons 12 rods, east on the highway 13 rods, and north 14¼ rods on the land of Jonathan Crane." In 1679, the town grants to Jonathan Crane two acres of land "against Thomas Bingham's to build upon," unless he can "find it in some more convenient place." Evidently Jonathan does not consider this a desirable spot, for in 1686, he buys of Josiah Read this corner lot. A small piece of adjoining land is granted him by the town, and he then records his home-lot as "one acre, 146 rods of land, beginning at the north-west corner at a small white oak, abutting west on the street 13 rods, abutting south on the land of Josiah Read 15½ rods, and east on a highway 26 rods," ("part purchase and part grant"). Here he builds his house, which is sold to Israel Lathrop in 1695.

Jonathan Crane (b. 1658), was the son of Benjamin Crane of Wethersfield, who is said, by some authorities, to have married in 1655, Mary, daughter of

William Backus; by others, in 1656, Elinor Breck, daughter of Edward Breck of Dorchester, Mass. We are unable to say which of these statements is correct. It is possible that Mary may have died, and Elinor may have been a second wife. Benjamin Crane is said to have lived in Westfield, and Wethersfield, Ct., and perhaps at Taunton, Mass. Jonathan was born at Wethersfield, and married in 1678, Deborah, daughter of Francis Griswold. He was by trade a blacksmith. In 1690, he purchased a large tract of land, in what was then called "Joshua's tract," and, with quite a number of Norwich people, went to found the town, now known as Windham. He was very prominent in all the affairs of the new settlement, was moderator at town meetings, one of the committee for building the meeting house, assisted in settling the town bounds, built the first grist-mill, kept the first tavern, was chosen ensign of the train-band, and next to Mr. Whiting, was the largest land operator in the town. Near the close of his life, he removed to Lebanon, probably to live with his son Jonathan. He died in 1734-5. His house in Norwich was sold in 1695-6 to Israel Lathrop. There is nothing in the records to show whether Israel occupied this house or not. We assume that he did live here for a while, until some time after his father's death, when he moved to the paternal homestead. He buys the land on the south of Josiah Read, though the deed of sale has not been found. In the highway survey of 1705, it is mentioned as "the orchard of Israel Lothrop." At that time, we think it is probable that he had moved to his father's house.

In 1722, Israel gives this house and three acres of land, and "the garden place on the north side of the highway against the house," to his son William, who in 1729, in exchange for land on Plain Hills, deeds these back to his father.

William Lathrop (b. 1688), married (1) 1712, Sarah, daughter of Simon Huntington, 2nd. He married (2) in 1731, Mary Kelly, and (3) in 1761, Phoebe French. After leaving the Crane house, he lived, till his death in 1778, on his farm at Plain Hills, and was a useful and highly respected citizen. He was a deeply religious man, and during the Separatist excitement, he, and his second wife, Mary Kelly, joined that sect. When summoned before Dr. Lord, for presuming to join with others in setting up a Separate meeting, he boldly gave these reasons:—

"1. The minister, denying the power of godliness, though not in word yet in practice.

2. Insisting on imprudencies, and not speaking up for that which is good.

3. Not praying for their meeting (the Separatist), and not giving thanks for the late glorious work. (The preaching of Mr. Whitefield).

4. Not a friend to lowly preaching and preachers, particularly not letting Mr. Jewett preach once, and once forbidding Mr. Crosswell (Separatist preachers).

5. Not having the sacrament for six months, in the most glorious part of the late times; and often enough since the church is in difficulty, and oftener now than ever."

These were Mrs. Lathrop's reasons:—

"1. As to communion in the church at the sacrament, I did not commune because I was in the dark, and thought I was not fit.

2. Another reason, because I was not edified.

3. Because the power of godliness, it seems to me, is denied here, and is elsewhere.

4. By covenant, I am not held here any longer than I am edified."

One of William Lathrop's sons, John (b. 1739), became the pastor of the old North Church in Boston. He is alluded to as

"John, old North, for little worth,
Won't sacrifice for gold,"

in the famous satirical poem on the Boston ministers supposed to have been written by Dr. Benjamin Church in 1774. This Rev. John Lathrop, or Lothrop (as his name was written), was the grandfather of John Lothrop Motley, the historian, and United States minister to Austria and England.

In 1730-1, Israel deeds this property on the corner, with "garden spott" on the north side of the highway, "with shop by the side of sd highway," to his son Ebenezer (b. 1702-3), who had married in 1725, Lydia, daughter of Deacon Thomas Leffingwell. This remained in Ebenezer's possession till his death, which occurred in 1781. The Lathrop memoir says: "He was a man of note in town, both in civil and military affairs." In 1740, he received his commission as Ensign;

in 1742, as Lieutenant; and in 1745, as Captain, by which title he is best known.

Ebenezer's first wife died in 1766 and he married (2) before 1771, Hannah Lynde, widow (1) of Capt. Joshua Huntington, and (2) of Col. Samuel Lynde of Saybrook, Ct. His will, shows him to be a man of large possessions. He wills the house to his son Jedidiah (b. 1748), who married (1) in 1772, Civil, daughter, of John and Lydia (Tracy) Perkins, who died in 1797. He married (2) in 1807, Anna Eames. He died in 1817. Jedidiah sells the old homestead in 1793, to Ebenezer Carew. In 1800, it is sold to Felix Huntington, Sen., who lives here till his death. Felix Huntington was by trade "a joiner" or carpenter and his shop was on the opposite corner, where now stands the house of Ira Peck.

In 1843, this old Lathrop house was purchased by William M. Converse, and was occupied for many years by his father, Augustus Converse, who came from Salem, Mass., in 1834, to end his days in Norwich. In 1877, it is sold to Capt. Joseph Reynolds, who tore down the large, square, gray house, which many still remember, and built the one at present owned and occupied by Samuel K. Lovett.

In 1771, Capt. Ebenezer Lathrop sold to Felix Huntington the south part of his home-lot (frontage 5 rods), next to Stony Lane, and here Felix builds a house and shop. Felix Huntington (b. 1749), was the son of Daniel and Rebecca (Huntington) Huntington. He married in 1773, Anna, daughter of Jacob and Mary (Brown) Perkins, who died in 1806, aged 50. In 1791, Jedidiah Lathrop sells to him additional land (frontage 2½ rods), north of Felix's shop, and Felix then sells the whole property

(frontage 7½ rods), with house and shop, to Dr. Joshua Lathrop, who gives it to his son Daniel, on the latter's marriage in 1793. Daniel Lathrop lived here until his removal to the house now occupied by the Misses Gilman. In 1810, he sells this house to James Stedman, who altered and modernized it, and whose heirs retained possession until a few years ago, when it was sold to George C. Raymond. The shop north of the house was probably used by Felix Huntington for a time as a joiner's shop. It is not mentioned in the deed of sale to James Stedman in 1810, so may have disappeared.

In 1785, Jedidiah Lathrop sells land north of the Felix Huntington house (frontage 4 rods), to Daniel Tracy (b. 1756), son of Josiah and Rachel (Allen) Tracy. He married in 1783, Lucy, daughter of Josiah Tracy, 2nd, and Margaret Pettis of Franklin. Daniel was a house carpenter, and built himself a house upon this lot. Two children were born to him in Norwich, Lucy (b. 1784), and Nancy (b. 1786). He then moved to Newton, Mass., and later to Dover, N. H., and the house was occupied for a time by Samuel Avery, who was living here in 1794. In 1798, it was sold to Stephen Backus of Brooklyn, Ct., who also buys of Jedidiah Lathrop additional land (4 rods frontage), on the south. Stephen Backus and his wife, Eunice, have one child born in Norwich, George Whitney (b. 1800). In 1802, he sells the house and land (frontage 8 rods), to Capt. Elisha Leffingwell (b. 1778), son of Elisha and Alice (Tracy) Leffingwell. Capt. Leffingwell married in 1808 Frances Thomas, daughter of Simeon and Lucretia (Deshon) Thomas, and had nine children. He was a sea captain, and with his oldest son, Thomas (b. 1811), sailed for South America on Oct. 24, 1825. The ship is supposed to have foundered at sea, and all on board were lost. In 1839, the house is sold to Charles Bliss, and later by the Bliss heirs to George Rudd, who metamorphosed the large, old, square house into a comparatively modern dwelling. It is now occupied by Mrs. Lyman.

CHAPTER XXXIV.

ON the opposite side of the street leading up Long Hill, was the home-lot of Thomas Sluman, which was registered as "home lot and pasture of twelve acres more or less, abutting west, east, north, and south on highway." As the bounds of the home-lot and pasture are never clearly defined, and the greater part of the land is used as pasture land for many years, we will not attempt to mark the limits of this home lot, but only locate the houses, which are later erected, on that part of the land nearest the main highways. The date of the home lot is 1663. In 1668, Thomas Sluman,* of whose antecedents we know nothing, married Sarah, daughter of Thomas Bliss. Six children are born to them, and the father died in 1683. In the same year, died Mrs. Solomon Tracy, and in 1686, Dr. Solomon Tracy, who was the administrator of the Sluman estate, married the widow Sluman. In 1688, he sold nine acres with the house, bounded south on the highway 45 rods, abutting west on his own land 37 rods, abutting north on a highway and commons 49 rods, abutting east on his own

---

*The son, Thomas Sluman (b. ——), moved to West Farms or Franklin, and resided near the Peck Hollow Station on the N. L. N. R. R., where he had a saw and corn-mill.—See Woodward's History of Franklin, Ct.

land 32½ rods to Christopher Huntington, who in the same year presents it to his son, Thomas, who has married in 1686–7, Elizabeth, daughter of Lt. William Backus. About 1692, Thomas Huntington removes to the then "nameless town of Windham," where he becomes a prominent citizen, and his descendants reside to this day. Two of his children were born in Norwich, Thomas and Jedidiah. In 1696–7, he sells his house and home lot to Thomas Leffingwell, who sells it in three portions : the west part (frontage 9 rods, 6½ feet), and the east (frontage 8½ rods), to Daniel Tracy, and the middle of the lot (frontage 27½ rods), to Christopher Huntington. In these sales no house is mentioned, so possibly it has disappeared. Daniel Tracy sells ere long his lots to Solomon, and the Solomon Tracy and Huntington families retain the property for many years.

In 1687, Dr. Solomon Tracy sold 21½ rods at the south-west corner of the Sluman lot, abutting north and east on his own land, south on the highway 6½ rods, and west on the highway 4½ rods, to Jonathan Crane. Here, the latter builds a barn. In the sale of the Crane property to Israel Lathrop, this land and barn are included. In 1722, Israel gives the land, then called "a garden spott," to his son William, who in 1729, gives it back to Israel, who then in 1731–2, deeds it to his son Ebenezer, "with shop by the side of sd highway." At Ebenezer's death in 1781, the garden where the old blacksmith shop stands is given to his son Jedidiah, who sells it in 1785, to Samuel Avery. Here is built the shop, where Samuel Avery and Maj. Thomas Tracy were associated together in business as the firm of Avery & Tracy ; and after the death of Maj. Tracy in 1805, Samuel Avery takes his son Henry into partnership, and the firm is known as Samuel Avery & Son. In 1818, Roger Huntington and Henry Avery are established here as the firm of Roger Huntington & Co. In 1843, David M. Lewis purchases the property, which he sells in 1856, to William Jackson, who alters the store into a house, in which he lives for many years.

About 1744, William Lathrop, Jun., buys of Ebenezer Lathrop, Simon Tracy and Isaac Huntington, land adjoining the "garden spott." Here he builds the house now owned by Owen Smith. William Lathrop (b. 1715), was a son of William and Sarah (Huntington) Lathrop. He married in 1745, Dorcas, daughter of Isaac and Rebecca (Lathrop) Huntington. They had no children, and he died in 1770, and lies buried near his father in the old Norwich Town grave-yard. Dorcas, his widow, died in 1804, and is buried in the East Chelsea burying-ground. After the death of Dorcas, her nephew, Oliver Fitch, inherited the house, and sold it in 1806 to Ezekiel Huntley, the father of Mrs. Sigourney.

Ezekiel Huntley (b. 1750), was the son of Elisha and Mary (Wallbridge) Huntley of West Farms (now Franklin). Mrs. Sigourney says that her grandfather Huntley emigrated from Scotland to this country early in life, and this may be true, for no record of his birth has been found, but as he came from Lyme to Norwich, we think he was possibly a descendant, but certainly a relative, of the Lyme family of that name. The grandmother, Mary Wallbridge, was probably a daughter of Ebenezer and Mary (Durkee) Wallbridge of Franklin, and was born in 1731-2. Mrs. Sigourney speaks of "the loveliness of character," and the piety of her grandmother, "ever industrious, peaceful, and an example of all saintly virtues." "At the age of seventy, not a thread of silver had woven itself with her lustrous black hair. Then a mild chill of paralysis checked the vital current," and gave to her granddaughter "the first picture of a serene death." *

Mrs. Sigourney says that her father resembled his mother in "his calm spirit and habitual diligence, as he did also in a cloudless longevity." She testifies to his mild and gentle nature, and that, throughout his long life, she never heard him utter a hasty or unkind word. He served in the army for a while during the Revolution, and in 1786, married Lydia Howard, who died within a year after marriage, of consumption, and Ezekiel married (2) Sophia (as Mrs. Sigourney writes it), or Zerviah (according to the records), Wentworth, daughter of Jared Wentworth of Norwich. Mrs. Sigourney describes her as young and beautiful, fourteen years younger than her husband, who was then forty years of age, and "belonging to a family which stretched its pedigree back through the royal governors of New Hampshire to the gifted Earl Strafford, the hapless friend of Charles I."

Lydia, the only child of Ezekiel and Zerviah Huntley, was born in 1791. She was baptized before she was two weeks old, as was then the custom. In

---

* Mrs. Sigourney's "Letters of Life."

earlier times, it was customary to carry the poor little infant to church on the day of its birth. Mrs. Sigourney remembers seeing a small white satin bag, in which was once ensconced a small baby, whose mother dreaded sending it to church on its entrance into the world, on the coldest day of the year.

The early years of Mrs. Sigourney's life were passed in the household of Mrs. Daniel Lathrop, where her father was occupied with the charge of the garden and grounds. After the death of Mrs. Lathrop, he purchased the house, where Mrs. Dorcas Lathrop formerly lived, and to this home, as Mrs. Sigourney says, the Huntley family made their removal "in the bloom and beauty of a most glorious June." Lydia Huntley was then a girl of fourteen, but evidently efficient and capable, for she superintended entirely the removal and arrangement of the furniture. The house had two parlors, a bedroom, a spacious kitchen, with a wing for the pantry and "milk room" on the first floor; on the second floor five chambers, with one in the attic, "and that delightful appendage to old fashioned mansions, a large garret."

The garden was "skirted by a small green meadow, swelling at its extremity into a knoll, where apples trees flourished, and refreshed by a clear brooklet." Lydia was installed as assistant or "prime minister" to her mother, who was "an adept in that perfect system of New England house-keeping, which allots to every season its peculiar work, to every day its regular employment, to every article its place." The mother and daughter papered walls, painted the wood-work of the parlors, and Mrs. Sigourney cut silhouettes, and "executed small landscapes and bunches of flowers in water colors to embellish the rooms." In a conspicuous place hung possibly her first large picture, "Maria," or the "crazy girl, described by the sentimental Yorick," who was "represented sitting under an immense tree, with exuberant brown tresses, a pink jacket, and white satin petticoat, gazing pensively at a small lap-dog, fastened to her hand by a smart blue ribbon. Sterne is seen at a distance, taking note of her with an eye glass, riding in a yellow-bodied coach, upon a fresh-looking turnpike road, painted in stripes with ochre and bistre."

"For a hall, in the second story, which was carpetless," Lydia cut "squares of flannel, about the size of compartments in a marble pavement, and sewed on each a pattern of flowers and leaves cut from broadcloth of appropriate colors. The effect of the whole was that of rich, raised embroidery." Without an idle moment, the mother and daughter were "up with the lark" wielding the broom and duster, keeping every room "in the speckless sanctity of neatness," spinning all their household linen, except the "Holland" sheets with which the guest-chamber was provided, making flannel sheets, weaving rag carpets, each spinning also a gown for herself out of fine cotton yarn, which had been "carded in long beautiful rolls" by the mother. "A portion of the yarn was bleached to a snowy whiteness, and the remainder dyed a beautiful fawn or salmon color. It was woven into small, even checks, and made a becoming costume, admired even by the tasteful." Lydia also "braided white chip and fine split straw for the large and pretty hats then in vogue." But the pride of her heart was the suit of clothes made for her father, for which she spun the finest thread "consistent with strength," each thread "carefully evened and smoothed with the fingers, ere it received the final twist, and was run upon the spindle." "The yarn was arranged in skeins of twenty knots, vernacularly called a run, each knot containing forty strands around the reel, which was two yards in circumference." An extra price was demanded for weaving, on account of the "awful fineness" of the thread. The material was then sent to the fulling-mill, and "when brought home from the cloth-dresser a beautiful, lustrous black, and made into a complete suit, surmounted by a handsome overcoat or surtout," the daughter's happiness was complete. The tenderest relations existed between father and daughter. It was a great pride and pleasure to Lydia, from the age of eight years, to make her father's shirts, to spin the yarn for his stockings, which, after the death of her grandmother, she felt it her prvilege to knit. She assisted him in the garden, and together, they set out two apple trees in the front yard. "To the rallying remarks of some of his more fashionable friends," Ezekiel replied that "it was better to fill the space with something useful, than with unproductive shade." To these trees he devoted "almost a florist's care," washing their trunks and boughs with soap-suds in the hot summer months, rubbing off the moss and excrescences which appeared in places, and then applying with a brush a solution of a quarter of a pound of nitre dissolved in warm water, and mixed with three gallons of lye from wood ashes, a pint of soft soap, and a handful of common salt."* In the spring the roots received a bath of "one quart of soap and of salt, one pound of flour of sulphur, with a sufficient quantity of soft water," and "the earth was opened in a circle around each tree to the depth of two inches, and a prescription of compost mingled with two quarts of wood ashes, one quart of salt, and the same quantity of pulverized plaster added, to quicken their appetite, and the whole neatly raked over." No wonder that bushels of fine greenings and russets rewarded all this care, and in the spring the fragrance of apple-blossoms filled the house.

Breakfast in this household was served at "sunrise, dinner at twelve," and the hour of supper "somewhat varied by the seasons." The table-fare was "simple," but undoubtedly, under the superintendence of these notable housekeepers, always "admirably prepared." The animals of this domain consisted of a cow, some poultry, and an animal, whom Mrs. Sigourney mentions as "a quadruped member of our establishment," "the animal to whom the Evangelists allude," "this scorned creature, the poor man's friend," "the adjunct of every economical household," "this stigmatized animal," but never once by the common name of pig.

On the Huntley premises was a small house, whose sole tenant was a widow, a weaver by trade, who desired to pay the rent in her own work. From her, Mrs. Sigourney learned to spin. "Wrinkled was her visage, yet rubicund with healthful toil; and when she walked in the streets, which was seldom, her bow-like body, and arms diverging toward a crescent form, preserved the attitude, in which she sprung the shuttle, and heaved the beam. Her cumbrous old-fashioned loom contained a vast quantity of timber, and monopolized most of the space in the principal apartment of her cottage. Close under her window were some fine peach trees, which she claimed as her own, affirming that she planted the kernels from whence they sprung. So their usufruct was accorded her by the owner of the soil. As the large rich fruit approached its blush of ripeness, her watchfulness became intense. Her cap, yellow with smoke, and face deepening to a purple tinge of wrathful emotion, might be seen protruding from her casement, as she vituperated the boys who manifested a hazardous proximity to the garden wall. Not perfectly lamblike was her temperament, as I judge from the shriek of the

* Mrs. Sigourney's "Letters of Life."

objurgations she sometimes addressed to them ; while they, more quiescent, it would seem, than boy-nature in modern times, returned no rude reply."

Lydia was in the habit of "carrying her pudding on Sunday noons, and baked beans on Saturday nights," and books for the only days in the year, in which she indulged in reading, "Sabba' day" as she called it, and the yearly Fast day. In conversation, the old woman "evinced a good measure of intelligence and shrewdness, with those Yankee features, keen observation of other people, and a latent desire to manage them. Her strongest sympathies hovered around the majesty and mystery of her trade, and her highest appreciation was reserved for those who promoted it. The kindness that dwelt in her nature was most palpably called forth" by the "quadruped member of the establishment" (the pig), to whom she made daily offerings, and exulted in his "increasing corpulence," hinting to the Huntleys a "personal claim, or future prospect of a dividend of bacon, on the principal of joint investment."

In 1810, about four years after her entrance into this new home, Mrs. Sigourney realized her earliest ambition "to teach a school." After great efforts to obtain pupils, she succeeded in securing two scholars, cousins, of the name of Lathrop, one eleven, the other nine years of age. One of the pleasantest rooms in the house was fitted up with "a new long desk, and benches neatly made of fair white wood," to which she added an hour-glass and a few other articles of convenience and adornment, and here for six hours of five days in the week, and three on Saturday, did she "sedulously devote to questioning, simplifying, illustrating, and impressing various departments of knowledge." The results of her efforts are set forth in a certificate, adorned with floral designs in water color, and presented to one of her pupils, who, during the quarter in which she attended school, had "read in the New Testament as far as the fifth chapter of John, read 60 of the Psalms, through the American Preceptor in course, and partly through the Columbian Orator, Proceeded in Arithmetic from Numeration to Compound Division; learnt the necessary rules and tables, and performed 452 Sums. Written 118 copies. Studied in Murray's Grammar as far as Punctuation; and in Morse's Geography to the State of Massachusetts; Learnt to repeat a dialogue; an hymn; a description of Modesty; and Reflections on the grave of a young man." A young lady from Massachusetts of the name of Bliss, being in town for a short time, also joined the school, during that interval, to pursue drawing, and painting in water colors. At the close of the quarter an elaborate examination was held, "with which the invited guests signified their entire approbation."

In order to perfect herself as a teacher, Lydia Huntley went with her most intimate friend, Nancy Maria Hyde, to Hartford, and there they attended the two best seminaries of the town, devoting themselves "to the accomplishments of drawing, painting in water-colors, embroidery of various kinds, filagree, &c." On returning to Norwich, they opened a private school on the "Little Plain," and later at the Landing, where they taught for several years.

In 1815, Lydia Huntley went to Hartford, to start, under the auspices of Daniel Wadsworth, a small school of fifteen pupils, later increased to twenty-five, which she carried on for four years. She also published in 1815, the first of her many volumes of prose and verse. In 1819, she returned to Norwich, to prepare for her marriage with Charles Sigourney, a wealthy merchant of Hartford, to whom she had become engaged in January of that year.

On the morning of June 16, 1819, the bridal procession started from the house of the Huntleys for Christ Church * in "Chelsea," or "the Landing," where the wedding was to take place at the early hour of eight. The ceremony was performed by the Rev. John Tyler, rector of the church, assisted by Rev. (afterward Bishop) Jonathan Wainwright of Hartford. After the ceremony, the wedding procession (as was the custom of the time), consisting of the bridal coach, drawn by white horses, and several carriages filled with friends, journeyed to Andover, forty miles distant, where an elaborate wedding dinner was served, after which the guests escorted the newly-wedded pair to their home at Hartford, took tea with them, and then departed with "cordial good wishes" for their future happiness, which were amply fulfilled in a happy domestic life, in the love and reverence which Mrs. Sigourney's talents and many deeds of benevolence inspired in Hartford, and the honors she received in this country and Europe, as one of the earliest and most esteemed of American poets. After "a beautiful

* Not the present Christ Church, but the small building now standing on the Salem Green, then located on Church Street, a little east of the present Trinity Church.

life," as Mrs. Sigourney testifies, in her "Letters of Life," she died in 1865 in the seventy-fourth year of her age.

At the age of eighty, Ezekiel Huntley and his wife went to reside with their daughter in Hartford, and the house was sold in 1830 to Erastus Waters, in 1837, to Nancy Davenport, and in 1839 to David M. Lewis. It is now owned, and has been much altered in appearance, by Owen Smith.

CHAPTER XXXV.

AT the turn of the road leading to Dr. Gulliver's on a part of the Sluman lot, stood as early as 1747, the house of Thomas Danforth. The first deed of this property has not been found, so we are unable to say whether he purchased or built the house. The land was bought of the Simon Tracy family. The house is still standing, unaltered probably since its first erection. It remained in the possession of the Danforth family until 1883, when it was sold to Mrs. Lasthaus. In 1769, adjoining land on the south is sold to John Danforth, on which he builds a house. In 1786, he deeds this house "which I now live in" to Daniel and Samuel Danforth. In 1797, Daniel quit-claims to Samuel, who in 1800, sells it to Andrew Huntington, and from that time it is owned and occupied by various persons, until sold in 1861, to Henry Skinner.

Thomas Danforth (b. 1703), was the descendant of an old and distinguished Massachusetts family. His great-grandfather, Nicholas Danforth of Framingham, Suffolk Co., England, was, according to Cotton Mather, "a gentleman of such estate and repute in the world, that it cost him a considerable sum to escape the knighthood, which King Charles I. imposed on all of so much per annum; and of such figure and esteem in the church, that he procured the famous lecture at

Framingham, where he had a fine manor." In 1634, he came to New England, and died at Cambridge, Mass., in 1637-8. His son, the Rev. Samuel Danforth, grandfather of the Norwich resident, was pastor of a church in Roxbury, Mass., and colleague of the Rev. John Eliot, "the apostle to the Indians." He was a very emotional preacher, and it is said that he "never finished a sermon without weeping." He was celebrated as a poet, astronomer, mathematician, and author of a series of almanacs. His wife was a daughter of Rev. John Wilson the distinguished pastor of the First Church in Boston, who was a son of Dr. William Wilson, Prebendary at Rochester, and a grand-nephew of Dr. Edmund Grindal, Archbishop of Canterbury.

The father of Thomas Danforth was the Rev. Samuel Danforth, 2nd, who for forty-four years was pastor of the church at Taunton, Mass., and married Hannah, daughter of Rev. James Allen of the old North Church, Boston. He is said to have left a large fortune to his children, of whom he had fourteen, but "it pleased God to take" four of them "all away at once, in one fortnight's time," in their childhood, with a disease called "bladders of the windpipe;" but "afterward, happily, the loss was made up" to him in the birth of ten more. The Rev. John Danforth of Dorchester, uncle of Thomas, was famous as a writer of elegies and epitaphs, of which this verse from one written on the death of a child of the Hon. Edward Bromfield of Boston, in 1709, is a specimen:—

> "Nature and Grace are mourners at this sight,
> But 'tis Religion gives to mourn aright
> Charming the musick in the Heavenly ears
> While Christ is bottling of your trickling tears."

Thomas Danforth (b. 1703), married (1) Sarah ———, and had three children, born in Taunton. He then came to Norwich, and married in 1742, Hannah Hall. Like his father, he had fourteen children, and four of these were all taken away "at once in a fortnight's time," but the Norwich records do not say whether the malady was also "bladders of the windpipe."

In 1773, the firm of Thomas Danforth & Son (pewterers), was dissolved. Where their shop or store stood, we do not know, perhaps on the lot purchased of Daniel Tracy, opposite Thomas Danforth's house, perhaps on the Green, where Thomas at one time owned a shop.

Of all the sons of Thomas Danforth, John (b. 1746), is the only one, the births of whose children are entered on the records. He married in 1767, Elizabeth Hartshorn, and had three sons, John, Samuel, and Daniel, and two daughters, Mary and Lydia. John studied medicine, and "his amiable disposition and integrity of heart, joined with his good proficiency in the healing science, gave a pleasing prospect of future usefulness," but he died, alas! in 1791, at the age of twenty-three. Thomas Danforth died in 1786.

Samuel Danforth (b. 1770), married in 1797, Lucy Hartshorn, and had three children. He carried on the trade established by his father, and in 1793, built a shop near the present residence of Ira Peck, which he occupied until about 1803, when he sold it to the firm of Avery & Tracy.

CHAPTER XXXVI.

JOHN Elderkin received from the town in 1667, a grant of six acres for a home-lot, abutting south on the Town street 36 rods, west on a highway 32 rods, north on a highway 29 rods, and east on a highway 32 rods. This is the land which Miss Caulkins mistakenly calls the Bradford lot. It is bounded on the north, east, and west, by the road, which, leading from "Peck's" corner past the Gulliver residence, comes out again into the main road by the Gen. Ebenezer Huntington house (now belonging to William Fitch). On receiving other land at the Falls, where he afterward resided, John Elderkin sold this lot, "abutting on the highway against Goodman Tracy's house on the south," to Samuel Lathrop, in 1668.

Samuel Lathrop was a son of the Rev. John Lathrop or Lothropp (as the name was formerly written), who came to America in 1634. Rev. John Lothropp was the son of Thomas Lowthroppe or Lothropp of Etton, Harthill Wapentake, East Riding, Yorkshire. He was born in 1584, was educated at Queen's College, Cambridge, where he was "matriculated in 1601, graduated B. A. in 1605, and M. A. in 1609."* In 1611, he became the curate of the parish church of Egerton, Co. Kent, where he remained until 1623, when, from conscientious scruples, he resigned his office in the Church of England, and became pastor of the First Independent Church of London, which had no regular place of worship, but met from house to house. With the greater part of his congregation he was arrested on April 22, 1632, by the spies of Archbishop Laud, and confined in Newgate prison, from which he was released in 1634, and sailed for New England, arriving in September of that year. He was pastor of the church at Scituate, Mass., and later at Barnstable, where he died in 1653.

* Lathrop Family Memoir by Rev. E. B. Huntington.

Nathaniel Morton, in his "New England Memorial," names the Rev. John Lothropp as among "the specialest" of the ministers who came to New England. Mr. Otis of Barnstable, an authority on all that relates to the early history of that town, says that "he was a man who held opinions in advance of his times;" that he "fearlessly proclaimed, in Old and New England, the great truth, that man is not responsible to his fellow man in matters of faith and conscience. Differences of opinion he tolerated. During the fourteen years that he was pastor of the Barnstable church, such was his influence over the people, that the power of the civil magistrate was not needed to restrain crime. No pastor was more beloved by his people, none ever had a greater influence for good. . . . To become a member of his church, no applicant was compelled to sign a creed, or profession of faith. He retained his freedom. He professed his faith in God, and promised that it should be his constant endeavor to keep His commandments, to live a pure life, and to walk in love with the brethren."

During the imprisonment of Mr. Lathrop in London, his first wife died, and in 1635, he married (2) Anna ——. He had fourteen children, of whom six were born in this country. Samuel was the only one of the children who came to Connecticut. The others remained in Massachusetts.

Samuel Lathrop, 2nd, was born in England, came to America with his father, was at Scituate, Boston, and Barnstable, at which latter place he married, in 1644, Elizabeth Scudder, a sister of John Scudder of Barnstable. He arrived at New London with the Winthrop colony, probably about 1646 or 1647, where he at once became an important citizen, and was chosen with John Winthrop and Thomas Miner, "to act in all Towne affaires, as judge in all cases under the value of 40s." His home-lot was north-west of Gov. Winthrop's, on the upper part of Williams Street and Main Street. His house stood "just beyond the bridge, over the mill-brook, on the east side of the highway toward Mohegan." In 1661, it was sold to Rev. Gershom Bulkeley, and was later known as the old Hallam homestead. Samuel had also a large grant of a farm on the west bank of the river, four or five miles from New London, called Namucksuck, which later belonged to his son Nathaniel. In 1657, when Uncas was besieged by the Narragansetts in the fort at the head of the Nahantick river, Lt. James

Avery. Mr. Brewster, Richard Haughton, Samuel Lothrop, and others, "succeeded in throwing themselves into the fort," and the enemy, alarmed at the appearance of the English, abandoned the siege.

In 1668, Samuel Lathrop removed to Norwich, where he officiated as townsman and constable, and was engaged, on the year of his arrival, in "repairing and heightening" the first old meeting-house, for his occupation was that of a carpenter. In that capacity, he was constantly associated with John Elderkin. In 1673, he assists him in building the new meeting-house in Norwich, and in 1679, together they contract to build another in New London.

The date of the death of the first wife of Samuel Lathrop is unknown. He married (2) in 1690, Abigail, daughter of Deacon John Doane of Plymouth, and died in 1700, leaving a nuncupative will; which divided the home lot between Israel and Joseph, the latter receiving the north part of the lot, and Israel, the south part and the house, at decease of wife Abigail, or at the time of her "changing her condition." The widow Abigail lived until 1735, outliving Israel. Miss Caulkins says: "On the completion of her century, Jan. 23, 1732, the Rev. Benjamin Lord preached a sermon in her room, at the house of her son." The Boston Weekly Journal prints this notice of her death: —

"Mrs. Abigail Lothrop died at Norwich, Jan. 23, 1735, in her 104th year. Her father, John Done, and his wife came to Plymouth in 1630, and there she was born the next year. She lived single till sixty years old, and then married Mr. John* Lothrop of Norwich, who lived ten years and then died. Mr. Lothrop's descendants at her decease were 365."

Israel Lathrop (b. 1659), married in 1686, Rebecca, daughter of Thomas Bliss, and in 1687, he buys the former house of Lt. Thomas Tracy. We assume that he occupies the Tracy house until his purchase of the Crane house in 1695-6, possibly then resides in the latter for a while, and after his father's death in 1700, takes possession of the homestead. Israel and Joseph Lathrop were married on the same day, April 8, 1686, Joseph to Mary Scudder, and Israel to Rebecca Bliss. With James Huntington, Israel was commissioned by the town, to lay out the east sheep walk, later known as the Landing, or Chelsea.

---
* Samuel Lothrop.

The Lathrop Family Memoir says: "Israel was a man of wordly thrift, and had a family of enterprising sons, who are said to have planted themselves "on seven hills* within the old nine-miles-square of Norwich." He died in 1733, and his wife in 1737. On his gravestone is inscribed: "Here lies buried ye body of Mr. Israel Lothrup, ye Husband of Mrs. Rebekah Lothrup, who lived a life of exemplary piety and left ye Earth for Heaven, March ye 28, 1733, in ye 73rd year of his age."

In the division of the home-lot between Joseph and Israel, Israel's share abuts south on the street 38 rods, 7 feet, west on the highway 27 rods, 9 feet, east on the highway 19 rods, 2½ feet, and north on Joseph Lathrop 32 rods, 4 feet. In 1730-1, Israel deeds one half of the house and lot to his son Jabez, and at his death in 1733, the house becomes the property of Jabez, but the land is divided between Jabez and Ebenezer. Jabez Lathrop (b. 1706-7), married (1) in 1728, Elizabeth Burnham, daughter of Eleazer and Lydia (Waterman) Burnham, who died in 1730. He married (2) in 1734, Delight, daughter of Judge Joseph and Dorothy (Thomas) Otis of Montville. She died in 1747, and he married (3) Lydia, widow of Dr. Joseph Wetherell of Taunton, Mass. Jabez had three daughters and four sons, and died in 1796.

---

* Israel, Jun., lived on Blue Hill, and John on Meeting-house Hill, Franklin; William and Jabez lived on Plain Hill; Ebenezer at the foot of Long Hill; Samuel settled at Bozrah, but where Benjamin resided, we do not know.

CHAPTER XXXVII.

IN 1738, Jabez Lathrop sells his share of his grandfather's home-lot, with house, barn, cider-press and mill, to Capt. Joshua Huntington, beginning at the southwest corner of the stone wall by the "Town Street" and abutting south on the street 16 rods, 11 feet, east on Ebenezer Lathrop's land 28½ rods, north on Joshua Huntington 17 rods, and west on the highway 28 rods, 5 feet. The house, now owned by Mrs. John White, is said to have been built by Joshua Huntington, about 1740. As a large price was paid for this property, and the house has many features which seem to indicate an earlier origin than 1740, it is possible, that, instead of destroying or removing the old Lathrop mansion, Joshua may have altered and remodeled it, but of this we have have no positive proof.

Joshua moves to the Lathrop lot, and gives to his son, Jabez, his former homestead on the Bradford land.

Capt. Joshua Huntington was born in 1698, and married in 1718, Hannah, daughter of Jabez and Hannah (Lathrop) Perkins. Miss Caulkins says: "He was a noted merchant, beginning business at nineteen, and pursuing it for twenty-seven years, during which time, it is said, that he traded more by sea and land than any other man in Norwich. He was one of the first to start the new settlement at the Landing, and received a grant of land, 20 feet square, on the west side of Rocky Point. He was highest on the list of subscribers to the bridge, built in 1737 over the Shetucket, between Norwich and Preston, and was prominent in all town affairs, and often served as representative to the General Assembly." "In the prime of life, activity, and usefulness, he took the yellow fever in New York, came home sick, and died the 27th of August, 1745, aged 47." His widow married (2) before 1747, Col. Samuel Lynde, a very influential and wealthy citizen of Saybrook, Ct., who died in 1754. She then married (3), between 1766 and 1771, Capt. Ebenezer Lathrop of Norwich. She died in 1788. Numerous relics of Hannah are still cherished among the families of her descendants, who hold her in high esteem, and her great-granddaughter, Mrs. George B. Ripley of Norwich, still retains the beautiful brocaded satin gown and quilted silk petticoat which her ancestress formerly wore.

After Joshua's death, the house is inherited by his widow, and his son Zachariah. This son was born in 1731, and died unmarried in 1761, evidently deeply mourned by his own family and a large circle of friends. His nephew, Jedediah, writes to his father of the pleasure he always took in his uncle's company and conversation. Zachariah is said to have planted the two beautiful elm trees now standing in front of the house.

In 1766, Mrs. Hannah Lynde, the mother of Gen. Jabez Huntington, deeds to him one-half of this house and land, and here Andrew (son of Gen. Jabez), who had married in that year, comes to live with his young wife, Lucy, the daughter of Capt. Joseph Coit.

Andrew Huntington (or Judge Andrew, as he was always called), was born in 1745, and married (1) in 1766, Lucy Coit, daughter of Capt. Joseph Coit, then of New London, later of Norwich. Two children were born to them, and the young wife died in 1776. Her father, Capt. Joseph Coit, records in his diary :—

"May 4th, 1776. At three o'clock in the morning dyed my dear daughter Lucy Huntington with the consumption, having been in the decline near seven months ; her end was even Glorious, her reason continued to the last, she had got the compleat victory over the fear of Death, and with uplifted hands and eyes bid it welcome, and a little before she expired, repeated with great emotion the words of Musculus's dying song:—

> "Cold death invades my heart, my life doth fly,
> Oh! Christ, my everlasting life, draw nigh.
> Why quiverest thou my Soul within my breast,
> Thine angels come to lead thee to thy rest.
> Quit cheerfully this drooping House of Clay,
> God will restore it at th' appointed day,
> Hast sin'd, I know it, let not that be urg'd
> For Christ thy sins with his own blood hath purg'd.
> Is death affrighting, true, but yet withal
> Consider Christ thro' death to life doth call.
> He triumph'd over Satan, sin, and death;
> Therefore with joy, resign thy dying breath."

Judge Andrew Huntington carried on the business of a merchant in his father's former store, west of his brother Zachariah's, and about 1790, in company with Ebenezer Bushnell, he started a paper manufactory at the Falls. During the Revolution, he was a commissary of brigade, and indefatigable in his efforts to furnish supplies to the army. He received his title from the office of Judge of Probate, which he held for many years. Mrs. Sigourney says: "He was of plain manners, and incorruptible integrity. His few words were always those of good sense and truth, and the weight of his influence given to the best interests of society."

On May 1, 1777, Judge Andrew married Hannah Phelps (b. 1762), daughter of Dr. Charles and Hannah (Denison) Phelps of Stonington, a young lady whom the Norwich Packet mentions as "possessed of the Beauties of Mind and Person in an eminent degree." She was of a much more lively nature than her husband, and was always a great social favorite from the time, when, as "a jolly young girl of fourteen," she "sticks her compliments" into a letter from Jonathan Bellamy to Aaron Burr, to later days, when she impresses Mrs. Sigourney with "that elegance of form and address which would have been conspicuous at any foreign court." Mrs. Sigourney adds: "She was especially fascinating to the children who visited her, by her liberal presentations of cake and other pleasant eatables, or which was equally alluring to some, a readiness to lend fine books with pictures." Many now living remember her wit, her charming manners, her never-failing hospitality. Young girls confided to her their joys and sorrows. Mrs. Sigourney read to her her earliest poems, sure of an appreciative and inspiring listener.

Her father, Dr. Charles Phelps, was a distinguished physician of Stonington. He was also a Judge of the County Court, and used to attend the sessions at Norwich. The Hon. Charles Miner thus describes him: "A fine, round, full-formed man,—very handsome, of courteous manners, dressed in fashionable style, flowing ruffles from his bosom, and ruffles over his hands—exceeding fluent,—an agreeable talker."

The bill for the wedding finery of Mrs. Andrew Huntington is still preserved, and may be interesting at this late date:—

CHARLES PHELPS, ESQ.

To WILLIAM HUBBARD, DR.

1777.
April. To 20 yards Brocade @ 46/6, . . . £46 10 0
" 8¼ yds Lute string @ 21/, . . . 8 13 3
" 7 yds Blown Lace @ 9, . . . 3 3 0
" 10 Do Thread Lace @ 5/4. . . . 2 13 4
" 25 yds Trimming @ 1/6, . . . 1 17 6
" 6 " White ribbon @ 3 . . . 0 18 0
" 1 pair White Silk Gloves, . . . 1
                                                                            ———————
                                                                            £64 15 1

After the death of his grandmother, Mrs. Hannah Lathrop, Judge Andrew acquired entire possession of the house. He died in 1824, and his wife Hannah, in 1838. In this latter year, the house is sold to Wolcott Huntington, who held it till his death in 1861. In 1883, Mrs. John White, its present occupant, became the owner. The view from this house extends over the lands of Christopher Huntington, Lt. Thomas Tracy, and Dea. Thomas Adgate, to the hill at the rear of the former Olmstead property.

At his father's death in 1733, the south-east part of the Lathrop lot was inherited by Capt. Ebenezer Lathrop, except the extreme south-east corner, where a small lot of land was granted in 1728, to Hezekiah Huntington, "to build a house on." This was possibly unenclosed common land at the time of the Elderkin grant, or perhaps, as was often the case, had been ceded to the town

by the Lathrop family, in exchange for other property. Hezekiah Huntington sells this land (frontage on the street 6 rods, 6 feet, on the lane 5 rods), to Ebenezer Lathrop, in 1755. At Ebenezer's death in 1776, the barn-lot facing on the lane, beginning 8 rods from the corner, is given to his son, Jedediah, and the land on the street, divided into four lots, is inherited in the following order by the daughters of Capt. Ebenezer: the one on the corner by Lydia, then comes Sibyl's lot, then Zerviah's, and next to the Andrew Huntington property, that of Zipporah. Zipporah's and Zerviah's lots are purchased and added to the Andrew Huntington lands in 1796 and 1797. The lot on the corner, where now stands the house of Ira Peck, with 8 rods frontage "on the highway," and 5 rods, 4½ links on the street, is sold in 1795, to Felix Huntington, who builds here a joiner's shop, which is sold in 1822 to Roger Huntington and Henry Avery. The next lot (frontage 5 rods, 11½ links), is sold to Samuel Danforth by Samuel and Sibyl Tracy in 1793. Samuel Danforth builds a "pewterer's" shop (of one story with gambrel roof and painted red), which is sold in 1803, to the firm of Avery & Tracy. In 1818, Roger Huntington and Henry Avery have a shop in this building. For a long time wooden troughs, or aqueduct pipes, were manufactured here. In 1830, these two buildings, the Danforth and Felix Huntington shops were sold to Henry Barrows, who alters the latter into a house, which he sells to Wolcott Huntington in 1850. In 1870, the Barrows house, and land on which it stands, is sold to Ira Peck, who builds the new house which he now occupies.

CHAPTER XXXVIII.

IN 1688, Samuel Lathrop, Sr., deeds to his son, Samuel, 2nd, "land, where his (Samuel, 2nd's), house stands," 3 rods in depth, abutting north on the highway 9 rods, and east, south, and west, on the Lathrop home-lot. The house built by Samuel Lathrop, Jun., is probably the one later known as the old "Grist" house. In 1689, Samuel Lathrop, Jun., inherits the Olmstead house, and moves there to live, and in 1692, calling himself "yeoman," he sells this house to his brother Joseph ("yeoman").

Joseph Lathrop (b. 1661), married (1) in 1686, Mary Scudder, probably a relative of his mother, Elizabeth. He married (2) 1696-7, Elizabeth, daughter of Isaac and Sarah (Pratt) Watrous of Lyme, Ct., and also takes a third wife in 1727, Martha (Morgan) Perkins, widow of Deacon Joseph Perkins of Newent, and daughter of Lt. Joseph Morgan of Preston. After the death of his father, he receives as his share of the property, the north part of the home-lot, adjoining his newly-purchased house. This land and house he deeds to his son Joseph in 1723, and Joseph, Jun., sells to Joshua Huntington in 1725, the house and west part of the land, bounded on the north and west by the highway, and south by Israel Lathrop's land. In the same year, he sells the land on the east to Daniel Tracy, who later sells it in two portions, in 1747 and 1763, to Thomas Danforth. Before 1806, part of this is taken off to enlarge the highway and the remainder is sold to the Rev. Joseph Strong in 1813. Joseph Lathrop, Sr., died in 1740. His son Joseph (b. 1688), married in 1735, Mary Hartshorn of Franklin. He moved to Waterbury, Ct., in 1743. In 1752, he is living in Bolton, Ct., and dies in 1757.

Joshua Huntington sells the house and land on which it stands, to Thomas Grist in 1726, beginning at the north-east corner by the brook, then running west, and by north 7 rods, then south 40° W., 11½ rods, 3 feet, then east by Israel

Lathrop's land 4 rods, thence bounded east by the land of Daniel Tracy, Jun. In 1761, Thomas Grist deeds one-half of this property to his son John, and at his death, it is divided between the children, John receiving one-half, and the four daughters, Anna, Hannah, Zillah, and Mary, the other half. The house is described by some old persons, who have a vivid recollection of it, as large and square, with a long lean-to, and lattice windows.

Thomas Grist is said to have come from England to Norwich about 1720, and to have married in 1721, Anna, daughter of Samuel and Ann (Calkins) Birchard. He had a family of nine daughters and two sons. He and Edmund Gookin are said to have been "the first Church of England men in the place," and services were held alternately at their houses, the Gookin house being situated at Bean Hill. At first only a few persons assembled, but as the number increased, it was decided to build a church at the Landing.

Thomas Grist was appointed one of the building committee, and subscribed £40 toward its erection. A lot of land, the present site of Christ's Church, was given by Capt. Benajah Bushnell, and the church was completed in 1749. In 1789, a more central location was considered desirable, and the church building was removed to a lot, presented by Phinehas Holden, on Church Street, a few rods east of the present Trinity Church. This later building was erected in 1828, and the old church edifice was in 1830, sold to the Episcopal Society of Salem, Ct. It was then moved to a site on the Salem Green, was afterward purchased by the town and is now the Salem Town House.

Thomas Grist was chosen to serve as one of the vestry-men of Christ Church. His grand-daughter, Theophila, was one the first children baptized by Rev. John Tyler, after his ordination. Mr. Grist was not only devoted to the interests of the Church of England, but to his native land as well, and it is said that during the Revolution, he and Richard Hyde, who was a strong patriot, were continually discussing and disputing the claims of both countries, and freely applying to each other the epithets of "tory" and "rebel." Thomas Grist died in 1781, aged 81 years, and was buried in the old Christ's Church grave yard, from which the stones have been removed.* His business seems to have been the

* A large number of these gravestones are preserved in the cellar of Christ Church.

making of "slays" and harnesses. Mary Grist, the last of the family, dies in 1824. In 1827, the property is sold to the Rev. Joseph Strong. The house, we have been told, remained standing until after 1853.

On the opposite side of the street from the Grist house stood the joiner shop of John Grist, which he sold in 1783 to Zephaniah Huntington. This is sold in 1793 to Joshua Huntington, whose heirs sell the land, from which the shop seems to have disappeared, to George W. Lee, in 1823.

CHAPTER XXXIX.

FOLLOWING the road, as it turns again toward the main street, next to the Grist house, we come to the land given by Gen. Jabez Huntington to his son Joshua. The house was built about 1771. After Col. Joshua Huntington's death, it was sold in 1823 to George W. Lee, and in 1859, by the Lee heirs to its present owner, Theodore McCurdy.

Col. Joshua Huntington (b. 1751), married in 1771, Hannah, daughter of Col. Hezekiah Huntington. At the beginning of the Revolution, he was already established in a prosperous business at the Landing, and had vessels of his own at sea, but at the first summons to arms, he hastened to Boston. At that time he had already served as lieutenant of militia. Though he felt that his business claims required his presence at home, he still remained with the army, and served for a while in New York. He was later engaged in securing ships for the service, and in fitting out privateers. He was agent for Wadsworth & Carter of Hartford, in supplying the French army at Newport with provisions, and had charge of the prizes sent by the French navy to Connecticut. He

Mrs. Sigourney says of him: "Col. Joshua Huntington had one of the most benign countenances I ever remember to have seen. His calm, beautiful brow, was an index of his temper and life. Let who would be disturbed or irritated, he was not the man. He regarded with such kindness, as the gospel teaches, the whole human family. At his own fair fireside, surrounded by living congenial spirits, and in all his intercourse with the community, he was the same serene and revered Christian philosopher." He was for a time High Sheriff of New London County.

Hannah, the wife of Col. Joshua, of whom it was said, "A memorial of her virtues will live as long as anyone remains, who had the happiness to know her," died in 1815. They had only one child, a daughter, Elizabeth (b. 1774), who married in 1800 the Hon. Frederick Wolcott of Litchfield, Ct.

In 1757, Hannah Lynde, widow of Capt. Joshua Huntington, sells to Charles Whiting the lot of land (frontage 5 rods), next to the present McCurdy residence,

on which he builds the house now occupied by Mrs. Isabella Williams. The Whiting heirs sell this house in 1785 to Mundator Tracy, who sells in 1810 to Henry Nevins, and in 1827 it is sold to Mrs. Elizabeth Anderson. It is now owned by William Fitch.

Charles Whiting (b. 1725), was the son of Charles and Elizabeth (Bradford) Whiting, and the great-great-grandson of Maj. William Whiting, a distinguished and wealthy citizen of Hartford. His grandfather, Col. William Whiting, was conspicuous in the French and Indian wars. On his mother's side, Charles Whiting was a descendant of Gov. William Bradford, and also of John and Priscilla Alden of Plymouth. His father lived for a time at Montville. Three of his sons, Charles, William Bradford, and Ebenezer settled in Norwich.

The Charles Whiting who built this house, married in 1749, Honor, daughter of Hezekiah and Honor (Deming) Goodrich of Wethersfield. He was a goldsmith or jeweller, and built a shop, a short distance from his house, on land leased from Daniel Tracy. He died about 1765. We believe that Mundator Tracy, who bought the house in 1785, lived here for a time, but the deeds do not allude to an occupancy.

Mundator Tracy (b. 1749), was the son of Deacon Simon and Abigail (Bushnell) Tracy. A Norwich Packet of 1773, announces the marriage of Mr. Mundator Tracy, "an accomplished gentleman, to Miss Caroline Bushnell, a young lady endowed with every qualification to make the connubial state happy." His wife, Caroline, was the daughter of Benajah and Hannah (Griswold) Bushnell. She died in 1785, and he married (2) in 1786, Nabby, daughter of Eleazer Lord. Mundator Tracy died in 1816, and his widow in 1821.

CHAPTER XL.

ON the west corner of the former Lathrop lot, was for a time located the shop of Zachariah, son of Capt. Joshua Huntington. After Zachariah's death in 1761, the shop and land, bounded south on the street 6 rods, and west "on the lane into the woods," passed into the possession of his brother, Jabez, who gives it to his son, Jedediah. The latter builds, about 1765, the house now standing on the lot, and lived here until his departure for New London in 1789. While Jedediah Huntington was with the army in 1776, the shop was for a time tenanted by Samuel Loudon, who offered for sale "a neat assortment of books, pictures, glazed and unglazed maps, &c."

Samuel Loudon had married sometime before 1768, Lydia, daughter of John and Hannah (Lee) Griswold of Lyme, and sister of Gov. Matthew Griswold, and of Mrs. Benajah Bushnell and Mrs. Elijah Backus of Norwich. He was a merchant in the city of New York, where he built in 1771 a large house and wharf. He writes to his brother-in-law, Elijah Backus, in March, 1776:—

"New York, 29 March, 1776.

I lately engaged in the Printing Business, as there was nothing to be done in the Merchantile, and as I have good encouragement to prosecute it, it will not do to leave the city till I'm obliged. I intend to keep my office by head Quarters where the posts meet, which will be in or near this city, and if there is apparent danger, to move my Family a little way into the Conntry. Our City is now Fortifying;—every street is strongly Barracadoed and entrenched, and Batterys in every part of the City, and they are making a Strong Fortification on a Hill behind the City, and opposite to it on Long Island. We are intrenching and Forming a strong Redoubt. Some thousands of the Citizens and Army are employed every day at the works; which make them go on very rapid. Some of the Troops from Boston are arrived here and many more expected. We will have a large Army here soon, which I hope will be able to repell the Forces which Britain may send."

Mr. Loudon probably fled from the city with the troops and many of the citizens in September of that year and came to Norwich, bringing with him a large stock of books, &c. He remained here only a few months, then returned to New York, where his wife died in 1788. After Gen. Jedediah Huntington moved to New London, his nephew, Joseph Huntington, son of Andrew, occupied the store for a time in 1790, and during a part of 1791. In 1792, Gen. Jedediah Huntington sold the house and store to his brother, Ebenezer, who had married in 1791, and the house remained in the possession of the family of Ebenezer until sold in 1886 to its present owner, William Fitch. In 1793, Ebenezer Huntington, whose main place of business was at the Landing, opened also a stock of goods in this shop. When this building disappeared, we are unable to say.

Gen. Jedediah Huntington (b. 1743), was the son of Gen. Jabez and Elizabeth (Backus) Huntington. After graduating at Harvard College "with distinguished honor," he entered into business with his father. At the beginning of the Revolutionary troubles, he became an ardent Son of Liberty, and captain of militia. In 1774, he was appointed colonel of the Twentieth Regiment of Militia. At the news of the British march on Lexington, he started at once with seventy

men for the scene of action. He fought at the battle of Bunker Hill, and Seth Miner, who was his orderly sergeant, used to relate how quietly and "unconcernedly" Col. Huntington moved amid the shower of cannon balls, with which the British were besieging the town.

After the battle of Bunker Hill, he went with the army to New York, stopping at Norwich to entertain Gen. Washington and Gov. Trumbull, who met by appointment to dine at his house. He was soon appointed Colonel of the Eighth Regiment, raised and drilled under his orders. Miss Caulkins says: "This regiment was the best equipped of any in the colony, and was distinguished by a British uniform, the Governor and Council having appropriated to them a quantity of English red-coats taken in a prize vessel."

Gen. Jedediah served in most of the important engagements of the war, both in New York and Pennsylvania, endured the hardships of Valley Forge, and helped repulse the British at Danbury, Ct., in 1776. At the battle of Long Island in that year, his men "fought with desperate bravery" and many were taken prisoners, and died "in the noted sugar-house and prison-ship at New York," of disease and starvation. Gen. Huntington was a member of the court martial which tried Gen. Charles Lee, was one of the court of inquiry to which was referred the cause of Major Andre, and also served on other important commissions.

In 1777, "at Gen. Washington's request," he was made a Brigadier-General, and at the close of the war received the brevet title of Major-General. He was one of the first founders of the Order of Cincinnati, and one of the delegates to the State convention which adopted the Constitution of the United States. After the war, he filled many important offices, some of which are enumerated in a newspaper announcement of his appointment as Treasurer of Connecticut in 1788:—

"Major-General Huntington, Esq., Vice President of the Order of Cincinnati, High Sheriff for the county of New London, Judge of Probate for the district of Norwich, first Alderman of the city of Norwich, one of the Representatives of the town in the State Legislature, and one of the State Electors, is now appointed by the General Assembly Treasurer for the State of Connecticut."

Jedediah married in 1766, Faith, daughter of Gov. Jonathan Trumbull of Lebanon, Ct., the famous war governor, and well known "Brother Jonathan."

They had one son, Jabez (b. 1767), who later became a prominent citizen of Norwich Landing, or Chelsea.

Faith Trumbull was born in Lebanon in 1742-3, and went to Boston to complete her education, "thence to return (as Stuart says in his life of Gov. Trumbull), with skill in embroidery, and with two heads and landscapes in oil of her own painting, with which to rouse the curiosity, and for the first time stimulate in the art of delineation, the till then wholly unpractised hand of her younger brother, the artist of future renown." She accompanied her husband to Boston, and her brother, John Trumbull, the artist, writes: "The novelty of military scenes excited great curiosity throughout the city, and my sister was one of a party of young friends, who were attracted to visit the army before Boston. She was a woman of deep and affectionate sensibility, and the moment of her visit was most unfortunate. She found herself surrounded not by "the pomp and circumstance of glorious war," but in the midst of all its horrible realities. She saw too clearly, the life of danger and hardship, upon which her husband and her favorite brother had entered, and it overcame her strong, but too sensitive mind. She became deranged, and died the following winter at Dedham, Mass. In writing of her death to his brother-in-law, Joseph Trumbull, Gen. Jedediah says: "Her obligingness and affection were without a parallel. The law of kindness was ever on her tongue and heart, but she is gone, and gone, I trust, to scenes of uninterrupted bliss. My tears must and will flow."

Gen. Jedediah's second wife, whom he married in 1778, was Ann, daughter of Col. Thomas Moore of New York. Her great grandfather, John Moore, an eminent lawyer of Pennsylvania, born in England about 1658, is said to be one of the sons of Sir Francis Moore. He emigrated to South Carolina, where he practised law for a while, then moved to Philadelphia, was soon after appointed attorney-general, later register-general and then collector of customs for Pennsylvania. His son, John Moore, settled as a merchant in New York, was one of the aldermen of the city, colonel of a regiment, and at the time of his death a member of the provincial council. Col. Thomas Moore (son of John Moore, 2nd), was "born in New York, received his education at Westminster School, London, engaged in commercial pursuits in his native city, at the approach of the Revolution

OLD HOUSES OF NORWICH.

retired with his family to West Point, and driven thence by violence, returned to the city, where he occupied a place in the custom house during the war." So says the Huntington Family Memoir, but, according to Miss Caulkins, Col. Moore came to Norwich, and occupied for a time the Arnold house, where he died in 1784. The newspaper notice of his death, and also the notice of his daughter's marriage in 1778, mentions them as "late of New York." Miss Caulkins writes: "The Moore family was large, and their dwelling had the reputation of being the seat of hospitality and festive enjoyment." Col. Moore was buried in Trinity Church grave-yard, New York city. Two of the sons, John, as a merchant, and Benjamin, as a physician, remained for some years in Norwich, but before 1793, they had removed from the town. Another son was Richard Channing Moore, the distinguished Bishop of Virginia. By his second wife, Gen. Jedediah had seven children, one of whom, Joshua, became the pastor of the old South Church in Boston. Daniel was settled over a church at North Bridgewater, Mass., and Thomas, who first studied for the medical profession, afterward became an evangelist of the Baptist denomination in Brooklyn, Ct. The daughters married prominent citizens of New London, Norwich, and New York.

In 1789, Gen. Jedediah Huntington was appointed collector of customs at New London, and entered on his office, as the record says, Aug. 11, 1789, "at 7 o'clock A. M." He held this office under four successive Presidents, and died in 1818, aged 75. He was buried in New London, but it was afterward found on reading his will, that his desire was to be interred in his native town, so the body was removed to Norwich, and now lies in the family tomb in the burying-ground near the Green*.

Miss Caulkins speaks of Gen. Jedediah's "sedate temperament, of his great energy, steadiness and dignity, of the neatness and precision of his personal appearance, and his polished, though reserved demeanor." He joined the church at the age of twenty-three, and was ever after a consistent Christian, and very liberal in his charities. According to contemporary testimony, "His munificence for its profusion, its uniformity, its long continuance, and for the discretion, by

---

*Gen. Huntington built for his residence in New London the house, now occupied by Elisha Palmer, on the corner of Broad and Washington Streets.

which it was directed, was without a parallel in his native state." He was one of the founders and the first President of the New London Branch of the American Board of Foreign Missions, organized in 1810.

Mrs. Sigourney describes him as "of small stature, but of correct and graceful symmetry. Firm in camps, and wise in council, in refined society he was gentleness itself." She compares the two brothers, Jedediah and Ebenezer, "to the two Gracchi, save that the elder had more gentleness of soul, and the younger less ambition for popularity, than their ancient prototypes."

In 1781, Gen. Jedediah gave an entertainment for the French officers, who were quartered at Lebanon, and these gay young men must have made a fine appearance in their brilliant hussar uniforms,* as they rode into town. The two Dillon brothers, a major and a captain, were particularly admired "for their fine forms and expressive features." One, or both of these brothers, "suffered death from the guillotine during the French Revolution."

The handsome Duke de Lauzun was one of this company, and what a contrast this simple entertainment in a small country town offers to the rest of his stormy career, his early years of dissipation, his life as an ambassador at the English court, and intimacy with the gay Prince of Wales, afterward George IV., then his later life as Duke de Biron, espousing the Orleans cause, and afterwards fighting against the Vendeans, until accused of favoring the enemy, he was tried, condemned, and executed on the last day of 1793. After dinner the company of officers went out on the lawn in front of the house and shouted huzzas for "Liberty," and exhorted the people assembled outside "to live free or die for liberty."

Gen. Lafayette made several visits to Norwich, once on a hurried ride to Newport, when the need of haste and the intense heat, necessitated a light attire. The good people of Norwich were rather scandalized to see him ride up to Gen. Huntington's door, dressed in a blue military coat, without vest or stockings, and, his boots being short, with the leg bare below the knee. He stopped only a short time for refreshment, and then proceeded to Newport.

* The cavalry of the Duke de Lauzun wore blue hussar jackets and high-crowned round hats; the infantry uniform was black and red.

At another time in 1778, he arrived with 2000 men of Gen. Glover's Irish Brigade, who encamped on the plain for three days, from Thursday to Sunday, while the General was entertained at the house of Gen. Huntington. This may have been the time, when at Lafayette's request, on the morning of their departure, Mr. Strong prayed with the soldiers, they forming three sides of a hollow square.

On Sunday, Aug. 22, 1824, Lafayette visited Norwich, and some old people, who remembered him, wept, and the General was also moved to tears. A young school girl describes this visit in her journal.:—

"After church walked to the Landing, as the arrival of Gen. La Fayette, the great benefactor of our country, was announced. He arrived in this country (in the ship Cadmus from France, accompanied by his son, George Washington, and his friend, M. De Vasseur). On Sunday, the 8th of August, he first landed on Staten Island, and on Monday entered the city of New York, where great preparations had been made for his reception. 6 steamboats went down to escort him up to New York; among them were the Oliver Ellsworth and Chancellor Livingston, the latter of which he came up in. He landed in Castle Garden, and from thence he proceeded to the City Hall, where rooms were prepared for him, and he received calls from 12 to 2 o'clock. The steamboats were decorated and a band of music on each. From N. Y., he proceeded to New Haven and New London and to-night he arrived in this city accompanied by an escort from New York and Norwich. Great numbers had assembled to welcome and to behold the great man, to whom our country is so greatly indebted. A line was formed on either side of the street and the procession passed through consisting of gigs and horsemen—his arrival was announced by three cheers, & followed by clapping of hands, & 13 cannon were discharged. I had the honour as most of the town did of being introduced to him and of shaking hands. He is of large stature, well proportioned, dark complexion, good looking and looks young for his age, which is 68 I could not but pity him, although he remarked 'that he was not fatigued, that it was such a mark of gratitude & affection, and he was also accustomed to fatigue.' He pronounced a benediction upon this country and its inhabitants. He sets out this evening for Plainfield on his way to Boston (where he is also to be received with great magnificence) & is to be at commencement at Cambridge on Wednesday, where his son was graduated." This was Lafayette's last visit to America. His death occurred in 1834.

The second occupant of this house, Gen. Ebenezer Huntington (b. 1754), was the son of Gen. Jabez Huntington, and his second wife, Hannah, daughter of Rev. Ebenezer Williams of Pomfret, Ct. He was at Yale College, and within two months of graduation, when the war commenced. With several other students, he asked permission to enter the army, was refused, ran off in the night to Wethersfield, enlisted, and left at once for Boston. "He continued firm throughout the contest, and rose through the different grades of command to that of Lieut.-Colonel in 1778, while yet in the early stages of manhood." He was at the surrender of Cornwallis, and his portrait figures in the painting of that scene by Col. John Trumbull. He served through the whole war, until the troops were disbanded in 1783.

After the war, in 1792, he was appointed Major-General of the State militia, which office he held for thirty years. In 1799, when a war with France was anticipated, he received from President Adams the appointment of Brigadier-General in the U. S. army. He served also in the war of 1812. In 1810, and in 1817, he was elected a member of Congress. He died in 1834. Mrs. Sigourney describes him as having "a fine figure, with military carriage, and a countenance, which was considered a model of manly beauty." She speaks of "the elegant manners," and "decision of character," which "were conspicuous in him, and unimpaired by age."

He married (1) in 1791, Sarah, daughter of Joseph Isham of Colchester, Ct. She died in 1793, and he married (2) in 1795, Mary Lucretia (daughter of Gen. Samuel McClellan of Woodstock, Ct.), who died in 1819. His son, Wolcott Huntington, lived in Norwich; his other sons settled in New Orleans, La. One daughter married the late George Perkins, a well-known lawyer of Norwich; another became the wife of Gabriel Denton of New Orleans. The four remaining daughters, who are well remembered as "the Ladies Huntington," lived for many years in the old family mansion. The last of the sisters died in 1885, and in 1886, the house was sold to its present owner, William H. Fitch.

CHAPTER XLI.

OPPOSITE the house of Samuel Lathrop, was the home-lot of Lt. Thomas Tracy, which, beginning at the brook by Christopher Huntington's, extended to a point three rods east of the cemetery lane. It consisted of nine acres, abutting north on the street 34½ rods, east on lands of Christopher Huntington and Thomas Adgate 56 rods, south on the Rev. James Fitch 16 rods, 14 feet, and west on Rev. Mr. Fitch and Simon Huntington 53½ rods.

From Chancellor Walworth's valuable "Genealogy of the Hyde Family," we learn that Lt. Thomas Tracy of Norwich, was the grandson of Richard Tracy of Stanway, Gloucestershire, England, and his wife, Barbara Lucy, a daughter of Sir William Lucy of Charlecote, Warwickshire. From the recent researches of Lt. Charles Stedman Ripley, U. S. N., we find that Lt. Thomas was a son of Sir Paul Tracy, second son of Richard Tracy, and not as was supposed of the latter's eldest son, Nathaniel.

Lt. Thomas Tracy was born about 1610 in Tewksbury, Eng., came to America in 1636, and received a grant of land at Salem, Mass., where his occupation was that of a ship-carpenter. About 1640, he went to Wethersfield, Ct., and is said to have married the widow of Edward Mason in 1641. Shortly after, he went to Saybrook, and in 1660, came with the first band of settlers to Norwich, bringing with him six sons and a daughter, and possibly his wife, as the date of her death has not been ascertained.

From the very beginning of the settlement, Thomas Tracy was called upon to fill important offices, as constable and townsman, was one of the first deputies chosen in 1661, an office which he held for many years; served also on Courts of Commission, and as Justice of the Peace. In 1666, he was appointed Ensign of the train-band, and in 1673, Lieutenant of the New London County Dragoons, enlisted to fight the Dutch and Indians.

After the death of his opposite neighbor, John Bradford, he married the widow, Martha, who died ere long, and he then succumbed to the charms of a third widow, Mary, relict of John Stoddard, and of John Goodrich of Wethersfield, and daughter of Nathaniel Foot. Lt. Thomas died in 1685, leaving an estate of £560. His real estate amounted to 5000 acres. John, the oldest son, received £140, the other sons, and son-in-law, Thomas Waterman, each £70. As the widow is not mentioned in the distribution, she had presumably died before her husband. To John Tracy had been assigned, at the time of the settlement, a home-lot at Bean Hill. Thomas and Jonathan had settled in Preston. In the division of Lt. Tracy's property, the east and west parts of the home lot were laid out to Daniel and Solomon. In 1687, the centre of the lot (frontage 16½ rods), with the house, is sold to Israel Lathrop, and entered on the records as the latter's home-lot, of three acres, bounded north on the highway 16½ rods, west on land of Solomon Tracy 53 rods, south on Mr. Fitch 7 rods, east on Daniel Tracy 41 rods, south on Daniel Tracy 2 rods, 13 feet, east on Daniel Tracy 14 rods, 4 feet, with highway to brook.

In 1692-3, the division of the property of Lt. Thomas Tracy is thus quaintly recorded in the second book of land deeds: "Cousen Richard Bushnell, I pray, enter the records of my fathers lands in the new booke, and then record to my brother, Daniel Tracy, a third part of the home lott that was my fathers," &c., &c. He also asks to have one-third recorded to Solomon. In 1688, Israel Lathrop sells land in the rear of his lot to Daniel Tracy, who sells a part to Solomon in 1692, which will account for seeming discrepancies in their several records, and also serve to date the entries of their lands.

Daniel's home-lot next to the brook, where he probably built his first homestead, is entered (evidently after 1692) as four acres, "bounded north on the highway 5 rods, 3 feet, bounded east on Christopher Huntington and Thomas Adgate 56 rods, a compassing line, bounded south on Mr. Fitch 7 rods, 6 feet, abutting west on Solomon Tracy 41 rods, abutting west on Israel Lathrop 14 rods, except an open passage to the brook."

Daniel Tracy (b. 1652), married (1) in 1682, Abigail, daughter of Deacon Thomas Adgate, and after her death in 1711, he married (2) 1712, Hannah, widow of Thomas Bingham, and daughter of William Backus, 2nd. In 1712, Daniel Tracy gives (not with the usual "good-will, and fatherly affection" of other parents of those days), but "of my own meare good pleasure to my loving son, Daniel, the one half of the homested of me the sd Daniel Tracy, containing four acres abutting on land in the present tenure of René Grignon and Thomas Adgate," &c., &c. This deed differing from all others on record in its peculiar wording, inclines us to believe, that Daniel was a most exact man and somewhat autocratic and dictatorial, evidently one who kept his family in subjection, as will appear later.

In 1728, at the rebuilding of Lathrop's bridge on the Shetucket, connecting Newent and Norwich, which had been destroyed in the freshet of 1727, a part of the frame-work gave way, and one hundred feet of the bridge, and forty men were precipitated into the water. The water was low, and they were thrown upon the rocks, and among those most seriously injured, was Mr. Daniel Tracy, who died the following day. The pamphlet, giving an account of the accident, says that "Mr. Tracy was not a person concerned in the affair, only as he was a benefactor to it, and went out that day to carry the people some provision, and happened to be on the bridge at that juncture of danger: a man that had always been noted for an uncommon care to keep himself and others out of probable danger, and yet now himself insensibly falls into a fatal one. And very remarkable is it, that to keep his son at home this day, and so out of danger by that occasion, he chooseth to go himself" (of his meare good pleasure, we suppose), "on the fore-named errand, and is taken in the snare which he thought more probable to his son." This son was then a married man, forty years of age; and Daniel Tracy was seventy-six. His foot-stone in the cemetery reads: "This worthy in a good old age died by a fall from a bridge."

Daniel Tracy, 2nd (b. 1688), inherited the house and home-lot. He married in 1710, Abigail, daughter of Ensign Thomas Leffingwell, and had five children, according to the records, and sixteen, according to the testimony of the grave-stone of one of these children, Hannah, wife of Simon Huntington.

How long Israel Lathrop occupied the house of Lt. Thomas Tracy has not been ascertained. In 1695-6, he purchased the Jonathan Crane house, but in 1705, after his father's death, he seems to be living in the paternal homestead across the street. It is possible that the Tracy house may have been destroyed by fire, which perhaps was the occasion for Israel's purchase of the Crane house. At the time of his death in 1733, there is no house upon this Tracy lot, which is then called "the orchard of Israel Lothrop," and in 1738, Jabez Lathrop, son of Israel, sells it to Daniel Tracy, which gives to Daniel a frontage of about 21 rods, 11 feet. We are unable to say whether Daniel then vacated the house in which he was living, and built the one (now standing on the lot, and occupied by Mr. Bacheler), as in the settlement of his estate, the measurements of the property, which might locate this house, are not given. Daniel died in 1771. It is possible that he inherited a portion of his father's decided character, as he was one of the proprietors, who, though much importuned, refused to "sell an inch of land" to facilitate the erection of the Second Church in 1760.

At the time of Daniel's death, his only surviving son, Samuel, was living at the Landing. This Samuel Tracy (b. 1723), married in 1750, Sibyl, daughter of Capt. Ebenezer Lathrop, and probably, shortly after his father's death, removed to Norwich Town. It is possible that he may have torn down the old house and built the new one, which was standing in the centre of the lot at his death, and was inherited by his son, Maj. Thomas Tracy, but we are inclined to believe that the present house was erected by Daniel Tracy, 2nd. About 1773, Samuel Tracy was one of the managers of the lottery for building the great Wharf Bridge at

Chelsea. He served for one year as town clerk, and for several sessions as representative to the General Assembly. He died in 1798 of the small-pox, and his widow and son, Thomas, inherited the house and home-lot.

Maj. Thomas Tracy (b. 1767), married Elizabeth, daughter of Samuel Avery. With the latter he formed a mercantile partnership in 1793, as the firm of Avery & Tracy. Maj. Tracy died in 1806, and his only child, a daughter, was born shortly after her father's death. This daughter, Ann Thomas Tracy, married in 1834, James T. Richards of New York, and had two children, who, dying young, the property was sold to Ferdinand Stedman in 1852. The house is now owned by Mrs. Bacheler.

Some time after 1750, Capt. Charles Whiting (goldsmith), builds a shop on the land of Daniel Tracy. In 1775, Charles Beaman, "Taylor and Habit Maker," appears in this shop "opposite Col. Jedidiah Huntington's," and advertises that he hopes to recommend himself "by the fashion and neatness of his garments that he fabricates," and promises "not to waste nor demand more materials than are indispensably necessary. Cabbage and extortion are his aversion." Being a stranger in the place he "expects no more favors than his honesty, abilities, and sincerity shall merit."

In 1784, Roswell Huntington advertised as a goldsmith and jeweller opposite the store of Gen. Jedediah Huntington. Whether this is the Roswell Huntington (b. 1763), son of Ebenezer and Sarah (Edgerton) Huntington, (a descendant of the first Simon), who afterwards moved to North Carolina, or another Roswell (b. 1754), (son of Samuel Huntington of Mansfield, Ct., and a descendant of Christopher Huntington), who married in 1777, Sarah Read of Windham, we are unable to say. In 1785, the Whiting heirs sell this shop, "standing on land of Samuel Tracy," to Mundator Tracy, son of Simon. The fact that the shop was standing on leased land makes it difficult to learn how soon it disappears. It is possible that Mundator may have added it to an adjoining shop, which he purchased soon after, and converted into a house.

CHAPTER XLII.

WE have now arrived at the home-lot of Dr. Solomon Tracy, which is recorded, evidently before 1692, as of three acres, abutting north on the street 13 rods, south on the Rev. James Fitch 5 rods, 4 feet, and measuring 53½ rods through the middle in length, abutting west on the land of Simon Huntington.

Dr. Solomon Tracy (b. 1650), married (1) 1676, Sarah, daughter of Simon Huntington. After her death he married in 1686, Sarah, widow of Thomas Sluman, and daughter of Thomas Bliss. He was the second physician of Norwich, and possibly acquired his medical knowledge from Dr. John Olmstead. He filled the offices of constable and townsman, was frequently elected representative to the General Assembly, serving in 1711 as Clerk of the House, and in 1717 as Speaker. In 1698, he was chosen Ensign of the train-band, and in 1701, Lieutenant. He died in 1732, and on his grave-stone is written:—

> THE DEAD IN SILENT
> LANGUAGE SAY
> TO LIVING THINKING
> READER HEARE.
> O LOVING FRIENDS
> DOE NOT DELAY
> BUT SPEEDILY FOR
> DETH PREPARE.

In 1721, Solomon Tracy ("yeoman"), and wife, Sarah, deed to Simon Tracy "for love," &c., "all our Norwich lands and buildings, &c., only reserving to our own use and benefit the dwelling house and barn dureing our natural life." Solomon Tracy, Jun., son of Dr. Solomon, removes to Canterbury.

Simon Tracy (b. 1679-80), married in 1708, Mary, daughter of Ensign

Thomas Leffingwell. In 1736, he deeds one-half of the house and home-lot to his son, Simon Tracy, Jun., and in 1769, the whole of the property (frontage 9 rods, 23 links), which Simon, 2nd, sells in that same year to Samuel Huntington. Simon Tracy, Sr., possibly goes to reside with his son, Simon, 2nd, on the Plain Hills road, where his other son, Moses, also has a house. Simon Tracy lived to be very old, and on a head-stone in the cemetery we may read that "the pious beloved and very aged Simon Tracy died 14th September, 1775, in the 96th year of his age." His wife died 1770, aged 88.

Simon Tracy, 2nd (b. 1710), married (1) in 1735, Elizabeth, daughter of Jabez Hyde, and (2) in 1743-4, Abigail, daughter of Dr. Caleb Bushnell. He died in 1793, aged 82. He had filled the offices of representative to the General Assembly and deacon of the church, and his obituary notice in the Packet says that he was "for many years employed in public trust both in church and state, and discharged the several duties of a man, a magistrate, and a Christian with integrity." In 1757, Simon Tracy, Sr, and his son, Simon, sell to Jabez Huntington, the east corner of their home-lot (frontage 3 rods). On this Jabez builds a shop, which he sells to Simeon and Jabez Perkins, who had served as his apprentices for several years, and now wished to set up in business for themselves. Jabez (b. 1728), and Simeon (b. 1734), were the grandsons of Jabez Perkins, who came with his brother, Joseph, from Ipswich, Mass., to Norwich, in the latter part of the seventeenth century, and settled in a part of the town, to which they are said to have given the name of Newent. Jabez, 3rd, was the son of Jabez and Rebecca (Leonard) Perkins, and Simeon, of Jacob and Jemina (Leonard) Perkins. Rebecca and Jemina were daughters of Elkanah Leonard of Middleboro', Mass., and step-daughters of Jabez Perkins, Sr.

Taking a cousinly interest in the two young men, for his mother was also a daughter of the first Jabez Perkins, Jabez Huntington had promised, at the end of Simeon's apprenticeship, to start them in business. The partnership did not last long. Jabez Perkins moved ere long to the Landing. Simeon had married in 1760, Abigail, daughter of Ebenezer Backus by his first wife, Abigail, sister of Gov. Jonathan Trumbull. Simeon's young wife died within a year after his marriage, leaving a young son, Roger, and the disconsolate husband, as is evidenced by a diary kept at this time, moved to Liverpool, Nova Scotia, about 1762. Here he had a prosperous career as judge of probate, town clerk, chief justice of the county courts, colonel of militia, and for nearly thirty years a member of the Provincial House of Representatives. He died in 1812, and a tablet, in the Court House of Liverpool, enshrines his memory as "the late first magistrate of this county, who for nearly half a century presided in this court with great Integrity, Uprightness, and Impartiality, to the great satisfaction of this community." In the inscription on his grave-stone, he is said to have been "benevolent to the poor, loyal to his king, and a sincere Christian." He married (2) Elizabeth, widow of John Hadley of Manchester, N. S., and daughter of Henry Young.

In 1766, Jabez and Simeon Perkins sell their shop to Jabez Huntington. In 1773, Samuel Avery was possibly located here, as he advertises in a shop "nearly opposite Col. Jabez Huntington's store." In 1784, it is the barber shop of Nathaniel Townsend, and it was possibly in this shop in 1777, that Nathaniel offers to pay "16 s. per pound in cash for long, brown, human hair." In 1787, he advertises that he has just procured a workman from Philadelphia, and in his shop may be procured "the newest fashions in cushions and head-dresses." It is said that Nathaniel Townsend used to boast that he had once shaved Talleyrand.

Though Prince Talleyrand was in this country in 1795, we do not know that he ever visited Norwich, and we think that possibly his younger brother, who was on the staff of the Marquis Chastellux, may have been one of the party of French officers, who were entertained by Gen. Jedediah Huntington in 1781, and on that occasion the younger Talleyrand might have visited the shop across the way.

Samuel Adams Drake, in his "Old Landmarks of Boston," describes the entry of this young Frenchman into Boston with the French troops in 1782. The Marquis Chastellux wished to take him back with him to France, but the young soldier, only eighteen years old, desired to remain. When the army entered Boston, "he[*] obtained a grenadier's uniform, and marched in the ranks of the Soissonais, with his haversack on his back, and his gun on his shoulder." He was "well known to the superior officers, who pretended not to recognize him,

[*] Samuel Adams Drake's "Old Landmarks of Boston."

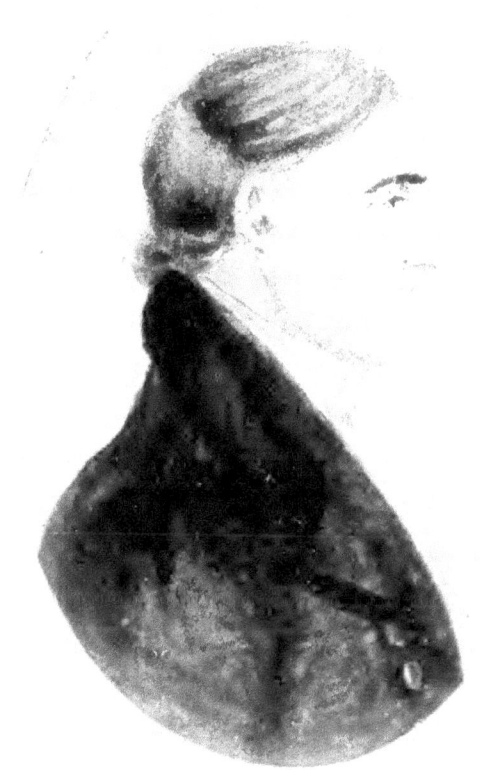

and his warlike ardor became the town-talk. He was christened Va - de - bon - cœur (go willingly), and was the subject of many attentions." Nathaniel Townsend not only dealt in wigs and false hair, but other goods as well, rum, maps, dry goods, &c. Before 1793, he moved to a shop near the Green, possibly as early as 1787, for in that year this shop is sold by the Huntington heirs to Mundator Tracy, who ere long converts it into a house, which he sells in 1815 to Luther Spalding, who then owns the Gov. Huntington house. The land is now part of the Charles Young property.

CHAPTER XLIII.

SAMUEL Huntington, who had purchased in 1769 the Simon Tracy house, was a son of Nathaniel Huntington of Windham, and a grandson of Joseph Huntington, who left Norwich in 1692 to become one of the founders of that town. Samuel was born in 1731, was apprenticed at the age of sixteen to the cooper's trade, and while he worked industriously at this, spent all his spare moments in study. At the age of twenty-two, he had determined to become a lawyer, and though not encouraged by his father, he had worked his way to the bar, and, before he was twenty-eight years old, had established himself as a lawyer in Norwich.

In 1761, he married Martha, daughter of the Rev. Ebenezer Devotion of Windham, and his wife Martha (daughter of Col. Simon Lathrop of Norwich). This connection, and his Huntington descent, brought him into close relation with some of the most prominent families of Norwich. He and his wife occupied for a time the old Solomon Tracy house, but shortly after the Revolution, he built the house now owned by Charles Young. This house has been greatly altered

since Gov. Huntington's day. At that time, with its tall pillars extending from the ground to the roof, it was said to have greatly resembled the house built by Gen. Jedediah Huntington in New London, on the corner of Broad and Washington Streets (now owned by Elisha Palmer).

As the Governor and his wife had no children of their own, they adopted a niece and nephew, Frances [Hannah] and Samuel, children of the Rev. Joseph Huntington of Coventry, Ct., and some of their young Windham relatives were constantly at the house. Among these were the Governor's nephew, Nathaniel (or Natty, as he was familiarly called), (b. 1751), son of the Rev. Nathaniel Huntington of Windsor, Ct., whose early death, in 1774, was deeply lamented; and "the beautiful Betsey Devotion," younger sister of Mrs. Huntington, who died in 1775, aged 24; of whom, Jonathan Bellamy, who seems to have felt her death keenly, writes, in a letter to Aaron Burr: "If a natural sweetness of disposition can scale Heaven's walls, she went over like a bird." The Rev. Dr. James Cogswell writes in his dairy, "A more amiable, accomplished, benevolent, discreet and religious young lady is rare to be found. She was of a beautiful form, had a sweetness in her countainance, and pleasantness in her conversation, which was quite graceful, knew how to behave to all persons, to all characters, of all ages, in all circumstances, so as to render herself agreeable to all. She was an ornament to her family, an honor to her Christian profession, and ye glory of her sex, but she is gone."

A number of young men studied law with Mr. Huntington, and were constantly at the house. This youthful element, and the warm hospitality of Gov. and Mrs. Huntington, made their home a centre of attraction for all the young people of the town, and it is said, that after games in the parlor, the young guests would often retire to the kitchen, and dance away until the curfew rang at nine o'clock.

Mrs. Huntington, it is said, was "plain in her manners but affable," and Gov. Huntington "though dignified in manner even to formality, and reserved in popular intercourse," "in the domestic circle was pleasing and communicative." Mrs. Huntington is described as dressing "very simply, often in a white short gown and stuff petticoat with stiffly-starched cap, and clean muslin apron, probably in the style of her mother, whose portrait is still preserved by her descendants, the family of the late John L. Devotion.

In the journal of the Marquis de Chastellux, who dines with Gov. Huntington in Philadelphia, in 1780, while Mr. Huntington was President of Congress,

Martha (Lathrop) Devotion
1715-1795
Mother of Mrs. Gov. Huntington.

he describes Mrs. Huntington as "a good-looking lusty woman, but not young," who "did the honors of the table, that is to say, helped everybody, without saying a word." The poor woman was probably longing to speak, but rendered mute by her ignorance of French. The Marquis also speaks of calling upon Mr. Huntington with the French Ambassador, and finding him in his cabinet, "lighted by a single candle," "this simplicity" reminding him "of Fabricius and the Philopæmens."

Gov. Huntington was of middle size, with a "swarthy" complexion, and a "vivid" and "penetrating" eye; "considering comfort and convenience" more than splendor in his domestic arrangements, "moderate and circumspect in all his movements," "never frivolous," but always "practical" in his conversation. One, who had been an inmate of his family for a long time, bears witness that he never showed the slightest symptom of anger, nor spoke an unkind word. As a judge, he was "impartial in his judgments," "dignified in his deportment," "courteous and polite to the gentlemen at the bar." He was "a constant attendant at public worship, and at conference-meetings, in the absence of the minister, often led the services."

His public life began in 1764, as a Representative to the General Assembly. In 1773, he was elected a member of the upper house, in 1774, Associate Judge of the Supreme Court of Connecticut, and in 1775, a member of Congress, which office he held till 1780. He was also elected a member of the Marine Court, was one of the signers of the Declaration of Independence, served as President of Congress from 1779 to 1781, and was then obliged to resign on account of ill-health. On retiring from Congress, he resumed his office of Judge of the Supreme Court. In 1782 and 1783, he was again elected to Congress, but resigned the office forever in this last year. In 1784, he was appointed Chief Justice of the Supreme Court; in 1785, Lieut. Governor; in 1786, Governor, which office he held till his death. He died in 1796 of dropsy of the chest. His wife had died in 1794, aged 56.

His funeral was attended by a large concourse of people from Norwich and the neighboring towns. The order of the funeral procession from his house to the church, was as follows: —

" A Band of Music.
The Drummers and Fifers of the Twentieth Regiment.
Four Military Companies in Uniform with Arms reversed.
The corps supported by Pall-Bearers.
Mourners.
Magistrates and Officers of the Peace.
About two hundred Officers in their Uniforms.
Aldermen and Council of the City.
Selectmen of the Town.
Clergy of different Denominations.
Citizens."

"A sermon was preached by the Rev. Joseph Strong from Acts 13, 36. After the solemnities of public worship, the procession continued to the burying ground," where the governor was laid to rest beside his wife, in the family tomb, not far from the home where they had so long resided.

In 1788, Dr. Mason Fitch Cogswell, afterward of Hartford, Ct., while on a journey through Connecticut, stopped at Norwich for a short visit at Gov. Huntington's. His father, the Rev. James Cogswell, had recently married the widow of the Rev. Ebenezer Devotion of Scotland, and Dr. Cogswell writes in his diary, "Had I been an own brother, Mrs. Huntington could not have treated me with more tenderness and affection, and I never saw the Governor so social and conversible." The latter entertains him with musical anecdotes, and Mrs. Huntington regales him freely with "flip and pompion pie." He spends several days in town, enjoying a round of entertainments among his old friends.

Samuel and Frances Huntington, the adopted children of the governor and his wife, were the son and daughter of the Rev. Joseph Huntington of Coventry, and his wife, Hannah Devotion, sister of Mrs. Huntington, so the children were doubly related to their adopted parents. Samuel Huntington (b. 1765), was educated by his uncle, graduated at Yale in 1785, and married in 1791, Hannah, daughter of Andrew Huntington and his first wife, Lucy Coit. He was admitted to the bar in Norwich, but after his uncle's death, he moved to Cleveland, Ohio, and in 1805 to Painesville. Here he was appointed a colonel of militia; in 1802 was one of the first delegates to the convention which formed the State constitution of Ohio. In 1803, he was appointed Judge of the Supreme Court; in 1804, Chief Judge; and in 1808, Governor of the State, which office he held for two years. He helped to found the town of Fairport, and during the war of 1812-14, was Paymaster of the Northwestern army.

"At the time that he migrated to Ohio, the State was a wilderness, and wild beasts were numerous. While travelling from the east to Cleveland, where he then lived, he was attacked, about two miles out of town, by a pack of wolves. He broke his umbrella to pieces, in his efforts to keep them off, but owed his safety to the speed of his horse."* He died in 1817, and his widow in 1818.

Frances Huntington (b. 1769), resided with her uncle till his death. A few months after, she married Rev. Edward D. Griffin, D. D., of Park Street Church, Boston, who afterward became President of Williams College. She was said to be "a lady of uncommon delicacy and excellence of character." She died in 1837.

This story is told by Mrs. Sigourney of Rev. Dr. Griffin, when President of Williams College. During the prevalence of a northeast storm, he called the theological students together, and addressing them in a solemn, impressive manner, said: "I am satisfied with your class, save in one respect. Of your proficiency in study, your general deportment, I have no complaint to make. Still there is one very sad deficiency. That to which I allude, young gentlemen, is a neglect of the duty of Christian laughter."

Then, drawing up to its full height of six feet his large, symmetrical person, and expanding his broad chest, he commanded, "Do as I do," and uttered a

---
* "Huntington Family Memoir."

Gov. Samuel Huntington

peal of hearty, sonorous laughter. After summoning each one separately to imitate his example, and observing how the corrugated muscles untwisted, and the brow cast off its wrinkling thought, he said, "There, that will do for the present."

On leaving town in 1801, Samuel Huntington sold the house to Asa Spalding, who, until this time, had resided on the Green, in what was formerly known as the "Perit" house.

Asa Spalding (b. 1757), was the son of Ebenezer Spalding of Canterbury. He graduated at Yale in 1778, studied law with Judge Adams of Litchfield, and settled as an attorney at Norwich in 1782. He married in 1787, Lydia, daughter of Nathaniel Shipman, who, after his death, married as second wife, Capt. Bela Peck. In 1786, he purchased the "Perit" house, in which he resided, until, in 1801, he removed to the Gov. Huntington house, which, as the Spalding Family Memoir says, "with its majestic porticoes and massive pillars, presented in 1811, the most imposing apearance of any structure in the town." Asa Spalding's death was a very sudden one. The inscription on his gravestone reads: "He died of a disease called by the Medical Faculty, Angina Pectoris."

Though blunt and peculiar in manner, as a lawyer he was eminently successful, and acquired a large fortune. On one occasion, while arguing a case before a judge of the Superior Court, after the hour for adjournment had arrived, the impatient judge, who had frequently presented the face of his watch to Mr. Spalding, in the hope of bringing his speech to an end, said angrily, "Excuse me, Mr. Spalding, but you have talked three-quarters of an hour, and have said nothing to the purpose as yet."

"Very well, your Honor," replied the imperturbable lawyer, "I expect to speak three-quarters of an hour longer, and before I get through, I hope I may say something to the purpose."

On one occasion, it is said, he was employed by the Hon. John Hancock of Boston, to collect a considerable claim, the payment of which was contested. The jury having returned a verdict for the defendant, Mr. Spalding procured an order for a new trial, and wrote to Mr. Hancock to attend court in person, believing that the prestige of his person would perhaps favorably influence the jury. At the appointed time, Mr. Hancock appeared in a coach, attended by a retinue of servants at the place of trial (the tale does not give the name of the place), and suffering at the time from an attack of gout, was borne into the court room, wrapped in flannels. The judges offered him a seat upon the bench, and the jury, overawed by his presence, returned a verdict for the plaintiff in full amount, with interest.

Two children were born to Asa Spalding, one of whom died in infancy, the other at twelve years of age. The house and land became the property of Asa's brother, Luther Spalding (b. 1762), who married in 1796, Lydia Chaffee of Canterbury, Ct. He studied law with his brother, and was at one time Judge of the County Court. He lived here till his death in 1838.

In 1854, Charles Spalding, son of Luther, sells the property to Charles Stedman. In 1860, it passed to Junius Kingsley; in 1863, to William M. Converse; in 1867, to Dr. William Cutler. It is now owned by Charles Young.

CHAPTER XLIV.

LEAVING the Tracy property, we now arrive at the home-lot of Simon Huntington, which is entered in the first book of records as "four acres, abutting east on the land of Thomas Tracy, south on land of Mr. James Fitch and north on the highway," also "four acres over the highway against his home lot" abutting south and west upon the highway, east on Mr. Bradford, north on the pasture of Mr. Fitch.

In the second book of records it is called, "the home lot lying on both sides of the highway." We will give the measurements of the house-lot as in this second record, leaving the land on the north side of the street for later consideration. This south division abuts north on the street 25½ rods, west on the street 13½ rods, south on land of Capt. Fitch 14 rods, the line then runs southeast 4 rods, abutting north-west on the Fitch lot, thence it runs south-west 2 rods, 4 feet, thence west 2 rods, then south 20 rods wanting 4 feet, abutting west on land of Capt. Fitch, then abuts south on land of Capt. Fitch 18 rods, and east on land of Lt. Thomas Tracy 43 rods. Now we find that the frontage of 25½ rods, (beginning at a point in the grounds of Charles Young, three rods east of the cemetery lane), brings us to the corner, near the house recently occupied by the Rev. Charles A. Northrop, and from here the western frontage of 13½ rods, continues along the road by the Green, as far as the house now occupied by Miss Grace McClellan. On this lot were situated the houses of the first and second Simon Huntington.

The first Simon Huntington of Norwich was born in England about 1629, and was probably four years of age, when he came with his parents, two brothers and a sister, to this country in 1633. His father having died of small-pox on the voyage, and his mother having married again, he lived for a while in the home of his step-father, Thomas Stoughton, at Windsor, Ct., then followed his brother Christopher to Saybrook, where he married in 1653, Sarah, daughter of John Clark. In 1660, he came with the first band of settlers to Norwich, where he took at once a prominent position, serving as constable, townsman, and deputy, and holding the office of deacon in Mr. Fitch's church from about 1680 to 1696. In 1695, he was appointed by the town "to keep an ordnary or house of publique entertaynement." We may read on two ancient-looking, roughly lettered stones in the old burying-ground, at the rear of their former home lot, that Simon died in 1706, aged 77, and his wife, Sarah, in 1721, aged 88. We have so little knowledge of these early settlers that every item is of interest. Even the dry inventory, which Miss Caulkins gives, of Simon's library, presents a picture of the good deacon, standing before his book shelves on Saturday night, pondering as to whether he will read "Rogers, His Seven Treatises," "The Practical Catechise," "Mr. Moody's Book," "Thomas Hooker's Doubting Christian," the New England Psalm Book, "Mr. Adams' Sarmon," "The Bound Book of Mr. Fitch and John Rogers," or "The Day of Doom," to prepare himself for the coming Sabbath. "William Dyer" has a doubtful sound, so we will leave that for week-day reading. His estate was valued at £275.

As Simon died intestate, the heirs sign an agreement, by which Daniel and James receive two-sixths of the real estate, on the condition that they are to "preveide sutable maintainence for our Honour'd Mother, Rellect to the Deseased, Dureing her natural life." Simon Huntington, Jun., was living on the north-west corner of the home lot (frontage 7½ rods), which had been deeded to him by his father in 1688-9. Joseph had moved to Windham, and Samuel to Lebanon. How soon Daniel (who had married Abigail Bingham, the year before his father's death), moved to a home of his own, we know not. We think it is evident that James, the youngest son, lived with his mother in the homestead, of which he eventually became the owner. In his inventory, his home-lot is given, as situated on the south side of the street, with a dwelling house and tan-yard, and a lot with barn and shop on the opposite side of the street.

James Huntington was born in 1680, and married in 1702-3, Priscilla Miller. He was a man of energy and enterprise, and in 1722, was appointed one of a committee, "to go down to the Landing Place, and lay out what may be needful for the town's use." In 1723, Simon Lathrop, Joshua and James Huntington, and Daniel Tracy each received a grant of land, " 20 feet square, on the west side of Rockie point," and these four men were among the first to open and develop that part of the town, later known as Chelsea. James Huntington and Israel Lathrop were the agents of the town in laying out the East Sheep Walk, as the lands now forming the City of Norwich were then called. In 1721, James Huntington was appointed Ensign of the first company or train-band. He died in 1727, and his widow, according to the testimony of her grave-stone, "after a patient and pious life, fell asleep in Jesus, January 19, 1742, in the 67th year of her age." Three sons and two daughters were living at the time of their parents' death. Peter married in 1734, and James and Nathaniel in 1735. James moved to Great Plains. Peter continued to reside on the home lot. We have not ascertained where Nathaniel resided.

It is possible that the property of the first Simon Huntington was not divided until long after his death, for in 1734 the heirs sign acquittances for their shares of the estate, and in 1737 there are various exchanges of different portions of the property. In that year, Joshua quit-claims to James and Peter, sons of the first James Huntington, " the east part of the home lot which was their father's lying on the south side of the street," "abutting north on the street 9½ rods," to a point "a little west of the house which was their father's, and from thence running south across the middle of the well . . . . with buildings," &c., and James and Peter deed to Joshua, the "west part of our honoured father's home lot, abutting north on the street 8 rods, and west on Ebenezer Huntington's land."

The fact that there is also a dwelling house on the west part of the lot, makes it seem a little doubtful as to which of the two was the house of the first Simon. At the time of James' death, but one house is mentioned as standing on the lot, and we may assume from the wording of Joshua's deed to James and Peter, that this was the one which James inherited from his father, and in which his son Peter afterward resided This other dwelling may have been built by the second James on his marriage in 1735, and was perhaps occupied by him until his removal to the Great Plain, but of this we have no proof, so we will leave the matter to be solved by some of James' descendants.

In 1752, Peter Huntington sells to Samuel Abbot a small lot of land (frontage 3 rods), in the north-east corner of the home lot, "on which I now dwell," beginning at the north-west corner of Simon Tracy's land. On this lot (now a part of the grounds of Charles Young), Samuel Abbot builds a house, in which he resides until his death in 1789. In 1792, it is sold to Gov. Huntington, and in 1801 passes with the rest of the Gov. Huntington property to Asa Spalding. It is said to have been occupied at one time by Luther Spalding, and also by Abner Basset. In 1860, it is sold to Junius Kingsley, and the house was shortly after moved across the street, and is now the residence of Russell Lewis.

Samuel Abbot (b. 1726), in Windham, Ct., was the son of John and Elizabeth (Phipps) Abbot of Franklin, Ct., who came from Stow, Mass., to Windham, Ct., about 1726, resided there for a time, but the year after Samuel's birth, purchased and moved to a farm in West Farms or Franklin, then a part of Norwich. In 1749, Samuel married Phoebe, daughter of John and Phoebe Edgerton. They had nine children. In 1758, he received his commission as Lieutenant; in 1774, was appointed Lieut. Colonel of the Twentieth Regiment of Infantry; and in 1776, was commissioned by the government to buy guns for the troops. He was one of the members of the Association against Illicit Trade. He died suddenly in 1789, and his widow, Phoebe, in 1792.

In the home of his father, James, which was probably also the house of the first Simon, Peter Huntington lived until his death in 1760. He was born in 1708-9, and married in 1734, Ruth, daughter of John and Ruth (Adgate) Edgerton, and half-sister of Mrs. Samuel Abbot. They had a large family of sons and daughters.

Simeon (b. 1740), the oldest son, becomes the next owner of the house, and marries (1) in 1777, Freelove, "the amiable and accomplished" daughter of Capt. Jonathan Chester. His wife died in 1787, and he married (2) in 1789, the widow Patience Keeney of Wethersfield, Ct., who survived him, dying in 1820. Simeon died in 1817. He was a blacksmith, and a very large and powerful man. At the beginning of the Revolution, on July 4, 1774, Francis Green, a merchant of

Boston, and a noted loyalist, while on a business tour through Connecticut, was most rudely received, and ordered to leave the town by the patriots of Windham, at whose tavern he intended to pass the night. He left at once for Norwich, and word was sent to arouse the town.

The Sons of Liberty were greatly excited at the news, and it was arranged that the moment Mr. Green appeared, Diah Manning should ring the church bell. In the morning, when Mr. Green's carriage arrived at Lathrop's tavern, a large crowd was ready to receive him, and he was allowed his choice, to depart at once or be sent out on a cart. Mr. Green pleaded for delay, attempted to address the people, but Simeon Huntington, calling him rascal, grasped him by the collar with no gentle hand, and a cart with a high scaffolding appearing in sight, Mr. Green thought it wise to get at once into his carriage, and with all possible speed leave the town, followed by "drums beating and horns blowing." On his arrival in Boston, he offered $100 reward for anyone who would give information that would lead to the conviction of "those villains and ruffians," particularly mentioning "one Simeon Huntington." The advertisement was republished in a handbill, which was sold about the town, and created considerable merriment.

In a letter from Col. Jedidiah Huntington to Gov. Trumbull, dated Sept.

9, 1775, he expresses a wish that Simeon Huntington would accept a second lieutenancy, then vacant, assigning as his reason, "I want officers of a military spirit." Simeon was later commissioned as Captain, by which title he is always known. After Simeon's death, the land, house, and barn are sold in 1819 to the First Ecclesiastical Society, who, retaining part of the land for the cemetery and lane, sell the rest to Lyman Roath,* and the latter in 1820, reserving to himself the house and barn, sells the land to David Nevins, who was then living in the present Dickey house.

---

* It is believed that Lyman Roath, who had at that time purchased land on the Scotland road, may have moved this house to that lot, and it may now form a part of the present residence of Edward Sterry.

CHAPTER XLV.

JOSHUA Huntington sells to Philip Turner in 1737-8, the house and land, (frontage 8 rods), which had been conveyed to him by James and Peter Huntington. In 1738-9, Philip Turner sells the land and house to John Manly, reserving for himself for seven years, the use of a shop and water, with "liberty to remove the shop," if he should desire. In 1741, John Manly sells to Thomas Danforth, house, land and a joiner's shop, and in 1742, Richard Charlton buys the same of Thomas Danforth, with the addition of another shop, which may possibly be the one formerly reserved for the use of Philip Turner, or perhaps a new shop built by Danforth.

Richard Charlton sells in 1755 the west part of this land, and one of the shops, to Simeon Carew, and the east part is sold in the same year to Charles Whiting. The house and the remaining shop are occupied by the Charlton family until 1834.

John Manly married in Windham in 1735, Mary Arnold, granddaughter of John Arnold, an early resident of Norwich, later of Windham. Two children were born to them in Norwich, John (b. 1738), and Sarah (b. 1742). In 1739, he purchased of Philip Turner this house and land, which he sells in 1741. In 1740, he purchased land and a shop on the Green, which he sells in 1743. At this later date, he is living in Mansfield, Ct.

Richard Charlton's antecedents are unknown to us. In a family Bible record he is said to have been born in England. As this record, however, is not correct in every particular, he may, after all, have been born in this country, and may claim descent from Henri Charlton, probably a French Huguenot, who came to Virginia in the ship George in 1623, aged 19 years. This Henri Charlton was possibly the progenitor of the Southern family of that name.

Richard Charlton married in 1741-2, Sarah, daughter of Thomas and Ann (Birchard) Grist, and had six children. In 1756, he prefaces his will, "being bound to a voige to sea." This was probably the Havana expedition, as in the family Bible record we find that he was blown up in a vessel at the rejoicings at the capture of Havana in 1757.

A "blew" coat with velvet cape at the good value for those days of £2, 10 s., another "blew" coat at £1, 10 s., two brown coats, one valued at £1, 8 s., a plush coat 3 s., and a red coat £1, 15 s., mentioned in his inventory, show that he was not indifferent to dress. An ivory book, value £1, is rather an unusual item of this inventory. A large number of pewter basins, plates, tankards, &c., which have probably long ago melted away, appear to form a part of his household stores. He leaves the "mantion" house to his wife, Sarah, and at her death in 1808, it passes to the son Charles.

Charles Charlton marries in 1775, Sarah, widow of Jesse Williams, and has two daughters and three sons. He is a shoemaker by trade, and advertises now and then in the shop adjoining his house for apprentices of fourteen or fifteen years of age, to whom he offers 40 s. for the first year, and £3 a year and their clothes for the following year. In 1797, his son Jesse advertises in the same shop as a tailor. About 1800, Jesse Charlton moves to East Windsor. In Stiles' History of Windsor he is mentioned as a man "of courteous manners, and genial character." After his departure, his brother Samuel occupies the house until 1834, when he sells it to David Nevins, and moves to a house he has built on Mediterranean Lane. The old Charlton house is moved to East Great Plain, where it now forms a part of the residence of Elias Woodworth.

In 1755, the east part of the Charlton lot (frontage 2½ rods), is sold to Charles Whiting, who sells it in 1760 to Jacob Perkins. The latter builds the house now owned and occupied by Aaron W. Dickey. In 1782, this is sold to Mrs. Martha Greene of Boston, who evidently, though the deed has not been found, transfers it to her son, Capt. Russell Hubbard, formerly of New London, whose house and shop in that place were burnt by Benedict Arnold in 1781. This house is included in Capt. Hubbard's inventory at his death in 1785. Shortly after the death of Capt. Hubbard, it becomes the property of David Nevins, but whether by purchase or inheritance through his wife, the daughter of Capt. Hubbard, we are unable to say. In 1848, the house is sold to George Fuller by Henry Nevins,

with the addition of the Simeon Huntington land (purchased in 1820), on the east, and the Charlton lot on the west, which was sold to David Nevins in 1834. After the death of George Fuller, his daughter, Mrs. Dickey, entered into possession of the property.

Jacob Perkins (b. 1731), was the son of Jacob and Jemina (Leonard) Perkins of Newent, then a part of Norwich. He married (1) in 1755, Mary Brown, daughter of James and Ann (Noyes) Brown of Newport, R. I. His second wife, (married in 1767), was Abigail, daughter of Ebenezer and Hannah (Haskins) Thomas of Norwich. His shop was on the opposite side of the street. In 1774, Jacob Perkins was Lieutenant of the first company or train-band of Norwich and later was commissioned as Captain.

Capt. Russell Hubbard (b. 1732) was the brother of Capt. William Hubbard, who at one time occupied the Col. Hezekiah Huntington house. He was first a sea captain, then a merchant on Bank Street, New London. During the Revolution he moved to Norwich. He married Mary Gray, daughter of Dr. Ebenezer Gray, first of

Newport, then of Lebanon, Ct., and his wife, Mary, the daughter of Thomas Prentice, and widow of Dr. Thomas Coit of New London. They had two sons: Thomas, the editor of the Norwich Courier, and Russell, a sea-captain, who died in 1800 unmarried; and four daughters: Mary, wife of David Nevins; Martha, who married David Wright of New London; Susannah, who married (1) Ebenezer Bushnell, and (2) Robert Manwaring; and Lucretia, whose first husband was Daniel Tracy, and second, Elijah Backus.

David Nevins (b. 1747), was a son of David Nevins of Canterbury, and his wife, Mary, daughter of Col. Simon Lathrop of Norwich. The father was said to be of Scotch origin, and to have come from Kingston, Massachusetts, to Connecticut. In 1757, he was "engaged in repairing a bridge over the Quinebaug between Canterbury and Plainfield, which had been partially destroyed in a severe freshet." "He was standing on one of the cross beams of the bridge, giving directions to the workman, and had his watch in his hand, which he had just taken out to see the time, when losing his balance, he fell into the swollen stream, was swept down by the current, and drowned before he could be rescued." Two of his children, Samuel and Betsey, died unmarried. His remaining children were married in Norwich: Mary in 1771, to Nathan Lord; Martha in 1774, to Capt. James Hyde; and David in 1777, to Mary Hubbard.

In the early years of the war, David Nevins, 2nd, "was employed as the the confidential messenger of the Norwich Committee of Correspondence, to obtain exact news from the seat of war." "His personal activity and daring spirit, combined with trustworthiness and ardent participation in the popular cause, peculiarly fitted him for the work. But the battle of Lexington carried him from all minor employments into the army. He joined the Eighth Company, Sixth Regiment, which was organized on Norwich Green in May, 1775. and was its color-bearer on Dorchester Heights."* In October, 1776, he was commissioned as Lieutenant and later as Captain. "He remained with the army during the siege of Boston, the occupation of New York, and the retreat through the Jerseys, returning home in the winter of 1777. He did not, however, relinquish the service of his country, but was several times again in the field upon

* Miss Caulkins' History of Norwich.

various emergencies during the war."* He died in New York in 1838, aged 90. He had twelve children. His daughter, Mary, whom the Hon. Charles Miner calls "the fairest rose that ever bloomed," died at the age of twenty-two. His sons became prominent citizens of New York and Philadelphia, and one of them, the Rev. William Nevins, was pastor of the First Presbyterian Church of Baltimore.

* Miss Caulkins' History of Norwich.

CHAPTER XLVI.

IN 1755, Richard Charlton sells to Simeon Carew, the west part of the land (frontage 2 rods, 10 feet), and one of the shops, which he had purchased in 1742 of Thomas Danforth. In 1763, Simeon sells the property to his brother Joseph, who buys of Azariah Lathrop additional land in the rear, and builds the house now occupied by the family of Louis Mabrey. In 1778, he sells the house to Col. Joseph Trumbull.

Joseph Trumbull (b. 1737), was the son of Gov. Jonathan and Faith (Robinson) Trumbull of Lebanon, Ct. He was educated at the Tisdale School in Lebanon, graduated from Harvard College in 1756, then embarked on a business career, under the direction of his father, who in 1763 sent him to England to buy goods, obtain contracts for building vessels, and form new business connections. On his return in 1764, he entered into a partnership with his father and Col. Eleazer Fitch of Windham, under the firm name of Trumble, Fitch and Trumble. The main store or office was in Norwich, where Joseph came to reside. After inquiries made at the Heraldry Office, during one of his visits to London, Joseph

found that the proper spelling of the last syllable of the family name was *bull* rather than *ble*, and on his return this form was adopted by his father.

In 1766, the new firm met with heavy losses. Many of their vessels were lost, and the firm was threatened with total bankruptcy. Joseph was again sent to London, and finally succeeded in making satisfactory arrangements with the English creditors. The Governor must have made frequent visits to Norwich, to attend to his business affairs and to see his children, Joseph, and Faith, wife of Jedediah Huntington. Miss Caulkins draws an interesting picture of the people of Norwich "running to their doors, and bowing and curtseying to the honored Governor and his wife as they rode by in their square-topped, two wheeled, one-horse carriage, almost as substantial in structure as a house." On some of these occasions, Mrs. Trumbull may have worn the famous scarlet cloak, said to have been presented to her by Count Rochambeau, Commander-in-Chief of the French Allied Army, and which, when a collection was at one time being taken up for the soldiers, in the Lebanon Meeting House, Madam Trumbull rose from her seat, and "advancing near the pulpit, laid on the altar as her offering to those who, in the midst of every want and suffering, were fighting gallantly the great battle for Freedom. It was afterward cut into narrow strips and employed as red trimming to stripe the dress of American soldiers."*

Gov. Trumbull was in Norwich on the afternoon of April 20, 1775, when the news arrived of the battle of Lexington. With what haste the huge chaise must have rattled back to Lebanon, where the Governor was busy for many days after, in equipping soldiers with ammunition and provisions for the seat of war. In 1775, Joseph Trumbull was appointed the first Commissary General of the American Army, an office of great and overwhelming responsibility, so intensified by the unwise measure of Congress in 1777, in appointing under-officers whom the heads of the department were not allowed to remove, that he felt obliged to resign his office. He writes to Congress, "The head of every department ought to have the control of it. In this establishment an *imperium in imperio* is created. If I consent to act I must be at continued variance with the whole department, and of course be in continued hot water. I must turn accuser, and

---
*Stuart's Life of Gov. Trumbull.

be continually applying to Congress, and attending with witnesses to support my charges, or I must sit down in ease and quiet, let the deputies do as they like, and enjoy a sinecure. The first situation I cannot think of, the last I never will accept. It never shall be said I was the first American pensioner. I am willing to do and suffer for my country, and its cause—but I cannot sacrifice my honor and my principles. I can by no means act under a regulation, which in my opinion will never answer the purpose intended by Congress, nor supply the army as it should be. I must beg Congress to appoint some person in my place, as soon as may be; until then, I will continue to furnish the army as heretofore." *

In this same year, 1777, he was married to Amelia Dyer of Windham; but their wedded happiness was very short. He continued in office, though in failing health, until April, 1778, when Col. Jeremiah Wadsworth of Hartford, was appointed to take his place, and Congress decided to rescind their unwise measure. Ill in body and mind, Joseph returns to Norwich, and in this same month, buys this house of Joseph Carew. In June, his father receives, while in Hartford, the news of his son's dangerous illness, and hastens to Norwich, finding him better, however, than he feared, but still "in a feeble condition easily overset." He writes to a friend, "The fatigues of his business, but chiefly the trouble, sorrow and grief for the treatment he received after all, broke his constitution; bro't him next door to death, and renders his recovery doubtful;—former health and strength never to be expected."

In July, Joseph is in his father's house at Lebanon, where he dies on Thursday the 23rd, at 4 o'clock A. M. This occurred "directly in the midst of the anxious preparations" the Governor was "making for the Rhode Island Expedition—preparations so pressing as to require a session of his own Council of Safety at Lebanon, on the very day of his son's funeral." "What a hint does this furnish us," as Stuart says, "of the sad urgency of the times, that the Governor's own Council are compelled in his own town,—sitting in his own office, not twenty paces from the corpse of his eminent son,"—"to forgo the courtesy of an adjournment,"—"denied the melancholy privilege of aiding a weeping father" "to wrap the athletic in his shroud and build his tomb." †

* † Stuart's Life of Gov. Trumbull.

The following epitaph is inscribed on the family tomb at Lebanon: "Sacred to the memory of Joseph Trumbull, eldest son of Governor Trumbull, and first Commissary Gen'l of the United States of America, a service to whose perpetual cares and fatigues he fell a sacrifice A. D. 1778, Æ. 42. Full soon indeed may his person, his virtues, and even his extensive Benevolence be forgotten by his friends and fellow-men. But blessed be God! for the hope that in His presence he shall be remembered forever."

His widow Amelia (b. 1750), the daughter of Col. Eliphalet and Huldah (Bowen) Dyer of Windham, married again in 1785, Col. Hezekiah Wyllys of Hartford, a descendant of Gov. Wyllys. She is said to have been very handsome and accomplished. The late William Weaver of Willimantic relates the following anecdote: "Col. Dyer had purchased, while in England, as a present for his wife, a splendid silk dress interwoven with gold, such as queens and princesses wore in those days. Mrs. Dyer considered it much too costly and splendid for her to wear, so it was given to Amelia, who created something of a sensation it is said, by appearing in this gorgeous gown in Philadelphia, among the wives and daughters of the dignitaries of the land."

In 1789, the house was sold to Newcomb Kinney. As this was about the time that Mr. Kinney was teaching in the brick school house on the Green, it is possible that he contemplated residing here, but if so he must have changed his mind, for in 1790, he sells the house to Asa Lathrop (b. 1755), son of Nathaniel Lathrop, 2nd, and his wife, Margaret. Asa Lathrop married in 1780, Elizabeth, daughter of Eleazer Lord, and died in 1835. His wife, Elizabeth, died in 1805. In 1810, Asa gives a quit-claim deed of this property to his children, "in return from them of a residence for life, in the house in which Eleazer Lord lived and died." In 1816, this Trumbull house is deeded by Asa's children to their aunt Nabby, wife of Mundator Tracy, and in 1820, she sells to Alice Baldwin this house on "Pork" Street, (as this street had been recently christened). After the death of Alice Baldwin (widow of the school-teacher William Baldwin), the house was sold by her heirs to Joseph B. Ayer in 1843, and in 1847, it was purchased by Mary Babcock, whose heirs are still in possession.

CHAPTER XLVII.

IN 1688-9, Simon Huntington, Sr., grants to his son, Simon, one acre of land, bounded south on Capt. Fitch's land 12½ rods, abutting east on the land of Simon Huntington, Sr., 15 rods, abutting north on the Town Street 7½ rods, and west on the street 13¾ rods. This is then recorded as the home-lot of Simon Huntington, Jun., who was born in Saybrook, 1659, and married in 1683, Lydia, daughter of John Gager of Norwich. Like his father, Simon, 2nd, played an important part in the history of the town, serving in many civil offices, and in 1696, succeeding Simon, Sr., in the office of deacon of the church, which he held until his death in 1736. In 1704, he calls himself Simon Huntington (cooper.) In 1706, he was granted liberty to keep "a house of public entertainment." His house, occupying a central position, was honored as the magazine for the defensive weapons of the town, and as late as 1720, a report, made to the town, states that it contained a half barrel of powder, 3 pounds of bullets, and 400 flints. He died in 1736, and leaves to his son, Ebenezer, "the dwelling house, and barn, and all land on that side of the way." To his widow, Lydia, he gives "the use of the dwelling house and land on each side of the waye with the buildings thereon, and to be at her dispose, and all my money I gave her, and if she wants more my sons must make it up that she may be comfortably provided for during her natural life, and the profit and income of all my fenced lands, two cows," &c., &c.

The Huntington Family Memoir says of Lydia: "Her grandfather was 'that right goodly man and skillful chyrurgeon,' who had come to America in 1630, with Gov. Winthrop. And most worthy did she show herself to be of such an ancestry; falling behind them, neither in the depth of her piety, nor in her skill in ministering to all 'aylements' both of the body and mind." Lydia did not long survive her husband, dying in 1737, nine months after his decease.

In 1768, Ebenezer Huntington wills to his son, Simon, "the old house down town." In 1773, Simon Huntington, son of Ebenezer, sells to Col. Samuel Abbot 11½ rods of land (frontage 36 feet, 9 inches). On this, Col. Abbot builds a shop, which is later occupied as a house by his son Daniel. In 1782, Simon Huntington sells to Thomas Carey, the old homestead, and a part of the home lot, and the latter sells to Joseph Carew. In another deed of the property, an old slaughter house is mentioned as standing on the lot in 1783. In 1785, Joseph Carew sells additional land to Col. Samuel Abbot (frontage 17 links). At this date, Daniel Abbot is living in the shop, which has probably been enlarged and made into a house. In the distribution of Col. Abbot's property, Daniel inherits this building, which is sold in 1799 to Gardner Carpenter, and then is owned at different times by various persons until 1828, when it is purchased by Alice Baldwin, and sold by her heirs, with the adjoining house in 1847 to Mary Babcock. The house is now owned by Richard H. Webb.

Between this house, and the house of Capt. Joseph Carew on the west, runs a brook, now quiet and sluggish, but in the early years of the town, probably a full and rapid stream.

Daniel Abbot (b. 1751), son of Col. Samuel Abbot, married Sarah, daughter of Elisha and Sarah (Smallie) Reynolds. He advertises frequently for green calfskins, &c., and was probably one of the many shoe-makers of the town.

Capt. Joseph Carew perhaps tears down the old Huntington house, and builds the one now standing on the lot, but it is also possible that instead of entirely destroying the old homestead, for which, being of Huntington blood, (though not a descendant of Simon, 2nd), he might have had some attachment, he may have altered, or added to the old framework, but this, of course, at this late day, we have no means of knowing. He also purchases the rest of the Huntington land, facing on the Green, except one small piece of one rod frontage, which is sold to Gardner Carpenter. The long, low, rambling house has the appearance of being of much older date than 1783. It was occupied by Capt. Joseph Carew until his death, and then by his daughter, Eunice, and son-in-law, Joseph Huntington.

It was later occupied by Capt. Carew's granddaughter, Sally Ann Huntington, who married the Hon. Jabez Huntington in 1833. In 1854, it was sold to Thomas Backus. In 1860, it came again into the possession of a descendant of Simon Huntington, 1st, Joseph Otis Huntington, son of Levi Huntington, 2nd. It has been occupied until recently as the First Church parsonage.

Capt. Joseph Carew (b. 1738), was the son of Joseph and Mary (Huntington) Carew. He married in 1765, Eunice, daughter of John and Phoebe Edgerton. He is said to have been a carpenter in early life, but in 1784 he was engaged in business as a merchant, probably in the shop which he built about 1765 on land purchased of Zachariah Huntington. From his marriage in 1765 to 1778, he probably lived in the house now occupied by the Mabrey family. In 1774, he was ensign of the first company or train-band of Norwich, and in 1781 he was serving in the army at West Point as captain of a company in Col. Canfield's Regiment. In 1783, he was a member of the Association against Illicit Trade. In 1793, he entered into a partnership with his son-in-law, Joseph Huntington, as the firm of Carew & Huntington, in the shop formerly occupied by Dudley Woodbridge on the Green. In 1800, the partnership was dissolved. He died in 1818. His wife, Eunice, had died in 1772. His only surviving child, Eunice (b. 1769), married in 1791, Joseph, son of Andrew and Lucy (Coit) Huntington.

Joseph Huntington was born in 1768. He was a prominent citizen and merchant, beginning in the shop on the corner of Gen. Jedidiah Huntington's house lot, then moving to the Woodbridge shop on the Green, where, first in

partnership with his father-in-law, Joseph Carew, then with his half-brother, Charles Phelps Huntington, and later with his own son, Joseph, he carried on a prosperous business for many years. He died in 1837, and his wife, Eunice, in 1848. One of his daughters, Sally Ann (b. 1811), married Jabez Williams Huntington, son of Gen. Zachariah, in 1833.

Jabez Huntington (b. 1788), graduated at Yale in 1806, and studied law under the celebrated teachers, Judge Reeves and Gould, in the famous Litchfield Law School, where he afterwards himself became an instructor. He remained in Litchfield, practising law for many years, was a Representative in the State Legislature in 1829, and a Member of Congress from 1829 to 1834. After his marriage in 1833, he resided in Norwich, when not engaged in official duties at Washington. He was appointed Judge of the Superior Court in 1834, and also of the Supreme Court of Errors.

On the death of the Hon. Thaddeus Betts, Senator from Connecticut in 1840, he was appointed to fill his place for the remainder of the term, and at its close in 1845, was again elected Senator. In 1847, he died very suddenly, and the following tribute to his memory, appeared in the American Obituary of 1847: "A statesman of more unbending integrity or more unswerving fidelity to the interests of the Union, never occupied a seat in the senate of the United States, and the records of that body, during the last eight years, bear ample testimony to the untiring industry, energy and distinguished ability, with which he discharged the responsible duties assigned him by his native state." His widow resided in the house for a few years after her mother's death, then went to reside with her sister Eunice, wife of Judge Henry Strong, at whose house she died in 1861.

CHAPTER XLVIII.

THE Huntington land on the north side of the street is recorded as of four acres—abutting east on Mr. John Bradford 47 rods, west on the highway 59 rods, 11 feet, north on the land of Mr. Fitch 17 rods, and south on the street 35 rods, 10 feet. The street line begins at Mediterranean Lane, and extends to a point about 13 rods, 10 feet, east of the brook. In 1683, John Arnold records his home-lot as one acre and thirty rods, bounded south and west on the highway, and east and north on the land of Simon Huntington. This is that part of the Huntington land which borders on Mediterranean Lane. It was deeded to John Arnold with the proviso that "whenever it is to be sold, Simon Huntington, or his heirs, have the refusall, giving as much as another for it." This John Arnold was accepted as an inhabitant in 1680, and Miss Caulkins thinks, though no record has been found to confirm the supposition, that he may have been the town school-master, as he afterward served in that capacity at Windham.

Before coming to Norwich, he had lived in Newark, N. J., and Killingworth, Ct. The fact that his eldest son was named Benedict, would imply a connection with William, the progenitor of the Rhode Island family of Arnolds, who also had a son named Benedict. He sold his house and land, according to agreement, to Simon Huntington in 1686,* and shortly after moved to Windham, where his name is found on the list of inhabitants in 1693. He settled in that part of Windham which is now known as Mansfield.

In 1699, Simon Huntington, Sr. (yeoman), "for love, good will," &c., deeds to his son, Samuel, "two acres, 'more or less,' lying on the southwest corner of

---

* It is possible that after 1686 he may have resided for a time, before moving to Windham, at West Farms, or Franklin, (as Dr. Woodward says), in the house later owned by Rev. Henry Willes. (See History of Franklin, Ct., by Dr. Ashbel Woodward.)

my home-lot, on the northward side of the Town Street with the Dwelling house upon it, abutting 22 rods on the street to the brook, abutting east on my land 16½ rods, abutting north on my land 13½ rods, and west on the highway 26½ rods."

Samuel Huntington (b. 1665), the third son of Simon Huntington, Sr., married in 1686, Mary, daughter of John Clark of Farmington, Ct. In 1700, he is filled with the desire to join the settlers who go to found the town of Lebanon, so in exchange for a quit-claim deed of the Maj. Fitch lot, on the other side of the Green, which he had purchased in company with his brother Simon, and which Miss Caulkins has mistaken for his home-lot, he cedes this land and house to his brother, and then sells the Fitch property to the town.

He was at that time highly esteemed in Norwich, and had filled the positions of townsman and constable, though still quite young. In 1709, after his removal to Lebanon, he was chosen as one of the committee to locate the Norwich meeting house, and wisely decided in favor of a site on the Plain. But the inhabitants would not agree to this, and persisted in building on the hill. Later, however, they erected a third church on the site chosen by this committee. Samuel was a large landed proprietor, both in Lebanon and Norwich, and held the office of Lieutenant in the Lebanon train-band. He died in Lebanon in 1717, and his wife in 1743.

The home-lot of John Bradford (frontage on the Town Street 19½ rods), is recorded as four and a half acres, abutting south and east on the highways, north on Commons, and west on Simon Huntington. This extended from the point 13 rods, 10 feet, east of the brook, to the lane (now street) on the east.

John Bradford was the son of Gov. William Bradford of Plymouth, and his first wife, Dorothy May. His mother was drowned by falling overboard from the deck of the Mayflower, in Provincetown harbor, in 1620. He lived for a while in Duxbury and Marshfield, serving as deputy in both places. He married Martha, daughter of Thomas Bourne of Marshfield. He was townsman in Norwich in 1671, and died in 1676. By 1679, his widow, Martha, was married to Lt. Thomas Tracy, and died before 1683. The house and home-lot passed into the possession of John's nephew, Thomas Bradford.

Thomas Bradford was the son of Deputy-governor Maj. William Bradford, and his wife, Alice, daughter of Thomas Richards of Weymouth. He married Ann, daughter of Nehemiah Smith. In 1691, he sells to Simon Huntington, Jun., his "home lot, with my now dwelling house and pasture in all 8½ acres." The home-lot abutted south on the Town Street 19½ rods, east on the highway and Commons 60 rods, north on Commons and Mr. Fitch's land 30 rods.

Miss Caulkins says that Thomas Bradford, in connection with his brother-in-law, Nehemiah Smith, Jun., purchased land on the west side of Nahantick Bay, called the Soldier-Farm, having been given by the Legislature to five of Capt. Mason's soldiers, for services in the Pequot war. On the north part of this land was a farm of 200 acres, where Thomas Bradford settled. His home was not far from the north-west corner of what was then known as New London, but would now lie in the town of Salem. He died in 1708. Two of Thomas Bradford's sisters married in Norwich. Alice became the second wife of Maj. James Fitch, and Melatiah married John Steele. His brother Joseph also came to Connecticut, married Ann, daughter of the Rev. James Fitch, and settled in Montville.

After the sale of Samuel Huntington's home-lot in 1700, and the Bradford lands in 1691, to Simon Huntington, Jun., the only land on this side of the street remaining in the possession of Simon Huntington, Sr., was that extending from the brook to the former Bradford lot, with a frontage of 13 rods, 10 feet. This was inherited at Simon's death in 1706, by his son James.

In 1719-20, Simon Huntington, 2nd, "in consideration of love," &c., deeds to his son, Joshua, the part of the Bradford lot nearest the lane, abutting 8 rods on the street, and to be 40 rods in length. No house is mentioned as standing on the land, but as this is after Joshua's marriage, we believe that either the house was still there and occupied by Joshua, or that the latter at this time built the house now standing on the lot, for in 1724 his house is mentioned as situated on this lane.

At the death of Simon Huntington, 2nd, in 1736, he gives to Joshua the rest of the Bradford land, and also divides the lot, extending from the brook to Mediterranean Lane, between Ebenezer and Joshua, giving the part next to Mediterranean Lane (with 12½ rods frontage on the Town Street), to Ebenezer, and the rest to Joshua. James and Peter Huntington have inherited their father's land, lying between the brook and the former Bradford property (frontage 13 rods, 10 feet), and in 1737, they sell to Joshua, who thus becomes the owner of the whole tract on the north side of the street, except Ebenezer's lot (12½ rods frontage), next to Mediterranean Lane.

In the will of Simon Huntington, 2nd, this lot of Ebenezer's is described as abutting 12½ rods on the highway, and running up hill to the "personage lot" ("the mulbury tree" standing on the line), and abutting west on the "personage" land. In 1746, Ebenezer deeds this land to his son Simon. In both these conveyances of the land there is no mention of any building, but a deed of neighboring property, dated 1782, alludes to a house on this lot, and a lady who was born in 1796 remembered perfectly a very old house, which stood here in her youth, and was then considered "haunted." This may have been the original Arnold house, occupied first by John Arnold, then by Samuel Huntington, and later probably by various occupants. In 1782, David Rogers was living here. The marriage of David Rogers and Elizabeth Sawyer is recorded in Norwich, and the birth of four children, Amos (b. 1763), Wheeler (b. 1766), Betsey (b. 1768), and Desire (b. 1771). We believe this family to be of New London origin.

In the division of Simon Huntington's estate in 1801, this land and house are set out to his daughter, Hannah Lyman, but there is evidently some unrecorded exchange of property, for it appears soon in the possession of Simon's son, Daniel, and is left by him to his daughter, Lucy, who marries Cyrus Miner. The Miner heirs sell in 1861 to the Whaley family, who build the new house now standing on the lot. A blacksmith's shop also stood back of the old Arnold house. This was probably occupied for a time by Benjamin Butler. In 1802, it had been converted into a house (size 12x25 feet), and soon after disappears.

In 1824, land, with a frontage of 1½ rods, adjoining the Arnold house, is sold to Lyman Roath, who builds a shop, which he sells in 1827 to Joseph Huntington. Before 1833, this building was used as a school house, was later occupied for some years as a law office by Jabez Huntington, the distinguished Member of Congress and Senator, and not many years ago served as the dwelling house of an old colored woman. The Rev. Theodore Weitzel, during his pastorate, established here a Lending Library for the boys of Norwich Town.

CHAPTER XLIX.

IN 1738, Joshua Huntington sells to André Richard (wig-maker), "51 rods of land on the Town Street, opposite the house that was my honored father's," beginning by the street, and running north 31° W. 11 rods, abutting west on Deacon Ebenezer Huntington's land, and taking in one-half of the mulberry tree, thence abutting north on the highway 6 rods "against ye parsonage lands," thence it runs east 13 rods, 5 feet, abutting on his own land, and thence south 3 rods, abutting on the street, "reserving to myself" (Joshua evidently was fond of mulberries), "¼ part of fruit of sd tree."

André Richard builds here a house, which he sells in 1740 to Aaron Fish of Groton. The "stump" of the mulberry tree is mentioned, showing that this had been cut down. In 1746-7, the house is sold to Daniel Needham. In 1754, the latter deeds the land and house "I now dwell in," to his son, Daniel Needham, Jun., who sells it in 1761 to Benjamin Butler.

André Richard was a Frenchman, and probably of a Huguenot family. His marriage to Hephzibah Grant is recorded in New London in 1726. He appears in Norwich about 1727, calling himself of "Old France," and buys land and a house near Bean Hill. He makes frequent purchases of property, and seems to often change his residence. After his sale of this house in 1740, no further mention of him has been found, and it is possible that he then left town. The births of three children are recorded in Norwich, Sarah (b. 1727-8), "Lucie" (b. 1730), and "Lowes," (Louis, or Louise), (b. 1735). His occupation was that of a wig-maker, in which trade as a Frenchman, he must certainly have excelled.

As Daniel Needham came from Salem, one would naturally suppose that he was a descendant of Anthony Needham, who was a citizen of Salem before 1658, but it seems to us more probable that he belonged to the Lynn family of Needhams, in which the name Daniel frequently appears. To Daniel and Isabella Needham, six children are born in Salem, and three, after their arrival in Norwich. The oldest son, Daniel (b. 1729 in Salem), marries in Norwich in 1751, Hannah Allen, and has three children : Hannah (b. 1752), Hannah, 2nd (b. 1753), and Daniel (b. 1757). The elder Daniel Needham deeds this house to his son, Daniel, in 1754, and the latter sells it in 1761 to Benjamin Butler. In 1768, Daniel Needham, Jun., buys another house near Bean Hill, which he sells in 1770. Whether he then leaves town or not, we are unable to say.

Benjamin Butler was a son of Thomas and Abigail (Craft) Butler of Windham. It is said that two brothers, Daniel and Thomas Butler, came from Massachusetts to Windham, but as we have been unable to find any descendants of the Massachusetts Butler families, who would answer to these two, we are inclined to believe that they are descended from Dea. Richard Butler of Hartford, Ct., as the names Thomas and Daniel appear frequently in the families of his descendants.

Benjamin Butler of Norwich (b. 1739), married in 1761, Diadema, daughter of Rev. Jedediah and Jerusha (Perkins) Hyde of Norwich. His first wife died in 1771, and he married (2) in 1774, Ruth, daughter of Peter and Ruth (Edgerton) Huntington. Though Chancellor Walworth calls him a physician, we have found nothing to prove that he practiced medicine, but judge from the items of his inventory, that his occupation was that of a blacksmith.

In 1776, he advertises in the Norwich Packet to sell blistered, German, English and Venus steel. He was a very eccentric man, witty and original, was also a strong Tory, and in 1776, was arrested and imprisoned on a charge of "defaming the Honorable Continental Congress." This charge was proved at his trial in New London, and he was prohibited from wearing arms, and declared incapable of holding office. "This sentence he treated with indifference. He died of a lingering illness in 1787."*

Miss Caulkins relates, how a few years before his death, while in perfect health, he selected a sapling, intending to have his coffin made of it when it

---

* Miss Caulkins' History of Norwich.

should grow sufficiently large, but finding that it increased in size too slowly, he had the coffin constructed of other wood, and kept it for a long time in his chamber. As he pined away, he would put his hands on his knees, and say, "See how the mallets grow." He prefaced his will, "My immortal part I resign to the Immortal God, my mortal to mortality." On the headstone of his grave is inscribed, at his own request, "Alas, poor human nature!" By his side, in the old grave-yard, lie his wife, Diadema, and his daughters, Rosamond and Minerva.

Benjamin Butler (b. 1764), the oldest son, was educated (as his advertisement, which appears in 1787 in a Norwich Packet of 1787, announced), "by the learned Doctor Philip Turner, in the Sciences of Physick and Surgery." He married in 1791, Hannah, daughter of Capt. William and Mary (Dolbeare) Avery of Groton. He practiced for a time, then relinquished his profession; was a merchant at the Landing in 1799; later a shipping merchant at New London; then went to New York, where his business was that of a broker, and finally moved to Oxford, N. Y. The other son, Thomas (b. 1769), was educated at Yale, but did not graduate. He studied law; married in 1792, Sarah, daughter of Joseph Denison of Stonington, at which place he resided for a time; then went from there to Oxford, N. Y., and finally settled, in 1817, on a farm at Plainfield, Ct. Jerusha, the oldest daughter (b. 1762), married Gideon Denison. The widow, Ruth, whom Benjamin mentions in his will as "an infirm person," died in 1797. In 1793, Gardner Carpenter buys the Butler house, and either tears it down or moves it away, and builds the present brick house, which, after his death, was sold in 1816 to Joseph Huntington, and in 1841, was again sold to Rev. Hiram P. Arms. When first built by Gardner Carpenter, the roof was more the shape of that of the house in which he formerly lived, on the opposite side of the Green (now occupied by Miss Grace McClellan), but Joseph Huntington, during his occupancy, added the upper wooden story. Gardner Carpenter also buys additional land on the west of Simon Huntington, and Joseph Huntington purchases still more, bringing the lot up to its present limits. The house is now owned by the Rev. William Clarke, son-in-law of the late Dr. Arms.

Joseph Huntington (b. 1792), was the son of Joseph and Eunice (Carew) Huntington. He married in 1816, Julia Stewart Dodge (b. 1799), daughter of

David Dow and Sarah (Cleveland) Dodge of New York City. He was for some years associated with his father in business in Norwich, but removed to New York in 1834, where he was very active in religious matters, and was a deacon of the Tenth Presbyterian Church. He died in New York in 1852, and his wife in 1859.

CHAPTER L.

IN the distribution of Capt. Joshua Huntington's property, the land between Gen. Jabez Huntington's home-lot on the east and the house lot of Daniel Needham, is set out to his children, Zachariah, and Lydia, wife of Capt. Ephraim Bill. Zachariah receives the west part, and in 1753, he sells to his brother, Jabez, the land next to the Needham lot (frontage 43 feet). Here Jabez builds a distillery and a cooper's shop, which were inherited in 1786 by his son, Andrew. In 1811, the distillery has disappeared, but the old cooper's shop remains, and is sold with the land to Joseph Huntington.

In 1760, Zachariah Huntington sells to William Bradford Whiting the land between the distillery lot and the brook (frontage 4 rods), and the latter builds the house now owned and occupied by Mrs. William Fitch. He also builds near the street a shoe-maker's shop. In 1771, William Bradford Whiting (then of Canaan, N. Y.), sells the land and buildings to his brother-in-law, Azariah Lathrop. In 1797, the latter sells the property to Zenas Whiting (frontage 3 rods, 22 links). In 1800, Zenas sells to Asa Spalding. In 1812, the property passes into the possession of Dr. Rufus Spalding, whose family occupy the house until

Harriet (Whiting) Backus.
1779—1804.
First Wife of Eleazer Fitch Backus

Col. William Bradford Whiting.
1731—1796

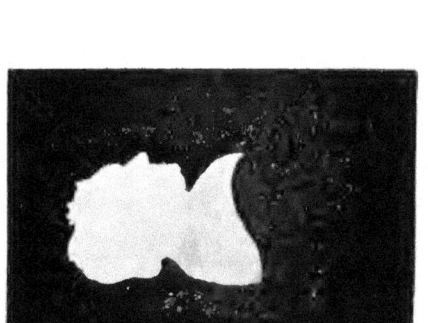

Amy (Lathrop) Whiting.
1735—1815.

after the doctor's death. In 1837, it is sold to Henry Lord; in 1848, to Dr. Jonathan Brooks; in 1853, to Edward Worthington; and in 1857, to the late William Fitch, whose widow still retains possession.

William Bradford Whiting (b. 1731), the first occupant of the house, was the son of Charles and Elizabeth (Bradford) Whiting of Montville, Ct., and a brother of Capt. Charles and Maj. Ebenezer Whiting of Norwich. He married (1) in 1754, Abigail, daughter of Thomas and Abigail (Huntington) Carew, who died in 1756. He married (2) in 1757, Amy, daughter of Nathaniel and Ann (Backus) Lathrop, who died in 1815. From the mention of the shoe-maker's shop, we may conclude that William Bradford Whiting was one of the many who were engaged in the shoe trade, which was then so profitable with the West Indies. We have found no mention of the shop after 1765, so it may have disappeared shortly after that date. Before 1771, William Bradford Whiting had left Norwich for Canaan, N. Y., and in that State he served as Colonel in the Revolutionary war, was a member of the State Senate for twenty years, and a Judge of the County Court for a long period. At this time it required great courage to start for the unknown and then frontier region of central New York, but the following anecdote, related by a descendant, will show that Col. Whiting had a wife well-fitted to be a help-mate to him in this pioneer enterprise: "One day when Col. Whiting was obliged to leave home and all of the men were absent, Mrs. Whiting decided to make soft soap, and was in the midst of operations when one of the girls called out that Indians were skulking around the edge of the clearing. (I do not know whether the 'girls' were daughters or servants. The Whitings had servants from Dumbleton, who came with Col. Whiting, to old Chloe, a slave, who lived in my grandfather's family as cook). A watch was set at the windows, the wooden shutters closed. Soon an Indian was seen trying to fire the house at one corner. A quantity of ammunition was stored in the house, and it was doubly in danger from fire. Mrs. Whiting seized the pot from the fire, ran upstairs and ladled a dipperful of boiling hot soap on the Indian's back as he knelt under the window. It is easy to fancy the yells as the lye burned in. Other Indians tried other parts of the house, but everywhere the hot soap was shot at them. Part of the kitchen furniture was used to keep up the fire. At all events, the house was kept till sundown and the return of Col. Whiting and his men." *

We may well believe this to be true of the handsome and determined old lady, whose portrait is on the opposite page, with her keen brown eyes, hair all tucked away under a white cap, gold beads around her neck; the soft white kerchief folded over the black silk dress, and the general air of spirit and sense pervading her face and attitude. The same descendant also writes of this portrait, which hung in her grandfather's house at Milford, Ct.: "The eyes of the portrait had the old-fashioned faculty of following one, (especially if naughty), about a room, and always, until a woman grown, it was my belief that they shed tears. When a quarter of a century later, I asserted that they did so, it was explained to me that during a certain 'line-storm,' a leak had been sprung in the ceiling of our dining-room, and the drops had fallen upon the old lady's face. It may be true, but I prefer to think she cried." †

Another treasured possession in this grandfather's house was the red camlet cloak worn by Amy (Lathrop) Whiting in her early frontier life. This had a hood, and a string with a bullet attached, to hold in the mouth and keep the hood in place, when riding on horseback, over the rough and untried roads.

The house of Col. Whiting had probably various tenants after his departure, until it was sold to Zenas Whiting.

Zenas Whiting (or Whiton, as the name was originally written), was a native of Hingham, Mass., where he was born in 1754. He was the son of Daniel and Jael (Damon) Whiton (or Whiting). He married (1) in 1778, Sarah Loring, and (2) in 1779, Leah Loring, and (3) Phoebe, widow of Ebenezer Raymond. "He served on the armed brig Hazard in 1776 and 1777. He was by occupation a carpenter, and had the reputation of being a man of genius, and of superior executive ability. He moved to Connecticut." ‡

We do not know the date of his arrival in Norwich, but he was living here in 1794, when he advertises for workmen to assist him in building a bridge over the Piscataqua at Portsmouth. From April 20th to Nov. 20th he was engaged on this work, which is thus described in the Norwich Packet of Jan. 8, 1795:—

* † Letter from Mrs. Clarence Deming of New Haven, Ct.
‡ History of Hingham, Mass.

Amy (Lathrop) Whiting

"The large and most elegant Bridge in North America, was built last summer over Piscataqua River in the State of New Hampshire. The length of said Bridge is 2,000 ft., without its Butments. One arch, 75 ft. in length, one, ditto, 245 ft., at their basis. This large piece of work was directed by Col. Thomas Thomson and John Pierce, Esq., and superintended by Mr. Zenas Whiting of Norwich, Connecticut, as Master Workman, much to his honor and credit, for it is viewed as one of the greatest pieces of Mechanical genius done in America;—one hundred Piers, from 20 to 25 ft. in length, from 10 to 25 tons of timber in a Pier."

The Norwich Packet of March 17, 1796, tells us, that "a Model of an Arch Bridge on an entire new construction, has been completed by the celebrated Architect Capt. Zenas Whiting of this City, and was sent off on Saturday last for Newport, to be embarked in a ship bound to Petersburg in Russia. Thus we see the great Tyrant of the North condescending to become dependent for mechanical invention, on the genius of this new hemisphere. The bridge which the Empress has it in contemplation to build, is to be erected over the river Neva, which divides the City of Petersburg, and is to be a single arch of eight hundred feet in length!" In 1802, Zenas Whiting was employed by Howland & Baxter, in connection with Timothy Lester, to build the machinery for their cordage and hemp-spinning mill. It is possible that he may have left Norwich shortly after, as we have found no further trace of him.

Dr. Rufus Spalding was a brother of Asa and Luther Spalding. He was born in Brooklyn, Ct., and married in 1782, Lydia, daughter of David Paine. He studied medicine with Dr. Elisha Perkins of Plainfield, Ct.; practiced first in Mansfield, Ct., and then at Holmes' Hole, Martha's Vineyard. During his stay at the latter place, he filled the offices of doctor, innkeeper, postmaster, justice of the peace, school-director, and village librarian. In 1812 he removed to Norwich, and died here in 1830.

CHAPTER LI.

IN 1761, after the death of Zachariah, Capt. Ephraim and Lydia Bill deed to Jabez all the land formerly belonging to Zachariah, lying between the Whiting house and a lot which they had sold to John Hughes in 1754. In 1765, Jabez sells to Joseph Carew land near William Bradford Whiting's shoe-maker's shop, 16½ feet in breadth, and 22½ feet in depth, and lying one rod north from the highway, with liberty of passing over Jabez' land to the highway. It is said that Joseph Carew was formerly a carpenter, but, if this is true, it is certain that he soon relinquished that occupation, and became a merchant, and probably in this store sold the variety of goods which he advertises: tools, glass, paint, rum, sugar, &c., &c. He remained here until 1793, when he entered into partnership with his son-in-law, Joseph Huntington, in the shop on the Green. In 1794, after the death of Gen. Jabez Huntington, his son, Zachariah, 2nd, sells to Joseph Carew the land in front of the shop, bounded 16½ feet on the street. On this land now stands a building, owned by Mrs. William Fitch, used formerly as a school-house, and now occasionally as a branch chapel of the Episcopal Church.

In 1794, land with a frontage of 24¾ feet, next to the Carew lot, is sold by Zachariah Huntington, 2nd, to Asa Lathrop, who is then living in the former Joseph Trumbull house on the opposite side of the street. Here stands, or is later built, his shoe-maker shop, which is sold to John Townsend in 1814. In 1836, this has either been converted into a house, or a new house has been built, which is then sold to Joseph Kinon. This is possibly the one now standing, occupied by the Gorman family.

Some time before 1786, a house must have been built on the adjoining land (frontage 4 rods, 19 links), which, at this date was occupied by the Gildon family, and set out in the distribution of Gen. Jabez Huntington's estate to his son, Zachariah. In 1800, Zachariah sells it to David Nevins. At that time it is tenanted by Richard Doyle. In 1792, Charles Gildon advertises as a leather-dresser, and leather breeches or glove maker, "opposite Capt. Joseph Carew's." His mother, Isabella Gildon, taught a small "dames" school for several years. She was the wife of Richard Gildon, and her son, Charles, was born in 1773.

In 1755, Jacob Perkins, Jun., buys of Zachariah Huntington, 1st, 20 rods of land (frontage 58 feet), on which he builds a shop and barn, which he sells in 1781. In 1782, the property is sold to Mrs. Martha Greene of Boston, and from her passed to her son, Capt. Russell Hubbard, and later to David Nevins, Capt. Hubbard's son-in-law.

In 1777, Capt. Jacob Perkins has vacated his shop, and an anonymous advertisement appears in the Packet, asking for "green sheep and Lamb Skins to be delivered at the hatter's shop formerly occupied by Capt. Jacob Perkins," and again for "Otter, Mink, Sables, Musquash, Red, Gray and Mungrel Fox Skins," &c., for the same unknown person. In 1784, Thomas Hubbard carries on a stocking manufactory in this shop of "Russell Hubbard & Son." In 1787, he moves to Leffingwell Row and is associated in business with Christopher Leffingwell.

In 1787, David Nevins moves his hat-factory to a shop "near Gov. Huntington's," and probably this is the shop. Thomas Hubbard also brings his stocking business here again for a while in 1791, then moves to his new quarters "west of the Meeting-house." David Nevins either continues to occupy this shop as his hat-factory, or, possibly in 1800, moves into the Gildon house. In 1823, a building was still standing here, called the Nevins hat-factory, but before 1848 it had been moved away, and now forms part of a house standing opposite the former residence of the late Alba Smith. In 1848, this land is sold to Russell Lewis, who still lives here in the "Abbot" house, which he moved from the opposite side of the street.

In 1797, Samuel Gaine, a hair-dresser from New York, informs the public that he has taken "the new shop, a few rods west from Capt. David Nevins hat-factory." He offers hard and soft pomatum for sale. We are unable to say which shop this may be, unless a new one has been built to take the place of Joseph Carew's old shop, or perhaps the Gildons have moved away, and their house may have been converted into a shop.

In 1746, John Hughes buys of Jabez Huntington, 22 rods of land (frontage 4 rods), and in 1754, of Ephraim and Lydia Bill, 30 rods of land (frontage 5½ rods). Of this land, John Hughes sells 16½ rods (frontage 3 rods), to Simeon Huntington in 1774, and here are built a store, a blacksmith shop, coal-house and cooper's shop. We have been unable to learn when the store was built, and who were its occupants. It is possible that this, or the Gildon house, may be the shop "next door to the Nevins hat factory" to which Simon Carew transfers his stock of books in 1796.

Simon Carew (b. 1776), was the son of Ebenezer and Eunice (Huntington) Carew. His earliest advertisement appears in 1793. In 1795, he has moved from his first stand to the building on the corner of the burying-ground lane. In the early part of 1796, he moves to this shop near the hat-factory, and in December of this same year, to the Landing.

The cooper's shop stood in the rear of the blacksmith's shop, and was sold by Simeon Huntington to Jeremiah Leach in 1791. Simeon Huntington occupied the blacksmith's shop.

Jeremiah Leach (b. 1749), son of Thomas and Sarah (Reynolds) Leach, married Eunice Hughes, daughter of Capt. John Hughes, and had two children, Jeremiah and Eunice, the latter marrying Jedidiah Story. A Jeremiah Leach married in 1799, Betsey "Gelding" (probably "Gildon") of Mansfield, and had a son, Charles (b. 1800). This might indicate a connection with the family of Richard and Isabella Gildon. We are unable to say whether this last Jeremiah is the father or son, or which of them occupied the cooper's shop, which in 1798 came again into the possession of Simeon Huntington, and was sold with the rest of his property in 1819 to John Townsend. We are unable to say when these buildings disappeared.

Probably about 1746, or soon after, John Hughes builds on the land purchased of the Huntington heirs, a house, which he deeds in 1802 to the family of his daughter and son-in-law, Nathaniel Townsend. We know nothing of John Hughes previous to his arrival in Norwich. In 1748, he married Zipporah Hartshorn (b. 1725), daughter of David and Abigail (Hebard) Hartshorn, and had four children. His only son, John, died in 1775. His daughter Eunice was married to

Jeremiah Leach, and Hannah, to Nathaniel Townsend. His wife Zipporah, died in 1799, and Capt. Hughes in 1803, aged 84. It is recorded on his grave stone, that he was "industrious and useful in life, until debilitated by age and infirmity."

Nathaniel Townsend (b. 1747), was the son of Jeremiah Townsend, first of Boston, later of New Haven, and his wife, Rebecca (Parkman) Coit, widow of Capt. Coit of Boston. He began life as a barber, combining with this a small mercantile business which gradually became more extensive—his stock of goods later including all the necessaries of life, and some of the luxuries. He also at one time carried on a bakery on the Green. He died in 1818. His wife died in 1788.

The Townsend family occupied the Hughes house for many years. In 1861, the house was burnt to the ground. The last of the family, Miss Rebecca Townsend, died not very many years ago. Two modern houses now occupy the lot.

In 1746, Jabez Huntington sells 17¾ rods of land (frontage 3¼ rods) to Nathaniel Shipman, who sells to Jabez Perkins in 1758. On this lot Jabez builds a house, and buys additional land (21 feet frontage), of John Hughes.

Jabez Perkins (b. 1728), was the son of Jabez and Rebecca (Leonard) Perkins of Newent. In 1751, he married Anna, daughter of Capt. Ebenezer

Lathrop. After her death in 1785, he married in 1786, the widow, Lydia Avery, of Groton, Ct. He died in 1795. In 1749, he had purchased land and a blacksmith's shop, in front of the house now occupied by Gardiner Greene, which he sells in 1761. Miss Caulkins says that he occupied at one time a house on the street leading by "Sentry" Hill. This was probably previous to his purchase of this land. At this date, 1758 he and his cousin Simeon were about to start in business in the shop across the street, which they relinquished about 1762. In 1765, Jabez buys a lot at the Landing, and builds a house, to which he soon removes, and his former house is sold in 1769. It is occupied for many years by Capt. Joseph Gale, whose son, Azor, buys it in 1798, and sells it in 1803 to Luther Spalding. In 1832, while tenanted by Diah Bailey, it is sold to Henry Armstrong. It is now occupied by Mrs. Jabez Wattles.

Joseph Gale (b. 1736), was a descendant of Edmund Gale of Cambridge, Mass., and a son of Joseph and Mary (Alden) Gale of Marblehead, Mass. His grandfather, Capt. Azor Gale, was captain of a vessel, and afterward a merchant at Marblehead. Joseph came to Norwich, and married in 1765, Sarah Huntington, whose parentage we have been unable to trace. She died in 1787, and he married (2) in 1795, Sarah (Leach) McDonald, widow of Alexander McDonald.

Joseph Gale is said to have been a tin-plate worker. He was a captain in the Sixth Regiment (Col. Parsons), of Gen. Putnam's brigade, at the siege of Boston in 1775. He was afterward a sealer of measures and a custom house officer. Capt. Glover used to say of him that he was the only honest official he ever knew, as he was the only one he couldn't bribe.* He had eight children. One of his daughters married Augustus, son of Azariah Lathrop. His eldest son, Azor, married Eunice, daughter of Ebenezer and Temperance (Edgerton) Lord, and granddaughter of the Rev. Benjamin Lord. Capt. Joseph Gale died in 1799.

Next to the Gale house stood the "long shop" of Gen. Jabez Huntington (probably the former shop of his father, Joshua), a long, low, one story and a half building, painted red, with the roof sloping to the street. Here for many years he carried on an extensive business, having also a warehouse at the Port or Landing. At the time of the Revolution, he was said to have owned twenty or

*Miss Caulkins' History of Norwich.

OLD HOUSES OF NORWICH.

more vessels engaged in foreign trade, but many of these were lost, and his health and mind were so seriously affected by those anxious years, that he was never again able to resume business, or entirely retrieve his losses. At his death in 1786, his sons, Andrew and Zachariah, inherited the shop. Zachariah, however, built for himself on the adjoining land another shop, long and narrow, with the gable end to the street, and Andrew established himself in his father's "long" shop. Both were prosperous and successful merchants, and, in addition to their mercantile trade, carried on many manufacturing enterprises.

In 1824, the heirs of Andrew Huntington sell their father's former store to Ichabod Ward, who sells to Henry Armstrong in 1828. At this latter date, no shop is mentioned in the deed, and it may possibly have been moved away. Before 1832 the house, now standing on the lot, was moved here from Bean Hill, and was then occupied by Henry Armstrong. We are unable to say when the Zachariah Huntington shop disappeared.

CHAPTER LII.

AS we now turn down the road leading to Dr. Gulliver's we come to the house, which has always been regarded as the oldest of the Huntington homesteads. We have found from the records, that this was the Bradford home-lot, which, with the Bradford house, were sold to Simon Huntington, Jun., in 1691; that the land next the lane was granted to Joshua by his father, Simon, in 1719; and that Joshua's house was standing on the lane in 1725, and the rest of the Bradford land came into Joshua's possession at the death of his father in 1736.

In 1745, Joshua gives to his son, Jabez, this house with barn and shop, and 23 acres of land, adjoining the town street, opposite the house of Simon Tracy; "beginning at the southeast corner, east from the shop, and bounded south on the street 16 rods, then north 15° E. 29 rods, to an apple tree marked ; thence runs west 15° N. 26½ rods to parsonage lands, then bounded west on parsonage 87 rods, to stones on the west side of the small brook, at the north-east corner of sd parsonage, thence runs east about 35° S. 40° W. 22 rods to a heap of stones on a ledge of rocks, thence runs south 18° W. 30 rods to a tree by a stone wall,

thence bounded north on the stone wall 2 rods, then bounded east 22 rods, then bounded east and south on the highway to the woods 35½ rods." It is possible that Joshua, who had purchased in 1738, another house for himself, gave this one to Jabez at the time of the latter's marriage in 1742, though it was not conveyed by deed until 1745.

There is a tradition in the family that at the time this house was built, an old building, supposed to have been the family homestead, was moved from its site near by, and added to the new structure. We are unable to say whether the present house was built in 1719, when the land was first given to Joshua, or after 1740 by Jabez. In the latter case, the addition must have been the former house of Joshua; in the former, the old Bradford homestead, which seems to us more probable, as this addition, the western end of the house, is evidently very ancient. Here, the old wooden shutters with small heart-shaped openings are still retained. The house, large and square, with projecting upper story, stands with its side to the street, and the long expanse of lawn extends up to the main street, where the shop of Jabez formerly stood. This is one of the houses in which, it is said, Lafayette was entertained during some of his visits to Norwich.

Gen. Jabez Huntington (b. 1719), was the son of Capt. Joshua and Hannah (Perkins) Huntington. He married (1) in 1741-2, Elizabeth, daughter of Samuel and Elizabeth (Tracy) Backus, who was born in 1721 and died in 1745. He then married (2) in 1746, Hannah, daughter of Rev. Ebenezer Williams of Pomfret, Ct. After his graduation at Yale College in 1741, he entered into commercial life at Norwich, and on his father's death in 1745, assumed entire control of the latter's business, as his brother, Zachariah, was then only fourteen years of age. He added largely to the ample fortune left him by his father, and at the beginning of the Revolution owned a large number of vessels engaged in foreign trade.

Pres. Daniel C. Gilman of Johns Hopkins University, in his historical discourse delivered at the Norwich bi-centennial celebration, says that Gen. Huntington was chosen in 1750 "to represent this town in the General Assembly, and for several years afterward he was either a member of the Lower House, over which he often presided, or was one of the Assistants. While attending the semi-annual meetings of the legislature, he would write home to his son, Joshua

Huntington, particular directions in respect to the farm and store, always closing his letters with a devout petition for the blessing of divine providence on all his family. When Governor Fitch, in 1765, presented to his council the stamp act, and proposed that they should administer to him the oath, which would require the execution of that obnoxious measure, Jabez Huntington, with his cousin Hezekiah, the other member from Norwich, voted, with a majority of the council, to do no such thing, and (when four of the councilors proceeded to administer the oath), indignantly left the chamber. In 1774, he was chosen moderator of the meeting in which Norwich declared itself in favor of liberty."

Though he could not but foresee that a war would greatly endanger his shipping, and perhaps lead to the utter ruin of his fortunes, not for a moment would Gen. Huntington allow his interests to interfere with his patriotism. He was one of the most active members of the Committee of Safety, and in 1776, he and Gen. Wooster were appointed the two Major Generals of the Connecticut militia. On the death of Gen. Wooster in 1777, Gen. Huntington was made sole Major General of the State. During the war, he was in constant correspondence with Washington, Lafayette, Hancock, Sherman, Trumbull, and many leading patriots of the time. Of his fortune he gave largely to the cause, and when ammunition was scarce, it is said that he at one time "permitted even the leaden weights, by which his windows hung, to be cast into bullets."

Though a strong athletic man, the great strain of these trying times upon his health and strength, led to a failure of both mental and physical powers. He retired from active service in 1779, and the last seven years of his life were passed in great mental and bodily suffering till his death in 1786. In his funeral sermon, it is said that he "devoted his all to the public good," and "sacrificed his ease, his health, and eventually his life, to serve and save his country."

Pres. Daniel C. Gilman describes the assembling of the Huntington family one morning in 1774, when the father told the children of his and their mother's decision to risk their fortune and comfort for the cause of freedom, and asked the sons, even the little ten year old Zachariah, if they would not also stand by their country in its hour of need, and one and all assented heartily, and as the Huntington Family Memoir says, "Their names were all identified with the

protracted struggle which resulted in the independence of the United States, and so well did they perform their part, assigned them in that memorable achievement, that the faithful historian of those days has been obliged to leave this testimony to their success: 'If the annals of the revolution record the names of any family which contributed more to that great struggle, I have yet to learn it.'"*

Gen. Jabez's first wife, Elizabeth Backus (b. 1720-1), was the daughter of Samuel and Elizabeth (Tracy) Backus. She had two sons, Jedediah and Andrew, and died at the early age of twenty-four. Her father, Samuel Backus, son of Joseph and Elizabeth (Huntington) Backus, was a prominent and wealthy citizen. Her mother, daughter of John and Elizabeth (Leffingwell) Tracy, was an ardent Separatist. Refusing to pay the minister's rate in 1752, she was seized one night and committed to jail for 13 days. The rate was then paid by her son-in-law, Jabez Huntington. Her grandson, Jedediah, used, at a later date, to pay her rate annually, that she might remain unmolested. The second wife, Hannah Williams (b. 1726), was the daughter of Rev. Ebenezer Williams of Pomfret, Ct., and his wife, Penelope Chester, daughter of John and Hannah (Talcott) Chester of Wethersfield, Ct. She lived to the age of 80, dying in 1807. Mrs. Sigourney writes: "It was beautiful to see how warmly she was welcomed, and what marked and sweet respect was paid her by all her descendants. Her person seemed the centre and crown of their enjoyments. Tenderly cared for, and honored, she dwelt under the roof of her youngest son, Gen. Zachariah Huntington, until her death, which I think was sudden, and from the effects of a severe influenza."

One of the daughters of Gen. Jabez Huntington, Elizabeth (b. 1757), "richly gifted," as Mrs. Sigourney writes, "both in person and mind," married in 1773 her cousin, Col. John Chester of Wethersfield, son of John and Sarah (Noyes) Chester. The Norwich Packet of that date chronicles the marriage of "the amiable Miss Elizabeth Huntington." Her husband, Col. John Chester, was a colonel in the army of the Revolution, and, as we read in the Huntington Family Memoir, "was much in public life, and always in highest esteem both for signal public service, and for his great personal worth." He especially distinguished himself at the battle of Bunker Hill.

* Pres. Daniel C. Gilman's Historical Discourse in "The Norwich Jubilee."

Gen. Zachariah Huntington (b. 1764), the youngest son of Gen. Jabez and Hannah (Williams) Huntington, married in 1786, Hannah, daughter of Thomas and Catherine (Havens) Mumford of Groton, Ct. Mrs. Sigourney describes him as "a model of manly symmetry and beauty. He was tall, with noble features, a pure complexion, and a fresh color upon cheek and lip." To her childish fancy he seemed, she says, "like one of the chieftains of the old Douglas blood, who ruled the Scottish Kings." *

Gen. Huntington, who "superintended a mercantile establishment, as well as the culture of his extensive grounds, took great delight in music. He possessed a scientific knowledge of it, with a voice of great power and melody. A desire to improve this important department of divine worship, induced him at one time, to become the leader of our choir in church. This voluntary service was appreciated by the people, and the labor connected with it, felt to be, on his part, both a condescension and a religious offering. When he gave out the name of the tune, which was then always done in a distinct enunciation, and we rose in our seats in the gallery, every eye turning to him for guidance, he seemed, with his commanding presence and dignified form, to our young minds a superior being."

"One of his requisitions was imperative, that the female portion of the choir should sing without their bonnets. That article of apparel being then the antipodes of the present fashion, and formidable both for size and protrusion, he affirmed not only intercepted the sound, but precluded striking the key-tone with accuracy. None of us would gainsay his wishes, and the simplicity of the times counted it no indecorous exposure." †

With his brother Ebenezer, Zachariah served in the war of 1812, attaining the rank of Brigadier-general. He died in 1850. His eldest son, Thomas Mumford Huntington, inherited the house, and married in 1819, Mary Bowers Campbell. He died in 1851, and the house is now the property of his daughter, Mary, widow of the late Dr. Timothy Childs, who resides in Florence, Italy. The second son, Jabez Williams Huntington was at one time a distinguished United States Senator. The only daughter, Elizabeth Mary (b. 1793), married John Griswold, a prominent merchant of New York, and died early in her married life. Mrs. Sigourney describes

* † Mrs. Sigourney's "Letters of Life."

her as "beautiful," "full of life and spirit," and ardently loved by her family and friends. She pays to her this tribute in a poem:—

> "With silent course,
> Unostentatious as the heaven-shed dew,
> Thy bounties fell; nor didst thou scatter gifts,
> Or utter prayers with pharisaic zeal,
> For man to note. Thy praise was with thy God.
> In the domestic sphere, where Nature rears
> Woman's meek throne, thy worth was eminent;
> Nor breathed thy goodness o'er cold stoic hearts.
> What gentleness was thine—what kind regard,
> To him thou lov'dst—what dove-like tenderness
> In voice and deed! Almost Disease might bear
> Its lot without complaining, wert thou near,
> A ministering angel."

CHAPTER LIII.

IN 1738, Joshua Huntington sells to Peter Morgan 26 rods of land "on ye south-east corner of my pasture, northeast from my dwelling house," the boundary line running north 6 rods, then west 4 rods, then south 6 rods to the highway, and on this Peter builds a house. In 1743, he buys of Joshua Huntington additional land (now the site of the Gulliver house), beginning at the south-east corner of his own land, then running north-east 6 rods, then north 2 rods, bounded on the highway, then west 5½ rods, bounded on Huntington land to the north-east corner of his first purchase, then running south 6 rods, bounded on his own land, to the first bound at the highway.

Peter Morgan (b. 1712), was the son of John and Ann (Dart) Morgan of New London, and grandson of Richard Rose Morgan, one of the first settlers of Waterford. He married in 1738 Elizabeth Whitmore of Middletown and had six children. He sold this land and the old house to Jabez Huntington in 1770, and moved to the Great Plain, where we believe he kept an inn, and died in 1786.

Gen. Jabez gave the old Morgan house and land to his daughter, Mary, who was married in 1778 to Rev. Joseph Strong, and the young couple built a new house near the old one, which latter was still standing in 1786. Mrs. Strong

Rev. Joseph Strong
1753—1834

received from her father a large amount of additional land, both in 1784 and at his death in 1786, and Dr. Strong also bought adjoining land, so that their domain covered many acres, but the house site was on the Morgan land. We do not know when the Morgan house disappeared. After the death of Rev. Joseph Strong, the homestead was inherited by his son, Henry Strong, and is now in the possession of the latter's daughter, Mary, wife of the late Dr. Daniel Gulliver. Mrs. Gulliver furnishes the following short sketch of the lives of her grandfather and father:—

"Joseph Strong, son of Rev. Nathan Strong of Coventry, Conn., and Esther Meacham, was born Sept. 21, 1753. He graduated at Yale College in 1772, at the age of 19. Having prepared for college when quite young, he returned to college after graduation, by his father's advice, and reviewed many of his studies, and afterward prepared for the ministry. He was called to the First Church in Norwich, as colleague of Rev. Dr. Lord, and 'the consideration of having so able and wise a friend was an influential motive to his engaging in this wide field of labor.' His ordination sermon was preached by his brother, Rev. Nathan Strong of Hartford, March, 1778, and the charge was given by his father.

This was his only settlement. He remained pastor of this church till his death, Dec. 18, 1834, having a colleague for nearly six years. The last church service he attended was in January, 1833, when he took part in the administration of the Lord's Supper.

His preaching was simple, earnest and solemn. He was peculiarly gifted in prayer, and always successful in selecting thoughts appropriate to the circumstances. Like many other good men at that time, he was not at first in favor of Sunday schools, but he lived to remember earnestly in his prayers the organization that 'cared for children.'

In his Half-Century sermon, while lamenting that the fruits of his labors had not been more abundant, he says: 'I do not recollect a single year of my ministry without some hopeful instances of awakening and conversion.'

He was a member of the corporation of Yale College for 18 years and faithfully performed the duties connected with this position. In 1807, he received the degree of D. D., from the college of New Jersey. Several of his sermons were printed,

Dr. Strong was tall and well-proportioned. His health was uniformly good, so that he was rarely absent from his pulpit by reason of sickness. Reserved and unostentatious, he was always ready to do everything in his power for the comfort and welfare of others.

He married Oct. 18, 1780, Mary, daughter of Jabez and Hannah (Williams) Huntington, who was born March 24, 1760. She was a woman of rare excellence of character. Possessing a cultivated mind, ready sympathy, and abounding charity, she was an acceptable substitute for her husband, in his absence, to those who sought counsel or aid from him. She died May 14, 1840.

Their children were: Joseph Huntington Strong (b. Nov. 27, 1780), Mary Huntington (b. Feb. 5, 1786), who married Aaron P. Cleveland in 1820, and died in 1843, and Henry, who died Nov 12, 1852.

Henry Strong was born Aug. 23, 1788. His preparation for college was made in his native town, and he was admitted to Yale at the age of 14. During the first two years of college life, he studied a part of the time at home, passing the regular examinations. He graduated in 1806. After graduation he taught a small school of young ladies in Norwich Town, and in after years he liked to recall his pupils individually, considering what a choice circle they formed. During this time, he commenced studying law with James Stedman, Esq. In 1808, he was called to take the position of tutor at Yale College, which he filled for two years, continuing his legal studies under Judge Chauncey. He was admitted to the bar in New Haven County in 1810, but commenced practice in his native town. Here, for more than forty years, he devoted his energies to his chosen profession.

His perception was acute, so that he quickly saw the rights of a case, and when he perceived that his client was in the wrong he would advise him to settle the matter with his opponent, rather than go to law about it. His questions were so searching that he was often asked, "Has the other side been to see you, Squire?"

After his death, a gentleman in a neighboring town, who had great respect for Mr. Strong, said to his wife, "It was not so much your husband's legal abilities that we valued, though we esteemed them highly as they deserved, but

Mary Johnston Strong

his unbending integrity." This characteristic commenced in early life, for his mother used to say that she could not recall an instance when he disobeyed or deceived her.

In a sermon, preached the Sabbath after his death, his pastor says: "Mr. Strong was a man free from all taint of personal ambition. He sought not the honor which cometh from men. He was solicited to allow himself to be put in nomination for some of the highest offices in the gift of the State, but except that in two or three instances he reluctantly accepted a seat in the State Legislature, he uniformly and resolutely declined all such overtures. He was invited to accept a chair of instruction, as professor of law, in his own Alma Mater. He refused to listen to the invitation. In the year 1848, however, the Corporation, without asking his leave, conferred upon him the honorary degree of Doctor of Laws, an honor which was richly deserved." Mr. Strong died Nov. 12, 1852. He married July 7, 1825, Eunice Edgerton Huntington, daughter of Joseph and Eunice (Carew) Huntington, who was born Sept. 13, 1797, and died June 19, 1865."

Miss Caulkins describes the Rev. Joseph Strong as "above the middle size and stature," with a calm dignity of address which impressed every one with respect. This dignity, however, was blended with great kindness and courtesy, and his manners, far from inspiring awe, were gentle and attractive. In his latter years, especially, it was delightful to listen to his conversation, flowing as it did in an easy graceful stream, enlivened with anecdotes, and enriched with sketches of character, curious incidents, and all the varied stores collected by an observant mind through long years of experience."*

"In the pulpit he was remarkable for the fluency and impressive solemnity of his prayers. The deep tones of his voice, combined with the devout humility of his address, and the free flow of adoration and praise with which he approached the Father of spirits, would hush an audience into deep attention, and waft them, as it were, into the immediate presence of the Most High."

Of Mary Huntington, wife of the Rev. Joseph Strong, Mrs. Sigourney writes: "A mistress was she of the minutiæ of that domestic science, which promotes household comfort and happiness. Proverbially plain was she in dress

---
* Miss Caulkins' History of Norwich.

and manner, condescending to the lowliest, and of so easy and cheerful a temperament, that her words were always mingled with smiles. In those days, a minister and his consort were expected to be patterns in all things to all people, and the closest critic perceived in her only those quiet unambitious virtues that pertain to woman's true sphere, and a cloudless piety. Her husband had erected a handsome parsonage within the precincts of Huntington Square; and they and their children formed an integral part of those weekly social gatherings which kept bright the chain of affection and the fountain of kindred sympathy. To be occasionally comprehended in those circles, and partake their 'feast of reason and flow of soul,' which comprised always a most liberal admixture of creature-comforts, was accounted a rare privilege." *

Jabez Huntington sells to Robert Lancaster in 1748, 30 rods of land (frontage 5 rods, 2 feet), north of the Morgan land. Here Robert built a house, which, owing to the slope of the land, had two stories in the front, approached by a long flight of steps, and only one in the rear. We do not know the parentage of Robert Lancaster, nor the date of his first appearance in Norwich. He died in 1770, aged 76, and was buried in the Christ Church grave-yard. It is possible that his nearness to the Grist house, where the Episcopal services were held for so many years, may have led to his attending the Episcopal Church.

His son, John (b. 1737-8), married in 1798, Anna (Bentley) Trapp, widow of Ephraim Trapp. John Lancaster buys of Simon Tracy in 1769, land on the opposite side of the street, where he builds a shop. In 1803, John Lancaster and his wife, Anna, deed to Ephraim Trapp one-half the land and house, but in 1809, Ephraim, who is mate on the ship of Capt. Edward Whiting, dies of a fever on the Island of St. Bartholomew, W. I., and his mother and step-father inherit his property. In 1830, Anna Lancaster deeds the house, shop, and land to Orimel Mabrey, who had married in 1817 her daughter, Anna Trapp. Orimel Mabrey still retained this property in 1850, when the house seems to have disappeared. In 1831, the land where the shop stood, on the opposite side of the street, was sold to George W. Lee, and later to Theodore McCurdy.

* Mrs. Sigourney's "Letters of Life."

CHAPTER LIV.

NOW returning to the Green, we find that the north line of the lot occupied by Miss Grace McClellan, marks the beginning of the home-lot of Maj. James Fitch, eldest son of the Rev. James Fitch, and his first wife, Abigail Whitfield. The land was a part of the house-lot of the Rev. Mr. Fitch, and was given by him to his son. It extended from the home-lot of Simon Huntington, 2nd, to the southern line of the burying-ground lane, covering a frontage of 37½ rods.

The record gives it as three acres, "more or less," abutting south on the home lot of the Rev. James Fitch 45½ rods, abutting east on the land of Lt. Thomas Tracy, 8 rods, 4 feet, abutting north on the land of Simon Huntington 18 rods, and east on the land of Simon Huntington 19 rods, 4 feet, then the line runs easterly over the brook, "it being two rods," "then the line runs two rods, 4 feet, north, and thence northwest 4 rods, thence west, abutting north on the land of Simon Huntington 14 rods, to the street, abutting northwest and west on the Town Green 37½ rods."

James Fitch, 2nd, was born in Saybrook in 1649, and married in 1676, Elizabeth Mason, (daughter of Maj. John Mason, and younger sister of his father's second wife), by whom he had four children, one of whom died in infancy. His wife died in 1684, and in 1687, he married Alice (Bradford) Adams, daughter of Dep. Gov. William Bradford, and widow of the Rev. William Adams of Dedham, Mass. Three children were born to them in Norwich, and five more in Canterbury.

During the time that Maj. Fitch resided in Norwich he took a leading part in all town affairs, and served as land-surveyor, registrar, captain of the train-band, and commissioner of boundaries. He was one of the first persons to receive, in 1687, a grant of land for a wharf and a warehouse at the "port" or "Landing," and was also allowed the exclusive right to establish a saw-mill. As a large land-owner, and the general agent of the Mohegan Indians in their transfers of property, he acquired great influence, and controlled all the land transactions of an extensive territory. He was appointed Captain in 1680, Assistant in 1690, and Sergeant Major of New London County in 1696.

As treasurer of New London County he seized, laid out, and offered for sale 600 acres of land in the Quinebaug region, to indemnify the State for the burning of the county-prison by the Indians. He sold this land to John, Daniel and Solomon Tracy, and Richard Bushnell of Norwich; and then, empowered by a deed from Owaneco, son of Uncas, Maj. Fitch laid claim to the rest of this region, against the counter-claims of Fitz-John and Wait Winthrop, sons of the Governor, who based their title on a deed from two resident Sachems; and great were the struggles and litigation of both parties, in their efforts to gain and dispose of these lands.

Maj. Fitch had many enemies, made partly by his domineering spirit, and partly through jealousy of his great landed possessions, which last gained for him the reputation, shared by Capt. John Chandler of Woodstock, of being "one of the biggest land grabbers" in Connecticut.

About 1697, he was accused of some very irregular land transaction, which caused his removal from the office of assistant, and he finally decided in 1698 to remove to Peagsconsuck, where he had already sold lands and an attempt at settlement had been made. The spot selected by Maj. Fitch for his house, and still marked (we have been told) by traces of a cellar, was below the river island, on a point called "Indian Neck," and is one of the most beautiful situations in Canterbury. Here he erected the first framed-house and barn within the limits of the town.

His own family of eleven children, and those of his wife, the widow of the Rev. William Adams, formed a large and doubtless lively household, and this attraction, combined with Maj. Fitch's position as disposer of almost all the lands in this region, made the house a place of great resort. Courts were also held here, and Miss Larned, the historian of Windham County, says that "a road was laid out from Windham to this noted establishment," which, "connecting with the

Greenwich path, formed the great thoroughfare to Providence."* Major Fitch gave to the town the name of Kent, but it was afterward changed to Canterbury.

Miss Caulkins says that the Major, according to tradition, and record, "could not always resist the temptation to convivial excess," but for this and also for his frequent outbreaks of temper against the government, he was always repentant, ready to acknowledge his fault and when possible to make amends.

Miss Larned says that "he was an ardent patriot, a firm friend of popular liberty, contending 'as strenuously against Gov. Saltonstall and the Council, for the rights and privileges of the Lower House;' as he did thirty years earlier against the encroachments of Andross, nor did he allow his personal feelings and prejudices to hinder him from promoting what he deemed the public good. He was a friend of progress, ready to initiate and carry on public improvements, a friend of education, endowing Yale College in 1701 with over six hundred acres of land, in what was afterward Killingly, and furnishing glass and nails for the first college edifice in New Haven."†

But his irascible disposition, and his efforts to establish his Indian claims, involved him in endless disputes, and his last years were sad and embittered. He died in 1727. The inscription on his grave stone, in the old Canterbury grave-yard reads: "He was very useful in his Military & in his Magistracy to which he was chosen, & served successively many years to the Great Acceptance & Advantage of this country being a Gentleman of good parts & very forward to promote ye civil & religious interest of it."

His second wife, Alice (Bradford) Adams (b. 1661), was the daughter of Dep. Gov. William Bradford of Plymouth and his first wife, Alice, daughter of Thomas Richards of Weymouth, Mass. She married (1) in 1680, as second wife, the Rev. William Adams of Dedham, Mass. He died in 1685, leaving his young widow with three children of her own, and a step son, Eliphalet, who came with her to Norwich, studied theology with the Rev. James Fitch, and settled as minister at New London in 1709. A posthumous child, Abiel, (?) was also born four months after her father's death.

The widow, Alice Adams, married in 1687, Maj. James Fitch, as second

*† Miss Ellen D. Larned's History of Windham County.

wife. He had already a family of three children, and eight more were born to them in Norwich and Canterbury. Alice lived to the age of 84, dying in 1745. The inscription on her grave-stone at Canterbury reads: "In memory of Mrs. Alice, dtr. to ye Hon. Wm. Bradford, Esq., Lieut-Gov. of ye Col. of New Plymouth, Relict of ye Hon. James Fitch, Esq. late of Canterbury, a person of rare qualities & excellent endowments, an example of virtue, & paten of piety. She after an exemplary life fell asleep in Jesus, Mar. 10, 1745, in ye 84th yr. of her age."

Elizabeth, the eldest daughter of the Rev. William and Alice (Bradford) Adams (b. 1680-1), was, after the death of her father, adopted and brought up by her childless uncle and aunt, Capt. John and Ann (Winthrop) Richards of Boston, Mass. On one of her visits to her mother in Norwich, she probably met for the first time Samuel Whiting, afterward minister of the First Church of Windham, then studying theology with the Rev. James Fitch of Norwich, was married to him in 1696, and though not yet sixteen years of age, went to Windham, as Miss Caulkins says, "to be set up as a model to the whole parish for sobriety of demeanor, discreet conversation and skilful housewifery." Rev. Samuel Whiting died in 1725, and in 1737, the widow, Elizabeth, married the Rev. Samuel Niles of Braintree, Mass., and died in New Haven in 1762, at the house of her son, Col. Nathan Whiting. Alice Adams, the second daughter (b. 1682), married the Rev. Nathaniel Collins of Enfield, Ct., in 1701. The son, William, was a helpless invalid. The other daughter, Abiel (?) (b. 1685), married the Rev. Joseph Metcalf of Falmouth, Barnstable Co., Mass.

CHAPTER LV.

IN 1698-9, Capt. Fitch, calling himself "of Peagsconsuck, (Gent.), sells his house and home-lot to Samuel and Simon Huntington, who perhaps had purchased it in order to control the disposal of property, so immediately in their neighborhood. In 1699-1700, Simon deeds his share to Samuel, who sells the property to the town committee, the latter purchasing it with a view to the settlement of the Rev. John Woodward.

In 1694, the Rev. James Fitch was rendered unable to preach by a stroke of palsy, and an effort was made by the people of Norwich to induce his son, Mr. Jabez Fitch, to be his father's successor; but though he preached on trial for more than a year, he declined to become the settled pastor; was later a fellow and tutor of Harvard college; was ordained at Ipswich in 1703, as colleague of the Rev. John Rogers; and was afterward minister at Portsmouth, N. H., where he died in 1746. Various candidates were then tried, but the town failed to procure a settled pastor.

In December, 1696, the people of Norwich feel that they "have reason to bless God," for having sent Mr. Henry Flint, a Harvard graduate of 1693, to "preach to them in order to a settling and carrying on the work of the ministry," and they agree to give him 20 s. per week and to "defray the chardges of his Board and horsmeat" "as long as he shall continue to be our Minister." But all their efforts to induce him to settle among them were in vain. Others were tried, and failed to please. In 1698, Rev. Joseph Coit, son of John Coit of New London, was engaged to supply the pulpit, but, when invited to settle, declared his "disagreement from Norwich church, and consequently he cannot walk with them, for how can two walk together, if they be not agreed." The church having confidence in its own infallibility, is concerned about Mr. Coit, who "doth sett up his own opinion in opposition to the Synod book, and a cloud of witnesses," and fears he "will be in great danger to wander from the way of peace and truth." Rev. Joseph Coit was settled in 1705 as minister at Plainfield, Ct, where he resided till his death in 1750, at the age of 77.

The next candidate finally accepted a call, and was ordained in 1699. This was the Rev. John Woodward (b. 1671), son of Peter Woodward of Dedham, Mass., who graduated from Harvard College in 1693. The town agree to give Mr. Woodward "the home-lot purchased of Mr. John Mason, 9 acres adjoining, on the south side of the river, 150 acres at the north-east end of Plain Hills, 2½ miles from town, also the use and improvement of the home-lot and pasture purchased of Stephen Gifford, also 12 acres of pasture land near the town, 6 acres lying within the little boggy meadow, £150 interest in the undivided lands belonging to the Township, and 30 cords of fire wood per year delivered at his door." The agreement continues, "If it shall please God to remove you by death, while you be a bachelor, within the term of 5 years next after your ordination, then the home lot, 9 acres, and also 50 acres of 150 acres shall be at the only use and dispose of yourselfe, your heirs . . . . at that time in which you shall enter upon the improvement of any part of sd tract of land, but after the term of five years, the remaining 100 acres shall be at your use and dispose," and "also we do propose and promise to give you yt house lot, together with the dwelling house barn &c which were Maj. Fitchs, which sd lot, house and barn shall be yours after the day of ordination, reserving to ourselves 1½ acres for a burying place at the lower corner of sd land, next to land in the present tenure of the Rev. James Fitch, also to give you 20 £ in money in order to the repair of sd dwelling house, also to clear the meadow lands on both sides of the river purchased of Mr. Fitch."

Then as "sallery" for his "incouragement," they agree to give him "60 £ per annum in our ordinary pay, and 10 £ in money annually till the term of four years," then "to make an addition of 10 £ in ordinary pay, and 5 £ in money, the same to begin Dec. 6, 1699," and it was to be understood that "pork should pass" with him at "3 d. per pound as pay, and beef at 2 d., provided there be no more beef carried than he hath occasion for."

No houses are mentioned as on the lots of Maj. Mason and Stephen Gifford, as it is probable that those formerly standing there had disappeared. The town at first contract with John Elderkin to build for £140 "a parsonage 40 foot in length, and 18 foot in width, 15 foot between joints, with a room on the back side 18 foot one way, and 15 foot the other way, and 15 foot between joints," but finding that Mr. Woodward preferred the former house of Maj. Fitch, it was finally decided to use that as a parsonage, and not to build a new one.

Rev. Mr. Woodward married in 1703, Sarah, daughter of Richard Rosewell of New Haven, and had seven children born in Norwich. In 1708, the council at Saybrook drew up their rules for church regulation, later known as the Saybrook Platform, which Mr. Woodward, who had been a delegate to the convention and secretary of the synod, was naturally desirous of having adopted by his church, which had always strongly adhered to the Cambridge Platform. The Legislature accepted the Saybrook Platform, and confirmed it as a law of the Colony, with the proviso, that any churches dissenting from these rules, might be allowed to regulate church discipline according to their consciences.

In reading this act of the Legislature to the church, Mr. Woodward omitted this last clause, and the two representatives, Richard Bushnell and Joseph Backus, arose and announced the whole law to the people. They then withdrew from the church, and with a number of warm sympathizers, held private Sabbath meetings. At the next session of the Legislature, they were expelled from the house. The majority of the church members adhered for a time to Mr. Woodward, but the increasing dissatisfaction, continued complaints on his part of insufficient salary, and the prospect of division into two ecclesiastical societies, finally compelled the calling of a council of ministers, who recommended his immediate dismissal, which was accordingly effected in 1716. The retiring minister sued the town for arrears of salary, which he did not, however, recover until 1721. He sold his house and lands in Norwich to the town committee, and removed to a farm in East Haven, where he died in 1746.

CHAPTER LVI.

IN 1717, the First Church committee, "a company in ye purchas of ye Estate of Mr. John Woodward," sell to Sarah Knight of Norwich, "(widdow), all yᵗ their Messuage or Tenement with ye land whereon ye same doth stand, situated in ye Town Plot," (frontage 32 rods, 3 ft.), "extending from ye southerly corner of Dea. Simon Huntington's land, down to ye highway laid out to ye Burying Place,"—"together with all ye singuler, ye houseing, outhousen, Barn, Buildings, Edifices, &c., orchard, yard, garden, Trees, well water, Brooks, Runs of water, water courses, stones, wayes, easements, rights, privilidges, members, and appurtenances," &c. Evidently Sarah, being a woman of business, meant to have all that was her right.

This Sarah Knight (b. 1666 in Boston), was the daughter of Capt. Thomas Kemble, a merchant of Charlestown, Mass., and his wife, Elizabeth Trarice, (perhaps daughter of Nicholas Trarice). Capt. Kemble lived in a house on North Square, Boston, later the residence of Samuel Mather. In 1673, he was sentenced to stand for two hours in the stocks, "for lewd and unseemingly conduct," in saluting his wife at the doorstep on the Sabbath day, after a three years absence. He died in 1688-9, and was buried in the Copp's Hill burying-ground. His daughter, Sarah, married, as second wife, Richard Knight, of whom little is known. He is said by one authority, to have been a brick-layer, by another a carver, and is supposed to have died between 1706 and 1714, leaving his widow, with one daughter, Elizabeth (b. 1689). Mrs. Sarah Knight "kept school in her father's house from 1701 till her death in 1708." So says one authority, but her journal, dated 1704, shows that at that time she was travelling through New England, and her appearance in Norwich in 1717, proves that she certainly did not die in 1708.

Her journal is most interesting, showing "Madam" Knight to have an education and mind far above the average, especially in those days, when many women, even of good family, could hardly write their own names. It was preserved in the family of Christopher Christophers of New London, whose wife, Sarah, inherited it among other effects of her relative, Madam Livingston, the daughter of Sarah Knight. It then passed by inheritance into the possession of Mrs. Ichabod Wetmore of Middletown, Ct., who allowed its publication in 1825, under the supervision of Theodore Dwight of New York. We can, perhaps, hardly realize what a difficult and hazardous undertaking was this journey of Madam Knight from Boston to New York 271 miles, through a wild and half-settled country, at this early date, which, as W. R. Deane says (in his annotated review of this journal in Littell's Living Age of June 26, 1858), was the very year in which died Peregrine White, the first child born in New England; "also the year of the publication of the first newspaper in America (the Boston News Letter); about the time of the establishment of the first daily paper in London; one year before the birth of Dr. Franklin, and twenty-seven years before the birth of Washington."

On Monday, Oct. 2nd, 1704, at three o'clock in the afternoon, Madam Knight starts on her long and perilous journey. She waits for a while at Dedham for the "post" to come along, but as he does not arrive, she finally proceeds to the tavern and negotiates for a guide to conduct her to the first stopping place. She succeeds in procuring one, of whom she writes:—

"His shade on his Hors resembled a Globe on a Gate post. His habitt, Hors, and furniture, its looks and goings Incomparably answered the rest." With this guide she travels through a dark and dismal Swamp, and after reaching her destination, is conducted to "a parlour in a little back Lento, wch was almost fill'd wth the bedstead, wch was so high that I was forced to climb on a chair to gitt up to ye wretched bed, that lay on it." There laying her head upon a "sadcoloured" pillow, she thought over the events of the past day. Finally the "post" appears, and she travels on with him. Crossing Providence Ferry, they come to a river, which is usually forded, but she, not daring "to venture," the post rode through, leading her horse, and she crossed in "a cannoo," "very small and shallow, so that when we were in, she seem'd redy to take in water, wch greatly terrified mee, and caused me to be very circumspect, sitting with my hands fast on each side, my eyes stedy, not daring so much as to lodg my tongue a hair's breadth more on one side of my mouth than tother, nor so much as to think on Lott's wife, for a wry thought would have oversett our wherry." The "Post" tells her of another rapid river, "so very firce a hors could sometimes hardly stem it," which they should have to cross, and all day she sees herself in imagination, "drowning, otherwhiles drowned, and at the best like a holy Sister Just come out of a Spiritual Bath in dripping Garments." When night came, "each lifeless Trunk, with its Shatter'd Limbs appear'd an Armed Enymie, and every little stump like a Ravenous devourer." Finally, after descending a hill in the darkness, she knew "by the Going of the Hors," that they were fording the dreaded river, "ralyed" all her courage, and "sitting as Stedy as just before in the Cannoo," arrived safely on the opposite shore. Riding through "dolesome woods," the guide far ahead, in the "Terrifying darkness," which was enough "to startle a more Masculine courage," and reflecting that her "Call to take this Journey was very Questionable," which she had not till then "prudently considered," she became much distressed in mind, but on arriving at the top of a hill, "the friendly Appearance of the kind Conductress of the night, just then Advancing above the Horizontall Line" inspired her with courage and a poem, which she jots down at the next stopping place. As a specimen of her poetical powers we will give the whole of this poem :—

> "Fair Cynthia, all the Homage that I may,
> Unto a Creature, unto thee I pay :
> In Lonesome woods to meet so kind a guide
> To Mee's more worth than all the world beside.
> Some joy I felt just now, when safe got or'e
> Yon Surly River to this Rugged shore,
> Deaming Rough welcome from these clownish Trees,
> Better than Lodgings with Nereidees.
> Yet swelling fears surprise ; all dark appears—
> Nothing but Light can dissipate those fears.
> My fainting vitals can't lend strength to say,
> But softly whisper, O I wish 'twere day.
> The murmur hardly warm'd the Ambient air,
> E're thy Bright Aspect rescues from dispair ;
> Makes the old Hagg her sable mantle loose,

> And a Bright joy do's through my Soul diffuse,
> The Boistero's Trees now lend a Passage Free,
> And pleasant prospects thou giv'st light to see."

In the light of the moon she sees in imagination "A Sumpteons city, fill'd wth famous Buildings and churches, wth their spiring steeples, Balconies, Galleries," &c., and "without a thou't of anything but thoughts themselves," she hears the "Post" sound his horn, and knows that they have arrived at the "Stage," where they were to lodge for the night. Here everything was neat and clean, and she has "chocolett" prepared, which she had brought with her; then goes to bed, but not being able to sleep, on the account of the discussion of some "Town tope-ers" in the next room, she finally rises, sets the candle on a chest by the bedside, and falls, as she says, "to my old way of composing my Resentments," in the following manner:—

> "I ask thy aid, O potent Rum,
> To charm these wrangling Topers Dum.
> Thou hast their Giddy Brains possest—
> The man confounded wth the Beast—
> And I, poor I, can get no rest.
> Intoxicate them with thy fumes:
> O still their Tongues till morning comes!"

And she adds, "I know not but my wishes took effect; for the dispute soon ended wth 'tother Dram; and so Good night!"

On Oct. 4th, they set out for Kingston in the company of a French doctor, and he and the "Post" rode so furiously, she could scarcely keep up with them. They were obliged to ride 22 miles before they could "bait their horses," but the "Post" encouraged her, by saying they should be "well accomodated at Mr. Devill's." "But I questioned whether we ought to go to the Devil to be helpt out of affliction. However like the rest of Deluded souls, that post to ye Infernal denn, wee made all possible speed to this Devil's Habitation; where alliting, in full assurance of good accomodation, wee were going in. But meeting his two daughters, as I supposed twins, they so neerly resembled each other, both in feature and habit, and look't as old as the divil himselfe, and quite as Ugly, we desired entertainm't, but could hardly get a word out of 'em, till with our

Importunity, telling them of our necesity, &c., they call'd the old Sophister, who was as sparing of his words as his daughters had bin, and no or none, was the reply he made us to our demands. Hee differed only in this from the old fellow in t'other Country; hee let us depart." After more adventures she arrives at "Stoningtown" and from there, guided by an old countryman and his two daughters, she comes to the New London ferry. Here there was a high wind, and Madam Knight says: "The Boat tos't exceedingly, and our Horses capper'd at a very surprizing Rate, and set us all in a fright; especially poor Jemina, who desired her father to say so Jack to the Jade, to make her stand. But the careless parent taking no notice of her repeated desires, she Rored out in a Passionate manner: Pray, suth, father, Are you deaf? Say so Jack to the Jade, I tell you. The Dutiful Parent obey'd; saying so Jack, so Jack as gravely as if hee'd bin to saying Catechise, after Young Miss, who with her fright look't of all coullers in yᵉ Rainbow."

At New London she arrives "at the house of Mrs. Prentices," and "waits on" the Rev. Gurdon Saltonstall, who invites her to stay the night at his house, where she was "handsomely and plentifully treated and Lodg'd, and made good the Great Character" she had before heard concerning him, viz., "that hee was the most affable, courteous, Genero's and best of men."

Mr. Joshua Wheeler is her escort to "Seabrook," and from there to New Haven. She writes about the customs of New Haven, and comments on the frequent "Stand aways," as she calls the divorces, which are then "too much in vougue" among the English, and also the Indians. She sees her relatives, the Prouts and Trowbridges, and from there travels to New York, and back to New Haven, comes again to New London, where she is entertained by Gov. Winthrop, and is accompanied across the ferry by Mary Christophers and Madam Livingston (the Governor's daughter), who little thought she was then travelling with her husband's future mother-in-law. Mr. Samuel Rogers escorts her part of the way, and Capt. John Richards of Boston was her companion on the latter part of the journey. On March 3rd, 1705, she joined "her aged and tender mother in Boston, and her dear and only child," having been five months from home. On the window-pane of her home in Boston was scratched with a diamond:—

> "Now I've returned, poor Sarah Knights,
>   Thro' many toils and many frights;
>   Over great rocks and many stones
>   God has preserv'd from fracter'd bones."

It is said that she first appeared in Norwich in 1698 with goods to sell, remained here a few years, then went back to Boston, and in 1717 again returned to Norwich. It is certain that for a time previous to 1717, she was residing in New London, where she may possibly have gone after the marriage of her daughter to Col. Livingston, which occurred in 1713. On the Norwich town records of 1717 we find that "The town grants liberty to Mrs. Sarah Knight to sit in the pue where she use to sit in the meeting house." She is said to have presented the church with a handsome silver goblet, to be used in the communion service. In 1718, Sarah Knight, with others, was "brought before" Richard Bushnell, Justice of the Peace, for selling strong drink to the Indians. She accused her maid, Ann Clark, of selling the liquor, but refusing to acquit herself by oath, was sentenced to pay a fine of 20 s.

Her daughter's husband, Col. Livingston, died in 1721, and in 1722 she sold her house in Norwich to Edmund Gookin of Sherborn, Mass., and moved to the Livingston farm, which she had previously purchased of her son-in-law. This farm stood on Saw Mill brook, near Uncasville, on the west side of the road to New London. Madam Knight was a pew-holder in the Montville Church, built in 1724. She was also called an inn-keeper. In company with Joseph Bradford, she purchased large quantities of land. She died in 1727. Madam Livingston died in 1735-6. The latter's inventory includes diamond rings, jewelry, valuable pictures, slaves, and a large amount of silver-plate.

Edmund Gookin, who purchased Madame Knight's house in 1722, resided here until 1733. He later purchased a house at Bean Hill, with which the history of his family is more closely identified, so we will reserve his history and lineage for our second volume.

CHAPTER LVII.

IN 1733, Edmund Gookin sells to Curtis Cleveland, the north part of his home-lot and buildings (frontage 2 rods, 1½ feet), "beginning at the north-west corner of my shop." This is possibly the "warehouse" of Sarah Knight. Curtis Cleveland either altered the shop into a dwelling house, or built a new one on the lot in which he lived for many years. Curtis was born in 1700. He was a descendant of Moses Cleveland of Woburn, Mass., and a son of Isaac Cleveland, who married in 1699, Elizabeth Curtis, and came from Woburn to Canterbury, Ct., or Plainfield, between 1699 and 1703. He shortly after moved to Norwich, where he was admitted an inhabitant in 1709. He was appointed bell-ringer in 1709-10, and a grant of land was voted to him in 1714, nearly opposite the warehouse of Ensign Thomas Leffingwell. He died probably in that year, and by 1715, his widow had married Clement Stratford, a mariner of New London, Ct. She died in 1742. Four children were born to Isaac and Elizabeth Cleveland. His daughter, Kesiah, became the wife of Sylvanus Jones, and his son, Curtis, married in 1733-4, Remembrance, daughter of Richard Carrier of Colchester, Ct., and had eight children. In 1761, Curtis Cleveland was still residing in this house on the Green, but died probably shortly after that date. His widow, Remembrance, died in 1790.

The house and land passed before 1776, into the possession of Joseph Peck, though the deed of transfer has not been found. It is possible that the latter built a new house on the lot, as at his death in 1776, he leaves to his widow, Elizabeth, "the use and improvement of the new dwelling house we live in, with use and improvement of the land where the said house stands (called the Cleveland lot)," but he gives the property to his step-son, Gardner Carpenter, on condition that the latter shall pay one-third of its value.

Gardner Carpenter (b. 1749), probably resides here with his mother, Elizabeth, until about 1793 or 1794, when he buys the Butler property opposite, and builds the brick house, now owned by Rev. William Clark. He was the son of Joseph and Elizabeth (Lathrop) Carpenter of Norwich. His shop was on the opposite side of the Green. He served as paymaster in the Seventeenth Connecticut Regiment, in 1776, and married in 1791, Mary, daughter of Benjamin and Mary (Carew) (Brown) Huntington. His death occurred in 1815. In 1816, the house (called "the red house)," on the Cleveland lot, was sold to Bela Peck, who in 1829, sells it to Orimel Mabrey. At present, it is owned by Miss Grace McClellan.

In November, 1733, Edmund Gookin sells the remaining part of his home-lot (frontage 30 rods, 1½ feet), to William Witter of Preston, who, in December of the same year, sells to André Richard the house and land next to the Cleveland lot (frontage 7 rods, 2 feet). In January, 1734, André Richard sells to Sylvanus Jones a part of this purchase (frontage 2 rods), "together with the east part of the house purchased of Mr. Witter, with chimney, and one-half the stones of the cellar—the Great Room called the kitchen, with Lentoo on the north side of the kitchen, with liberty to separate them from the house off my land, and to remove the same." André either builds an addition to the remaining part of the old Fitch house, or builds a new house and shop, which he sells in December, 1734, to William Darby of Canterbury, Ct., with the land (81 rods), "abutting west on the Green 5 rods, 2 feet," south on the Jones lot, and north on the Cleveland land.

Wiliam Darby was an early settler of Canterbury, but now moves to Norwich, and probably resides in this house until about 1737-8, when he sells the property to Susanna Ramé (shop-keeper), of Boston, Mass., who conveys it to her son-in-law and daughter, William and Elizabeth (Ramé) Fountain, "late of Boston, now of Norwich."

Capt. William Fountain (for his calling was that of a sea captain), was possibly the son of Aaron and Hannah (———) Fountain of Fairfield, Ct., and grandson of Aaron Fountain, who lived in New London about 1683, and married (Miss Caulkins claims) Susanna, daughter of Samuel Beebe, but a Stamford record says that his wife was "Mary, daughter of Samuel Beebe of New London." It is possible that the latter may have been a second wife. This Aaron Fountain's house stood on the Great Neck, now Waterford, and he left New London in the latter part of the century for Fairfield, Ct. Wm. A. E. Thomas of Hartford, Ct., who has made many researches in the Fountain genealogy, believes him to be the son of Edward Fountain, who came to New England in 1635 in the ship Abigail, at the age of 28. The family is of French origin, the name being originally Fontaine, and is a branch probably of the same family to which the Rev. James Fontaine of Virginia belonged.

The Ramé lineage we have not been able to trace, but think that Elizabeth may have been a descendant of George Ram, who also came in the Abigail from London in 1635, aged 25, and her father may possibly have been a Simon Ramé who was in New York in the latter part of the seventeenth and beginning of the eighteenth century. Mrs. Caroline F. Blackman of Norwich, a granddaughter of Capt. William and Elizabeth (Ramé) Fountain, says that her great-grandmother's name was Basset, and we think she may possibly be Susanne Basset (b. 1689), daughter of Francis and Marie Madeleine (Nuquerque) Basset, French Huguenots, who fled from Marennes, France, to this country, and lived for a while both in New York and Boston. Susanne Ramé was a widow in 1737.

Family tradition tells of the large property sacrificed in France for the sake of their religion, of their trials and persecutions. It is said that Elizabeth Ramé was sent back to France for a while to be educated, and also to learn if anything could be recovered of their former estates, but found that they had been confiscated by the government, and that nothing could be secured unless she abjured the Protestant faith and became a Romanist.

Mrs. Blackman remembers how her grandmother would often narrate to her grandchildren, the trials her ancestors endured, telling of the strict surveillance exercised over the Huguenot households, how the Bible was fastened open by straps under the seat of a chair and how during family worship, watchers were stationed at the windows, and when the gendarmes were seen approaching, the chair was at once placed in position, with one of the family seated in it. She also remembers boxes, sent by the friends in France, containing silk gowns and many luxuries, and her grandmother would often say, "How little my friends know of our real needs in this new country!" In February, 1738-9, the house was sold to Thomas Danforth, and the Fountain family removed to the Landing, or Chelsea, where they afterward resided. In November, 1739, Thomas Danforth sells the house, shop, and land to Philip Turner (later known as Capt. Philip Turner), (b. 1715), who came from Scituate, Mass., to Norwich, and married in 1739, Anne, (b. 1715), widow of Thomas Adgate, 3rd, and daughter of Daniel and Abigail (Bingham) Huntington. Philip Turner was the son of Philip and Elizabeth (Nash) Turner, and great-grandson of Humphrey Turner, a prominent citizen of Scituate, Mass. Miss Caulkins writes of "the enviable popularity Capt. Turner" soon acquired among his new associates, performing the duties of constable, selectman, and captain of the troop of horse, a spirited band of young men, in whose parades and exercises he took great pride. He was active in all works for public improvement, and was one of the chief agents of the town in opening the two avenues to the Landing, and in the laying out of Water Street. In 1752, he was a member of the General Assembly. But alas! this active and useful career was cut short by his death in 1755, at the age of thirty-nine. His widow married for a third time, in 1757, Capt. Joshua Abel. Five children were born to Anne and Philip Turner, of whom, the second son, Philip, became a distinguished surgeon.

After the death of Capt. Turner, the house was sold in 1757 to Joseph Peck. The shop is not mentioned in the deed of sale, so may have disappeared.

Joseph Peck (b. 1706), was the son of Benjamin Peck, a wealthy resident of Franklin, and a great-grandson of Henry Peck, who came in 1633, in the ship Hector to Boston, and later in 1638 with Gov. Eaton, the Rev. John Davenport and others to make a settlement at New Haven. Joseph married in 1729, Hannah, daughter of Richard and Thankful (———) Carrier of Colchester, Ct. She died in 1741-2, and he married (2) in 1742, Elizabeth Edgerton, who died in 1753. In 1754, he married for a third wife, Elizabeth, widow of Joseph Carpenter of Norwich, and daughter of Nathaniel and Ann (Backus) Lathrop. It is shortly after this marriage that he buys this house of Capt. Philip Turner. He possibly enlarges the house, and keeps a tavern here until shortly before his death in 1776. At that time he is not living in the inn, but in the house next door.

This inn was one of the three celebrated taverns on the Green, and some old people still remember the large old elm which stood in front of the house, among the boughs of which was built a platform or arbor, approached by a wooden walk from one of the upper windows. From this high station, the orators of the day held forth on public occasions, and here tables were set, and refreshments served.

"On June 7, 1768, an entertainment was given at Peck's tavern, adjoining Liberty Tree, to celebrate the election of Wilkes to Parliament. The principal citizens, both of town and Landing, assembled on this festive occasion. All the furniture of the table, such as plates, bowls, tureens, tumblers and napkins were marked "No. 45." This was the famous number of the "North Briton," edited by Wilkes, which rendered him so obnoxious to the ministry. The Tree of Liberty was decked with new emblems, among which, and conspicuously surmounting the whole, was a flag emblazoned with "No. 45, Wilkes and Liberty."

"In September of that year, another festival was held at the same place, in mockery of the pompous proceedings of the Commissioners of Customs, appointed for the colonies by the British ministry. These Commissioners had published a list of holidays to be observed by all persons in their employ, and among them was "September 8th," the anniversary of the date of their commission. The citizens of Norwich were resolved to make it a holiday also. At the conclusion of the banquet, toasts were drank, and at the end of everyone was added:—

"And the 8th of September."

Thus:—

"The King and the 8th of September."
"Wilkes and Liberty and the 8th of September"
"The famous 92, and the 8th of September."

Songs were also sung with this chorus; nor did the assembly disperse without indignant speeches made against 'British mis-government' and the disgrace of wearing a foreign yoke."*

In 1774, John Wheatley, who had formerly kept a boot and shoe shop on the opposite side of the Green, moved to the Peck Tavern, "lately kept by Joseph Peck," and it is perhaps about this time, that the latter moved to the Cleveland house next door.

John Wheatley (b. 1748), was the son of Capt. John Wheatley, who married in 1743, Submit, widow of Aaron Cook, and daughter of Benjamin Peck of Franklin. Capt. John Wheatley served as paymaster in the expedition to Havana; was living in 1760 at Bozrah, and in 1768 at a place called "Coase." We have found no record of the marriage of John Wheatley, 2nd. He was a Second Lieutenant in Col Samuel Selden's Regiment in the Revolutionary war, was taken prisoner at the battle of Harlem Heights in Sept., 1776, and died soon after. His estate was settled by his widow, Jane, and his brother, Andrew Wheatley. In December, 1776, "De O Dad Liddle" (as the Packet announces), is keeping the tavern, and offers "brown sugar, and molasses" for sale.

Deodat Little (b. 1750), was the son of the Rev. Ephraim Little of Colchester, Ct., and his wife, Elizabeth Woodbridge, daughter of the Rev. Samuel and Mabel (Russell) (Hubbard) Woodbridge of East Hartford, Ct. Deodat's mother, Elizabeth Woodbridge, "ye vertuous consort of ye Rev^d Mr. Ephraim Little," as her gravestone announces,

"So Pious, Prudent, Patient, and Kind,
Her Equall mayn't be left behind,"†

died when Deodat was only four years old. Deodat married possibly previous to his arrival in Norwich, as the baptisms of several of his children are recorded here. In 1781, he was a resident of New London, and afterward lived both in East Windsor and Ellington, Ct.

In 1784, Jonathan Trott, "a fiery old patriot" (as the Hon. Charles Miner calls him), was keeping the tavern. Mr. Miner writes in his letter, declining the

---
* Miss Caulkins' History of Norwich.
† From "The Woodbridge Record," compiled by Donald G. Mitchell from papers left by the late Louis Mitchell, formerly of Norwich, Ct.

invitation to the Norwich Bi-Centennial celebration: "Consciousness of memory is first awakened to the shouts of triumph, and the thundering of cannon at the old Peck house, when peace was declared in 1784." An old lady, living in 1865, remembered the great crowds of people assembling on the plain, "their joyous greetings and congratulations, the shaking of hands, the waving of flags, firing, drumming, shouting, and the large bonfires at night. The following Sabbath, the church was filled with a dense crowd, all in their best array, smiling and happy. The choir of singers appeared with brilliant decorations, and sung an ode adapted to the occasion, in the tune of Worcester, of which the following was the opening stanza:"—

> "Behold a radiant light!
> And by divine command,
> Fair Peace, the child of Heaven descends
> To this afflicted land." *

When peace was again declared after the war of 1812, Norwich (according to Miss Caulkins), was in a tumult of excitement. "Rockets flew up from the hills, salutes were fired from the ships in the river, and these were echoed from the fortresses at New London, and these again were responded to from the British blockading squadron at the mouth of the river." †

A letter written by a Norwich citizen in March, 1815, mentions a commemoration ball given at Norwich in that month, at which 180 persons were present, and another at New London, where there were 500 guests, including 40 English officers. A dinner was also given at Norwich Town, where 100 persons "sat down at the table, and ratified the peace with all the requisite formalities." The letter also alludes to a ball, which Admiral Hotham was expected to give in the following week, on his ship Superb, but we are unable to say whether this took place or not.

In 1787, the year in which Capt. Bela Peck was married to Betsey Billings, we think that he probably moved with his bride to his father's former tavern. In that year, Newcomb Kinney advertises that he will open a school "in a large, convenient room in Capt. Bela Peck's house." In 1829, the house was occupied by

* † Miss Caulkins' History of Norwich.

Samuel Claghorn. In 1851, the heirs of Bela Peck sell the house to Nathan D. Morgan. It is now occupied by Edwin LaPierre.

Jonathan Trott was possibly identical with a Jonathan Trott who was a jeweller in Boston in 1772, and whose genealogy is given by Edward Doubleday Harris in the N. E. Historical and Genealogical Register for January, 1889. He married Lydia (b. 1736), daughter of John and Lydia (Richards) Proctor of Boston and New London. His daughter, Abigail, married Dr. Philemon Tracy in 1785. A son, John Proctor Trott, married in 1796 Lois Chapman, daughter of Joseph and Elizabeth (Abel) Chapman, and another son, George Washington Trott, married (1) in 1806 Sally Marvin, daughter of Gen. Elihu Marvin, and (2) Lydia Chapman, sister of his brother's wife. Miss Caulkins writes of the long sixteen days' journey, which Lydia Chapman made in the month of February, 1800, when, "the only female in a considerable party of emigrants," she went out with her younger brothers to the Wyoming Valley, Penn., to join her father, who had emigrated to that region shortly before. "Not a murmur escaped her, and her noble patience and cheerful hope animated and sustained her companions." Her husband, George W. Trott, was afterward a physician in Wilkesbarre, Pa.*

---

* Miss Caulkins' History of Norwich.

CHAPTER LVIII.

IT is possible that the "Great Room" or kitchen, and "the Lentoo" of the old Fitch or Knight house were added in 1734 to the house, then erected by Sylvanus Jones, on land purchased of André Richard, but of this we have no positive proof.

Sylvanus Jones (b. 1707), was the son of Caleb Jones, one of the first settlers of Hebron, Ct., and his wife Rachel, daughter of John Clark of Farmington, Ct. He married in 1730 Kesiah, daughter of Isaac and Elizabeth (Curtis) Cleveland, and died in 1791. He had eight children, and at his death, his son, Ebenezer, becomes the owner of the house and land.

Ebenezer Jones (b. 1744), married in 1765, Elizabeth Rogers, and had three daughters, one of whom, Lucy (b. 1766), marries Henry J. Cooledge, and another, Rachel (b. 1771), becomes in 1793 the wife of Asa Lathrop, Jun. Louisa, daughter of Lucy (Jones) Cooledge, marries in 1832 Charles Avery of New London, and her daughter, Mrs. Harriet Robinson, now owns and occupies the house.

We do not know the occupation of Sylvanus, but Ebenezer was a cooper, and Mr. Miner pictures him "with his adz and double driver, holding it in the middle, and playing it rapidly on the empty barrel, as he drives the hoop, sounding a reveille to the whole neighborhood regular as the strains of Memnon." His shop stood south of the house and a little back from the street.

To enter into all the exchanges of property between the Jones lot and the burying-ground lane, would be not only tiresome, but very bewildering, so we will make the account as brief as possible. In 1739, William Witter sells to Thomas Danforth, land adjoining the Jones lot (frontage 10 rods); in 1737, to Joshua Prior, the next frontage of 4 rods; in 1739, to Jonathan Wickwire, the next 2 rods of frontage; and to Joshua Prior in 1734, the land beyond this, abutting west on the Green 7 rods, and south on the highway to the "burying-place."

In 1742, Thomas Danforth sells to Philip Turner the north part of his purchase (frontage 4 rods). In 1740, he sells the next three rods of frontage, with a shop upon it, to John Manly, and in 1744, his remaining 3 rods of frontage, with another shop (which he has probably built), to William Morgan, Jun., of Groton, Ct. Philip Turner sells the upper part of the land purchased of Thomas Danforth (frontage 30 feet), to George Wickwire in 1753. On this, the latter has built a house, which he sells in 1765, to Ebenezer Jones. This is later occupied as a shoe-shop by Asa Lathrop, Jun., the son-in-law of Ebenezer Jones, and again as a dwelling by Eliphaz Hart, who is living in it in 1823, when it is sold by Lucy Cooledge to Capt. Bela Peck.

George Wickwire (b. 1727-8), was the son of Peter and Patience (Chappell) Wickwire of New London, North Parish (or Montville). The family of Jonathan Wickwire (an uncle of George), also appeared at this time in Norwich. George Wickwire married in 1749-50, Elizabeth Culver, perhaps a daughter of John Culver. John Wickwire, the grandfather of George, was an early settler at Montville. His wife was Mary, daughter of George Tongue, who kept an inn at New London, on the bank between the present Pearl and Tilley Streets. One of the daughters of George Tongue married Fitz John Winthrop. At her death, she left legacies "to sister Wickwire's children."

The remainder of Philip Turner's purchase (about 2 rods frontage), comes into the possession of William Morgan in 1747. John Manly's land and shop (frontage 3 rods), is sold in 1746 to William Morgan, who, as we learned before, had acquired possession of the Danforth shop and land in 1744. The land purchased of William Witter by Joshua Prior, comes into Morgan possession in 1740. William Morgan came from Groton to Norwich, either in the latter part of 1744 or the beginning of the year 1745, and built a house between this time and 1752. At this latter date, James Noyes Brown is occupying the house. In 1752, the Danforth and Manly shops have disappeared. In 1750, William Morgan sells land (frontage 3 rods, 15½ feet), and a barn at the north of his lot, just south of where the Wickwire house later stood, to Daniel Needham, who in 1752 sells it to James Noyes Brown (formerly of Newport, R. I.), who also buys of William Morgan the lower part of the Morgan lot (frontage 64 feet), on which he builds a shop.

James Noyes Brown belonged to an old Rhode Island family. He was the gr.-gr.-grandson of Chad Brown, and through his mother and paternal grandmother was the descendant of four Rhode Island governors: Jeremiah Clark, Peleg and John Sanford, and William Coddington. His mother was the granddaughter of the Rev. James Noyes of Stonington, Ct.

James Noyes Brown was married at Newport, R. I., in 1751 to Robe Carr, and came to Norwich about 1752 with his widowed mother, Ann (Noyes) Brown, and possibly a sister, Mary, who married in 1755, Jacob Perkins of Norwich. A son and namesake was born and died in 1753, and his wife and mother died in 1754, the former in August, the latter in October, and in December of that year he married Mary, daughter of Joseph and Mary (Huntington) Carew. A second son, also named James Noyes Brown, was born in 1755, and died in April, 1756, and the father died in November of that year. The widow, Mary, married in 1767, Benjamin Huntington.

In 1757, William Morgan* sells his house and remaining land to Nathan Stedman, who also buys the Brown lots. In 1764, Nathan Stedman sells his house and home-lot to Azariah Lathrop, "bounded north on George Wickwire, south on Jonathan Goodhue," and in 1770, Ebenezer Jones, who purchased in 1765, the

* The genealogies of William Morgan and Nathan Stedman will be given in the history of the west end of the town, where they later resided.

Wickwire house and land, sells also a small piece of the land on the south (frontage 10 feet) to Azariah.

Azariah Lathrop either altered and enlarged the old Morgan house, or built a new one, in which resided for a time his son, Dr. Gurdon Lathrop (b. 1767),

who graduated at Yale in 1787, and married in 1791, Lucy, daughter of Dr. Philip and Lucy (Tracy) Turner.

Gurdon Lathrop was a merchant in 1791, in the former shop of Dudley Woodbridge, across the green. In the same year he moves to the "Perit" store on the corner of the burying-ground lane, and again to a new shop near his dwelling house. He was later either a druggist or doctor (as he bore that title), and moved to New York, where he died in 1828.

Gerard Lathrop (b. 1778), fourth son of Azariah, married in 1809 Mary Ely, daughter of the Rev. Zebulon Ely of Lebanon, Ct. At the death of Azariah Lathrop in 1810, "the large mansion house" (the one now owned by Mrs. Peter Lanman), is willed to Gerard, and the land on the north to Gurdon, who sells it to his brother in 1811.

Gerard Lathrop had seven children, three of whom were born in Norwich. In 1814, he conveys his property in Norwich to his brother-in-law, Rev. Ezra Stiles Ely of Philadelphia, and later resides in Savannah and New York City. The house had then for many years a variety of tenants. Capt. Elisha Leffingwell resided here for a time. In 1823, it was sold to Capt. Bela Peck. In 1853, it passed into the possession of the Lanman family, and is still owned by the widow of Peter Lanman, who occasionally resides here. When the property of Gerard Lathrop was conveyed to Rev. E. S. Ely in 1814, there was standing on the lot a "red shop," the property of Abigail, widow of Azariah Lathrop. We think this was possibly the former shop of James Noyes Brown. It has since disappeared It probably stood on the site of the house now occupied by Anthony Peck.

CHAPTER LIX.

THE land (frontage 3½ rods), on which now stands the store of Herbert Hale, is sold in 1736, by Joshua Prior (who, in 1734, purchased it of William Witter), to Alexander Stewart, and by Stewart to Jonathan Wickwire in 1737. Jonathan Wickwire purchased in 1739, the land north of this (2 rods frontage), on which he must have built a house. In 1740, he sells both these lots of land, with a house and shop, to William Morgan. An old well, with crotch pole, &c., belongs to the property, but stands on "the common," south-west of the house. William Morgan sells this house and shop to Jonathan Goodhue in 1742.

In 1735, Joshua Prior sells the land (frontage 3½ rods), on the corner of the lane to the "burying-place;" to Samuel Waterman, and here the latter has already built a shop. In 1736, Samuel Waterman sells the land to William Hyde, and after this date the shop is no longer mentioned, though the land is several times bought and sold. In 1745, it is purchased by William Morgan, who sells it in the same year to Jonathan Goodhue.

Samuel Waterman (b. 1712), is the son of John and Judith (Woodward) Waterman. After 1736, we have no further knowledge of him. His parents resided in the house, formerly the home of the Rev. Mr. Fitch.

Jonathan Goodhue we believe to be the son of Joseph and Abigail Goodhue, of Ipswich, Mass., and a descendant of Dea. William Goodhue of that town. He probably came to Norwich about 1742, when he purchased this house and shop of William Morgan. He also leased of Joseph Waterman in 1747, for a term of fifty years, the island in the river at the north part of "No-man's Acre," near Bingham's mill-dam, where he erected works for grinding scythes. He died in 1760. The Goodhues of Ipswich were profoundly religious people, and so was Jonathan, if we may judge from the inventory of his library, which included such works as Flavel's "Meditations," the "Imitation of Christ," Vincent on the Day of Grace, the "Day of Doom," Dr. Edwards' Book of Prayer, &c., &c. Four children were born in Norwich, and one of the sons, David Goodhue, (then of Simsbury, Ct.), sells the house and land to John Perit in 1771.

John Perit was a descendant of Peter or Pierre Peyret (or Peiret), one of the first Huguenot pastors in America, who was the grandson and namesake of a Protestant officer, who distinguished himself by bravery at the siege of Mas d' Azil. He came to America about 1687 in the ship Robert from London. Family tradition says that he escaped from France by being carried aboard ship concealed in a meal-sack. He was a preacher for seventeen years in the French church at New York, died in 1704, and lies buried in Trinity Church grave-yard, where a stone, with the following inscription, in both Latin and French, marks his resting-place :—

Ci - git - le - reverent - Mr Pierre - Peirete - M : D - St . Ev - qui - chasse - de - France pour la - religion - a preche - la - parole - de - Dieu - dans - l' Eglise - Francoise - de - cette - ville - pendant - environ - 17 - ans - avec - l appro - bation - generale - et - qui - apres - avoir vescu - comme - il - avoit - preche - jusques - a - l age - de - 60 - ans - il - remit - avec une - proffonde - humilite - son - esprit - entre - les - mains - de - Dieu - le - 1 - Septembre - 1704.

Hic - jacet - reverd - Dom - Petrus - Per - rieterus - V - D - M - qui - ex - Gallia - religi - onis - causa - expulsis - verbum - Dei - in - hujus - civitatis - ecclesia - Gallicana - per - annos - 17 - cum - generale - approbatione - proedicavit - quique - cum - vitam - proedi - cationibus - suis - conformem - duxeret - usque - ad - 60 - aetatis - suae - annum - tan - dem - in - manus - Domini - spiritum - hu - militer - deposuit - 1 - mens - Sept - ann - Dom - 1704.

The wife of the Rev. Pierre Peiret was Marguerite de Grenier la Tour, des Verriers de Gabre. His son, Peter Peiret, joined the French colony at Milford, married Mary Bryan, daughter of Capt. Samuel and Martha (Whiting) Bryan of Milford; and in 1709, acted as clerk of the expedition to Canada under Col. William Whiting, writing the journal and letters, and drawing up the orders for the troops. He died before 1715, and letters of administration were granted to the widow, Mary "Pieritt," with the guardianship of the two minor children: Peter, aged 8, and Margaret, aged 6 years.

The third Peter Perit married in 1734 Abigail Shepherd, daughter of John and Abigail (Allen) Shepherd. He built the wharf, now called the "Town Wharf" in Milford, and sent a ship to Bordeaux, France, after a cargo of wine. She made a good voyage, and got safely as far as Newport, R. I., but in attempting to pass through Fisher's Island Sound, was wrecked, and her valuable cargo lost.*

John Perit of Norwich was the son of Peter Perit, 3rd, and was born about 1738. He served as ensign of the Third Company, Second Regiment, in the

French war in 1761, and in 1762 as Second Lieutenant. Shortly after he came to Norwich, and in 1771 bought the Goodhue property. Whether the old gambrel-

---

* Lambert's History of New Haven Colony.

roofed building on the corner of the burying-ground lane was included among the buildings mentioned in the deed of sale, or was later built by John Perit, we are unable to say, but in this building, he for some years carried on a mercantile business. It is probable that in 1775 he raised an independent company to march to the relief of Boston, for the General Assembly in that year grant to the men in Boston under the command of Capt John Perit, the same pay as the regularly commissioned troops. In 1779, he marries Ruth Webster, who came with her father, Pelatiah Webster, to visit in Norwich in 1776. The latter was a citizen of Philadelphia, and a distinguished writer on financial and political matters, who, for his strong and outspoken patriotism was imprisoned for a time by the British during their occupation of Philadelphia, and a part of his property confiscated. In 1786, John Perit leaves Norwich, resides for a while in Scotland, Conn., and dies in Philadelphia in 1795. He left five children: John Webster Perit, who married Margaretta Dunlap of Philadelphia, and resided in that city; Pelatiah, who for many years was President of the Chamber of Commerce in New York City; Rebecca, who married Joshua Lathrop, and resided in Le Roy, N. Y.; and Maria, who married Charles P. Huntington of Norwich. The widow, Ruth (Webster) Perit, married in New Haven in 1799, Col. Christopher Leffingwell of Norwich, and died in the latter place in 1840.

In 1786, the Perit house is sold to Asa Spalding, who resides here until he moves to the Gov. Huntington house in 1801. In 1815, Luther Spalding sells the house, office and barn to the State for county uses, and the land between the house and Perit shop for a jail lot. The jail, erected at that time, remains standing until the courts are moved to the Landing, and is then shortly after burnt to the ground. The Perit house becomes the home of the jailer and, from a tree in front, hangs a sign of two crossed keys. In 1835, the county house and jail lot are sold to William Cleveland, who builds for his son-in-law, George D. Fuller (the husband of his daughter Susan), the store now occupied by Herbert W. Hale. The Perit house passes into the possession of Henry Harland, whose heirs retain it for a while. It is then sold, and of late years has had many occupants.

We think that in 1789, Alexander McDonald may have occupied the Perit

OLD HOUSES OF NORWICH.

shop, as a bookseller and book-binder, but it is possible that his location "a few rods north of the court house" may refer to the Woodbridge shop. Gurdon Lathrop establishes himself in the Perit shop for a while in 1791, after leaving the Woodbridge shop across the green. His stock consists of a general assortment of goods, from groceries, hardware, "Russel, Calimanco, and Lasting Shoes," shawls, dress goods, &c., to annotated editions of the Bible. In 1793, this shop is sold to Asa Spalding. In 1794, Gurdon Lathrop moves to a new shop two doors from the corner, and Simon Carew transfers his stock of books from a former stand to the Perit shop in 1795. In 1801, Joseph and Charles P. Huntington are for a while located here. In 1817, the shop comes into the possession of William Cleveland, and after his death, this and the adjoining land and store are deeded by the Cleveland heirs to George D. Fuller. At the present time, the upper part of this building is occupied as a dwelling and the meat-market of Lucius Fenton is located in the basement.

The lane, leading by the market, was laid out in 1699, as an approach to the one and a half acres, which were at the same time "set apart" for "the burying place." In 1704, the town grants liberty to Mr. Woodward "to flood the burying place till the town sees cause to fence it in by itself." According to Miss Caulkins, "the first persons interred in this lot were Dea. Simon Huntington, who died in 1706, and his grandson, Simon, who died of the bite of a rattlesnake, received while mowing in an adjoining lot in 1707. In 1714-15, a committee is appointed to lay out the burying place. In 1734, the inhabitants declare by their vote that the Burying Place, adjoining to the Lott that was Mr. Gookins, shall be laid open to the Common from and after the 1st of September next." Miss Caulkins says in her History of Norwich, "that in 1778 some French troops, on the route from Providence to the south, halted in Norwich for 10 or 15 days on account of sickness. They had their tents spread upon the plain, while the sick were quartered in the court house. About 20 died, and were buried each side of the lane that led into the old burying yard. No stones were set up, and the ground was even smoothed over, so as to leave no trace of the narrow tenements below."

In Dr. Lord's sermon, preached in 1778, he alludes to "20 French prisoners from New York who died here in a few weeks." This may have occurred at the time when Gen. Glover's Irish brigade, under the command of Lafayette, remained for three days in town in that year, though the Packet makes no allusion to any deaths at the time.

In 1796, additional land was purchased of Azariah Lathrop, and again in 1819, of the estate of Simeon Huntington. At this latter date, the other entrance lane was laid out, adjoining the property of Charles Young. In the beginning of this century, two Indians died suddenly on the same day, one a Mohegan, the other a Pequot. The funeral services were held on the square opposite the courthouse, and graves side by side were prepared for them in this burying-ground, but when the time for interment arrived, the Mohegan Indians refused to allow one of their race to lie beside a hated Pequot. So strong was the feeling among those rival races, even at that late day.

John Perr

CHAPTER LX.

OCCUPYING all the land on the south side of the Green, was the home-lot of Maj. Mason of 8 acres, "more or less," abutting north, north-west and east on the highways, south on the river and west on the land of Thomas Waterman. No measurements are given in the record, nor in the sale of the land to the town in 1698. The street line, beginning by the river, extended along the road leading from the present railroad depot, then by the Green, and the Bean Hill road, to a point beyond the residence of Mrs. Hoffman.

Maj. John Mason, the pioneer of the Norwich settlement to whom the people looked for counsel and protection, was born in England about 1601. He is said to have been a relative of John Mason, the New Hampshire patentee, but his parentage and birthplace are unknown. The first knowledge we have of him is in 1630, when he was serving as a lieutenant in the army of the Netherlands It is possible that at that time he was associated with the future commander of the Parlimentary army, Sir Thomas Fairfax, who, as a young man of 18, served for several months in the Netherlands in the spring and summer of 1630. About fifteen years after, in 1645, Sir Thomas Fairfax was made commander-in-chief of the Parliamentary forces, and wrote to Maj. Mason offering him the position of Major General, which honor Major Mason declined.

In 1632, Major Mason appeared at Dorchester, Mass., and is commissioned by the Massachusetts Colony, in company with Capt. John Gallup, to search for a pirate named Dixey Bull, who had been committing depredations on the coast. In 1634, he was one of a committee to plan the fortifications of Boston harbor, and was placed in charge of a battery on Castle Island. In 1635, he was a Representative to the General Court from Dorchester, and shortly after comes to Connecticut, with the colony that settled Windsor in 1636. In April, 1637, the

Pequot Indians made an attack on Wethersfield, and the General Court, alarmed for the safety of the new settlements, declared war against them on May 1st.

By May 10th, an army of 90 men had been raised, which, under the command of Maj. Mason, sailed to Saybrook, and arriving on the 17th, was there wind-bound for two days. The Court instructions were to land at the mouth of the Pequot river, but Mason, finding that the Indians had heard of this intention, concluded to act according to his own judgment, go on to Narragansett and approach them from the rear, though in his written account of the expedition, he advises others not "to act beyond their commission, or contrary to it; for in so doing, they run a double hazard." He also counsels the government "not to bind up" their military leaders "into too narrow a compass. For it is not possible for the wisest and ablest senators to forsee all accidents and occurrences, that fall out in the management and pursuit of a war."

At Saybrook, they were joined by Capt. Underhill and 19 men, and 20 of the former band were sent back to guard the settlements. The small army of 90 men sailed from Saybrook on Friday, the 19th, reaching their landing place on Saturday, the 20th. They kept the Sabbath day aboard ship, and were prevented from landing on Monday by a storm, but on Tuesday evening, the 23rd, Capt. Mason and Capt. Underhill with 77 men disembarked, leaving the others in charge of the vessels. They were joined by 60 Mohegans and several hundred Narragansetts, in all about 500 Indians, who, with the exception of Uncas and a Niantic Sachem named Wequash, all deserted before they reached their destination, where they arrived on the 25th.

The Pequot fort, which they were going to attack, covered a circular area of one or two acres, and was surrounded by a palisade 10 or 12 feet high, formed of trunks of trees, driven into the ground. There were two openings, on opposite sides, obstructed by light bushes or underbrush. Into these two entrances, on the 26th of May, two hours before daylight, Captains Mason and Underhill forced their way, each with sixteen men, the others remaining outside. The barking of a dog gave the alarm, and with the cry of "Owanux! Owanux!" the Indian name for Englishman, the startled Indians rushed from their wigwams. There was a confused firing of muskets and arrows, and Capt. Mason, seeing the need of immediate and decisive action, seized on a brand from one of the wigwams, and set fire to the mats, with which they were covered. The flames, fanned by a north-east wind, spread rapidly, driving Capt. Underhill and his men from the enclosure, and Capt. Mason also retired outside the fort, to be ready to intercept the Indians as they emerged. But out of 700 Indians, who were estimated to be in the fort at this time, only seven escaped and seven were taken captive. The rest were either shot or perished in the flames.

As Capt. Mason says: "Thus did the Lord judge among the heathen, filling the place with dead bodies." Of the English, two were killed and twenty wounded. There were many providential escapes. Lt. Bull had an arrow shot into a hard piece of cheese in his pocket, which as the Captain writes, "may verify the old saying, 'A little armor would serve, if a man knew where to place it.'" The only surgeon had remained on board the ship, and there was no one to attend to the wounded. Major Mason writes: "Our provisions and munition were spent; we in the enemies country," — "our pinnaces at a great distance," and "when they would come, we were uncertain."

But as they were debating what to do, they suddenly saw the ships sailing into Pequot harbor. Sassacus, and about 300 Pequots, appeared from the neighboring fort, and hovering in the rear of the English, obliged them to fight their way to the vessels, carrying their wounded comrades. After they were safely on board the vessels, there was some misunderstanding with Capt. Patrick, and Capt. Mason with twenty of his men landed, and returned on foot to Saybrook. They arrived the same day at the Connecticut river, where, as Capt. Mason says, they were "nobly entertained by Lieut. Gardiner with many great guns." On the next day they reached Saybrook, where they were "entertained with great triumph and rejoicing, and praising God for his goodness to us," for as the Captain adds: "It is He that hath made his work wonderful, and therefore ought to be remembered."

The remainder of the Pequots, with their Sachem, Sassacus, set out to join the Indian tribes in central New York, but as they killed some white people on the way, Mason was sent to intercept them. He surrounded them in a swamp at Fairfield and killed or captured all but 70, who escaped to join the Mohawks.

Thus, by his prompt and brave action, Capt. Mason secured for the Connecticut settlers immunity from Indian attack for a period of nearly forty years.

On his return to Hartford, he was appointed chief military officer of the colony, with the rank of Major, which was equivalent to Major General, his only duty being to "traine the military men in every plantation ten days in every yeere, soe as it be not in June or July." The salary was £40 per annum. In 1654, he was ordered to hold a general review of all the train-bands once in two years.

When Saybrook was transferred to the Connecticut Colony, Capt. Mason was appointed commander of the fort, and moved there in 1647. In the winter of that year, the fort, which was built of wood, caught fire, and was burnt to the ground, with the dwelling house connected with it. Captain Mason, his wife, and one of his children, barely escaped the flames.

The New Haven colony contemplated at one time, making a settlement on the Delaware river, and urged Major Mason to be the leader of the expedition, but the Connecticut colony interposed, and prevailed upon him not to leave them. Not being able to secure the services of Major Mason, the New Haven people were obliged to relinquish their enterprise. By Uncas and the Mohegan Indians, Maj. Mason was loved and revered as a firm friend and protector, but to the other Indian tribes he was often severe, and as Roger Williams writes, "terrible." In public affairs, he was always a prominent figure, serving as Judge of the Courts, member of the Legislature, Commissioner, as arbitrator and agent in all Indian affairs, Deputy Governor for eight years, and Assistant. Miss Caulkins divides his life into four periods:—

"Lieutenant and Captain at Dorchester, . . . 5½ years.
Conqueror of the Pequots, Magistrate and Major, } at Windsor, . . . 12 years.
Captain of the fort and Commissioner of the United Colonies, } at Saybrook, 12 years.
Deputy Governor and Assistant at Norwich, . . 12 years."

On January 30, 1672, as Rev. Simon Bradstreet of New London writes in his journal : "Major John Mason, who had severall times been Deputy Govern^r of Connecticut Colony, dyed. He was aged about 70. He lived the two or three last years of his life in extream misery, with ye stone or strangury, or some such disease. He dyed with much comfort, and assur' it should be well with him."

Trumbull, the historian, describes Maj. Mason as "tall and portly, full of martial fire" as one who "shunned no hardships, or dangers, in the defence and service of the colony."

Norwich may well be proud of her founder, so brave and fearless, yet withal so modest, that he "forbears to mention" any especial matters relating to his own personal action in the encounter with the Pequots, "ascribing all blessing and praise" to God for the success which crowned his undertaking; so wise and prudent in counsel, that he advises that "matters of moment should be handled with ripe advice, poised consultation, and solid conclusions;" though sometimes severe, yet always just in his judgments, and in religious controversies, suggesting that "we look up to God to help us see our evil, and great folly in our needless strife, and contention, and that we unfeignedly and heartily repent and speedily reform."

At last, worn out with pain and suffering, when he can no longer labor for the public good, he resigns his honors and offices, ending his last letter to the General Assembly: —

"Beseeching the God of Peace, who brought again from the dead the Lord Jesus, the great Shepherd of His Sheep, to make us perfect in every good word and work to do his will, into whose hands I commend you, and your mighty affairs, who am your afflicted yet real servant. JOHN MASON."

It is believed that Maj. Mason was twice married, as on the old Church Book of Windsor, among the list of deaths occurring before 1639, is mentioned "the Captain's wife," and at that time he was the only person in the settlement who bore that title. In July, 1639, he was married to Anne Peck (b. 1619), daughter of the Rev. Robert Peck of Hingham, Mass.

This Rev. Robert Peck (b. 1580), was the son of Robert Peck, a wealthy citizen of Beccles, Suffolk Co., England. He graduated at Magdalen College, Cambridge, in 1599, and was ordained rector of St. Andrew's Church, Hingham,

Co. Norfolk, England, in 1605. For "having catechised his family, and sung a psalm in his own house on a Lord's day evening, when some of his neighbors attended," he was so persecuted by the Bishop of the diocese that he fled to New England "with his wife, two children, and two servants," and became the Teacher of the church at Hingham, Mass. When the persecutions in England had ceased, he returned in 1641, and resumed his rectorship of St. Andrew's Church in Hingham, where he died in 1658. His wife, Anne, and his son, Joseph, returned with him, the former dying in 1648, and he married (2) Mrs. Martha Bacon, widow of James Bacon, Rector of Burgate. His daughter, Anne, remained in New England, as the wife of Major Mason.

In the funeral sermon preached "upon the occasion of the Death and Decease of that piously affected, and truely Religious Matron, Mrs. Anne Mason," her son-in-law, Rev. James Fitch, calls upon us to "mark and behold her godly life and happy end." "It is a rare thing to behold such constant freshness of spirit, and affectionate esteeming of communion with God. O with what weakness, and trembling difficulty, and danger to health and life, did she many times come to the public ordinances, but she would purposely conceal her sickness, oftentimes from her near relations, lest in tenderness to her, they should hinder her from going to the publick ordinances. In respect of secret prayer, she had been so acquainted with that ordinance from a child, that she could not charge and accuse herself of any neglect, not so much as one time in thirty years." "Were I able to rehearse the many spiritual, weighty and narrow questions and discourses, I have heard from her, it would fill up a large book." "The Lord having gifted her with a measure of knowledge, above what is usual in that sex—as she had opportunities, by reason of her usefulness to the afflicted, so the Lord supplied her with a word in season. I need not tell you what a Dorcas you have lost— men, women and children are ready with weeping to acknowledge what works of mercy she hath done for them."

The date of her death is unknown, but it is supposed that she died either in or before 1672, the year of her husband's death. They were both probably laid to rest with the other settlers, who died previous to 1700, in the old burying-ground near Bean Hill, but no stones have been found to mark their resting-place.

Priscilla, Major Mason's eldest daughter by his second wife, married in 1664, Rev. James Fitch as second wife; the second daughter, Rachel, became in 1678, the second wife of Charles Hill of New London. Anne married Capt. John Brown of Swansey, and Elizabeth, Capt. James Fitch.

Samuel (b. 1644), married for his second wife, his cousin, Elizabeth Peck, daughter of Joseph Peck, 2nd, of Rehoboth, Mass. Like his father, he was chosen Assistant, and also bore the title of Major. He settled early at Stonington, where he died in 1705.

Daniel Mason, the third son (b. 1652), married (1) in 1676, Margaret, daughter of Edward and Elizabeth (Weld) Denison of Roxbury, Mass., and (2) in 1679, Rebecca Hobart, daughter of the Rev. Peter Hobart of Hingham, Mass. In 1679, he filled the office of schoolmaster in Norwich, but soon after went to Stonington, where he died in 1736-7, aged 85.

The Major's house and home-lot passed into the possession of his second son, John Mason, 2nd, (b. 1646), who early entered into public life, serving as deputy to the General Court in 1672, 1674 and 1675. He received his commission as Lieutenant of the train-band in 1672, and in 1675, was appointed Captain. In this latter year he was severely wounded in the great swamp fight, lingered until September of the next year, when he died at the age of 30. He was chosen Assistant the very year of his death. In the probate of his estate he is called "the worshipful John Mason." He married Abigail, daughter of the Rev. James and Abigail (Whitfield) Fitch and left two children: Anne, who married John Denison of Stonington, and John (b. 1673), afterward known as Capt. John Mason, 3rd. It is possible that the widow, Abigail, went to Lebanon to join her relatives after her husband's death, or perhaps her son may have moved there later.

In 1698, Capt. John Mason, 3rd, (yeoman), of Lebanon, sells the house and home-lot to the town of Norwich. In 1699, when the committee were looking about for a parsonage, though this land is granted to Mr. Woodward, no house is mentioned as standing on the lot, and it may possibly have been burnt or destroyed. If the Major's old home had been standing, it is probable that it would have been used for a parsonage.

Uncas had given to Major Mason, some time previous to the settlement of Norwich, a deed of all the Mohegan lands which were then not occupied by the tribe, and Capt. Mason later surrendered this to the General Court. After the death of Major Mason, his relatives claimed that this deed was only the conveyance of land which the Major held in trust for the Indians, and prevailed upon the latter to urge their claims to the property.

In the meantime a large part of these lands had been deeded to various settlers, and many courts were held in Stonington and Norwich to bring the contest to a settlement. No sooner, however, did the Courts of Commission decide in favor of the Colony, than the Masons would at once appeal to the King. However, in 1767, the English government gave a final decision in favor of the Colony and against the Indians.

Capt. John Mason, 3rd, married (1) Anne, daughter of his uncle Samuel, and (2) in 1719, Anne (Sanford) Noyes, widow of Dr. James Noyes, and daughter of Gov. Peleg Sanford of Rhode Island. He moved from Lebanon to Stonington, then to Montville, where for a while he served as teacher of the Indians, made several journeys to England, and finally died in 1736, in London, where he had gone with Mahomet, grandson of Owaneco, for prosecution of the Indian claims.

CHAPTER LXI.

THE whole church were so united in their approbation of Mr. Benjamin Lord, who was called to preach "on tryal" in 1716, that they extended to him a unanimous call to be their pastor, with the offer of £100 per annum, the use of the parsonage land formerly purchased of Stephen Gifford, and wood sufficient for his use to be dropped at his door, "provided he settle himself without charge to the town." He accepted the call, and was ordained Nov. 20, 1717. He proceeded "to settle himself" by purchasing the Mason home-lot and erecting a house on a site* near the present residence of John Sterry.

At his ordination, the Saybrook Platform was distinctly renounced, and from this time the relations of pastor and people were most harmonious. As Dr. Lord writes: "From a Massah and Meribah, a place of Temptation and Strife, this, in a good measure, became a Salem or place of Peace." In 1721, 1735, and 1740, there were great revivals in the church. In 1744, the pastor and the majority of the people voted to adopt the Saybrook Platform, and again the church became greatly excited, and thirty members, one of whom was Deacon Joseph Griswold, left the church and formed the order known as Separatists. Others joined them, and soon they established a distinct church.

From 1740 to 1772, Dr. Lord was a member of the Corporation of Yale College, and in 1774, he received the degree of D. D. He preached his half-century sermon on Nov. 29, 1767, from II. Peter 1: 12-15. He was then 74 years old. In the fifty-fourth year of his ministry, at his request, a colleague was provided in Joseph Howe, who, however, left in 1773 to become the pastor of the New South Church of Boston. Another colleague was procured in 1777: Joseph Strong of Coventry, Ct. In 1778, Dr. Lord delivered his sixty-first anniversary

---
* See pencil sketch of the Green.

sermon. Both this and his first sermon were published. The sermon preached on his sixty-fourth anniversary was never printed. In his eighty-seventh year his eyesight failed, but he was still able to write his sermons, which his granddaughter, Caroline, used to read over repeatedly to him, so that he was able to deliver them with ease, and some of these were considered by many as among the best of all his discourses. His mind was clear till the last, and, though feeble, he was still able to appear in the pulpit, and occasionally, with the help of his colleague, conduct the services. He preached for the last time "on the Thanksgiving subsequent to the restoration of peace to America, seemingly by a special Providence gratified in living to such a memorable period, which he had often expressed his wish to see." He died March 31, 1784, in the ninetieth year of his age, and the sixty-seventh of his ministry.

His funeral sermon was preached by the Rev. James Cogswell of Windham, from I. Cor. 4: 1. Mr. Cogswell alludes to the beauty of Dr. Lord's character in old age, when "his meekness, humility, philanthropy, and heavenly mindedness were apparently increased, and he seemed to

> ' Stand with his starry pinions on,
> Drest for the flight, and ready to be gone.' "

His funeral was "attended by a respectable number of his own profession, the gentlemen of the Superior Court, and their officers, together with a large concourse of people of almost every denomination, whose very countenance loudly expressed the general loss."* We learn from his obituary in the Norwich Packet, that "his talent at expounding the scriptures, and representing them in their true analogy was singular. The solemn, animated, and commanding manner of his public address was a distinguished part of his character, and exceeded by nothing, unless it was that spirit of prayer, which on every occasion dwelt upon his lips."

"His first prayer, at morning service on the Sabbath, occupied the full run of the hour-glass at his side." How full of interest must this prayer have been to that part of the congregation, which came from the outlying districts, for in it was condensed all the news of the week, public and town events, " deaths, acci-

---
* Norwich Packet.

dents and storms." "In war time, his supplications and thanksgivings were so particular and specific, as to give the congregation the best information, that had been received of the progress of affairs. Notes were sent up to the pulpit, not only in cases of sickness and death, but by persons departing on a journey or voyage, and also on returning from the same. It is said that a petition was once sent up to the pulpit for public prayer in behalf of a man, gone, going or about to go to Boston."*

According to the testimony of the Rev. Joseph Strong, "Dr. Lord was assiduous in visiting the sick and afflicted, a Barnabas to the dejected and feeble-minded, and very skilful in discriminating characters, and making proper applications, and giving suitable advice in soul-troubles."

Dr. Lord was small in stature, and in his old age his figure was bent, yet his face was said to have been attractive and pleasing. He had bright, keen, blue eyes, and was very neat and careful in his dress. He wore an imposing white wig, and silver buckles at his knees and on his shoes. A portrait of him is still extant in the possession of his gr.-gr.-grandson, John Bliss of Brooklyn, L. I., which represents him with hand raised as if in the act of preaching.

Of his wig this tale is told, how John Rogers, the founder of the sect of Rogerenes, who regarded it as his duty to inveigh against the clergy, and especially the observance of the Sabbath, followed Dr. Lord to church one day, using abusive and insulting language, and when Dr. Lord arrived at the church-door, and taking off his hat disclosed his carefully adjusted wig, Rogers exclaimed: "Benjamin! Benjamin! Dost thou think that they wear white wigs in heaven?"

Though Dr. Lord lived to be so old, he was far from strong, and suffered all his life from pain and disease. His first wife, the daughter of Rev. Edward Taylor of Westfield, was also a great invalid. They were married for twenty-eight years, and during sixteen of these she was confined to her bed, and for eight years of that time unable to feed herself. Yet with all these trials, Dr. Lord was still able to attend to all his church duties, and in addition to his long weekly sermons, to prepare for publication eighteen pamphlets or sermons, preached on special occasions.

* Miss Caulkins' History of Norwich.

On his eighty-first birthday he writes in his diary: "It is a wonder to many, and especially to myself, that there are any remains of the man, and the minister at this advanced age, and that I am still able to preach with acceptance to my numerous assembly. It is much that I have survived two former climacterics, in which many have died, and ministers not a few, and still more, that I have lived to this greater climacteric, nine times nine. But the climax is at hand— the certain crisis. Death has not gone by me, not to come upon me."

On his eighty-third birthday he alludes to his being the oldest preaching minister in the State, yet considers himself but "a babe and dwarf in religion," in proportion to its high demands. On the eighty-fifth anniversary of his birth he writes: "Oh, my soul hast thou on the garment of salvation, both inherent and imported righteousness, the one to qualify for heaven, the other to give the title! Art thou the subject of that effectual calling, which is both the fruit and proof or evidence of election?" *

His tombstone in the old burying ground bears the following inscription: "In memory of the Revd Benjn Lord D. D. Blessed with good natural abilities, improved from a liberal Education and refined by Grace, he early dedicated himself to the sacred office, tho' incumbered through life with much bodily infirmity, he executed the social duties of his charge, in a manner which was acceptable and usefull. In 1714, he had conferr'd upon him the highest honors of Yale College, after having been the faithfull Pastor of the 1st Ch. of Ch^t in Norwich for 67 years, he departed this life, March 31st, 1784, Æ 90 – tho' now unconscious in Death may the living hear (or seem to hear) from him the following address.

'Think, Christians, think!
You stand on vast Eternity's dread brink
Faith and Repentance, Piety and Prayer
Despise this world, the next be all your care,
Thus while my Tomb the solemn silence breaks,
And to the eye, this cold dumb marble speaks.
Tho' dead I preach, if e'en with ill success
Living I strove th' important truths to press,—
Your precious, your immortal souls to save,
Hear me at least, O hear me from my Grave.'"

---
* Miss Caulkins' History of Norwich. First Edition.

As we turn from this inscription to the portrait, where the hand is raised, as if in admonition, we can still "hear (or seem to hear)" the old pastor, with his slow, impressive manner, preaching to the people, of whom he said, " I have lived in their hearts, and they in mine." The marble slab, with its conventional grotesque cherub's head carving, has been removed from this tombstone, and ground to powder within the last two years.

The Hon. John T. Wait gives this little anecdote, to show that the good parson did not entirely despise the things of this world. He was invited out to dine on a Thanksgiving day, at the house of one of his deacons, who was troubled with a slight impediment of speech. Beginning to hesitate in his blessing, which was rather lengthy, Dr. Lord at once turned his plate over, and said, " Deacon, this is no time to hesitate, when the turkey is cooling."

Ann Taylor (b. 1697), the first wife of the Rev. Benj. Lord, was the daughter of Rev. Edward Taylor of Westfield, and his second wife Ruth Wyllis. Through her mother, she was descended from two Connecticut governors: Gov. John Haynes and Gov. George Wyllis. The second wife of Dr. Lord was Elizabeth, widow of Henry Tisdale of Newport, R. I., who died in New York shortly after her marriage. His third wife was Abigail Hooker, possibly daughter of Nathaniel and Mary (Standley) Hooker, and great-granddaughter of Rev. Thomas Hooker. She died in 1792, aged 86.

It will be interesting to know how a minister's wife attired herself a little more than 100 years ago, so here are a few items of Abigail's inventory. For gowns, she had among others, "a brown damask," a green "tabby," and a black "taffety," a "grogram," and a black "padusoy," and a "green full suit," and a "reddish-colored silvereth." She had 26 aprons in all, among which were 12 Holland aprons and one of black silk ; of cloaks, to choose from, she had one of black satin, one small black "padusay," and one black velvet fringed cloak. She had also a flowered gauze shade, a crimson cloth riding-hood trimmed with red, two lutestring hoods with gauze, a velvet hood with lace, a black silk bonnet and a gauze scarf, besides 23 caps. Then she had fans of black gauze, of paper, ivory, and bone, six silvered girdles, gloves of black silk, leather, and white-leather, and white mitts, red and blue silk stockings, silk clogs, three strings of gold beads, and a pair of stays,

In his will, the Rev. Benjamin Lord gives to his widow the use of the house for life, and he then divides the house and home-lot (frontage 8 rods, 4 links), between his sons, Benjamin and Ebenezer, the west half to the former, the east part to the latter. The east end of the former Mason lot, where the new school-house now stands, with a frontage of 17 rods on the highway to the river, and of 4 rods, 4 links, on the Green is given to his daughter, Elizabeth. The west part, where the Sterry house now stands, had been sold to Nathaniel Lathrop. Benjamin Lord, 2nd, dies in 1787. He was a farmer, and lived at that time on Plain Hills. Ebenezer Lord died in 1800, and his son, Ebenezer, then occupied the house. Lucy (Lord) Avery, widow of Richard Avery, and daughter of Benjamin Lord, 2nd, resided here in 1825. She married in 1826, Capt. Erastus Perkins. In 1830, the Lord heirs sell the property to William Cleveland, grandfather of President Grover Cleveland. He builds a shop east of the house, where he carries on the business of a goldsmith, until his death in 1837. The house remained in the possession of his heirs, though occupied at times by other tenants, until 1852, when it was burnt to the ground. In the old drawing of the Green, we have a picture of this house and shop.

Joseph Howe, the young colleague provided at Dr. Lord's request in 1772, was born in Killingly, Ct., in 1747. He was the son of the Rev. Perley and Damaris (Cady) Howe of Killingly. He graduated at Yale College in 1765, for a while had charge of the public school in Hartford, and was afterward a tutor at Yale until 1772. In that year he was called to Norwich, and preached alternately with Dr. Lord for a part of 1772 and 1773. While at Yale, we learn from Sprague's "Annals of the American Pulpit," that he was distinguished for his literary accomplishments, and especially for his remarkable powers of elocution, not less than for his fine moral and social qualities."

While at Norwich, he received a call to the New South Church of Boston, which he accepted, leaving for this new field in May, 1773. The poem "Boston Ministers" heralds his arrival in Boston:—

> "At New South now, we hear of Howe,
> A genius, it is said, Sir,
> And there we'll hail this son of Yale—
> There's not a wiser head, Sir."

In the early part of 1775, he fled with many other inhabitants of Boston and sought a refuge in Norwich. "But the anxiety and agitation had affected his health, and after a few weeks, he went to New Haven for change of air, and on his way back stopped at Hartford, where he was taken seriously ill, and died in three weeks, in August, 1775."

"In person, he was tall and slender—his head was rather inclined forward, not from any defect in his form, but from a habit which he had of letting his eyes fall, while engaged in meditation. His complexion was fair, and though his features were somewhat irregular, and by no means strikingly agreeable, his expression was strongly indicative of high intellectual and moral qualities. His efforts in the pulpit were of the most impressive and fascinating kind. In almost every department of literature and science, he had made himself at home. He was distinguished for benevolence and generosity, mildness and courtesy, humility and modesty. One of his most attractive qualities was that he seemed unconscious of the applause which his character and his efforts elicited."*

Miss Ellen D. Larned in her history of Windham County, writes of the Rev. Joseph Howe: "His memory was fondly cherished through all the generation that had known him, and years later, when many of his contemporaries had passed into oblivion, his character was portrayed in that of the model hero, in one of the first original popular tales published in America, 'The Coquette, or the History of Eliza Wharton.'"

---

* Sprague's "Annals of the American Pulpit."

CHAPTER LXII.

IN 1737, Rev. Benjamin Lord sells to Nathaniel Lathrop "8 rods of land of my home lot (formerly John Woodward's,)" with a frontage on the Green of 3 rods, 12½ feet, and on the highway leading to Bean Hill of 15 rods, 7 feet. Nathaniel Lathrop (b. 1693), was the son of Samuel and Hannah (Adgate) Lathrop. In the division of Samuel's property, he receives the farm at Namucksuck, a few miles north of New London, where he resides until 1735, when he moves to Norwich. He married in 1717, Ann, daughter of Joseph and Elizabeth (Huntington) Backus, and had nine children.

On the land purchased of Dr. Lord, he built the house, which became the well-known Lathrop tavern. From here, was started the first line of coaches to Providence in 1768. He also had a shop on the Green, which he was ordered to remove in 1757. He dealt largely in "Flower of Mustard Seed," which he advertises in 1773. He died in 1774, aged 81. His obituary in the Packet says: "He was of a hospitable and charitable disposition, and made the principles of Religion the Rule of his actions, and died a Real Believer in the Promises of the Gospel." His wife died in 1761.

His son, Azariah (b. 1728), succeeded him as landlord of the tavern. He had married in 1764 Abigail, daughter of Isaac and Rebecca (Lathrop) Huntington, and had seven children. He also carries on the trade in "Flower of Mustard Seed," advertising as late as 1791. In 1787, he buys additional land on the east (frontage 2 rods), of Benjamin Lord, and here builds a shop.

Azariah Lathrop was one of the wealthiest citizens of Norwich, and his tavern was one of the best known and prosperous. The Hon. John T. Wait gives various anecdotes of this popular landlord—how when the guests of the inn complained of the cold, used to tell them that "there was plenty of fire in the bar." At one time, card-playing was prohibited by law, so when Azariah approached a room, where it was possible that some of the guests might be indulging in this forbidden amusement, he used to cough loudly, then knock, and when the door was opened, stood with his back turned to the room, that he might truly say he had "never seen anything of the kind in his tavern." His sons were highly respected citizens, and both they and his daughters married into the prominent families of the town. Azariah died in 1810, aged 82, leaving the house to his widow, and son, Augustus, and the shop to his son, Charles. Augustus Lathrop died in 1819, and in 1821, the administrator of the estate sells the tavern to Bela Peck. It was shortly after partly destroyed by fire. In 1829, the land was sold to the Union Hotel Company, who erected the large brick house now standing, which was used for some years as a hotel, but when the courts were moved to the Landing, lost its popularity, was later occupied as a boarding school, and was finally sold to John Sterry, who now occupies it as a summer residence. Charles Lathrop sold his part of the lot to William Cleveland in 1829.

In this tavern were held the winter assemblies, in the room built by Mr. Lathrop with a spring floor for this special purpose. The Hon. Charles Miner says that there was "no formal supper on these occasions, but tea, coffee, tongue, ham, cakes and every suitable refreshment in abundance. Collier with his inimitable violin; Manning with his drum. Order the most perfect, never for a moment, that I heard or saw of, infringed. Contra-dances occupied the evening. The stately minuet had gone out of fashion, and the cotillion not yet introduced. At one o'clock the assembly closed." William Pitt Turner, in a Packet of 1789, satirizes these assemblies and the young beaux of Norwich:—

> "Adieu, adieu to Sans Soucie,
> Cries all the Lads with merry glee,
> The girls, I'm sure if they complain
> Of N ---- h boys, 'twill be in vain.
> For they this winter, strange tho' true,
> Have spent of shillings not a few;
> The fair to please, night-errants stout,
> They've turned their purses wrong side out;
> And to maintain their dancing-sett
> All head and ears, they've run in debt;
> Some to the Cobler for their shoes,
> Some to the Merchant for their cloaths,
> Of jackets, stocks, and cambrick ruffles,
> Silk stockings, hats and plated buckles."

He then proceeds to mention the beaux of the assembly, giving their initials and possibly alludes to himself as:—

> "A Druggist too, that retails Crocus
> Who's noddle's full of hocus pocus,
> With hair that like a fire brand red,
> Or like a gay woodpecker's head,
> Belongs to this great lib'rel ball
> And always meets at ev'ry call."

He alludes to the music furnished by "Cuffee," and to "the dancing master Griffiths," and to "the Landing bucks," who,

> "With heads just fit for barber's blocks,
> Mount their old pacing mares, & prance
> To this expensive merry dance."

In this tavern in 1774, Jabez Smith advertises as "a teacher of Psalmody," and of the "scale, fife, and German flute." In 1797, a Mr. Marriott informs the people of Norwich that he intends to amuse them at Mr. Lathrop's tavern, with a performance entitled "Brush upon Brush, or a Pill for the Spleen," price of admittance 1s. 6d. Again Moulthorp and Street exhibit here these wax works, among which figure, "The Beauty of Norwich," "David bearing the head of Goliath," "Maj. Andre taking leave of his Honoria," &c., &c.

CHAPTER LXIII.

THE early courts which met in Norwich were held either in private houses, or the meeting-house. In 1720, money was raised, and an unsuccessful attempt was made to have the county court hold some of its sessions here. In 1735, another effort was more fortunate. Norwich was made a half-shire town, and a court-house, whipping-post, and pillory were erected on the south corner of the parsonage lot. The key of the court-house was given into the custody of Capt. Joseph Tracy in 1736, and a room in the attic was made to hold the town's stock of ammunition, and a fine of 5 s. imposed on any man, "who shall smoke it in the time of sessions of any town meeting." In 1745, the care of the town house was committed to Philip Turner; in 1755, to Benjamin Lord.

This court-house was so dilapidated in 1759, that it was voted to build a new one 48 or 50 feet × 26 or 28 feet in size, on the south-east corner of the plain, in front of the old one. The building was finished in 1762. A powder-house was also built in 1760, on the hill near the path leading to the meeting-house. This was blown up in 1784. A train of powder, laid by some unknown person, was discovered one-half hour before the explosion, but not a person could be found courageous enough to extinguish it. Everyone was warned to get out of the way. The stone powder-house was blown to atoms. Only one of the stones could be afterward identified, and this descended through the roof of a house and two floors, and landed in the cellar. A bag of canister shot entered one of the windows of the parsonage. The meeting-house was greatly damaged, also some of the neighboring houses, and all the window panes in the vicinity were shattered.*

Shortly after the erection of the new court-house, Samuel Huntington, then a young attorney just entering into business, petitioned the town for liberty to use and improve the north-east chamber in the court-house for a writing-office, "except in Term-time, at a Reasonable rent," and if the town will grant his request and give him the key, "he will promise to take all proper care," &c., &c.

In this court-house, in 1767, was read the famous Boston circular, and a committee of prominent citizens was formed to draw up a report for the next meeting. This consisted of an agreement not to import or to use articles of foreign manufacture or produce, such as tea, wines, liquors, silks, china, &c. Linens, low-priced broadcloths, and felt hats were excepted. It was also voted to encourage all domestic manufactures. One clause reads: "And it is strongly recommended to the worthy ladies of this town, that for the future, they would omit tea-drinking in the afternoon; and to commission-officers, to be moderate and frugal in their acknowledgments to their companies, for making choice of them as officers, which at this distressing time will be more honorable than the usual lavish and extravagant entertainments heretofore given." This report, however, closes with the determination to remain "loyal subjects to our Sovereign Lord the King, holding firm and inviolable our attachment to and dependence on our mother country."

Homespun dresses and Labrador tea became the fashion. The latter was made from the dried leaves of the *Ceanothus Americanus*, now well known under the name of New Jersey tea.

* Miss Caulkins' History of Norwich. First Edition.

In 1774, a circular from the Boston Committee of Correspondence, calling for resistance to the oppressive laws of the mother country, brought out so vast an audience, that they were obliged to adjourn from the court-house to the meeting house for better accommodation. A Standing Committee of Correspondence was appointed of five of the leading citizens:—

CAPT. JEDIDIAH HUNTINGTON.   CHRISTOPHER LEFFINGWELL, ESQ.
DR. THEOPHILUS ROGERS.   CAPT. WILLIAM HUBBARD.
CAPT. JOSEPH TRUMBULL.

All through the Revolution, the Norwich citizens, with but few exceptions, were staunch in their patriotism, and numerous and enthusiastic meetings were held in this court-house. To all appeals for aid to the army, the people of Norwich made a generous and immediate response.

In 1784, "a new," and as a correspondent of the Norwich Packet says, "a most pompous" City Hall was erected in New London, and the question was raised, whether if £5000 of the county money must be laid out in county buildings, whether Norwich, "who pays double the tax of New London, in justice ought not to have some proportion of the money agreeable to the tax? or so far at least as to paint and repair the Court House, build a house for the Goal Keeper, and remove the old one."

However, the Norwich Court-House was destined to last for many years longer, though in 1793, the courts complained loudly of its ruinous condition. The town thought the county should pay the expense of repairs or build a new one. In 1798, the house was thoroughly repaired and painted, and money raised to move it from the Green. In this year, Eleazer and Elizabeth Lord, who had inherited from the Rev. Benjamin Lord the land on the north-east corner of his home-lot, sold to the town land "to extend as far south as shall be necessary for the purposes of placing a county court-house south of a line drawn from the north-west corner of Ebenezer Lord's dwelling house to the west side of Eleazer Lord's north door of his dwelling house," &c. To this lot the court-house was moved and remained standing until 1891.

Between the years 1809 and 1833, the attempts made to move the courts to the Landing were strenuously opposed by the town. Three times the matter was brought before the General Assembly, who, in 1833, referred it to the New London County Representatives, who finally decided on removal. The town then sent in a petition, asking to be separated from the city, which was granted.

The whipping-post and pillory were in frequent requisition in the early years of the town. In 1773, the Packet mentions the punishment of three negroes, one with 6 lashes, the other with 8, for striking some white people; and two white men, convicted of burglary, receive, one 15 lashes, and the other 6. A man arrested in this year for horse-stealing is sentenced to receive 15 stripes, to be imprisoned one month in the workhouse, and to pay a fine of £10, costs and damage. Another, for burglary, receives 6 stripes, and pays 20 s. fine and £15 costs. For manslaughter, an Indian is branded in the hand, receives 39 lashes, and forfeits his goods.

In 1785, one of "the light-fingered gentry" receives at the post "the discipline of the whip," and a man, convicted of horse-stealing, receives his chastisement, as he "sets on the wooden horse." In 1787, another sufferer for horse-stealing "rides the wooden horse" for an hour, is whipped 25 stripes, fined £10, imprisoned for 6 weeks, and is then sold to pay the costs. However, his punishment is so far ameliorated, that he "rides the horse," and receives 15 stripes on one day and the balance of 10 stripes on the first Monday of the next month. A man convicted of forgery is sentenced to stand in the pillory for three public days, for the space of fifteen minutes each day.

The penalties for breaking the seventh commandment were very severe. The offenders, if church members, were obliged to appear before the church, and make public confession of their fault, and were also censured and punished by the civil authorities. In 1743, a man and a married woman of well-known and respected families were, for this offence, sentenced "to be branded in the forehead with the letter A on a hot iron," "to were a halter about the neck on the outside of the garment" during their "abode in this colony," "so it may be visible," to pay the cost of prosecution which, in the woman's case, amounted to £3 9 s. 9 d., in the man's, to £4 17 s. 3 d., to be whipped "on the naked body," the woman to receive "23 strips," the man 25, and "to stand committed until this sentence be performed."

The court-house also served as a theatre. On Dec. 15, 1791, the tragedy of "Douglas," and Foote's farce, "The Mayor of Garrat," were given by "Messrs. Solomon & Murry;" and on Dec. 22, of the same year, the comedy of "The Citizen, or Old Square Toes Outwitted," and "The Female Madcap," and a ballad farce called "The Elopement." The tickets for admission were 1 s. 6 d.

On February 19, 1792, "The Poor Soldier" and "The Mock Doctor," were given for 9 d. a ticket, children half-price. On February 16 of the same year a number of young ladies and gentlemen of the city took part in the tragedy of "Gustavus," and the comedy called "The Mistakes of a Night." The entertainment began at 6 o'clock.

In March of that year, a part of the tragedy of "Ulysses" was given, and a comedy called "Flora, or Hob in the Well," a part of the tragedy of "Sophonisba" and a farce called "The Miser, or Thieves and Robbers," the exercises to begin at 7 o'clock.

Mrs. Sigourney describes the singing school held in the court-house: "Behind a broad table, where in term time the lawyers took notes of evidence, or rectified their briefs, sat we girls of the novitiate, technically called 'the young treble.' In the gallery, raised a few steps above, sat the older and more experienced singers. When discords occurred, the master, standing in a listening attitude, with more knowledge of music than of grammar, would exclaim, 'There its them young treble.'"*

In the court-house were often held the dancing-classes, under a variety of teachers. The first dancing master of whom we have any knowledge, Mr. Griffiths, in 1787, held his classes not in the court-house but in "the house of the widow Billings." As there were two of that title in town, it is difficult to say which was intended, but we believe it to have been the house of the widow Mary Billings, which was on the "Cross highway." Mr. Griffiths advertises to teach "Minuets and a Duo Minuet (which are entirely new), Cotillion Minuet, and new Country Dances, with the real step for dancing," and his terms were $6 for the first quarter, $4 for the second. In 1793, a Providence dancing master appears in town, and in 1797, John C. Devero (or Devereux), whom Mr. Charles Miner describes "as an Irish gentleman of a titled family, whom the war had embarassed,"

* "Letters of Life."

who, "with a noble spirit of independence, rather than sit down in indigence and despair," opened a dancing school in the court-house at Norwich, and also had classes in Bozrah, Franklin, and two or three neighboring towns. Mr. Miner says that Mr. Devereux afterward became one of the wealthiest citizens of Utica, N. Y., and president of the United States Branch Bank.

Mrs. Sigourney's first dancing master was a Frenchman, "whose previous history not even Yankee perseverance could elicit. He bore the sobriquet of Colonel, and was disturbed at the name of Bonaparte. He was tall, gaunt, well-stricken in years, and impassable beyond aught what we had seen of his mercurial race. His style of instruction betrayed his military genius. He would have made an excellent drill sergeant. We were under a kind of martial law. During the hours of practice, not a whisper was heard in our camp. The girls received elementary instruction mornings, and when a particular grade of improvement was attained, met and mingled with the other sex for two hours in the evening. Being his own musician, and executing with correctness on the violin, he required a strict adaptation of movement to measure. At his cry of 'Balancez' we all hopped up in a line, like so many roasted chestnuts. Low obeisances, lofty promenades to solemn marches, and the elaborate politeness of the days of Louis Quatorze were inculcated. Many graceful forms of cotillion he taught us, and some strange figures called horn-pipes, in which he put forth a few of his show pupils on exhibition days. They comprised sundry absurd chamois leaps, and muscle wringing steps, throwing the body into contortions. He gave out words of command as if at the head of a regiment. As imperative was he, as Frederick the Great, and we as much of automatons as his soldiers."* Every separate term closed with a ball, when beaux and belles of a more advanced age joined in the festivities. On these occasions, only, the dancing lasted beyond 9 o'clock.

In 1823, a Mr. Fuller was the dancing master, and taught his pupils "how to enter, and leave a room, to walk gracefully and to take the long allemand." Contra-dances such as "Chester Castle," "The Hay Dance," "Turnpike Gate," "Life let us cherish," "Opera Reel," "Durang's Hornpipe" and "Patty Carey," seem at this time to have superseded the more graceful minuet.

* Mrs. Sigourney's "Letters of Life."

After the courts were moved to the Landing, the old court-house was sold in 1835 to be used as a school-house, and served in that capacity until 1891, when a new school-building was erected, and the old structure was destroyed.

CHAPTER LXIV.

AT the south-east corner of the Green, near the residences of the Rev. Mr. Fitch and Maj. Mason, stood the earliest meeting-house of Norwich. This was probably a plain, rough, barn-like structure without steeple, porch, or gallery. In 1668, a rate was collected to pay Samuel Lathrop, for "repairing and heightening" it, and in 1673, thirteen years after its erection, the town contracted with John Elderkin and Samuel Lathrop, for "the building of" a new house of worship. This was to have a "gallery, and trough to carry the water from the roof." The site chosen was on the hill, overlooking the greater part of the township.

At this time, before King Philip's war, when Indian attacks were constantly expected, the inhabitants may have thought (as Miss Caulkins suggests), that on this lofty site, commanding an extensive outlook, the building might serve "as a watch-tower, and garrison-post, as well as a house of worship." So great was the dread of Indian invasion, that the settlers carried their muskets to church, and stacked them outside. A guard was set to watch, and the militia sat near the door to be ready in case of alarm.

The new meeting-house was finished in 1675. The estimated cost was £428, but John Elderkin claimed that the expense had much exceeded this sum, and for compensation the town gave him a grant of land near the mouth of Poquetanneck Cove. To James Fitch, who had generously furnished nails to the value of £12, a grant of 200 acres was given, 100 of which were situated "on the other side" of the Shetucket, and 100 "in the crotch" of that river and the Quinebaug. In the winter time, when the winds howled and whistled around this church in its exposed position, how cold and cheerless it must have been, and how little could have availed the foot-muffs and heated stones to keep the congregation warm.

In 1689, Lt. Leffingwell, Ensign William Backus, Dea Thomas Adgate, and Sergt. Waterman were appointed a committee "to consider and contrive to the enlargement of the meeting-house." A lean-to was added, in which several new pews were made.

In 1697, Samuel Post, John Waterman, Daniel Huntington, Jabez Hyde, Caleb Abel, Caleb Bushnell, Thomas Leffingwell, John Gifford, John Tracy, Joseph Bushnell and Samuel Abel were allowed "to build a seat on the east side of the Meeting-house on the Leanto beams, for their convenient sitting on the Lord's Dayes."

At a town meeting March 28, 1698, the seats were divided into eight classes, and Lt. Leffingwell, Lt. Backus, Dea. Simon Huntington, Dea. Thomas Adgate, and Sergt. John Tracy were directed to seat the people according to rank, the seats varying "in dignity," in the following order:—

"1. The square pue, the first in Dignity.

2. The New Seate and the fore seate in the broad alley the next and alike in Dignity.

3. The second seate in the broad ally, and the first long seate next and alike in Dignity.

4. The third seate in the broad ally next in Dignity.

5. The fourth seat in the broad ally next in Dignity.

6. The first Long seate in the Leanto and the fore seate in the Gallery, the first seate in the Lower teer in the leanto and the fifth seat in the broad ally next and alike in Dignity.

7. The sixth seate in the broad alley, and the second long seate in the leanto next and alike in Dignity.

8. The second seate in the lower teer in the leanto, and the seventh seate in the broad alley next and alike in Dignity."

In 1705, it was agreed "to claboard and shingle, when claboards and shingles are wanting, to repaire the staircase and stairs, to mend the piramid, and to close the leanto roofs, where they join to the border of the meeting-house," and to be at no further charge at present. From these changes, we can form some idea of the architecture of this early church building. At this date, according to the old highway survey, the first old meeting house was still standing on the corner of the plain.

In 1708, Capt. René Grignon, who had recently come to Norwich, presented the town with a bell, which is supposed to have been brought from France to Oxford, Mass., by a band of French exiles, who had settled that town, and were finally driven from thence by Indian attacks. Capt. Grignon, who was one of these Huguenot exiles, then brought the bell with him to Norwich. The town "thankfully accept it," and decree "that it shall be hung in a usable place, and shall be ringed at all times as is customarie in other places where there are bells." It must have been a great satisfaction to the Norwich settlement to receive this gift from Capt. Grignon, as the New London church had already possessed a bell since 1691. It was decided to hang it on the hill, suspended from a scaffolding on the ridge west of the meeting-house, near the path, by which the inhabitants of the west end of the town came "cross lots" to meeting. In 1709-10, Isaac Cleveland was engaged for £5 10 s. per year, "to ring the bell on publick days, and at 9 o'clock in the evening as is customary."

In 1709-10 it was voted to build a new meeting-house, either 50 feet square or not to exceed in dimension 55 feet × 45, and a great discussion arose as to the proper site, some preferring the old situation on the hill, others the more accessible plain. It was finally referred to a committee of three of the principal citizens of Lebanon,* who decided for the plain. The frame was set up, but the inhabitants were still dissatisfied. Another meeting was called, at which only

* Capt. William Clark, William Halson (perhaps Halsey) and Samuel Huntington.

Ground Plan of the Norwich Town Church 1756-1761

Front (Pulpit area)

Pew	Occupants
Pulpit / Deacon's Seat	
No 1, 14£	Isaac Huntington
No 2, 17£	Asa Lathrop / Asa Lord
No 3, 17£	Benj Wheat
No 4, 16£	E. Lord / Jr. Waties / E. Bill / S. Wetmore
No 5, 13£	Noah Abel / Jabez Dean / Enoch Myers
No 6, 7£	Jeremiah Huntington
No 7, 6£	Moses Tracy / Daniel Douglass
No 8, 7£	John Huntington
No 9, 7£	Charles Winship

North Door

Pew	Occupants
No 10, 6£	Ebenezer Case / Joshua Prior
No 11, 6£	Aaron Chapman / Caleb Norman
No 12, 5£	Eleazer Burnham
No 13, 5½£	Joseph Winship
No 14, 10£	Richard Hyde / Stedman / Daniel Burnham
No 15, 15£	
No 16, 19£	Perkins Marsh
No 17, 21£	Joshua Lathrop
No 18, 23£	Daniel Lathrop
No 19, 23£	Jabez Huntington
No 20, 21£	Hannah Lynde
No 21, 19£	Zachariah Huntington
No 22, 15£	William Lathrop / John Bliss
No 23, 10£	Asa Turner / Simeon Huntington

Great Door 6ft 5in

Pew	Occupants
No 24, 4£	N. Parrish
No 25, 6£	Oliver Arnold / Cary Lunn
No 26, 7£	Elisha Tracy
No 27, 7£	Tom Danforth / Gideon Fitch
No 28, 7£	Ebenezer Backus
No 29, 6£	Abigail Backus / Mattew Adgate
No 30, 7£	

South Door

Pew	Occupants
No 31, 13£	Francis Griswold
No 32, 16£	Eben Huntington / Simon Huntington
No 33, 17£	Hez Huntington
No 34	For the Minister's Family

Interior pews

No 35, 23£	No 36, 21£	No 37, 20£	No 38, 19£	No 39, 18£
Scales				

No 35, 22£ Richard Bushnell	No 36, 21£	No 37 £20	No 38, 19£ John Hughes	No 39, 18£
No 56, 9£	No 57, 21£ William Morgan	No 58, 23£ Thomas Lathrop		
No 55, 19£ Mattew Adgate	No 66, 20£ John Louden			
No 54, 18£ Samuel Gifford / John Abel				
No 53, 14£ Tom Carew				
No 52, £12.0 Starr	No 51, 12£ Agate / Philip Turner / Bela Turner	No 50, 9£ Samuel Starr		

No 40, 14£	No 41, £12.0.0 Daniel Bichard / Peter Huntington
No 42, 12£ Joseph Reynolds	No 43, 9£ Nash Shipman / Samuel Abbot
No 60, £12.100 Barnabas Bushnell Perkins Bushnell	No 61, 12£ Benjamin Lord / Eleazer Lord Jr
No 44, £10.100	

No 62, 19£ Simon Tracy / Simon Tracy Jr	No 45, £18.100 Berachel Arnold
No 63, 21£ Daniel Tracy / Samuel Tracy	No 46, £20.10.0 John Leffingwell
No 64, 21£ Simon Lathrop	No 47, £20.10.0 Ebenezer Lathrop
No 65, 19£ T. Leffingwell	No 48, £18.100 Samuel Leffingwell
No 66, 12£ Samuel Bushwith / Peter Morgan	No 49, £10.00 Benajah Leffingwell
No 67, £12.10	

Robert Roath (No 39, 18£)
Azariah Lathrop (No 69, 9£)

Plan of the Gallery of the Norwich Town Church

	Pew	£ s d	Occupants
No. 1	3£ 5		
No. 2	5£		
No. 3	5£		
No. 4	5£		James Thomas, Philip Turner
No. 5	5£		
No. 6	4£		
No. 7	5£ 0		Simeon Huntington, Ebenezer Crew, Isaac Tracy
No. 8	6£ 0		James Huntington, Ebenezer Hartshorn, James Backus
No. 9	6£ 0		Seth Huntington
No. 10	6£ 0		James Calkins
No. 11	6£ 0		
No. 12	6£ 0		John Huntington
No. 13	6£		
No. 14	6£ 0		
No. 15	5£		
No. 16	5£		
No. 17	5£		
No. 18	5£		
No. 19	5£		
No. 20	5£		

4 feet wide

Daniel Lathrop
Joseph Lathrop
Gurdon Huntington
Henry Lathrop 2d
Joseph Lothwell

twenty-eight persons voted, and of these twenty-seven were in favor of the hill, so there it was finally built, near the site of the old church, which last building was sold in 1714-15, to Nathaniel Rudd of West Farms, for £12 5 s. 6 d. The difficulty and expense of moving this edifice from its elevated site must have been great, and Nathaniel complained to the town, that he was "sick of his bargain," so the price was reduced to £5 10 s. The old pews, pulpit, and canopy were carried to West Farms or Franklin, and were later used in the Franklin meeting house which was erected in 1718.

The new church was completed in 1713. Lands were granted to all who had contributed labor or money toward its erection. Ensign Thomas Waterman, "for his labor and cost in providing stones for steps at the meeting house doors," received 22 acres at the Landing Place. Miss Caulkins describes one of the fixtures of this 1707 meeting-house, "an hour-glass, set in a frame, and made fast to the pulpit (cost 2 s. 8 d.) This hour-glass was placed in 1729 under the particular charge of Capt. Joseph Tracy, who was requested to see that it was duly turned, when it ran out in service time, and that the time was kept between the meetings, the bell man being charged to attend his orders herein."

In 1748, it was voted to build a fourth church, which was not, however, begun until 1753. In 1752, it was voted to "remove all incumbrances from the west side of the meeting-house plain under the site of ye Great Rock by ye Town Street," and here, where the present church stands, the frame of the fourth meeting house was built, the bell hung, and the clock set in its place, but a sufficient sum not having been raised to complete it, it remained in an unfinished state for several years. It was not completed until 1770. It is said that the Rev. Mr. Whitefield preached in this church, while in its unfinished condition, and fifteen years after, when he again came to Norwich, it was still unaltered. He publicly reproved the congregation for their neglect, and efforts were made to complete the work. The galleries were built, the stone steps set up, and finally in 1769, a vote was passed to "colour" the meeting-house. It is said to have been "a square building, with doors on three sides, and a front porch, or platform. The house was furnished with pews, except there were slips in front of the pulpit for aged men and strangers, with low benches in the aisles for the children.*" On the front of the pulpit canopy was the motto in large letters, "Holiness becometh God's house." In 1791, this motto was removed, as a correspondent in the Norwich Packet explains, "out of complaisance and in conformity to an act of the General Assembly, to secure the rights of conscience to Christians of every denomination."

On the Sabbath, Miss Caulkins says, "the deacon lined the psalm, and the congregation, under the guidance of one or two leaders, who faced them from the front of the pulpit, sung in their seats. Choir singing was considered a great innovation, and the new tunes were frowned upon as too lively and worldly, by the older people, who missed the old time quavers."

Mrs. Sigourney writes: "It was the custom of the church to employ a competent teacher† for several months in the year, to train the young people in the melodies of Sabbath worship." For the rest of the time, the choir were instructed by the regular choir leader. From the simple tune of "Lebanon," they were led on gradually to "complex music, elaborate anthems, and some of the noble compositions of Handel." "After the reading of the psalm or hymn on Sundays," the leader "rose in his place, enunciating audibly the name of the tune to be sung, giving the key-tone through the pitch-pipe, then raising high his hand to beat the time." "The taste of the congregation was for that plain, slow music, in which the devotion of their fathers had clothed itself." The leader had a great love "for those brisk fugues, where one part leads off, and the rest follow with a sort of belligerent spirit."

"One Sabbath morning," Mrs. Sigourney narrates, "he gave out a tune of a most decidedly lively and stirring character, which we had taken great pains in practicing. Its *allegro, altissimo* opening,

> 'Raise your triumphant songs
> To an immortal tune,'

startled the tranquillity of the congregation, as though a clarion had sounded in their midst. The music, being partly antiphonal, comprehended several stanzas. On we went complacently, until the two last lines,

---

* In 1778, John Bliss was paid £37 11s. 6d. for work on the bell and tower of the church.
† The Hon. Charles Miner mentions "Roberts, the famed singing master," who "infused his own impassioned soul" into the singers.

> 'No bolts to drive their guilty souls
> To fiercer flames below.'

Off led the treble having the air, and expending con spirito, upon the adjective 'fiercer,' especially its first syllable, about fourteen quavers, not counting semis and demis. After us came the tenor, in a more dignified manner, bestowing their principal emphasis on 'flames.'

'No bolts, no bolts' shrieked a sharp counter of boys, whose voices were in the transition state. But when a heavy bass, like claps of thunder, kept repeating the closing word 'below' and finally all parts took up the burden, till in full diapason, 'guilty souls,' and 'fiercer flames below' reverberated from wall to arch, it was altogether too much for Puritanic patience. Such skirmishing had never before been enacted in that meeting-house. The people were utterly aghast. The most stoical manifested muscular emotion. Our mothers hid their faces with their fans.

Up jumped the tithing man, whose office it was to hunt out and shake refractory boys. The ancient deacons slowly moved in their seats at the foot of the pulpit, as if to say, 'Is not there something for us to do in the way of church government?' As I came down from the gallery, a sharp, gaunt Welsh woman seized me by the arm, saying, 'What was the matter with you all, up there? You began very well, only too much like a scrame. Then you went gallivanting off like a parcel of wild colts, and did not sing the tune that you begun not at all.'"* How the shrill-voiced old lady who could not sing, should know what the new tune was, or ought to be, Mrs. Sigourney was not given to understand.

In 1745, a new clock was placed in the belfry. In 1772, Watts' version of the Psalms was introduced into the service. In 1783, the society, using as a nucleus the £500 left by Dr. Daniel Lathrop in 1782 for the support of the ministry, started a subscription, and a large sum was raised, the pew-holders were induced to relinquish their rights, so that the pews might be sold yearly, and enough money was thus collected to accomplish what had been so long desired, the abolishing of the minister's rate. The first annual sales of pews took place in 1791.

---

* Mrs. Sigourney's "Letters of Life."

In 1792, the church, with but "one dissenting voice," voted to have an organ. This "one dissenting voice was that of a man, who," the Weekly Register says, "had lived a bachelor to the age of 43," and was incapable of having "any music in his soul." It seems he believed that "instrumental music was apt to excite ideas of levity." The efforts to procure an organ at this time were, however, unsuccessful, and the change was not made until some years later.

In 1801, the church and the neighboring store and house were burnt to the ground, and with money raised partly by subscription, and partly by a lottery, the present church was built. A copy of the subscription paper for the building of this meeting-house is now in the possession of Mrs. George B. Ripley of Norwich. The first names on the list are Dr. Joshua Lathrop and sons, who contribute $300. The other subscriptions range from $100 to $5. The sum of $2,016½ was raised in this manner and there were also some conditional subscriptions. John Backus gives $66 "with $34 more added, provided that $3,000 is obtained on this subscription." Simon Huntington will give $20, "on condition the incumbrances be removed." Elisha Tracy adheres to his former declaration "made to the committee and others," that "in case the House is put in the Center of Travel, he will give $333.34, in case the house is put on the Hill he will build ½ of the House, cost what it will. Provided the House is built under the Hill & the bell hung on the Hill he will give $100, if neither of these conditions are complied with, he thinks buying a Pew is all he ought to do."

"For having the Meeting House on, or nigh where it stood before, there were 58 votes; for having it on the Rocks 27." Fifty-four persons were in favor of "having the Bell on the Meeting House," and twenty-four for "having a crotch built on the Rocks for hanging the Bell." The building committee were Elisha Hyde, John Backus, Christopher Leffingwell, Zachariah Huntington, Dr. John Turner, Ebenezer Huntington and Thomas Lathrop.

Miss Caulkins describes the laying of the corner-stone by Gen. Ebenezer Huntington on the 18th of June: "Only a few words were uttered, but they were of solemn import: 'May the house raised on this foundation, become a temple of the Lord, and the dwelling place of the Holy Spirit.' A throng of spectators murmured their assent, and young people standing above on the rocks, waved their green boughs. Dr. Strong, the pastor, then offered prayer."*

In the style of church architecture, this edifice displayed a great advance over all other churches in this part of the State. "It had groined arches, massive

pillars to support the gallery and a central dome painted sky-blue; but it retained the old form of a high contracted pulpit, and square pews. In 1845, the interior was entirely remodelled, and since that period it has been a second time renovated and improved." Its earlier appearance is given in the sketch of the Green.

At the beginning of this century, there was a great rage for Lombardy poplars, which, according to a newspaper article of 1802, "not only gave the country a gay and pleasant aspect, but also purified and refreshed the air." A Rhode Island gentleman established a nursery of them, and offered, when they were sufficiently grown, to distribute them gratis to anyone who would set them out for the public good. About 1803, they were thickly planted about the church and plain. On July 21, 1824, a young girl writes in her journal, "This morning,

* Miss Caulkins' History of Norwich.

when I came to school, saw that the beautiful poplars which were by the meeting-house had been cut down."

In 1810, stoves were first used in the church. In 1824, the bass-viol gave place to the organ. The first Sabbath School was held in the court-house in 1820. In 1852, the present chapel was presented by Mrs. Harriet Peck Williams. The regularly ordained pastors of this church from the settlement of the town to the present day, are as follows:—

    Rev. James Fitch,   1660 – 1694.
    Rev. John Woodward,   1699 – 1716.
    Rev. Benjamin Lord,   1717 – 1784.
    Rev. Joseph Strong,   1784 – 1834.
      (Colleague pastor from 1778 – 1784).
    Rev. Cornelius Everest,   1834 – 1836.
      (Colleague pastor from 1829 – 1834).
    Rev. Hiram P. Arms,   1836 – 1873
      (Pastor Emeritus from 1873 – 1882).
    Rev. William C. Scofield,   1873 – 1875.
    Rev. Charles Theodore Weitzel,   1876 – 1885.
    Rev. Charles Addison Northrop, ordained, 1885.

CHAPTER LXV.

BETWEEN the chapel and Mediterranean Lane, was formerly situated the home-lot of Stephen Gifford. Though it is generally supposed that he was one of the original settlers of the town, his name is not included in the list, which we believe to have been made by Dr. Lord. He was born about 1641, so at the time of the settlement was about nineteen years of age. In 1667, he married Hannah, daughter of John and Rhoda —— Gore of Roxbury, Mass. She died in 1670-1, and in 1672, he married another Hannah, daughter of John and Hannah (Lake) Gallup of Stonington, Ct. In 1686, he was chosen one of the constables of the town. He lived to be very old, dying in 1724, and was buried in the old burying-ground near the Green, where his grave-stone and that of his wife, who died in the same year (1724), still remain.

In 1697, Stephen Gifford sells to the town "all that my home lott, with the house, orchard and fences about it . . . scittuated lying and being in the town of Norwich,"—"contayning six acres more or less, abutting on the Town Common eastwardly 20 rodds, abutting on a highway into the woods Northeasterly 20 rodds, abutting Northerly on land of Abraham Dayns 30 rodds, abutting westerly 44 rods, abutting southwardly on the Commons 24 rods—as also six acres more or less adjoineing to the sd home lott abutting southeasterly on the sd home lott 20 rodds to the corner of the stone wall, abutting Northwest on Commons 60 rodds, abutting northeast on Commons 60 rods to the highway abutting east by the highway to the first corner."

Stephen Gifford moves to the Great Plain, and in 1699 this land is granted to the Rev. Mr. Woodward on his settlement in Norwich, and is afterward known as the "parsonage lot." The house is not mentioned in the deed of settlement, and had possibly either been destroyed by fire, or removed from the lot. In

1714-15, the town allows Mr. Woodward "to fence in the Gifford lot leaving convenient room about the new meeting-house."

After Mr. Woodward's departure, the land is granted to the next pastor, the Rev. Benjamin Lord. In 1735, the first court-house is built on the south corner of this lot. In 1759, it was voted to treat with Mr. Lord about "the sail" of a part of the "parsonage" lands. This matter was, however, not arranged until many years after. Many lots were leased or sold to various persons by Rev. Mr. Lord, but the only records of lease are to be found in private account books, and the few deeds of sale on record give such indefinite measurements and bounds, that it is difficult to locate the lots, or to tell in what manner they were occupied. The Chelsea Church Society laid claim to a share of the parsonage land, but the property was finally adjudged to the First Church Society. The first purchasers were then induced to resign their lands to the church, and between the year 1786 and 1799, new leases for a period of 999 years were granted to them.

The land next to the church, on which the chapel stands, belonged to the town, but was not a part of the original Gifford or "parsonage" lot. Here in 1762, twenty-six rods of land were laid out to Ebenezer Lord, "where his house and shop stand," beginning at the south corner of his shop, "then running northwest on the line of his shop, and on the stone-wall 9½ rods to a point, thence bounded northeast on the land called Parsonage 11 rods, thence abutting southeast, the front of sd house and shop in the line 4 rods, 13 feet, to the first corner."

Ebenezer Lord was the son of Rev. Benjamin Lord, and his first wife, Ann Taylor. He was born in 1731, and married in 1760, Temperance Edgerton, daughter of John and Phoebe Edgerton. The house and shop were sold in 1774 to Dudley Woodbridge. Whether Ebenezer at this time went to reside with his father or not we do not know, but at the death of his father in 1784, he inherited one-half of the house and resided there till his death in 1800.

Dudley Woodbridge (b. 1747), son of Dr. Dudley and Sarah (Sheldon) Woodbridge of Stonington, Ct., was the descendant of a long line of ministers: the Rev. John Woodbridge of Andover and Newbury, Mass.; the Rev. John of Killingworth (now Clinton), and Wethersfield, Ct.; and the Rev. Ephraim of Groton, Ct. He was also a gr.-gr.-gr.-grandson of Gov. Thomas Dudley of Massachusetts, and a gr.-gr.-grandson of Gov. William Leete of Connecticut. He graduated at Yale College in 1766, married in 1774, Lucy, daughter of Elijah and Lucy (Griswold) Backus, and purchased in that same year the house and shop of Ebenezer Lord, where he lived till his removal to the west between 1789 and 1790. His brother, Samuel, was for a short time associated with him in business. In 1782, the first post-office was established in Norwich, and Dudley Woodbridge was appointed postmaster, which office he held until 1789. The mails had previously been delivered by post riders. On his removal to Marietta, Ohio, about 1790, he adopted the profession of law, which he had previously studied at Yale. He died at Marietta in 1823. His son William (b. in Norwich in 1780) became Governor of Michigan, and United States Senator. Elizabeth, the sister of Dudley Woodbridge, married Daniel Rodman. His brother William also settled in Norwich, and after the death of his father, his mother and sister, Lucy, came here to reside.

In 1790, Gurdon Lathrop occupied this store as a general trader. In 1791, he moves to the opposite side of the Green, and the store is sold to Joseph Huntington. In 1793, the latter forms a partnership with his father-in-law, Joseph Carew, under the firm name of Carew & Huntington. Like the store of Tracy & Coit, these shops are stocked with goods of every description, groceries, books, shoes, dress goods, hardware, &c. The wonder is how the town could support so many establishments. In October, 1800, the firm of Carew & Huntington was dissolved, and Joseph Huntington associated with himself his younger half-brother as the firm of Joseph & Charles P. Huntington.

The house of Dudley Woodbridge was also sold in 1791 to Roger Griswold (b. 1762), the son of Gov. Matthew and Ursula (Wolcott) Griswold of Lyme, Ct., who graduated at Yale College in 1780, studied law with his father, was admitted to the bar of New London County, and settled at Norwich in 1783. He married in 1788, Fanny Rogers, daughter of Col. Zabdiel and Elizabeth (Tracy) Rogers. In 1794, he was elected Member of Congress, and moved from Norwich to Lyme. He served in Congress for ten years, and in 1801 declined the office of Secretary of War which was offered to him by President Adams. He filled the offices of Judge of the Supreme Court from 1807 to 1809, Lieut. Governor from 1809 to 1811, and of Governor from 1811 to 1812.

In 1807, while arguing a case, he experienced the first attack of a painful and alarming disease of the heart, which, recurring at intervals, obliged him in the summer of 1812 to come to Norwich for change of air, and to be under the care of Dr. Philemon Tracy, in whose skill he had great confidence. But nothing could check the progress of his disease, and he died in October, 1812, at fifty years of age. He had ten children, three of whom were born in Norwich. He is described as "a very handsome man, with flashing black eyes, a commanding figure, and majestic mien, seeming even by outward presence born to rule."

On his tomb-stone we may read that he was "not less conspicuous by honorable parentage and elevated rank in society than by personal merit, talents and virtue. He was respected at the University as an elegant and classical scholar, quick discernment, sound reasoning, legal science and manly eloquence raised him to the first eminence at the bar. Distinguished in the National Councils among the illustrious statesman of the age. Revered for his inflexible integrity and pre-eminent talents, his political course was highly honorable. His friends viewed him with virtuous pride. His native state with honest triumph. His fame and honors were the just rewards of noble actions, and of a life devoted to his country. He was endeared to his family by fidelity and affection, to his neighbors by frankness and benevolence. His memory is embalmed in the hearts of surviving relatives and of a grateful people. When this monument shall have decayed, his name shall be enrolled with honor among the great, the wise, and the good."

Mrs. Roger Griswold long survived her husband, dying in 1863, aged 96. In the family of Gov. Roger Griswold's mother, Ursula Wolcott, the office of Governor seemed almost hereditary, as her father, brother, husband, son, and nephew were all Governors of the State of Connecticut.

In 1797, an attempt was made to burn the carriage house of Roger Griswold, which was then "improved" by Capt. Elisha Tracy. There had been so many acts of incendiarism at this time, that the Mayor, John McC. Breed, offered a reward of $500, for the discovery of the criminal. In 1800, Roger Griswold sells his house to Jesse Brown, "near the store" of the latter. The destruction of this house, and of the Huntington store in the following year, 1801, is thus described in the Norwich Packet:—

On the night of February 5th, 1801, "between the hours of nine and ten o'clock, the Inhabitants of this town were awakened by the alarming cry of Fire, and the ringing of the Bell. The Fire when first discovered, burst forth from the large store of J. & C. P. Huntington, and in a short time . . . . that valuable building was wrapped in the destructive element. By this time the inhabitants had collected from all parts of the town, and made every effort to quell its further progress. But alas! it seemed to put all their exertions at defiance, and spread with unconquerable fury—it communicated to the Meeting House next, and first caught in several places on the steeple, so that the Engines which were kept constantly playing to the best advantage on the most contiguous buildings, were of little use to preserve this Stately Dome from the destruction which now followed. The flames ascended to its Spire and continued to expand until the House was enveloped in one general blaze. A scene more dread, terrific, and sublime the eye could never behold! . . . . A handsome dwelling house owned by Mr. J. Brown next the Store . . . . now met the same fate. The large house owned by Mr. Lathrop was happily preserved, tho several times on Fire." "Mr. Brown's elegant dwelling house, in which he resides," was saved, and some of the goods in Messrs. Huntington's store. The Packet thanks "our fellow citizens at the Port" for assistance rendered. The fire was supposed to be of incendiary origin.

The enterprising firm of Jos. & Charles P. Huntington moved their goods to the store, "a few rods N. E. from the Court House," possibly the one formerly owned by John Perit. In May, they invite the attention of the public by a column-long advertisement of goods for sale, including paints, dyes, dress goods, groceries, hardware, china, &c. In August, they move to the large, new brick store, which they have built on the site of the old Woodbridge shop. After a few years, this firm is dissolved. Charles P. Huntington establishes a store of his own, and Joseph Huntington later takes his son, Joseph, into partnership. In 1841, the brick store is sold to Bela Peck, and in 1852, it is converted into the present chapel, and presented to the church by Harriet Peck Williams, wife of Gen. William Williams.

In 1787, lot No. 1 of the parsonage lands is leased to Dudley Woodbridge, and, in 1795, again to Roger Griswold. This land lies between the Griswold, or former Woodbridge house, and the Brown tavern, and is "bounded beginning at the highway at the south corner of Jesse Brown's land, then leased to him for a house lot, then runs by said land, abutting on it 9 r. 12 l., then S. 49½° W. 9 r. 20 l. to the Common lands behind the Meeting House, then runs in a straight line, abutting on the Griswold house lot to the highway 1 r. 2 l. distant from the first bound." This is now included in the grounds of the Rock Nook Home.

CHAPTER LXVI.

THE first deed of lot No. 2 of the Parsonage land (frontage 5 rods, 18 links), to Jesse Brown is dated 1787. In 1796, he also leases one-half of lot No. 3 (frontage 3 rods, 8 links). We know nothing of his antecedents. He married in 1769, Anna Rudd, daughter of Nathaniel and Mary (Backus) Rudd of Franklin, Ct., who was the mother of his six children. In 1772, he purchased a house and land in Bozrah which he sold in 1774. During the Revolution he officiated as the Governor's post, bringing, in October, 1777, the latest news of the Continental Congress, then in session at Yorktown, and of the occupation of Philadelphia by the British under Lord Howe. In 1781, he married Lucy Rudd, daughter of Daniel and Mary (Metcalf) Rudd, and cousin of his first wife.

In 1790, Jesse Brown was licensed to keep a tavern, which was famed, it is said, for its good dinners, and was greatly patronized by merchants from the West Indies. His stages were constantly bringing table delicacies from Boston and Hartford. Miss Caulkins says that "many were the excursions and gallant hunting parties with hounds and servants which started from this tavern one hundred years ago." Here, on Wednesday evening, Aug. 1, 1797, arrived Pres. John Adams and wife, and the Matross company came out to welcome them in full uniform, and fired a federal salute of sixteen guns. They proceeded the next day to Providence, a large company on horseback attending them out of town. Jesse Brown established stage lines between Hartford and Boston, by way of Norwich, in 1790, and in 1793 between Boston and New York, by way of Providence and Norwich. The Hartford line, "Old Industry," was advertised in 1797, as running once a week. The New York and Boston stages made two weekly trips in winter and three in summer, arriving at Norwich on Sunday, Wednesday and Friday in the latter season. The stage left Providence on Sunday morning at eight o'clock, and arrived in Norwich at noon, "the stage horn sounding just as the audience issued from the church after morning service." In truth, times were changing even then from the early days, when every Sunday traveller had to give an account of himself, or go to jail. The fare from Boston to Providence was $3, from Providence to New London $4, for the remainder of the road 4½ cents per mile. Fourteen pounds was the limit of luggage allowed. All in excess of this, was charged at the rate of "100 pounds as a passenger." Five days was the length of time allowed for the journey from New York to Boston.

One of the daughters of Jesse Brown, Ann Brown, married in 1802, John Vernet of St. Pierre, Martinique, who afterward built in 1809 the house, later known as the Lee house, on Washington Street, now occupied by Charles Sturtevant. He sold the house in 1811 to Benjamin Lee of Cambridge, Mass., and moved with his father-in-law and family to Wilkesbarre, Penn., where Jesse Brown died in 1818. Mr. Vernet introduced into the garden of the Brown tavern about the year 1809, a species of grape, never before cultivated in this region. It was propagated from this vine into other gardens, was highly prized, and popularly called the Vernett grape. It is not known where Mr. Vernet obtained it, but it is supposed to be identical with the Isabella. The original vine planted by Mr. Vernet, was still flourishing at the time Miss Caulkins wrote her history.

At the Brown tavern appeared in 1791, Dr. I. Greenwood, who "with an experience of fifteen years extensive practice," advertises "to set teeth which will vie

Mother's Grave
(Executed by Charlotte and Harriet Peck.)

in beauty and duration with the most brilliant natural ones, with or without extracting the stumps, or causing the least pain, transplants them, grafts natural teeth to remaining roots in the gum," &c., &c. He at first intends remaining four days, but being "honored with more applications" than he could attend to in so short a time, his stay extends to several months. Jesse Brown, Jun., married in 1801, Lucy, daughter of Erastus Perkins, and was for a time associated in business at the Landing with the Howlands, as the firm of Howland & Brown, which partnership was dissolved in 1806. Jesse Brown, Jr, died in 1811. In 1814, the house is sold to William Williams of New London, and in 1817 to Capt. Bela Peck, who resides here till his death in 1850.

Bela Peck (b. 1758), was the son of Joseph Peck, and his third wife Elizabeth (Lathrop) Carpenter, widow of Joseph Carpenter and daughter of Nathaniel and Ann (Backus) Lathrop. At the time of Joseph Peck's death in 1776, Bela was only 18 years of age, and according to the terms of his father's will, the tavern, though left to him, was to be rented for a term of years. He probably resided with his mother until his marriage to Betsey Billings in 1787. At that time, or shortly after, he moved to the former Peck tavern to reside. In 1805, his only son, William Billings Peck, died while a student at Yale College. The illustration on the opposite page is a copy of a memorial piece of embroidery and painting, executed by the two sisters of William Peck. The faces are said to be family likenesses. It was quite customary at the time to have these mourning pieces made for departed friends.

In 1817, Capt. Peck purchased the former Brown tavern, to which he soon removed. In 1818, his wife died, and he married (2) in 1819, Lydia, widow of Asa Spalding. He resided in this house until his death in 1850, at the age of 93. He inherited a good fortune from his father, which he also largely increased, and was "noted for his business sagacity, and strong common sense." The Peck Library in the Slater Memorial building was given by Mrs. Harriet (Peck) Williams to the Norwich Free Academy, as a tribute to the memory of her father. In 1855, this house was purchased by Moses Pierce, who lived here for some years, and then presented it to the United Workers as a home for poor children, and the old tavern much altered and modernized, is now known as "The Rock Nook Home."

CHAPTER LXVII.

THE other half of lot No. 3 of the Parsonage land is leased to Joseph Carpenter, 2nd, in 1788. Joseph Carpenter, 1st, comes from Woodstock, Ct., to Norwich and marries in 1746, Elizabeth, daughter of Nathaniel and Ann (Backus) Lathrop. He died in 1749, leaving two sons, Joseph (b. 1747), and Gardner (b. 1748-9). The widow, Elizabeth, marries in 1754, Joseph Peck, who kept the Peck tavern. As early as 1769, Joseph Carpenter, 2nd, was established in business as a goldsmith in a shop belonging to his step-father, for which he pays a yearly rent of £1 10s. This may have been one of the shops then owned by Joseph Peck, in the rear of the jail.

In 1772, Joseph Carpenter, 2nd, buys boards, &c., of Joseph Carew, and pays to James Wentworth £11 for "stoning the seller" and for the underpinning of a shop. In 1773, he pays for "stepstones" and shingle nails, and buys of John Danforth eight scaffold poles, so we may assume that about this time he builds the

John Verner

shop now owned by his grandson, Joseph Carpenter, 3rd. In 1774, and for some years after, he pays rent to Rev. Benjamin Lord for land "my shop stands on." After the parsonage lands are ceded to the church, he receives in 1787 a 999 years' lease of this land, then known as lot No. 4 (frontage 4 rods, 9 links). It is said that he occupied one side of this shop, while his brother, Gardner, carried on a mercantile business in the other part. The building has never been altered, and retains to this day its gambrel roof and old-fashioned shutters, and all the features of a shop of the olden time. Joseph's stock in trade consisted of gold necklaces and beads, stone earrings and rings, teaspoons, smelling bottles, "specktacals" or "specticls," "stone nubs," bonnet pins, "tortashell" buttons, "brass holberds," "cristols," "nee buckls," stock buckles, clocks, watches, &c. He also advertises in January, 1776, that he has for sale engravings of "four different views of the Battles of Lexington, Concord, &c., copied from original Paintings taken on the Spot." The price is 6 shillings per set for the plain engravings, and 8 shillings for the colored ones.

In 1775, Joseph Carpenter married Eunice Fitch, and had six children. From 1777 to 1778, he leases a house of Seth Miner. From 1779 to 1782, he occupies a house belonging to Joseph Peck. These buildings we are unable to locate exactly. In or before 1788, the church lease to him the north half of lot No. 3, and here, next to his shop, he builds the house now owned by his great-grandson, Joseph Carpenter, 3rd. About 1790-1, he builds the house near the Chelsea Parade, which has been recently sold to Mrs. Gardiner of New London. His death occurred in 1804.

Gerard Carpenter (b. 1779), son of Joseph, married in 1819, Rebecca E. Hunter, and lived in this house on the Green, till his death in 1861. He served as Lieut. Colonel in the war of 1812.

Approached by a lane, between the shop of Joseph Carpenter and the school-house, there stood high up on the hillside, a house (now disappeared) which was at one time occupied by Seth Miner. All the land lying back from the street, comprising lots Nos. 7, 8, 9, 10, 16 and part of No. 14, were leased to him by the First Church Society, the earliest deeds dated 1787 and 1789, but Seth Miner may have resided here at a much earlier date, possibly at the time of the Revolution.

His son, the late Hon. Charles Miner of Wilkesbarre, Penn., in his letter of Norwich reminiscences, alluding to the patriotic excitement of that period writes:—

"My father, a house carpenter, and his journeyman dropped their tools on the alarm. As the broad axe rung, the journeyman said, 'That is my death knell.' Breathing the common spirit, he hied away cheerfully and returned no more." Mr. Miner says that his father was orderly sergeant under Col. Jedediah Huntington at the battle of Bunker Hill.

Seth Miner (b. 1742), was the son of Hugh Miner of New London. He married at Norwich in 1767, Anna Charlton, daughter of Richard and Sarah (Grist) Charlton, and had five children. For a number of years he served as keeper of the jail which stood near his house. He was an investor in the Delaware Land Company, and when the time arrived for his sons to go out into the world to seek their fortune, the eldest son, Asher (b. 1778), after serving seven years as an apprentice in the office of the "New London Gazette, or Commercial Advertiser," and one year as a journeyman in New York, resolved to go to Pennsylvania and look up his father's landed interests.

His brother, Charles (b. 1780), after an apprenticeship in the New London Gazette office, also went to Pennsylvania in 1799. After wandering about for a while, he went to Wilkesbarre to enter into partnership with his brother, who was then editing "The Luzerne County Federalist," the first number of which was issued in 1801. It is said that the press on which this paper was published was brought from Norwich on a sled. Asher afterward relinquished his interest in the paper to Charles, and went to Doylston, Pa., where in 1804, he established the "Pennsylvania Correspondent, or Farmer's Advertiser," which afterward became the "Buck's County Intelligencer." He also for a time edited another newspaper called "The Star of Freedom."

In 1807 and 1808, Charles Miner was elected to the Legislature. In 1816, he went to West Chester, Pa., and there started "The Village Record." In 1824, he was again joined by his brother, Asher, who formed with him another editorial partnership. From 1824 to 1828, Charles Miner was sent to Congress, having for his colleague, James Buchanan, afterward President. In 1834, the brothers returned to Wilkesbarre, where Asher died in 1841. Among other publications of Charles was a newspaper called "The Gleaner," which he issued for a time, and a history of Wyoming, which, as one of the early residents of that region, he must have been well qualified to write. He died in 1865, aged 80.

In writing his recollections of Norwich to the committee of the Norwich Bi-Centennial Celebration, he speaks of his old home, "the Red House on the hill." He tells of "the snug little room fourteen feet square, with a fire-place, called the Judges' Chamber," which the Chief Judge, the Hon. William Hillhouse, Judge Noyes, and Judge Coit used often to occupy during a period of twenty or more years while the court was in session. Seated around the fire-place, "with their long pipes, the ends coated with sealing wax," "the old gentlemen were often as merry as kittens passing their jokes, as their pipes threw up columns of smoke without intermission to the ceiling." "Their thoughts ran on early life, as old men's, I suspect, are apt to do, and they talked of their sweet-hearts. Judge Noyes was acknowledged to have been most of a beau, and claimed to have been a favorite with the fair. But the Chief Judge reminded him that at a certain gathering he had run away with Noyes's partner. At one time Noyes told, with great glee, the well-known story, seemingly justified by the swarthy complexion of Hillhouse, that several of the Montville and Mohegan mothers being out huckleberrying had left their children together in the shade, when, being alarmed by a bear, they ran, each seizing the first infant she could catch up, and fled. It so happened Mrs. Hillhouse, by a fortunate mistake, had gotten the papoose of Queen Uncas."

On Saturday night "the family is called together," and "after a chapter read from the sacred volume, Judge Noyes, gifted in prayer, standing, his hand resting on the top of his chair, the back of it being from him, commences (solemn and softly, as one deeply sensible that he was in the presence of, and presuming to adress the Supreme), with the Creation, the fall of Adam, and his expulsion from Paradise, his wickedness,—the flood,—the Covenant with Noah,—with Abraham,—with David—dwelling on the great and sublime Covenant of Redemption— becoming more and more animated and sonorous as he warmed with the subject, walking his chair more and more rapidly, until he came to the Advent of our Saviour, and near an hour had expired, the good old man would strike his chair against the back of the parlor with a force that would make the windows shake again."*

This Judge William Noyes was the son of Moses and Mary (Ely) Noyes of Lyme, Ct., and grandson of the Rev. Moses Noyes, the first minister of Lyme. He married in 1756 Eunice Marvin (b. 1735), of Lyme, Ct. Judge Noyes "was a tall, grave man, the terror of Sabbath-breakers," who "never allowed a traveler to pass through Lyme on the Lord's Day without some extraordinary excuse." He was regarded by his four grown-up sons with such respect that when on horseback they "never presumed to ride on a line with him, but always at a respectful distance behind."†

Judge Benjamin Coit (b. 1731), son of Col. Samuel and Sarah (Spalding) Coit of Griswold, Ct., was, like his father, an influential citizen, Representative in the State Legislature and Judge of the County Court. He married (1) 1753, Abigail Billings, daughter of Capt. Roger Billings of Preston, Ct., and (2) 1760, Mary (Tyler) Boardman, widow of Elijah Boardman, and daughter of Capt. Moses Tyler of Preston. Judge Coit died suddenly while on a visit to North Stonington in 1812.

Judge William Hillhouse (b. 1728), was the son of the Rev. James and Mary (Fitch) Hillhouse of Montville, Ct. The Rev. James Hillhouse was born about 1688, at Free Hall, County Londonderry, Ireland, was educated at the University of Glasgow, came to America in 1720, and in 1721 was installed as minister of the North Parish of New London, now Montville. He married Mary, daughter of Daniel Fitch, and granddaughter of the Rev. James Fitch of Norwich.

Judge Hillhouse was "a leading patriot of the revolution," "a member of the council of safety for Connecticut and major of the first regiment of cavalry raised in that state. He was afterward a magistrate, or assistant, of the state for 24 years, and for many years the chief judge of the county court for the county of New London. He was frequently a member of the State legislature, and was a member of the congress of the confederation."‡ He died in 1816.

---

* Letter from Hon. Charles Miner to the Bi-Centennial Committee.
† From an article on Lyme, Ct., by Mrs. Martha J. Lamb, in Harper's Monthly for February, 1876.
‡ Chancellor Walworth's "Genealogy of the Hyde Family."

Between 1811 and 1815, Seth Miner sells the property, and in 1818 it comes into the possession of Capt. Bela Peck. The house soon after disappeared, and the land now forms part of the grounds of the Rock Nook Home. In 1839, Charles Miner paid a visit to Norwich, but the house was no longer in existence. But "he went up the hill on the slope of which it had stood," Miss Caulkins says, "to look for the brown thrasher's nest that he left there more than forty years before."

CHAPTER LXVIII.

THE early laws required that every town of thirty inhabitants should have a school to teach reading and writing, and that in every county town a Latin school should be established. In 1677, it was voted in a town meeting at Norwich, that "a schoole" should be kept "for nine months according to law," and that John Birchard should be the school-master, and receive £25 in provision pay for his services, each scholar to pay 9 s. for the nine months, and the remainder to be paid by the town rate. In 1679, "Mr." Daniel Mason was engaged for the same length of time.

A school-house was built in 1683 by John Hough and Samuel Roberts, and Miss Caulkins believes that, at this time, John Arnold officiated as school master.* In 1697, Richard Bushnell served for a while in that capacity, and in 1698, David Hartshorn. In 1700, Norwich is indicted "for want of a school to instruct children," and the town at once negotiate with David Knight to repair the school-

* A later affidavit of John Arnold's testifies to his having taught school in several towns.

house. In 1702-3, Mr. Solomon Tracy engages to repair it. In 1709, the town votes to "have a school-master according to law," and Richard Bushnell is again employed.

In 1712, it was voted that "a good and sufficient school-master be appointed to keep schooll the whole yeare and from yeare to yeare, one halfe the time in the Town Platt, the other halfe at the farms in the several quarters." In 1714, a rate of 40 s. on a thousand pounds is voted "for ye maintaining of ye school provided ye schoolers of ye Town Platt pay to ye school-master what fails in ye sum agreed for, and ye farmers have liberty to send their chilldren free of cost." In 1745, the Town appointment for schools was as follows:—

"School at the Landing Place to be kept 3 months, 17 days.
Two schools in the Town Plot one at each end, 5½ months each.
School at Plain Hills, ... 2 months 19 days.
School at Waweekus Hill, ... 1 month 16 days.
School at Great Plain, ... 2 months 18 days.
School at Wequanuk, ... 2 months 15 days.
School on the Windham Road, . . . 2 months 11 days."

"If any of these schools should be kept by a woman, the time was to be doubled, as the pay of the mistress was but half that of the master."*

We are unable to determine the site of any of these early school-houses. The one "at the east end of the Town Plot" may have stood near the Green, and possibly on the site of the old red brick building formerly used as a school-house. The date of the erection of this latter building is unknown.

Few of the names of the early school-teachers have come down to us. In 1774, Thomas Eyre advertises to teach an evening school at the rate of 1 s. per week for a class of not less than ten pupils. He will give special attention to Algebra and Geometry, and "the three useful though neglected rules" in Arithmetic, "Vulgar and Decimal Fractions, the Progressional Series, and the Extraction of the Roots."

* Miss Caulkins' History of Norwich.

One Jared Bostwick (school-teacher), died "greatly lamented in August, 1778, at the age of 27." A friend mourns his loss in the Norwich Packet as—

> "A friend sincere whose heart did aim
> In virtue's path at honest fame—
> While modest wit and sense refined
> With radiance sweet adorn'd his mind
> Such virtues, Bostwick! warm'd thy breast,
> Such sentiments thy soul possest."

In the latter part of 1783, a school was opened in the brick school-house "a few rods north of the court house," "upon the most extensive plan and liberal construction," "for the reception of a large number of young Gentlemen and Ladies, Lads and Misses: where is taught by experienced Instructors, in the most modern manner, every branch of literature, viz., reading, writing, arithmetic, the learned languages, rhetoric, logic, geography, mathematicks," &c. A Mr. Goodrich was the instructor. In addition to all these accomplishments, the pupils were taught "the rules of decency, decorum, and morality." Andrew Huntington and Dudley Woodbridge were the committee.

"The exhibitions of this school were deemed splendid, and great was the applause when Miss Mary Huntington came upon the stage dressed in green silk brocade a crown glittering with jewels encircling her brow, and reading Plato to personate Lady Jane Grey, while young Putnam, the son of the old general, advanced with nodding plumes to express his tender anxieties for her in the person of Lord Guilford Dudley."*

At his death in 1782, Dr. Daniel Lathrop left £500 "for the interest to be Annually Improved for the support of a school for all the Inhabitants of the whole Town, at some Convenient place near where the Meeting House now stands, the school to be kept by an able Master for the Instructing Youth in Reading, Writing English, also for teaching Arithmatick, also teaching the Lattin Tongue—no Children to be sent to said school but such as can read in class—the school to be kept 11 months in Each Year, and 8 hours in each day from the 20th of March to the 20th of September, and from the 21st of September to

---
* Miss Caulkins' History of Norwich. First Edition.

the 20th of March, 6 hours in each day that is to say as nearly that space of Time in each day as may Reasonably be expected."

No action was taken on this until 1784, and then it was decided to take the brick school-house on the Green for its accommodation, and here probably presided the following teachers, in the order mentioned by the Hon. Charles Miner, who was born in 1780, and received his early schooling in this building:—

     CHARLES WHITE.
     NEWCOMB KINNEY.
     MR. HUNT.
     ALEXANDER MCDONALD.
     WILLIAM BALDWIN.

Miss Caulkins, however, mentions an Ebenezer Punderson as the first instructor in this newly-endowed school. This Ebenezer Punderson was probably born shortly before the Revolution. His grandfather was the Rev. Ebenezer Punderson, who married Hannah Miner in 1732, was ordained minister of the Episcopal Church at Poquetannock in 1738, was pastor of Christ Church in Norwich from 1749 to 1751, then went to New Haven, and in ten years later to Rye, N. Y., where he died in 1771, aged 63. His widow, Hannah, died in 1792, aged 80. A stone table, erected to their memory, formerly stood in front of Christ Church, but has lately been removed.

Ebenezer (b. 1735), son of the Rev. Ebenezer Punderson, married Prudence Geer in 1757. In 1771, he purchased property on Poquetannock Cove and resided there, though owning a farm, store and wharf at Groton. He was evidently a regular attendant at Christ Church where several of his children were baptized. When accused in 1775, of drinking the then prohibited tea, he replied, according to the Norwich Packet, "to use his own words, that he has drank tea, and means to continue that practice," and that "Congress was an unlawful combination, and that the petition from Congress to his Majesty was haughty, violent and rascally." The Committee of Inspection immediately ordered that "no Trade, Commerce, Dealings or Intercourse whatsoever be carried on with said Punderson," which had the effect of bringing him to his senses. In less than a week he appears before the Committee, and begs that "they and all his neighbors will forgive him, that he was sorry that he drank any Tea since last March," and is determined "that he will drink no more until its use is no longer prohibited." He regrets also "all expressions used against Congress," and promises that he will never again do anything "inimical to the Freedom, Liberty and Privileges of America." It is probable, however, that his life in Norwich was no longer a pleasant one, and in 1777, Miss Caulkins says, "his property was confiscated, and he left town to join the enemy."

No record of the third Ebenezer Punderson's service as teacher in this school has been found, except the brief mention by Miss Caulkins. We know, however, that an Ebenezer Punderson was officiating as jailer in 1786 in the prison near the school-house.

Mr. Miner writes: "Among the earliest teachers within my recollection was Charles White, a young gentleman from Philadelphia, handsome and accomplished. Of his erudition, I was too young to judge, but popular he certainly was among the ladies." In July, 1784, the Packet mentions "a public scholastic performance" exhibited in the court-house by the scholars "under the tuition of Mr. White." "The genius of the scholars, and the taste and good judgement of the Instructor, which were exhibited in the various representations during the day, gave universal satisfaction to the spectators. Between the different representations the harmony of vocal and instrumental music inhanced the pleasures of the day, and rendered it compleat."

Mr. Miner also alludes to "the high degree of emulation awakened" by Newcomb Kinney especially in writing. "A sampler was pasted up before six or seven scholars near the ceiling, on fine paper, on a double arch sustained by Corinthian columns, the upper corners of each sheet bearing a neatly painted quill, with the motto, 'Vive la Plume.' Within each half arch near the upper part, in fine hand, a poetical quotation, as suggested by fancy, probably from Hannah More's 'Search After Happiness,' then highly popular. Beneath, in larger hand, successive lines in beautiful penmanship, filling the whole. The Piece painted in water colors, the pride of mothers—master and scholars."

In October, 1787, Newcomb Kinney advertises that he has opened a school in a large, convenient room in Capt. Bela Peck's house, where he will teach "Reading, Writing, English Grammar, Composition, Geography, with the use of the terrestial globe, Book-Keeping by single and double entry, Arithmatic, Geometry, Trigonometry, Navigation, and Surveying by actual survey." He will also obtain board for pupils "in reputable houses at 6 s. per week, and will accept country produce or West India goods in payment."

Newcomb Kinney (b. 1761), was the son of Joseph and Jemina (Newcomb) Kinney. He married in 1786, Sally Branch, daughter of Samuel and Hannah (Witter) Branch of Preston. It is probable that the committee of the brick school-house, rather than have so formidable a competitor on the Green, engaged his services as teacher of the Lathrop school. In 1789, he buys the former Joseph Trumbull house near the Green, perhaps with a view to residing permanently at Norwich Town, but sells it in 1790. He later resided at the Landing, where he kept the most popular of taverns. The old Frenchman, in McDonald Clarke's verses, is supposed to allude to this favorite landlord, when he says:—

"Norwich von very fine place,
And Kinney he von fine man."

It may have been in the year 1790, that Alexander McDonald became the teacher of this school. He was born about 1752, and may possibly have been a son of Alexander and Ann (Wilson) McDonald of Newport, R. I., who were married in 1747. In 1783, Alexander McDonald of Norwich marries Sarah Leach, daughter of Thomas and Sarah (Reynolds) Leach. In 1785, he publishes at the Landing his "Youth's Assistant," a guide to Arithmetic, which is highly praised by many of the chief instructors of the day. In 1786, he advertises as a bookseller and bookbinder at Chelsea, and also, in connection with Hezekiah Woodruff, opens a school in Chelsea Hall, and offers to obtain good board for pupils at 6 s. per week. In 1788, he moves his bookstore to No. 2 Leffingwell Row at Norwich Town, and in 1789, to the shop a few rods north of the Court-House, probably the former "Perit" shop. He died in 1792, aged 40, possibly while still a teacher in the brick school-house. It is probable that he left no children, as no births of that name have been found in the records. His widow married Capt. Joseph Gale in 1795.

William Baldwin is the best remembered of all the teachers in the town plot. Mrs. Sigourney describes him as "somewhat stricken in years," having "held his office from early manhood." "He was a thorough scholar and austere. Not being addicted to social pleasures, he was considerably past his prime, before he entered the marriage relation, and he still retained the temperament of a recluse. Never having had opportunity to wreathe his features into a smile for a babe of his own, they were not often moved to that form by the children of others. Indeed, according to the system of Rochefoucauld, he seemed to take it for granted that every boy was a rogue, until proved to the contrary. Neither was slight proof sufficient to overcome his scepticism. He was of a tall, spare form, with a keen black eye. Everyone in school could imitate his frown, his measured gait, and precision of speech."

"Boys, I shall be compelled to punish you severely, if there is either persistence in or repetition of such conduct."

"Little did the dominie suppose that in the familiar talk of the scholars the irreverent cognomen of 'Uncle Billy' was applied to him. The more observant, who, according to Goldsmith,

'— are skill'd to trace
The day's disaster in the morning's face.'

would sometimes say pantomimically 'Uncle Billy is chewing a tough Greek root to-day. Look out for breakers.'"

"To the female branch of his dominion he was eminently taciturn. I doubt whether I ever addressed him save in replies to his questions on the lessons, or what sprung collaterally from the business of the school. Still there was no mixture of dislike in our reserved intercourse. On the contrary, I felt an innate sense of his approbation, which sustained my complacency. He elevated me as an honor to the especial office of monitor of the reading classes. This was no sinecure, as the classes were large; and when they were marshalled for this exercise, I was expected to stand opposite each one, as they read, and criticize elocution and emphasis, having the power to make them repeat their allotted portion as often as I deemed necessary. On the whole, I enjoyed myself, and improved under the stern old master, and felt a sort of pride in his strictness, which I think scholars generally do, notwithstanding what they may say to the contrary."*

William Baldwin (b. ab. 1761), married in 1802, Alice, daughter of Benjamin and Mary (Carew) (Brown) Huntington. He died in 1817, and his wife died in 1833.

* From Mrs. Sigourney's "Letters of Life."

CHAPTER LXIX.

WHILE William Baldwin continued to teach in the brick school-house, Mrs. Sigourney "was removed from his regency to share the benefits of a school unique in those times," and, as she writes, "I am inclined to think, not easily paralleled in any. A young gentleman of superior talents, education, and position in society, having been compelled by some infirmity of health to abandon his choice of the clerical profession, consented to take charge for one year of a select circle of twenty-five pupils." *

This teacher was Pelatiah Perit (b. 1785), son of John and Ruth (Webster) Perit. He graduated at Yale College in 1802. The location of this school we have been unable to determine, but think it quite possible that Col. Christopher Leffingwell, who had recently married (in 1799) the mother of Pelatiah Perit, may have placed at his disposal an upper room in the two-storied part of Leffingwell Row, which we know was later used as a school-room.

Mrs. Sigourney considered it a "rare privilege" to attend this school, and writes of Mr. Perit: "He had but recently completed his collegiate course, and it seems a scarcely credible fact that, ere he had reached his twentieth birthday, he should have judgment to conduct such an institution, and to impress every varying spirit with respect and obedience. Yet so it was. The secret of his sway was in his earnest piety and consistent example."

"The order of the school was perfect. The classes were excellently well taught, as were also the English studies. Among the latter, I recollect geography was quite a favorite, probably because it was deepened by our construction of maps and charts, in which we were strenuous for accuracy and some degree of elegance. The former we decorated by painted vignettes and devices, and for

---

* Mrs. Sigourney's "Letters of Life."

the latter had immense sheets manufactured at the paper mill on purpose for us. These being divided into regular parallelograms by lines of red ink, we wrote on their left the name of every country on the habitable globe, filling its even line of regular compartments according to their designation over the top—Length and Breadth, Latitude and Longitude, Boundaries, Rivers, Mountains, Form of Government, Population, Universities, and Learned Men, where they existed, and whatever circumstance of history was reducible to so narrow a compass. The search after these facts, the conciseness of style requisite, and the fair chirography which were held indispensable, were all valuable attainments. This could not be an exercise common to the whole school, from the large space required for accommodation. I recollect being one of six—three of each sex,—who had permission to pursue it, and to have each a table spread for that purpose in a large vacant apartment. So much was our conscientiousness cultivated by this admirable instructor, that we, in conformity to our promise, comported ourselves with the same gravity as if in his presence, holding no conversation save what was necessary to test and condense the knowledge drawn out from the text-books on separate papers, and criticized ere they were copied."

"He also suggested an excellent employment for the intervals of Sunday,—the selection of passages of Scripture on subjects given us by himself. Our zeal to bring a large number, neatly copied, on Monday morning, prevented the idle waste of consecrated time, and promoted an intimate acquaintance with the treasures of the sacred volume. . . . . I have never attended a school where the religious sentiment was so perfectly cultivated, ... not by the constant repetition of precept, still less by the enforcement of peculiar doctrines, ... but by the influence of an earnest, consistent, pious example. The deep feeling of the morning prayer often moistened the eyes of the most unthinking; and the same spirit caught from the closing orison followed them home. . . . . The future course of Mr. Pelatiah Perit fully verified its opening promise. . . . . Wherever he was, and in whatever he engaged, his influence was for God and goodness."

In 1809, he married Jerusha Lathrop, daughter of Thomas and Lydia (Hubbard) Lathrop, and entered into business in New York. From 1817 to 1832, he was a member of a firm of shipping merchants. In 1821, his wife died, and in 1823, he married her cousin, Maria Coit, daughter of Daniel Lathrop and Elizabeth (Bill) Coit. From 1852 to 1863, he was President of the Chamber of Commerce. He was also President of the Seaman's Savings Bank. During the cholera epidemic, he assisted in nursing the sick, and gave large sums of money to aid the sufferers. He resided for many years at Bloomingdale, N. Y., and later moved to New Haven, where he died at his house on Hillhouse avenue in 1864. His wife died in 1885.

The school was next "taken in charge by the Rev. Daniel Haskell, a gentleman of somewhat more mature years, and also a graduate of Yale College. He was decidedly a religious character, a ripe scholar, and of great amenity of manners, and disposition. The belles-lettres studies were admirably taught by him, and he gave critical attention to the correct expression of written thought. He read to us portions of the best standard authors, in his own elegant elocution, and encouraged us freely to criticize both style and sentiment."

"Into the idioms and refinements of our own language he carefully led us. The 'Exercises of Lindley Murray' he especially rendered delightful in daily lessons, throwing us back continually upon definition and derivation, until the roots of words, and their minute shades of meaning, became beautiful as thought-pictures. So much did he inspire us with his own favorite tastes, that parsing the most difficult passages of the poets, remarkable either for elision or amplification, was coveted as a sport. The culture of memory was also a prominent object with him, for being a natural metaphysician, he scanned the intellect as a map, and wrought in each department. He occasionally read slowly to us pages from rare or antique works, historical, descriptive, or didactic, and, closing the book, required the substance or analysis in our own language. This was given orally at the time, and might also, if we chose, be presented in writing, subject to his correction."

"Our course of study, which was arduous, he sustained and quickened by emulation. The gift of books signalized the close of each term, of which there were four in the year, and a silver medal was semi-annually awarded. These premiums were so definitely adjusted to different grades of proficiency, or exemplary deportment, that there was no possibility of partiality, and so wisely balanced by the kind feelings cultivated among us, as never to create jealousy or dislike. I well remember our added meekness of manner when in the reception of these coveted prizes, and am sure that it was the fruit of his teachings. He faithfully developed not the intellect alone, but the affections. . . . Under the charge of this learned and amiable man, there was a perceptible growth of 'whatsoever was lovely and of good report.'"

"His sway sweetly illustrated the beauty of rule and the beauty of obedience. Our grief at the termination of the school was more deep and passionate than aught I have ever seen on a similar occasion. He was to us all the 'man greatly beloved.' We were as Niobes at the parting interview, when gathering us around him that last sad morning, he read once more in his voice of music from the Holy Book, gave us solemn and tender counsels, and kneeling down, commended us to the blessed care of the 'Father of Lights, with whom is no variableness, neither shadow of turning.'

> "Thou who didst bend to guide the timorous mind,
> Wise as a father, as a brother kind;
> With gentle hand its wayward cause withheld,
> Allured, not forced--encouraged, not compelled,
> Till the clear eye look'd up, devoid of fears,
> I bless thee for thy love, through all this lapse of years."

This Rev. Daniel Haskell was born in Preston, in 1784, and graduated at Yale College in the same class with Pelatiah Perit in 1802. After leaving Norwich, he taught in the Bacon Academy, Colchester, in 1806-7, then studied theology, was settled as pastor at Middletown and Litchfield, Ct., and afterward at St. Albans and Burlington, Vt., from 1810-21, and was then elected President of the University of Vermont, which position he retained until 1824. During the latter part of his life he was afflicted with a mental disorder, from which he, however, recovered, and later resumed his literary work. He received the degree of LL. D., from Olivet College, Michigan. He was the author of a Gazetteer of the United States, and a book called "A Chronological View of the World," and also assisted in editing McCulloch's Geographical Dictionary.

CHAPTER LXX.

SOME time before 1795, a part of lot No. 5 (frontage 1 rod, 16½ links), just beyond the school-house, was leased to Gardner Carpenter. On this he builds a store (or store-house), which, after his death, is sold in 1816 to Nathaniel and John Townsend. In the deed it is called "the red store." In 1846, John Townsend sells it to Charles Charlton, who alters the store into a house, which is now occupied by his widow.

The lease of the other half of No. 5 to Nathaniel Townsend, "on which his traiding or barber's shop now stands," is dated 1795, but he was probably in possession of the property sometime before, certainly as early as 1793. The line is described as "running N. 5½° W. 4 r. 18 l." (abutting on Mediterranean Lane), "to the narrow alley which leads to the jail," "then by sd lane N. 4 r.—then south 35° E 4 r. 11¾ l. by land leased to Gardner Carpenter to the highway, then by sd highway 1 r. 17½ l." In 1793, Nathaniel Townsend advertises that he has "hired a regular bred Baker from Boston and proposes to the inhabitants of Norwich to send his Bread Carriage round from the upper part of the town, and through Chelsea every day except Sundays (designated by Slay Bells), about 4 o'clock afternoons, with all those different kinds of Bread which those that are pleased to patronize this undertaking shall require. Butter & Groat Biscuit, Crackers, Gingerbread, Sugar & Ginger Cookies, Rusk, Buns, &c.—for sale in large or small quantities at his Bake House in front of the Goal." He later sold in the same place a varied stock of goods, paper-hangings, dry-goods, groceries, &c., so possibly the bakery enterprise was soon relinquished. The shop, which resembled in many features the one owned by the Carpenters, remained until after 1868, in the possession of the Townsend family. It was then sold, and destroyed, and the house now standing on the lot was built.

We believe this shop to be the one in which John Wheatley carried on the business of boot and shoe-making in 1774, near the Printing office, and made "the best of materials, good work and quick despatch, the cardinal points of his compass." He moved in the next year, across the Green to keep the Peck tavern, and Nathaniel Patten, with an utter disregard of the points of the compass, establishes his book store here "at the east end of the plain near the Printing office." He has one of the largest and most varied assortments of books ever offered in town for sale, and advertises also iron-mould drops, a tincture to take stains out of mahogany, Tooth-drops, Venetian Tooth Powder, Lip Salve, Eye Water, &c. He will "bind, gold and letter books," and "metamorphose old books into New at least the difference will not be perceptible to those who do not open them."

In 1775, his store is robbed and he announces that he intends to leave town, but is still residing here in 1776, when he advertises for rags for making wrapping paper.

In 1797, a Nathaniel Patten, possibly a son of the first Nathaniel, advertises in Norwich as of the firm of Sterry & Patten. This second Nathaniel Patten marries in 1796, Faith Foster. These probably belonged to the Patten family of Cambridge, Mass.

We think this may be the shop in which Gideon Denison advertises in 1783 to sell a large and varied assortment of goods. He also wishes to buy horses for the Surinam market. We are unable to say when this shop was built.

CHAPTER LXXI.

THE early jail (or "goal," as it was then written), stood, it is said, on the south-east corner of the Green. About 1759, a new jail was erected back of the old brick school house on the parsonage land. In February, 1786, this jail "took fire," as the Norwich Packet says, "and alarmed the inhabitants, who collected in great numbers, but notwithstanding their sacrificing exertions, the whole of this lonesome building was burned to the ground." The Packet adds: "It is wished by many that the inhabitants would provide themselves with two good fire engines, which are the best preservatives against that worst of all masters, fire." It was shortly after this, that Thomas Harland made his first fire engine.

In 1774-5, Sims Edgerton was the jailer, and to his care was committed in November, 1775, Dr. Benjamin Church, gr.-grandson and namesake of the noted Indian fighter. Dr. Church had written songs and delivered orations in favor of American freedom, and had also been a member of the Provincial Congress in 1774, and yet was convicted of treasonable correspondence, arrested, and sent under close guard to Norwich for safe keeping. A high picket fence was built around the jail, and "even within this inclosure, Dr. Church was not permitted to walk but once a week, and then with the sheriff at his side. In May, 1776, he was sent to Watertown, and shortly after was allowed to sail for the West Indies, but the vessel was never again heard of." Various tories and suspected persons were sent to the Norwich prison from time to time, and many escaped. In 1778, John Barney, Jun., was the prison-keeper; in 1783, Darius Peck; in 1784-5, and at various other times, Seth Miner served in that capacity. Ebenezer Punderson was the successor of Seth Miner in 1786.

Rewards of $5 or $10 were frequently offered for the arrest of escaped prisoners, confined for debt, murder, burglary, treason and counterfeiting, in which latter crime old offenders were detected by their "cropt and branded ears." In 1782, a company of English sailors, who were imprisoned here, ran away to New London, seized a new coasting vessel, and made good their escape. In 1800, seventeen French prisoners were brought here, captured as they were fleeing from the Island of St. Domingo. They were allowed to wander about freely in the town, treated considerately, and soon released in 1801. One of these prisoners, Jean Pierre Boyer, afterward President of the Haytien republic, remembered, with substantial rewards, kindnesses he had received while in Norwich.

After the burning of the prison in 1786, a new building was erected on the same site, but in 1815, the "Perit" house on the opposite side of the Green was purchased for the county house, and a jail was built on the adjoining lot a short distance back of where now stands the store of Herbert W. Hale. This lasted until the courts were moved to the Landing, in 1833, and was then shortly after burnt to the ground.

Back of the jail, and surrounded by paths leading from the jail and main highways, was a small lot of land which was sold by James Huntington to Joseph Peck in 1760, and was deeded back to the town by Bela Peck in 1783. At that time there stood on the lot a shop "improved by Darius Peck," and another "occupied by a chaise-maker."

In 1773, this latter building was the printing office of the Norwich Packet, which was transferred to a shop west of the church in 1775, and William Lax, an Englishman and a wheelwright, moves "to where the Printing office formerly kept on the Plain. He repairs carts, coach and chaise wheels," and during the Revolution built up quite a reputation as a maker of gun carriages. He died in 1779. In 1775, Darius Peck, who was also a wheelwright, moved "from the east side of the plain" to the other shop on this land "back of where the Printing office formerly kept." In one of these two shops in the rear of the jail, Joseph Carpenter was possibly located in 1770, when he pays to Joseph Peck £1 10 s for one year's rent of shop.

The Norwich Packet or Weekly Advertiser was the first newspaper published in Norwich. It was started in October, 1773, by the firm of Robertsons & Trumbull, the partners being Alexander and James Robertson, and John Trumbull.

Their first printing office, according to the advertisement, was rather indefinitely located "near the Court House," but from the advertisements of adjoining shops, we think that it probably stood in the rear of or near the jail. In 1775, the firm moved to another stand west of the Meeting House.*

The brothers, Alexander and James Robertson, were born in Scotland, and were the sons of a printer. They emigrated to America, and established themselves about 1768 at New York, where they published "The New York Chronicle." In 1770, they opened a printing office at Albany, and also in 1773, at Norwich, where, besides "The Norwich Packet," they printed many books, pamphlets, tales, sermons, political tracts, military manuals, school books, hymn books, &c. During the Revolution, they were suspected of sympathizing with the British, and though there was no evidence of this feeling in the columns of the Packet, which freely admitted all patriotic communications, they, however, finally acknowledged their lack of sympathy with the Revolutionists and moved to New York, in 1776.

A grave-stone in the old burying-ground marks the resting place of Amy, wife of James Robertson, who died in Norwich, in June, 1776, shortly before their departure from the town. After the capture of New York by the British, the brothers published in that city "The Royal American Gazette," and later James Robertson issued in Philadelphia "The Royal Gazette." They finally removed to Nova Scotia, where at Port Roseway (Shelburne) in November, 1784, Alexander Robertson died, in the 42nd year of his age, as the Norwich Packet announces, "a gentleman of probity, benevolence, and philanthropy, much esteemed, and now greatly lamented by a very numerous and respectable acquaintance." After the death of his brother, James Robertson returned to Scotland.

* We will reserve the Trumbull genealogy and the later history of The Packet for our second volume, which describes that part of the town, in which this second office is located.

CHAPTER LXXII.

DARIUS Peck (b. 1749-50), was a son of Jonathan and Bethiah (Bingham) Peck of Norwich. He married (1) in 1772, Hannah Warner of Windham, Ct., and (2) Mary Frances, and had ten children. He died about 1804. He was among the first to enlist in the army of the Revolution, was appointed Ensign in 1777, commissioned as Lieutenant in 1778, and retired from the service in 1779. Between 1772, the date of his marriage, and 1781, he builds the house (long known as the Dr. Tracy house), standing on the slope of the hill at the foot of Mediterranean Lane. He also occupied, as a wheelwright, a shop which stood between his own house and the Miner house, and back of the jail.

In 1781, he sells this property to Gideon Denison, and also a blacksmith's shop which he owned in the rear of the old Arnold house. From one of the bills of sale we learn that his dwelling house was originally painted red.

Gideon Denison (b. 1753), was the son of Gideon Denison of Saybrook, Ct., and gr.-gr.-grandson of Capt. George Denison and his wife, "Lady" Ann Borodell of Stonington, Ct. He married in 1780, Jerusha, daughter of Benjamin and Diadema (Hyde) Butler, lived for a while in Norwich, his business being that of a merchant, and his shop near the Green. He moved from Norwich to Havre de Grace, Md., where he died. His widow, Jerusha, died in Washington. He had five children, of whom one, Minerva, married Capt. John Rodgers, U. S. N. Elizabeth became the wife of Capt. John D. Henley, and Louisa, of Capt. Alexander Wadsworth, all distinguished naval officers. Gideon Denison sells his house in 1782, to his father-in-law, Benjamin Butler, who leaves it by will to his son, Thomas.

The next occupant was Dr. Philemon Tracy (b. 1757), son of Dr. Elisha and Elizabeth (Dorr) Tracy, who, though he resided in the house for some years previously, did not purchase the property until 1801. He studied medicine with his father, and also with Dr. Philip Turner, and practiced in Norwich for more than fifty-five years. He received from Yale College the honorary degree of Doctor of Medicine. He married in 1785, Abigail, daughter of Jonathan and Lydia (Proctor) Trott of Norwich.

Mrs. Sigourney thus describes Dr. Philemon Tracy: "I think I see now that cautious Mentor-like person, so grave and courteous, his countenance marked with deep thought and kindness—Dr. Philemon Tracy. I remember him among my benefactors. From his father he inherited medical skill and fame, monopolizing the principal practice of the city. Yet let the pressure of his business be ever so great, he studied a new case as a faithful clergyman does a sermon. He happily avoided the extremes which my Lord Bacon has designated: 'Some physicians are so conformable to the humor of the patient, that they press not the true treatment of the disease, and others so bound by rules as to respect not sufficiently his condition.' But the practice of our venerated Norwich healer was to possess himself of the idiosyncrasy of constitution as well as of the symptoms of disease, to administer as little medicine as possible, and to depend much on regimen, and rousing the recuperative powers to their wonted action. His minute questions and long deliberation inspired confidence, while the sententious mode of delivering his prescriptions gave them a sort of oracular force."*

Mrs. Sigourney again writes of him: "I well remember his dignified

---

* Mrs. Sigourney's "Letters of Life."

deportment, his originality in conversation." From an old bill of Dr. Tracy's we will give a few homely items, as illustrative of his fees and practice:—

To ANDREW HUNTINGTON in acct. PHILEMON TRACY, Dr.

1796.
July 20. To extracting Tooth for Lucy, . . 1 s. 6 d.
1800.
Nov. 2. To a visit to his wife, Bleeding & Box of Pills, 4 s. 6 d.
1801.
July 1. To Bitters prepared, ... 2 s.
July 21. To Columbo & Vit. Tart. &c pp" . . . 2 s. 9 d.
Oct. 21. To a visit to Abner & Puke, . . . 3 s. 4 d.
"   "   "   "   "   "   " & Pills, . . . 3 s.
Oct. 23. "   "   "   "   " Pills & Blisters, . . 4 s. 6 d.
Nov. 1. "   "   "   "   " & Bark, . . . 3 s. 6 d.

Dr. Philemon Tracy died in Norwich, in 1837, aged eighty. He became blind several years before his death. His daughter, Harriet Frances Tracy, witty and talented, died in 1830. Two of his sons, Phinehas, and Albert Haller Tracy, became members of Congress: one from Batavia, N. Y., the other from Buffalo. Another son, Edward, was Judge of the Superior Court in Macon, Ga. The only remaining son, Richard Proctor (b. 1791), studied medicine at Yale College, and succeeded to his father's practice. He never married, and lived in the old homestead till his death in 1871. He was talented, eccentric, and peculiar, but highly esteemed as a physician, and like all the other members of this family, renowned for his witty and original sayings. He was the last of his family to occupy the old homestead, which was sold after his death. It is now occupied by George Williams.

Next to the Tracy house comes lot No. 10, formerly part of the lands of Seth Miner, and beyond this, lot No. 11, at one time in the possession of Ebenezer Jones. This was later leased by the Church Society to Samuel Charlton, and the two houses now standing there, were built by John and Samuel Charlton. The second of the houses was sold by John Charlton in 1839 to Chauncey K. Bushnell. In 1868, it was in the possession of Luther Matthewson.

Beyond lot No. 11, we come to lot No. 12, which was early leased to Parmenas Jones, and the house built, which still remains in the possession of the Jones family.

Parmenas Jones (b. 1752), was a son of Sylvanus and Kesiah (Cleveland) Jones. He married (1) in 1777, Eunice Herrick, and (2) in 1788, Rosanna Weeks. Beyond the Jones house we come to lot No. 13 (frontage 6 rods), leased to Daniel Abbot in 1787. On this land he builds a barn, and sells the property in 1792 to William Osborn. This may be the William Osborn who advertises in 1785 as a painter and gilder on the road west of the meeting-house. In 1802, William Osborn sells to Isabella Gildon, the land and former barn ("converted into a house"), in which he then resides. The house has since that time had many occupants.

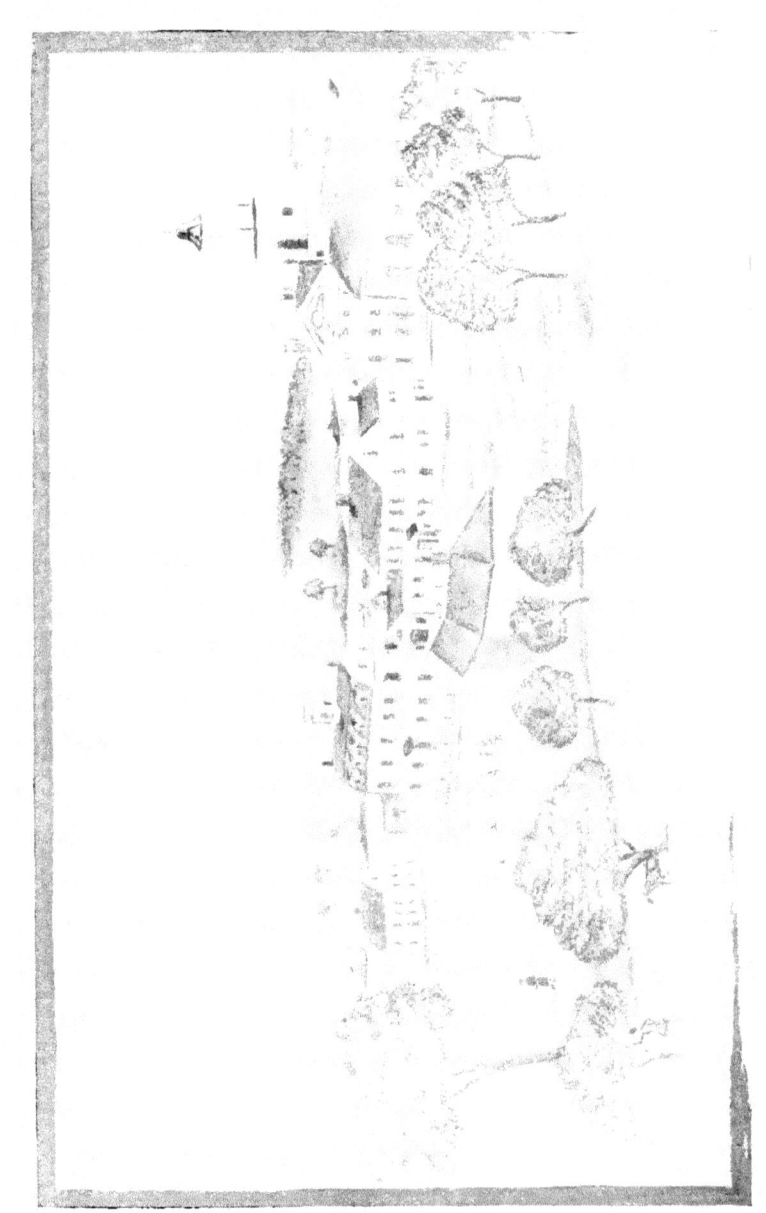

Pencil Sketch of the Plain about 1840.

CHAPTER LXXIII.

IN the first settlements, a plot of ground was usually left open in the centre of the town for public use, about which clustered the church, the parsonage, and public buildings. This centre of the town plot in Norwich was called "ye Green," "ye Meeting-House Green," and later "the Parade," "the Training Field," and "the Plain." What an event it must have been in the history of the town when the first train band, with Francis Griswold as Lieutenant, and Thomas Tracy as Ensign, assembled here in 1666. Under the special supervision of Major Mason, who, from the windows of his house at the south of the Green, could watch their evolutions, what a proficiency these "trainers" must have attained, for the old Major would hardly allow his Norwich company to fall behind the other train bands of the colony at the regular biennial reviews.

According to the laws of Connecticut, a band of thirty-two persons was entitled to a lieutenant, ensign and two sergeants, but no captain was allowed until the number of privates had increased to sixty-four. John Mason, 2nd, son of Major Mason, was the first captain of the Norwich train-band, and he received his appointment in 1675. What an impetus it must have given to the annual training when the new "drums, holbarts, and one pr. of collours" were purchased in 1708, and two companies were formed, the first with the popular Richard Bushnell as Captain, Solomon Tracy as Lieutenant, and Thomas Leffingwell, 2nd, as Ensign; and the second officered by Capt. Samuel Griswold, Lt. Joseph Backus, and Ensign Thomas Waterman.

In 1729, it was voted by the town "that the Plain in the Town Platt, called the Meeting House plain, with all its contents and extents of it as it now lyeth, shall be and remain to be and lye common for public use for the whole town forever without alteration." The first old meeting-house which was built on the south-east corner of the plain was still standing in 1705, but probably soon after disappeared.

In 1737, Nathaniel Lathrop requests permission "to build a shop on the plain," and it was then resolved by the inhabitants that "there shall no shop, barn, house, or any other building be erected, built, or sett up in or upon the above sd plain or any part thereof without special liberty from this Town." But it is possible that the town relented, and that later the privilege of building was granted to Nathaniel, as in 1757, it is voted "to remove all incumbrances off the lands late in possession of Nathaniel Lothrop, on the west side of the meeting house plain that the land may be fit for public use." Between 1760-62 the court-house was built upon the plain, and remained there until 1798.

On this Green, Capt. Philip Turner paraded and exercised his troop of horse, and Richard Bushnell, 2nd, who, under the captaincy of Philip Turner, had served as cornet, later succeeded him in command. Fines were imposed for non-appearance on Training day. On April 8, 1750, John Bliss, "Clerk of ye first company or Train band of Norwich," was ordered by Capt. Ebenezer Lathrop, to levy fines on all who did not "appear and answer to their names on the forth day of September, 1749, on ye Common place of parade," and "if any neglect or refuse to pay" he is "to distrain their goods or chattels" and for want of these "to seize ye body or bodys of such person or persons, and commit them unto ye Common Goal."

At the time of the Stamp Act excitement, Miss Caulkins says, that a liberty pole was erected on the Green adorned with standards and appropriate devices and crowned with a cap, and under it was built a tent or booth called the Pavilion.* Here the citizens met to celebrate the repeal of the Stamp Act with great rejoicings, and the effigy of Jared Ingersoll, the unpopular stamp distributor, was burnt on the high hill overlooking the plain. During the Revolution, this liberty pole was the rallying place for the citizens, and here they met daily, to make speeches and discuss the state of affairs.

* Miss Caulkins' History of Norwich.

In 1774, a field review of four companies was held on the plain, with the following officers:—

First Company.

JEDIDIAH HUNTINGTON, Captain.
JACOB PERKINS, JR., Lieutenant.
JOSEPH CAREW, Ensign.

Second Company.

SAMUEL WHEAT, Captain.
JOSEPH ELLIS, Lieutenant.
ISAAC GRISWOLD, Ensign.

Third Company.

ISAAC TRACY, JR., Captain.
JACOB WITTER, Lieutenant.
ANDREW TRACY, Ensign.

Fourth Company or Chelsea Company.

GERSHOM BREED, Captain.
BENJAMIN DENNIS, Lieutenant.
THOMAS TRAPP, Ensign.

"One of the words of command in training at this time was 'Blow off the loose corns,' and before and after the command to 'Poise arms' came 'Put your right hand to the fire-lock,' or 'Put your left hand to the fire-lock.' An odd kind of aspirate was sometimes used after a command, thus: 'Shoulder! hoo!'"*

The English colors were also used, "displaying the Cross of St. George in a field of red or blue, and sometimes the St. Andrew's Cross united with it in reference to the union of England and Scotland." It was perhaps of this grand training of 1774, that Miss Caulkins tells the tale of the artillery company, composed of strong patriots, who bore the banner of the State, while the light infantry appeared with the royal colors. In marching through the streets, the artillery encountered the infantry, and planting their cannon in the way, refused to let

---

* Miss Caulkins' History of Norwich.

them pass until they had lowered the royal standard, which from this time was never used again.

In 1777, Congress ordered that the flag, representing the thirteen original States, should have thirteen stripes, alternate red and white, with a union of thirteen stars, white on a blue field. In 1794, the number of stars and stripes was changed to fifteen. This was the flag of the war of 1812, for which was written the song called "The Star Spangled Banner." In 1818, the number of stripes was changed to the original thirteen, while it was ordered that the blue field should contain as many stars as there were States in the Union.

In 1774, the General Court ordered that the Norwich companies should form the Twentieth regiment of infantry, and Jedediah Huntington was appointed colonel, Samuel Abbot, lieutenant, and Zabdiel Rogers, major, and a regimental training was ordered for the first Monday in May, but by that time, most of the men were already in service at Boston, and no review took place.

On the Sunday following the Battle of Bunker Hill, toward the close of the morning service, the noise of a galloping horse was heard, and the church bell was violently rung. The audience rushed out upon the Green, and gathered around to hear the courier read the dispatches from the seat of war. That evening the bell was rung, cannons were fired, bonfires blazed, speeches were made, and many pledged themselves to join the army.

After the war was over, and independence was declared, how gay must have been the scenes enacted here on the yearly "training" day, when all the houses and taverns around were filled with guests, every table set with training or election cake, and wine, beer, or cider, and throngs of people straggling over the plain, and through the streets, among whom, the Mohegan Indians, with their queen, Betty Uncas, and their brooms, blankets and papooses were most conspicuous as they "lined the fence from Lord's to Lathrop's tavern." How the small boys enjoyed themselves, hovering as closely as possible to the military until, charged upon by a row of muskets, they scattered in all directions.

The first train-bands wore probably a modification of the Puritan or Roundhead costume. To the early colonial soldier was generally furnished the scarlet uniform of the British, but at the beginning of the Revolution, when the army was called hurriedly into the field, a great variety of dress and equipment prevailed. Even the officers were so poorly supplied, that Gen. Washington ordered that the general officers should be distinguished by ribbons across the breast, and later that the field officers should wear various colored cockades. He also requested that the troops should wear as much as possible hunting shirts and breeches, fastened garter fashion about the legs, but this was not generally adopted.

After the alliance with the French in 1779, stores of cloth were procured of the shade known as "Dutch blue," and it was ordered that this should be the army color, the Connecticut light horse or cavalry having their uniforms faced and lined with white, the artillery with red, and the general officers with yellow. The familiar continental or cocked hat was worn, the face was clean-shaven, with the hair clubbed or queued, and powdered. In 1781, the stock of blue cloth was exhausted, and none could be procured at any price. It was not until after 1782, that the army was completely uniformed.

In April, 1793, Adj. Gen. Ebenezer Huntington issues the orders of the Captain General for the militia of the State. The generals are to wear blue coats, faced and lined with buff, buff underdress, yellow buttons and epaulettes, and the aids-de-camp and brigade majors the same as the generals, except when they hold commissions in the line, in which case, they wear the uniform of the corps to which they belong. The officers of the regiments of foot are to wear blue coats, faced with red, and lined with white, white underdress, white buttons, and white epaulettes. The sergeants have the same uniform as the commissioned officers, and are designated by a white worsted "nott" on each shoulder. The "musick" are to be attired in red coats, faced with blue, and lined with white, trimmed with blue livery lace, white underdress, white buttons, and a blue worsted "nott" on each shoulder. The corporals and privates are to wear white frocks and overalls. All on horseback are to be armed with swords and pistols, and the troops are to have black cockades.

In August of the same year, the officers and men of the artillery regiments are ordered to wear blue coats, faced and lined with red, buff underdress, and yellow buttons, the officers to wear yellow belts, the sergeants a red worsted "nott" on each shoulder, and the corporals, one on the left shoulder. The "musick" are required to wear red coats faced and lined with blue, and trimmed with blue livery lace, yellow buttons and buff underdress, and a blue worsted "nott" on each shoulder. The Captain General is to be adorned with a deep blue ribbon across the breast, the Lieut. General with one of pink. The Major General has two stars on the strap of each epaulette, the Brig. General and Adj. General one star, and the latter wears one blue and one black feather on his hat. The hats of the aids-de-camp are adorned with white and black feathers, and the brigade-majors with blue and black.

In this year, the Twentieth regiment, commanded by Lt. Col. Joseph Williams, was reviewed by Maj. Gen. Gordon, and inspected by Brigade-Major Joseph Perkins. It consisted of one matross company, one light infantry, one grenadier, and eight infantry companies attended by Capt. Edgerton's troop of Horse. The Weekly Register thus expatiates on the scene: "Tho' mankind look forward with avidity to the season when 'swords shall be beaten into ploughshares, and spears into pruning hooks, and the nations learn war no more,' yet for beauty, order, regularity of movement and the true Sublime perhaps no place or situation short of the Heavenly Jerusalem can furnish scenes equal to military arrangements."

Mr. Charles Miner describes a review of long ago, when the Matross company, commanded by Roger Griswold, paraded in front of the meetinghouse, the light infantry near the Perit house, the common militia company stood facing west on the lower point of the Green—and the out-of-town companies were assigned positions by the adjutant on their arrival. He comments on "the fine soldier-like bearing of Gen. Marvin on his stately war steed," "accompanied by his aids in splendid uniform and nodding plumes." "The march was down east, and round the square. The band and brigade of drums and fifes under Collier and Manning alternating." After the parade was over, games were usually the order of the day, in which Capt. Griswold took the lead in cricket, Capt. Edward Slocum in wrestling, and John Post would show his agility by climbing the steeple. After the shades of evening had gathered, the sounds of revelry proceeded from Lathrop's tavern. "The officers have dined, and prefer punch, such as Lathrop only could make, to indifferent wine. The choicest Antigua, loaf sugar by the pailful, lemons, oranges, limes. Merrier fellows with tempered mirth never wore cockade or feather."

A more amusing, if not quite so imposing occasion, was the annual election of their governor by the colored people of the town. One of the first of these dignitaries was Boston Trow-trow, who died 1772, aged 66. After his death Samuel Hun'ton (named after his master, Gov. Huntington), was annually elected to the office for many years. "As he rode through the town on his master's horse adorned with plated gear, his aids on each side, à la militaire, himself puffing and swelling with pomposity, sitting bolt upright, and moving with a slow, majestic pace as if the universe was looking on. When he mounted or dismounted, his aid flew to his assistance, holding his bridle, putting his feet into the stirrup, and bowing to the ground before him. The Great Mogul in a triumphal procession never assumed an air of more perfect self-importance than the negro governor at such a time."* Provisions, and decorations, and liquors were freely furnished for this occasion, and the colored people made speeches, counted votes, and ended with a drunken frolic and often a fight. The last of these governors was Ira Tosset.

In old times, as well as now a-days, the plain was the center of boyish sports. In the winter, as Mr. Miner relates, the boys sometimes built "a semi circular fort of vast snow balls, eight or ten rods apart. When the snow was soft and would adhere, all hands were summoned to the work. A line of balls as big as could be rolled, was laid in a crescent; outside that, another as large. Then with skids, a row on the top, then a third row as large as could be raised on the summit, to crown the work, making a formidable breastwork. Lockers were cut out in the inside to hold great quantities of balls, made ready for action. When both sides were prepared, a proclamation was made, and then came "the tug of war." The Jabez Choate, whom Mr. Miner remembers, as the head of all the sports, "a favorite," "brave & clever," "who when he moved, moved like an engine," was perhaps, a son of Jabez and Eunice (Culver) Choate, and was born in 1771. He was a relative of the celebrated Rufus Choate.

During the war "the plays of the boys were battles with the regulars—

---

*Miss Caulkins' History of Norwich.

the charge—the ambuscade—the retreat—'The regulars are coming!' Then the rally and renewed charge. Their songs:—

> Don't you hear the general say
> Strike your tents and march away."*

The old Green, or "Training Field," though no longer a business centre, is still the rallying place for the boys of Norwich Town, and every part of it is endeared by many tender associations to the old inhabitants. The Hon. John T. Wait, alluding to the affection cherished for the Green, by some who have long since passed away, tells of one resident, who, remonstrating with a neighbor, about to move to Wequonnock, said: "Why, ———, I'd rather live all my life on Norwich Town Green, and then be hung at 'the Cross Keys,' than go to Wequonnock, and die a natural death."

---

* Letter of Hon. Charles Miner in "The Norwich Jubilee."

PART II.

GENEALOGIES.

A line, drawn across a genealogical page, indicates either a not absolutely verified descent, or that one or two generations are missing.

ABBOT.

I.

1. GEORGE ABBOT, b.   d. 1647. m.
   (From England to Rowley, Mass.)

II.

2. GEORGE, b.   in England. d. 1689. m. 1658 Sarah Farnum (or Farnham) b. ab. 1638. d. 1728.
   poss. sister of Ralph Farnham of Andover, Mass.
   She m. (2) (as second wife) 1689 Henry Ingalls of Andover, b. ab. 1627. d. 1719, son of Edmund Ingalls of Lynn, Mass.
   (To Andover, Mass.)

III.

3. JOHN. b. 1662. d. 1717–18. m.   Jemina   b.   d.   1754.
   (To Sudbury and to Watertown, Mass.) She m. (2) bef. 1721 John Beels. b.   d. 1740.

IV.

4. JOHN. b. 1701 d.   at Lexington, Mass. Elizabeth Phipps. b.   d.
   dau. of Solomon and Sarah (Sewell) Phipps of Cambridge, Mass.
   (From Stow, Mass., to Windham, Ct., ab. 1726. To West Farms or Franklin, Ct., in 1727.)

V.

5. (Col.) SAMUEL, b. 1726, at Windham, Ct. d. suddenly 1788. m. 1749 Phebe Edgerton, b. 1732. d. 1793.
   dau. of John and Phebe (Harris)(Frank)(Prentis) Edgerton.
   (To Norwich, Ct.)

VI.

Children of (Col.) Samuel (5) and Phebe (Edgerton) Abbot.

6. DANIEL. b. 1751. d.   m.   Sally Reynolds. b.   d.   dau. of Elisha and Sarah (Savillie or Smalley) Reynolds.
7. JEDEDIAH. b. 1755. d. 1760.
8. JOHN. b. 1757. d.
9. PHEBE. b. 1760. d. 1764.
10. EUNICE. b. 1762. d.   m.   Joshua Hobart. b.   d.
    (To New York.)
11. PHEBE. b. 1764. d.   m. 1783 Ephraim Baker, (or Barker?)
    (To Colrain, Ct., and Sheffield, Mass.)
12. SAMUEL. b. and d. 1766.
13. ELIZABETH. b. 1769. d.
14. PHEBE. bapt. 1771. d.
    (To Colrain, Ct., in 1800.)

VII.

Children of Daniel (6) and Sally (Reynolds) Abbot.

15. SAMUEL. (bapt. 1775. d.
16. SAMUEL.)
17. LORINDA. b. ab. 1777. d. 1800. m.   Eleazer Motier of Brooklyn, L.I. b.   d.
18. CLARA. bapt. 1782. d.

[407]

ADGATE.

I.

1. (Dea.) THOMAS ADGATE. b. ab. 1620. d. 1707. m. (1) ( ) Adgate (From Saybrook, Ct., to Norwich, Ct., 1660.) m. (2) ab. 1660 Mary (Marvin) Bushnell, b. 1629. d. 1713. dau. of Matthew Marvin and widow of Richard Bushnell.

II.

Children of (Dea.) Thomas (1) and ( ) Adgate.

2. ELIZABETH. b. 1651. d. m. 1672 Richard Bushnell.
3. HANNAH. b. 1653. d. 1695. m. 1675 Samuel Lathrop.

Children of (Dea.) Thomas (1) and Mary (Marvin) (Bushnell) Adgate.

4. ABIGAIL. b. 1661. d. 1711. m. 1682 Daniel Tracy.
5. SARAH. b. 1663. d. 1705-6. m. 1681 Christopher Huntington.
6. REBECCA. b. 1666. d. 1748. m. 1687 Joseph Huntington.
7. (Dea.) THOMAS. b. 1669-70. d. 1760. m. (1) 1692 Ruth Brewster. b. 1671. d. 1734. dau. of Benjamin and Anna (Dart) Brewster
   m. (2) 1749 Elizabeth (Morgan) Starr. b. 1678. d. 1763.
   dau. of Capt. James Morgan and widow of Capt. Jonathan Starr of Groton, Ct.

III.

Children of (Dea.) Thomas (7) and Ruth (Brewster) Adgate.

8. RUTH. b. 1692. d. 1729. m. 1714 John Edgerton, 2nd. b. 1690. d. son of John and Mary (Reynolds) Edgerton
   He m. (2) 1731 Phebe (Harris) (Frank) Prentis. dau. of Joseph Harris of New London, and widow first of John Crank, and second of Stephen Prentis.
9. MARY. b. 1694. d. 1676. d. 1739-40. m. 1718 Benjamin Lathrop.
10. REBECCA. b. 1696. d. 1781. unm.
11. HANNAH. b. 1699. d. m. 1733 (as second wife) John Durkee. b. 1659. d. of Norwich, Ct. son of John and Elizabeth (Parsons) Durkee of Gloucester, Mass.
12. THOMAS. b. 1702-3. d. 1736. m. 1731 Anne Huntington. b. 1745. d. 1759.
    She m. (2) 1739 Capt. Philip Turner.
    She m. (3) 1757 Capt. Joshua Abel.
13. MATTHEW. b. 1706. d. 1787. m. (1) 1727 Hannah Hyde. b. 1704. d. 1766. dau. of William and Anne (Bushnell) Hyde.
    m. (2) 1773 Abigail (Culverhouse) Waterman. b. 1719. d. 1777. widow of John Waterman.
14. MARTHA. b. 1710. d. 1755. m. 1731 Eleazer Waterman.
15. LUCY. b. 1714. d. 1717-18.

[408]

ADGATE.—Continued.

IV.

Children of Thomas (12) and Anne (Huntington) Adgate.

16. THOMAS. b. 1734. d. 1779 at New London. m. 1753 Ruth Leffingwell. b. 1736. d.   dau. of Capt. John and Mary (Hart) Leffingwell.
17. JOSATHAN. b. 1736. d. 1760.

Children of Matthew (13) and Hannah (Hyde) Adgate.

18. BENJAMIN. b. 1727. d. 1750. unm.
19. LUCY. b. 1731. d. 1813 at Canaan, N. Y. m. 1754 Joseph Lord.
20. ANDREW. b. 1733. d. 1754. unm.
21. DANIEL. b. 1735. drowned 1794. m. 1760 Phebe Waterman. b.   d. 1793 at Philadelphia. dau. of John and Anne (Ryder) Waterman.
22. MATTHEW. b. 1737. d. 1815. m. (1) 1762 Lucy Waterman. b. 1737. d. 1762. dau. of Asa and Lucy (Hyde) Waterman.
    m. (2) 1767 Eunice Baldwin. b.   d. 1787. dau. of Samuel Baldwin of Canaan, N. Y.
    m. (3) 1795 Janet (   )Williams. b.   d.   widow of   Williams.
    m. (4) 1815   )Norton. b.   d.   widow of Col. Rufus Norton of Chesterfield, N. Y.
23. ELIJAH. b. 1739. d. 1775. m. 1761 Abiah Perkins. b. 1738. d. 1766.
24. JABEZ. b. 1741. d. 1744. unm.
25. WILLIAM. b. 1744. d. 1779. m. 1767 Eunice Waterman. b. 1744 d. 1843. dau. of John and Abigail (Calverhouse) Waterman.

V.

Children of Daniel (21) and Phebe (Waterman) Adgate.

26. ANDREW. b. 1762. d. 1793 at Philadelphia of yellow fever.
27. PHEBE. b. 1765. d.
28. ASA. b. 1762. d. 1763.

Children of Matthew (22) and Lucy (Waterman) Adgate.

Children of Matthew (22) and Eunice (Baldwin) Adgate.

29. ASA, 2nd. b. 1767. d. 1832 at Chesterfield Falls N. Y. m. (1) 1795 Anna Allen. b. 1774. d. 1813. dau. of Jabez Allen of N. Y.
    m. (2) 1819 Anne Waterman. b. 1790. d. 1837.
30. ASHER. b. 1770. d. 1800. m. 1791 Delight Merril of Canaan, N. Y.   d. 1826. of New Lebanon, N. Y.
31. LUCY WATERMAN. b. 1772. d. 1837. m. 1800 Stephen Patterson. b.   d. 1821. dau. of Daniel Hawley of Canaan, N. Y.
32. MARTIN. b. 1776. drowned 1824 m. 1801 Hannah Hawley. b.

ADGATE.—Continued.

33. LUTHER. b. 1780. d. 1854. m. (1) 1807 Sarah Wright.   b.   d. 1809. dau. of Capt. Isaac Wright of Chesterfield, N. Y.
    m. (2) 1812 Anne Lord. b. 1785. d. 1820 at Essex, N. Y. dau. of Maj. Joseph and Lucy (Abel) Lord of Canaan, N. Y.
    m. (3) 1824 Mrs. Eliza (Wright) Willard. sister of his first wife.
34. HANNAH. b. 1782. d.   m. 1811 Benjamin Bacon. b.   d. 1815. of Canaan, N. Y.

Children of Elijah (23) and Abiah (Perkins) Adgate.

35. ABIGAIL. b. 1761. d. 1788. m. 1783 Lynde Lathrop. b. 1762. d. 1837. son of Elijah and Susannah (Lord) Lathrop.
    He m. (2) 1795 Polly L'Hommedieu. b.   d.
36. JABEZ. b. 1764. d.

Children of William (25) and Eunice (Waterman) Adgate.

37. DANIEL. b. 1768. d.   unm. at Philadelphia.
38. LUCY. b. 1769. d. 1781.
39. ESTHER. b. 1771. d.
40. WILLIAM. b. 1775. d.   at Philadelphia.

[410]

# ARNOLD.

I.

1. JOHN ARNOLD. b.   d.   m.   Mary
   (From Newark, N. J. to Killingworth, Ct.)
   (" Killingworth " Norwich, Ct.)
   (" Norwich   " Windham, Ct., ab. 1693)
   (Settled at "The Ponds" or Mansfield.)

II.

Children of John (1) and Mary (   ) Arnold.

2. BENEDICT. b.   at Newark. d.
3. JOHN. b.   at Newark. d. 1745. m. 1702 Elizabeth Cross. b. 1683. d.   dau. of Peter and Mary (   ) Cross.
4. SAMUEL. b.
5. STEPHEN. b.   at Newark. d.   m.   Sarah   b.   d.
6. BOWLEY. b. 1679–80 at Killingworth, Ct. d.   m. 1702 Elizabeth Lathrop. b. 1678. d.
   dau. of John and Ruth (Royce) Lathrop of Wallingford, Ct.
7. MARY. b. 1688 at Norwich. d.   m.   John Angell of Mansfield, Ct. b.   d.
8. ROBERT. b. 1690 at Norwich. d.   m. 1715–76 Mary Sargeant. b.   d. 1747. dau. of Ensign John Sargeant.
9. ELIZABETH. b. 1692 at Norwich. d. 1716. m. 1711 Thomas Huntington. b. 1688. d. 1755.
   son of Dea. Thomas and Elizabeth (Backus) Huntington of Mansfield, Ct.
   He m. (2) 1733 Mehetabel Johnson. dau. of James Johnson of Andover.
10. MEHITABLE. b. 1694 at Windham. d.   m.   James Royce of Mansfield, Ct. b.   d.

[411]

AVERY.

I.

1. CHRISTOPHER AVERY. b. d. 1679. m.
(To New England in 1630 or 1631.)
(To Gloucester, Mass.)
(Selectman in 1646, 1652 and 1654.)
(To Boston, Mass., in 1658.)
(To New London, Ct., betw. 1663-5.)

II.

2. (Capt.) JAMES. b. ab. 1620. d. 1700. m. (1) 1643 Joanna Greenslade. b. ab. 1622. d. aft. 1693.
m. (2) 1698 Abigail ( ) (Cheesebrough) Holmes. b. d. aft. 1714 widow first of Samuel Cheesebrough, second of Joshua Holmes.

(To New London, Ct., from Gloucester, Mass., 1650-1.)
(Built house at Groton, Ct., known as "The Hive of the Averys.")
(Was Ensign, Lieutenant and Captain, and served as Deputy twelve times betw. 1658-80.)

III.

3. (Capt.) THOMAS. b. 1651. d. 1737. m. 1677 Hannah Miner. b. 1655. d. 1692. dau. of Thomas and Grace (Palmer) Miner of Stonington, Ct.
(To Montville, Ct.)

IV.

4. SAMUEL. b. 1680. d. 1750. m. 1702 Elizabeth Ransford. b. d. 1761. dau. of Jonathan Ransford (or Rainsford).
(Saybrook, Ct.)

V.

5. JOHN. b. 1723. d. 1790. m. 1745 Prudence Miner. b. 1719. d. 1790. dau. of Thomas and Hannah (Avery?) Miner.
(Montville, Ct.)
6. SAMUEL. b. 1752-9. d. 1844. m. 1780 Candace Charlton. b. 1748. d. 1816.
(Norwich, Ct.)

VI.

Children of Samuel (6) and Candace (Charlton) Avery.

7. ELIZABETH. b. 1781. d. 1822. m. 1804 Maj. Thomas Tracy. b. 1767. d. 1806.
8. HENRY. b. 1783. d. 1783.
9. SAMUEL. b. 1784. d. m. Chloe b. d.
10. HENRY. b. 1786. d. m.
11. EUNICE. b. 1789. d. 1792.

AVERY.

I.

1. CHRISTOPHER AVERY. b. d. 1679. m. (Groton, Ct.)
(See genealogy of Samuel Avery on preceding page.)

II.

2. (Capt.) JAMES. b. ab. 1620. d. 1700. m. (1) 1643 Joanna Greenslade. b. ab. 1622. d. aft. 1693.
m. (2) 1693 Abigail (   ) (Cheesebrough) Holmes. b.   d. aft. 1714.
(Groton, Ct.) widow first of Samuel Cheesebrough, and second of Joshua Holmes

III.

3. JOHN. b. 1654. d.   m. 1675 Abigail Cheesebrough. b. 1656. d.   dau. of Samuel and Abigail (   ) Cheesebrough of Stonington, Ct.
(Groton, Ct.)

IV.

4. JOHN. b. aft. 1683. d.   m. 1705 Sarah Denison.
(Groton, Ct.)

V.

5. JOHN. b. 1706. d.   m. ab. 1730 Lydia Smith. b.   d.   perhaps dau. of Samuel and Elizabeth (Ely) Smith of Saybrook, Ct

VI.

6. JABEZ. b. 1733. d. 1779. m. (1) 1755 (?) Lydia.
(Resided in Norwich, Ct.) m. (2) 1761 Lucy Bushnell. b. 1733. d. 1789. dau. of Capt Richard and Lucy (Perkins) Bushnell.

VII.

Children of Jabez (6) and Lucy (Bushnell) Avery.

7. JABEZ. b. 1763. d.   m. 1789 Eunice Huntington. b. 1766. d. 1790.
8. RICHARD. b. 1764. d.   m. 1789 Lucy Lord. b. 1769. d. 1841.
   She m. 2) 1826 Capt. Erastus Perkins.
9. LUCY. b. 1766. d. 1856. m. 1788 Bela Lethingwell. b. 1766. d. 1746 at Charleston, S. C. son of Matthew and Clarity (Bushnell) Lethingwell.
10. HASSAH. b. 1767. d.
11. JOHN. b. 1769. d.   m. 1794 (?) Lucy Woodworth of Montville, Ct.
12. GURDON. b. 1771. d.
13. CALEB. b. 1773. d.   m.   Prudence Avery. b. 1777. d.   perhaps dau. of Ephraim and Abigail (Bill) Avery of Montville, Ct.

[413]

BACKUS.

I.

1. WILLIAM BACKUS. b.   d. bef. 1664.   m. (1) Sarah Charles (?) b.   d.   dau. of John Charles of Branford, Ct.
   m. (2) bef. 1660 Ann (   ) Bingham. b.   d. 1670. widow of Thomas Bingham.

II.

Children of William (1) and Sarah (Charles) Backus.

2. (Lt.) WILLIAM. b.   d. ab. 1721.   m. bef. 1660 Elizabeth Pratt. b. 1641. d. 1730. dau. of Lt. William and Elizabeth (Clark) Pratt of Saybrook, Ct.
3. STEPHEN. b.   d. bef. 1700.   m. 1666 Sarah Spencer. b.   d.   poss. dau. of Jared and Hannah (   ) Spencer of Haddam, Ct.
4. SARAH. b.   d.   m.   John Reynolds.
5. MARY. b.   d.   m. 1655 Benjamin Crane.
6.   b.   d.   m.   John Bayley (?) b.   d.

III.

Children of (Lt.) William (2) and Elizabeth (Pratt) Backus.

7. WILLIAM. b. 1660. d. 1742.   m. (1) 1681 Elizabeth
   (To Windham, Ct., ab. 1692.)   m. (2) 1692 Mary Dunton. b. 1662. (?) d. 1757. poss. dau. of Samuel Dunton of Reading, Mass.
8. JOHN. b. 1661-2. d. 1744.   m. 1691-2 Mary Bingham. b. 1672. d. 1747. dau. of Thomas and Mary (Rudd) Bingham.
   (To Windham, Ct., ab. 1692.)
9. SARAH. b. 1663. d.   m. 1681-2 Edward Culver. b.   d.   son of Edward and Ann (   ) Culver of New London, Ct.
   (To Lebanon from Norwich ab. 1698.)
10. SAMUEL. b. 1665. d.
11. JOSEPH. b. 1667. d.   m. 1690 Elizabeth Huntington. b. 1669. d.
12. NATHANIEL. b. 1669. d. 1728.   m. (1) 1693-4 Lydia Edgerton. b. 1675. d.   dau. of Richard and Mary (Sylvester) Edgerton.
                                  m. (2) 1702 Elizabeth Tracy. b. 1676. d. 1739. dau. of John and Mary (Winslow) Tracy.
13. ELIZABETH. b.   d. 1728.   m. 1686-7 Capt. Thomas Huntington.
14. HANNAH. b.   d.   m. (1) 1691-2 Thomas Bingham, 2nd. b. 1667. d. 1710. son of Thomas and Mary (Rudd) Bingham.
                                  m. (2) 1712 Daniel Tracy.

Children of Stephen (3) and Sarah (Spencer) Backus.

15. SARAH. b. 1668. d.   m. 1691-2 David Knight. b.   d. 1744.
16. STEPHEN. b. 1670. d. 1707.   m. (?)
17. MARY. b. 1672. d. 1752.   m. 1697 Thomas Hyde. b. 1672. d. 1755. son of Samuel and Jane (Lee) Hyde.
    (West Farms or Franklin.)

[414]

BACKUS.—Continued.

18. RUTH. b. 1674. d.   m.   Robert Green. b.   d.   of Canterbury, Ct.
19. LYDIA. b. 1677. d.   m. 1702 David Birchard. poss. an unrecorded son of John Birchard or identical with Daniel, son of John. b. 1680.
20. TIMOTHY. b. 1682. d.   m. 1708–9 Sarah Post.   poss. dau. of John and Sarah (Reynolds) Post.
21. ELIZABETH. b. 1686. d.   m. 1713–14 Nathaniel Bond of Canterbury, Ct. b. 1686. d.   poss. son of Nathaniel and Bethiah (Fuller) Bond of Watertown, Mass.
22. REBECCA. b.   d.   m. 1706 William Baker. b.   d.

IV.

Children of Joseph (11) and Elizabeth (Huntington) Backus.

23. JOSEPH. b. 1691. d.   m. 1721–2 Hannah Edwards. b. 1696. d. 1747. dau. of Richard and Mary (Talcott) Edwards of Hartford, Ct.
24. SAMUEL. b. 1693. d. 1749. m. 1715–16 Elizabeth Tracy. b. 1698. d. 1769. dau. of John and Elizabeth (Leffingwell) Tracy.
25. ANN. b. 1695. d. 1701. m. 1717 Nathaniel Lathrop.
26. (Rev.) SIMON. b. 1700–1. d. 1746. m. 1729 Eunice Edwards. b. 1705. d. 1788.   dau. of Rev. Timothy and Esther (Stoddard) Edwards of East Windsor, Ct.
27. JAMES. b. 1703. d.
28. ELIZABETH. b. 1705. d. 1787. m. 1725 Cyprian Lord.
29. SARAH. b. 1709. d. 1792. m. 1732 Isaac Bingham. b. 1709. d. 1792. son of Nathaniel and Sarah (Lobdell) Bingham.
30. EBENEZER. b. 1712. d. 1798. m. (1) 1741 Abigail Trumbull. b. 1719. d. 1744.
            m. (2) 1745 Eunice Dyer. b. 1727. d. 1751. dau. of Col. Thomas and Lydia (Backus) Dyer of Windham, Ct.
            m. (3) 1753 Sarah Clark. b.   d.   dau. of Benjamin and Miriam (Kilby) Clark of Boston, Mass.

V.

Children of Samuel (24) and Elizabeth (Tracy) Backus.

31. SAMUEL. b. 1716–17. d.   m. 1743 Phebe Calkins. b. 1721. d.   dau. of Hugh and Phebe (Abel) Calkins
32. ANN. b. 1718. d. 1759. m. 1712 as second wife (Capt.) Joshua Abel. b. 1708. d. 1785. son of Lt. Samuel and Elizabeth (Skinner) Abel.
33. ELIZABETH. b. 1720–1. d. 1748. m. 1741–2 (Gen.) Jabez Huntington.
34. (Rev.) ISAAC. b. 1723–4. d. 1806. m. 1749 Susanna Mason. b. 1725. d. 1800. dau. of Samuel Mason of Rehoboth, Mass.
    (Minister of the Baptist Church at Middleboro, Mass.)
35. ELIJAH. b. 1726. d. 1796. m. (1) 1753 Lucy Griswold. b. 1729. d. 1795. dau. of John and Hannah (Lee) Griswold of Lyme, Ct.
            m. (2) 1794 Margaret (Grant) Tracy. b.   d. 1815. widow of Jared Tracy.
36. SIMON. b. 1728–9. d.
37. EUNICE. b. 1731. d. 1754. m. 1752 John Post. b. 1729. d.   son of Nathaniel and Abigail (Birchard) Post.
            He m. (2) 1757 Abigail Leffingwell. b. 1734. d.   dau. of Samuel and Hannah (Bishop) Leffingwell.
38. (Maj.) ANDREW. b. 1733. d.   m. 1759 Lois Pierce. b. 1732. d.   dau. of Thomas and Mary (   ) Pierce of Plainfield, Ct.
    (To Plainfield, Ct.)

BACKUS.—Continued.

39. ASA. b. 1736. d. 1788. m. 1762 Esther Parkhurst. b. d. poss. of Plainfield, Ct.
40. LUCY. b. 1738. d. m. 1764 Benajah Leffingwell.
41. (Dea.) JOHN. b. 1740. d. 1814.

Children of (Maj.) Andrew (38) and Lois (Pierce) Backus.

42. STEPHEN. b. 1759. d. m. 1798 Eunice Whitney. b. d.
    (To Norwich, Ct., ab. 1798.)
43. (Dr.) THOMAS. b. 1762. d. m. 1793 at Norwich, Ct., Lydia Lathrop. b. d.
44. SIMON. b. 1765. d. 1788.
45. SILVENUS (or SYLVANUS.) b. 1765. d.
46. EUNICE. b. 1770. d.
47. POLLY. b. 1773. d. m. (?) 1796 John Lester.
48. LUCY. b. 1777.

Children of Stephen (42) and Eunice (Whitney) Backus.

49. GEORGE WHITNEY. b. 1800. d.

[416]

BILLINGS.

I.

1 WILLIAM BILLINGS (or BILLING.) b.   d. 1713   m. 1658 at Dorchester, Mass, Mary
   (From Taunton, Eng., to New England.)
   (Said to have been one of the original proprietors of Lancaster in 1654.)
   (At Dorchester, Mass, in 1658.)
   (To Stonington, Ct.)

II.

2 WILLIAM. b.   d. 1733. m.   Hannah   b.   d.
   (To Preston, Ct.)

III.

Children of William (2) and Hannah (   ) Billings.

3. MARY.   b. 1689. d.   m. 1713 John Boardman. b.   d.
4. JOSEPH.   bapt. 1692. d.   m. (1) Comfort   b.   d.
                                 m. (2) Sarah   b.   d.
5. PRUDENCE. bapt. 1694. d.
6. (Rev.) WILLIAM. b. 1697. d. 1733. m. 26, 1724 Bethiah Otis. b. 1703. d.   dau. of Joseph and Dorothy (Thomas) Otis of Montville, Ct.
    (Settled in a part of Windham, now Hampton, in 1723.)   She m. (2) Rev. Samuel Mosely of Hampton, Ct.
7. SAMUEL.   b. 1699. d. 1727. m. 1725 Hannah Williams. b.   d.
8. DOROTHY. b. 1702. d.   m. 1720 Thomas Edwards.   b.   d.
9. RACHEL.   b. 1704. d.   m.   Kennedy.   b.   d.
10. SARAH (?) b. 1705. d.
11. HANNAH.   b. 1705-6. d.   m. 1739-4 Eleazer Putnam of Preston. b. 1695 (?) d. 1745-6 poss. son of Eleazer and Hannah (Boardman) Putnam of Danvers, Mass.
12. (Capt.) ROGER. b. 1708. d.   m. 1729 Abigail Denison. b. 1708. d.   dau. of William and Mary (Avery) Denison of Stonington, Ct.
13. ICHABOD. b. 1710. d.
14. ELIZABETH b. 1712-13. d. 1791. m. 1733 Theophilus Avery of Groton, Ct. b. 1708. d. 1799, son of Edward and Joanna (Rose) Avery.

[117]

BILLINGS—Continued.

IV.

Children of (Capt.) Roger (12) and Abigail (Denison) Billings.

15. ABIGAIL. b. 1729–30. d. 1760. m. 1753 Benjamin Coit. b. 1731. d. 1812. son of Col Samuel and Sarah (Spalding) Coit. He married (2) 1760 Mary (Tyler) Boardman. b. ab. 1730. d. 1809. dau. of Capt Moses Tyler and widow of Elijah Boardman.
16. JOHN. b. 1732. d. m. 1757 Eunice Gallup. b. 1738. d. dau. of Capt. Joseph and Eunice (Williams) Gallup of Stonington, Ct.
17. (Capt.) WILLIAM. b. 1734. d. 1774. m. 1757 Mary (Leffingwell) Richards. b. 1731. d. 1805. widow of Nathaniel Richards and dau. of Benajah and Joanna (Christophers) Leffingwell.
18. PELEG. b. 1738. d. m. Mary b. d.
19. DOROTHY. b, 1741 d.
20. BENJAMIN. b. 1743. d.
21. (Capt.) HENRY. b. 1746. d. 1797 at Port au Paix. m. 1770 Lucretia Leffingwell. b, 1749. d. sister of William's wife. She m. (2) 1795 Dea. Thomas Brown of Hebron, Ct.
22. SABRA. b. 1751. d. m. Elias Brown. b. d.
23. MARY. b. 1755. d. 1823. m 1771 Darius Denison. b. 1747. d. 1829. son of William and Prudence (Denison) Denison. (Stonington, Ct.)

V.

Children of (Capt.) William (17) and Mary (Leffingwell) (Richards) Billings.

24. NATHANIEL. b. 1758. d.
25. ABIGAIL. b. 1760. d. 1761.
26. ABIGAIL, 2nd. b. 1762. d. m. 1804 James Busby.
27. BETSEY. b. 1764. d. 1818. m. 1787 (Capt.) Bela Peck. He m. (2) 1819 Lydia (Shipman) Spalding. widow of Asa Spalding and dau. of Nathaniel and Elizabeth. (Leffingwell) Shipman.
28. RICHARD LEFFINGWELL. b. 1768. d. 1795.

[418]

BIRCHARD.

I.

1. THOMAS BIRCHARD, b.   d.   m.   Mary   b.   d. 1655.
(In Truelove from England in 1635.)
(At Boston, Mass., in 1637.)
(At Hartford, Ct., 1639.)
(At Saybrook, Ct., 1650-1.)

II.

2. JOHN. b. ab. 1628. d. 1702. m. (1) 1653 Christian Andrews. b,   d.
(To Norwich, Ct, in 1660.) m. (2) (?)   Jane (Lee) Hyde. b.   d. 1723, widow of Samuel Hyde and Jno. of Thomas Lee of Lyme, Ct.
(To Lebanon, Ct., ab. 1695.)

III.

Children of John (2) and Christian (Andrews) Birchard.

3. THOMAS. b. 1654. d. 1658.
4. CATHERINE. b. and d. 1656.
5. JOHN. b. 1657. d. 1658.
6. JOHN, 2nd. b. 1659. d. 1662.
7. SARAH. b. 1661. d. 1664.
8. b. SAMUEL. 1663. d.   m. 1695 Ann Caulkins. b. 1670. d.   dau. of David and Mary (Bliss) Caulkins of New London, Ct.
(To New London, Ct.)   She m. (2) 1720-1 Josiah Rockwell of Norwich. b. 1662. d. 1728-9.
9. JAMES. b. 1665. d. aft. 1745. m. 1695 Elizabeth Beckwith. b. 1679 (?) d. 1754. perhaps dau. of Matthew Beckwith, 2nd, of Lyme, Ct.
(Lived in Norwich, Ct.)
10. ABIGAIL. b. 1667. d.   m. 1690 John Calkins. b. 1661. d.   son of John and Sarah (Royce) Calkins.
(To Lebanon, Ct.)
11. THOMAS. b. 1669. d.   m. 1708 (?) Sarah Webb. b.   d.
(Lebanon, Ct.)
12. JOHN. b. 1671. d. 1735. m. 1708 Hannah Loomis. b. ab. 1677. d. 1740.
(Lebanon, Ct.)
13. JOSEPH. b. 1673. d.
14. BENJAMIN. b. and d. 1675.
15. MARY. b. 1677. d.
16. DANIEL. b. 1680. d.
17. DAVID. (?) b.   d.   m. 1702 Lydia Backus. b. 1677. d.
(Norwich, Ct.)

BIRCHARD—Continued.

IV.

Children of Samuel (8) and Ann (Caulkins) Birchard.

18. SAMUEL. bapt. 1697 in New London. d.
19. ANN. bapt. 1701 in New London. d.   m. 1721 Thomas Grist.
20. ABIGAIL. (?) bapt. Hartford 1704.

Children of James (9) and Elizabeth (Beckwith) Birchard.

21. ELIZABETH. b. 1697. d.   m.
22. JAMES. b. 1699. d.   m. 1723 Deborah Marks. b.   d.
23. SARAH. b. and d. 1701.
24. MATTHEW. b. 1702. d.   m. 1725 Ruth Hartshorn. b. 1706. d.   dau. of Jonathan and Mary (Richards) Hartshorn.
25. JOHN. b. 1704. d.
    m. (1) 1728 Jane Hyde. b. 1704. d. 1755. dau. of Thomas and Mary (Backus) Hyde.
    m. (2) 1755 Mrs. Mary Burrell. b.   d. 1774.
    m. (3) 1774 Sarah (Hewitt) Hyde. b. 1708 at Mansfield, Mass. d. 1777. widow of Eleazer Hyde.
26. PHEBE. b. 1705. d.
27. SARAH. b. 1707. d.
28. JONAH. b. 1709. d.   m. 1731 David Hartshorn. b.   d.
29. REBECCA. b. 1717. d. 1719.
30. DANIEL. b. 1718. d.   m. 1745 Elizabeth Cooley. b.   d.   of Springfield, Mass.

V.

Children of John (25) and Jane (Hyde) Birchard.

31. JEMINA. b. 1729. d. 1789. m. 1752 (as second wife) Jedediah Lathrop. b. 1718. d. 1792. son of Israel and Mary (Fellows) Lathrop. (To Bozrah, Ct.)
32. EZRA. b. 1731. d.   m. 1756 Martha Barret. b. 1740. d.   dau. of Ezekiel and Mary (Lathrop) Barret.
33. JOHN. b. 1733. d.   m. 1759 Ann Barker. b. 1743. d. 1822.
34. GIDEON. b. 1735. d.   at Utica, N. Y. m. 1757 Eunice Abel. b. 1737. d.   dau. of Capt. Joshua and Jerusha (Frink) Abel. (To Whitestown, N. Y.)
35. PHEBE. b. 1736-7. d.   m. 1760 Jacob Worthington. b. 1735-6. d. 1793. perh. son of Daniel and Elizabeth (Loomis) Worthington of Colchester, Ct. (Bozrah, Ct.)
36. PHINEHAS. b. 1738. d.   m. 1764 Lydia Farnham. b.   d.
37. JANE. b. 1740.
38. MATTHEW. b. 1743. d.   m. 1774 Anne Pelton. b.   d.   of Bozrah.

[420]

BIRCHARD.—Continued.

39. LOIS, b. 1744, d. 1769, m. 1767 Joseph Chapman, b. 1729, d.   son of Joseph and Elizabeth (Ormsby) Chapman.
    He m. (2)   Elizabeth Abel, b. 1749, d.   dau. of Capt. Joshua and Anne (Rackins) Abel.
40. ELIZABETH, b. 1746, d.   m. (?) 1775 Benjamin Corning, b. 1748–9, d.   son of Nehemiah and Mary (Pride) Corning. (Bozrah, Ct.)
41. LUCY, b. 1748, d.   m. (?) 1775 William Edgerton, b. 1744, d.   son of Joseph and Elizabeth (Haskins) Edgerton.

VI.

Children of Gideon (34) and Eunice (Abel) Birchard.

42. ELISHA, b. 1755, d.   m.   Thankful   b.   d.
    (To Whitestown, N. Y.)
43. EUNICE, b. 1760, d. 1796, m. 1773 Thomas Langrell Thomas, b. 1757, d. 1827, son of Ebenezer and Deborah (Hyde) Thomas.
    He m. (2) 1799 Anne (Post) Blake, b. 1766, d. ab. 1818, widow of Henry Blake, and
        dau. of Abner and Lucy (Hyde) Post.
44. ROGER, b. 1762, d. 1782.
45. JEDEDIAH, b. 1765, d.
46. GIDEON, b. 1767, d.
47. LOIS, b. 1770, d. 1779.
48. JERUSHA, b. 1773, d. 1792, unm.
49. ERASTUS, b. 1780.

BLISS.

I.

1. THOMAS BLISS. b. ab. 1580–5. d. 1650. m. 1612–15 Margaret Lawrence. b. d. 1684
   (Came from Belstone Parish, Co. Devonshire, Eng., to Braintree, Mass., in 1635.)
   (To Hartford, Ct.)
   (Widow and other children to Springfield, Mass., after Thomas' death.)

II.

2. THOMAS. b. d. 1688. m. 1644 Elizabeth b. d.
   (From Hartford to Saybrook, Ct.)
   (To Norwich in 1660.)

Children of Thomas (2) and Elizabeth ( ) Bliss.

III.

3. ELIZABETH. b. 1645. d. 1689. m. 1663 Edward Smith. b. d. 1689.
4. SARAH. b. 1647. d. 1730. m. (1) 1668 Thomas Shuman.
   m. (2) 1686 (Dr.) Solomon Tracy.
5. MARY. b. 1649. d. m. 1672–3 David Calkins of New London. b. d. 1717. son of Hugh Calkins, Sr.
6. THOMAS. b. 1652. d. 1681–2.
7. DOLINDA (or DELIVER, or DELIVERANCE). b. 1655. d. m. 1682 Daniel Perkins. b. d. dau. of John and Elizabeth (Drake) (Gaylord) Elderkin.
8. SAMUEL. b. 1657. d. 1731. m. 1681 Ann Elderkin. b. 1661. d. 1748. dau. of John and Elizabeth (Drake) (Gaylord) Elderkin.
9. ANNE. b. 1660. d. 1714–15. m. 1658 Josiah Rockwell. b. 1662. d. 1725. son of Josiah Rockwell of Preston.
   He m. (2) 1720–1 Ann (Calkins) Birchard. dau. of David Calkins and widow of Samuel Birchard.
10. REBECCA. b. 1663. d. 1737. m. 1656 Israel Lothrop.

Children of Samuel (8) and Ann (Elderkin) Bliss.

IV.

11. THOMAS. b. 1682. d. 1719 of a rattlesnake bite. m. 1708 Mary Loomer. b. ab. 1687. d. dau. of Stephen and Mary (Miller) Loomer of New London, Ct.
12. SAMUEL. b. 1684. d. 1763. m. 1715 Sarah Packer. b. d. 1775. dau. of John Packer of Groton, Ct.
13. ELIZABETH. b. 1686–7. d. 1757. m. 1710 (as second wife) (Capt.) Daniel White. b. 1671. d. 1726 of Hatfield, Vt., and Windsor, Ct.
14. (Rev.) JOHN. b. 1690. d. 1741. m. 1709–10 Anna b. d.
    (Settled at Hebron, Ct. Dismissed 1735. Episcopal Lay Reader from 1734–1741.)
15. PELETIAH. b. 1697. d. 1765. m. 1725 Mrs. Martha (Avery) Comstock. b. 1707. d. widow of Peter Comstock and dau. of Samuel and Hannah (Miner) Avery of Montville, Ct.
16. THANKFUL. b. 1699–1700. d. m. 1719 Joseph Willoughby. b. d.

[422]

BLISS.—Continued.

V.

Children of Samuel (12) and Sarah (Packer) Bliss.

17. JOHN. b. 1717. d. 1809. m. 1747 Sarah Huntington. b. 1721. d. 1806.
18. DESIRE. b. 1719. d. 1805. m. George Dennis. b. 1718. d. son of Ebenezer Dennis of New London.
19. THANKFUL. b. 1721. d. 1793. m. 1746 Benjamin Denais. b. ab. 1722. d. 1746. son of Ebenezer Dennis of New London.
20. FREELOVE. b. 1723. d. 1807. m. 1754 Nehemiah Corning. b. d.
21. MINDWELL. b. 1726. d. 1765. m. 1746 Daniel Rockwell. b. 1724. d. son of Daniel and Tabitha (Hartshorn) Rockwell.

VI.

Children of John (17) and Sarah (Huntington) Bliss.

22. JOHN. b. 1748-9. d. 1815. unm.
23. ELIAS. b. 1750-1. d. 1833. unm.
24. ZEPHANIAH. b. 1753. d. 1827. m. 1794 Temperance Lord. b. 1764. d. 1839.
25. SARAH b. 1757. d. 1786. m. 1784 Frederick Huntington. b. d.
26. WILLIAM. b. 1766. d. m. 1813 Lydia Wells. b. 1785. d. dau. of James Wells.

VII.

Children of Zephaniah (24) and Temperance (Lord) Bliss.

27. JOHN. b. 1795. d. m. 1830 Abby Williams. b. 1802. d. 1885.
28. CHARLES. b. 1797. d. 1868. m. 1820 Elizabeth B. Clement. b. 1792. d. 1877. dau. of Peabody and Elizabeth (Shipman) Clement.
29. SARAH. b. 1799. d. 1875. unm.
30. ANNA. b. 1811. d. 1822. unm.
31. GEORGE. b. 1804. d. 1857. unm.
32. LYDIA. b. 1806-7. d. 1884. unm.

[423]

BRADFORD.

I.

1. (Gov.) WILLIAM BRADFORD. b. 1588-9. d. 1657. m. (1) Dorothy May. b. drowned in Provincetown Harbor 1620.
m. (2) 1623 Alice (Carpenter) Southworth. b. 1590. d. 1670.
(From Austerfield, Co. Yorkshire, Eng., to Holland in 1608.) dau. of Alexander Carpenter and widow of Edward Southworth.
(To Plymouth, N. E., in Mayflower in 1620.)

II.

Children of (Gov.) William (1) and Dorothy (May) Bradford.

2. JOHN. b. d. 1678 s. p. m. Martha Bourne. b. d. 1689. ( ) Bourne of Marshfield, Mass.
dau. of Dea. Thomas and Martha (

3. (Dep. Gov.) WILLIAM. b. 1624. d. 1703-4. m. (1) Alice Richards. b. d. 1674. ( ) Richards of Weymouth, Mass.
She m. (2) bef. 1679 Lt. Thomas Tracy. dau. of Thomas and Wealthian ( ) Wiswall. b. d. (widow.)
m. (2) ( ) (Said to be a dau. of Thomas Fitch of Norwalk, Ct.)
m. (3) Mary (Atwood) Holmes. b. d.
widow of Rev. John Holmes of Duxbury, Mass., and dau. of John and Sarah
(Masterton) Atwood of Plymouth, Mass.

4. MERCY. b. 1627. d. m. 1648 Benjamin Vermayes. b. d. of Boston and of Plymouth, Mass.
5. JOSEPH. b. 1630. d. m. 1664 Jael Hobart. b. 1643. d. 1730. dau. of Rev. Peter Hobart of Hingham, Mass.

III.

Children of (Gov.) William (3) and Alice (Richards) Bradford.

6. JOHN. b. 1652-3. d. 1736. m. 1674 Mercy Warren. b. 1653. d. 1747. dau. of Joseph and Priscilla (Faunce) Warren of Plymouth, Mass.
7. WILLIAM. b. 1655. d. 1687. m. 1679 Rebecca Bartlett. b. d. dau. of Benjamin and Sarah (Brewster) Bartlett of Duxbury, Mass. (?)
(Lived in Kingston, Mass.)
8. THOMAS. b. d. 1708. m. ab. 1681 Ann Smith. b. d. dau. of Nehemiah and Ann (Bourne) Smith of Norwich, Ct.
(Lived at Norwich and at Montville, Ct.)
9. (Lt.) SAMUEL. b. 1668. d. 1714. m. 1689 Hannah Rogers. b. 1668. d. dau. of John and Elizabeth (Peabody) Rogers of Plymouth, Mass.
(Lived at Duxbury, Mass.)

BRADFORD.—Continued.

10. ALICE. b. 1661. d. 1745. m. (1) 1679 (as second wife) Rev. William Adams. b. 1650. d. 1685. of Dedham, Mass. son of William Adams of Ipswich, Mass.
    m. (2) 1687 Maj. James Fitch of Norwich, Ct.
    (lived at Dedham, Mass., and at Norwich and Canterbury, Ct.)
11. HANNAH. b. 1662. d. 1738. m. (1) 1682 Joshua Ripley. b. 1658. d. 1739. son of John and Elizabeth (Hobart) Ripley of Hingham, Mass. (lived in Windham, Ct.)
12. MERCY. b. d. 1729. m. 1689 Samuel Steele. b. 1652. d. of Hartford, Ct. son of John and Mary or Mercy (Warner) Steele of Farmington, Ct.
13. MELATIAH. b. d. m. John Steele of Norwich, Ct., perh. brother of Samuel Steele. b. 1650. (?) d.
14. MARY. b. d. m. William Hunt of Weymouth, Mass.
15. SARAH. b. 1655. d. m. Kenelm Baker b. 1655. d. son of Samuel and Elinor (Winslow) Baker of Marshfield, Mass.

Children of (Gov.) William (3) and ( ) (Wiswall) Bradford.

16. (Lt.) JOSEPH. b. 1674. d. 1747. m. (1) 1698 Anne Fitch. b. 1675. d. 1715.
    Said to have m. (2) 1715–16 Mary (Sherwood) Fitch. widow of Daniel Fitch. b. d. 1752.
    (To Lebanon and Mohegan or Montville, Ct.)

Children of William (3) and Mary (Atwood) (Holmes) Bradford.

17. ISRAEL. b. 1678. d. m. 1701 Sarah Bartlett. b. d. dau. of Benjamin and Ruth (Pabody) Bartlett.
18. EPHRAIM. b. 1690. d. m. 1710 Elizabeth Bartlett. b. d. dau. of Benjamin and Ruth (Pabody) Bartlett.
19. DAVID. b. d. 1739. m. 1714 Elizabeth Finney. b. 1691. d. dau. of John and Mary (Rogers) Finney of Plymouth, Mass.
20. HEZEKIAH. b. d. m. Mary Chandler. b. 1704. (?) d. perh. dau. of Joseph and Martha Hunt Chandler of Duxbury, Mass.

IV.

Children of Thomas (8) and Ann (Smith) Bradford.

21. JOSHUA. b. 1682 at Norwich. d. m. 1711–12 Mary Brooks.
22. JAMES. b. 1684 at Norwich. d. m. (1) Edith b. d. (To Canterbury, Ct.) m. (2) Susanna b. d.
23. JERUSHA. bapt. 1693 at Montville. d. 1739. m. 1710 Hezekiah Newcomb of Lebanon, Ct. b. ab. 1693. d. 1772.
    He m. (2) Hannah
24. WILLIAM. bapt. at Montville 1695. d.

[425]

BROWN.

I.

1. GUID BROWN, b.   d. bef. 1650.   m.   Elizabeth   b.   d. aft. 1650.
   (Providence, R. I.)

II.

2. JAMES, b.   d. bef. 1693.   m.   Elizabeth Carr, b.   d. aft. 1697, dau. of Robert Carr.
   (Newport, R. I.)   She m. (2) Samuel Gardiner.

III.

3. JAMES, b.   d. 1759.   m. (1)   Ann Clarke, b.   d.   dau. of James and Hope (Power) Clarke.
   (Newport, R. I.)   m. (2)   Catharine   b.   d. aft. 1754.

IV.

4. JAMES, b. 1709, d. 1765.   m.   Ann Noyes, b. 1704, d. 1754 in Norwich, Ct.
   (Newport, R. I.)   dau. of Dr. James and Ann (Sanford) Noyes of Stonington, Ct.

Children of James (4) and Ann (Noyes) Brown.

V.

5. JAMES NOYES, b.   d. 1759.   m. (1) 1751 at Newport, R. I., Robe Carr, b.   d. 1754 at Norwich, Ct.
   (To Norwich, Ct.)   m. (2) 1754 at Norwich, Ct., Mary Carew, b. 1734, d. 1777.
   She m. (2) 1767 Benjamin Huntington.

6. MARY (?) b. ab. 1739, d. 1759.   m. 1755 (Capt.) Jacob Perkins. He m. (2) 1767 Abigail Thomas.
   (Perhaps others.)

Children of James Noyes (5) and Robe (Carr) Brown.

VI.

7. JAMES NOYES, b. and d. 1753.

Children of James Noyes (5) and Mary (Carew) Brown.

8. JAMES NOYES, 2nd, b. 1755, d. 1759.

[426]

BROWN.

I.

1. JESSE BROWN. b.   d. 1815, in Wilkesbarre, Pa.   m. (1) 1769 at Bozrah, Ct., Anna Rudd. b. 1749. d.
                                                                dau. of Nathaniel and Mary (Backus) Rudd of Franklin, Ct.
                                                      m. (2) 1784 Lucy Rudd. b. 1750. d. 1830.
                                                                dau. of Daniel and Mary (Metcalf) Rudd of Franklin, Ct.

II.

Children of Jesse (1) and Anna (Rudd) Brown.

2. PHILENA. b. 1770. d. 1775.
3. BETSEY. b. 1772 at Bozrah. d. 1792. m. 1791 Peleg Tracy. b. 1760. d.   son of Andrew and Mary (Clement) Tracy.
                                                                He m. (2) 1793 Hannah Leffingwell.
4. RUSSELL. b. 1774 at Bozrah. d. 1795.
5. JESSE. bapt. 1776 at Bozrah. d. 1811. m. 1801 at Hebron, Ct., Lucy Perkins. b. 1771. d. 1842.
6. WILLIAM. bapt. 1779 at Bozrah. d. ab. 1809. unm.
7. ANN. bapt. 1780 at Bozrah. d. 1859 in Wilkesbarre, Pa. m. 1802 John Vernet. b. 1794 in Varchviller, Loraine, France.
                                                                d. 1827 in Port au Prince, Hayti.

III.

Children of Jesse (5) and Lucy (Perkins) Brown.

8. JESSE HOWARD. b. 1802. d.   m.   Bailey.
9. WILLIAM PERKINS. b. 1803. d.
   (To New York.)
10. VERNET. b. 1805. d. 1807.
11. EDWARD WHITING. b. 1806. d.
12. ANN VERNET. b. 1807. d.   m.
    (To Texas.)
13. ELIZA HALLAM. b.   d.   m.   Franklin. b.   d.   of New Orleans, La.

[427]

BUSHNELL.

I.

1. RICHARD BUSHNELL. b.   d. ab. 1652 at Saybrook, Ct. m. 1648 Mary Marvin, b. 1629, d. 1713, dau. of Matthew and Elizabeth (   ) Marvin of Norwalk, Ct. She m. (2) ab. 1669 Dea. Thomas Adgate.

II.

Children of Richard (1) and Mary (Marvin) Bushnell.

2. JOSEPH, b. 1651, d. 1746. m. 1673 Mary Leffingwell, b. 1654, d. 1745.
3. RICHARD, b. 1652, d. 1727. m. 1672 Elizabeth Adgate, b. 1651, d.
4. MARY, b. 1654, d. 1745. m. 1672 Ensign Thomas Leffingwell.
5. MERCY, b. 1657, d.   m. (1) 1678 Jonathan Rudd, b.   d. 1689, son of Lt. Jonathan Rudd of Saybrook, Ct.
   m. (2)   Dea. Joseph Cary of Windham, Ct.

III.

Children of Joseph (2) and Mary (Leffingwell) Bushnell.

6. MARY, b. 1675, d.
7. JOSEPH, b. 1677, d.
8. JONATHAN, b. 1679, d. 1757. m. (1) 1709–10 Mary Calkins, b.   d.   dau. of David and Mary (Bliss) Calkins of New London, Ct.
   m. (2) 1731 Mary (Loomer) Bliss, b. 1657, d.   widow of Thomas Bliss, and dau. of Stephen and Mary (Miller) Loomer of New London, Ct.
   m. (3)   Hannah   b.   d.
9. DANIEL, b. and d. 1681.
10. DEBORAH, b. 1682, d. 1770. m.   John Lane, b.   d.   of Killingworth, Ct.
11. HANNAH, b. 1684, d.
12. NATHAN, b. 1686, d. 1770. m. (1) 1713 in Norwich, Ct., Anne Cary, b.   d.
    (To Lebanon, Ct.) m. (2) 1715 in Norwich, Ct., Mehitable Allen, b.   d.
13. REBECCA, b. 1687, d.   m. 1707–? Job Barstow, b. 1679, d.   son of John and Lydia (Hatch) Barstow of Scituate, Mass.
14. ABIGAIL, b. 1690, d.   m. (1) 1711 Joseph Cary, b.   d. ab. 1722, son of Dea. Joseph Cary of Windham, Ct.
                               m. (2)   Jacob Warren of Plainfield, Ct. b.   d.
15. RACHEL, b. 1692, d.   m. 1714 Timothy Allen, b. 1691, d. 1755, of Norwich, later of Windham, Ct. son of Samuel and Rebecca (Cary) Allen of Bridgewater, Mass.
16. JERUSHA, b. 1695, d.   m. 1715 John Hutchins.

[428]

BUSHNELL.—Continued.

III.

Children of Richard (3) and Elizabeth (Adgate) Bushnell.

17. ANNE, b. 1674. d. 1745. m. 1695 William Hyde, b. 1670. d. 1755. son of Samuel and Jane (Lee) Hyde.
18. (Dr.) CALEB, b. 1679. d. 1724–5. m. 1699-1700 Anne Leffingwell, b. 1680. d. 1762.
19. BENAJAH, b. 1684. d. 1762. m. 1709 Zerviah Leffingwell, b. 1680. d. 1779.
20. ELIZABETH, b. 1685. d. 1760. m. 1709 Jabez Hyde, b. 1677. d. 1742. son of Samuel and Jane (Lee) Hyde.

IV.

Children of Jonathan (8) and Mary (Calkins) Bushnell.

21. MARY, b. 1711. d. 1770. m. 1730–7 Samuel Bliss, b. 1712. d. 1804. son of Thomas and Mary (Loomer) Bliss.
22. LYDIA, b. 1713. d. bef. 1742. m. 1739 Robert Perkins, b. 1697. (?) d. poss. son of Thomas and Sarah (Wallis) Perkins of Topsfield, Mass.
    He m. (2) 1742 Rebecca Arnold of Middletown, Ct. b. d.
23. JONATHAN, b. 1715. d. 1800. m. (1) 1743–4 Ruth Hill, b. d. 1744. dau. of Jonathan and Mary (Sharswood) Hill.
    m. (2) 1745 Lydia Burnham, b. 1709. d. dau. of Eleazer and Lydia (Waterman) Burnham.
24. HANNAH, b. 1717. d. 1717. m. 1747 Simeon Loew, (?) b. d.
25. ABIGAIL, b. 1720. d. m. 1741 Joseph Bushnell.
26. DAVID, b. 1721–2. d. 1760. m. 1740 Mary Leffingwell.
27. JOHN, b. 1724. d.
28. ELIZABETH, b. 1726. d. m. 1740 David Smith, (?) b. d.
29. ELIJAH, b. 1728. d.

IV.

Children of Nathan (12) and Anne (Cary) Bushnell.

30. NATHAN, b. 1714. d. m. 1737 Margery Jackson, b. d.

Children of Nathan (12) and Mehitable (Allen) Bushnell.

31. JOSEPH, b. 1719. d. m. 1741 Abigail Bushnell, b. 1720. d.
32. SAMUEL, b. 1721. d. m. 1743 Zerviah Lyman, b. d.
33. AARON, b. 1723. d.
34. MEHITABLE, b. 1725. d.
35. DANIEL, b. 1728. d.
36. EBENEZER, b. 1730. d. 1790. m. 1750 Elizabeth Tiffany, b. d. 1790.
    (Lebanon, Ct.)
37. ANN, b. 1733. d.
38. REBECCA, b. 1735. d.

BUSHNELL.—Continued.

IV.

Children of (Dr.) Caleb (18) and Anne (Leffingwell) Bushnell.

39. ANNE. b. 1705. d. 1706. m. 1726 Samuel Starr. b. 1699. d. 1780. son of Jonathan and Elizabeth (Morgan) Starr of Groton, Ct.
40. MARY. b. 1707. d. 1795. m. 1730 Dr. Joseph Perkins as second wife.
41. (Capt.) RICHARD. b. 1710. d. 1774. m. 1731 Lucy Perkins. b. 1709. d.
    m. (2) Prudence b. d. 1795.
42. ELIZABETH. b. 1715. d. 1742. m. 1731 John Perkins.
43. ABIGAIL. b. 1718. d. 1774. m. 1733-4 Simon Tracy, 2nd.
44. ZIPPORAH. b. 1723. d. m. 1758 Nathan Hebard. b. d. of Windham, Ct.

IV.

Children of Benajah (19) and Zerviah (Leffingwell) Bushnell.

45. ELIZABETH. b. 1711. d. m. 1730 Isaac Tracy. b. 1706. d. 1779. son of John and Elizabeth (Leffingwell) Tracy.
46. BENAJAH. b. 1714-15. d. 1787. m. (1) 1740 Hannah Griswold. b. 1715. d. 1772.
    (Y. C. 1735.) dau. of John and Hannah (Lee) Griswold of Lyme, Ct.
    m. (2) 1774 Betsey Webster. b. d. of Lebanon, Ct.
47. ABISHAI. b. and d. 1720.
48. ZERVIAH. b. 1721. d. 1786. (?) m. 1750-1 Phinehas Holden of Norwich. b. 1715. d. 1791.
    son of Samuel and Susanna ( ) Holden of Cambridge, Mass.
    He m. (2) 1788 Hannah Tracy. b. ab. 1764. d. 1831.
    She m. (2) Pepper.

V.

Children of Ebenezer (36) and Elizabeth (Tiffany) Bushnell.

49. EBENEZER. b. 1757. d. 1800 at Havana. m. (1) 1780 Tryphena Clark. b. 1760. d. 1785.
    dau. of Dr. John and Jerusha (Huntington) Clark of Lebanon, Ct.
    m. (2) 1786 Susanna Hubbard. b. 1786. d. 1814.
    She m. (2) 1803 Dea. Robert Manwaring.
50. ELIZABETH. b. 1761. d.
51. JERUSHA. b. 1768. d. 1833. m. 1804 (as second wife) Dea. Daniel Strong. b. 1752. d. 1826. of Lebanon, Ct.

[43]

BUSHNELL.—Continued.

V.

Children of Benajah (46) and Hannah (Griswold) Bushnell.

52. ELIZABETH, b. 1741, d. 1752.
53. BENAJAH, b. 1744, d.   Lucy Abel,   dau. of Noah and Anne (Marshall) Abel.
54. JADLEEL, b. 1745, d.   m. 1768 Lydia Bushnell, b. 1747, (?) d.   perhaps dau. of Jonathan and Lydia (Burnham) Bushnell.
55. CAROLINE, b. 1747, d. 1755.   m. 1773 Mundator Tracy, b. 1749, d. 1810,
56. EUSEBIUS, b. 1749, d.   m. 1772 Borodill Latimer, b. 1755, d.   dau. of Col. Jonathan and Lucretia (Griswold) Latimer of Montville, Ct.
    (To Lyme, Ct.)
57. CLARISSA, b. 1751, d.
58. ABISHAI, b. 1752.
59. EZRA, b. 1755, d. 1777, unm.
60. ELIZABETH, b. and d. 1756.
61. ZERVIAH, b. 1757, d. 1759.
62. HANNAH, b. 1760, d. 1774.
63. ZERVIAH HOLDEN, b. 1762, d.
64. MATTHEW, b. 1764.
65. CLARISSA, b. 1765.

VI.

Children of Ebenezer (49) and Tryphena (Clark) Bushnell.

66. HEZEKIAH, b. 1782, d.   m. (?) 1744 Charlotte Bailey.
    (To Susquehannah, Pa.)

Children of Ebenezer (49) and Susanna (Hubbard) Bushnell.

67. THOMAS, b. 1778, d.
68. LYDIA, b. 1779, d.
69. HARRIET, b. 1780, d.
70. LEONARD, b. 1782, d.
71. TRYPHENA, b.   d.

[43]

BUTLER.

I.
1. (Dea.) RICHARD BUTLER. b. d. 1684. m. (1) Elizabeth Bigelow. b. d. 1691.
   (In Cambridge, Mass., in 1632.)   m. (2)
   (To Hartford, Ct., bef. 1643.)

II.
2. (Sergt.) THOMAS. b. 1656-7. d. 1688. m. Sarah Stone. b. d. dau. of Rev. Samuel Stone of Hartford, Ct.
   (Son of first wife of Dea. Richard Butler.)

III.
3. THOMAS. b. d. m. 1691 Abigail Shepherd. b. d. dau. of John and Rebecca (Greenhill) Shepherd of Cambridge, Mass.

IV.
4. THOMAS. b. d. 1777. m. 1732 Abigail Craft of Windham, Ct. b. d. 1743-4.
   (To Windham, Ct.)   m. (2) 1744-5 Deborah Meacham of Windham. b. d. 1747-9.
                              m. 1749 Thankful Luce. b. d.

V.
5. BENJAMIN. b. 1739. d. 1777. m. (1) 1761 Diadema Hyde. b. 1740. d. 1777. dau. of Rev. Jedediah and Jerusha (Perkins) Hyde.
   (To Norwich, Ct.)   m. (2) 1784 Ruth Huntington. b. 1735. d. 1797.

VI.
Children of Benjamin (5) and Diadema (Hyde) Butler.

6. JERUSHA. b. 1762. d. m. 1780 Gideon Denison.
   (To Havre de Grace, Md.)
7. (Dr.) BENJAMIN. b. 1764. d. 1839. m. 1791 Hannah Avery. b. 1772. d. 1829.
   (To New London, Ct., and afterward to Oxford, N. Y.) dau. of Capt. William and Mary (Dolbeare) Avery of Groton, Ct.
8. ROSAMOND. b. 1766. d. 1783.
9. THOMAS. b. 1769. d. 1822. m. 1792 Sarah Denison. b. 1773. d. 1839. dau. of Joseph and Mary (Babcock) Denison.
   (To Stonington, Ct., and then to Oxford, N. Y., afterward to Plainfield, Ct.)
10. MINERVA. b. 1771. d. 1784.

It is said that Thomas Butler, the father of Benjamin, came with his brother Daniel from Massachusetts to Windham, but I can find no Thomas or Daniel Butler in the Massachusetts families, who would answer to these, but Thomas and Abigail Butler of Hartford had a son Thomas, also a son Daniel, and these may have been the later residents of Windham.

CAREW.

I.

1. THOMAS CAREW. b. 1677. d.   m.   Anna Tompson. b. 1677. d.
   dau. of Benjamin and Susanna (Kirtland) Tompson of Roxbury and Braintree, Mass.
   (Came perhaps in 1679 in ship Benjamin from Barbadoes.)

II.

2. THOMAS. b. 1701 at Boston. d. 1701. m. 1724 Abigail Huntington. b. 1703. d. 1777.
3. JOHN. b. 1704 at Boston.
4. JOSEPH. b.   d. 1740. m. 1730-1 Mary Huntington. b. 1709. d.
5. PALMER. b.   d.   m. 1739 Hannah Hill. b. 1704-5. d.
   dau. of Charles and Abigail (Fox) Hill of New London, Ct.
6. ANNA. b. 1712 at Braintree, Mass. d.
7. MARY. b.   d.   m. 1720-1 at Bedham, Xehemiah Fales.

Children of Thomas (2) and Abigail (Huntington) Carew.

8. DANIEL. b. 1726. d.
9. ABIGAIL. b. 1727-8. d. 1750. m. 1754 William Bradford Whiting.
10. ELIPHALET. b. 1740. d.   m. 1742 Mary Huntington. b. 1739. d. 1814.

Children of Joseph (4) and Mary (Huntington) Carew.

   Elizabeth Starr. b. 1735. d. 1821. dau. of Samuel and Ann Lefflingwell Starr.
11. SIMEON. b. 1731. d. 1809. m.   m. 1754 (as second wife) James Noyes Brown.
12. MARY. b. 1734. d. 1777. m. 1757-8. d. 1765.
    m. (2) 1767 Benjamin Huntington.
13. Capt. JOSEPH. b. 1735. d. 1812. m. 1762 Eunice Edgerton. b. 1738. d. 1772. dau. of John and Phebe Harris (Otis) Perkis Edgerton.
14. BENJAMIN. b. 1738-40. d.   m. 1769 Sarah Hubbard. b.   d.
15. ANNE. b. 1741. d. 1779. m. 1764 Elijah Huntington.
16. EBENEZER. b. 1743-4. d. same year.
17. EBENEZER. b. 1745. d. 1804. m. (1) 1771 Eunice Huntington. b. 1747. d. 1772.
    m. (2) 1779 Mehitable Gardiner. b. 1753. d.
    dau. of Samuel and Abigail Gardiner Gardiner of New London, Ct.
18. DANIEL. b. 1747. d. 1813. m. 1773 Lucy Perkins. b. 1750. d. 1832.

Children of Palmer (5) and Hannah (Hill) Carew.

19. SAMUEL. b. 1735. d.   m. (?) 1794 in Providence, Amy Mawney.
20. HANNAH. b. 1737-8.
21. PALMER. (?) b. 1739. d. 1742. m. 1760 Sarah Chapman. b.   d.
22. RUTH, bapt. 1743.

[433]

CAREW.—Continued.

IV.

Children of (Capt.) Joseph (13) and Eunice (Edgerton) Carew.

23. JOSEPH. b. and d. 1768.
24. EUNICE. b. 1769. d. 1848. m. 1791 Joseph Huntington.

Children of Ebenezer (17) and Eunice (Huntington) Carew.

25. ANNE. b. 1772. d. 1851. unm.
26. CHARLES. b. 1774. d. 1842.
27. SIMON. b. 1776. d.
28. EBENEZER. b. 1778. d. m. 1815 Sally Eels. b. 1781. d. dau. of Edward and Mercy (Denison) Eels of Stonington, Ct.
29. ELIZABETH LATHROP. b. 1780. d. 1781.

Children of Ebenezer (17) and Mehitable (Gardiner) Carew.

30. EUNICE HUNTINGTON. b. 1787. d. 1860. m. 1810 James Stedman. b. 1779. d. 1856. of Norwich, Ct., son of Thomas and Mehitable (Griffin) Stedman of Hampton, Ct. (Y. C. 1801.)
31. MARIA. b. 1788. d. 1789.
32. ABIGAIL GARDINER. b. 1790. d. 1871.
33. THOMAS. b. 1793. d. 1861 (?)
34. MARIA. b. and d. 1794.
35. GARDINER. b. and d. 1797.

Children of Daniel (18) and Lucy (Perkins) Carew.

36. LUCRETIA. b. 1776. d. 1778.
37. LUCRETIA. b. 1778. d.
38. DANIEL. b. 1781. d. 1838.
39. LUCY. b. 1783. d. 1800. m. 1800 James Tillinghast of Providence.

CARPENTER.

I.
1. WILLIAM CARPENTER. b. 1576. d.   m.   b.   d.
(To New England from Southampton in 1638, aged 62; on ship Bevis from Harwell.)
(To Weymouth, Mass.)

II.
2. WILLIAM. b. 1605 in England. d.   m.   Abigail   b. 1605. d. 1685
(To Rehoboth, Mass., 1643-4.)

III.
3. JOHN. b.   d. 1695.   m.   Hannah   b.   d.

IV.
4. EPHRAIM. b. 1670. d.   m. 1711 Rebecca   b.   d.
(To Woodstock, Ct.)

V.
5. (Capt.) JOSEPH. b. 1715 in Woodstock. d. 1749 of yellow fever on return voyage from Jamaica. Buried at sea off New London, Ct.
(To Norwich, Ct.)
m. 1740 Elizabeth Lathrop. b. 1724. d. 1817.
She m. (2) 1754 Joseph Peck.

VI.
Children of Joseph (5.) and Elizabeth (Lathrop) Carpenter.

6. (Capt.) JOSEPH. b. 1745. d. 1809. m. 1773 Eunice Fitch. b. 1755. d. 1847. dau. of Ebenezer and Mary Hazelton Fitch.
7. GARDNER. b. 1747-8. d. 1815. m. 1790 Mary Huntington. b. 1768. d. 1832.

VII.
Children of Joseph (6.) and Eunice (Fitch) Carpenter.

8. BETSEY. b. 1776. d.   m. (1) 1814 Jason Walter.
9. GERARD. b. 1779. d. 1841. m. 1809 Rebecca E. Hunter. b. 86. (?) 90. d. 1879.
10. ANNE. b. 1782. d. 1832. unm.
11. CHARLES AUGUSTUS. b. 1785. d.
12. MARY ANN. b. 1788. d. 1828. m. 1819 Capt. Walter Lester. b. 1783. d. 1828. son of Caleb, Jr. and Sarah Hyde Lester.
m. 1833 Mary Elizabeth Carpenter. b. 1792. d. 1883.
13. DANIEL. b. 1793. d. 1837. m.

CARPENTER.—Continued.

Children of Gardner (7) and Mary (Huntington) Carpenter.

14. GEORGE. b. 1795. d.   m.
15. MARY ELIZABETH. b. 1797. d. 1883. m. 1833 (as second wife) (Capt.) Walter Lester. b. 1782. d. 1851.
16. GARDNER. b. 1802. d.
17. HENRY. b. 1804. d. unm. in Poughkeepsie, N. Y.
18. JOHN. b. 1807. d.
19. CHARLES. b. 1810. d.

CASE.

I.

1. (?) JOHN CASE.   b.   d.   m.   Desire Manton. b.   d.
(From Martha's Vineyard to Windham, Ct.)

II.

2. JOHN. b.   d.   m. 1727 Hannah Ormsby. b.   d.   probably dau. of John and Susanna Ormsby.
(To Norwich, Ct.)

Children of John (2) and Hannah (Ormsby) Case.

3. JOHN, b. 1728-9. d.
4. EBENEZER, b. 1730-1. d.   m. 1762 Prudence Cooley, b.   d.   of Windham, Ct.
5. SIMEON, b. 1733. d. 1755.   m. 1759 Mehitable Allen, b. 1732. d. 1782 of Pomfret, Ct.
6. HANNAH, b. 1735. d. 1736.
7. HANNAH, b. 1737. d.
8. JERUSHA, b. 1740. d.   m. (?) 1759 Samuel Waterhouse.

III.

Children of Ebenezer (4) and Prudence (Cooley) Case.

9. JERUSHA, b. 1763. d.   m.   James Wilson. b.   d.
10. PRUDENCE, b. 1765. d.
11. ASAHEL, b. 1769. d. 1822. m. (?) 1790 Roxana Sloan, b. ab. 1775. d. 1840.
12. LUTHER, b. 1771. d.
13. ESTHER, b. 1774. d.   m. 1799 David Bede.
14. BETSEY, b. 1776. d.   m. 1795 Burton Peavy.
15. CALVIN, b. 1779. d.   m. 1799 Molly Kilgrove, b.   d.   Asahel Maynard, b.   d.   of Burlington, N. J.
16. HANNAH, b.   d.

IV.

Children of Simeon (5) and Mehitable (Allen) Case.

17. JOHN, b. 1760. d. 1761.
18. SIMEON, b. 1761. d. 1830.
19. SAMUEL, b. 1762. d. 1791.   m. 1788 Susana Cowdrey, b. ab. 1762. d. 1848.
20. JOHN, b. 1764. d. 1777.
21. DANIEL, b. and d. 1766.
22. MEHITABLE, b. 1767. d.
23. MARY,
24. WILLIAM, } b. 1769. d. in two days.
25. ELIZABETH,

29

CASE.—Continued.

V.

Children of Asahel (11) and Roxanna (Sloan) Case.

26. ABBY. b. 1792. d.
27. ASAHEL. b. 1794. d.
28. ELEANOR S. b. 1796. d. m. 1819 Varney Parkison.
29. MARY. b. 1800. d.
30. LOUISA. b. 1802. d. 1809.
31. LUTHER. b. 1804. d. m. 1832 Elizabeth Palmer. b.   d.

Children of Calvin (15) and Mary (Killgrove) Case.

32. POLLY. b. 1799. d.
33. NANCY. b. 1801. d. m. 1821 John Gardner Smith. b.   d.   son of Potter and Anna (Leach) Smith.
34. LUTHER. b. and d. 1803.
35. SALLY. b. 1804. d.
36. CALVIN. b. 1806. d.
37. EBENEZER. } b. 1808. d. 1808.
38. MARY.   }   d.
39. GEORGE. b. 1810. d. 1811.
40. JOHN SIMEON. b. 1812. d.
41. GEORGE FRANCIS. b. 1814. d.

Children of Samuel (19) and Susanna (Cowdrey) Case.

42. SUSANNA. b. 1789. d. 1820.
43. JOHN. b. 1788. d.
44. SAMUEL. b. 1791. d. m. 1812 Sally Bailey. b. 1793. d.   dau. of Samuel and Cynthia (Meach) Bailey.

[438]

CHAPMAN.

I.

1. WILLIAM CHAPMAN. b.   d. 1699. m.
   (At New London, Ct., in 1657.)

II.

2. JOSEPH. b. 1667. d. 1725. m. ab. 1705 Mercy Taylor. b.   d. 1725.
   (Adm. inhabitant of Norwich in 1715.)

III.

Children of Joseph (2) and Mercy (Taylor) Chapman.

3. JOSEPH. b. 1708. d. 1739. m. (1) 1727 Mary Taylor. b. 1702. d. 1727.
   m. (2) 1728 Elizabeth Ormsby. b.   d.   perhaps dau. of John and Susanna ( ) Ormsby.
4. MARY. b. 1709. d.
5. MOSES. b. 1711. d.
6. SARAH. b. 1713-14. d.
7. EZEKIEL. b. 1715-16. d.
8. AARON. b. 1718. d.   m. 1739 Kesiah Rood. b. 1716. d.   dau of George and Hannah (Bush) Rood.
9. DANIEL. b. 1720-1. d.   m. (2) 1742 Mary Books of New London.
   (Was a Captain in the French war.)
10. SIMON. b. 1723. d.   m. (1) 1744 Rebecca DeWolf. b.   d. 1755.
    m. (2) 1755 Alice Rouse. b.   d.

IV.

Children of Aaron (8) and Kesiah (Rood) Chapman.

11. MARY. b. 1742. d. 1744.
12. EZEKIEL. b. 1741. d.
13. MARY. b. 1743. d.
14. AARON. b. 1745. d.
15. SARAH. b. 1747-8. d.
16. ELIAS. b. 1751. d.
17. CALEB. b. 1753. d.
18. JOSEPH. b. 1755. d.
19. JOSEPH. b. 1757. d.

[439]

CHARLTON.

I.

1. RICHARD CHARLTON. b. ab. 1715 in England (according to a family record). d. 1757. (Blown up on a vessel at the rejoicings at the capture of Havana.) (To Norwich, Ct., bef. 1741.)
    m. 1741-2 Sarah Grist. b. 1722. d. 1808. dau. of Thomas and Ann (Birchard) Grist.

Children of Richard (1) and Sarah (Grist) Charlton.

II.

2. SARAH. b. 1742-3. d.
3. ANN. b. 1744. d. 1804. m. 1767 Seth Miner.
4. ELIZABETH. b. 1746. d. bef. 1757.
5. CANDACE. b. 1748. d. 1810. m. 1781 Samuel Avery.
6. CHARLES. b. 1752. d. 1818. m. 1775 Sarah Williams. b. 1746. d. 1812. dau. of Nathan and Elizabeth (Haley) Williams of Stonington, Ct., and probably widow of Jesse Williams of Norwich.
7. SAMUEL. b. 1756. d. in the prison ship at New York, during the Revolution.

Children of Charles (6) and Sarah (Williams) Charlton.

III.

8. JESSE. b. 1776. d. 1859. m. (1) 1809 Rebecca M. Thomas of Hartford, Ct. b. 1778. d. 1829.
    m. (2) 1830 Harriet Jones. b. 1791. d. 1841.
    (To East Windsor, Ct., ab. 1800.)
9. ELIZABETH. b. 1778. d. 1825. m. 1796. Gen. Stephen B. Allyn. b. 1774. d. 1822 of yellow fever at Demerara.
10. SARAH. b. 1780. d. 1854. m. 1810 Nathaniel Rockwell. b. 1772. d. 1847. son of Nathaniel Rockwell of East Windsor, Ct. (To East Windsor, Ct.)
11. CHARLES. b. 1782. d.
12. SAMUEL. b. 1785. d. 1865. m. 1807 Dolly Kelping. b. ab. 1790. d. 1882.

Children of Samuel (12) and Dolly (Kelping) Charlton.

IV.

13. MARIA. b. 1808. d. 1809.
14. EMILY. b. 1810. d.
15. CHARLES HENRY. b. 1812. d.   m. 1839 Sarah Morgan. b.   d.
16. JOHN. b. 1814. d.
17. MARIA. b. 1817. d. 1821.
18. ELIZA ANN. b. 1819. d.
19. FREDERICK. b. 1822. d.
20. JAMES DUNTON. b. 1824. d.   m. 1848 Lydia Ladd.
21. HOWARD. b. 1826. d.

CLEVELAND (or CLEAVELAND).

I.

1. MOSES CLEVELAND. b.   d. 1701-2. m. 1648. Ann Winn. b.   d.   dau. of Edward Winn of Woburn, Mass. (Came with his master, a joiner, from Ipswich, Co. Suffolk, Eng., to Woburn, Mass., ab. 1648-9.)

II.

Children of Moses (1) and Ann (Winn) Cleveland of Woburn, Mass.

2. MOSES, b. 1651. d.   m. 1676 Ruth Norton, b.   d.
3. HANNAH, b. 1653. d.   m. 1677 Thomas Henshaw of Woburn, Mass. b.   d. 1700.
4. AARON, b. 1654-5. d.   m. (1) 1675 Dorcas Wilson, b.   d. 1714.
   m. (2)   Prudence   b.   d. 1716.
   (Ancestor of Pres. Grover Cleveland.)
5. SAMUEL, b. 1657. d.   m. (1) 1680 Jane Keyes, b. 1659. d. 1681. dau. of Solomon and Frances (Grant) Keyes of Chelmsford, Mass. (To Canterbury, Ct.)
   m. (2)   Persis Hildreth, b. 1660. d.   ) Hildreth of Chelmsford, Mass.
           dau. of Richard and Sarah (Fosdick.
6. MIRIAM, b. 1659. d.   m.
7. JOANNA, b. 1661. d. 1667.
8. EDWARD, b. 1663. d.
   (Prob. to Canterbury, Ct.)
9. JOSIAH, b. 1666-7. d. 1709. m.   Mary
   (To Canterbury, Ct.)
10. ISAAC, b. 1669. d. 1714. m. 1699 Elizabeth Curtis, b.   d. 1742.
    (To Canterbury, Ct.)   She m. (2)   Clement Stratford of New London, Ct. b.   d.
    (To Norwich, Ct.)   He m. (1) 1712 Sarah Haughton.
        Keyes.
11. JOANNA, b. 1670. d.   m.   Elizabeth
12. ENOCH, b. 1671. d.

III.

Children of Isaac (10) and Elizabeth (Curtis) Cleveland.

13. CURTIS, b. 1700. d.   m. 1733-4 Remembrance Carrier. b. 1715. d. 1790.   ) Carrier of Colchester, Ct.
            dau. of Richard and Thankful (
14. KESIA, b. 1700. d. 1777. m. 1730 Sylvanus Jones.
15. ANN, b. 1703.
16. MIRIAM, b. 1705.

CLEVELAND (or CLEAVELAND).—Continued.

IV.

Children of Curtis (13) and Remembrance (Carrier) Cleveland.

17. GIDEON. b. 1734. d. 1742-3.
18. IRENE. bapt. 1737. d.
19. JOANNA b. 1737. d.
20. ISAAC. b. and d. 1739.
21. ISAAC. b. 1740-1. d.
22. GIDEON, 2nd. b. 1743. d.
23. ANNE. bapt. 1746. d.
24. ANNE. b. 1751. d.
25. BELA. b. 1758. d.

COBB.

I.

1. (Elder) HENRY COBB. b.   d. 1679. m. (1) 1631 Patience Hurst. b.   d. 1649, dau. of Dea. James Hurst of Plymouth, Mass.
   (To Plymouth, Mass.)   m. (2) 1649 Sarah Hinckley. b.   d.   dau. of Samuel Hinckley of Scituate, Mass.
   (At Scituate in 1633.)
   (At Barnstable in 1639.)

II.

2. HENRY. b. 1655. d.   m. 1690 Lois Hallet. b.   d.   dau. of Joseph Hallet.
   (1795 to Stonington, Ct.)

III.

3. HENRY. b. 1710. d.   m.

IV.

4. NATHAN. b. 1734. d. 1805. m. 1757. Katharine Copp. b. 1730. d. 1793. dau. of Jonathan and Margaret Stanton Copp.
   (To Norwich, Ct.)

Children of Nathan (4) and Katherine (Copp) Cobb.

5. HENRY. b. 1760. d. 1761.
6. (LL.) HENRY STANTON. b. 1761. d.   m. 1791 Mary Cobb. b. 1769. d.   dau. of Ebenezer and Mary (Brown) Cobb of Stonington, Ct.
7. KATHARINE. b. 1762. d.
8. JERUSHA. b. 1764. d.
9. MARGARET. b. 1766. d.
10. MARY. b. 1768. d.

Children of (LL.) Henry Stanton (6) and Mary (Cobb) Cobb.

11. FRANCES. b. 1793. d.
12. CATHARINE. b. 1794. d. 1795.
13. HENRY HALLET. b. 1796. d.
14. ALFRED. b. 1797. d.
15. CATHARINE. b. 1800. d.
16. MARY. b. 1803 at Stonington, Ct. d.
17. NATHAN. b. 1805 at Stonington, Ct. d.

COIT.

I.

1. JOHN COIT. b. ab. 1596. d. 1670. m. Mary Gaines (or Jenners), b. ab. 1596. d. 1676.
dau. of (   ) and (   ) Jenners.
(To America between 1630-38.)
(In Salem, Mass. in 1638. Removed to Gloucester in 1644. To New London ab. 1650.)

II.

2. JOSEPH. b.   d. 1704. m. 1657 Martha Harris. b.   d. 1710. dau. of William and Edith (   ) Harris of Wethersfield, Ct.
(To New London ab. 1650.)

III.

3. JOHN. b. 1670. d. 1744. m. 1695 Meletabel Chandler. b. 1673. d. 1758. dau. of John and Elizabeth (Douglas) Chandler of Woodstock, Ct.

IV.

4. JOHN. b. 1696. d.   m. (1) 1719 Grace Christophers. b. 1698. d. 1745.
dau. Judge Richard and Grace (Turner) Christophers of New London.
m. (2) 1748 Hannah (Gardiner) Potter. b.   d.
widow of Thomas Potter of Newport, R. I., and dau. of Henry Gardner.
5. (Capt.) JOSEPH. b. 1698. d. 1787. m. (1) 1732 Mary Hunting. b.   d. 1733.
(   ) Hunting of East Hampton, L. I.
(To Norwich ab. 1775.)
dau. of Rev. Nathaniel and
m. (2) 1739-40 Lydia Lathrop. b. 1718. d. 1794.
6. SAMUEL. b. 1700. d. young. (?)
7. THOMAS. b. 1702. d. 1725. m. 1723 Mary Prentis (or Prentice). b.   d.   dau. of Thomas and Mary (   ) Prentis of N. L.
She m. (2) 1727-8 Dr. Ebenezer Gray of Lebanon, Ct.
8. ELIZABETH. b. 1704. d.   m. 1720 Samuel Gardiner. b. 1695. d.   son of John and Mary (King) Gardiner of Gardiner's Island.
9. MARTHA. b. 1706. d. betn. 1782 and 1785. m. (1) 1730 Daniel Hubbard.
m. (2) 1744 Thomas Greene. b. 1705-6. d. 1764.
son of Nathaniel and Ann (Gould) Greene of Boston, Mass.

V.

Children of John (4) and Grace (Christophers) Coit.

10. JOSEPH. b. 1725. d. 1756. m.   Sarah Mosier. b.   d.   (   ) Mosier of Montville.
dau. of (   ) and (   ) Prentice.
She m. (2)

[444]

COIT.—Continued.

V.

Children of (Capt.) Joseph (5) and Mary (Hunting) Coit.

11. JONATHAN. b. and d. 1735.

Children of (Capt.) Joseph (5) and Lydia (Lathrop) Coit.

12. LYDIA. b. 1741. d. 1778. m. 1764 William Hubbard.
  He m. (2) 1779 (?) Joanna Perkins.
      dau. of James and Joanna (Masereene) Perkins of Boston, Mass.
  m. (3) ab. 1788 Alice (Skinner) Deming, widow of Maj. Jonathan Deming of Colchester, Ct.

13. ELIZABETH. b. 1743. d. 1790. m. 1764 Christopher Leffingwell.
  He m. (1) Elizabeth Harris and (3) Ruth (Webster) Perit.

14. LUCY. b. 1746. d. 1776. m. 1766 Andrew Huntington.
  He m. (2) 1777 Hannah Phelps. b. 1760. d. 1838.

15. LUCRETIA. b. 1748. d. young, unmarried.

16. (Dr.) JOSEPH. b. 1750. d. 1779. m. 1775 Elizabeth Palmes. b. ab. 1751. d. 1803.
  dau. of Dr. Guy and Lucy (Christophers) (Douglas) Palmes of New London, Ct.
  She m. (2) 1780 (as second wife) Capt. William Coit. b. 1735. d. 1821.
      son of Col. Samuel and Sarah (Spalding) Coit.

17. THOMAS. b. 1752. d. 1832. m. (1) 1778 Frances Mary Baker. b. ab. 1757. d. 1778.
  (Norwich and Canterbury.) m. (2) 1782 Sarah Chester. b. 1754. d. 1834. dau. of Hon. John and Sarah (Noyes) Chester of Wethersfield, Ct.

18. DANIEL LATHROP. b. 1754. d. 1833. m. 1786 Elizabeth Bill. b. 1767. d. 1840. dau. of Capt. Ephraim and Lydia (Huntington) Bill.

19. JERUSHA. b. 1758. d. 1776.

20. (Hon.) JOSHUA. b. 1758. d. 1798. m. 1788 Ann Borodill Hallam. b. 1764. d. 1844.
  dau. of Nicholas and Elizabeth (Latimer) Hallam of New London
  (II. C. 1778)
  (M. C. 1793-95)
  (New London.)

VI.

Children of Joseph (10) and Sarah (Mosier) Coit.

21. RICHARD. b. 1746. d.

22. JOSEPH. b. 1748. d. 1807. unmarried.
  (Partner with Uriah Tracy in firm of Tracy & Coit.)

23. SARAH. b. 1749-50. d.

[445]

COIT.—*Continued.*

VI.

Children of Daniel Lathrop (18) and Elizabeth (Bill) Coit.

24. DANIEL WADSWORTH. b. 1787. d.   m. 1834 Harriet Frances Coit. b. 1805. d. 1879. dau. of Levi and Lydia (Howland) Coit.
25. LYDIA. b. 1789. d. 1864. m. 1811 Prof. James L. Kingsley of Yale College. (New Haven.)
26. HENRY H. b. 1791. d. 1879. m. 1819 Mary Breed. b. 1795. d. 1859. dau. of Shubael and Lydia (Perkins) Breed. (Liverpool, O., and Euclid, O.)
27. MARIA. b. 1793. d. 1885. m. (as second wife) 1823 Pelatiah Perit. (New York and New Haven.)
28. ELIZA. b. 1796. d. 1865. m. 1820 William C. Gilman. b. 1795 at Exeter, N. H. d. 1863. (New York and Norwich.)
29. JOSHUA. b. 1800. d.   unm. (Y. C. 1819.) (New Haven.)

[446]

CRANE.

I.

1. BENJAMIN CRANE. b.   d. 1693. m. (according to Hinman) 1655 Mary Backus. b.   d.   dau. of William Backus.
   (At Medfield, Mass., 1649.)   m. ("   " Savage.) 1656 Ellinor Breck. b. 1630. d.
   (Freeman, Wethersfield, Ct., 1658.)   dau. of Edward Breck of Dorchester, Mass.
   (1664 perhaps at Taunton, Mass.)

II.

2. JONATHAN. b. 1658. d. 1734-5. m. 1677 Deborah Griswold. b. 1661. d.   dau. of Lt. Francis Griswold.
   (To Norwich, Ct., about 1678-9.)
   (To Windham, Ct., " 1691.)
   (Later to Lebanon, Ct.)

III.

Children of Jonathan (2) and Deborah (Griswold) Crane.

3. SARAH. b. 1680. d.   m.   Nathan Hebard. b.   d.   of Windham, Ct.
4. JONATHAN. b. 1684. d.   m. 1707 Mary Hebard. b.   d.   dau. of Robert Hebard.
   (To Lebanon, Ct., in 1714.)
5. JOHN. b. 1675. d.   m. (1) 1708 Sarah Spencer. b.   d.
                           m. (2) 1716 Prudence Belding. b.   d.
6. MARY. b. 1679. d.   m.   Jacob Simons (?) or   Lathrop (?)
7. HANNAH. b. 1692. d.   m.   Caleb Coman. b.   d.
8. JOSEPH. b. 1695. d.
9. ISAAC. b. 1697. d.   m. 1719 Ruth Waldo.
10. ELIZABETH. (b. 1695. d.
11. DEBORAH.   (d.
12. ABIGAIL. b. 1700. d.   m.   David Knight. (?) b.   d. 1744.

DANFORTH.

I.
1. NICHOLAS DANFORTH. b.   d. 1637-8. m.   Elizabeth Symmes. b.   d. 1629.
(From Framingham, Co. Suffolk, England, to New England in 1634.)
(To Cambridge, Mass.)

II.
2. (Rev.) SAMUEL. b. 1626. d. 1674. m. 1651 Mary Wilson. b. 1633. d. 1713.
(H. C. 1643.)   dau. of Rev. John Wilson, pastor of the First Church of Boston, Mass., and Elizabeth,
   possibly dau. of Sir John Mansfield.
She m. (2)   Joseph Rock, of Boston, Mass.
(Settled at Roxbury, Mass., 1650, as colleague of Rev. John Eliot.)

III.
3. (Rev.) SAMUEL. b. 1656. d. 1727. m. 1687 Hannah Allen. b. 1669. d. 1771.
(H. C. 1683.)   dau. of Rev. James Allen of the First Church, Boston, Mass, and Elizabeth (Houchins) Endicott.
(Settled at Taunton, Mass, in 1687.)

IV.
4. THOMAS. b. 1703. d. 1756. m. (1)   Sarah   b.   d.
   m. (2) 1742 Hannah Hall. b. ab. 1720. d. 1795.
(To Norwich, Ct.)

V.
Children of Thomas (4) and Sarah (   ) Danforth.

5. THOMAS. b. 1731 at Taunton, Mass. d.
6. ELIJAH. b. 1732 at Taunton, Mass. d.
7. JOHN. b. 1735 at Taunton, Mass. d. 1739.
8. EDWARD. b. 1738 at Norwich, Ct. d.

Children of Thomas (4) and Hannah (Hall) Danforth.

9. JOHN. b. 1742. d. 1799. m. 1767 Elizabeth Hartshorn. b. 1746. d.   dau. of David and Sarah (Birchard) Hartshorn.
10. SARAH. b. and d. 1743.
11. JONATHAN. b. 1744. d. 1751.

DANFORTH.—Continued.

12. ELIZABETH. b. 1745. d. 1753.
13. DANIEL. b. 1746. d. 1746–7.
14. DANIEL. b. 1747–8. d. 1751.
15. SAMUEL. b. 1749. d. 1751.
16. ELIPHALET. b. 1750. d. 1751.
17. JOANNA. b. 1752. d.
18. BETHIAH. b. 1753. d.

VI.

Children of John (9) and Elizabeth (Hartshorn) Danforth.

19. (Dr.) JOHN. b. 1768. d. 1791.
20. SAMUEL. b. 1770. d.   m. 1797 at Mansfield, Ct., Lucy Hartshorn. b. ab. 1777. d. at Hartford, Ct., 1813.
21. DANIEL. bapt. 1777. d.
22. LYDIA. bapt. 1780. d.   m. 1808 Samuel Cogsdall.
23. MARY. bapt. 1788. d.   m. 1808 John Nichols.

VII.

Children of Samuel (20) and Lucy (Hartshorn) Danforth.

24. JOHN. b. 1797. d.
25. HARRIET. b. 1800. d. 1802.
26. SAMUEL. b. 1801. d.

DARBY.

I.

1. WILLIAM. b.   d.   m. 1718 Elizabeth Spalding. (?) b.   d.
   (From Canterbury, (?t., to Norwich ab. 1734.)
2. ELIZABETH. b. 1719 in Canterbury. d. 1790.   m. 1735 James Huntington, 2nd.
3. MARY. b. 1721 in Canterbury. d.
4. JOHN. b. 1723 in Canterbury. d.
5. MARTHA. b. 1725 in Canterbury. d.
6. WILLIAM. b. 1727 in Canterbury. d.   m. 1749 Abigail Cleveland. b.   d.
7. JEDIDIAH. b. 1730 in Canterbury. d.   m. 1755 Lucretia Cleveland. b.   d.
   (Resided in Canterbury.)
8. RUTH. b. 1732 in Canterbury. d.
9. BLANCHARD. b. 1734 in Canterbury. d. 1791.   m. 1763 Priscilla Longbottom. b.   d.
   (Resided in Norwich.)
10. ABIGAIL. b. 1736–7 at Norwich. d.

II.

Children of Blanchard (9) and Priscilla (Longbottom) Darby.

11. BETTY. b. 1763. d.
12. BLANCHARD. b. 1765. d.   m. 1790 Lucy Cleveland. b.   d.
13. ERASTUS. b. 1766. d.
14. LUCY. b. 1769. d.
15. ANNE. b. 1771. d.
16. RUFUS. b. 1774. d. 1830.   m. 1799 Polly Jones. b. ab. 1773. d. 1858.
17. ROSWELL. b. 1776. d.

III.

Children of Rufus (16) and Polly (Jones) Darby.

18. HARRIET. } b. 1800. d.   m. 1825 Charles Billaby.
19. HARRY. } 1819. d.
20. BETSEY. b. 1802 d.   m. 1827 Diah Bailey. b. 1803. d.   dau. of Samuel and Cynthia (Meech) Bailey.
21. POLLY. b. 1803. d. 1819.
22. RUFUS. b. 1805. d.   m. 1831 Betsey Perry.
23. EDMUND. b. 1807. d.   m. 1830 Harriet Bailey. b. 1799. d.
24. WILLIAM JONES. b. 1809.
25. LEVI. b. 1811. d.

[450]

DENISON.

I.

1. (Dea.) WILLIAM DENISON. b. ab. 1586 in England. d. 1654 in Roxbury, Mass. m. Margaret b. d. 1645. (From Bishops Stortford, Hertfordshire, Eng, to Roxbury, Mass, in 1631.)

II.

2. (Capt.) GEORGE. b. ab. 1618. d. 1694 at Hartford. m. (1) 1640 at Roxbury, Mass, Bridget Thompson. b. d. 1643. dau. of John Thompson of Preston, Northamptonshire, Eng.
m. (2) 1645 "Lady" Ann Borodell (or Boralil or Borrowdale.) b. ab. 1615-16. d. 1712. whose wid., Alice, came with children to Roxbury, Mass. dau. of John Borodell of Ireland.

III.

3. GEORGE. b. 1653. d. 1711. m. Mercy Gorham. b. 1659 at Barnstable, Mass. d. 1725. (Stonington and Westerly, Ct.) dau. of Capt. John and Desire (Howland) Gorham of Barnstable, Mass.

IV.

4. SAMUEL. b. 1680. d. m. Mary (Lay) Miner. b. d. (Lay). (Moved to Saybrook, Ct., in 1710.) widow of Christopher Miner and dau. of and

V.

5. GIDEON. b. 1724. d. m. 1752 Elizabeth b. d. (Saybrook, Ct.)

VI.

6. GIDEON. b. 1753. d. m. 1780 Jerusha Butler. b. 1762. d. (Norwich, Ct., and Havre de Grace, Md.)

VII.

Children of Gideon (6) and Jerusha (Butler) Denison.

7. HENRY. b. 1782 at Norwich. d.
8. A daughter d. young d. 1784 at Norwich.
9. MINERVA. b. 1784 at Norwich. d. 1777 at Rock Island, Ill. m. Com. John Rodgers, U. S. N. b. 1771. d. 1838.
10. LOUISA. b. 1786 at Havre de Grace. d. ab. 1829. m. Capt. Alexander Wadsworth, U. S. N. b. d.
11. ELIZABETH. b. 1778 at Havre de Grace, Md. d. m. Com. John D. Henley, U. S. N. b. d.

FITCH.

I.

1. (Rev.) JAMES FITCH. b. 1622. d. 1702. m. (1) 1648 Abigail Whitfield. b. d. 1659. dau. of Rev. Henry Whitfield of Guilford, Ct.
m. (2) 1664 Priscilla Mason. b. 1641. d. aft. 1710. dau. of Mtj. John and Anne (Peck) Mason.

II.

Children of (Rev.) James (1) and Abigail (Whitfield) Fitch.

2. (Maj.) JAMES. b. 1647. d. 1727. m. (1) 1676 Elizabeth Mason. b. 1654. d. 1684. dau. of Maj John and Anne (Peck) Mason.
m. (2) 1687 Alice (Bradford) (Adams) b. 1661. d. 1745. widow of Rev. William Adams of Dedham, Mass.
and dau. of Dep. Gov. William and Alice (Richards) Bradford of Plymouth, Mass.
(Lived in Norwich and Canterbury, Ct.)
3. ABIGAIL. b. 1650. d. m. Capt. John Mason.
4. ELIZABETH. b. 1651-2. d. 1689. m. 1674 Rev. Edward Taylor. b. 1642. d. 1729. of Westfield, Mass.
He m. (2) 1692 Ruth Wyllys. b. d. 1730. dau. of Samuel and Ruth (Haynes) Wyllys of Hartford, Ct.
5. HANNAH. b. 1653. d. m. 1677 Thomas Mix. b. 1655. d. possibly son of Thomas and Rebecca (Turner) Mix of New Haven, Ct.
6. SAMUEL. b. 1655. d. after 1725. m. . b. d.
(Preston, Ct.)
7. DOROTHY. b. 1658. d. 1691. m. 1683 (as second wife) Nathaniel Bissell of Windsor, Ct. b. 1640. d. 1713-14. son of John Bissell of Windsor.

Children of (Rev.) James (1) and Priscilla (Mason) Fitch.

8. DANIEL. b. 1665. d. m. 1698 Mary Sherrod (or Sherwood). b. d. 1752.
She is said to have m. (2) 1717 Lt. Joseph Bradford of Montville, Ct.
9. (Capt.) JOHN. b. 1667-8. d. 1743. m. 1695 Elizabeth Waterman. b. 1675. d. 1751.
(Windham, Ct.)
10. JEREMIAH. b. 1670. d. 1730. m. Ruth Gilford. b. 1670. d.
(To Lebanon and to Coventry, Ct., in 1703.)
11. (Rev.) JABEZ. b. 1672. d. 1746. m. 1704 Elizabeth Appleton. b. ab. 1681. d. 1745.
(H. C. 1694.) dau. of Hon. John and Elizabeth (Rogers) Appleton of Ipswich, Mass.
(Settled at Ipswich, Mass., 1703. At Portsmouth, N. H., 1725.)
12. ANNE. b. 1675. d. 1715. m. 1695 Lt. Joseph Bradford.
(Montville, Ct.)
13. (Capt.) NATHANIEL. b. 1679. d. 1759. m. (1) 1701 Anne Abel. b. 1681. d. 1728.
dau. of Joshua and Mehitable (Smith) Abel of Norwich, Ct.
m. (2) Mindwell Tisdale. b. d. of Lebanon, Ct.
14. JOSEPH. b. 1681. d. 1741. m. (1) 1703 Sarah Mason. b. d. dau. of Maj. Samuel Mason of Stonington, Ct.
m. (2) 1721 Anne Whiting. b. 1698. d. 1778.
dau. of Rev. Samuel and Elizabeth (Adams) Whiting of Windham, Ct.
15. ELEAZER. b. 1683. d. ab. 1747 s.p. m. Martha Brown. b. 1681. d. dau. of Capt. John and Anne (Mason) Brown of Swanzey, Mass.
(Lebanon.)

FITCH.—Continued.

III.

Children of (Maj.) James (2) and Elizabeth (Mason) Fitch.

16. JAMES. b. and d. 1677–8.
17. JAMES, 2nd. b. 1679. d. yg.
18. JEDEDIAH. b. 1681. d.   m.   Elizabeth   b.   d.
    (To Nantucket, Mass.) (?).
19. SAMUEL. b. 1683. d.   m.   Mary   b.   d.
    (To New Jersey.) (?)
20. ELIZABETH. b. 1684. d.

Children of (Maj.) James (2) and Alice (Bradford) (Adams) Fitch.

21. ABIGAIL. b. 1687–8. d.   m. 1713 Capt. John Dyer of Canterbury, Ct. b.   d.
22. EBENEZER. b. 1689–90. d. 1724. m. 1712 Bridget Brown. b.   d.   poss. dau. of Eleazer Brown of Canterbury, Ct.
    (From Canterbury, Ct., to Windsor. Ct.)   She m. (2)   John Perry of Ashford, Ct.
23. DANIEL. b. 1692–3. d. 1752. m. 1718–19 Anna Cook. b.   d. 1735. poss. dau. of Stephen Cook of Canterbury, Ct.
    (Canterbury, Ct.)
24. JOHN. (?) b. 1695. d.
25. BRIDGET. (?) b. 1697. d.
26. JERUSHA. b. (699. (?) d. 1780. m. 1717–18 Daniel Bissell. b. 1694. d. 1770. son of Daniel and Margaret (Dewy) Bissell of Windsor, Ct.
    (Canterbury, Ct.)
27. WILLIAM. (?) b. 1701. d.
28. (Col.) JABEZ. b. 1702. d. 1784. m. (1) 1722 Lydia Gale. b.   d. 1753. poss. dau. of Richard Gale of Canterbury, Ct.
    m. (2)   Elizabeth Darby. b.   d.
    m. (3) 1782. (?)   ( ) King. b.   d.   widow of   King.
29. LUCY. b.   d.   m. 1749 Henry Cleveland. b. ab. 1695. d.   son of Josiah and Mary ( ) Cleveland of Canterbury, Ct.
30. THEOPHILUS. b.   d. 1751 "sudd'ly." m. 1734 Mary Huntington. b. 1705. d.
31. ALICE. b.   d.

Children of Samuel (6) and ( ) Fitch.

32. HEZEKIAH. b.   d.
33. BENJAMIN. b.   d. 1725. m. 1713 Hannah Read. b. 1697. (?) d.   poss. dau. of Josiah and Grace (Holloway) Read.
34. JABEZ. b.   d.   m. 1719 Anna Knowlton. b.   d.   poss. dau. of Thomas Knowlton.
35. JONATHAN. b.   d.   m. (1) 1783 Elizabeth Baskell. b.   d. 1725.
    m. (2) 1729 Elizabeth Choate. b.   d. 1779.
    poss. dau. of Stephen and Mary (Williams) Choate of Ipswich, Mass.

FITCH.—Continued.

III.

Children of Daniel (8) and Mary (Sherwood) Fitch.

36. ABONIJAH. b. 1700. d.   m. (1)   Sarah Fitch. (?) b.   d.
    m. (2) 1744 Anne (Hyde) Gray. b.   d.
    widow of Simon Gray and dau. of Samuel and Elizabeth (Calkins) Hyde of Lebanon, Ct.
37. JAMES. b. 1702-3. d. 1789. m. 1727-8 Ann Denison. b. 1707. d. 1792.
    dau. of Capt. Robert and Joanna (Stanton) Denison of Montville, Ct.
38. LEMUEL. b. 1703-4. d.   m.   Mary Bigelow. b.   d.
39. MARY. b. 1707. d. 1768. m. (1) 1726 Rev. James Hillhouse. b. ab. 1687 at Free Hall, Co. Londonderry, Ireland. d. 1740 at Montville, Ct.
    son of John and Rachel (   ) Hillhouse.
    m. (2) 1744 Rev. John Owen. b. ab. 1698. d. 1753.
    (Groton, Ct.) (H. C. 1723.)
    m. (3)   Rev. Samuel Dorrance. b.   d.
    (Voluntown, Ct.)
40. DANIEL. bapt. 1710. d. 1755. m.   Rachel   b.   d.

Children of (Capt.) John (9) and Elisabeth (Waterman) Fitch.

41. ELIZABETH. b. 1696. d.
42. MIRIAM. b. 1699. d. 1741 s. p. m. 1740 Hezekiah Ripley. b. 1695. d. 1779.
    son of Joshua and Hannah (Bradford) Ripley of Windham, Ct.
    He m. (2) 1746 Mary Skinner. b. ab. 1694. d. 1778.
43. PRISCILLA. b. 1703. d.
44. JOHN. b 1705. d. 1700. m. 1731 Alice Fitch. b.   d.   dau. of Ebenezer and Bridget (Brown) Fitch (?) of Windsor, Ct.

Children of Jeremiah (10) and Ruth (Gifford) Fitch.

45. LUCY. b. 1699. d. bef. 1736. (?)   Daniel Whitmore. b.   d.
46. RUTH. b 1699. d.   m.   m. (2) 1736 Humphrey Davenport. b.   d.
47. HANNAH. b. 1701. d.
48. ABNER. b. 1703. d.
49. JEREMIAH. b.   d.
50. GIDEON. b.   d.   m. 1736 Sarah Calkins. b. 1716. d.   dau. of Hugh and Phebe (Abel) Calkins.
51. ELISHA. b.   d.
52. STEPHEN. (?) b. ab. 1712. d.
53. JAMES. b.   d.
54. JOSEPH. b.   d.
    (To East Windsor, Ct.)

FITCH.—Continued.

Children of (Rev.) Jabez (11) and Elizabeth (Appleton) Fitch.

55. ELIZABETH. b. 1705. d.   m.   John Wibird. b.   d.
56. MARGARET. b.   d.   Gibbs. b.   d.   of Watertown, Mass.
57. MARY. b.   d.   m.   Francis Cabot. b.   d.   of Salem, Mass.
58. ANN. b.   d.   m.   (as second wife) Rev. Nathaniel Gookin. b.   d.   of Northampton, Mass.
59. JOHN. b.   d.
    (H. C. 1728.)
60. JAMES. b.   d.

III.

Children of (Capt.) Nathaniel (13) and Anne (Abel) Fitch.

61. ANNE. b. 1702. d.   m. (?) 1722 John Partridge. b.   d.   dau. of Joseph and Hannah (Higley) Trumbull of Lebanon, Ct.
62. JOSHUA. b. 1704. d.   m. ab. 1730 Mary Trumbull. b. 1713. d.   d. 1735.
63. NATHAN. b. 1705. d. 1750. m. 1725 Hannah Huntington (?) b.   d.
64. NEHEMIAH. b. 1708. d.   m. 1731 Elizabeth Veitch. b.   d.
65. JAMES. b. 1709. d.   m.   Anne Abel. b.   d.
66. JOHN. b. 1712. d. 1742. m. 1734 Hannah Scott. b.   d.
67. NATHANIEL. b. 1714. d.
68. MEHITABLE. b. 1717. d.   m.   Whiting. b.   d.
69. ELIZABETH. b. 1718. d. 1747. m. 1746 Daniel Bissell. b. 1693. d. 1776.
    (Lebanon, Ct.)   Son of John and Sarah (White) Loomis) Bissell of Windsor and of Lebanon, Ct.
70. RACHEL. b. 1720. d. 1721.
71. ABEL. b. 1722. d.   m. 1747. Ruth Woodworth. b. 1730. d. 1751 of Bozrah, Ct., dau. of Joshua and Ruth (Brown) W[oodworth].
72. CALEB. b. 1725. d.

Children of Nathaniel (13) and Hinkwell (Tisdale) Fitch.

73. JABEZ. b. 1730. d. 1730.
74. EZEKIEL. b. 1732. d.
75. ISAAC. b. 1734. d.

Children of Joseph (14) and Sarah (Mason) Fitch.

76. SARAH. b. 1705. d.
77. MASON. b. 1707. d. 1734.
    (Y. C. 1726.)
78. (Capt.)JOSEPH. b. 1710. d.   m. 1738 Zerviah Hyde. b. 1720. d.   dau. of Capt. Daniel and Abigail (Wattles) Hyde.

FITCH.—Continued.

Children of Joseph (14) and Anne (Whiting) Fitch.

79. SAMUEL. b. 1723-4. d. 1784 in England. m. Elizabeth Lloyd. b. 1722. d. dau. of Henry and Rebecca (Nelson) Lloyd of Lloyd's Neck (Queen's Village, L. I.) (Y C. 1742.)
80. (Col.) ELEAZER. b. 1726. d. 1796 at Chambly, Canada. m. 1746 Amy Bowen. b. d. (To Windham, Ct., and to St. John's, Canada.)
81. ASAHEL. b. 1728. d. prob. unm. in Canada.
82. ICHABOD. b. 1734. d. m. (?) 1758 Lucy Lathrop. b. 1735. d.
83. ANNE. b. 1737. d.
84. THOMAS. b. 1739. d. 1746-7.

FOUNTAIN (or FONTAINE).

The following account of the first three and part of the fourth generations of the Fountain family of Connecticut is inserted at the request of William A. E. Thomas of Brooklyn, L. I., who has for several years been looking up the Fountain genealogy.

I.

1. AARON FOUNTAIN (or FONTAINE). b.　　d.　　m.　　Mary Beebe. b.　　d.　　dau. of Samuel Beebe of New London, Ct.
(Residing in New London in 1683.)
(His house stood " on the Great Neck, now Waterford." Moved to Fairfield, Ct., about 1700.)
(Mr. Thomas believes Aaron to be the son of Edward Fountain who came to New England in the ship Abigail on June 30, 1635, at the age of 25.)
(Samuel Beebe died in 1712. His age in 1708 was 78, according to a deposition of that date. At his death he left a widow, Mary. His first wife was Agnes, or Anna, dau. of William Keeny. In a list of his children given by Miss Caulkins, Susanna is mentioned as the wife of Aaron Fountain, and Mary as the wife of Richard Tozer, but on the Stamford records Mary, the wife of Aaron Fountain, is called the dau. of Samuel Beebe of New London.)

II.

Children of Aaron (1) and Mary (Beebe) Fountain.

2. MARY. b.　　d. Nov. 19, 1732.　m. Oct 2, 1702 John Mills of Stamford, Ct. b.　　d. Dec. 1, 1723.　son of Richard Mills.
(They were married in Fairfield by Peter Burr, Assistant.)
3. AARON. b.　　d.　　m.　　Hannah
(Hannah, wife of Aaron Fountain, was baptized and received to full communion May 29, 1696.)

III.

Children of John and Mary (2) (Fountain), Mills.

4. SARAH. b. Sept. 27, 1703.　d.
5. ROBERT. b.　　d.
6. MARY. b. Nov. 24, 1706.　d.
7. JOHN. b. Feb. 18, 1707.　d. young.
8. JOHN. b. Feb. 20, 1709-10.　d.　　m. Oct. 30, 1728, Tabitha Dibble. b.　　d.
9. WILLIAM. b. Feb. 28, 1712.　d.
10. JAMES. b.　　d.
11. ABIGAIL. b. Mar. 2, 1719-20.　d.

FOUNTAIN (or FONTAINE).—Continued.

III.

Children of Aaron (3) and Hannah ( ) Fountain.

12. SAMUEL. bapt. May 29, 1698. d.
13. AARON. bapt. June 5, 1698. d.   m.   Elizabeth   b.   d.
14. MOSES. bapt. June 5, 1698. d.   m. Aug. 13, 1719, Elizabeth ( ) Gregory (widow) of Norwalk, Ct. b.   d.
15. HANNAH. bapt. June 5, 1698. d.
16. (Capt.) (?) WILLIAM. bapt. May 26, 1700. d.   m. (?)   Elizabeth Rame, b.   d.   and Susanna (Basset) Rame of Boston, Mass. (To Norwich, Ct.) (?)   dau. of
17. JOHN. bapt. May 9, 1702.
18. JAMES. (?) b.   d. ab. 1710 at Greenwich, Ct.
19. ABIGAIL (?) b.   d.   m. about 1735 Samuel Philleo. b.   d.

IV.

Children of Aaron (13) and Elizabeth ( ) Fountain.

20. HANNAH. b. Apr. 2, 1729. d.   m. (1) Jan. 1, 1749-50 Abel Sherwood. b. Dec. 20, 1720. d. betn. Apr. and Nov. 1761, in the army. (Ancestress of P. T. Barnum.)   son of David and Sarah (Meeker) Sherwood.
    m. (2) bef. Feb. 12, 1762, Elisha Perry. b.   d.   son of Capt. Elisha and Anna (Saunders) Perry.
    (He served both in the French war and the Revolution.)

21. MARY. b. June 5, 1722. d.
22. TIMOTHY. b. June 27, 1725. d.
23. ABEL. b. Apr. 24, 1734. Killed in the French war, 1756.
24. SARAH. b. Nov. 23, 1737. d.

IV.

Children of Moses (14) and Widow Elizabeth (Gregory) Fountain.

25. MOSES. b. Sept. 7, 1720. d.
26. JOSEPH. b. Dec 4, 1723. d.
27. SAMUEL. b. Mar. 7, 1725-6. d.   m. Dec., 1748 Abigail Stuart. b.   d.   dau. of John Stuart.
28. MATTHEW. b. Mar. 4, 1730-1. d.   m.   Elizabeth Hoyt. bapt. Mar. 30, 1735-6. d. ( ) Hoyt.   dau. of Zerbabel and Dorothy

(It is said that he went to Nova Scotia after the Revolution.)

[458]

FOUNTAIN (or FONTAINE).—Continued.

IV.

Children of (Capt.) William (16)(?) and Elizabeth (Rams) Fountain.

29. ELIZABETH, b. 1737, d.
30. WILLIAM, b. 1738, d.
31. MARY, b. 1741, d.   m   Capt. John Bradlick, b. 1732, d.
    poss. son of Capt. John and Lucretia (Christophers) Bradlick of New London, Ct.
32. ELIZABETH, b. 1743-4, d.
33. ANN, b. 1746, d.   m. 1776 Capt. John Chapman, b.   d.
34. SIMON PETER, b. 1748, d.

GALE.

I.
1. EDMUND GALE. b.   d. 1642 at Boston. m.   b.   d.
(Of Cambridge, Mass.)

II.
2. EDMUND GALE. b.   d.   m.   Sarah Dixey. b.   d.   dau. of Capt. William Dixey of Beverly, Mass.
(Salem and Marblehead, Mass.)

III.
3. (Capt.) AZOR GALE. b.   d. 1727. m.   Mary Roots. b.   d.   dau. of Thomas and Elizabeth (Gale) Roots of Boston, Mass.
(Marblehead, Mass.)

IV.
4. JOSEPH. b.   d. bef. 1775. m. 1730 Mary Alden. b.   d.   dau. of William and Mary (Drury) Alden.
(Marblehead, Mass.)

V.
5. (Capt.) JOSEPH. b. 1730. d. 1799. m. (1) 1765 Sarah Huntington. b. ab. 1742. d. 1787.
                          m. (2) 1795 Sarah (Leach) McDonald. b. 1793. d.   widow of Alexander McDonald.
(To Norwich, Ct.)

VI.
Children of (Capt.) Joseph (5) and Sarah (Huntington) Gale.

6. AZOR. b. 1766. d.   m. 1793 Eunice Lord. b. 1767. d. 1819.
                       She m. (2) 1805 Samuel Bailey.
7. SARAH. b. 1768. d.   m. 1793 Jedediah Boutell. b.   d.
(To Troy, N. Y.)
8. JOSEPH. b. 1770. d.   m.
(To the South.)
9. WILLIAM. b. 1776. d.   m. 1801 at New London, Ct., Elizabeth Barr. b.   d.
10. MARY. b. 1779. d. 1780.
11. JOHN. b. 1781. d. 1833. m. the widow of his brother Joseph.
(To Alabama.)
12. MARY. b. 1783. d. 1839. m. 1809 Augustus Lathrop.
13. JAMES. b. and d. 1786.

VII.
Children of Azor (6) and Eunice (Lord) Gale.

14. SARAH EDGERTON. b. 1793. d. 1810.
15. LYDIA LORD. b. 1800. d. in infancy.
16. CHARLES. b. 1796. d.   m. 1822 Ann W. Marshall. b. 1800. d.   dau. of Thomas and Freelove (Edgerton) Marshall.

[460]

GIFFORD.

I.

1. STEPHEN GIFFORD, b. 1641, d. 1724. m. (1) 1667 Hannah Gore, b. 1645, d. 1670-1, dau. of John and Rhoda ( ) Gore of Roxbury, Mass.
   m. (2) 1672 Hannah Gallup, b. 1644, d. 1724, dau. of John and Hannah (Lake) Gallup of Stonington, Ct.

Children of Stephen (1) and Hannah (Gore) Gifford.

2. SAMUEL, b. 1668, d. 1714. m. Mary Calkins, b. 1669, d. 1748, dau. of John and Sarah (Royce) Calkins. (To Lebanon, Ct.) in 1692. Later to Norwich.)
3. HANNAH, b. 1670-1, d. m. 1691 Samuel Calkins, b. 1663, d. son of John and Sarah (Royce) Calkins. (To Lebanon, Ct.)

Children of Stephen (1) and Hannah (Gallup) Gifford.

4. JOHN, b. 1673, d. 1747. m. 1705 Martha Gallup, b. d. 1775, dau. of John and Elizabeth (Harris) Gallup.
5. RUTH, b. 1676, d. m. Jeremiah Fitch. (To Lebanon, Ct.)
6. STEPHEN, b. 1679, d.
7. AQUILA, b. 1682, d.

II.

Children of Samuel (2) and Mary (Calkins) Gifford.

8. HANNAH, b. 1696, d. m. 1714-15 Samuel Leffingwell, b. 1692, d. son of Nathaniel and Mary (Smith) Leffingwell.
9. MARY, b. 1701, d. 1760. m. 1723 Daniel Waterman, b. 1701, d. 1773. son of Thomas and Elizabeth (Allen) Waterman.
   He m. (2) 1703 Elizabeth Haskell, b. d.
10. SAMUEL, b. 1694, d. 1753. m. 1720 Experience Hyde, b. 1700, d. dau. of John and Experience (Abel) Hyde.
11. JEREMIAH, b. d. 1701-2.
12. LYDIA, b. 1704, d. 1780. m. 1723-4 Samuel Abel, 2nd, b. 1792, d. 1775, son of Dr. Samuel and Elizabeth (Sluman) Abel.
13. RUTH, b. 1706, d. m. 1727 John Hewitt, b. d. 1760.
14. SARAH, b. 1712, d. m. 1733 Nehemiah Waterman, b. 1709-10, d. 1796, son of Thomas and Elizabeth (Allen) Waterman. (To Bozrah, Ct.)
15. JEREMIAH, b. 1708, d. m. 1730 Martha Hough, b. d. 1745.

III.

Children of John (4) and Martha (Gallup) Gifford.

16. JOHN, b. 1710, d. 1742. m. 1739 Martha Arnold, b. d.
17. ELIZABETH, b. 1716, d.
18. MARTHA, b. 1721-2, d. 1764-5. m. 1742 Samuel Gifford, b. 1720, d. son of Samuel and Experience (Hyde) Gifford.
    He m. (2) 1765 Ann Lord, "Jr." b. 1724 (?) d. perhaps dau. of Rev. Benjamin and Ann (Taylor) Lord.

GILDON (or GELDING).

1. RICHARD GILDON. b.   d.   m.   Isabella   b.   d.
   (Norwich, Ct.)

Children of Richard (1) and Isabella (   ) Gildon.

2. CHARLES. b. 1773 at Norwich. d.
3. LUCINDA. bapt. 1778 at Bozrah, Ct. d.   m. 1796 Zaddock Pratt. b.   d.   of Mansfield, Ct.
4. SAMUEL. bapt. 1778 at Bozrah, Ct. d.

GOODHUE.

I.

1. (Dea.) WILLIAM. b.   d. 1699-1700. m. (1)   Margery Watson. b.   d. 1668.
   (Freeman 1636 at Ipswich, Mass.)
   m. (2) 1670 Mary (   ) Webb (widow). b.   d.
   m. (3) 1683 Bethiah (Ray) (Lothrop) Grafton. b.   d. 1680.
   dan. of Daniel and Bethiah (   ) Ray of Salem, Mass.
   and widow first of Capt. Thomas Lothrop and second of Joseph Grafton of Salem.
   m. (4) 1689 Remember (   ) Fiske. b.   d. 1702.
   widow of John Fiske of Wenham, Mass.

II.

2. (Dea.) WILLIAM. b.   d. 1712. m. 1666 Hannah Dane. b.   ) Dane of Andover, Mass.
   (Ipswich, Mass.)
   dan. of Rev. Francis and Elizabeth (

III.

3. JOSEPH. b. 1670. d.   m.   Abigail   b.   d.
   (Ipswich, Mass.)

IV.

4. JONATHAN. b. 1722. d. 1700. m.   Elizabeth   b.   d.
   (To Norwich, Ct.)

V.

Children of Jonathan (4) and Elizabeth (   ) Goodhue.

5. DAVID. b. 1744-5 d.
   (To Simsbury, Ct.)
6. JONATHAN. b. 1751. d.
7. ELIZABETH. b. 1755. d.
8. ABIGAIL. b. 1757. d.

GREENLEAF.

I.

1. EDMUND GREENLEAF. b. 1600. d. 1671. m. (1) Sarah Dole. b. d.
   m. (2) widow Hill.
   (To Newbury, Mass., from England in 1635.)
   (Kept a tavern and was by trade a silk-dyer.)
   (Moved to Boston in 1650.)

II.

2. (Capt.) STEPHEN. b. 1630. drowned 1690 at Cape Breton. m. (1) 1651 Elizabeth Coffin. b. d. 1675.
   dau. of Tristram and Dionis (Stevens) Coffin of Nantucket.
   m. (2) 1679 Esther (Weare) Swett. b. ab. 1630. d. 1718.
   wid. of Capt. Benjamin Swett and dau. of Peter Weare of Newbury, Mass.
   (Newbury, Mass.)

III.

3. STEPHEN. b. 1652. d. 1743. m. 1676 Elizabeth Gerrish. b. 1654. d.
   dau. of Capt. William and Joanna (Goodale) (Oliver) Gerrish of Newbury, Mass.
   (Newbury, Mass.)

IV.

4. (Rev.) DANIEL. b. 1680. d. 1763. m. 1701 Elizabeth Gookin. b. 1681. d.
   dau. of Samuel and Mary ( ) Gookin of Cambridge, Mass.
   (H. C. 1699.)
   (Ordained at N. Yarmouth, Mass., 1708. Later a resident of Boston.)

V.

5. (Dr.) DANIEL. b. 1702. d. 1795. m. (1) 1726 Silence (Nichols) Marsh. b. 1702. d.
   widow of David Marsh and dau. of Israel and Mary (Sumner) Nichols of Hingham, Mass.
   (To Bolton, Worcester Co., Mass.)
   (1726–1732 at Hingham, Mass.) m. (2) Dolly Richardson. b. d.

VI.

6. DAVID, b. 1737. d. 1800. m. 1763 Mary Johnson. b. 1742. (?) d. perhaps dau. of Stephen and Mary (Kinne) Johnson of Norwich, Ct.
   (Lived at Norwich and at So. Coventry, Ct.)
   (1772 at Lancester, Worcester Co., Mass.)

[464]

GREENLEAF.—Continued.

VII.

Children of David (6) and Mary (Johnson) Greenleaf.

7. MARY. b. 1764 at Norwich. d. 1845.
8. DAVID. b. 1765 at Norwich. d. 1834. m. 1757 Nancy Jones. b. 1765. (?) d.   perhaps dau. of Rufus and Anne (Hartshorn) Jones.
9. DANIEL. b. 1767 at Norwich. d. 1842. m. 1791 Abigail Forsyth at New London, Ct.
10. SARAH. b. 1769 at Norwich. d. 1792.
11. NANCY. b. 1771. d.
12. SUSANNA. b. 1772. d. 1812.
13. JOHN. b. 1774. d. 1831.
14. NABBY. b. 1777. d. young.
15. WILLIAM. b. 1779. d.

GRIFFING.

I.

1. (Sergt.) EBENEZER GRIFFING. b. ab. 1673. d. 1723. m. (1) (?)
   m. (2) 1702 Mary (Harris) Hubbell. b. d. widow of Ebenezer Hubbell of New London, Ct., and dau. of Gabriel Harris.
   (To New London ab. 1698.)

II.

2. JOHN. b. d. m. 1725 Elizabeth Truman. b. d. possibly dau. of Joseph and Mary (Shapley) Truman.
   (New London.)

III.

3. JOHN. b. 1726. d. m. 1750 Mary Rogers. b. d.
   (New London.)

IV.

4. JAMES. b. 1751. d. m. Hannah b. d.
   (New London.)

V.

5. JEREMIAH. b. 1773. d. 1825. m. 1793 Betsey Spinck. b. ab. 1773. d. 1857.
   (To Norwich, Ct.)

VI.

Children of Jeremiah (5) and Betsey (Spinck) Griffing.

6. RICHARD. b. 1794. d. m. 1815 Daniel Leach. b. d.
7. LYDIA. b. 1796. d. m. (2) bef. 1829 Lucius Wilson of Saratoga, N. Y.
8. BETSEY. b. 1794. d.
9. JAMES. b. 1802. d.
10. JEREMIAH. b. 1804. d.
11. MARY ANN. b. 1808. d.
12. CHARLES THOMPSON. b. 1810. d.
13. WILLIAM. b. 1813. d. m. (2) 1832 Mary Ann Dory. b. d.

[466]

GRIST.

I.

1. THOMAS GRIST. b. 1699-1700. d. 1781. m. 1721 Anne Birchard, bapt. 1701. d.

II.

Children of Thomas (1) and Anne (Birchard) Grist.

2. SARAH. b. 1722. d. 1808. m. 1741-2 Richard Charlton. b. d.
3. ANNE. b. 1723-4. d. unm.
4. ELIZABETH. b. 1727. d. m. Leach. b. d.
5. HANNAH. b. 1729. d. unm.
6. LUCE. b. 1731. d. 1757.
7. GEORGE. b. 1732. d. 1757.
8. JOHN. b. 1734. d. m. 1767 Delight Lathrop. b. 1744. d.
9. ZILLAH. b. 1736. d. 1801. m. (?) 1791 William Russell. b. d. of Litchfield, Ct.
10. THEOPHILA. b. 1738. d. 1769.
11. MARY. b. and d. 1740.
12. MARY. 2nd. b. 1742. d. 1824. unm.

III.

Children of John (8) and Delight (Lathrop) Grist.

13. THEOPHILA. bapt. 1769. d. 1806. m. 1790 Philip Huntington. b. d.
14. GEORGE. bapt. 1771. d.
15. EUNICE. } bapt. 1777. d.
16. CHARLOTTE. }
17. JOHN BIRCHARD. } bapt. 1784. d.
18. THOMAS LATHROP. }

GRISWOLD.

I.

1. MATTHEW GRISWOLD. b. 1597. d. 1693. m. ab. 1636 Anne Wolcott. b. ab. 1620. d. ——. dau. of Henry and Elizabeth (Saunders) Wolcott of Windsor, Ct. (From Kenilworth, Eng., to Windsor, Ct.) (To Saybrook ab. 1639.)

II.

2. MATTHEW. b. 1653. d. 1716. m. (1) 1683 Phebe Hyde. b. 1663. d. 1704. dau. of Samuel and Jane (Lee) Hyde of Norwich, Ct. m. (2) 1705 Mary (DeWolf) Lee. b. 1656. d. 1724. prob. dau. of Belthazar DeWolf and widow of Thomas Lee.

III.

3. JOHN. b. 1690. d. 1764. m. 1713 Hannah Lee. b. 1695. d. 1773. dau. of Ensign Thomas and Mary (DeWolf) Lee of Lyme, Ct.

IV.

4. (Gov.) MATTHEW. b. 1714. d. 1799. m. 1743 Ursula Wolcott. b. 1724. d. 1788. dau. of Gov. Roger and Sarah (Drake) Wolcott of Windsor, Ct.

V.

5. (Gov.) ROGER. b. 1762. d. 1812. m. 1788 Fanny Rogers. b. 1767. d. 1863. dau. of Col. Zabdiel and Elizabeth (Tracy) Rogers of Norwich, Ct. (Y. C. 1780.) (From Lyme to Norwich, Ct., ab. 1783.) (To Lyme ab. 1795.)

VI.

Children of (Gov.) Roger (5) and Fanny (Rogers) Griswold.

6. AUGUSTUS HENRY. b. 1789 at Norwich. d. 1836. m. 1820 Elizabeth Lansdale. b. 1793. d. 1847. dau. of Thomas Lansdale of Boxhill, Co. Sussex, Eng.
7. CHARLES CHANDLER. b. 1791 at Norwich. d. 1839. m. 1820 Ellen Elizabeth Perkins. b. 1799. d. ——. (Y. C. 1808.) dau. of Judge Elias and Lucretia Shaw (Woodbridge) Perkins of New London, Ct.
8. MATTHEW. b. 1762 at Norwich. d. ——. m. 1827 Phebe Hubbard Ely. b. 1804. d. ——. dau. or Col. Seth and Phebe (Marvin) Ely of Lyme, Ct.

[468]

GRISWOLD.—Continued.

9. FRANCES ANN. b. 1795 at Norwich. d.   m. 1818 Judge Ebenezer Lane. b. 1793. d.
   son of Ebenezer and Marian (Griswold) (Chandler) Lane of Northampton, Mass.
   (H. C. 1811.)

10. ROGER WOLCOTT. b. 1797 at Lyme. d.   m. 1823 Juliet Griswold. b.   d. 1855.
    (Y. C. 1817.)
    (To Ashtabula, O.)   dau. of Thomas and Ethelinda (Caulkins) Griswold of Lyme, Ct.

11. ELIZA WOODBRIDGE. b. 1799. d.   m. 1832 Charles Leicester Boalt. b.   d.   son of John and Ruth (Lockwood) Boalt of Norwalk, Ct.
    (To Norwalk, O.)

12. MARIAN. b. 1801. d.   m. 1820 as second wife) Thomas Shaw Perkins. b. 1793. d. 1744.
    son of Judge Elias and Lucretia Shaw (Woolbridge) Perkins of New London, Ct.
    His first wife was Cornelia Leonard. b.   d.
    dau. of Timothy and Mary (Baldwin) Leonard of Lansingburg, N. Y., who d. s. p.

13. WILLIAM FREDERICK. b. 1804. d. 1851.   m. 1831 Sarah Noyes. b.   d.   dau. of William and Hannah (Townsend) Noyes of Lyme, Ct.
14. ROBERT HARPER. b. 1806. d.   m. 1840 Helen Powers. b. 1832. d.   dau. of Edward and Julia (Collins) Powers of Guilford, Ct.
15. JAMES. b. 1808. d. 1810.

[469]

HARLAND.

I.

1. THOMAS HARLAND. b. 1735. d. 1807. m. 1779 Hannah Clark. b. 1754. d. 1816. dau. of Elisha and Hannah (Leffingwell) Clark. (From London, Eng, to Boston, Mass., in 1773.)
(From Boston to Norwich, Ct., in the same year.)

II.

Children of Thomas (1) and Hannah (Clark) Harland.

2. MARY. b. 1780. d. 1859.
3. THOMAS. b. 1781. d. 1806.
4. HANNAH. b. 1783. d. 1784.
5. HANNAH. b. 1785. d. 1803.
6. FANNY. b. 1787. d. 1859.
7. HENRY. b. 1789. d. 1841. m. 1822 Abigail L. Hyde. b. 1800. d. 1888. dau. of Judge John and Sarah R. (Leffingwell) Hyde.
8. EDWARD. b. 1793. d. 1817.

HOWE.

I.

1. JAMES HOWE, b. 1598, d. 1702. m. Elizabeth Dane. b. d. 1693. dau. of John Dane of Roxbury and Ipswich, Mass. (To New England 1636-7.) (To Roxbury, then to Ipswich, Mass., where he lived and died.) (Son of Robert Howe of Broad Oak and Bishops Stortford, Essex Co., Eng.)

II.

2. JAMES. b. d. 1701. m. 1657 Elizabeth Jackson. b. d. 1692, being hung as a witch. dau. of William and Deborah (Jackson) of Rowley, Mass.
3. JOHN. b. 1642. d. 1697.
4. MARY. b. d. 1730. m. 1659 Dea. Nehemiah Abbot. b. d. 1707. of Rowley and Topsfield, Mass. (Rowley and Topsfield, Mass.)
5. REBECCA. b. d. m. 1671 Stephen Barnard. b. d. son of Robert Barnard of Andover, Mass. (Andover, Mass.)
6. ABRAHAM. b. 1646. d. 1717-18. m. 1677 Sarah Peabody. b. 1659. d. 1732. dau. of Lt. Francis and Mary (Foster) Peabody of Ipswich, Mass. of Lynn and Rowley and Andover, Mass.
7. SARAH. b. d. m. 1666 John Bridges. b. d. son of Edmund and Alice (Bridges). (Rowley, Mass.)

III.

Children of Abraham (6) and Sarah (Peabody) Howe.

8. LOVE. b. 1678. d.
9. INCREASE. b. 1680. d.
10. Capt. SAMPSON. b. 1682. d. 1734. m. 1709 Alice Perley. b. 1689. d. 1746. dau. of John Perley of Boxford, Mass. (To Killingly, Ct., about 1708.)
11. ABRAHAM. b. 1689. d.
12. ABIAH. b. 1689. d.
13. ISRAEL. b. 1692. d.
14. MARK. b. 1695. d. m. 1722 Hepzebeth Perkins. b. d.

HOWE.—Continued.

IV.

Children of (Capt.) Sampson (10) and Alice (Perley) Howe.

15. (Rev.) PERLEY. b. ab. 1710. d. 1753. m. Damaris Cady. b. 1717. d. 1775. dau. of Justice Joseph and (   ) Cady of Killingly, Ct. (Killingly, Ct.) She m. (2) Rev. Aaron Brown of Killingly. b.   d. 1775. (Y. C. 1749.)
16. (Lt.) SAMPSON. b.   d.   m. 1737 Sarah Sabin. b. 1716. d. 1752. dau. of Hezekiah Sabin of Killingly, Ct.
17. ALICE. b.   d.   m.   Newell. b.   d.

V.

Children of (Rev.) Perley (15) and Damaris (Cady) Howe.

18. ELLIS. b.   d. young.
19. ELIZABETH. b.   d.
20. SARAH. b.   d.   m. 1765 Damaris Burch.
21. ISAAC CADY. b.   d.
22. (Capt.) PERLEY. b.   d.   m. (1) 1764 Tamar Davis. b. 1745. d. 1771. dau. of Dea. Daniel and Tamar (Towne) Davis of Killingly, Ct.
    m. (2) Abigail DeWolfe. b.   d.
23. DAMARIS. b. 1745. d.   m. 1768 Timothy Holton (or Houghton).
24. (Rev.) JOSEPH. b. 1747. d. 1775. unm.
    (Y. C. 1765.) (Colleague of Rev. Benj. Lord at Norwich, Ct., in 1772-3, then pastor of the New South Church, Boston, Mass., 1773-5.)
25. REBECCA. b. 1749. d. 1769. unm.
26. SAMPSON b. 1751 d. 1824. m. 1774 Huldah Davis. b. 1754. d. 1810. dau. of Dea. Daniel and Tamar (Towne) Davis of Killingly, Ct.

HUBBARD.

I.

1. WILLIAM HUBBARD, b. ab. 1595, d. 1670, m. Judith Knapp, b. d. dau. of John and Martha (Blois) Knapp. (Grad. Cambridge, 1620.) (Came from Tendring Hundred, Co. Essex, to America, in ship Defence in 1635.)

II.

2. (Rev.) WILLIAM, b. 1621, d. 1704, m. Margaret Rogers, b. d. dau. of Rev. Nathaniel and Margaret (Crane) Rogers of Ipswich, Mass. (H. C. 1642.) m. (2) Mary ( ) Pearce, b. d. widow of Samuel Pearce. (Historian. Author of "King Philip's War," "Hist. of New England," "Present State of New England.") (Settled at Ipswich, Mass. Ordained 1657.)

III.

3. JOHN, b. 1648, d. 1710, m. ab 1679 Ann Leverett, b. 1652, d. dau. of Gov. John and Sarah (Sedgwick) Leverett. (Boston merchant.)

IV.

4. (Rev.) JOHN, b. 1677, d. 1705, m. 1701 Mabel Russell, b. 1677, d. 1730, dau. of Rev. Daniel and Mabel (Wyllys) Russell. (H. C. 1695.) She m. (2) 1707 Rev. Saml. Woodbridge of East Hartford, Ct., b. 1683, d. 1746. (Settled at Jamaica, L. I.) (H. C. 1701) son of Rev. Benj and Mary (Ward) Woodbridge.

V.

5. DANIEL, b. 1706, d. 1741, m. 1734 Martha Coit, b. 1706, d. betw. 1752–5. (Y. C. 1727.) dau. of John and Mehetabel (Chandler) Coit of New London. (Settled as a lawyer at New London.) She m. (2) 1744 Thomas Greene, b. 1705–6, d. 1764. (High Sheriff of the County.) Son of Nathaniel and Ann (Gould) Greene of Boston, Mass. (Thomas G. m. (1) Elizabeth Gardiner, b. d. dau. of John and Mary (King) Gardiner of Gardiner's Island.)

VI.

Children of Daniel (5) and Martha (Coit) Hubbard.

6. (Capt.) RUSSELL, b. 1732, d. 1773, m. 1755 Mary Gray, b. 1722, d. dau. of Dr. Ebenezer and Mary (Prentice (?)) Gray of Newport, R. I., and of Lebanon, Ct. (New London and Norwich, Ct.)
7. JUDITH, b. 1734, d.
8. DANIEL, b. 1738, d. 1760 at St. Croix, W. I. m. 1757 Mary Greene, b. 1733, d. 1803, dau. of Thomas and Elizabeth (Gardiner) Greene of Boston, Mass. (Boston, Dunearn, S. A., and West Indies.)
9. ELIZABETH, b. 1738, d. 1797, m. 1760 Benjamin Greene, b. 1735, d. 1754, son of Benjamin and Mary (Chandler) Greene of Boston, Mass.
10. (Capt.) WILLIAM, b. 1740, d. 1801 at New York, m. (1) 1764 Lydia Coit, b. 1741, d. 1775, dau. of James and Joanna (Mosecrove) Perkins of Boston, Mass. (To Norwich, Boston, and Colchester, Ct.) m. (2) 1777, Joanna Perkins, b. d. 1775. m. (3) ab. 1779 Alice (Skinner) Deming, b. ab. 1747, d. 1824, widow of Maj. Jonathan Deming of Colchester, Ct.

[473]

HUBBARD.—Continued.

VII.

Children of (Capt.) Russell (6) and Mary (Gray) Hubbard.

11. MARY. b. 1756. d. 1820. m. 1777 Capt. David Nevins. d. 1838.
12. THOMAS. b. 1758. d. 1807. m. 1781 Mary Hallam. b. 1760. d. 1825. dau. of Amos and Sarah (Denison) Hallam of New London, Ct. (New London and Norwich, Ct.) She m. (2) 1809 Capt. Erastus Perkins.
13. LUCRETIA. b. 1762. d. 1787 at New London, Ct. m. (1) 1782 Daniel Tracy.
    m. (2) 1784 Elijah Backus, 2nd. b. 1759. d. 1811. son of Elijah and Lucy (Griswold) Backus.
    He m. (2)   Hannah Richards of New London, Ct.
    (To New London, Ct., and to Marietta, O.)
14. RUSSELL. b. 1764. d. 1800 at sea. unm.
15. MARTHA. b. ab. 1766. d. 1830. m. 1786 David Wright of New London, Ct. b. ab. 1757. d. 1795 of yellow fever.
16. SUSANNA. b. 1768. d. 1814. m. (1) 1789 Ebenezer Bushnell.
    m. (2) 1803 (as third wife) Dea. Robert Manwaring. b. 1745. d. 1807 at Norwich. son of Christopher and Deborah (Denison) Manwaring of New London, Ct.
    (From New London to Montville and then to Norwich, Ct.)

Children of (Capt.) William (10) and Lydia (Coit) Hubbard.

17. LYDIA. b. 1765. d. 1791. m. 1783 Thomas Lathrop.
    He m. (2) 1791 Hannah Bill
18. WILLIAM. b. 1767. d. 1789.
19. JOSEPH. b. 1770. d. 1790.
20. LUCRETIA. b. 1770. d. 1775.
21. DAVID GREENE. b. 1773. d. 1825. m. 1799 Lucy Manwaring. b. 1773. d.
    (Boston, Mass.) dau. of David and Martha (Saltonstall) Manwaring of New London, Ct.

Children of (Capt.) William (10) and Joanna (Perkins) Hubbard.

22. JAMES PERKINS. b. 1780. d. 1789.
23. DANIEL. b. 1781. d.
24. (Judge) SAMUEL. b. 1785. d. 1847. m. (1) 1815 Mary Ann Greene. b. 1790. d. 1827. dau. of Gardiner and Elizabeth (Hubbard) Greene of Boston, Mass.
    m. (2) 1828 Mary Anne (Coit) Blatchford. b. 1798. d.   widow of Rev. Henry Blatchford of New York, Salem, Mass, and Maryland, and dau. of Elisha and Rebecca (Manwaring) Coit of New York City.
    (Lawyer. To Biddeford, Me., and later to Boston, Mass.)

VIII.

Children of Thomas (12) and Mary (Hallam) Hubbard.

25. THOMAS. b. 1783. d. 1817 at Batavia, Java.
26. RUSSELL. b. 1785. d. 1857. m. 1811 Abby Williams. b. 1787. d. 1863. dau. of Gen. Joseph and Abigail (Coit) Williams.
27. AMOS HALLAM. b 1791. d. 1865. m. 1821 Eliza Lanman. b. 1800. d. 1872. dau. of Hon. James and Mary Anne (Chandler) Lanman.

[474]

HUGHES.

I.

1. (Capt.) JOHN HUGHES. b. ab. 1719. d. 1763. m. 1748 Zipporah Hartshorn, b. 1725. d. 1799. dau. of David and Abigail (Hebard) Hartshorn of Franklin. (To Norwich, Ct.)

II.

Children of (Capt.) John (1) and Zipporah (Hartshorn) Hughes.

2. EUNICE. b. 1749. d.   m.   Jeremiah Leach.
3. ELIJAH. bapt. 1751. d.
4. HANNAH. b. 1752. d. 1754.
5. JOHN. b. 1755. d. 1775 at Cambridge, Mass.
6. HANNAH. b. 1757. d. 1801. m. 1774 Nathaniel Townsend.

[475]

HUNTINGTON.

I.

Line of Simon Huntington, 2nd.

1. SIMON HUNTINGTON. b.   d. 1633.   m.   Margaret Baret. b.   d.
   (To New England in 1633.)   She m. (2) 1635-6 (as second wife) Thomas Stoughton. b.   d. 1661.
   (Died on the voyage, of small pox.)   of Dorchester, Mass., and Windsor, Ct.

II.

Children of Simon (1) and Margaret (Baret) Huntington.

2. CHRISTOPHER. b.   d. ab. 1691. m. 1652 Ruth Rockwell. b. 1633. d.   dau. of William Rockwell of Windsor, Ct.
3. (Dea.) SIMON. b. 1629. d. 1706. m. 1653 Sarah Clark. b. ab. 1633. d. 1721. dau. of John Clark of Windsor, later of Saybrook, Ct.
4. ANN. b.   d.
5. THOMAS. b.   d. bef. 1664. m. (1)   Swain. b.   d.   dau. of William Swain of Branford, Ct.
   (To Newark, N. J., in 1667.)   m. (2)   Hannah Crane. b.   d.   dau. of Jasper Crane of New Haven, and Branford, Ct.

III.

Children of (Dea.) Simon (3) and Sarah (Clark) Huntington.

6. SARAH. b. 1654. d. 1705. m. 1676 Dr. Solomon Tracy. He m. (2) 1690 Sarah (Bliss) Sluman, widow of Thomas Sluman.
7. MARY. b. 1657. d.   m.   (as second wife) Dea. Caleb Forbes of Preston. b.   d. 1710.
   He m. (1) 1681 Sarah Gager. b. 1651. d.
                                         dau. of John and Elizabeth (Gore) Gager.
8. (Dea.) SIMON. b. 1659. d. 1736. m. 1683 Lydia Gager. b. 1663. d. 1737. dau. of John and Elizabeth (Gore) Gager.
9. (Dea.) JOSEPH. b. 1661. m. 1747. Rebecca Adgate. b. 1666. d. 1748.
   (To Windham, Ct.)
10. ELIZABETH. b. 1664. d. in infancy.
11. (Lt.) SAMUEL. b. 1665. d. 1717. m. 1686 Mary Clark. b.   d. 1743.   dau of John Clark of Farmington, Ct.
    (To Lebanon, Ct.)
12. ELIZABETH. b. 1669. d.   m. 1690 Joseph Backus.
13. NATHANIEL. b. 1672. d. young.
14. DANIEL. b 1675-6. d. 1741. m. (1) 1705-6 Abigail Bingham. b. 1679. d. 1734. dau. of Thomas and Mary (Rudd) Bingham.
    m. (2)   Rachel Wolcott. b.   d.   perhaps dau. of Henry and Rachel (Talcott) Wolcott of Windsor, Ct.
    She m. (2) 1742 Joseph Bingham. b. 1687. d. 1765. of Windham.
                                                son of Thomas and Mary (Rudd) Bingham.
15. (Ensign) JAMES. b. 1680. d. 1727. m. 1702-3 Priscilla Miller. b. 1675. (?) d. 1742. perhaps dau. of George Miller of New London, Ct.

[476]

HUNTINGTON.—Continued.

IV.

Children of (Dea.) Simon (8) and Lydia (Gager) Huntington.

16. SIMON.   b. 1680. d. 1707 from the bite of a rattlesnake.
17. SARAH.   b. 1687–8. d. 1730. m. 1712 William Lathrop.
18. (Dea.) EBENEZER. b. 1692. d. 1768. m. 1717 Sarah Lothingwell. b. 1697–9. d. 1779.
19. Capt. JOSHUA. b. 1698. d. 1745. m. (1) 1718 Hannah Perkins. b. 1701. d. 1788.
    She m. (2) bef. 1748 Col. Samuel Lynde of Saybrook, Ct. b. 1689. d. 1754.
    son of Nathaniel and Susanna (Willoughby) Lynde.
    m. (3) bef. 1771 Capt. Ebenezer Lathrop.

Children of (Dea.) Joseph (9) and Rebecca (Adgate) Huntington.

20. JOSEPH. b. in Norwich, 1688. d. 1783. m. 1719 Elizabeth Ripley. b.   d. 1774.
21. NATHANIEL. b. 1691 in Norwich. d. 1767. m. 1723 Mehetabel Thurston. b. 1700. d. 1771. of Bristol, R. I.
22. JONATHAN. b. 1695 in Windham. d. 1773. m. (1) 1734 Elizabeth Rockwell. b. 1713. d. 1751.
    dau. of Joseph and Elizabeth (Drake) Rockwell of Windsor, Ct.
    m. (2) 1754 Mrs. Sarah Norton. b.   d. 1788.
23. DAVID. b. 1697. d. 1771. m. 1725 Mary Mason. b. 1707. d.
    dau. of Hezekiah and Anne (Bingham) Mason of Lebanon, Ct. and Windham, Ct.
    She m. (2) 1776 Ebenezer Wright of Mansfield, Ct.
24. SOLOMON. b. 1700. d. 1752. m. 1727 Mary Buckingham. b. 1705. d. 1775. dau. of Thomas and Margaret (Griswold) Buckingham.
25. REBECCA. b. 1712. d.   m. 1734 John Crane. b. 1709. d.   son of John and Sarah (Spencer) Crane of Windham, Ct.
26. SARAH. b. 1705. d.   m. 1728 Ebenezer Wright. b.   d.
27. MARY. b. 1707. d.   m. 1731 Theophilus Fitch of Canterbury, Ct.

Children of (Lt.) Samuel (11) and Mary (Clark) Huntington.

28. ELIZABETH. b. 1687–9. d. 1764. m. 1710 Moses Cark. b.   d. 1749 son of Paul and Hannah (Pratt) Cark of Lebanon, Ct.
29. SAMUEL. b. 1691. d. 1754. m. 1722 Puelah Metcalf. b. 1702. d. 1791. dau. of Jonathan and Hannah (Avery) Metcalf of Lebanon, Ct.
30. CALEB. b. 1693–4. d.   m. 1729 Lydia Griswold. b. 1699. d.   dau. of Capt. Samuel and Susannah (Huntington) Griswold.
31. MARY. b. 1696 in Norwich. d. 1712.
32. REBECCA. b. 1697–9. d.   m. 1717 Joseph Clark. b. ab. 1692. d. 1769.
33. SARAH. b. 1700. d.
34. JOHN. b. 1703. d.   m.   Mehitable Metcalf. b. 1709. sister of Samuel's wife.
35. SIMON. b. 1705. d. 1753. m. 1735 Sarah Huntington. b. 1712. d. 1791. dau. of Dea. Ebenezer and Sarah Lathrop Huntington.
    She m. (2) 1773 Capt. Daniel Throop of Lebanon, Ct.

[477]

HUNTINGTON.—Continued.

IV.

Children of Daniel (14) and Abigail (Bingham) Huntington.

36. ABIGAIL. b. 1702. d. 1777. m. 1724 Thomas Carew.
37. MARY. b. 1709. d. m. 1730-1 Joseph Carew.
38. DANIEL. b. 1711. d. 1753. m. (1) 1740 Sibyl Buil of Milford, Ct. b. d. 1744.
    (Y. C. 1733.) m. (2) 1746 Rebecca Huntington. b. 1726. d. 1774.
39. ANNA. b. 1715 d. 1759. m. (1) 1731 Thomas Adgate.
    m. (2) 1739 Capt Philip Turner.
    m. (3) 1757 Capt. Joshua Abel. b. d.
40. JONATHAN. b. 1719. d. 1801. m. 1746 Eunice Lathrop. b. 1725. d. 1803.

Children of Daniel (14) and Rachel (Wolcott) Huntington.

41. (Hon.) BENJAMIN. b. 1736. d. m. 1765 Anne Huntington. b. 1740. d. 1790.
    (Y. C. 1761.) dau. of Col. Jabez and Sarah (Booth) (Wetmore) Huntington of Windham, Ct.
    (M. C. and Judge of Superior Court.)

Children of (Ensign James (15) and Priscilla (Miller) Huntington.

42. JERUSHA. b. 1704-5. d. 1771. m. 1729. Abner Hyde. b. 1706. d. 1787. son of Thomas and Elizabeth (Backus) Hyde.
    He m. (2) 1733 Mehetabel Smith. b. ab. 1713. d. 1792. dau of Capt. Obadiah and Martha (Abel) Smith.
43. JAMES. b. 1706-7. d. 1785. m. 1735 Elizabeth Parby. b. 1719. d. 1790.
44. PETER. b. 1708-9. d. 1760. m. 1734 Ruth Edgerton. b. 1715. d. 1761. dau. of John and Ruth (Adgate) Edgerton.
45. JACOB. b. 1711. d. 1726.
46. NATHANIEL. b. 1713. d. m. (1) 1735 Mary Brown of Stonington, Ct. b. d.
    m. (2) Elizabeth Jones, b. d. perh. dau. of Ephraim Jones of New London, Ct.
    m. (3) Pembroke. b. d.
47. ELIZABETH. b. 1716. d. 1759. m. 1732 Thomas Hyde. b. 1699. d. 1782. son of Thomas and Elizabeth (Backus) Hyde.

V.

Children of (Dea.) Ebenezer (18) and Sarah (Leffingwell) Huntington.

48. SARAH. b. 1715. d. 1791. m. (1) 1735 Simon Huntington.
    m. (2) 1753 Capt. Daniel Throop of Lebanon, Ct. b. d.
49. (Rev.) SIMON. b. 1719. d. 1801. m. (1) 1751 Hannah Tracy. b. 1727. d. 1753.
    (Y. C. 1741.) m. (2) 1759 Zipporah Lathrop. b. 1733. d. 1814.
50. LUCY. b. 1722 d. 1751. m. 1743 Dr. Elisha Tracy.
51. LYDIA. b. 1735. d. 1803. m. 1754 Dr. Jabez Fitch. b. 1725. d. 1806 of Canterbury, Ct. son of Jabez and Lydia (Gale) Fitch.
    He m. (2) 1754 Elizabeth Dorr.
    m. (3) 1781 Lois (Hinckley) Huntington, widow of Nehemiah Huntington.

HUNTINGTON.—Continued.

V.

Children of (Capt.) Joshua (19) and Hannah (Perkins) Huntington.

52. (Gen.) JABEZ. b. 1719. d. 1786. m. (1) 1741-2 Elizabeth Backus. b. 1720-1. d. 1745. (Y. C. 1741.)
    m. (2) 1746 Hannah Williams. b. 1726. d. 1807. dau. of Rev. Ebenezer and Penelope (Chester) Williams of Pomfret, Ct.
53. JEDIDIAH. b. 1721-2. d. 1725.
54. ANDREW. b. 1724. d. 1739.
55. LYDIA. b. 1727. d. 1798. m. 1746 Capt. Ephraim Bill. b. 1719. d. 1802. son of Samuel and Hannah ( ) Bill of New London, Ct.
56. ZACHARIAH. b. 1731. d. 1761. unm.

Children of Nathaniel (21) and Mehetabel (Thurston) Huntington.

57. (Rev.) NATHANIEL. b. 1724. d. 1756. m. Jerusha Ellsworth. b. d. (Y. C. 1747.) (Settled at Windsor, Ct.)
58. ABIGAIL. b. 1727. d. m. 1750 Richard Kimball, Jun., of Scotland, Ct. b. d.
59. MEHETABEL. b. 1729. d. m. prob 1748 Zebulon Webb, of Windsor, Ct. b. d.
60. (Gov.) SAMUEL. b. 1731. d. 1796. m. 1701 Martha Devotion. b. 1739. d. 1794. dau. of Rev. Ebenezer and Martha (Lathrop) Devotion of Windham, Ct.
61. (Rev.) JONATHAN. b. 1733. d. 1794. m. 1757 Sarah Huntington. b. 1738. d. 1793. dau. of Simon and Sarah (Huntington) Huntington of Lebanon, Ct. (Pastor of Church at Worthington, Mass.)
62. (Rev.) JOSEPH. b. 1735. d. 1794. m. 1764 Hannah Devotion (sister of brother Samuel's wife). b. 1742. d. 1771. (Y. C. 1762.)
    m. (2) Elizabeth Hale. b. ab. 1745. d. 1800. of Glastonbury, Ct.
63. ELIPHALET. b. 1737. d. 1799. m. 1762 Bindi Rudd. b. 1745. d. dau. of Jonathan and Esther (Taylor) Rudd of Windham, Ct.
64. (Rev.) ENOCH. b. 1739. d. 1809. m. 1794 Mary Gray. b. 1744. d. 1803. dau. of Samuel Gray of Windham, Ct. (Y. C. 1759.) (Pastor of Church at Middletown, Ct.)
65. SIBYL. b. 1742. d. 1773. m. 1763 Rev. John Eels. b. d. of Glastonbury, Ct. son of Rev. Nathaniel Eels of Stonington, Ct.
    He m. (2) Sarah Wells. b. d. of Wethersfield, Ct.

Children of Daniel (38) and Sibyl (Bull) Huntington.

66. SIBYL. b. 1742. d. 1820 unm in Stratford, Ct.
67. (Dr.) DANIEL. b. 1744. d. 1819. m. Tomlinson. b. d. (To Woodbury, Ct.)

HUNTINGTON.—Continued.

v.

Children of Daniel (38) and Rebecca (Huntington) Huntington.

68. LEVI. b. 1747. d. 1802. m. 1772 Anna Perkins. b. 1754. d. 1799. dau. of Jabez and Anna (Lathrop) Perkins.
69. FELIX. b. 1749. d. 1822. m. 1773 Anna Perkins. b. 1756. d. 1806. dau. of Capt. Jacob and Mary (Brown) Perkins.
70. REBECCA. b. 1752. d. 1753.

Children of Jonathan (40) and Eunice (Lathrop) Huntington.

71. EUNICE. b. 1747. d. 1775. m. 1771 Ebenezer Carew.
72. LUCRETIA. b. 1748. d. 1826. unm.
73. JONATHAN. b. 1751. d.
74. DANIEL. b. 1753. d. 1811 s.p. m. Elizabeth ( ) Moore. b. ab. 1753. d. 1811. (widow)
75. LUCY. b. 1755. d. 1833. m. 1776 Ebenezer Hyde. b. 1753. d. 1781 in N. Y., on "Jersey," prison ship, son of Elijah and Ruth (Tracy) Hyde.
76. ELIPHALET. b. 1757. d. 1759.
77. ABIGAIL. b. 1761. d. 1845. m. John Pierce. b. d.
78. RUFUS. b. 1763. d. 1832. unm.
79. HANNAH. b. 1765. d. 1845. m. Dr. John Turner.
80. ELIPHALET. b. 1768. d. 1802. m. Daniels. b. d.

Children of James (43) and Elizabeth (Darby) Huntington.

81. WILLIAM. b. 1736-7. d. 1816. m. (1) 1763 Anne Pride. b. 1740-1. d. 1776. perh. dau. of John and Abigail ( ) Pride.
    m. (2) 1777 Lois Durkee. b. 1752. d. dau. of Andrew and Eunice (Armstrong) Durkee.
    m. (3) 1791 Elizabeth Waterman. b. d.
    (To Lebanon, Ct., and later to Middlebury, Vt. Served in the Revolution.)
82. MARY. b. 1739. d. 1814. m. 1762 Eliphalet Carew.
83. JARED. b. 1740-1. d. 1819. m. 1776 Amy Gorton. b. d. 1829.
    (To Mansfield, Ct.)
84. JAMES. b. 1743. d. m. Hannah Curtis. b. d.
    (To Royalton, Vt.)
85. JOHN. b. 1745. d. 1815. m. 1773 Abigail Abel. b. 1752. d. 1814. dau. of Capt. Joshua and Ann (Backus) Abel.
86. ELIZABETH. b. 1748. d. 1799. m. 1767 Ezra Huntington.
87. ABIGAIL. b. 1753. d. m. Hon. David Hough of Lebanon, N. H. b. 1753. d.
    (To Lebanon, N. H., in 1778.) son of Capt. David and Desire (Clark) Hough of Bozrah, Ct.
88. NANCY. b. 1755. d. 1848. m. 1772 Frederick Calkins. b. d.
    (To Chelsea, Vt.)

HUNTINGTON.—Continued.

V.

89. ROGER. b. 1755. d.   m.   Polly Dyer. b.   d.
    (To Hartford, Vt. Served in the Revolution.)
90. SIBYL. b. 1760. d. 1852. m.   Dudley Hammond. b.   d.
    (To Chemung, N. Y.)
91. EUNICE. b. 1766. d. 1799. m. 1789 Jabez Avery. b.   d.

Children of Peter (44) and Ruth (Edgerton) Huntington.

92. RUTH. b. 1735. d. 1797. m. 1754 (as second wife) Benjamin Butler.
    He m. (1) 1701 Diadema Hyde. b. 1740. d. 1777.
    dau. of Rev. Jedidiah and Jerusha (Perkins) Hyde.
93. JERUSHA. b. 1737. d. 1777. unm.
94. (Capt.) SIMON. b. 1740. d. 1817. m. (1) 1777 Freelove Chester. b. ab. 1755. d. 1777. dau. of Capt. Jonathan and Freelove (Waterman) Chester
    m. (2) 1789 Patience ( )Keeno (or Keeney) of Wethersfield, Ct. b.   d. 1820.
    widow of Edward Keeney (?)
95. ZEBDIAIAH. b. 1742. d. 1826. unm.
    (Commissary of brigade in the Revolution.)
96. (Capt.) ELISHA. b. 1745. d. 1810. m. 1769 Anna Ryan.
    (Sea captain.)
97. PETER. b. 1747. d. 1799. m. 1785 (as second wife) Ebenezer Hyde. b. 1748. d. 1816. son of James and Sarah (Marshall) Hyde.
    He m. (1) 1775 Chloe Ellsworth and 1 (3) 1779 Elizabeth Peck.
98. (Capt.) FREDERICK. b. 1750. d.   m. (1) 1784 Sarah Bliss. b. 1757. d. 1780.
    (Was a sea captain.)   m. (2) 1787 Lydia Andrews. b.   d.
    (Moved to Hudson, N. Y.)
99. REUBEN. b. 1753. d. 1804. m. (1)   Carey. b.   d.
                                  m. (2)   Provost. b.   d.
                                  m. (3)   Frazier. b.   d.
100. LEFFREY (or LIBBEREY). b. 1756. d.   m. 1774 Edna Cement. b.   d.
     (To Plainfield, Vt.)

VI.

Children of (Rev.) Simon (49) and Hannah (Tracy) Huntington.

101. SAMUEL. b. 1751. d. 1812. m. 1772 Philura Tracy. b. 1751. d. 1810.
102. HANNAH. b. 1753. d. 1836. m. 1779 Rev. Eliphalet Lyman. b. 1754. d. 1836.   of Woodstock, Ct.

HUNTINGTON.—Continued.

VI.

Children of (Rev.) Simon (49) and Zipporah (Lathrop) Huntington.

103. ROGER. b. 1759. d. 1780 from a penknife wound.
104. DANIEL. b. 1762. d. 1805. m. 1777 Polly Edgerton. b.   d. 1811.
105. EBENEZER. b. 1764. d. 1853. m. 1806, Eunice Huntington. b. 1779. d.
    dau. of Capt. Andrew and Ruth (Hyde) Huntington of Lebanon, Ct.
106. ERASTUS. b. 1769. d. 1840. m. (1) 1800 Nabby Hyde. b. 1786. d. 1811. dau. of Abiel and Mary (Hosmer) Hyde.
    (Y. C. 1791.)   m. (2) 1815 Sarah Williams. b. 1785. d.   dau. of Gen. Joseph and Abigail (Coit) Williams.

Children of (Gen.) Jabez (52) and Elizabeth (Backus) Huntington.

107. (Gen.) JEDIDIAH. b. 1743. d. 1818. (?) m. (1) 1766 Faith Trumbull. b. 1743. d. 1775.
    (H. C. 1763.)   dau. of Gov. Jonathan and Faith (Robinson) Trumbull of Lebanon, Ct.
              m. (2) 1778 Ann Moore. b.   d.
    dau. of Col. Thomas L. and Elizabeth (Channing) Moore of New York.
108. (Judge) ANDREW. b. 1745. d. 1824. m. (1) 1766 Lucy Coit. b. 1746. d. 1776.
          m. (2) 1777 Hannah Phelps. b. 1760. d. 1832.
    dau. of Dr. Charles and Hannah (Denison) Phelps of Stonington, Ct.

Children of (Gen.) Jabez (52) and Hannah (Williams) Huntington.

109. (Col.) JOSHUA. b. 1751. d. 1821. m. 1771 Hannah Huntington. b. 1759. d. 1815.
110. HANNAH. b. 1753. d. 1791.
111. (Gen.) EBENEZER. b. 1754. d. 1834. m. (1) 1791 Sarah Isham. b.   d. 1793. dau. of Joseph Isham of Colchester, Ct.
    (Y. C. 1775.)   m. (2) 1795 Lucretia Mary McClellan. b. 1773. d. 1819.
    dau. of Gen. Samuel and Rachel (Abbe) McClellan of Woodstock, Ct.
112. ELIZABETH. b. 1757. d. 1834. m. 1773 Col. John Chester. b. 1749. d. 1809.
              son of Hon. John and Sarah (Noyes) Chester of Wethersfield.
113. MARY. b. 1760. d. 1840. m. 1778 Rev. Joseph Strong of Norwich.
114. (Gen.) ZACHARIAH. b. 1764. d. 1850. m. 1786 Hannah Mumford. b. 1767. d.
    dau. of Thomas and Catharine (Haveus) Mumford of Groton, Ct.

Children of (Rev.) Nathaniel (57) and Jerusha (Ellsworth) Huntington.

115. NATHANIEL. b. 1751. d. 1774 in Norwich, Ct.
    (Y. C. 1772.)
116. JERUSHA. b. 1753. d.
117. EUNICE. b. 1754. d. prob. 1755.

HUNTINGTON.—Continued.

VI.

Children of (Rev.) Joseph (62) and Hannah (Devotion) Huntington.

118. JOSEPH. b. 1767. Killed in a duel, 1794. m. 1788 Mirza Dow. b.   d. 1855 in Coventry, Ct.
    (To Charleston, S. C.)
119. (Gov.) SAMUEL. b. 1765. d. 1817. m. 1791 Hannah Huntington. b. 1770. d. 1818.
    (Y. C. 1785.)
    (Moved to Painesville, Ohio.)
120. FRANCES. b. 1769. d. 1857. m. 1796 Rev. E. D. Griffin of Park Street Church, Boston, afterward President of Williamstown College, son of George and Eve (Dorr) Griffin of East Haddam, Ct.

Children of (Rev.) Joseph (62) and Elizabeth (Hale) Huntington.

121. SEPTIMUS. b. 1773. d. 1776.
122. ELIZABETH. b. 1774. d. 1843. m. 1794 Amasa Jones. b.   d. 1842. of Coventry, Ct. son of Col. Joel Jones of Hebron, Ct.
    (To Wilkesbarre, Penn., in 1816.)
123. GEORGE W. b. 1776. d. 1777.
124. SEPTIMUS G. b. 1778. d. 1844. m. 1810 Mary Tyler Morse. b.   d.   of Wrentham, Mass.
    (Moved in 1819 to Shelby Co., Indiana.)
125. HANNAH. b. 1779. d. 1794.
126. HENRY. b. 1781. d. 1806. num.
127. LUCRETIA. b. 1783. d.   m. 1806 Joseph G. Norton. b.   d. 1844. of Hebron, Ct.
    (To Buffalo, N. Y., in 1823.)
128. PENELOPE. b. 1788. d. 1794.
129. JAMES. b. 1790. d. 1794.

Children of Felix (64) and Anna (Perkins) Huntington.

130. LUCY. b. 1774. d. 1822. m. 1795 Augustus Perkins. b. 1773. d.   son of John and Bethiah (Baker) Kingsley Perkins.
131. REBECCA. b. 1776. d. 1838. m. (as second wife) Augustus Perkins (her brother-in-law).
132. SARAH. b. 1778. d. 1787 &c. m.   Cyrus Williams. b.   d.   of Stockbridge, Mass.
133. MARY E. b. 1774. d. 1801.
134. JAMES. b. 1775. d. 1822. m. 1809 Zerviah Tyler. b. 1786. d.   dau. of Rev. John and Hannah (Tracy) Tyler.
135. CHARLOTTE. b. 1775. d. 1786.
136. CHARLOTTE. b. 1787. d.   unm.
137. FELIX A. b. 1779. d. 1802. m. 1811 Frances Snow. b. ab. 1790. d. 1829.
    (To New York City in 1825.)
138. WILLIAM. b. 1796. d.   unm.
    (To Charlotte, C. H., Va.)

HUNTINGTON.—Continued.

VI.

Children of John (85) and Abigail (Abel) Huntington

139. JESSE. b. 1774. d. 1851. unm.
140. ANNA. b. 1776. d.   unm.
141. RICHARD. b. 1777. d. 1784.
142. NABBE. b. 1780. d. 1804. unm.
143. LUCRETIA. b. 1783. d. 1850. m. 1801 Epaphras Porter. b. ab. 1779. d. 1861.
144. RUFFARD. b. 1786. d. 1855. m. 1830 Ellen Owens. b. 1794 in N. Wales, England. d.
     (To Utica, N. Y.)
145. JOHN. b. 1789. d.
     (To Zanesville, O.)
146. WILLIAM HENRY. b. 1793. d. 1846. m.   Stuart. b.   d.
     (To Sidney, O.)
147. CHARLES. b. 1795. d.   unm.
     (To New York City and to Ohio.)

VII.

Children of (Capt.) Simon (94) and Freelove (Chester) Huntington.

148. PETER CHESTER. b. 1777. d. 1836. m. 1805 Rachel Waring. b.   d. 1862.   dau. of Jonathan Waring of Athens, N. Y.
     (To Hudson, N. Y., later to Lebanon, Ct.)
149. SIMEON. b. 1779. d. 1777.
150. JERUSHA. b. 1771. d.   m. 1803 William Tilley.
     (To Hudson, N. Y.)
151. EDWARD. b. 1773. d. 1792.
152. MARTHA. b. 1775. d. 1794.
153. FREELOVE. b. 1777. d.   m. 1812.   James Lathrop. b. 1788.   Lost at sea.   son of Simon and Mary (Wetmore) Lathrop.
     (To New York City.)

Children of Samuel (101) and Philura (Tracy) Huntington.

154. ROGER. b. 1784. d. 1852. m. (1) 1814 Ann Denison. b. 1785. d. 1819. dau. of Benajah and Dinis (Read) Denison of Norwich, Ct.
                                m. (2) 1820 Amelia Matilda Lambert. b. 1798. d. 1883. dau. of Louis and Lydia (Fosdick) Lambert of Boston, Mass.
155. HANNAH TRACY. b. 1790. d.   m. 1810 Solomon Dickinson. b.   d.   of Hatfield, Mass.
156. GILBERT. b. 1796. d. 1841. m. 1836. Mary Ann M. Clement. b. 1796. d.   dau. of Peabody and Elizabeth (Shipman) Clement.

HUNTINGTON.—Continued.

VII.

Children of Daniel (104) and Polly (Edgerton) Huntington.

157. BETSEY, b. 1793, d.   m. 1812 Asher Bennett, b.   d.
158. LYDIA, b. 1796, d. 1856, m.   Joseph Bailey, b.   d.   of Bozrah, Ct.
159. LUCY TRACY, b. 1799, d. 1845, m.   Cyrus Miner, b. 1796, d. 1845.
160. (Rev.) SIMON, b. 1801, d. 1850, m.   Sarah Smith, b.   d.
    (Methodist preacher.)
    (To Canada.)
161. DANIEL LATHROP, b. 1804, d.   m. 1829 Mary Ann Lothrop, b. 1809, d.   dau. of Simon and Amelia (Greene Davis) Lothrop.
    (Lived at Yantic, Ct.)

Children of (Gen.) Jedidiah (107) and Faith (Trumbull) Huntington.

162. JABEZ, b. 1767 at Lebanon, Ct., d. 1848, m. (1) 1792 Mary Lanman, b. ab. 1773, d. 1809, dau. of Peter and Sarah (Coit) Lanman.
    (N. C. 1784.)   m. (2) 1810 Sarah Lanman, b. 1768, d. 1854, (sister of 1st wife.)

Children of (Gen.) Jedidiah (107) and Ann (Moore) Huntington.

163. ELIZABETH MOORE, b. 1777, d. 1823, unm.
164. ANN CHANNING, b. 1780, d. 1857, m. 1800 Peter Roberts, b.   d.   of New London, Ct.
    (To New London, Ct.)   son of Peter and Catherine (Mansfield) Roberts.
165. FAITH TRUMBULL, b. 1782, d. 1835, m. 1812 Benjamin Huntington, b. 1777, d. 1850,
                                                son of Judge Benjamin and Anne (Huntington) Huntington of New York City.
                                                [No. 124]   Mrs. Mary Ann (Kempton) Wales, b. 1795, d. 1841, of New York City.
166. HARRIET SMITH, b. 1784, d. 1814, m. 1810 Jesse DeWitt, b. ab. 1781, d. 1815, of Norwich, Ct.
167. (Rev.) JOSEPH, b. 1788, d. 1819, m. 1819 Susan Mansfield, b. 1791, d. 1823, dau. of Rev. Achilles Mansfield of Killingworth, Ct.
    (Y. C. 1809.)
    (Pastor of Old South Church, Boston.)
168. (Rev.) DANIEL, b. 1788, d. 1858, m. (1) 1812 Mary Hallam Saltonstall, b.   d. 1822, dau. of Capt. Gurdon Saltonstall.
    (Y. C. 1807.)   m. (2) 1823 Alma French, b.   d. 1837, dau. of Benjamin French of Boston, Mass.
                                                m. (3) 1841 Sarah Sayr Rainey of New London.
    (Pastor of Cong. Church at North Bridgewater, Mass.)
169. (Rev.) THOMAS, b. 1793, d.   m. (1) 1818 Elizabeth Colfax, b. 1795, d. 1830,
                                                m. (2) 1831 Taddine Clark, b. 1795, d.   of Brooklyn, Ct.
    (Pastor of Baptist Church in Brooklyn, Ct.)

[485]

HUNTINGTON.—Continued.

VII.

Children of (Judge) Andrew (108) and Lucy (Coit) Huntington.

170. JOSEPH. b. 1768. d. 1837. m. 1791. Eunice Carew. b. 1769 d. 1848.
171. HANNAH. b. 1770. d. 1818. m. 1791 Gov. Samuel Huntington.
(To Painesville, O.)

Children of (Judge) Andrew (108) and Hannah (Phelps) Huntington.

172. LUCY. b. 1778. d. 1846. m. 1746 Col. Elisha Tracy. b. 1766. d. 1842.
173. CHARLES PHELPS. b. 1779. d. 1850. m. (1) 1802 (?) Charlotte Lathrop. b. 1781. d. 1805.
m. (2) 1806 Maria Perit. b. 1783. d. 1854

Children of (Col.) Joshua (109) and Hannah (Huntington) Huntington.

174. ELIZABETH. b. 1774. d. 1812. m. 1800 Hon Frederick Wolcott. b. 1767. d. 1837. son of George Oliver and Lorraine (Collins) Wolcott of Litchfield, Ct.
He m. (2) Sally Worthington (Goodrich) Cooke (widow).

Children of (Gen.) Ebenezer (111) and Sarah (Isham) Huntington.

175. ALFRED ISHAM. b. 1793. d. 1854. m. Caroline Sius. b. d.
(To New Orleans, La.)

Children of (Gen.) Ebenezer (111) and Lucretia Mary (McClellan) Huntington.

176. WOLCOTT. b. 1796. d. 1861. m. 1837 Jane E. Watkinson of Middletown, Ct. b. 1809. d. 1899. dau. of John R. Watkinson.
177. LOUISA M. b. 1797. d. 1877.
178. GEORGE WASHINGTON. b. 1799. d. 1870. of New Orleans, La.
(To New Orleans, La.)
179. EMILY. b. 1801. d. 1874.
180. NANCY LOVETT. b. 1803. d. 1877.
181. WALTER. b. 1804. d.
182. SARAH ISHAM. b. 1806. d. 1855.
183. ELIZABETH MARY. b. 1808. d. 1845. m. 1830 Gabriel W. Denton. b. d. of Norwich, Ct.
184. MARIA HANNAH. b. 1810. d. 1881. m. 1837 George Perkins. b. d. of Norwich, Ct.

HUNTINGTON.—Continued.

VII.

Children of (Gen.) Zachariah (114) and Hannah (Mumford) Huntington.

185. THOMAS MUMFORD. b. 1786. d. 1751. m. 1819 Mary Bowers Campbell. b. 1792. d.
186. (Hon.) JABEZ WILLIAMS. b. 1788. d. 1875. m. 1833 Sally Ann Huntington. b. 1811. d. 1861.
    (N. C. 1809.)
    (M. C. and U. S. Senator.)
187. ELIZABETH MARY. b. 1793. d.   m. 1814 John Griswold. b. 1783. d.   of New York City,
    son of John and Sarah (Johnson Griswold of Lyme, Ct.
    He m. (2)   Louisa Wilson of Newark, N. J.

Children of (Gen.) Samuel (119) and Harriet (Huntington) Huntington.

188. FRANCIS. b. 1793 in Norwich. d. 1822. m. 1821 Sally White. b.   d.
    (To Painesville, O.)
189. MARTHA DEVOTION. b. 1795 in Norwich. d.   m. 1813 John H. Mathews, M. D. of Painesville, O. b.   d.
190. JULIAN CLAUDE. b. 1796 in Norwich. d.   m. 1823 Adeline Parkman. b. ab. 1795. d. 1834.
    (To Painesville, O.)
191. COLBERT. b. 1797. d.   m. 1833 Ellen Paine. b. 1809. d.
    (To Painesville, O.)
192. SAMUEL. b. 1799 in Norwich. d. 1804.
193. (Dr.) ROBERT GILES. b. 1800 in Norwich. d. 1836. m. 1829 Mary L. Fitch. b.   d.
    (To Ellsworth, O.)

VIII.

Children of Joseph (170) and Eunice (Carew) Huntington.

194. JOSEPH CAREW. b. 1792. d. 1852. m. 1816 Julia Stewart Dodge. b. 1769. d. 1859. dau. of David Dow and Sarah (Cleveland) Dodge
195. LUCY COIT. b. 1794. d. 1802. m. 1827 Stephen B. Cleveland. b. 1792. (?) d. 1857 at Cincinnati, O.
    (To Bloomfield, N. J.)   son of Rev. Aaron and Elizabeth (Clement) Breed Cleveland. (?)
196. EUNICE EDGERTON. b. 1795. d.   m. 1825 Judge Henry Strong.
197. BENJAMIN FRANKLIN. b. 1800. d. 1801.
198. OLIVER ELLSWORTH. b. 1802. d.   m. 1830 Mary Ann Strong. b.   d.
    (To Cleveland, O., 1837.)
199. ANDREW BACKUS. b. 1805. d. 1846. m. 1829 Jane Eliza Norris. b. ab. 1804. d. 1861.
200. HANNAH PHELPS. b. 1808. d.   m. 1829 John T. Adams. b.   son of Richard and Mary Rebecca (Merrills) Adams.
    He m. (2)   Elizabeth (Leo) Dwight. b.   d.
201. LYDIA COIT. b. 1808. d. 1826.
202. SALLY ANN. b. 1811. d. 1801. m. 1833 Hon. Jabez Huntington.
203. GEORGE FREDERIC. b. 1813. d. 1819.

[487]

HUNTINGTON.

I.

Line of Christopher Huntington.

1. SIMON HUNTINGTON b.   d. 1633.   m. Margaret Baret. b.   d.   d. 1661. of Dorchester, Mass., and Windsor, Ct.
   (To New England in 1633.)   She m. (2) 1635-6 Thomas Stoughton. b.
   (Died on the voyage, of small-pox.)

II.

Children of Simon (1) and Margaret (Baret) Huntington.

2. CHRISTOPHER. b.   d. 1691. m. 1652 Ruth Rockwell. b. 1633. d.
   dau. of William and Susanna (Chapin or Cajin) Rockwell of Windsor, Ct.
3. (Dea.) SIMON. b. 1629 d. 1706. m. 1753 Sarah Clark. b ab. 1633. d. 1721. dau. of John Clark of Windsor, later of Saybrook, Ct.
4. ANN. b.   d.
5. THOMAS. b.   d. bef. 1694.   Swain. b.   d.   dau. of William Swain of Branford, Ct.
   (To Newark, N. J., in 1667.)   m. (1)
   m. (2) Hannah Crane. b.   d.   dau. of Jasper Crane of New Haven and Branford, Ct.

III.

Children of Christopher (2) and Ruth (Rockwell) Huntington.

6. CHRISTOPHER. b. 1653. d. 1654.
7. RUTH. b. 1653. d. young.
8. RUTH. b. 1655. d. 1673. m. 1681 Samuel Pratt. b. 1655. (?) d.   prob. son of Lt. William and Elizabeth (Clark) Pratt of Saybrook, Ct.
9. (Dea.) CHRISTOPHER. b. 1660. d. 1735. m. (1) 1681 Sarah Adgate. b. 1663. d. 1705-6.
   m. (2) 1706 Judith (Stevens) Brewster. b.   d.   and Sarah (Smith) Stevens
   widow of Jonathan Brewster and perh. dau. of   of Hingham, Mass.
10. (Capt.) THOMAS. b. 1664. d. 1732. m. 1686-7 Elizabeth Backus. b.   d. 1728.
    (To Windham ab. 1692.)
11. JOHN. b. 1666. d. 1696. (?) m. 1686 Abigail Lathrop. b. 1665. d.
12. SUSANNAH b. 1668. d. 1727. m. 1685 Capt. Samuel Griswold. b. 1665. d. 1740. son of Lt. Francis Griswold.
    He m (2) Hannah   b.   d. 1752.
13. LYDIA. b. 1672. d.
14. ANN. b. 1675. d.   m. 1697 Jonathan Bingham. b. 1674. d. ab. 1751. son of Dea. Thomas and Mary (Rudd) Bingham of Saybrook, Ct.
    (To Windham, Ct.)

HUNTINGTON.—Continued.

IV.

Children of Dea. Christopher (9) and Sarah (Adgate) Huntington.

15. RUTH. b. 1672. d. 1725. m. (1) 1705-? Ralph Wyecock. b. 1683. d. 1748. of Windham, Ct.
son of Capt. Eleazer Wheelock of Mandon, Mass.
He m. (2)   Mary Standish. b.   d.   dau. of Capt. Josiah Standish of Preston, Ct.

16. CHRISTOPHER. b. 1686. d. 1759. m. (1) 1717-18 Abigail (Abel) Lathrop. b. 1689-90. d. 1739.
(To Franklin, Ct.)   widow of Barnabas Lathrop, and dau. of Caleb and Margaret (Post) Abel.
m. (2) 1733 Elizabeth Ensworth of Canterbury, Ct. b.   d. 1734-5
m. (3) 1740 Mary Brewster. b.   d. 1749.
m. (4) 1750-1 Mrs. Mary (Gaylord) of Hebron, Ct. b.   d. 1761.

17. ISAAC. b. 1688. d. 1764. m. 1715-16 Rebecca Lathrop. b. 1695. d. 1774.
18. (Old) JABEZ. b. 1691. d. 1752. m. (1) 1724 Elizabeth Edwards. b. 1697. d. 1733.
dau. of Rev. Timothy and Esther (Stoddard) Edwards of East Windsor, Ct.
m. (2) 1735 Sarah (Booth) Wetmore. b. 1700. d. 1753.
widow of Rev. Izrahiah Wetmore.

19. MATTHEW. b. 1694. d.   m. (1) 1719 Mary Morgan. b.   d. 1720-1.
m. (2) 1721 Elizabeth Wheeler. b.   d. 1725.
m. (3) 1726 Lydia Leonard. b.   d.

20. (Old) HEZEKIAH. b. 1696. d. 1773. m. (1) 1719 Hannah Frink. b. 1695. (?) d. 1740.
perhaps dau. of Sergt. Samuel and Hannah (Miller) Frink of Stonington, Ct.
m. (2) 174—? Dorothy (James) Williams. b. 1706-7. d. 1774. widow of John Williams of Bristol, R. I.
and dau. of Nathaniel and Dorothy (Rainsford) Pother of Bristol, R. I.

21. SARAH. b. 1699-1700. d.   m. (as second wife) 1724 Thomas Bingham. b. 1692. d.
son of Thomas and Hannah (Backus) Bingham.
He m. (1) 1713 Hannah Edgerton.

22. JEREMIAH. b. 1702. d. 1703.

Children of Dea. Christopher (9) and Judith (Stevens) Huntington.

23. JUDITH. b. 1707. d. 1752. m. 1725 Samuel Lathrop.
24. JOHN. b. 1709. d. 1794. m. (1) 1735 Civil Tracy. b. 1712. d. 1747-9.
m. (2) 1749 Mary Tracy. b. 1718. d. 1780.

25. ELIZABETH. b. 1712. d. 1776. m. 1733 Capt. Matthew Hyde. b. 1716. d. 1792. son of John and Experience (Abel) Hyde.
He m. (2) 1776 Hannah Pember. b. 1759. d. 1739. dau. of John and Hecter (Wood) Pember.

26. JEREMIAH. b. 1715. d. 1794. m. (1) 1744 Sarah Reynolds. b. 1725. d. 1747.
m. (2) 1747-8 Hannah Watrous. b. 1725. d.
(At close of Rebellion to Lebanon, N. H.) dau. of Ensign Isaac and Elizabeth (Brewster) Watrous of Lyme, Ct.

HUNTINGTON.—Continued.

IV.

Children of (Capt.) Thomas (10) and Elizabeth (Backus) Huntington.

27. THOMAS. b. 1688. d. 1755. m. (1) 1711 Elizabeth Arnold. b. 1692. d. 1716.) Arnold of Norwich and Windham, Ct.
    dau. of John and Mary (
    m. (2) 1733 Mehetabel Johnson. b. d. of Lebanon, Ct. d. 1740. dau. of James Johnson of Andover.

28. JEDIDIAH. b. 1692–3. d. 1780.
29. ELIZABETH. b. 1695 in Windham. d. m. 1722 Caleb Chappell. b. d. d. 1784. dau. of James Hovey of Mansfield, Ct.
30. ELEAZER. b. 1697 in Windham. d. 1747–9. m. 1718–19 Deborah Hovey. b. d.
31. RUTH. b. 1699. d. 1757. m. 1723. Samuel Lincoln of Windham, Ct. b. d.
32. LYDIA. b. 1701–2. d. m. 1730 Dea. Nathaniel Wales. b. d. 1744. of Windham, Ct.
33. WILLIAM. b. 1705. d. m. 1734–5 Mary Bassett. b. 1707–8. d. 1740. dau. of Nathaniel and Joanna (Borden) Bassett of Mansfield, Ct.
34. CHRISTOPHER. b. 1707. d. 1714.
35. SIMON. b. 1710. d. m. 1734 Amy Standish. b. 1709–10. d. 1795. dau. of Israel and Elizabeth (Richards) Standish of Preston, Ct.

Children of John (11) and Abigail (Lathrop) Huntington.

36. ABIGAIL. b. 1687. d. m. (?) Shebar Hall. b. d. of Mansfield, Ct.
37. JOHN. b. 1688. d. 1692.
38. JOHN. b. 1691. d. 1737. m. 1723 Thankful Warner. b. d. 1739.
    (To Tolland, Ct.)
39. HANNAH. b. 1693–4. d. 1761. m. 1714 Joseph Rockwell of Windsor. b. 1695. d. 1746.
    probably son of Joseph and Elizabeth (Drake) Rockwell
40. MARTHA. b. 1696. d. m. (1) 1717 Noah Grant. b. 1693. d. 1727 of Tolland, Ct.
    son of Samuel and Grace (Miner) Grant of Windsor, Ct.
    m. (2) 1728–9 Peter Buel. b. d. of Coventry, Ct.

V.

Children of Isaac (17) and Rebecca (Lathrop) Huntington.

41. REBECCA. b. 1717. d. 1725.
42. ISAAC. b. 1719. d. 1799 s. p. m. 1749–50 Lucy Edgerton. b. 1723. d. 1800. dau. of John and Ruth (Adgate) Edgerton.
    (To Bozrah, Ct.)
43. SARAH. b. 1721. d. 1808. m. 1747 John Bliss.
44. NEHEMIAH. b. 1722–3. d. 1780. m. 1748–9 Lois Hinckley. b. 1727. d. 1790. dau. of Gershom and Mary (Bird) Hinckley of Lebanon, Ct
    She m. (2) 1782 Dr. Elisha Tracy.
45. DORCAS. b. 1724–5. d. 1804. m. 1745 William Lathrop.

[490]

HUNTINGTON.—Continued.

V.

46. REBECCA. b. and d. 1725.
47. REBECCA. b. 1727. d 1774. m. 1747 Daniel Huntington, 2nd.
48. MARY. b. 1728 (?) d. 1798. m. 1750 Ebenezer Fitch. b. 1725. d. 1797.
49. SAMUEL. b. 1730. d. 1737.
50. JOSEPH. b. 1732. d. 1803.
51. ELIJAH. b. 1734. d. 1814. m. (1) 1764 Anna Carew. b. 1741. d. 1779. dau. of Joseph and Mary (Huntington) Carew.
    m. (2) 1771 Lydia Baldwin. b. 1741. d.   dau. of Thomas and Anna (Bingham) Baldwin.
52. BENJAMIN. b. 1736. d. 1801. m. 1767 Mary (Carew) Brown. b. 1734. d. 1777. widow of James (Noyes) Brown.
    She m. (1) 1754 James Noyes Brown.
53. ABIGAIL. b. 1739. d. 1829. m. 1764 Azariah Lathrop.

Children of (Col.) Hezekiah (20) and Hannah (Frink) Huntington.

54. HANNAH. b. 1720. d. 1744. unm.
55. ANNE. b. 1722. d 1754. m. 1747 Prosper Wetmore. b. 1722. d. 1788. son of Rev. Israhiah and Sarah (Booth) Wetmore of Stratford, Ct.
    He m. (2) 1756 Keturah Cheesebrough. b. 1734. d. 1757. of Stonington, Ct.
56. EUNICE. b. 1724. d. 1732.
57. HEZEKIAH. b. 1726. d. 1747.
    (Y. C. 1744.)
58. ELIAS. b. 1729. d. 1739.
59. ABIGAIL. b. 1731. d.   m. (1) 1748 Thomas Frink. b.   d.
    m. (2)   Rev.   Conant. b.   d.
60. ELIJAH. b. 1733-4. d. 1734
61. EUNICE. b. 1735. d. 1766. m. 1757 Capt. John Williams. b.   Lost at sea 1764.
62. DOROTHY. b. 1737. d.   m. 1764 Rev. Abiel Leonard. b. 1740. d. 1778.   of Woodstock, Ct.
    son of Rev. Nathaniel and Priscilla (Rogers) Leonard of Plymouth, Mass.
    (H. C. 1759.)
    He m. (2) 1766 Mary Green of Bristol, R. I.
63. GIDEON. b. 1739. d. 1797. m. 1764 Lydia Lathrop. b. 1740. d. 1816.
    dau. of Capt. Ebenezer and Lydia (Leffingwell) Lathrop.
    She m. (2) 1775 Elisha Lathrop. b. 1745. d. 1790. son of Elisha and Abigail (Avery) Lathrop.
64. LUCY. b. 1741. d.   m.   Samuel Williams. b.   d.

Children of (Col.) Hezekiah (20) and Dorothy (Paine) (Williams) Huntington.

65. HANNAH. b. 1759. d. 1815. m. 1771 Col. Joshua Huntington.

[49]

HUNTINGTON.—Continued.

V.

Children of John (24) and Civil (Tracy) Huntington.

66. (Rev.) JOHN. b. 1736. d. 1766. unm. (Settled at Salem, Mass.)
67. SOLOMON. b. 1738. d. 1798. m. Dimis Fuller. b. d. 1800 (?) in East Haddam, Ct. (To Hebron, Ct.)
68. (Dea.) ANDREW. b. 1740. d. 1830. m. 1764 Lucy Landphere. b. 1741. d. dau. of Solomon and Mary (Palmer) Landphere. (To Griswold, Ct.)
69. EZRA. b. 1742. d. m. (1) 1767 Elizabeth Huntington. b. 1748. d. 1796.
    m. (2) 1797 Mary (Rudd) Dean. b. d. 1804.
    m. (3) 1805 Betsey (Hyde) Lathrop. b. 1755. d. 1835 at Ashford, Ct., widow of Azel Lathrop and dau. of Phinehas and Anne (Rogers) Hyde of Franklin, Ct. Mary Ward. b. 1753. d. 1825. of Attleborough, Mass.
70. THOMAS. b. 1744-5. d. 1835. m. (Y. C. 1768.) (To Ashford and Canaan, Ct.)
71. WILLIAM. b. 1746-7. d. 1814. m. 1770 Mary Cutler. b. d. (To Hampton, Ct.)
72. (Dea.) CALEB. b. 1748-9. d. 1842 s. p. m. 1795 Anna Huntington. b. 1762. d. 1851. dau. of Oliver and Anna (Lynde) Huntington of Lebanon, Ct.

Children of Jeremiah (26) and Sarah (Reynolds) Huntington.

73. ASA. b. 1745. d. 1746.

Children of Jeremiah (26) and Hannah (Watrous) Huntington.

74. SARAH. b. 1748. d. 1846. m. 1775 Jonathan Freeman. b. 1745-6. d. 1808. son of Edmund Freeman of Mansfield, Ct.
75. JEREMIAH. b. 1751. d. 1831. m. Bates. b. d. (To Shaftesbury, Vt.)
76. ASA. b. 1753. d. m. Mary Marsh. b. d. (To Canaan, Ct.)
77. SAMUEL. b. 1755. d. unm. in Virginia.
78. ELIAS. b. 1756-7. d. m. Mary (Eaton) West. b. d. widow of Seth West. (To Lebanon, N. H.)
79. CHRISTOPHER. b. 1759. d. at the South.
80. ANDREW. b. 1761. d. 1845. m. 1787 Lydia Davis. b. 1759. d. of Lebanon, N. H. (To Pittsford, N. Y., in 1830.)
81. HANNAH. b. 1764. d. 1832. m. 1798 Rev. Noah Worcester (as second wife). b. 1758. d. 1837.
82. HEZEKIAH. b. 1766. d. 1830. m. Esther Slade. b. d. dau. of Samuel Slade of Hanover, N. H. (To Hanover, N. H., and Haverhill, N. H.)

HUNTINGTON.—Continued.

VI.

Children of Benjamin (52) and Mary (Carew) (Brown) Huntington.

83. MARY. b. 1768. d. m. 1791 Gardner Carpenter.
84. PHILIP. b. 1770. d. 1825. m. 1796. Theophila Grist. b. 1769. d. 1866.
85. ALICE. b. 1773. d. 1833. m. 1802 William Baldwin. b. ab. 1761. d. 1818, s. p. son of and Margaret (Fuller) (2) (Lathrop) Baldwin.
86. DANIEL. b. 1776. d. 1805 s. p. m. 1803 Sarah Potter. b. 1780. d. 1859. of New London, Ct.

Children of Ezra (69) and Elizabeth (Huntington) Huntington.

87. CHARLES. b. 1767. d. 1775.
88. (Dr.) ASHER. b. 1770. d. 1833. m. Lucy Andrews. b. d.
   (To Preston, Ct., and to Chenango, N. Y.)
89. JOEL. b. 1772. d. 1850. m. (1) 1801 Mary S. Bingham. b. d.
   (To Manlius, N. Y.) m. (2) 1813 Laura Cheeney. b. d.
90. SILAS. b. 1774. d. 1799.
91. CHARLES. b. 1775. d.
92. (Dr.) ABEL. b. 1777. d. 1858. m. Frances Lee. b. d. dau. of George Lee.
   (To East Hampton, L. I.)
93. CHARLES. b. 1779. d. 1859. m. 1819 Martha Hyde. b. 1773. d. 1839. dau. of Abel and Margaret (Tracy) Hyde.
   (To Columbus, N. Y., and to Hartsville, and to Chittenango, N. Y.)
94. BETSEY. b. 1781. d. m. Wheelock Bingham.
95. ANNE. b. 1784.
96. (Rev.) DAVID. b. 1788. d. 1855. m. (1) 1813 Ann Dows of Charlton, N. Y.
   (C. C. 1808.) m. (2) Catharine Calegan of Charlton, N. Y.
   m. (3) Lydia Blakeslee Allen of Harpersville, N. Y.
   (To Charlton, N. Y., and Harpersville, N. Y.)

VII.

Children of Philip (84) and Theophila (Grist) Huntington.

97. BENJAMIN. 1796. d. 1871. m. 1830 Margaretta Petit. b. 1808 in Philadelphia. d. 1866. dau. of John and Margaretta (Dunlap) Perit of Philadelphia, Pa.

[493]

HUNTLEY.

I.

1. ELISHA HUNTLEY. b.   d.   m. 1749 Mary Wallbridge. b. 1731-2. d. 1800.
   (From Lyme to Bozrah, Ct.)   dau. of Ebenezer and Mary (Durkee) Wallbridge of Franklin, Ct.

Children of Elisha (1) and Mary (Wallbridge) Huntley.

II.

2. EZEKIEL. b. 1750. d. 1837. m. (1) 1786 Lydia Howard. b.   d. 1787.
   m. (2) 1790 Zerviah Wentworth. b. 1767. d. 1834. dau. of Jared and Abigail (Wilson) Wentworth.

Children of Ezekiel (2) and Zerviah (Wentworth) Huntley.

III.

3. LYDIA. b. 1791. d. 1865. m. 1819 Charles Sigourney. b.   d.   of Hartford, Ct.
   son of Charles and (Frazier) Sigourney of Boston, Mass.

[494]

HUTCHINS.

I.

1. JOHN HUTCHINS. b.   d. 1695. m.   Frances   b.   d. 1694.
(Remov. from Newbury to Haverhill, Mass.)

II.

Children of John (1) and Frances (   ) Hutchins.

2. WILLIAM. b.   d.   m. (1) 1657 Mary Edmunds. b.   d.   dau. of William Edmunds of Lynn, Mass.
   m. (2) 1661 Sarah Hardy. b.   d.   dau. of Thomas Hardy of Ipswich, Rowley and Bradford, Mass.
   m. (3) 1685 Elizabeth (Eaton) Growth. b.   d.   widow of John Growth of Hampton and dau. of John Eaton.

3. JOSEPH. b. 1640. d. 1679. m. 1669 Johanna Corliss. b.   d.   Corliss of Haverhill, Mass.
   perhaps dau. of George and Joane (   )

4. BENJAMIN. b. 1641. d.   m. (?) 1694 Sarah Lampry. b.   d.
5. LOVE. b. 1645. d. 1739 at Kingston. m. 1665 Samuel Sherburne. b. 1638. d.   son of Henry Sherburne of Portsmouth.
6. ELIZABETH. b.   d.
7. (EBS.) SAMUEL. b.   d. 1712-13. m. 1672 at Andover, Mass., Hannah Johnson. b.   d.   of Hampton.

III.

Children of William (2) and Sarah (Hardy) Hutchins.

8. WILLIAM b. and d. 1662.   m. (?)

Children of Joseph (3) and Johanna (Corliss) Hutchins.

9. JOHN. b. 1671. d.   m. (?)   Sarah Page. b. 1680. d.
   perh. dau. of John and Sarah (Davis) Page of Haverhill, Mass.

10. JOHANNA. b. 1673. d. 1677.
11. FRANCES. b. 1676. d.
12. MARY. b. 1677-9. d.
13. ANDREW. b. and d. 1681.
14. SAMUEL. b. 1682. d. 1772 at Norwich, Ct. m. (?)   at Haverhill, Mass., Hannah Merrill. b.   d. 1744.
15. JOSEPH. b. 1689. d.

[495]

HUTCHINS.—Continued.

IV.

Children of John (9) and Sarah (Page) Hutchins.

16. JOHN. b. 1699. d.
17. SARAH. b. 1701. d.
18. RICHARD. b. 1703. d.
19. JAMES. b. 1705. d.
20. JEREMIAH. b. 1707-8. d.
21. DAVID. b. 1710. d.
22. MARY. b. 1712. d.
23. JONATHAN. b. 1715. d.
24. NATHANIEL. b. d.
25. ELIZABETH. b. 1721. d.

Children of Samuel (2) (14) and Hannah (Merrill) Hutchins.

26. SAMUEL. b. 1716 at Haverhill. d. m. Mary b. d.
    (To Norwich, Ct.)
27. HANNAH. b. 1717 at Haverhill. d. m. Swain. b. d.
    (Norwich, Ct.)
28. NATHAN. b. 1722 at Haverhill. d.
    (Norwich, Ct.)
29. ABIGAIL. b. 1724 at Haverhill. d. m. Fales. b. d.
    (Norwich, Ct.)

These are the only records we have found of the early Hutchins families of Haverhill, Mass. The Norwich notes are supplied from the will of Samuel Hutchins, formerly of Haverhill, Mass, who died in Norwich, May 15, 1778, aged 96 years, 9 months and 2 days, which does not quite agree with the date of birth, Aug. 20, 1682, of Samuel, son of Joseph and Johanna (Corliss) Hutchins, but for convenience sake, and as it is possible that the age at death may not be entirely correct, we have assumed that the latter may have married Hannah Merrill.

[496]

HUTCHINS.

Norwich Early Records of the Hutchins Family.

1. (1) JOHN HUTCHINS. b.   d.   m. 1715 Jerusha Bushnell. b.   d. 1744.
(Norwich, Ct.)

Children of John (1) and Jerusha (Bushnell) Hutchins.

2. JERUSHA. b. 1718. d. 1736-7.
3. ABIGAIL. b. 1720. d. 1750. m. 1743 David Knight, Jr. b.   d.   of Windham, Ct.
   He m. (2) 1757 Jane Clark. b.   d.
4. JOHN. b. 1722. d.
5. ELIZABETH. b. 1724. d.   m. 1745 Jonathan Knight. b.   d.
6. JOSEPH. } b. 1726-7. d.
7. BENJAMIN. }   d.   m.   Judith   b.   d.
8. JOSHUA. b. 1731. d.
9. SAMUEL. b. 1733-4. d.   m.

A Benjamin Hutchins also appears in Norwich and marries in 1739 Prudence Starkweather. b.   d.
John Meech of Preston also marries in 1723 Sarah Hutchins.

[497]

HYDE.

I.

1. WILLIAM. b.   d. 1681. m.
   (Probably to Hartford, Ct., ab. 1636.)
   (To Saybrook, Ct., in   .)
   (To Norwich, Ct., in 1660.)

II.

Children of William (1) and (   ) Hyde.

2. HESTER. b, prob. in England. d. 1703. m. 1652 at Saybrook John Post. b. ab. 1627. d. 1711. son of Stephen Post of Newtown, Hartford, and Saybrook.
   (To Norwich, Ct., in 1660.)

3. SAMUEL. b. ab. 1637 at Hartford, Ct. d. 1677. m. 1659 Jane Lee. b.   d.   (Brown) Lee of East Saybrook, now Lyme, Ct.
   (To Norwich, Ct., in 1660.)   dau. of Thomas and

III.

Children of Samuel (3) and Jane (Lee) Hyde.

4. ELIZABETH. b. 1660 at Norwich. d. 1736 at Lyme, Ct. m. 1662 Lieut. Richard Lord. b. 1647 in Saybrook. d. 1727 at Lyme, Ct. son of William Lord.
   (To Lyme, Ct.)

5. PHEBE. b. 1663. d. 1704 at Lyme, Ct. m. 1683 Matthew Griswold. b. 1653 at E. Saybrook, now Lyme. d. 1716. son of Matthew and Anne (Wolcott) Griswold.
   (To Lyme, Ct.)
   He m. (2) 1705 Mary (DeWolf) Lee, widow of Thomas Lee, and dau. of Balthazar DeWolf.

6. SAMUEL. b. 1665. d. 1742. m. 1690 Elizabeth Calkins. b. 1673. d.   dau. of John and Sarah (Royce) Calkins.
   (To Windham and Lebanon, Ct.)

7. JOHN. b. 1667. d. 1727. m. 1698 Experience Abel. b. 1674. d. 1763. dau. of Caleb and Margaret (Post) Abel.

8. WILLIAM. b. 1670. d. 1759. m. 1695 Anne Bushnell. b. 1674. d. 1745.

9. THOMAS. b. 1672. d. 1755. m. 1697 Mary Backus. b. 1672. d. 1752. dau. of Stephen and Sarah (Spencer) Backus.
   (To West Farms, now Franklin.)

10. SARAH. b. and d. 1675.

11. JABEZ. b. 1677. d. 1762. m. 1709 Elizabeth Bushnell. b. 1685-6. d. 1766.
    (To West Farms, now Franklin.)

IV.

Children of Jabez (11) and Elizabeth (Bushnell) Hyde.

12. ELIZABETH. b. 1711. d. 1741. m. 1735 Dea. Simon Tracy. b. 1710. d. 1793.
    He m. (2) 1744 Abigail Bushnell. b. 1718. d. 1774.

13. (Judge) JABEZ. b. 1713. d. 1805. m. 1736 Lydia Abel. b. 1719. d. 1803. dau. of Benjamin and Lydia (Hagen) Abel.
    (Franklin).

HYDE.—Continued.

IV.

14. ABIGAIL. b. 1715. d. 1804. m. 1742 Jonathan Barstow. b. 1712. d. bef. 1750. son of Job and Rebecca (Bushnell) Barstow. (Franklin.)
15. PHINEHAS. b. 1720. d. m. 1744 Anne Rogers. b. 1726. d. 1776. dau. of Dr. Theophilus and Elizabeth (Hyde) Rogers. (Franklin.)
16. JOSEPH. b. 1724. d. 1754. unm.

V.

Children of Jabez (13) and Lydia (Abel) Hyde.

17. EZEKIEL. b. 1738. d. 1808. m. 1768 (1) Rachel Tracy. b. 1740. d. 1781. dau. of John and Margaret (Hyde) Tracy.
    m. (2) 1782 Mary Gosen. b. d. s. p. (Franklin.)
18. (Judge) JABEZ. b. 1740. d. 1835 at Rush, Pa. m. 1775 Martha Pettis. b. 1742. d. 1816. dau. of Joshua Pettis (To Rush, Pa., in 1800.)
19. LYDIA. b. 1744. d. 1822. m. John Lathrop. b. 1739. d. 1803. son of John and Elizabeth (Abel) Lathrop. (Franklin.)
20. ELIZABETH. b. 1746. d. 1746. m. 1774 Phinehas Leffingwell. b. 1742. d. 1777. son of Capt. John and Mary (Hart) Leffingwell.
21. ANDREW. b. 1748. d. 1835. m. (1) 1775 Mary Tracy. b. 1750. d. 1784. dau. of John and Margaret (Hyde) of Hoosick, N. Y. b. 1758. d. 1820 s. p.
    m. (2) Edrah (Hyde) Rogers of Hoosick, N. Y. b. 1758. d. 1820 s. p.
    widow of Dr. Stephen Rogers and dau. of Capt. Thomas and Lydia (Backus) Hyde.
22. PHEBE. b. 1752. d. 1834. m. 1772 John Gager. b. 1764. d. 1854. son of John and Lydia (Avery) Gager. (Franklin.)
23. SOLOMON. b. ab. 1753. d. 1815. m. Susanna Rogers. b. ab. 1753 at Goshen, Ct. d. 1820. dau. of Nathaniel Rogers of Goshen, Ct. (Franklin.)
24. JOSEPH. b. ab. 1755. d. 1809. m. 1780 Susanna Waterman. b. 1762. d. 1810. dau. of Nehemiah and Susanna (Abel) Waterman. (Franklin.)
25. BENJAMIN. b. ab. 1757. d. 1839. m. 1772 Elizabeth Hyde. b. 1760. d. 1829. dau. of Capt. Thomas and Edrah (Backus) Hyde. (To Rome, N. Y. in 1811.)
    (To Tabery, N. Y., ab. 1815.)
26. DICK. b. 1759. d. 1848. m. 1777 Oliver Backus. b. 1755. d. 1820. son of Jabez and Esther (Lathrop) Backus. (Bazrah, O.)
27. AMBROSE. b. 1762. d. 1747 at Platsala. m. 1790 Phebe Hyde. b. 1770. d. 1845. dau. of Capt. Thomas and Edrah (Backus) Hyde. (To Pittsfield, Mass., and to Berlin, Columbia and Pharsalia, N. Y.)

HYDE.—Continued.

VI.

Children of Ezekiel (17) and Rachel (Tracy) Hyde.

28. EZEKIEL. b. 1769. d. 1770.
29. EZEKIEL. b. 1771. d. 1805 unm. at Wilkesbarre, Pa.
30. (Judge) JOHN. b. 1773. d. 1847. m. 1798 Sarah Russell Leffingwell. b. 1778. d. 1855. dau. of Daniel and Elizabeth (Whiting) Leffingwell. (Norwich Town.)

VII.

Children of (Judge) John (30) and Sarah Russell (Leffingwell) Hyde.

31. RACHEL TRACY. b. 1799. d.
32. ABIGAIL LEFFINGWELL. b. 1800. d. m. 1822 Henry Harland.
33. ELIZABETH WHITING. b. 1803. d.
34. SARAH RUSSELL. b. 1805. d. 1841. unm.
35. SAMUEL LEFFINGWELL. b. 1807. d. m. 1831 Harriet Tyler Brewer. (To New York City.)
36. MARY M. b. 1809. d.
37. JOHN EZEKIEL. b. 1811. d. m. Amelia Bailey of New Orleans, La. (To New Orleans, La.)
38. ARCHIBALD CRARY. b. 1813. d. (To Victoria, Texas.)
39. STEPHEN HENRY. b. 1816. d. 1837 at New Orleans. unm.
40. JANE LEE. b. 1818. d. 1829. unm.

[500]

JONES.

I.

1. THOMAS, b. , d. 1654 in England, of the small-pox. m. (1) Mary widow Carter. b. , d. .
   (At Guilford, Ct., in 1639.) m. (2) , b. , d. 1650.

II.

2. (Capt.) SAMUEL, b. , d. 1794. m. 1666 Mary Bushnell, b. , d. perhaps dau. of Francis Bushnell of Saybrook, Ct.
   (To Saybrook, Ct.)

III.

3. CALEB, b. , d. 1711–12. m. Rachel Clark, b. , d. dau. of John Clark of Farmington, Ct.
   (To Hebron, Ct.) She m. (2) 1713–14 Israel Phelps of Enfield, Ct.

IV.

4. SYLVANUS, b. ab. 1707–8, d. 1791. m. 1730 Kesiah Cleveland, b. 1709, d. 1777, dau. of Isaac and Elizabeth (Curtis) Cleveland.
   (To Norwich, Ct.)

Children of Sylvanus (4) and Kesiah (Cleveland) Jones.

5. PERSIS, b. 1731–2, d. 1790.
6. RUFUS, b. 1732, d. . m. 1757 Anne Hartshorn, b. 1734–5, d. dau. of David and Abigail (Hebard) Hartshorn.
7. AZARIAH, b. 1735, d. . m.
8. PARMENAS, b. 1742, d. 1743.
9. EBENEZER, b. 1744, d. . m. 1765 Elizabeth Rogers, b. , d.
10. ELIZABETH, b. 1746, d. 1751.
11. TRYPHENA, b. 1749, d. 1751.
12. PARMENAS, b. 1752, d. . m. (1) 1777 Eunice Herrick, b. , d.
    m. (2) 1788 Rosanna Weeks, b. , d.

V.

Children of Ebenezer (9) and Elizabeth (Rogers) Jones.

13. LEVY, b. 1766, d. . m. 1788 Henry J. Coolege, b. ab. 1760, d. 1803 in Savannah, Ga.
14. RACHEL, b. 1771, d. . m. 1793 Asa Lathrop, Jun. b. , d. 1805 s. p.
15. MARY, b. 1775, d. 1794.

VI.

Children of Parmenas (12) and Eunice (Herrick) Jones.

16. RICHARD, bapt. 1779, d.

Children of Parmenas (12) and Rosanna (Weeks) Jones.

17. SALLY, bapt. 1789, d.
18. EUNICE, b. 1790, d.
19. SYLVANUS, b. 1792, d.
20. ELIZABETH WILLIAMS, b. 1793, d.
21. EBENEZER, b. 1796, d. 1797.
22. MARY WEEKS, b. 1798, d.

KINNEY.

I.
1. HENRY KINNEY. b. ab. 1624. d. 1712. m. Ann   b.   d
   (Was born in Holland of Puritan parentage. Of Salem, Mass., in or before 1656.)

II.
2. THOMAS. b. 1655. d. 1657. m. Elizabeth Knight. b.   d.
   (Salem, now Danvers, Mass.)

III.
3. JOSEPH. b. 1680 at Salem. d. 1745 at Preston, Ct. m. 1704 at Salem, Keziah Peabody. b. 1686 at Topsfield, Mass. d.   at Preston, Ct.
   (To Preston, Ct., in 1706.) dau. of Jacob and Abigail (Towne) Peabody of Topsfield, Mass.

IV.
4. JOSEPH. b. 1717 at Preston, now Griswold. d.   in Vermont. m. (1)   at Preston Sarah Blunt. b.   d. 1754.
   (Preston, Ct.) m. (2) 1755 at Norwich Jemina (Newcomb) Lamb. b. 1730 at Lebanon, Ct. d.   in Vermont (?)
   dau. of Hezekiah and Jerusha (Bradford) Newcomb and widow of Jonathan Lamb of Norwich, Ct.

V.
5. NEWCOMB. b. 1761 at Preston. d. 1846 at Norwich. m. 1786 at Norwich Sallie Branch. b. 1764 at Preston. d. 1824 at Norwich.
   (Rep. 1807, 1815, 1818, 1819, and 1825. Norwich, Ct.) dau. of Samuel and Hannah (Witter) Branch of Preston.

VI.

Children of Newcomb (5) and Sallie (Branch) Kinney.

6. JOSEPH. b. 1787. Killed at battle of Bridgewater, July 25, 1814.
   (Capt. in 25th Regt., U. S. A. Buried at Buffalo.)
7. CHARLES. b. 1789. d. 1794.
8. JACOB WITTER. b. 1791. d. 1854. m. 1813 Harriet Clark. b. 1794 at Preston. d. 1857 at Norwich.
   dau. of Capt. Elijah and Eunice (Morgan) Clark of Preston.
9. GEORGE. b. 1793 at N. d. 1888. m. 1819 at New York Eliza Gibbs Cahoone. b. 1802 at Newport, R. I. d. 1875 at Norwich, Ct.
   dau. of William and Sarah (Gibbs) Cahoone of N. Y.
10. CHARLES. b. 1795 at N. d. 1829 at N. unm.
11. HAPPY. b. 1791 at N. d. 1867 at N. m. 1841 Jedediah Huntington. b. 1794. d.
    son of Deu. Jabez and Mary (Latimau) Huntington of N.
12. JOHN. b. 1800 at N. d. 1866 at Stockton, Cal. m.   Laura Sophia Story. b. 1804. d.
    dau. of Samuel and Sophia (Corning) Story of N.
13. SALLY MIRAH. b. 1803. d. 1824. unm.
14. WILLIAM BRANCH. b. 1804. d. 1867.
15. HARRIET NEWCOMB. b. 1808. d. 1832. m. 1831 Holdridge Dewey. b.   d.   of Lockport, N. Y.

[502]

KNIGHT.

I.

Genealogy of Sarah (Kemble) Knight.

1. Thomas Kemble (Kemball or Kimball), b. 1622, d. 1689, m.   Elizabeth Trarice, b.   d.   ) Trarice
possibly dau. of Nicholas and Rebecca (   ) of Charlestown, Mass.

II.

2. Sarah, b. 1666, d. 1727, m.   Richard Knight, b.   d.   of Boston, Mass.
(Boston, Mass.)
(To Norwich and New London, Ct.)

III.

3. Elizabeth, b. 1679, d. 1735–6, m.   (as second wife) Col. John Livingston, b.   d. 1720–1, of New London, Ct.
He m. (1)   Mary Winthrop, b.   d. 1712–13,
dau. of Gov. Fitz John and Elizabeth (Tongue) Winthrop.

[503]

LANCASTER.

WILLIAM LANCASTER. b.   d.
(To Providence, R. I. Left there ab. 1670.)

1. ROBERT LANCASTER. b. ab. 1694-5.   d. 1770.   m.   Elizabeth   b.   d.

Children of Robert (1) and Elizabeth (   ) Lancaster.

2. JAMES. b. 1734. d.
3. ELIZABETH. b. 1736. d. aft. 1813. unm.
4. JOHN. b. 1737-8. d.   m. 1798 Anna (Bentley) Trapp. b. ab. 1754. d. 1831. widow of Ephraim Trapp.
5. MERCY. (?) b. 1742. d. 1807.
6. MARY. b. 1743-4. d.
7. ANNA. b. 1745-6. d.
8. WILLIAM. b. 1749. d.

LATHROPP (or LATHROP.)

I.

1. (Rev.) JOHN LOTHROPP (or LATHROP.) b. 1584. d. 1653. m. (1)   m. (2) 1635 Anna (   ) b.   d. 1657–8. (?) possibly a dau. of William Hammond of Watertown, Mass., and widow of
   (To New England in 1634.)
   (To Scituate, Mass., in 1634.)
   (To Barnstable, Mass., in 1639.)

II.

2. SAMUEL. b.   d. 1699–1700. m. (1) 1644 Elizabeth Scudder. b.   d.   perh. dau. of Thomas and Elizabeth Scudder (   ) of Salem, Mass.
   (Removed to New London ab. 1640–7.)
   (To Norwich in 1668.)   m. (2) 1690 Abigail Doane. b. 1632. d. 1734. dau. of John and Abigail (   ) Doane of Plymouth, Mass.

III.

Children of Samuel (2) and Elizabeth (Scudder) Lathrop.

3. JOHN. bapt. 1645–6. d. 1688. m. 1669 Ruth Royce. b.   d.   dau. of Robert Royce of New London, Ct. (To Wallingford, Ct.)
4. ELIZABETH. b. 1648. d.   m. (1) 1669 Isaac Royce. b.   d.   brother of Ruth Royce.
   (To Wallingford, Ct.)   m. (2)   Joseph Thompson of Wallingford, Ct. b.   d.
5. SAMUEL. b. 1650. d. 1732. m. (1) 1675 Hannah Adgate. b. 1653. d. 1695.
                              m. (2) 1697 Mary (Reynolds) Edgerton. b. 1664. d. 1727–8. widow of John Edgerton and dau. of John and Sarah (Backus) Reynolds.
6. SARAH. b. 1655. d. 1706. (?) m. 1681 Nathaniel Royce. b. 1650. d. 1739. son of Robert Royce.
7. MARTHA. b. 1657. d. 1719. m. 1677 John Moss. b. 1650. d. 1717. son of John Moss of Wallingford, Ct. (Wallingford, Ct.)
8. ISRAEL. b. 1659. d. 1733. m. 1686 Rebecca Bliss. b. 1663. d. 1737.
9. JOSEPH. b. 1661. d. 1740. m. (1) 1686 Mary Scudder. b.   d. 1695.
                              m. (2) 1696–7 Elizabeth Watrous (or Waterhouse). b. 1672. d. 1726. dau. of Isaac and Sarah (Pratt) Watrous of Lyme, Ct.
                              m. (3) 1727 Martha (Morgan) Perkins. b. 1680–1. d. 1754. widow of Dea. Joseph Perkins and dau. of Lt. Joseph and Dorothy (Parke) Morgan of Groton, Ct.
10. ABIGAIL. b. 1665. d.   m. 1686 John Huntington.
11. ANNE. b. 1667. d. 1745. m.   William Hough. b. 1657. d. 1705. son of William and Sarah (Calkins) Hough of New London, Ct.

[505]

LATHROP.—Continued.

IV.

Children of Samuel (5) and Hannah (Adgate) Lathrop.

12. HANNAH. b. 1677. d. 1721. m. (1) 1698 Jabez Perkins. b. 1677. d. 1741-2.
    He m. (2) 1722 Charity (Hodges) Leonard.
13. ELIZABETH. b. 1679. d. 1708. m. 1701 John Waterman. d.
    He m. (2) 1709 Judith Woodward.
    m. (3) 1721 Elizabeth Bassett.
14. THOMAS. b. 1681. d. 1774. m. 1708-9 Lydia Abel. b. 1688. d. 1752. dau. of Joshua and Bethiah (Gager) Abel.
15. MARGARET. b. 1683. d. 1698.
16. SAMUEL. b. 1685. d. 1753. m. 1715 Deborah Crow. b. 1691-4. d. 1794. ( ) Crow of Hartford, Ct.
    perhaps dau. of Nathaniel and Deborah
    (She is said to have died aged 104.)
17. (Col.) SIMON. b. 1689. d. 1774. m. (1) Mary Lathrop } twin sisters. b. 1696. d. daus. of Israel and Rebecca (Bliss) Lathrop.
    m. (2) 1714 Martha Lathrop } d. 1775.
18. NATHANIEL. b. 1693. d. 1774. m. 1717 Ann Backus. b. 1695. d. 1761.

Children of Israel (8) and Rebecca (Bliss) Lathrop.

19. ISRAEL. b. 1687. d. m. (1) 1710 Mary Fellowes. b. d.
    m. (2) 1747 Sarah Tuttle. b. d.
20. WILLIAM. b. 1688. d. 1778. m. (1) 1712 Sarah Huntington. b. 1687-8. d. 1730.
    m. (2) 1731 Mary Kelly. b. d. 1769.
    m. (3) 1761 Phebe French. b. 1702 (?) d.
    possibly widow of Maj. John French of Franklin and dau. of Thomas and Mary (Backus) Hyde.
21. JOHN. b. 1690. d. ab. 1752. m. 1715 Elizabeth Abel. b. 1695. d. dau. of Joshua and Bethiah (Gager) Abel.
22. SAMUEL. b. 1692. d. m. 1712 Elizabeth Waterman. b. 1696. d. 1773. Burnt to death. dau. of Thomas and Elizabeth (Allyn) Waterman.
23. REBECCA. b. 1695. d. 1774. m. 1715-16 Hon. Isaac Huntington.
24. MARY. } b. 1696. d. m. Col. Simon Lathrop.
25. MARTHA. } d. 1775. m. 1714 Col. Simon Lathrop.
26. BENJAMIN. b. 1699. d. m. (1) 1718 Mary Adgate. b. 1694. d. 1739-40.
    m. (2) 1741 Mary (Worthington) Jones. b. 1701. d. 1770.
    widow of Daniel Jones of Colchester and dau. of William Worthington of Colchester, Ct.
27. (Capt.) EBENEZER. b. 1702-3. d. 1784. m. (1) 1725 Lydia Leffingwell. b. 1706. d. 1766.
    m. (2) bef. 1771 Hannah (Perkins) (Huntington) Lynde. b. 1701. d. 1788.
    dau. of Jabez and Hannah (Lathrop) Perkins and widow of Capt. Joshua Huntington and Col. Samuel Lynde.

[506]

LATHROP.—Continued.

IV.

28. JABEZ. b. 1706-7. d. 1796. m. (1) 1728 Elizabeth Burnham. b. 1710. d. 1730. dau. of Eleazer and Lydia (Waterman) Burnham.
    m. (2) 1734 Delight Otis. b. 1706. d. 1747. dau. of Judge Joseph and Dorothy (Thomas) Otis of Montville, Ct.
    m. (3) Lydia ( ) Wetherell. b. d. widow of Dr. Joseph Wetherell of Taunton, Mass.

Children of Joseph (9) and Mary (Scudder) Lathrop.

29. BARNABAS. b. 1686. d. 1710. m. 1709-10 Abigail Abel. b. 1692. d. 1739. dau. of Caleb and Margaret (Post) Abel.
    She m. (2) 1717-18 Christopher Huntington.
30. JOSEPH. b. 1688. d. bef. 1757. m. 1735. Mary Hartshorn. b. 1701. d. dau. of Jonathan and Mary (Richards) Hartshorn.
    (To Waterbury, Ct., before 1752.)
31. ABIGAIL. b. 1693. d. m. 1719 Jacob Hazen. b. 1691-2. d. 1755. son of Thomas and Mary (Howlett) Hazen.

Children of Joseph (9) and Elizabeth (Waterous) Lathrop.

32. MEHITABLE. b. 1697. d. 1731-2. m. bef. 1719 William Bushnell. b. 1689. d. son of William Bushnell of Saybrook, Ct.
    m. (2) 1722 Lt. Thomas Stoughton. b. 1695. d. 1749. of East Windsor, Ct.
    son of Capt. Thomas and Abigail (Edwards-Lathrop) Stoughton.
33. SAMUEL. b. 1699. d.
34. ELIZABETH. b. 1700-1. d.
35. SARAH. b. 1702. d.
36. TEMPERANCE. b. 1794. d. m. 1727 (as second wife) John Bishop. b. d. 1754. poss. son of Thomas Bishop of Ipswich, Mass.
    He m. (1) 1715 Mary Bingham. b. 1697-. d. 1724. dau. of Thomas and Hannah (Backus) Bingham.
37. SOLOMON. b. 1706. d. 1733. m. 1727-9 Martha (Perkins) Todd. b. 1706. d.
    widow of Thomas Todd and dau. of Dea. Joseph and Martha (Morgan) Perkins.
    She m. (3) 1739 Matthew Loomis. b. 1703. d. of Bolton, Ct.
    poss. son of James and Mindwell ( ) Loomis.
38. RUTH. b. 1709. d
39. ESTHER. b. 1712. d.
40. ZERVIAH. b. 1715. d. m. 1739 William Bradford. b. d. of Canterbury, Ct. son of Lt. James Bradford.

V.

Children of Thomas (14) and Lydia (Abel) Lathrop.

41. (Dr.) DANIEL. b. 1712. d. 1752. m. 1744 Jerusha Talcott. b. 1717. d. 1805.
    (Y. C. 1733.) dau. of Gov. Joseph and Abigail (Clarke) Talcott of Hartford, Ct.
42. LYDIA. b. 1718. d. 1794. m. 1739-40 Capt. Joseph Coit.
43. (Dr.) JOSHUA. b. 1723. d. 1807. m. (1) 1745 Hannah Gardiner. b. 1730. d. 1760.
    (Y. C. 1743.) dau. of David and Rachel (Schellinx) Gardiner of Gardiner's Island.
    m. (2) 1761 Mercy Eels. b. 1743. d. 1833.
    dau. of Rev. Nathaniel and Mercy (Cushing) Eels of Stonington, Ct.

LATHROP.—Continued.

V.

Children of (Col.) Simon (17) and Martha (Lathrop) Lathrop.

44. MARTHA. b. 1715. d. 1795. m. (1) 1738 Rev. Ebenezer Devotion. b. 1714. d. 1771. of Scotland, Ct. (Y. C. 1732.)
    m. (2) 1773 (as second wife) Rev. James Cogswell of Scotland, Ct. b. 1720. d. 1807. son of Samuel and Ann (Mason) (Denison) Cogswell of Saybrook, Lebanon and Canterbury. (Y. C. 1742)
    He m. (1) 1745 Alice Fitch.
    m. (3) Mrs. Irena Hebard.

45. SIMON. b. 1718. d. 1740 at St. Eustatia.
46. ELIJAH. b. 1720. d. 1814. m. 1745 Susanna Lord. b. 1724. d. 1808. dau. of Richard and Elizabeth (Lynde) Lord of Lyme, Ct.
47. HANNAH. b. 1722. d. m. Truman.
48. EUNICE. b. 1725. d. 1803. m. 1746 Jonathan Huntington.
49. MARY. b. 1729. d. m. (1) 1746 David Nevins of Canterbury, Ct.
    m. (2) William Bingham. b. 1737-8. d. of Canterbury, Ct. son of Gideon and Mary (Cary) Bingham.
50. RUFUS. b. 1731. d. 1805. m (1) Hannah Choate. b. 1739. d. 1785. dau. of Francis and Hannah (Perkins) Choate of Essex, Mass.
    m. (2) bef. 1788 Zerviah Lothrop. b. 1738. d. 1795.
51. ELIZABETH. b. 1733. d. 1763.
52. LUCY. b. 1735. d. m. 1758 Ichabod Fitch.

Children of Nathaniel (18) and Ann (Backus) Lathrop.

53. ANNE. b. 1720. d.
54. NATHANIEL. b. 1722. d. 1755. m. Margaret Fuller. (?) b. ab. 1730. d. 1810.
    She m. (2) Baldwin.
55. ELIZABETH. b. 1724. d. 1815. m. (1) 1746 Joseph Carpenter.
    m. (2) 1754 Joseph Peck.
56. ZEBADIAH. b. 1725. d. 1793. m. Clorinda Backus. b. 1730. d. 1803. dau. of Rev. Simon and Eunice (Edwards) Backus.
57. AZARIAH. b. 1728. d. 1810. m. 1764 (as second wife) Abigail Huntington. b. 1739. d. 1820.
58. AMY. b. 1735. d. 1815. m. 1757 (as second wife) Col. William (Bradford) Whiting. b. 1731. d. 1796.
59. CHLOE. b. 1737. d. 1746.
60. ASA. b. 1718. d. 1761.
61. LUCY. b. d. 1747.

[508]

LATHROP.—Continued.

V.

Children of William (20) and Sarah (Huntington) Lathrop.

62. WILLIAM, b. 1715, d. 1776. m. 1745 Dorcas Huntington, b. 1724-5, d. 1794.
63. JOSHUA, b. and d. 1717.
64. EZRA, b. 1719, d. 1753. m. 1740 Esther Clark, b.   d.
   She m. (2) 1754 (as second wife) Jabez Backus, b. 1712, d.
   son of Nathaniel and Elizabeth (Tracy) Backus.
   m. (3) 1764 Ebenezer Baldwin, b. 1710, d. 1794, son of Thomas and Abigail (Lay) Baldwin.
65. JEREMIAH, b. 1721, d. 1753. m. 1746 Lydia Armstrong, b. 1727, d. 1755, dau. of Joseph and Lydia (Worth) Armstrong.
66. JAMES, b. 1724, d. 1729.
67. ANDREW, b. 1727, d. 1803. m. (1) 1755 Deborah Woodworth, b. 1734, d. 1760, dau. of Stephen and Aletheá (Smith) Woodworth.
   m. (2) 1763 Abigail Fish, b. ab. 1738, d. 1812.

Children of William (20) and Mary (Kelly) Lathrop.

68. EBENEZER, b. 1732, d.   m. 1757 Phebe Ayres, b. 1731, d.   dau. of Timothy and Abigail (Hartshorne) Ayres.
69. JONATHAN, b. 1734, d. 1817. m. 1758 Theoda Woodworth, b. 1738, d. 1810, dau. of Stephen and Aletheá (Smith) Woodworth.
70. (Rev.) JOHN, b. 1739, d.   m. (1) 1774 Mary Wheatley, b. ab. 1743, d. 1775, dau. of John Wheatley of Boston, Mass.
   (Pastor of Old North Church, Boston, 1768.)   (Sayer, b. ab. 1751, d. 1786,
   m. (2) 1779 Elizabeth (   ) widow of   Sayer and dau. of Rev. Samuel Checkley, Sen., of New South Church, Boston, Mass.
71. ZACHARIAH, b. 1742, d. 1817. m. 1767 Mehitable Cleveland, b.   d. 1825.

Children of (Capt.) Ebenezer (27) and Lydia (Leffingwell) Lathrop.

72. SIBYL, b. 1720, d.   m. 1752 Samuel Tracy, b. 1723, d.
   (N. C. 1741)
73. LYDIA, b. 1728, d. 1730.
74. ANNE, b. 1730-1, d. 1785. m. 1751 Jabez Perkins.
75. ZIPPORAH, b. 1733, d. 1814. m. 1756 Rev. Simon Huntington.
   He m. (1) 1751 Hannah Tracy, b. 1727, d. 1754.
76. SARAH, b. 1735, d. 1792. m. 1756 Capt. William Coit, b. 1735, d. 1821, son of Col. Samuel and Sarah (Spalding) Coit
   He m. (2) 1780 Elizabeth (Palmes) Coit, widow of Dr. Joseph Coit.
77. ZEBADIAH, b. 1738, d. 1795. m. (1) 1764 Gordon Huntington.
   (as second wife) Rufus Lathrop.
78. LYDIA, b. 1740, d. 1819. m. (2) 1775 Elisha Lathrop, b. 1745, d. 1799, son of Elisha and Abigail (Avery) Lathrop, d. 1774.
   He m. 1787 Lydia
79. EBENEZER, b. 1743, d. 1804. m. 1779 Deborah Lathrop, b. 1745, d. 1814, dau. of Elisha and Abigail (Avery) Lathrop.
80. ZEPHENIAH, b. 1746, d.   m. 1769 Hannah Lathrop, b. 1742, d.   dau. of Ezra and Charity (Perkins) Lathrop.
81. JEDEDIAH, b. 1748, d. 1817. m. (1) 1772 Oned Perkins, b. 1751, d. 1795, dau. of John and Lydia (Tracy) Perkins.
   m. (2) 1797 Anna Eames, b.   d.

LATHROP.—Continued.

V.

Children of Jabez (28) and Elizabeth (Burnham) Lathrop.

82. ELIZABETH.   b. 1730.   d.   m. 1750 Capt. Joseph Winship.

Children of Jabez (28) and Delight (Otis) Lathrop.

83. JABEZ.   b. 1736.   d. 1757.
84. REBECCA. b. 1738.   d.
85. ISAAC.   b. 1740.   d. 1776.   m. 1764 Lucy Pike.
86. HEZEKIAH. b. 1742.   d.
87. DELIGHT. b. 1744.   d.
88. DAVID.   b. 1749.   d. 1747.

VI.

Children of (Dr.) David (41) and Jerusha (Talcott) Lathrop.

89. DANIEL.   b. 1745–6. }
90. JAMES.   b. 1748.   }   d. 1757.
91. JOSEPH.   b. 1749.   }

Children of (Dr.) Joshua (43) and Mercy (Eels) Lathrop.

92. THOMAS. b. 1762. d. 1847. m. (1) 1773 Lydia Hubbard. b. 1745. d. 1790.
                                 m. (2) 1791 Hannah Bill. b. 1769. d. 1862. dau. of Capt. Ephraim and Lydia (Huntington) Bill.
93. LYDIA.   b. 1764. d. 1818. m. 1783. Rev. David Austin. b. 1759. d. 1831. son of David Austin of New Haven, Ct.
94. DANIEL. b. and d. 1766.
95. DANIEL. b. 1769. d. 1825. m. 1793 Elizabeth (Tracy) Turner. b. 1771. d. 1850.
     (Y. C. 1777.)
96. JOSHUA. b. and d. 1773.

Children of Nathaniel (54) and Margaret (Fuller) (?) Lathrop.

97. BURREL.   b. 1749.   d. 1773.
98. HANNAH.   b. 1750–1.
99. EUNICE.   bapt. 1753.
100. ASA.   b. 1755.   d. 1835.   m. 1780 Elizabeth Lord.   b. 1757.   d. 1805.

LATHROP.—Continued.

VI.

Children of Zebediah (56) and Clorinda (Backus) Lathrop.

101. JOSEPH, b. ab. 1755, d. 1778 at West Point during Revolution, aged 23.
102. ZEBEDIAH, b. ab. 1758, d. 1804, m. 1783 Sarah Starr, b. 1759, d. 1849, dau. of William Starr, of Middletown. (To Middletown, Ct.)
103. SIMON BACKUS, b. 1760, d. 1805, m. 1792 Molly Culver, b.   d.
104. ASA, b.   d. 1808 s.p., m. 1793 Rachel Jones, b. 1774, d.   in St. Mary, Ga.
105. EUNICE, b.   d. 1820 in New Canaan, N. Y., unm.
106. NATHANIEL, b. 1768, d. 1847 at Stockbridge, Mass.

Children of Azariah (57) and Abigail (Huntington) Lathrop.

107. (Dr.) GURDON, b. 1767, d. 1828, m. 1791 Lucy Turner, b. 1769, d.   (N. C. 1777.)
108. CHARLES, b. 1770, d. 1831, m. 1793 Joanna Leffingwell, b. 1771, d. 1854. (N. C. 1788.)
109. NABBY, b. 1772, d. 1805, m. 1793 William B. Whiting, b. 1766, d. 1810. (To Albany, N. Y.)
110. CHARLOTTE, b. 1774, d. 1777.
111. BURRELL, b. 1776, d.   m. (1) 1808 in Savannah Mary Rosalie Boulineau, dau. of George Boulineau of the West Indies.
    m. (2) 1840 Mary (   ) Simpson, widow of William F. Simpson.
    (To Savannah, Ga.)
112. GERARD, b. 1778, d.   m. 1809 Mary Ely, b. 1774, d.   dau. of Rev. Zebulon and (   ) Ely of Lebanon, Ct.
113. CHARLOTTE, b. 1781, d. 1805, m. 1802 Charles P. Huntington, b. 1779, d. 1850.
    He m. (2) 1809 Maria Perit, b. 1783, d. 1854.
114. AUGUSTUS, b. 1785, d. 1819, m. 1809 Polly Gale, b. 1783, d. 1839.

Children of Jedediah (81) and Civil (Perkins) Lathrop.

115. LYDIA, b. 1774, d.   m. 1792 Alexander Gordon, b.   d.
116. ROSWELL, b. 1776, d. 1783.
117. EBENEZER, b. 1781, d.
118. CIVIL, b. 1783, d.   m. 1806 Caleb Worden, b.   d.

LATHROP.—Continued.

VII.

Children of Thomas (92) and Lydia (Hubbard) Lathrop.

119. JOSHUA. b. 1777. d. 1856. m. 1809 Rebecca Hunt Perit. b. 1789. d. 1862.
(To Le Roy, N. Y.)
120. JERUSHA. b. 1779. d. 1821. m. 1809 Peletiah Perit. b. 1775. d. 1805.
(To New York.) He m. (2) 1823 Maria Coit. b. 1793. d. 1855

Children of Thomas (92) and Hannah (Bill) Lathrop.

121. LYDIA AUSTIN. b. 1792. d.   m. 1816 (as second wife) Aaron (Porter) Cleveland, son of Aaron and Abiah (Hyde) Cleveland.
He m. (1)   Abby Salisbury of Boston, Mass.
He m. (3) 1820 Mary H. Strong. b.   d.
122. MARY. b. 1795. d. 1809 at Bethlehem, Pa.
123. EMILY. b. 1797. d. 1899. m. 1819 Col. George L. Perkins. b. 1788. d. 1888. son of Capt. Hezekiah and Sarah (Fitch) Perkins.
124. WILLIAM. b. 1801. d. 1825. unm.
125. HANNAH GARDINER. b. 1806. lives in Norwich. m. 1825 George Burbank Ripley. b. 1801. d.   son of Dr. Dwight and Eliza (Coit) Ripley.

Children of Daniel (95) and Elizabeth (Turner) Lathrop.

126. JANE ELIZA. b. 1795. d. 1843. m. 1815 Jonathan G. W. Trumbull.
127. FRANK TURNER. b. 1797. d. 1832 s. p. m. Elizabeth Macalester. b.   d.
dau. of Charles and Anna (Sampson) Macalester of Philadelphia, Pa.
128. ANN MATILDA. b. 1802. d. 1839
129. CORNELIA SOPHIA. b. 1804. d. 1849. m. 1825 George G. Willis.

Children of Asa (100) and Elizabeth (Lord) Lathrop.

130. LUCY LORD. b. 1772. d. 1774. unm.
131. BETSEY. b. 1774. d. 1850. unm.
132. PEGGY FULLER. b. 1786. d. 1863. unm.
133. NABBY LORD. b. 1788. d. 1835. unm.
134. ELEAZER LORD. b. 1792. d.   m. 1820 Jerusha Thomas. b. 1795. d.   dau. of Thomas Langrel and Eunice (Birchard) Thomas.
135. WILLIAM BALDWIN. b. and d. 1793.
136. BURREL. b. 1795. d. 1840.
137. WILLIAM BALDWIN. b. and d. 1795.

Children of (Dr.) Gurdon (107) and Lucy (Turner) Lathrop.

138. JOHN. bapt. 1803. d.   unm.
(Was a merchant in Savannah, Ga.)
139. ABBY MARIA. b. ab. 1793. d. 1829. m.   Capt. Edward Whiting.
He m. (1)   Mary Perkins. b. 1778. d. 1823.
m. (3) McKee.

[512]

LATHROP.—Continued.

VII.

Children of Gerard (112) and Mary (Ely) Lathrop.

140. ABIGAIL HUNTINGTON, b. in Norwich 1810. d. m. Donald McKenzie.
141. WILLIAM GERARD, b. in Norwich 1812. d. 1872. m. 1837 Charlotte Jennings, b. 1815. d. dau. of Nathan and Maria (Miller) Jennings of Windham, Ct.
    (Resided later in Boonton, N. J.)
142. MILLS ELY, b. in Norwich 1814. d.
143. MARY CORNELIA, b. 1820. d. m. 1840 J. D. Vermilye, President Merchants' Bank, New York.
144. CHARLES CHRISTOPHERS, b. 1817 in New York. d. m. in 1850 Mary Augusta Andrus of Newark, N. J.
145. CHARLOTTE ELIZA, b. 1822 in New York. d.
146. EZRA STILES ELY, b. d. in infancy.

Children of Augustus (114) and Mary (Gale) Lathrop.

147. AZARIAH, b. 1810. d. 1862. m. (1) 1836 Jane Fish, b. d. 1842. dau. of Nathan and Ruby (Baldwin) Fish.
    (To Williamantic, Ct.) m. (2) 1845 Lucy Fish. (sister of his first wife.)
148. AUGUSTUS FREDERIC, b. 1811. d. 1828.
149. JOHN, b. 1813. d. 1840 s. p. m. 1846 Laura E. Tilton.
150. MARY BROCKDEN, b. 1814. d. m. 1855 Lyman Baker.
    (To New London, Ct.)
151. NABBY WHITING, b. 1814. d. 1804. unm.
152. JAMES STEDMAN, b. 1816. d. m. 1845 Juliette Stanley of Meriden, Ct.
153. SARAH GALE, b. 1818. d. 1849. m. 1845 Charles Champlin.
154. CHARLOTTE AUGUSTA, b. 1820. d. m. 1843 Henry W. Morgan.

VIII.

Children of Eleazer L. (134) and Jerusha (Thomas) Lathrop.

155. CHARLES THOMAS, b. 1732. d.
    (To Jamaica, N. Y.)
156. WILLIAM BALDWIN, b. 1724. lives in Norwich. m. 1751 Rhoda R. Smith, b. d. dau. of John P. Smith, of Franklin, Ct.
157. BURDET L. b. 1835. d. 1837.
158. ELIZABETH LORD, b. 1821. d. m. 1844 Edward Denison, b. 1822. d. son of Samuel and Mary (Cleveland) Denison of Stonington, Ct.
159. MARY LEFFINGWELL, b. 1826. d. 1820. unm.
160. HANNAH LORD, b. 1828. d. 1855 s. p. m. 1852 William B. Lathrop, b. d. son of John and Eunice (Bacon) Lathrop.
    (To Petersburg, Va.)
161. CORNELIA EVERETT, b. 1830. d. 1834. unm.
162. JANE ELIZA, b. 1838. d. 1845.

LEACH.

I.

1. THOMAS LEACH. b. ab. 1652. d. 1732. m. (1) Abigail Haughton. b. d. bef. 1693.) (Charles) Haughton.
(To, New London, Ct., ab. 1682.) dau. of Richard and Katharine (
m. (2) Mary Minor. b. 1664-5. d.) (Willey) Minor.
dau. of Clement and Frances (
m. (3) 1706 Mercy ( ) Crocker. b. d. widow of John Crocker.

II.

2. THOMAS. b. d. m. 1712-3 Mary (or Mercy) Munsell. b. d.
(New London, Ct.) She m. (2) 1736 Lt. Jeremiah Chapman. b. d.

III.

3. THOMAS. b. 1715. d. 1793. m. 1739 Sarah Reynolds. b. 1720. d. 1768. dau. of Joseph and Hannah (Bingham) Reynolds.
(To Norwich, Ct.)

Children of Thomas (3) and Sarah (Reynolds) Leach.

IV.

4. ELIJAH. b. 1744. d. 1830. m. 1768 Elizabeth Tracy. b. 1744. d. ab. 1827. dau. of Perez and Elizabeth (Hyde) Tracy.
5. LOIS. b. 1746. d. m. John Harris. b. d.
6. JEREMIAH. b. 1749. d. 1812. m. Eunice Hughes. b. 1749. d.
7. SARAH. b. and d. 1752.
8. JEDEDIAH. b. 1754. d. m. 1779 at Canterbury, Ct., Phebe Kasson. b. d
9. JOSEPH. b. 1757. d.
10. THOMAS. b. 1760. d.
11. SARAH. b. 1763. d. m. (1) 1783 Alexander McDonald. b. ab. 1752. d. 1792.
m. (2) 1795 Capt. Joseph Gale.

Children of Jeremiah (6) and Eunice (Hughes) Leach.

V.

12. PHILIP. bapt. 1775. d. m. 1800 Jedediah Story. b. d.
13. EUNICE. bapt. 1777. d.
14. JEREMIAH. bapt. 1780. d. m. (2) 1799 Betsey Gelding (or Gildon) of Mansfield, Ct.

[514]

LEFFINGWELL.

I.

1. (Lt.) THOMAS LEFFINGWELL. b. ab. 1622. d. aft. 1714. m. Mary White. b. d. 1710-11.
   (To Norwich, Ct., in 1659-60.)

Children of (Lt.) Thomas (1) and Mary (White) Leffingwell.

2. RACHEL. b. 1648. d. m. 1681 Robert Parke. b. d. son of dea. Thomas and Dorothy ( ) Parke of Preston, Ct.
3. (Ensign) THOMAS. b. 1649. d. 1723-4. m. 1672 Mary Bushnell. b. 1654. d. 1745.
4. JOSATHAN. b. 1650. d.
5. JOSEPH. b. 1652. d.
6. MARY. b. 1654. d. 1745. m. 1673 Joseph Bushnell.
7. NATHANIEL. b. 1656. d. 1697. m. 1682 Mary Smith. b. d.
   She m. (2) John Clark. b. d. 1708-9.
   m. (3) Ens. Phillip Bill of Groton, Ct. b. 1652. d. 1739. son of Phillip Bill of Groton, Ct. d. 1699-1.
8. SAMUEL. b. d. 1691. m. 1687 Ann Dickinson. b.

Children of (Ensign) Thomas (3) and Mary (Bushnell) Leffingwell.

9. (Dea.) THOMAS. b. 1674. d. 1733. m. 1698 Lydia Tracy. b. 1677. d. 1757.
10. ELIZABETH. b. 1676. d. 1737. m. 1697 John Tracy. b. 1672. d. 1728. son of John and Mary (Winslow) Tracy.
11. ANNE. b. 1680. d. m. 1699-1700 Dr. Caleb Bushnell.
12. MARY. b. 1682. d. 1770. m. 1707 Simon Tracy.
13. ZERVIAH. b. 1680. d. 1779. m. 1709 Benajah Bushnell.
14. (Capt.) JOHN. b. 1688. d. 1773. m. (1) 1710 Sarah Abell. b. 1691. d. 1730. dau. of Joshua and Bethia (Gager) Abell.
    m. (2) 1730 Mary Hart. b. d.
    She m. (2) 1759 Col. John Dyer of Canterbury, Ct. b. d.
15. ABIGAIL. b. 1691. d. 1777. m. 1710 Daniel Tracy.
16. BENAIAH. b. 1693. d. 1756. m. 1729 Joanna Christophers. b. 1705. d. 1754. dau. of Judge Richard and Grace (Turner) Christophers.
17. HEZEKIAH. b. 1695. d. 1699.

Children of Nathaniel (7) and Mary (Smith) Leffingwell.

18. NATHANIEL. b. 1684-5. d. 1710. m. 1707 Mary Rudd. b. 1689. d. 1734. dau. of Jonathan and Mercy (Bushnell) Rudd.
    She m. (2) James Norman. b. d. 1743.
19. JOSATHAN. b. 1687-? d. 1699.
20. DANIEL. b. 1689-90. d. m. 1711 Sarah Bill. b. d. dau. of Ensign Philip and Elizabeth (Lester) Bill
21. SAMUEL. b. 1692. d. m. 1714-15 Hannah Gifford. b. 1696. d.

LEFFINGWELL.—Continued.

III.

Children of Samuel (8) and Ann (Dickinson) Leffingwell.

22. SAMUEL. b. 1690-1. d. 1753. m. 1725 Judith Huntington. b. 1707. d. 1752.

IV.

Children of (Dea.) Thomas (9) and Lydia (Tracy) Leffingwell.

23. SARAH. b. 1698-9. d. 1770. m. 1717 Dea. Ebenezer Huntington.
24. THOMAS. b. 1703-4. d. 1793. m. 1728-9 Elizabeth Lord. b.   d.   dau. of Benjamin and Elizabeth (Pratt) Lord of Lyme, Ct.
25. LYDIA. b. 1706. d. 1766. m. 1735 Capt. Ebenezer Lathrop.
26. ZERVIAH. b. 1709. d. 1751. m.   Eleazer Lord.
27. HEZEKIAH. b. 1712. d. 1725.
28. SAMUEL. b. 1722. d. 1797. m. (1) 1743 Hannah Buck. b. 1724. d. 1761. dau. of Daniel Buck of Wethersfield, Ct.
    m. (2) 1762 Sarah Russell. b. 1730. d. 1763. dau. of Joseph and Sarah (Paine) Russell of Bristol, R. I.
    m. (3) 1764 Abigail Burnham. b. 1727. d. 1811.
    dau. of Jonathan and Mary (Chester) Burnham of Glastonbury, Ct.

Children of Benajah (16) and Joanna (Christopher) Leffingwell.

29. RICHARD. b. and d. 1727.
30. JOANNA. b. 1729. d. 1729-30.
31. BENAJAH. b. 1730. d. 1731.
32. MARY. b. 1731. d. 1805. m. (1) 1751 Nathaniel Richards. b. 1729. d.   son of Capt. George and Hester (Hough) Richards N. London, Ct
    m. (2) 1757 Capt. William Billings.
33. (Col.) CHRISTOPHER. b. 1734. d. 1810. m. (1) 1760 Elizabeth Harris. b. 1738. d. 1762.
    dau. of John and Elizabeth (Champlin) Harris of New London, Ct.
    m. (2) 1764 Elizabeth Coit. b. 1743. d. 1796.
    m. (3) 1799 Ruth (Webster) Perit. b. 1755. d. 1840.
    widow of John Perit and dau. of Pelatiah Webster of Philadelphia.
34. SARAH. b. 1735. d. 1790. m. 1757 Jonathan Starr. b. 1733. d.   son of Samuel and Ann (Bushnell) Starr.
    He m. (2) 1790 Mary (Perkins) Bishop.
    widow of Daniel Bishop and dau. of Dr. Joseph and Mary (Bushnell) Perkins.
35. BENJAMIN. b. 1737. d. 1804. m. 1764 Lucy Backus. b. 1738. d.   dau. of Samuel and Elizabeth (Tracy) Backus.
36. HEZEKIAH. b. 1740. d.   m. (1) 1761 Lydia Wetherell. b. ab. 1741. d. 1785. dau. of Dr. Joseph Wetherell of Taunton, Mass.
    m. (2) 1785 Cynthia Williams of Deerfield, Mass.
37. JOSEPH. b. 1742. d. 1746.
38. ELISHA. b. 1743. d. 1804. m. 1766 Alice Tracy. b. 1745. d. 1807.
39. RICHARD. b. 1745. d. 1768.
40. JOANNA. b. and d. 1748.
41. LUCRETIA. b. 1749. d.   m. (1) 1770 Capt. Henry Billings.
    m. (2) 1795 Dea. Thomas Brown of Hebron, Ct. b.   d.

[516]

LEFFINGWELL.—Continued.

IV.

Children of Samuel (22) and Judith (Huntington) Leffingwell.

42. HANNAH. b. 1726. d. 1781. m. 1751 (as second wife) Elisha Clark.

He m. (1) 1741 Mary Cleveland. b.   d.
dau. of Aaron and Abigail (   ) Cleveland
m. (2)   Lydia Hum. b. 1739. d. 1814.
of East Haddam, Ct.

43. JUDITH. b. 1728-9. d.
44. JOANNA. b. 1730-1. d.
45. SAMUEL. b. 1732. d. 1755. unm.
46. CYRUS. b. 1734. d.
47. (Dea.) JEREMIAH. b. 1736. d. 1814. m. 1760 Sarah Wright of Mansfield, Ct. b. 1732. d. 1814.
dau. of Ebenezer and Sarah (Huntington) Wright.
48. EUNICE. b. 1739. d.   m. (?) 1759 Rufus Baldwin. b. 1734-5. d.   son of Thomas and Anna (Bingham) Baldwin.
49. SARAH. b. 1742. d.
50. ASA. b. 1745. d.   m. 1771 at Canterbury, Elizabeth Smith. b.   d.
51. RUFUS. b. 1750. d. 1753.

V.

Children of Thomas (24) and Elizabeth (Lord) Leffingwell.

52. ELIZABETH. b. 1729-30. d.   m. 1750 Nathaniel Slapman. b.   d. 1805.

He m. (1) 1747 Ruth Reynolds. b. 1727-8. d. 1755.

53. THOMAS. b. 1732. d. 1814. unm.
54. ANDREW. b. 1734. d. 1775.
55. MARTIN. b. 1738. d. 1776.
56. LYDIA. b. 1741. d. 1725. m. (1) 1760 Nathaniel Backus. b. 1727. d. 1775. son of Nathaniel and Hannah (Bellows) Backus.
m. (2) 1769 Rev. Levi Hart of Preston, Ct. b. 1738. d. 1808. son of Thomas Hart of Southington, Ct.
He m. (1) 1769 Rebecca Bellamy. b. 1747. d. 1778.
dau. of Rev. Joseph and Frances (Sherman) Bellamy of Woodbury, Ct.

57. OLIVER. b. 1751. d. 1771 at sea.

LEFFINGWELL.—Continued.

v.

Children of Samuel (28) and Hannah (Buck) Leffingwell.

58. HANNAH. b. and d. 1744.
59. MEHITABLE. b. and d. 1745.
60. ELIZABETH. b. and d. 1747.
61. DANIEL. b. and d. 1748.
62. MARAH. b. and d. 1749.
63. DANIEL. b. 1752. d. 1774. m. 1772 Elizabeth Whiting. b. 1750. d. 1831. dau. of Col. John and Philena (   ) Whiting
64. JUDITH. b. and d. 1754.
65. HANNAH. b. 1755. d. 1756.
66. LYDIA. b. 1757. d.
67. ASA. b. 1758. d.
68. SARAH. b. 1762. d.

Children of Samuel (28) and Sarah (Russell) Leffingwell.

69. ELIZABETH. b. and d. 1760.
70. BETSEY. b. 1761. d. 1762.

Children of (Col.) Christopher (33) and Elizabeth (Harris) Leffingwell.

71. WILLIAM. b. 1765. d. 1834. m. (1) 1786 Sally Maria Beers. b. 1765. d. 1830.
   dau. of Isaac and Mary (Mansfield) Beers of New Haven, Ct.
   m. (2) Hannah Chester. b. 1779. d.   dau. of Leonard and Sarah (Williams) Chester.
72. ELIZABETH. b. 1767. d. 1830. unm.
73. LYDIA. b. 1769. d. young.
74. LUCRETIA. b. 1770. d.   m. 1796 James Cornell. b.   d.
75. JOANNA. b. 1771. d. 1854. m. 1793 Charles Lathrop.
76. LYDIA. b. 1773. d. bef. 1801. m. 1793 John Whiting.
      He m. (2) 1809 Rhoda Ellsworth.
77. CHRISTOPHER. b. 1775. d.   m.   Margaret   b.   d.
   (To Ohio.)
78. DANIEL. b. 1779.
79. JERUSHA. b. 1782. d. 1814. unm.
80. FANNY. b. 1783. d. 1804. m. 1802 Samuel Whiting. b.   d.

[518]

LEFFINGWELL.—Continued.

V.

Children of Elisha (38) and Alice (Tracy) Leffingwell.

81. DYER. b. 1767. d. 1770.
82. LUCY HUNTINGTON. b. 1768. d. 1853. m. 1796 Dea. Simeon Abel. b. 1767. d. 1849. son of Simeon and Martha (Crocker) Abel of Bozrah.
83. DYER. b. 1770. d. 1821. m. (1) 1796 Hannah Waterman. b. 1774. d. 1813. dau. of Arinah and Hannah (Leffingwell) Waterman. (To Middletown, Vt.) m. (2) widow Eunice (Sutherland) Brewster.
84. SALLY. b. 1772. d. m. 1798 Roswell Culver. b. 1775. d. son of Jonathan and Hannah ( ) Culver. (To Buffalo, N. Y.)
85. ALICE. b. 1775. d. 1849. m. 1795 Henry Tracy. b. 1773. d. 1849. son of Capt. Frederick and Deborah (Thomas) Tracy.
86. (Capt.) ELISHA. b. 1778. lost at sea 1825. m. 1808 Frances Thomas. b. 1784. d. dau. of Simeon and Lucretia (Peshon) Thomas.
87. NANCY. b. 1781. d. 1835. m. 1814 Dea. Nehemiah Huntington. b. 1782. d. 1852. son of Elijah and Lydia (Baldwin) Huntington of Bozrah. He m. (2) 1841 Anna (Hinckley) Hough. b. d. widow of Jirah I. Hough. dau. of Timothy and Salome (Strong) Hinckley of Lebanon.
88. LUCRETIA. b. 1782. d. 1810. m. 1803 Elijah Huntington. b. 1777. d. son of Elijah and Lydia (Baldwin) Huntington of Bozrah. He m. (2) 1821 Olive Stark. b. 1797. d. 1862. dau. of Joshua Stark of Bozrah.
89. MARTIN. b. 1785. d. at sea 1810 s. p. m. 1819 Mary Thomas. b. 1789. d. dau. of Thomas Langrel and Eunice (Birchard) Thomas.
90. PHILENA. b. 1791. d. unm.

VI.

Children of Daniel (63) and Elizabeth (Whiting) Leffingwell.

91. HANNAH. b. 1773. d. m. 1793 Peleg Tracy (as second wife). b. 1766. d. son of Andrew and Mary (Clement) Tracy. (To Pennsylvania.) He m. (1) 1791 Betsey Brown. b. 1772. d. 1732. dau. of Jesse and Anna (Rudd) Brown.
92. NABBY. b. 1774. d.
93. BETSEY. b. 1777. d. m. 1800 Joseph Chapman. b. 1768. d. son of Capt. Joseph and Loïs (Birchard) Chapman. (To Pennsylvania.)
94. SARAH RUSSELL. b. 1779. d. m. 1795 John Hyde. b. 1773. d. 1847. son of Ezekiel and Rachel (Tracy) Hyde.

Children of William (71) and Sally M. (Beers) Leffingwell.

95. ISAAC BEERS. b. 1787. d. 1791.
96. WILLIAM. b. 1788. d. 1833. m. (1) Sarah S. Dunham. b. d.
97. CAROLINE MARY. b. 1790. d. 1877. m. Augustus Russell Street.
98. ISAAC BEERS. } b. 1792. d. 1793.
99. SALLY MARIA. } b. 1792. d. 1869. m. Timothy Dwight Williams. b. 1794. d. 1857. son of Gen. Joseph and Abigail (City) Williams of Norwich. (New York City.)
100. LUCIUS WOOSTER. b. 1794. d. 1875. m. (1) 1819 Olive Douglass Starr. b. 1796. d. 1834. dau. of Christopher and Olive (Perkins) Starr.
    m. (2) Catharine Scott. b. d. 1841.
    m. (3) Emily Ward. b. 1814. d. 1895.
101. EDWARD. b. 1803. d. 1888.

LEFFINGWELL.—Continued.

VI.

Children of Capt. Elisha (86) and Frances (Thomas) Leffingwell.

102. THOMAS. b. 1811. Lost at sea, 1825.
103. EDWARD HENRY. b. 1812. d. 1836.
104. JOHN ELISHA. b. 1821. d.
105. FRANCES HARRIET. b. 1805. d. 1814.
106. LUCRETIA. b. and d. 1814
107. FRANCES LUCRETIA. b. 1815. d.
108. MARY ELIZABETH. b. 1818. d. m. 1844 Orrin W. Avery of Colchester, Ct.
109. HARRIET MATILDA. b. 1820. d.
110. SARAH JANE. b. 1823. d.

LINCOLN.

I.

1. STEPHEN. b.   d. 1658. m.   Margaret   b.   d. 1642.
(From Windham or Wymondham, Co. Norfolk, Eng., to Hingham, Mass., in ship Diligent in 1638, with mother Joan.)

II.

2. STEPHEN. b.   d. 1692. m. 1660 Elizabeth Hawke. b. 1639. d. 1713. daughter of Matthew and Margaret Hawke. (Was a carpenter.) (Hingham, Mass.)

III.

3. DAVID. b. 1668. d. 1714. m. 1692-3 Margaret Lincoln. b. 1669. d. 1740. dau. of Benjamin and Sarah (Fearing) Lincoln. (Yeoman and Constable in Hingham, Mass.)

IV.

4. ISAAC. b. 1701-2. d. 1760. m. 1729 Kesia Stone. b. 1701. d. 1703. dau. of Rev. Nathaniel and Reliance (Hinckley) Stone of Harwich, Mass. (H. C. 1722.) and gr. dau. of Gov. Thomas Hinckley of Barnstable, Mass.
(Taught a grammar school in Hingham.)

V.

5. (Capt.) JAMES. b. 1731. d. 1804. m. 1756 Susanna Humphrey. b. 1737. d. 1801. dau. of Ebenezer and Sarah (Ward) Humphrey. (Constable and Captain in War of Revolution.) (Hingham, Mass.)

VI.

6. JAMES b. (?) 1757 in Hingham, Mass. (?) d. 1807 at Norwich. m. 1779 Hannah Hanley. b.   d.
(From Boston, Mass., to Norwich in 1778.)

Children of James (6) and Hannah (Hanley) Lincoln.

VII.

7. HANNAH. b. 1779. d. 1830. m. 1801 Capt. James Day. b. ab. 1770. d. at sea 1827.

The above line of descent may not be correct, but as this is the only James Lincoln who has been found to answer to the James Lincoln of Norwich, it is inserted, in order that the descendants may, if possible, rectify all errors.

LITTLE.

I.

1. THOMAS LITTLE. b.   d. 1671. m. 1633 Ann Warren. b.   d.   dau. of Richard and Elizabeth (Jouatt) (Marsh) Warren of Plymouth, Mass.
(From Devonshire, Eng., to Plymouth, Mass., in 1630.)
(Was a lawyer.)
(Moved to Marshfield, Mass., ab 1650.)

II.

2. EPHRAIM. b. 1650. d. 1717. m. 1672 Mary Sturtevant. b. 1651. d. 1718. dau. of Samuel and Ann ( ) Sturtevant of Plymouth, Mass.
(Marshfield, Mass.)

III.

3. DAVID. b. 1654 (?) d.   m.   b.   d.
(Scituate, Mass.)

IV.

4. (Rev.) EPHRAIM. b.   d. 1757. m. 1737 Elizabeth Woolbridge. b. 1715. d. 1754. dau. of Rev. Samuel and Mabel (Hubbard) Woodbridge.
(N. (?. 1728.)
(Settled at Colchester, Ct.)

V.

5. DEODAT. b. 1750. d.   m.   b.   d.
(Lived at Norwich, New London, E. Windsor and Ellington, Ct.)

VI.

Children of Deodat (5) and   (   ) Little.

6. DEODAT. bapt. at Norwich 1776.
7. LUCRETIA. bapt. at Norwich 1777.
8. ANNE. bapt. at Norwich 1780.

[522]

LORD.

I.

1. THOMAS LORD. b. ab. 1585. d.   m.   Dorothy   b. ab. 1589. d. 1675–6.
(To New England in 1635 to Newtown, afterwards Cambridge.)
(To Hartford, Ct., in 1636, with Rev. Thomas Hooker.)

II.

2. WILLIAM. b. 1623. d. 1678. m. (1)
                           m. (2) 1664 Lydia Brown. b.   d.
(To Saybrook or Lyme ab. 1645.)

III.

3. BENJAMIN. b. 1667. d. ab. 1719. m. 1693 Elizabeth Pratt. b.   d. 1714. dau. of Ensign John and Sarah (Jones) Pratt of Saybrook, Ct.

IV.

Children of Benjamin (3) and Elizabeth (Pratt) Lord.

4. (Rev.) BENJAMIN. b. 1692. d. 1784. m. (1) 1720 Ann Taylor. b. 1696. d. 1748.
(Y. C. 1714.)   dau. of Rev. Edward and Ruth (Wyllys) Taylor of Westfield, Mass.
(Settled as minister at Norwich in 1717.) m. (2)   Elizabeth (   ) Tisdale. b.   d.   widow of Henry Tisdale of Newport, R. I.
                       m. (3)   Abigail Hooker. b. ab. 1707. d. 1792.
                             poss. dau. of Nathaniel and Mary (Standley) Hooker of Hartford, Ct.

5. ELEAZER. b. 1699 at Saybrook, Ct. d. 1780. m. (1)   Zerviah Leffingwell. b. 1709. d. 1751.
(To Norwich, Ct.)   m. (2) 1754 Abigail (   ) Mumford. b. ab. 1710. d. 1780.
                       widow of Thomas Mumford of Groton, Ct.

6. CYPRIAN. b. 1702. d.   m. 1725 Elizabeth Backus. b. 1705. d. 1787. dau. of Joseph and Elizabeth (Huntington) Backus
(To Norwich, Ct.)

7. ELIZABETH. b.   d.   m. 1728–9 Thomas Leffingwell, 4th.
(To Norwich, Ct.)

8. ANDREW. b.   d.
9. ABM. b.   d.

V.

Children of (Rev.) Benjamin (4) and Ann (Taylor) Lord.

10. BENJAMIN. b. 1722. d. 1725.
11. ANN. b. 1724. d.   m. (2) 1745 Samuel Gifford.
12. BENJAMIN. b. 1727. d. 1757. m. 1751 Lucy Leffingwell. b. 1734. d.   dau. of Capt. John and Mary (Hart) Leffingwell.
13. ELIZABETH. b. 1729. d.   m. 1753 Eleazer Lord, Jun.
14. EBENEZER. } b. 1731. d. 1800. m. 1760 Temperance Edgerton. b. 1738–9. d. 1804. dau. of John and Phebe (Harris) (Trask) (Prentice) Edgerton.
15. JOSEPH. }   d. 1731. d. 1762. m. 1754 Lucy Aigate. b. 1734. d. 1813 in Canaan, N. Y.
(Y. C. 1753.)

LORD.—Continued.

V.

Children of Eleazer (5) and Zerviah (Leffingwell) Lord.

16. ELEAZER. b. ab. 1729. d. 1809. m. 1753 Elizabeth Lord. b. 1729. d. 1803.
17. ZERVIAH. b. 1731. d. m. 1748 Howlet Hazen. b. 1723. d. son of Jacob and Abigail (Lathrop) Hazen.
    (To Wilkesbarre, Pa.)
18. LYDIA. b. 1733. d.
19. ASA. b. 1736. d. m. 1759 Abigail Mumford. b. d. perh. dau. of Thomas and Abigail ( ) Mumford of Groton, Ct.
20. NATHAN. b. 1738. d. m. (1) 1764 Abigail Ingraham. b. d. 1770.
    m. (2) 1771 Mary Nevius. b. 1751. d.
    m. (3) (?) Mary Hyde. b. 1754. d. dau. of Thomas and Elizabeth (Huntington) Hyde.

VI.

Children of Benjamin (12) and Lucy (Leffingwell) Lord.

21. ELIZABETH. b. 1753. d. 1839. m. 1774 Judge Prosper Rudd. b. 1753. d. 1833. son of Samuel and Lurena (Fitch) Rudd.
    (To Western, Oneida Co., N. Y., in 1802.)
22. WYLLIS b. 1756. d. m. Sarah Farnham. b. d. dau. of Capt. John and Elizabeth (Chapman) Farnham.
23. GURDON. bapt. 1758. d.
24. LUCY. b. 1760. d. 1841. m. (1) 1789 Richard Avery.
    m. (2) 1826 Capt. Erastus Perkins.
25. DANIEL. bapt. 1762. d. m. (?) Anna Choate (?) b. d.
26. CAROLINE. bapt. 1764. d.
27. MARY. b. d. m. 1779 Simeon Woodworth.
28. ANDREW. bapt. 1772. d.
29. ABIGAIL HOOKER. bapt. 1775. d.

Children of Ebenezer (14) and Temperance (Edgerton) Lord.

30. EBENEZER. b. 1761. d.
31. WILLIAM. b. 1763. d. m. 1785 Lydia Durkee. b. d.
32. TEMPERANCE. b. 1764. d. 1730. m. 1794 Zepheniah Bliss.
33. EUNICE. b. 1767. d. m. 1793 Azor Gale.
34. ANNA. bapt. 1769. d. m. 1796 John Hamilton. b. 1764. (?) d. son of Jonas Hamilton. (?)
35. BENJAMIN. bapt. 1770 d. m. Fanny Buell. b. d.
    (To Rutland, Vt.)
36. OLIVER. bapt. 1772. d.
37. LUCRETIA. bapt. 1777. d. m. Joseph Harris. b. d.
38. LYDIA. bapt. 1780. d.

LORD.—Continued.

171.

Children of Joseph (15) and Lucy (Algate) Lord.

39. HANNAH, b. 1755, d. 1841. m. (1) 1774 Isaac Abel, b. 1753, d. 1783, son of Capt. Joshua and Anne (Backus) Abel.
    m. (2) 1791 Wheeler Coit, b. 1738-9, d. ―――― son of Col. Samuel and Sarah (Spalding) Coit.
40. BENJAMIN ADGATE, b. 1757, d. ―――― s. p. in West Indies.
41. ANNE, b. 1760, d. 1802. m. 1784 Lupton Warner, b. 1758, d. 1836, son of William and Rebecca (Lupton) Warner of Canaan, N. Y.
42. (Maj.) JOSEPH, b. 1762, d. 1844. m. 1784 Lucy Abel, b. 1766, d. 1840, dau. of Joshua and Lucy (Edgerton) Abel. (To Canaan, N. Y., ab. 1790.)

Children of Eleazer (16) and Elizabeth (Lord) Lord.

43. NABBY, b. 1754, d. 1821. m. 1776 Mundator Tracy.
44. ELIZABETH, b. 1757, d. 1805. m. 1780 Asa Lachrop.

[525]

LOUDON.

I.

1. SAMUEL LOUDON. b.   d.   m.   Lydia Griswold. b. 1742. d. 1788. dau of John and Hannah (Lee) Griswold of Lyme, Ct.
   (New York City.)
   (To Norwich for a few months in 1776.)

II.

Children of Samuel (1) and Lydia (Griswold) Loudon.

2. LYDIA. b.   d.
3. MATTHEW GRISWOLD. bapt. at Norwich 1777. d.
4. SAMUEL. b.   d. 1795 at New York.

[526]

MANNING.

Line of Frederick and Rockwell Manning.

I.

1. WILLIAM MANNING. b.   d.   m.   Susanna   b.   d. 1650.
   (Cambridge, Mass., 1634.)

II.

2. WILLIAM. b. ab. 1614. d. 1690–1. m.   Dorothy   b. ab. 1612. d. 1692.
   (Merchant and prominent citizen of Cambridge, Mass.)

III.

3. SAMUEL. b. 1644. d. 1710–11. m. (1) 1664 Elizabeth Stearns. b.   d.   dau. of Isaac Stearns of Watertown, Mass
   (Removed to Billerica.)   m. (2) 1673 Abiah Wright. b.   d.
   (Representative 1695–6.)
   (Town Clerk for six years.)

IV.

4. SAMUEL. b.   d. 1755. m.   Deborah   b.   d. 1727. (?)
   (Removed to Cambridge 1692.)
   (In 1695 his father conveyed to him land, house, warehouse and wharf which he had inherited from his father, William.)
   (Samuel, 2nd, removed to Windham ab. 1724.)

V.

5. (Capt.) JOHN. b. 1691–7. d. 1760. m.   Abigail Winship. b. 1695. d. 1770.
   (To Windham, Ct., ab. 1727.)   dau. of Joseph and Sarah (Harrington) Winship of Cambridge, Mass.
   (Commissioned Captain in 1744.)

VI.

6. JOSIAH. b. 1725 at Hopkinton, Mass. d. 1809. m. 1746 Mary Cook. b. 1729 at Windham, Ct. d. 1790.
   (Lived near Manning's bridge at Franklin, Ct.)   dau. of Samuel and Leah (Ripley) Cook.

[527]

MANNING.—Continued.

VII.

Children of Josiah (6) and Mary (Cook) Manning.

7. FREDERICK, b. ab. 1758, d. at Windham, Ct., 1810, m. 1781 Anne Young, b. 1757, d. at Ovid, N. Y. ab. 1830. (Windham, Ct.)
8. ROCKWELL, b. ab. 1761, d. 1800, m. 1783 at Canterbury, Ct., Sarah Ainsworth, b. ab. 1761, d. 1851, of Canterbury. (Norwich and Canterbury, Ct.) (And perhaps others.)

These dates of Josiah, Frederick and Rockwell Manning are furnished by George E. Manning of North Franklin, Ct., who is now compiling a history of the Manning family.

VIII.

Children of Rockwell (8) and Sarah (Ainsworth) Manning.

9. MASSER, b. 1783, d.   m.
10. SALLY, b. 1788, d.   m.

MANNING.

Line of Samuel Manning.

I.

1. WILLIAM MANNING. b.   d.   m. Susanna   b.   d. 1650.
   (Cambridge, Mass., 1634.)

II.

2. WILLIAM. b. ab. 1614. d. 1690-1. m. Dorothy   b. ab. 1612. d. 1692.
   (Merchant and prominent citizen of Cambridge, Mass.)

III.

3. SAMUEL. b. 1644. d. 1710-11. m. (1) 1664 Elizabeth Stearns. b.   d.   dau. of Isaac Stearns of Watertown, Mass.
   (Removed to Billerica.)   m. (2) 1673 Abiah Wright.
   (Representative 1695-6.)
   (Town Clerk six years.)

IV.

4. SAMUEL. b.   d. 1755. m.   Deborah   b.   d. 1727. (?)
   (Removed to Cambridge 1692.)
   (In 1695 his father conveyed to him land, house, warehouse and what he had inherited.)
   (Samuel, 2nd, removed to Windham bef. 1724.)

V.

5. (Capt.) JOHN. b. 1690-7. d. 1750. m.   Abigail Winship. b. 1698. d.
   (To Windham, Ct.)   dau. of Joseph and Sarah (Harrington) Winship of Cambridge, Mass.

VI.

6. SAMUEL. b. 1723. d. 1773. m. 1746 Anne Winslip. b. 1727. d. 1792.
   (To Norwich, Ct.)

VII.

Children of Samuel (6) and Anne (Winslip) Manning.

7. EUNICE. b. 1747. d. 1750.
7. SAMUEL. b. 1749. d.   m. (?) (?) Mary Gates of Preston.
9. ANNE. b. 1751. d. 1753.
10. ANNE. b. 1753. d. 1754.
11. EUNICE. b. 1756. d. 1750. m.   John Obey Waterman. b.   d.
    prob. a descendant of John and Ann (Obey) Waterman of Providence, R. I.
12. ROGER. b. 1758. d.
13. PAUL. b. 1760. d. 1815. m. 1784 Anna Gifford. b. 1762. d. 1751. dau. of James and Susanna (Hubbard) Gifford.

[529]

MANNING.—Continued.

VIII.

Children of Diah (13) and Anna (Gifford) Manning.

14. SAMUEL. b. 1785. d. m. 1809 Polly Sisson.
15. WILLIAM. b. 1791. d.
16. ASA. b. 1795. d. m. Betsey Butler. b. d. of Windham, Ct.
17. JOSEPH TERRY. b. 1801. d.
18. EUNICE. b. 1786. d. m. 1811 DeLafayette Wilcox.
19. JOANNA. b. 1788. d.
20. ELMIRA. b 1799. d.

MARSH.

I.

1. JOHN MARSH. b.   d. 1688. m. (1) 1649 Anne Webster. b.   d. 1662. dau. of Gov. John Webster of Hartford, Ct., and Hadley, Mass.
    m. (2) 1664 Hepzibah (Ford) Lyman. b.   d. 1683.
    widow of Richard Lyman and dau. of Thomas Ford of Windsor, Ct.

II.

2. DANIEL. b. ab. 1653. d. 1725. m. 1676 Hannah (Sears) Crow. b.   d.
    widow of William Crow of Hadley, Mass., and dau. of William Sears of Farmington, Ct.
    (Lived at Hadley, Mass.)

III.

3. EBENEZER. b. 1658. d. 1772. m. (1) 1710 Mary Parsons. b. 1688 (?) d. 1759.
    perhaps dau. of Jonathan and Mary (Clark) Parsons of Northampton, Mass.
    (Hadley, Mass.) m. (2) Miriam b. 1702. d. 1785.

IV.

4. (Dr.) JONATHAN. b.   d. 1766. m. 1747 Sarah Hart. b.   d.   of Farmington, Ct.
    (Settled at Norwich, Ct.)

V.

Children of (Dr.) Jonathan (4) and Sarah (Hart) Marsh.

5. SARAH. b. 1749. d.   m. 1769 Dr. Samuel Lee of Windham, Ct. b. 1744. d. 1805.
6. ABIGAIL. b. 1751. d.   m. 1776 John Ripley. b. 1738. d. 1823. son of John and Mary (Backus) Ripley of Windham, Ct.
7. (Dr.) JONATHAN. b. 1754. d. 1795. m. 1776 Alice Fitch. b. 1755. d.   dau. of Capt. John and Alice (Fitch) Fitch of Windham, Ct.
8. HANNAH. b. 1757. d.   m.   Dr. Joshua Sumner of Windham, Ct.
9. MARY. b. 1759. d. 1835. m. 1783 Dr. Benjamin Dyer. b. 1753. d. 1833. son of Col. Eliphalet and Hulldah (Bowen) Dyer of Windham, Ct.
10. JOSEPH. b. 1762. d.   m. 1790 Eunice Huxley. b.   d.   dau. of Phinehas and Mary (Pierce) Huxley.

VI.

Children of (Dr.) Jonathan (7) and Alice (Fitch) Marsh.

11. LUCY. b. 1777. d.   m. 1801 Warham Shepherd.
12. MARY. b. 1784. d. 1854. m. 1811 Bela B. Hyde. b. 1784. d. 1853.
    son of Benjamin and Elizabeth (Hyde) Hyde of Franklin and afterw. of Taberg, N. Y.
    (To Rome, N. Y.)
13. SALLY. b. 1779. d.

[53]

MARSH.—Continued.

VI.

Children of Joseph (10) and Eunice (Huxley) Marsh.

14. FANNY, b. 1792. d. unm.
15. JONATHAN, b. 1794. d.
16. HART, b. 1796. d.
17. JOSEPH, b. 1799. d. m. 1823 Lora M. Fitch of Windham. b. d.
18. PHINEHAS, b. 1801. d. 1803.
19. JULIA, b. 1803. d.
20. ABBY, b. 1805. d. unm.
21. PHINEHAS, b. 1807. d.
22. EUNICE, b. 1811. d. m. Joseph Griffin.
23. HANNAH, b. 1813. d. m. Laurens Brewster.
24. OLIVER RIPLEY, b. 1816. d.

MASON.

I.

1. (Maj.) JOHN MASON. b. ab. 1600. d. 1672. m. (1) (it is said)   b.   d.   in Windsor, Ct.
(To Dorchester, Mass. about 1630.)   m. (2) ab. 1639-40 Anne Peck. b. 1619. d.   ) Peck of Hingham, Mass.
(To Windsor, Ct., in 1635.)   dau. of Rev. Robert and Anne (and Hingham, Eng.
(To Saybrook, Ct., in 1647.)
(To Norwich, Ct., in 1660.)

II.

Children of (Maj.) John (1) and (   ) Mason.

2. ISABELLA (?) b.   d. 1665. m. 1650 John Bissell. b.   d.   son of John Bissell of Windsor, Ct.
(To Lebanon and Coventry, Ct.)   He m. (2) 1669

Children of (Maj.) John (1) and Anne (Peck) Mason.

3. PRISCILLA. b. 1641. d. aft. 1714. m. 1664 Rev. James Fitch.
4. (Maj.) SAMUEL. b. 1644. d. 1705. m. (1) (2) 1670 Judith Smith. b. 1650-1. d.
(Stonington, Ct.)   dau. of Capt. John and Sarah (Woodward) Smith of Hingham, Mass.
     m. (2) 1694 Elizabeth Peck. b. 1657. d.   dau. of Joseph Peck of Rehoboth, Mass.
She m. (2)   Abigail Fitch. b.   d.   Dea. Gershom Palmer. b.   d. 1715. of Stonington, Ct.
5. (Capt.) JOHN. b. 1646. d. 1676. m.   Abigail Fitch. b.   d.
(Norwich, Ct.)
6. RACHEL. b. 1648. d. 1678. m. 1678 Charles Hill. b.   d. 1684.
7. ANNE. b. 1650. d.   m. 1672 Capt. John Brown. b. 1650. d.   of Swansey, Mass. son of John Brown of Swansey.
8. DANIEL. b. 1652. d. 1736-7. m. (1) bef. 1676 Margaret Denison. b. 1650. d.   dau. of Edward and Elizabeth (Weld) Denison of Roxbury, Mass.
     m. (2)
     m. (3) 1679 Rebecca Hobart. b. 1654. d. 1727. dau. of Rev. Peter Hobart of Hingham, Mass.
9. ELIZABETH. b. 1654. d. 1684. m. 1676 Capt. James Fitch.

III.

Children of (Maj.) Samuel (4) and Judith (?) (Smith) Mason.

10. JOHN. b. 1670. d. 1705. unm.
11. ANNE. b.   d.   m.   Capt. John Mason, 3rd.
12. SARAH. b.   d.   m. 1703 Joseph Fitch. b. 1680. d. 1741.
He m. (2) 1721 Anne Whiting. b. 1695. d. 1775.
dau. of Rev. Samuel and Elizabeth (Adams) Whiting of Windham, Ct.

MASON.—Continued.

III.

Children of (Maj.) Samuel (4) and Elizabeth (Peck) Mason.

13. SAMUEL. b. 1695. d. 1701.
14. ELIZABETH. b. 1697. d. 1725. m. 1720 Rev. William Worthington. b. 1695. d. 1756. of Stonington, Ct. son of William and Mehitable (Graves) Worthington of Colchester, Ct. He m (2) 1726 Temperance Gallup. b. 1701. d. of Stonington, Ct. dau. of William and Sarah (Cheesebrough) Gallup.
15. HANNAH. b. 1699. d. 1724. unm.

Children of (Capt.) John (5) and Abigail (Fitch) Mason.

16. (Capt.) JOHN. b. 1673. d. 1736 in London, Eng. m. (1) 1701 Anne Mason. b. d. m. (2) 1719 Ann (Sanford) Noyes. (?) b. d. widow of Dr. James Noyes of Stonington, Ct. and dau. of Gov. Peleg Sanford, of R. I.
17. ANNE. b. d. m. (1) 1699 John Denison. b. 1669. d. 1699. of Saybrook, Ct. son of Capt. John and Phebe (Lay) Denison of Stonington, Ct. m. (2) 1701 Samuel Cogswell. b. 1677 at Saybrook, Ct. d. 1752 at Canterbury, Ct. (Resided at Saybrook, Lebanon, and Canterbury, Ct.)

Children of Daniel (8) and Margaret (Denison) Mason.

18. DANIEL. b. 1674. d. 1705. m. 1704-5 Dorothy Hobart. b. 1679. d. 1733. dau. of Rev. Jeremiah and Elizabeth (Whiting) Hobart of Haddam, Ct. She m. (2) 1707 Rev. Hezekiah Brainard of Haddam, Ct. b. 1682. d. 1727. son of Daniel and Hannah (Spencer) Brainard.

Children of Daniel (8) and ( ) Mason.

19. HEZEKIAH. b. 1677. d. 1726. m. (1) 1699 Anne Bingham. b. 1677. d. 1724. dau. of Thomas and Mary (Rudd) Bingham. m. (2) 1725 Sarah Robinson. b. d. (To Windham, Ct.)

MASON.—Continued.

III.

Children of Daniel (8) and Rebecca (Hobart) Mason.

20. PETER. b. 1680. d. m. 1703 Mary Hobart. b. d.
    (To Stonington, Ct.)
    (To Montville, Ct.)
21. REBECCA. b. 1682. d. m. 1707 (as second wife) Elisha Chesebrough. b. 1697. d. 1727. , Chesebrough, son of Samuel and Abigail (
22. MARGARET. b. 1683. d.
23. SAMUEL. b. 1686. d. m. (1) 1712 Elizabeth Fitch. b. d. 1715.
    (To Stonington, Ct.) m. (2) 1720 Rebecca Lippincott. b. d.
24. ABIGAIL. b. 1689. d.
25. PRISCILLA. b. 1691. d.
26. NEHEMIAH. b. 1693. d. 1762. m. 1722 Zerviah Stanton. b. 1701. d. 1771.
    (Owner of Mason's Island, Stonington, Ct.) dau. of Joseph and Margaret (Chesebrough) Stanton of Stonington, Ct.)

IV.

Children of (Capt.) John (16) and Anne (Mason) Mason.

27. JOHN. b. 1702 at Lebanon, Ct. d.
28. RACHEL. b. 1700 at Stonington, Ct.
29. SAMUEL. bapt. 1707 at Stonington.
30. JEMIMA. bapt. 1709 at Stonington.
31. JAMES. bapt. 1713. d. m. 1735 Sarah Denison. b. d. Martha Brown. b. 1722. d. 1805 s. p.
32. ELIJAH. bapt. 1715 at Stonington, Ct. d. 1765. m.   dau. of Ebenezer and Sarah (Hyde) Brown of Lebanon, Ct.
    (Lebanon, Ct.)

Children of (Capt.) John (16) and Anne (Sanford) (Noyes) Mason.

33. PELEG SANFORD. b. 1720. d. m. 1742 Mary Stanton. b. d. of Charlestown, R. I.
    (To Lebanon, Ct.)

MINER.

I.
1. THOMAS MINER. b. 1608. d. 1690. m. 1634 Grace Palmer. b. d. dau. of Walter Palmer of Charlestown, Mass, later of Stonington, Ct. (To Charlestown, Mass., in 1632.) (To New London, Ct., ab. 1645.)

II.
2. CLEMENT. b. 1642. d. 1700. m. (1) 1662 Frances ( ) Willey. b. d. 1673. widow of Isaac Willey.
   m. (2) 1678 Martha Wellman. b. 1652. d. 1681. dau. of William and Elizabeth (Spencer) Wellman.
   m. (3) Joanna b. d. 1700.

III.
3. CLEMENT. b. 1668. d. 1747. m. 1698 Martha Monld. bapt. 1675. d. dau. of Hugh and Martha (Coit) Mould.

IV.
4. HUGH. b. 1710. killed 1753. m. 1731 Damaris Champlin. b. ab. 1713. d. 1753.

V.
5. SETH. b. 1742. d. m. 1767 Anna Charlton. b. 1744. d. 1804. (To Norwich, Ct.)

VI.
Children of Seth (5) and Anna (Charlton) Miner.

6. ELIZABETH. b. 1768 in Norwich. d. unm.
7. ANNA. b. 1770 in Norwich. d. unm.
8. SARAH. b. 1773. d. 1775.
9. CHARLOTTE. b. and d. 1774.
10. ASHER. b. 1777 in Norwich. d. 1841 at Wilkesbarre, Pa. m. (1) 1800 Mary Wright. b. d. dau. of Thomas Wright of Wilkesbarre, Pa.
    m. (2) 1835 Thomasin H. Boyer.
11. (Hon.) CHARLES. b. 1780 in Norwich. d. 1865 in Wilkesbarre, Pa. m. 1804 Letitia Wright (niece of his brother Asher's wife) (To Wilkesbarre, Pa.)

[536]

MINER.—Continued.

VII.

Children of Asher (10) and Mary (Wright) Miner.

12. ANNA MARIA, b. 1801. d. 1855. m. 1819 Dr. Abraham Stout.
13. THOMAS WRIGHT, b. 1803. d. 1855. m.   Lucy Bowman.
14. ROBERT, b. 1805. d. 1842. m. 1826 Eliza Abbott.
15. ELIZABETH R. b. 1808. d. 1835. m. 1834 (2d) Kinnard.
16. SARAH, b. 1810. d. 1841.
17. CAROLINE, b. and d. 1812.
18. CHARLES, b. 1814. d. 1829.
19. SAMUEL GREEN, b. 1816. d. 1847. m.   Julia Titus.
20. ASHER, b. 1818. d. 1826.
21. MARY W. b. 1820. d. 1839.
22. HELEN, b. 1822. d. 1841.
23. JOSEPH WRIGHT, b. 1825. d. 1850.

Children of (Hon.) Charles (11) and Letitia (Wright) Miner.

24. SARAH KIRKBRIDE, b.   d. 1774. num. (was blind).
25. ANNE CHARLTON, b.   d.   m.   Joseph Lewis.
26. MARY LAXTON, b.   d.
27. CHARLOTTE, b.   d.
28. LETITIA WRIGHT, b.   d   unm.
29. ELLEN ELIZABETH, b. 1814. d.
30. WILLIAM PENN, b. 1816. d.   unm.
31. FRANCIS COLE, b.   d.
32. EMILY HALLENBACK, b.   d.   unm.
33. CHARLES TOWNSEND, b.   d.   unm.

MORGAN.

I.
1. RICHARD ROSE MORGAN. b.   d. 1698.   m.   Hopestill   b.   d. 1712.
   (At Waterford, Ct., in 1679–80.)

II.
2. JOHN. b.   d.   m. 1697 Ann Dart. b. 1675. d.   dau. of Richard and Bethiah ( ) Dart of New London, Ct.

III.
3. PETER. b. 1713. d. 1780. m. 1738 Elizabeth Whitmore. b.   d. 1786. of Middletown, Ct.
   (T., Norwich, Ct.)

IV.
Children of Peter (3) and Elizabeth (Whitmore) Morgan.

4. TERIZAH. b. 1740–1. d. 1753.
5. LOIS. b. 1743. d.
6. ZEBEKIAH. b. 1744–5. d.   m. 1769 Ruth Dart. b.   d.
7. DARIUS. b. 1746. d.   m.   Sarah   b.   d.
8. TERIZAH. b. 1754. d.   m.   John Allen. b.   d.
9. EUNICE. b. 1758. d. 1786.

[538]

NEEDHAM.

I.

1. EDMUND NEEDHAM. b.   d. 1677. m. Joan   b. ab. 1609. d. 1675.
   (At Lynn, Mass., 1639.)

II.

2. DANIEL. b. ab. 1638. d. 1717. m. 1659 Ruth Chadwell. b. ab. 1640. d. 1719. perh. dau. of Thomas Chadwell of Lynn, Mass.
3. EZEKIEL. b.   d.   m. 1669 Sarah King. b.   d.   dau. of Daniel King of Lynn, Mass.
4. HANNAH. b.   d.   m.   Dalton.   b.   d.
5. MARY. b.   d. 1671. m.   Samuel Hart of Lynn. b.   d.
                                          He m. (2) 1674 Mary Whiting (or Witteridge),
6. ELIZABETH. b.   d. 1662. m.   Joseph Mansfield. b.   d.   of Lynn.

III.

Children of Daniel (2) and Ruth (Chadwell) Needham.

7. DANIEL. b. 1665. d.   Curtis. b.   d.
8. JOHN. b.   d.   m.
9. JUDITH. b. 1667. d.   m.
10. EZEKIEL. b. 1670. d.
11. MARY. b. 1672. d. 1711-12. unm.
12. ELIZABETH. b. 1674-5. d.   m.   Seers. b.   d.
13. EDMUND. b. 1677. d.   m. 1702-3 Hannah Hood. b.   d.
    (Marblehead, Mass.)
    (Currier.)
14. DANIEL. } b. 1680. d.   m.
15. RUTH.   }   d. 1680.
16. RUTH. b. 1682. d.

Children of Ezekiel (3) and Sarah (King) Needham.

17. EDMUND. b. 1670. d.
              b. and d. 1673.
18. SARAH. b. 1674. d.
19. EZEKIEL. b. 1676. d. soon.
20. EZEKIEL. b. 1677. d.
21. DANIEL. b. 1680. d.
22. RALPH. b. 1682. d.

[539]

NEEDHAM.—Continued.

IV.

Children of Edmund (13) and Hannah (Hood) Needham.

24. DANIEL. b. 1703. d.   m. 1728-9 at Boston, Mass., Isabella Armstrong. b.   d.
    (Joiner.)
    (Moved to Salem, Mass. (?) and later to Norwich, Ct.)
25. BATHSHEBA. b. 1705. d.   m.   Thomas Hoaller. b.   d.   of Marblehead, Mass.

Though Edmund and Hannah (Hood) Needham are given as the possible parents of Daniel N. of Norwich, still there was another Daniel, son of Edmund's brother, Daniel, who might be identical with the Norwich resident.

V.

Children of Daniel (24) and Isabella (Armstrong) Needham.

26. DANIEL. b. 1729 in Salem. d.   m. 1751 at Norwich, Hannah Allen. b.   d.
27. MARY. b. 1731 in Salem. d.   m. 1751 at Norwich, William Curtis. b.   d.
28. THOMAS. b. 1734 in Salem. d.
29. JOHN. { b. 1739 in Salem. d.
30. JANE.
31. WILLIAM. b. 1740 in Salem. d.
32. MARGARET. b. 1742 in Norwich. d.
33. ISABELLA. b. 1744-5 in Norwich. d.
34. ELIAS. b. 1747 in Norwich. d.   m.   Mercy   b.   d.
    (To Stephensburg, Ky.)

VI.

Children of Daniel (26) and Hannah (Allen) Needham.

35. HANNAH. b. 1752. d. 1753.
36. HANNAH. b. 1753. d.
37. LUCRETIA. bapt. 1756. d.
38. DANIEL. b. 1757. d.
39. LUCRETIA. bapt. 1760. d.

[540]

NEVINS.

I.

1. DAVID NEVINS. b.   drowned in the Quinebaug River 1757-8.   m. 1740 Mary Lathrop. b. 1729. d.
   (From Kingston, Mass. to Canterbury, Ct.)   She m. (2) William Bingham. b. 1737. d.   of Canterbury, Ct.
                                                                       son of Gideon and Mary (Cary) Bingham.

II.

2. (Col.) DAVID. b. 1745-?. d. 1830. m. 1777 Mary Hubbard. b. 1750. d. 1820.
3. SAMUEL. b. 1748-9. d.
4. MARY. b. 1751. d.   m. 1771 (as second wife) Nathan Lord.
5. ELIZABETH (or BETSY) b. 1753. d. 1792.
6. MARTHA. b. 1755. d. 1823. m. 1774 Capt. James Hyde. b. 1752. d. 1809. son of James and Sarah (Marshall) Hyde.
7. CYNTHIA. b. 1757. d. 1759.

Children of (Capt.) David (2) and Mary (Hubbard) Nevins.

8. MARY. b. 1777. d. 1809.
9. HENRY. b. 1779. d. 1835. m. 1805 Lucretia Manwaring. b. 1783. d. 1834. dau. of Dea Robert and Elizabeth (Rogers) Manwaring.
10. DAVID. b. 1781. d. 1782.
11. DAVID. b. 1783. Lost at sea on passage from Jamaica to N. Y., 1809.
12. RUSSELL HUBBARD. b. 1785. d. 1853 at N. Y.
13. FRANCES. b. 1789. d.   m. 1810 Charles Thomas. b. 1784. d. 1835. son of Thomas Langrell and Eunice (Birchard) Thomas.
14. SAMUEL. b. 1788. d.   m. 1810 Eliza West of Phila. b.   d.
15. JAMES. b. 1790. d.   m. 1814 Ackash Willis of Phila. b.   d.
16. ELIZABETH. b. 1792. d. 1858. m. 1812 Elihu Townsend of N. Y.
17. RUFUS. b. 1794. d. 1839. m. 1815 Jane Tenbrook of Newark, N. J.
    (To New York.)
18. RICHARD. b. 1795. d. 1831. m.   Louisa Macalester. b.   d.   dau of Charles and Anne (Sampson) Macalester of Philadelphia.
19. (Rev.) WILLIAM. b. 1797. d. 1835. m. 1822 Mary Lloyd Key of Baltimore, Md.
    (To Baltimore, Md.)

[541]

NORMAN.

Possibly Descended from the Salem or Marblehead Normans.

I.

1. JAMES NORMAN. b.   d. 1743.   m. (1) (? aft. 1730 Mary (Rudd) Leffingwell. b. 1686.   d. 1734.
   (To Norwich ab. 1715.)   dau. of Jonathan and Mercy (Bushnell) Rudd and widow of Nathaniel Leffingwell.
   (Was captain of a vessel in 1715,
   and a clothier in 1724.)   m. (2)   Elizabeth   b.   d.
                                           She m. (2) (?) John Bartlett. b.   d.

II.

Children of James (1) and (   ) Norman.

2. CALEB.   b.   m.   Elizabeth   b. ab. 1736. d. 1786.
3. MARY.   b.   d.   m. 1752 Eleazer Burnham. b. 1722-3. d.   son of Eleazer and Lydia (Waterman) Burnham.
4. JOSHUA. b.   d   m. 1760 Content Fanning.   b.   d.

III.

Children of Caleb (2) and Elizabeth (   ) Norman.

5. JAMES. (?) bapt. 1762. Killed in Revolution 1776.
6. JOHN (?) b.   d.   m. 1786 Mary Preston.
7. JABEZ. (?) bapt. 1765. d.   m. bef. 1793 Abigail   b.   d.
   (To Bridgeport, Ct.)
8. JOEL ARNOLD. bapt. 1768. d.
9. ELIZABETH. bapt. 1770. d.
10. MARY. bapt. 1772. d.
11. JAMES. bapt. 1777. d.

NORMAN.—Continued.

III.

Children of Joshua (4) and Content (Fanning) Norman.

12. CATHERINE. b. 1761. d.   m. 1777 Asa Peabody. b.   d.
13. JOSHUA. b. 1764. d. 1777.
14. ELINOR. b. 1766. d. 1792.
15. LUCY. b. 1768. d.   m. 1797 Henry Gordon. b.   d.
16. MARY. b. 1770. d.
17. HANNAH. b. 1772. d.
18. JOSEPH. b. 1774. d. 1775.
19. NATHANIEL (?) bapt. 1777. ; d. 1833 at Paris, N. Y. m. 1799 Lydia Frink. b. 1779 at Lisbon. d. 1804.

PARISH.

In the early part of the eighteenth century the following persons of the name of Parish appeared in Norwich, perhaps (as Miss Caulkins says) children of John Parish of Stonington, Ct.:

LIVIA PARISH. m. 1705 Christopher Tracy.
ELIZABETH PARISH. m. 1713-14 Francis Tracy.
SARAH PARISH. m. 1709 David Tracy.
BENJAMIN PARISH. m. 1705 Mary Tracy.
MARY PARISH. m. 1725 Jonathan Brewster.
RACHEL PARISH. m. 1719 Joshua Parke.

The births of these children of John Parish are also recorded:

{ MARY. b. 1704.
ABIGAIL. b. 1708.
DOROTHY. b. 1710.

I.

1 SAMUEL PARISH. b.   d. 1735. m. (1) Mary   b.   d. 1725.
   (Adm. inhab. of Norwich 1716.)   m. (2) 1724 Mary Rood. b.   d.

II.

Children of Samuel (1) and Mary (   ) Parish.

2. SOLOMON. b. 1710. d.   m.   Dinah   b.   d.
3. NATHANIEL. b. 1712-13. d. 1767. m. 1739 Kesiah Armstrong. b. 1717. d. 1781. dau. of Benjamin and Sarah (   ) Armstrong.
4. NEHEMIAH. b. 1715. d.
5. REBECCA. b. 1718. d.
6. JOHN. b.   d. 1725.

[544]

PARISH.—Continued.

II.

Children of Samuel (1) and Mary (Rood) Parish.

7. SAMUEL. b. 1727-8. d.
8. EBENEZER. b. 1730. d.
9. LEMUEL. b. 1732. d.
10. MARY. b. 1734. d.
11. JUDITH. b. 1737. d.

III.

Children of Nathaniel (3) and Kesiah (Armstrong) Parish.

12. ANDREW. b. 1740. d. 1794. m. 1763 Lydia Corning. b. d.
13. ELIZABETH. b. 1743. d. 1744.
14. ELIZABETH. b. 1745. d. m. 1770 Elisha Corning. b. d.
15. KESIAH. b. d.
16. NATHANIEL. b. d. m. Lucy b. ab. 1745. d. 1821.
17. ELIJAH. b. 1750. d.

IV.

Children of Nathaniel (16) and Lucy ( ) Parish.

18. NATHANIEL. b. d. m. 1821 Clarissa Woodworth. b. d.

PECK.

I.

1. HENRY PECK. b. d. 1651. m. Joan b. d.
(Came on ship Hector, to Boston, Mass., in 1637.)
(To New Haven, Ct., in 1638, with Gov. Eaton and Rev. John Davenport.)

II.

2. BENJAMIN. bapt. 1647. d. 1730. m. 1670 Mary Sperry. b. 1650. d.   ) Sperry of New Haven, Ct.
   dau. of Richard and Dennis (

III.

3. BENJAMIN. b. 1671. d. 1742. m.   Mary   b.   d. 1725.
(To Franklin, Ct., about 1700.)

IV.

Children of Benjamin (3) and Mary (   ) Peck.

4. DINAH. b. 1700. d.   m.   Jacob Willes. b.   d.
5. ELIZABETH. b. 1704. d. 1720.
6. JOSEPH. b. 1706. d. 1776. m. (1) 1729 Hannah Carrier. b. 1708. d. 1741-2.   ) Carrier of Colchester, Ct.
   dau. of Richard and Thankful (
   m. (2) 1742 Elizabeth Edgerton. b.   d. 1753.
   m. (3) 1754 Elizabeth (Lathrop) Carpenter. b. 1724. d. 1817. widow of Joseph Carpenter
   and dau. of Nathaniel and Ann (Backus) Lathrop.
7. MARY. b. 1708-9. d.   m. 1729 Phebe Hatch. b.   d.
8. BENJAMIN. b. 1710. d.   m. 1736 Martha Carrier. b.   d.
9. JOHN. b. 1712-13. d. 1743. m.   m: bef. 1738 Elizabeth   b.   d.
10. EBENEZER. b. 1715-16. d.
11. JONATHAN. b. 1717-18. d. 1780. m. 1741-2 Bethiah Bingham. b.   d.
12. DANIEL. b. 1719. d.   m. 1763 Jerusha (Tracy) Hyde. b. 1723. d. 1764.
    widow of Rev. Jedidiah Hyde and dau. of Capt. Joseph and Mary (Abel) Tracy.
13. SUBMIT. b. 1722. d.   m. (1) 1739 Aaron Cook. b. 1715 (?) d.   ) Cook of Windsor, Ct.
    perh. son of Nathaniel and Lydia (
    m. (2) 1743 John Wheatley.
14. PHEBE. b.   d.

[546]

PECK.—Continued.

V.

Children of Joseph (6) and Hannah (Carrier) Peck.

15. SIMEON. b. 1730. d. 1731.
16. JOSEPH. b. 1731. d. m. (1) 1752 Joanna Rudd. b. 1729. d. 1753. dau. of Jonathan and Joanna (Gregory) Rudd.
    m. (2) 1750 Susanna Brockway. b. d. 1761. of Lyme, Ct.
    m. (3) 1763 Rachel Fitch. b. 1735. d. 1764. dau. of Daniel and Rachel ( ), Fitch of Montville, Ct.
    m. (4) 1764 Mrs. Zerviah Hastings. b. d.

17. SIMEON. b. 1732-3. d. m. 1755 Ruth Willis. b. 1733. d. dau. of Rev. Henry and Martha (Kirtland) Willis of Franklin, Ct.
18. JAHLEEL. b. 1734. d.
19. GIDEON. b. 1736. d. 1740.
20. HANNAH. b. 1739. d.
21. GIDEON. b. 1741-2. d. m. (1) 1763 Irena Tracy. b. 1741. d. dau. of Josiah and Rachel (Allen) Tracy.
    m. (2) 1749 Sarah Edgecomb. b. d.

Children of Joseph (6) and Elizabeth (Lathrop) (Carpenter) Peck.

22. (Capt.) BELA. b. 1758. d. 1829. m. (1) 1777 Betsey Billings. b. 1764. d. 1815.
    m. (2) 1819 Lydia (Shipman) Spalding. b. 1760. d. 1835.
    widow of Asa Spalding and dau. of Nathaniel and Elizabeth (Latimer) Shipman.
23. CYNTHIA. b. 1761. d. 1797.

Children of Jonathan (11) and Beulah (Bingham) Peck.

24. PHINEAS. b. 1743. d. 1813. m. 1778 Elizabeth Barstow. b. 1745. d. 1823. dau. of Jonathan and Abigail (Hyde) Barstow.
25. BETHIAH. b. 1745. d. m. 1768 Hezekiah Edgerton. b. 1743. d. son of Hezekiah and Ann (Abel) Edgerton.
26. LUCY. b. 1747. d. m. (as second wife) Jason Gager. b. 1733. d. son of John and Jerusha (Barstow) Gager.
27. (Dea'con) DARIUS. b. 1749-50. d. 1804. m. (1) 1772 Hannah Warner. b. d. 1775. of Windham, Ct.
    m. (2) 1793 at Franklin, Mary Frances. b. d.
28. SYBIL. b. 1752. d. 1836. m. 1781 Isaac Hyde. b. 1750. d. 1810. son of Abel and Mehitable (Safford) Hyde.
29. ELNER. b. 1754. d. m. 1775 (?), Elisha Edgerton. b. 1755. d. son of Elisha and Zeruiah (Abel) Edgerton.
    (To Coventry, Ct.)
30. JOHN. b. 1756. Lost at sea.
31. JONATHAN. b. and d. 1757.
32. JAHLEEL. b. 1760. d. 1837. m. 1782 Olive Hyde. b. 1763. d. 1852. dau. of Capt. Thomas and Eleda (Burleigh) Hyde.
    (Served in the Revolution.)
    (To Hoosick, Mass., Hoosick, N. Y., Bennington, Vt. and Monkton, Vt.)

PECK.—Continued.

VI.

Children of (Capt.) Bela (22) and Betsey (Billings) Peck.

33. WILLIAM BILLINGS. b. 1788. d. 1805 at Yale College.
34. CHARLOTTE. b. 1790. d. 1819. m. 1803 Ebenezer Learned. b. 1780. d. 1858. of New London, Ct. son of Amasa and Grace (Hallam) Learned.
He m. (2) 1820 Lydia Coit. b. 1777. d. 1877. dau. of Joshua and Ann (Boradell) (Hallam) Coit.
35. HARRIET. b. 1795. d. 1860. m. 1812 Gen. William Williams. b. 1788. d. 1870. son of Gen. William and Eunice (Prentice) Williams of Stonington, Ct.

Children of (Ensign) Darius (27) and Hannah (Warner) Peck.

36. BRADFORD. b. 1773.
37. DARIUS. b. 1775. d. at sea.
38. JOHN. b. 1778. d. in the West Indies.
39. JOSEPH. b. 1782. d. m. Polly Collins. b. d.
    (To Columbia, Ct., and later to South Hartford, Penn.)
40. HENRY. b. d. in Charleston, S. C.
41. WARNER. b. d. on Staten Island.
42. HANNAH. b. d. m. Gurdon Fitch. b. d.
    (To Cleveland, Ohio.)
43. ELISHA. b. 1796. d. 1868. m. 1817 Lucy Hinckley. b. d.
    (To Waterville, N. Y.)
44. ANNA. b. d. m. Henry Parks. b. d.
45. LUCY. b. d. m. Alfred Young. b. d.
    (To New Haven, Ct.)

[548]

PERIT (PEIRET or PEYRET).

I.

1. (Rev.) PETER PEIRET. b.   d. 1704. m.   Marguerite Latour. b.   d.
(Pastor of Huguenot Church in New York.)
(To America in Ship Robert from England in 1687.)

II.

Children of (Rev.) Peter (1) and Marguerite (Latour) Peiret.

2. PETER. b.   d. bef. 1745. m. bef. 1717 Mary Bryan. b. 1685. d. 1752.
   (To Milford, Ct.)   dau. of Capt. Samuel and Martha (Whiting) Bryan of Milford, Ct.
3. MADELEINE. b.   d.
4. SUSANNA. b. 1692. d.
5. GABRIEL. b. 1693-4. d.
6. FRANÇOIS. b. 1695-6. d.
7. ELIZABETH. b. 1700. d.

III.

Children of Peter (2) and Mary (Bryan) Peiret.

8. PETER. b. 1717. d. 1791. m. 1744 Abigail Shepherd. b. 1718. d. 1764. dau. of John and Abigail (Akin) Shepherd (or Sheperd.)
9. MARGARET. b. 1719. d.   b.
10. MARY. b.   d.   (not mentioned in probate records of 1745.)
11. ABIGAIL. b.   d.

IV.

Children of Peter (8) and Abigail (Shepherd) Perit.

12. EDWARD. b. and d. 1757-9.
13. JOHN. b. ab. 1755. d. 1775. m. 1771 Ruth Webster. b. 1755. d. 1830. dau. of Preserved Webster.   ) Webster of Philadelphia.
    She m. (2d) 1779 d. Christopher Leffingwell of Norwich.
14. MARY. b.   d.   m. 1771 Ralph Isaacs.
15. ABIGAIL. b.   d.
16. ANTHONY. b. ab. 1744. d. 1814. m. (1st) 1773 Mary Sargent. b. ab. 1757. d. 1774.
    m. (2) ——— Betsy Quintard. b.   d.
17. PETER. b.   d. bef. 1794.
18. JOB. b. ab. 1751. d. 1794. m. 1773 Sarah Sanford. b.   d.
19. SAMUEL. b.   d.
20. THADDEUS. b. ab. 1755. d. 1800. m. (1) 1782 Sophia Webster. b. 1760. d. 1784. dau. of Preserved and Ruth ( ) Webster of Philadelphia.
    m. (2) 1787 Desire Sanford. bapt. 1762. d. 1845. dau. of Benjamin Sanford.

PERIT, (PERRET OR PEYRET).—Continued.

V.

Children of John (13) and Ruth (Webster) Perit.

21. JOHN, b. 1751, d. 1845, m. 1803 Margaretta Dunlap, b.   d.
    (Child Pelatiah.)
22. MARIA, b. 1753 in N. d. 1754, m. 1780 Charles P. Huntington.
23. PELATIAH, b. 1755 in N. d. 1865, m. (1) 1789 Jerusha Lathrop, b. 1783, d. 1821.
    (to New York City m. (2) 1823 Maria Coit, b. 1793, d. 1885.
    and New Haven, Ct.)
24. REBECCA, B. 1759, d. 1862, m. 1800 Joshua Lathrop.
    (To Le Roy, N. Y.)

[55]

PERKINS.

I.

1. JOHN. b. 1590. d. 1654. m. Judith   b.   d.
   (From England to Boston, Mass., in 1631.)
   (To Ipswich, Mass., in 1633.)

II.

2. (Sergt.) JACOB. b. 1624. d. 1699–1700. m. (1) 1647–8 Elizabeth Lovell. b. 1624. d. 1685–6. prob. dau. of Thomas Lovell of Ipswich, Mass.
   m. (2)   Damaris (   ) Robinson. b.   d. 1716.
   widow of Nathaniel Robinson of Boston, Mass.

III.

Children of (Sergt.) Jacob (2) and Elizabeth (Lovell) Perkins.

3. ELIZABETH. b. 1649. d.   m. 1667 Thomas Borman of Ipswich, perhaps son of Thomas Borman, first of Ipswich, later of Barnstable, Mass.
4. (Sergt.) JOHN. b. 1652. d. 1717. m. (1)   Mary Fiske. b. 1655. d. 1695. dau. of Capt. Thomas Fiske of Wenham, Mass.
   (To Wenham, Mass.)   m. (2) 1696 Elizabeth Prythatch. b.   d. 1710–11.
                                   m. (3)   Mary (White) (?) Hooper. b.   d.   widow of Samuel Hooper of Marblehead, Mass.
5. JUDITH. b. 1655. d.   m. 1673 Nathaniel Browne. b. 1645. d. 1717.
6. MARY. b. 1658. d.   m. (1)   Thomas Wells.
                                    m. (2)   John Annable.
7. (Sergt.) JACOB. b. 1662. d. 1705. m. (1) 1684 Elizabeth Sparks. b.   d. 1692. dau. of John and Mary (Sinnet) Sparks.
                                     m. (2) 1693 Sarah Treadwell. b. 1673. d. 1738. perhaps dau. of Thomas and Sarah (Titcomb) Treadwell
8. MATTHEW. b. 1665. d. 1735. m. 1695–6 Esther Burnham. b. 1669. d. 1749. dau. of Lt. Thomas and Mary (Tuttle) Burnham.
   (Was a weaver.)
   (To Norwich, Ct., but returned to Ipswich.)
9. HANNAH. b. 1670. d.
10. (Dea.) JOSEPH. b. 1674. d. 1726. m. 1700 Martha Morgan. b. 1680–1. d. 1754. dau. of Lt. Joseph and Dorothy (Parke) Morgan of Preston.
    (To Norwich, Ct.)   She m. (2) 1727 Joseph Lathrop
11. JABEZ. b. 1677. d. 1741–2. m. (1) 1698 Hannah Lathrop. b. 1677. d. 1721.
    (To Norwich, Ct.)   m. (2) 1722 Charity (Hodges) Leonard. b. 1682. d.   widow of Ekenah Leonard of Middleboro, Mass.
                               and dau. of Elder Henry and Esther (Gallup) Hodges of Taunton, Mass.

[55]

PERKINS.—Continued.

IV.

Children of (Dea.) Joseph (10) and Martha (Morgan) Perkins.

12. ELIZABETH. b. 1701. d. 1703.
13. (Dr.) JOSEPH. b. 1704. d. 1794. m. (1) 1728 Lydia Pierce. b. 1705–6. d. 1729–30. dau. of Timothy and Lydia (Spalding) Pierce.
    (Y. C. 1727.) m. (2) 1730 Mary Bushnell. b. 1707. d. 1795.
14. MARTHA. b. 1706. d. m. (1) 1727 Thomas Todd. b. 1701. d.
    poss. son of John and Elizabeth (Broclebank) Todd of Rowley, Mass.
    m. (2) 1728–9 Solomon Lathrop. b. 1706. d. 1733.
    m. (3) 1739 Matthew Loomis of Bolton, Ct. b. d.
15. (Capt.) JOHN. b. 1709. d. 1761. m. (1) 1731 Elizabeth Bushnell. b. 1715. d. 1742.
    m. (2) 1743 Lydia Tracy. b. 1719. d.
16. JERUSHA. b. 1711. d. 1741. m. 1733 Rev. Jedediah Hyde.
    He m. (2) 1742 Jerusha Tracy, dau. of Capt. Joseph and Mary (Abel) Tracy.
    She m. (2) 1763 Daniel Peck.
17. MATTHEW. b. 1713. d. 1773. m. 1739 Hannah Bishop. b. 1724. d. 1809. dau. of Samuel and Sarah (Forbes) Bishop.
18. DEBORAH. } b. 1715. d. 1772. m. 1741–2 Benajah Carey. b. 1718–19. d. 1773. of Seabed, Ct. son of John and Hannah (Thurston) Carey.
19. ANN. d. 1731.
20. HANNAH. b. 1717. d. 1793–5. m. 1737 Lemuel Bingham. b. ab. 1713. d. 1788. son of Samuel and Faith (Ripley) Bingham.
21. SIMON. b. 1720. d. 1725–6.
22. WILLIAM. b. 1722. d. m. Elizabeth Buck. b. 1723. d. dau. of Rev. David and Elizabeth (Perkins) Buck of Southington, Ct.

Children of Jabez (11) and Hannah (Lathrop) Perkins.

23. JABEZ. b. 1699. d. 1739. m. 1725 Rebecca Leonard. b. 1705–6. d. 1788.
    dau. of Elkanah and Charity (Hodges) Leonard of Middleborough, Mass.
24. HANNAH. b. 1701. d. 1775. m. (1) 1715 Capt. Joshua Huntington. b. 1698. d. 1745.
    m. (2) bef. 1745 Col. Samuel Lynde. b. 1689. d. 1754. son of Nathaniel and Susanna (Willoughby) Lynde.
    m. (3) bef. 1771 Capt. Ebenezer Lathrop.
25. ELIZABETH. b. 1703. d. 1763. m. (1) 1722 at Franklin, Ct., Rev. Daniel Buck. b. d. 1059. of Southington, Ct.
    (Southington and Norwich, Ct.) son of David and Elizabeth Hubbert (or Hubbard) Buck of Wethersfield, Ct.
    m. (2) John Deming. b. 1694 (?) d. 1793. perh. son of Samuel and Sarah (Kirby) Deming of Wethersfield, Ct.
26. MARY. bapt. 1705. m. 1723 Rev. Daniel Kirtland of New-ent. b. 1701 at Saybrook, Ct. d. 1773.
    (Y. C. 1720.) son of John and Lydia (Pratt) Kirtland.
27. JACOB. b. 1705–6. d. 1776. m. 1730 Jemina Leonard. b. 1714. d. 1770.
    dau. of Elkanah and Charity (Hodges) Leonard of Middleborough, Mass.
28. LUCY. b. 1709. d. m. 1731. Capt. Richard Bushnell, 2nd.
29. JUDITH. b. 1714–15. d. m. (Col.) Ephraim Leonard. b. 1705–6. d. 1776. of Taunton, Mass.
    (Taunton, Mass.) son of Maj. George and Ann (Tisdale) Leonard.
    He m. (2) Melatiah Ware (widow.)
    m. (3) Anna ( ) Woodworth) Ruggles, widow of Elisha Woodworth and Rev. Timothy Ruggles.

[552]

PERKINS.—Continued.

IV.

Children of Jabez (11) and Charity (Leonard) Perkins.

30. CHARITY. b. 1724-5. d.   m. 1743 Ezra Lathrop. b. 1718. d.   son of Samuel and Deborah (Crow) Lathrop.

V.

Children of Jabez (23) and Rebecca (Leonard) Perkins.

31. JEREMIAH. b. 1725. d. 1768. m.   Temperance Hazen. b. 1727. d.   dau. of Jacob and Abigail (Lathrop) Hazen.
32. Daughter. b. and d. 1729.
33. Son. b. and d. 1727.
34. (Capt.) JABEZ. b. 1728. d. 1795. m. (1) 1751 Anne Lathrop. b. 1730-1. d. 1775.
    m. (2) 1780 Lydia (   ) Avery (widow). b. ab. 1733. d. 1810.
35. ELKANAH. b. 1730. d. 1740.
36. REBECCA. b. 1730. d. young.
37. SAMUEL. b. 1732. d. 1739.
38. HANNAH. b. 1733. d. 1808. m. 1760 Jabez Fitch. b. 1736-7. d.   son of Jabez and Anna (Knowlton) Fitch.
39. CHARITY. b. 1734. d. 1736.
40. CHARITY. b. 1737. d.   m.   Samuel Lovett. b. 1737. d.   son of Samuel and Esther (   ) Lovett.
41. SAMUEL. b. 1738. d. 1705 at St. Eustatia s. p.

Children of Jacob (27) and Jemina (Leonard) Perkins.

42. (Capt.) JACOB. } b. 1731. d. 1814. m. (1) 1755 Mary Brown. b. ab. 1736. d. 1759. dau. of James and Ann (Noyes) Brown.
43. JEMINA.   m. (2) 1767 Abigail Thomas. b. 1740. d.   dau. of Ebenezer and Heulah (Haskins) Thomas.
                                           m. 1775. d. 1773. m. 1759 Benjamin Burnham. b. 1729. d. 1799. son of Benjamin and Mary (Kinsman) Burnham.
44. TIMOTHY. b. 1733. d. 1772.
45. (Col.) SIMEON. b. 1734-5. d. 1812 at Liverpool, N. S. m. (1) 1755-60 Abigail Backus. b. 1742. d. 1769. dau. of Ebenezer and Abigail (Franklin) Backus.
    (To Liverpool, N. S., ab. 1762.)
                                           m. (2) 1775 Elizabeth (Young) Hadley. b. ab. 1747. d. 1825 at Ithaca, N. Y. widow of John Hadley of Manchester, N. S., and dau. of Henry Young.
46. MARY. b. 1735. d. young.
47. DANIEL. b. 1736. d. 1777 of smallpox.
48. ABIAH. b. 1738. d. 1766. m. 1760 Elijah Adgate. b. 1739. d. 1775.
49. LUCY. b. 1740. d. 1756.
50. ELKANAH. b. 1742. d. 1744.
51. ZEBULON. b. 1743. Lost at sea 1765.
52. JABEZ. b. 1745. d. 1832. m. 1777 Mary Backus. b. 1750. d. 1813. dau. of Nathaniel and Elizabeth (Waterman) Backus.

PERKINS.—Continued.

V.

53. JUDITH. b. 1747. d. 1803. m. 1772 (as second wife) Gamaliel Ripley. b. 1740. d. 1799. son of Rev. David and Lydia (Carey) Ripley of Windham, Ct. He m. (1) 1764 Elizabeth Hebard. b. d. 1705.
54. ZEPHANIAH. b. 1749. d. 1773.
55. (Capt.) HEZEKIAH. b. 1751. d. 1822. m. 1784 Sarah Fitch. b. 1760. d. 1838. dau. of Col. Eleazer and Amy (Bowen) Fitch of Windham, Ct.
56. MARY. b. 1753. d. 1794. m. (?) John Manning. b. d. of Lebanon, Ct.
57. (Capt.) EBENEZER. b. 1756. d. 1831. m. Eunice b. ab. 1746. d. 1829.

VI.

Children of Jabez (34) and Anna (Lathrop) Perkins.

58. (Capt.) ERASTUS. b. 1752. d. 1853. m. (1) 1777 Anne Glover. b. ab. 1753. d. 1807.
    m. (2) 1809 Mary (Hallam) Hubbard. b. 1760. d. 1825. widow of Thomas Hubbard and dau. of Amos Hallam of New London.
    m. (3) 1826 Lucy (Lord) Avery. b. 1760. d. 1841. widow of Richard Avery.
59. ANNA. b. 1754. d. 1799. m. 1772 Levi Huntington.
60. (Capt.) JABEZ. b. 1757. Lost in a hurricane at sea, 1780.
61. HANNAH. b. 1760. d. 1783.
62. ASHER. b. 1764. d. 1784.
63. LYDIA. b. 1767. d. 1861. m. 1789 Shubael Breed. b. 1759. d. 1840. son of Gershom and Dorothy (McClaren) Breed.

Children of Jabez (34) and Lydia ( ) (Avery) Perkins.

64. HANNAH. b. 1783. d.

Children of (Capt.) Jacob (42) and Mary (Brown) Perkins.

65. LUCY. b. 1758. d. 1832. m. 1773 Daniel Carew.
66. ANNA. b. 1759. d. 1808. m. 1773 Felix Huntington.

Children of (Capt.) Jacob (42) and Abigail (Thomas) Perkins.

67. JEREMIAH. b. 1770. d. (To Cuba and to Michigan.)
68. SAMUEL. b. ab. 1772. d. 1794 at Surinam.
69. ABIGAIL. b. d. m. Rev. John Sherman. b. d. of Mansfield, Ct.
70. MARY. b. d. m. (1) Storrs. b. d.
    m. (2) Parker of Trenton, N. J. b. d.
71. SARAH. b. d.
72. JACOB. b. d. unm.
73. ZEPHANIAH. b. ab. 1781. d. 1803 at Surinam. (To New Orleans, La.)

PERKINS.—Continued.

VI.

Children of (Col.) Simeon (45) and Abigail (Backus) Perkins.

74. ROGER. b. 1760. d. at sea 1781.

Children of Simeon (45) and Elizabeth (Young) (Hall 1) Perkins.

75. ABIGAIL. b. 1770. d. 1819. m. 1795 Joshua Newton. b.   d.
    (Collector H. M. Customs at Liverpool, N. S.)
76. JOHN PERKINS. b. 1778. d. 1849. m. 1804 Elizabeth Thomas. b.   d.   dau. of John and Anna Roberts Thomas of Liverpool, N. S.
    (To Norwich, Ct., ab. 1819.)
77. LUCY. b. 1780. d. 1817 at New York. m. 1805 Daniel L. Bishop. b. 1777. d.   son of Samuel and Mercy (Johnson) Bishop.
78. ELIZABETH. b. 1783. d. 1856. m. 1824 (as second wife) Daniel L. Bishop.
79. EUNICE. b. 1785. d. 1813. unm.
80. MARY. b. 1786. d. 1814. unm.
81. SIMEON LEONARD. b. 1788. d. 1822. m. 1817 Hephzibah Dean. b.   d. 1846. dau. of Isaac Dean.
    at New Orleans, La. m.   Dr. Hennes. b.   d.
82. CHARLOTTE. b. 1790. d.

PRIOR.

I.

1. BENJAMIN PRIOR, b.   d.   m. 1697 Bethiah Pratt, b. 1679, d.   dau. of Jonathan and Abigail (Wood) Pratt of Plymouth, Mass. (Duxbury, Mass.)

II.

2. JOSHUA, b. 1709, d. 1784, m. 1735 Mary Burnham, b. 1714, d. 1789, dau. of Eleazer and Lydia (Waterman) Burnham of Norwich. (To Norwich, Ct.)

III.

Children of Joshua (2) and Mary (Burnham) Prior.

3. MARY,   d.
4. ELIZABETH,   d.   m. 1760 Amos Rogers, b.   d.
5. LYDIA,   d.
6. ELISHA, bapt. 1740, d.
7. JOSHUA,   d.   m. 1762 Sarah Hutchins, b.   d.   of Killingly, Ct.
8. JOSEPH,   d.
9. BENJAMIN,   d.   m. 1771 Rachel Hutchins, b. 1757, d.   of Plainfield, Ct.
10. JOHN, bapt. 1750, d.   m. 1776 Ditte Fillmore,   dau of Capt. John and Dorcas (   ) Fillmore.
11. SIMEON, bapt. 1754, d. (To Norwich, Mass.)

IV.

Children of Joshua (7) and Sarah (Hutchins) Prior.

12. ABIGAIL, b. 1763, d. 1766.
13. SARAH, b. 1767, d.
14. LUCY, b. 1768, d.
15. LUCY (2) bapt. 1775, d.

PUNDERSON.

I.

1. JOHN PUNDERSON. b.   d. 1681. m.   Margaret   b.   d.
(To N. E. from Yorkshire in 1638.)
(To New Haven 1639.)

II.

2. (Dea.) JOHN. b. 1643. d. 1730. m. Damaris Atwater. b.   d.   dau. of David Atwater.

III.

Children of John (2) and Damaris (Atwater) Punderson.

3. ABIGAIL. b. 1671. d.
4. JOHN. b. 1673. d.
5. HANNAH. b. 1676. d.
6. THOMAS. b. 1677. d.
7. DAMARIS. b. 1680. d.
8. MARY. b. 1683. d.
9. DAVID. b. 1686. d.
10. SAMUEL. b. 1691. d.
11. EBENEZER. b. 1694. d.

V. (?)

12. (Rev.) EBENEZER. b. ab. 1705 (?) d. 1771 (?) m. 1732 Hannah Minor. b. ab. 1712. d. 1792.
(Y. C. 1724.)
(From Pittsfield, Mass., to Groton, Ct., 1729.)
(Pastor of N. Groton Church 1729-1734.)
(To Poquetanock ab. 1738.)
(Rector of Episcopal Church at Poquetanock, Norwich and Hebron till 1751.)
(To New Haven in 1751.)

[557]

PUNDERSON.—Continued.

VI. (?)

Children of (Rev.) Ebenezer (12) and Hannah (Miner) Punderson.

13. HANNAH. b. 1733. d 1775. m. Solomon Avery of Groton, Ct. b. 1729. d. 1798 in Pennsylvania, son of Humphrey and Jerusha (Morgan) Avery of Preston, Ct.
14. EBENEZER. b. 1735. d. m. 1757 Prudence Geer. b. d.
15. CYRUS. b. 1737. d. m. Catharine

VII. (?)

Children of Ebenezer (14) and Prudence (Geer) Punderson.

16. PRUDENCE b. 1758. d. m. Polly b. d.
17. EBENEZER. (?) b. d.

VIII.

Children of Ebenezer (17) and Polly ( ) Punderson.

18. BETSEY. bapt. Christ Church 1792. d.
19. FRANK. bapt. Christ Church 1797. d.

[558]

READ.

WILLIAM READ, b.   d.   m.   Susanna   b.   d. 1656
(Boston, Mass.)

1.

1. JOSEPH (2) READ, b.   d. 1712, ab. m.   Ruth Perry, b.   d.   perhaps dau. of Robert Perry of New London, Ct.

II.

Children of Joseph (2) (1) and Ruth (Perry) Read.

2. JOSIAH, b.   d. 1717, m. 1699 Grace Holloway, b.   d. 1727, dau. of William Holloway of Marshfield, Mass.
   (Moved to Norwich, 1679.)
3. JOHN, b. ab. 1645, d. 1728, m.   Hannah Holloway, b.   d.   dau. of William Holloway of Marshfield, Mass.
   (To Windham, Ct., ab. 1695.)
4. HEZEKIAH, b.   d.

III.

Children of Josiah (2) and Grace (Holloway) Read.

5. JOSIAH, b. 1665, d. 1752, m. 1697 Elizabeth Amsden, b. 1677-8, d. 1749,
   dau. of Isaac and Jane (Rutter) Amsden of Cambridge and Marlborough, Mass.
6. WILLIAM, b. 1670, d. 1752, m. 1699 Anna Stark, b.   d.
7. ELIZABETH, b. 1672, d. March 1692. m. Jan. 1692 William Brewster, b. 1669, d.   son of Benjamin and Anna (Dart) Brewster.
8. EXPERIENCE, b. 1675, d.
9. JOHN, b. 1679, d.   m. 1713 Lydia Caswell, b.   d.
10. JOSEPH, b. 1684, d.   m. 1708 Mary Guggie, b.   d.
11. SUSANNA, b. 1687, d.
12. HANNAH, b. 1689, d.   m. (?) 1713 Benjamin Fitch.

[559]

REYNOLDS.

I.

1. JOHN REYNOLDS (RENALDS or RANALS). b.   d. 1702. m.   Sarah Backus. b.   d.

II.

Children of John (1) and Sarah (Backus) Reynolds.

2. JOHN. b. 1655. Killed by Indians in 1675.
3. SARAH. b. 1656. d. 1703. m. 1685 John Post. b. 1657. d. 1691. son of John and Hester (Hyde) Post.
4. SUSANNAH. b. 1658. d.
5. JOSEPH. b. 1660. d. 1722-9. m. 1688 Sarah Elgerton. b. 1667. d. 1714. dau. of Richard and Mary (Sylvester) Elgerton.
6. MARY. b. 1664. d. 1727-8. m. (1) 1689-90 John Elgerton. b. 1662. d. 1692. (brother of Joseph's wife).
   m. (2) 1697 (as second wife) Samuel Lathrop, 2nd.
7. ELIZABETH. b. 1666. d.   m. (1) 1687 Jonathan Fowler (alias Smith). b. 1650. d. 1691. son of Capt. William and Mary (Tapp) Fowler of Milford, Ct.
   m. (2)   Lyman.
8. STEPHEN. b. 1669. d. 1687.
9. LYDIA. b. 1671. d.   m. 1693-4 Benjamin Miller. b.   d.   possibly son of George Miller of New London, Ct.

III.

Children of Joseph (5) and Sarah (Elgerton) Reynolds.

10. JOHN. b. 1691. d. 1742. m. 1720 Lydia Lord. b. 1694. d. 1786. dau. of Capt. Richard and Elizabeth (Hyde) Lord of Lyme, Ct.
11. MARY. b. 1693-4. d. 1751. m. bef. 1717 Robert Warren. b. 1694. d. 1756.
12. JOSEPH. b. 1695-6. d. 1756. m. 1717 Hannah Bingham. b. 1699-7. d. 1787. dau. of Thomas and Hannah (Backus) Bingham.
13. STEPHEN. b. 1698. d. 1731-3. m. 1725 Mary Sanford. b.   d.   perh. dau. of Samuel (or Thomas) Sanford of Milford, Ct.
14. DANIEL. b. and d. 1701.
15. LYDIA. b. 1702-3. d.   m.
16. DANIEL. b. 1705. d. 1706-7.
17. SARAH. b. 1707. d.   m. 1725 John (or Jonathan) Calkins. b.   d.

REYNOLDS.—Continued.

IV.

Children of John (10) and Lydia (Lord) Reynolds.

18. DEBORAH. b. 1721. d.   m. (1) 1741 Joshua Bishop. b. 1717. d.   son of Samuel and Sarah (Forbes) Bishop.
    m. (2)   Daniel Whitmore of Middletown, Ct. b.   d.
19. ANN. b. 1723. d. 1771. m. 1747 Capt. Thomas Fanning. b. ab. 1723. d. 1790.
20. SARAH. b. 1725. d. 1747. m. 1744 Jeremiah Huntington.
21. RUTH. b. 1727–8. d. 1755. m. 1747 Nathaniel Shipman. b.   d. 1805.
    He m. (2) 1756 Elizabeth Leffingwell.
22. JOHN. b. 1730. d. 1752. Killed on Long Island by horse running against a tree.
23. JOSEPH. b. 1732. d. 1792. m. 1755 Phebe Lee. b. 1736. d. 1818. dau. of Elisha and Hephzibah (   ) Lee of Lyme, Ct.
24. ABIGAIL. b. 1734. d.   m. 1751 Daniel Kelly. b. 1726. d.   son of Joseph and Lydia (Pikens) Kelly.
25. LYDIA. b. 1736. d. 1815. m.   Dea. Seth Ely. b. 1734. d. 1821. son of Richard and Phebe (Hubbard) Ely of Lyme, Ct.
26. ELIZABETH. b. 1738–9. d.   m. betw. 1762–72 Col. John Sumner of Middletown, Ct.

V.

Children of Joseph (23) and Phebe (Lee) Reynolds.

27. RUFUS. b. 1756. d. 1782.
28. SARAH. b. 1758. d. 1789.
29. PHEBE. b. 1760. d. 1832. unm.
30. JOHN. b. 1762. d.   m.   Hannah Halsey of Long Island. b.   d.
31. SARAH. b. 1764. d. 1843. unm.
32. JOSEPH. b. 1766. d. 1844. m. (1) 1790 Hannah Ingles of Philadelphia. b. 1734. d. 1816. dau. of George and Elizabeth (Morgan) Ingles.
    m. (2) 1818 Anna (or Nancy) Colt. b. 1782. d.   dau. of Barwell and Anna (Tracy) Colt.
33. ENOCH. b. and d. 1767.
34. ELISHA. b. 1769. drowned at sea 17   .
35. ANNE. b. 1771. d. 1786.
36. ABIGAIL. b. 1774. d. 1854. m. 1795 Capt. Giles L'Hommedieu. b. ab. 1768. d. 1859.
37. ENOCH. b. 1776. d. 1838. m. 1800 Sally Canfield. b.   d.   of Middletown, Ct.
    (To Lucerne, Pa., and to Washington, D. C.)
    (Was an officer in the Treasury Department for many years.)
38. CHARLES. b. 1779. d. 1828 at Richmond, O. m.   Mary Sage. b. ab. 1789. d. 1837. of Middletown, Ct.

SLUMAN.

I.

1. THOMAS SLUMAN. b.   d. 1683.   m. 1668 Sarah Bliss. b. 1647. d. 1730.
   (To Norwich in 1663.)
   She m. (2) 1686 Dr. Solomon Tracy.

II.

Children of Thomas (1) and Sarah (Bliss) Sluman.

2. SARAH. b. 1669. d. 1703. m. 1689 Hugh Calkins (or Caulkins), 2nd. b. 1659. d. 1722. son of Hugh Calkins.
3. MARY. b. 1671.
4. THOMAS. b. 1674. d.   m. 1702-3 Sarah Pratt. b. 1684. (?) d.   prob. dau. of John and Sarah (Jones) Pratt of Saybrook, Ct.
   (To Franklin, Ct.)
5. ELIZABETH. b. 1677. d. 1741. m. 1696 Dr. Samuel Abel. b. 1672. d. 1704. son of Caleb and Margaret (Post) Abel.
6. ABIGAIL. b. 1679-80. d. 1748. m. 1705 Caleb Abel, 2nd. b. 1677. d.   son of Caleb and Margaret (Post) Abel.
   (To Lebanon, Ct.)
7. REBECCA. b. 1682. d.   m. 1703 John Abel. b. 1678. d.   son of Caleb and Margaret (Post) Abel.
   (To Lebanon, Ct.)

SPALDING.

I.
1. EDWARD SPALDING. b.   d.   m. (1) Margaret   b.   d.
   (To New England ab. 1630 or 1633.)   m. (2) bef. 1643 Rachel   b.   d.
   (To Braintree, Mass.)

II.
2. BENJAMIN. b. 1643. d. bef. 1708. m. 1668 Olive Farwell. b.   d.   ) Farwell of Concord, Mass., and Chelmsford, Mass.
   dau. of Henry and Olive (
   (To north part of Canterbury, Ct., now called Brooklyn.)

III.
3. EDWARD. b. 1672. d. 1749. m.   Mary Adams. b.   d.

IV.
4. (Capt.) EBENEZER. b. 1717. d. 1744. m. 1743 Mary Fassett. b.   d.

V.
(Of 7re of ((Capt.) Ebenezer (4) and Mary (Fassett) Spalding.

1. Mary. b. 1717. d. 1720. m. 1742 Roger Ogle. b.   d.   of Brooklyn, Ct.
2. EBENEZER. b. 1716. d. 1756.
3. SAMUEL. b. 1720. d. 1724.
4. JOSEPH. b. 1722. d. 1724.
5. JENNETT. b. 1774. dau. unknown. m.   Mary Baker. b.   d.   dau. of Simeon Baker of Canterbury, Ct.
6. LYDIA. b. 1726. d. 1784.
7. SAMUEL. b. 1727. d. 1801. m. Abigail   b. 1729. d. 1785. dau. of Nathaniel and Elizabeth (Jenkins) Shipman
   of Brooklyn.   m. (2) 1790 Capt. Ben Peck.
8. Ebenezer. b.   d.   m.   Lydia Chaffee. b.   d.   dau. of Jos. (?) Paine of Canterbury. Ct.
9. JOSEPH. b. 1732. d. 1736. m.   Lydia Chaffee. b.   d. 1745. of Canterbury, Ct.

SPALDING.—Continued.

VI.

Children of Asa (12) and Lydia (Shipman) Spalding.

15. MARIA ELIZABETH. b. 1797. d. 1809.
16. ASA. b. and d. 1811.

Children of (Dr.) Rufus (13) and Lydia (Paine) Spalding.

17. SOPHIA. b. 1782. d. 1851. m. Henry Allen. b. d. of Holmes' Hole, Mass.
18. SALLY. b. 1784. d. m. Capt. Thomas West. b. d. 1803.
19. SOPHRONIA. b. 1786. d. 1803.
20. ALICE FASSET. b. 1788. d. m. 1806 Benjamin Chase. b. d. of Holmes' Hole, Mass.
21. LYDIA PAINE. b. 1791. d. m. 1831 Elderkin Potter. b. d. of Ohio.
22. PHILURA PAINE. b. 1793. d. 1844. m. 1811 Samuel Claghorn. b. d. 1840. of Holmes' Hole, Mass. (To Norwich, Ct.)
23. HARRIET BYRON. b. 1795. d. 1861. m. 1820 Capt. Abner Bassett. b. d. 1870. (To Norwich and New London, Ct.)
24. RUFUS PAINE. b. 1798.
25. LUTHER PAINE. b. 1800.
26. SOPHRONIA MARIA. b. 1804. d. 1859. m. 1826 William Quimby. b. d. of Warren, Ohio.

Children of Luther (14) and Lydia (Chaffee) Spalding.

27. GEORGE. b. 1797. d. 1858. m. 1824 Helen M. Cowles. b. d. of Farmington, Ct.
28. MARY. b. 1802. d. 1803.
29. CHARLES. b. 1812. d. m. 1837 Juliet Hubbard. b. d. dau. of Russell and Abigail (Williams) Hubbard.
30. ELIZA ANN. b. 1813. d. 1838.

SPOONER.

I.

1. WILLIAM SPOONER. b.   d. 1684-5. m. (1)   Elizabeth Partridge. b.   d. 1648.
    m. (2) 1652 Hannah Pratt, m.   d.   ) Pratt of Plymouth, Mass.
    dau. of Joshua and Bathsheba (
    (From Colchester, Co. Essex, Eng., to N. E. in 1637.)
    (To Plymouth, Mass., bef. 1643.)
    (Moved in 1660 to Acushnet.)

II.

2. JOHN. b. bef. 1648. d. aft. 1734. m. (1)
    m. (2)
    (To Dartmouth.)

III.

3. JOHN. b. 1668. d. 1728. m. 1695 Rosamond Hammond. b. 1664. d. 1727. dau. of Samuel Hammond of Rochester.

IV.

4. THOMAS. b. 1718. d. 1767. m. 1742 Rebecca Paddock. b. 1718. d. 1772. dau. of Judah and Alice (Alden) Paddock.
    (Carpenter.)
    (Moved from New Bedford to New London.)

V.

5. JUDAH PADDOCK. b. 1748 in New London. d. 1807 at Rutland, Vt. m. 1772 Deborah Douglas. b. 1753. d. 1823 at Winsted, L. I.
    dau. of Capt. Nathan and Anne (Dennise Douglas
    of New London, Ct.

Children of Judah Paddock (5) and Deborah (Douglas) Spooner.

VI.

6. NANCY. b. 1771. d. 1812. m. (1)   Dr. Charles Bouldine of New London. b.   d.
    m. (2)   Thomas Miller of Wallingford, Vt. b.   d.
7. REBECCA. b. 1773. d. 1788. m.   Jacob Cooper of Springfield, Mass., afterward of Suffield, Ct. b.   d.
8. HANNAH. b. 1775. d. 1825. m. (1)   Thomas Hale. b.   d.
    m. (2)   Turner. b.   d.
9. DEBORAH. b. 1777. d. 1723. m. (1)   Oliver Bowman. b.   d.
    m. (2)   Andrew Leach of Pittsford, Vt. b.   d.
10. FANNY. b. 1780. d. 1783.
11. (Col.) ALDEN. b. 1783. d. 1849 at Brooklyn, N. Y. m. (1) 1807 at Sag Harbor, Rebecca Jermain. b. 1780. d. 1824
    (To Brooklyn, L. I.)   dau. of John and Margaret (Pierson)Jermain.
    m. (2) 1831 Mary Ann Wetmore. b. 1794. d.
    dau. of Prosper and Catherine (McEwen) Wetmore
12. FRANCES BOWMAN. b. 1798. d. 1862. m. 1820 Sylvester Rand of Wainscot, L. I.

STERRY.

I.

1. ROGER STERRY. b. d. m. 1670 Hannah (Palmer) Huet, (or Hewitt,) bapt. 1634. d. widow of Capt. Thomas Hewitt and dau. of Walter and Rebecca (Short) Palmer of Stonington, Ct. (Stonington, Ct.)

II.

2. SAMUEL. b. d. 1734. m. (1) 1703 Hannah Rose. b. d. 1724. perh. dau. or widow of Timothy Starkweather of Preston.
   m. (2) 1724 Mehetabel Starkweather. b. d. (To Preston, Ct.)

III.

Children of Samuel (2) and Hannah (Rose) Sterry.

3. HANNAH. b. 1704-5. d.
4. SAMUEL. b. 1706. d.
5. CYPRIAN. b. 1707. d. 1772. m. Elizabeth (?) Brown. b. 1703-9. (?) d. dau. of John Brown of Preston.
6. ROBERT. b. 1711. d. 1789. m. (1) Rosabillah b. 1711. d. 1738.
   m. (2) Lydia Olney. b. d. (To Providence, R. I.)
7. ZERVIAH. b. 1713. d.

Children of Samuel (2) and Mehetabel (Starkweather) Sterry.

8. SARAH. b. 1727. d. 1729.
9. ROGER. b. 1730. d. m. 1748 Abigail Holms. b. d. of Stonington, Ct.

IV.

Children of Roger (9) and Abigail (Holms) Sterry.

10. SAMUEL. b. 1749. d. 1751-2.
11. MARY. b. 1751. d. 1752.
12. MARY. b. 1753. d. m. 1773 Daniel Kimball. b. d.
13. ARTHUR. b. 1757. d. 1761.
14. MEHETABEL. b. 1758.
15. COSSIDER. b. 1761. d. 1817. m. (1) 1780 Sabra Park. b. 1763. d. 1794. dau. of Silas and Sarah (Ayer) Park. (Norwich.) m. (2) Mary (Norman) Hazen. b. d. (widow.)
16. ROGER. b. 1764. d. m. (?) Luvina b. d.
17. (Rev.) ASAHEL. b. 1766. d. 1833. m. 1792 Rebecca Bromley. b. 1770. d. 1833. dau. of Bethuel and Arabella (Herrick) Bromley of Preston, Ct. (Norwich.)
18. ABIGAIL. b. 1769. d.

[566]

STERRY.—Continued.

V.

Children of Consider (15) and Sabra (Parks) Sterry.

19. SALLA, b. 1753, d. 1851.
20. POLLY, b. 1755, d. 1844.
21. ELIZABETH, b. 1777, d. 1845.
22. ERASTUS, b. 1779, d. 1810.
23. WILLIAM, b. 1793, d. 1813.

Children of Consider (15) and Mary (Norton) (Hazen) Sterry.

24. ABBY HOLMS, b. 1797, d.   s. p.   m.   Tisdale Adams, b.   d.
25. HENRIETTA, b.   d.
26. SABRA, b.   d.
27. MARY ANN, b. 1801, d.   m.   Elisha Congdon, b.   d.
    (To Michigan.)
28. JANE, b. 1802, d. 1860, m. b. E. 1820 Peleg Hunt,   b.   d
29. SAMUEL ADAMS, b. 1805, d.   at sea on passage to Havti.
30. THOMAS JEFFERSON, b. 1808, d.
31. JAMES MADISON, b. 1809, d. 1866, m. 1832 Lucy B. Prentice, b. 1809, d. 1892, of Windham, Ct.
32. GEORGE CLINTON, b. 1812, d. 1877, m. 1832 Mary B. Mason, b.   d.   of Bozrah, Ct.
33. DeWITT CLINTON, b. 1815, d. 1838.
34. HARRIET HALE, b. 1817, d. 1820.
35.   b. 1819, d. young.

Children of (Rev.) John (17) and Rebecca (Brawley) Sterry.

36. JOHN HOLMS, b. 1768, d. 1826, m. (1)   Eliza Hewitt, b. 1767, d. 1806, of Ct.
                                m. (2)   Emily Standish, b. 1768, d. 1883.
37. MARJORY, b. 1769, d. 1845, m. 1812 Andrew Weldon, b. 1752, d. 1803.
38. REBECCA, b. 1769, d. 1870, m. (1)   William Smith, b. 1795, d. 1827.
                                m. (2)
                                in 1821
39. ROBERT, b. 1808, d. 1808, m. (1) Sarah M. Brewster, b. 1769, d. 1825.
40. GEORGE WASHINGTON, b. 1807, d. 1824.
41. CAROLINE, b. 1809, d. 1811.
42. EDWARD AUGUSTUS, b. 1811, d. 1827, m. 1833 Catherine A. Whittlesey, b. 1810, d. 1874.
43. MARIA LOUISA, b. 1817, d. 1881, m. 1839 Alpheus Mosier, b.   d.
44. WILLIAM PALMER, b. 1819, d. 1879, m. 1851 Nancy Haines, b.   d.
45. FRANCIS ASBURY PERKINS, b. 1824, d.   m. 1841 Betsey A. Bliss, b.   d. 1875.

[567]

STRONG.

I.

1. (Elder) JOHN STRONG. b. 1605. d. 1699. m. (1)
   m. (2) 1630 Abigail Ford. b. ab. 1608. d. 1688.
      dau. of Thomas Ford of Dorchester, Mass., later of Northampton, Mass.
   (From Taunton, Somersetshire, Eng.)
   (To Dorchester, Mass., 1630.)
   (To Hingham, Mass., 1635.)
   (To Taunton, Mass., 1638.)
   (To Windsor, Ct., aft. 1645.)
   (To Northampton, Mass., 1659.)

II.

2. THOMAS. b. 1637. d. 1689 aged about 56. m. (1) 1660 Mary Hewett. bapt. 1640. d. 1670-1.
      dau. of Rev. Ephraim and Isabel ( ) Hewett (or Huet) of Windsor, Ct.
   m. (2) 1671 Rachel Holton. b. d. dau. of Dea. William Holton of Northampton, Mass.
   She m. (2) 1698 Nathan Bradley of East Guilford, now Madison, Ct.

III.

3. ELNATHAN. b. 1666. d. 1727. m. 1712 Patience Jenner. bapt. 1682. d.)Jenner of Woodbury, Ct.
   (Was a farmer at Southbury, Ct.) She m. (2) Jonathan Law of Killingworth, Ct. b. d.

IV.

4. (Rev.) NATHAN. bapt. 1717. d. 1795. m. 1746 Esther Meacham. b. 1725. d. 1793.
   (Y. C. 1742.) dau. of Rev. Joseph and Esther (Williams) Meacham of Coventry, Ct.
   (Settled at Coventry, Ct., 1745, as pastor of Second Cong. Church.)

V.

5. (Rev.) JOSEPH. b. 1753. d. 1834. m. 1780 Mary Huntington. b. 1760. d. 1840. dau. of Gen. Jabez and Hannah (Williams) Huntington.
   (Y. C. 1772.)
   (Settled at Norwich as colleague of Dr. Lord in 1778.)
   (Pastor of Church 1784-1834.)

VI.

Children of (Rev.) Joseph (5) and Mary (Huntington) Strong.

6. JOSEPH H. b. 1781. d. 1855. m. 1805 Lucretia Fanning. b. 1783. d. 1865. dau. of Thomas and Lydia (Tracy) Fanning.
7. CHARLES. b. 1783. d. 1835.
8. MARY HUNTINGTON. b. 1786. d. 1843. m. (as third wife) 1820 Aaron Porter Cleveland of Boston, Mass. b. 1782. d.
      son of Rev. Aaron and Abiah (Hyde) Cleveland.
9. HENRY. b. 1788. d. 1852. m. 1825 Eunice Edgerton Huntington. b. 1797. d. 1865.
   (Y. C. 1806.)
   (Distinguished as a lawyer.)

TOWNSEND.

I.

1. THOMAS TOWNSEND, b. ab. 1594, d. 1677, m. Mary Newgate (or Newdigate), b. —, d. 1692, sister of John Newdigate of Boston, Mass.
(To Lynn, Mass., in 1635.)

II.

2. SAMUEL, b. 1637, d. 1704, m. Abigail Davis, b. ab. 1641, d. 1727, dau. of Samuel Davis.
(To Rumney Marsh, Chelsea, Mass.)

III.

3. ISAAC, b. 1672, d. 1712, m. 1703 Anne Ruger, b. ab. 1670, d. 1729, dau. of Edmund Ruger of Boston, Mass.
(To Boston, Mass.)

IV.

4. JEREMIAH, b. 1711, d. 1803, m. (1) 1734 Hannah Kneeland (or Cleland), b. ab. 1711, d. 1744, dau. of John Kneeland (or Cleland) of Boston, Mass.
m. (2) 1749 Rebecca (Parkman) Coit, b. ab. 1721, d. 1778, widow of Capt. Nathaniel Coit of Boston, Mass.

V.

5. NATHANIEL, b. 1747, d. 1834, m. 1774 Hannah Hughes, b. 1758, d. 1801, dau. of John and Zipperah (Hartshorn) Hughes.
(To Norwich, Ct.)

VI.

Children of Nathaniel (5) and Hannah (Hughes) Townsend.

6. FANNY, b. 1775, d. 1836.
7. JOHN HUGHES, b. 1778, d. 1785.
8. CHARLES, bapt. 1780, d. —.
9. HENRY, b. —, d. —.
10. REBECCA PARKMAN, b. —, d. —.

[569]

TRACY.

I.

1. (Lt.) THOMAS TRACY. b. ab 1610. d. 1685. m. (1) 1641 ( ) Mason. b. d. widow of Edward Mason.
   m. (2) Martha (Bourne) Bradford. b. d. widow of John Bradford,
   and dau. of Dea. Thomas and Martha) Bourne of Marshfield, Mass.
   m. (3) ab. 1683 Mary (Foster) Goodrich. b. ab. 1623. d. widow, first of John Stoddard,
   then of John Goodrich and dau. of Nathaniel and Elizabeth (Deming) Foote of Wethersfield, Ct.

II.

Children of (Lt.) Thomas (1) and widow (Mason) Tracy.

2. JOHN. b. 1642. d. 1702. m. 1670 Mary Winslow. b. 1646. d. 1721. dau. of Josiah and Margaret (Bourne) Winslow of Marshfield, Ct.
3. (Lt.) JONATHAN. b. 1644. d. 1711. m. (1) 1672 Mary Griswold. b. 1656. d. 1711. dau. of Lt. Francis Griswold.
   (Preston, Ct.) m. (2) 1711 Mary Richards. b. d. 1723.
   She m. (2) 1717 Eleazer Jewett. b. d.
4. THOMAS. b. ab. 1646. d. ab. 1724. m. bef. 1675.
5. MIRIAM. b. 1649-50. d. m. 1668 Thomas Waterman.
6. (Dr.) SOLOMON. b. 1650-1. d. 1732. m. (1) 1676 Sarah Huntington. b. 1654. d. 1683.
   m. (2) 1686 Sarah (Bliss) Shuman, widow of Thomas Shuman. b. 1647. d. 1739.
7. DANIEL. b. 1652. d. 1722. m. (1) 1682 Abigail Adgate. b. 1661. d. 1711.
   m. (2) 1712 Hannah (Backus) Bingham. b. d. widow of Thomas Bingham,
   and dau. of Lt. William and Elizabeth (Pratt) Backus.
8. SAMUEL. b. ab. 1654. d. 1693. unm.

III.

Children of John (2) and Mary (Winslow) Tracy.

9. JOSIAH. b. and d. 1671.
10. JOHN. b. 1672. d. 1726. m. 1697 Elizabeth Leffingwell. b. 1676. d. 1737.
11. ELIZABETH. b. 1676. d. 1739. m. 1792 (as second wife) Nathaniel Backus.
12. (Capt.) JOSEPH. b. 1682. d. 1765. m. 1705 Mary Abel. b. 1685. d. 1751. dau. of Caleb and Margaret (Post) Abel.
13. WINSLOW. b. 1688. d. dau. of Joshua and Hannah (Bradford) Ripley.
    m. 1714 Rachel Ripley. b. 1693. d.

[57]

TRACY.—Continued.

III.

Children of (11.) Jonathan (3) and Mary (Griswold) Tracy.

14. JONATHAN. b. 1675. d. 1794. m. 1799 Anna Palmer. b. d.
15. HANNAH. b. 1677. d. m. 1695 Thomas Davison. b. d. 1724.
16. CHRISTOPHER. b. 1680. d. 1724-5. m. 1705 Livia Parish. b. d.
17. MARY. b. 1682. d. m. 1705 Benjamin Parish. b. d.
18. MIRIAM. b. 1685. d. m. 1707 Issue Cork. b. d.
19. DAVID. b. 1687. d. m. 1709 Sarah Parish. b. d. 1727-9.
20. FRANCIS. b. 1690. d. 1755. m. 1713-14 Elizabeth Parish. b. d.
21. SARAH. b. 1692. d. 1693.
22. SAMUEL. b. 1697. d. m. 1733 Esther Richmond. b. d. dau. of John and Elizabeth ( ) Richmond of Westerly, R. I.

Children of Thomas (4) and ( ) Tracy.

23. NATHANIEL. b. 1675. d. 1751. m. 1796 Sarah Miner. b. 1679 (?) d. perh. dau. of Joseph and Mary (Avery) Miner of Stonington, Ct.
24. SARAH. b. 1677. d. m. (?) Joseph Miner. b. d. brother of Nathaniel's wife.
25. JEREMIAH. b. 1682. d. m. 1713 Mary Witter. b. 1691. d. dau. of Ebenezer and Dorothy (Morgan) Witter.
26. DANIEL. b. 1685. d. 1794.
27. THOMAS. b. 1687. d. 1755. m. Abigail b. d.
28. (Gra.) JEDIDIAH. b. 1692. d. 1779. m. (1) 1714 Margaret Rix. b. d. 1727.
    m. (2) 1728 Merey (Safford) Parke. b. 1697. d. 1775. widow of Ezekiel Parke and dau. of John Safford.
29. DEBORAH. } b. 1697. d. m. 1720 Eliashab Adams. b. d. 1733.
30. JERUSHA. } d. m. 1718 Thomas Rix. b. d.

Children of (Dr.) Solomon (6) and Sarah (Huntington) Tracy.

31. LYDIA. b. 1677. d. 1757. m. 1698 Dea. Thomas Leffingwell.
32. SIMON. b. 1679-80. d. 1775. m. 1707-8 Mary Leffingwell. b. 1682. d. 1779.

Children of (Dr.) Solomon (6) and Sarah (Bliss) (Sluman) Tracy.

33. SOLOMON. b. 1688. d. 1751. m.
    (To Canterbury, Ct.)

Children of Daniel (7) and Abigail (Adgate) Tracy.

34. DANIEL. b. 1688. d. 1771. m. 1710-11 Abigail Leffingwell. b. 1691. d. 1777.

TRACY.—Continued.

III.

Children of Daniel (7) and Hannah (Backus) (Bingham) Tracy.

35. ELIZABETH, b. 1712-13, d. 1715.
36. SAMUEL, b. 1714-15, d.

IV.

Children of (Capt.) Joseph (12) and Mary (Abel) Tracy.

37. JOSEPH, b. 1706, d. 1757, m. 1739 Ann Hinckley, b. 1716, d. 1801, dau. of Gershon and Mary (Buel) Hinckley of Lebanon, Ct.
38. MARY, b. 1708, d.   m. (?)   Benjamin Wentworth, b. 1698, d. 1764, perhaps son of Paul Wentworth.
39. MARGARET, b. 1710, d. 1765, m. 1733 William Waterman.
40. (Dr.) ELISHA, b. 1712, d. 1783, m. (1) 1743 Lucy Huntington, b. 1722, d. 1754.
    m. (2) 1754 Elizabeth Dorr, b. 1735, d. 1781, dau. of Edmund and Mary (Griswold) Dorr of Lyme, Ct.
    m. (3) 1781 Lois (Hinckley) Huntington, b.   d. 1790, widow of Nehemiah Huntington.
41. ZERVIAH, b. 1714, d.   unm.
42. LYDIA, b. 1716, d.   m. 1741 Elisha Hyde, b. 1714, d. 1759, son of William and Anne (Bushnell) Hyde.
43. IRENE, b. 1719, d.   m. 1743 Daniel Burnham, b. 1715, d.   son of Eleazer and Lydia (Waterman) Burnham.
44. PHINEHAS, b. 1720, d.   unm.
45. JERUSHA, b. 1723, d. 1764, m. (1) 1742 Rev. Jedediah Hyde, b. 1712, d. 1761, son of William and Anne (Bushnell) Hyde.
    She m. (2) 1763 Daniel Peck.
46. ELIZABETH, b.   d.   m. Andrew Abel, b. 1717, d. 1796, son of Benjamin and Lydia (Hazen) Abel.

Children of Winslow (13) and Rachel (Ripley) Tracy.

47. JOSHUA, b. and d. 1715.
48. PEREZ, b. 1716, d. 1501, m. 1740 Elizabeth Hyde, b. 1724, d. 1805, dau. of Capt. William and Anne (Basset) Hyde.
49. JOSIAH, b. 1718, d.   m. (1) 1740 Rachel Allen, b. 1719, d. 1761, dau. of Timothy and Rachel (Bushnell) Allen.
    m. (2) 1762 Esther (Richards) Pride, b.   d.   wid. of Micajah Pride.
50. ELIPHALET, b. 1720, d.   m. 1743 Sarah Manning, b. 1723-4 (?) d.   perh. dau. of Samuel and Irene (Ripley) Manning of Windham, Ct.
51. NEHEMIAH, b. 1722, d.
52. SAMUEL, b. 1724, d.
53. SOLOMON, b. 1728, d.   m. 1755 Anne Edgerton, b. 1733, d.   dau. of Samuel and Margaret (Abel) Edgerton.

TRACY.—Continued.

IV.

Children of Simon (32) and Mary (Leffingwell) Tracy.

54. SIMON. b. 1709. d. 1709-10.
55. SIMON. b. 1710. d. 1793. m. (1) 1735 Elizabeth Hyde. b. 1711. d. 1741.
    m. (2) 1743-4 Abigail Bushnell. b. 1718. d. 1774.
56. CIVIL. b. 1712. d. 1743-?. m. 1735 John Huntington, dau. of Capt. John and Sarah (Abel) Leffingwell.
57. MOSES. b. 1714. d.   m. 1737 Sarah Leffingwell. b. 1718. d.
58. MARY. b. ab. 1715. d. 1786. m. 1749 John Huntington (former husband of sister Civil).
59. JOB. b. 1716-7. d. 1719.
60. LYDIA. b. 1719. d.   m. 1743 (as second wife) John Perkins.

(Children of Daniel (34) and Abigail (Leffingwell) Tracy.

61. ABIGAIL. b. 1710. d. 1725.
62. DANIEL. b. 1718. d. 1728.
63. SAMUEL. b. 1723. d. 1798 of smallpox. m. 1750 Sibyl Lathrop. b. 1726. d. 1802.
64. HANNAH. b. 1727. d. 1753. m. 1751 Simon Huntington. b. 1719. d. 1801.
65. DANIEL. b. and d. 1730.
    (And others.)

V.

Children of (Dr.) Elisha (40) and Lucy (Huntington) Tracy.

66. LUCY. b. 1741. d.   m. 1763 Dr. Philip Turner.
67. ALICE. b. 1745. d.   m. 1770 Elisha Leffingwell.
68. LUCRETIA. b. 1747. d. 1825. unm.
69. LYDIA. b 1749. d. 1825. m.   Alvan Fosdick. b.   d.
70. PHILURA. b. 1751. d. 1816. m. 1782 Samuel Huntington.

Children of (Dr.) Elisha (40) and Elizabeth (Dorr) Tracy.

71. PHOEBE AR. b. 1755. d. 1775 in the army at Roxbury, Mass.
72. (Dr.) PHILEMON. b. 1757. d. 1837. m. 1785 Abigail Trott. b. 1759. d. 1835.
73. ELIZABETH. b. 1760. d. 1773.
74. CHARLOTTE. b. 1762. d. 1820. unm.
75. MARY. b. 1764. b. 1837. unm.
76. (Col.) ELISHA. b. 1766. d. 1842. m. 1790 Lucy Coit Huntington. b. 1772. d. 1840.
77. DEBORAH DORR. b. 1770. d. 1824. unm.
78. JOSEPH WINSLOW. b. 1769. d. 1770.

TRACY.—Continued.

V.

Children of Josiah (49) and Rachel (Allen) Tracy.

79. IRENE. b. 1741. d. m. 1763 Gideon Peck.
80. NEHEMIAH. b. 1744. d. He m. (2) 1769 Sarah Edgecomb. b. d.
81. DANIEL. b. 1746. d. 1747–8. m. Miriam Waterman. b. d.
82. ANNE. b. 1748. d.
83. JERUSHA. b. 1751. d.
84. CALVIN. b. 1753. d. 1755.
85. DANIEL. b. 1756. d. m. 1783 Lucy Tracy. b. 1762. d. 1807. dau. of Josiah and Margaret (Pettis) Tracy of Franklin. (Norwich, Boston and Dover, N. H.)
86. CALVIN. b. 1759. d. m. 1781 Elizabeth Huntington. b. 1763. d. dau. of Barnabas and Anna (Wright) Huntington. (To Coventry, Ct., then to W. New York, and last to Ohio.)

Children of Josiah (49) and Esther (Richards) (Pride) Tracy.

87. RACHEL. b. 1763. d. 1777.
88. MEHITABLE. b. 1765. d. m. 1782 Abel Edgerton. b. 1760. d. son of Capt. Elisha and Zerviah (Abel) Edgerton. (To Coventry, Ct.)

Children of Simon (55) and Elizabeth (Hyde) Tracy.

89. ELIZABETH. b. 1738. d. unm.
90. JABEZ. b. 1740. d. 1828. m. (1) 1763 Zipporah Hebard. b. d. 1769. dau. of Nathan and Zipporah (Bushnell) Hebard of Windham, Ct.
    m. (2) 1776 Hannah Edgerton. b. 1753. d. 1799. dau. of John and Elizabeth (Prentis) Edgerton.
91. MARY. b. 1741. d. 1803. m. 1766 Dea. Jonathan Rudd of Windham, Ct. b. 1743. d. son of Jonathan and Esther (Taylor) Rudd.

Children of Simon (55) and Abigail (Bushnell) Tracy.

92. ABIGAIL. b. 1744. d. 1746.
93. ABIGAIL, 2nd. b. 1746. d.
94. MUNDATOR. b. 1749. d. 1816. m. (1) 1773 Caroline Bushnell. b. 1747. d. 1785.
    m. (2) 1786 Nabby Lord. b. 1754. d. 1821.
95. SIMON. b. 1752. d. 1755.

[574]

TRACY.—Continued.

V.

Children of Samuel (63) and Sibyl (Lathrop) Tracy.

96. DANIEL. b. 1751. d. 1753.
97. SIBYL. b. 1753. d. 1793. m. Wheeler Coit. b. 1738-9. d.   son of Col. Samuel and Sarah (Spalding) Coit.
    He m. (1) 1765 Mehitable Lester. b. 1749. d. 1774. dau. of Timothy and Mehitable (Belcher) Lester of Preston, Ct.
    m. (3) 1793 Hannah (Lord) Abel. b. 1755. d. ab. 1841. widow of Isaac Abel and dau. of Joseph and Lucy (Abgate) Lord.
98. LYDIA. b. 1755. d. 1757. m. 1777 Thomas Fanning. b. 1750. d. 1813. son of Thomas and Anna (Reynolds) Fanning.
    He m. (2) 1789 Lydia Coit. b. 1760. d. 1789. dau. of Capt. William and Sarah (Lathrop) Coit.
    He m. (3) 1793 Lucy (Coit) Ledyard. b.   d.
99. DANIEL. b. 1758. d. 1782. m. 1782 Lucretia Hubbard. b. 1762. d. 1777.
    She m. (2) 1784 Elijah Backus, 2nd.
100. ZERUIAH. b. 1760. d.
    (To Windham, Ct.)
101. (Pr.) EBENEZER. b. 1762. d.   m. (2) 1800 Anna Vera Kirtland. b. 1793. d.   dau. of Daniel Kirtland of Norwich, Ct.
    (To Middletown, Ct.)
102. ABIGAIL. b. 1765. d.   m. 1795 Capt. John Fanning. b. 1758. d.   son of Thomas and Anna (Reynolds) Fanning.
103. (Maj.) THOMAS. b. 1767. d. 1860. m. 1804 Elizabeth Avery. b. 1781. d. 1822.

VI.

Children of (Dr.) Philemon (72) and Abigail (Trott) Tracy.

104. PHINEHAS LYMAN. b. 1789. d.   m.   Harriet Lay. b.   d.   dau. of John Lay of Cassill, N. Y.
    (N. C. 1807.)
    (M. C. from Batavia, N. Y.)
105. (Judge) EDWARD DORR. b. 1791. d.   m. (1)   Susan Campbell. b.   d. 1834.
    m. (2) 1835 Caroline Campbell. b.   d.
106. (Dr.) RICHARD PROCTOR. b. 1791. d. 1871. unm.
    (N. C. 1816.)
107. ALBERT HALLER. b. 1793. d. 1859. m. 1825 Harriet (Foote) Norton. b.   d.
    (Buffalo, N. Y.)   dau. of Ebenezer and Abigail (Kibbe) Norton of Canandaigua, N. Y.
    (M. C.)
108. FRANCES. b. 1795. d. 1802.
109. HARRIET FRANCES. b. 1788. d. 1830. unm.

TRACY.—Continued.

VI.

Children of Daniel (85) and Lucy (Tracy) Tracy.

110. LUCY. b. 1774 at Norwich. d. m. Dr. Wheeler Palmer. b. d. 1800 at Richfield Springs. (Otsego, N. Y.)
111. NANCY. b. 1776 at Norwich. d. m. 1805 at Franklin. Atkyus Clark. b. d. of Boston, Mass. (To Boston, Mass.)
112. FRANCES. b. d. unm.
113. AUGUSTA. b. d.
114. LUCRETIA. b. d.

Children of Munlator (94) and Caroline (Bushnell) Tracy.

115. SIMON. b. 1781. d. 1799 unm.
116. JEDEDIAH. b. 1784. d. m. 1812 Mercy M. Doane. b. d.
117. CLARISSA. b. 1776. d. 1781.
118. PHEBE. b. 1779. d. m. 1812 Simeon Woodworth. b. d.

Children of (Maj.) Thomas (105) and Elizabeth (Avery) Tracy.

119. ANN THOMAS. b. 1806. d. 1843. m. 1834 James T. Richards. b. ab. 1807. d. 1835. son of Charles and Lydia (Fanning) Richards.

VII.

Children of James T. and Ann Thomas (Tracy) (119) Richards.

120. THOMAS TRACY. b. 1835. d. 1851.
121. ELIZABETH TRACY. b. 1837. d. 1845.

TROTT.

I.

1. THOMAS TROTT. b. ab. 1614. d. 1696. m. Sarah ——— b. ——— d. 1712.

II.

2. SAMUEL. b. 1660. d. 1724. m ——— Mercy Leal. b. ab. 1670. d. 1761. dau. of Benjamin and Bathsheba (———) Beal. (Dorchester, Mass.)

III.

3. THOMAS. b. ——— d. 1777. m. 1727 Waitstill Payson. b. ——— d. 1744. (Blacksmith.)

IV.

4. JONATHAN. b. ——— d. ——— m. (?) 1725 Lydia Proctor. b. 1736. d. 1805. (Jeweller in Boston, Mass., in 1772.) (?) dau. of John and Lydia (Richards) Proctor of Boston, Mass., and New London, Ct. (Moved to Norwich and kept the Peck Tavern.)

Children of Jonathan (4) and Lydia (Proctor) Trott.

5. LYDIA. b. 1755. d. 1825. unm.
6. ABIGAIL. b. 1759. d. 1835. m. 1775 Dr. Philemon Tracy.
7. JOHN PROCTOR. b. ——— d. ——— m. 1796 Lois Chapman. b. 1772. d. ——— dau. of Joseph and Elizabeth (Abel) Chapman. (To New London, Ct.)
8. GEORGE WASHINGTON. bapt. 1777. d. ——— m. (1) 1799 Sarah Rogers Marvin. b. 1781. d. 1805. dau. of Gen. Elihu and Elizabeth (Rogers) Marvin. m. (2) ——— Lydia Chapman. b. 1776. d. ——— dau. of Joseph and Elizabeth (Abel) Chapman.

Children of John Proctor (7) and Lois (Chapman) Trott.

9. JOHN. b. 1797. d. ———
10. ELIZABETH. b. 1798. d. ——— m. 1823 Brig. Gen. Jirah Isham of New London, Ct. b. 1777 at Colchester. d. 1842
11. THOMAS P. b. 1799. d. ———
12. LOUISA. b. 1801. d. ———
13. LYDIA. b. 1803. d. ———
14. STASIRA G. b. 1804. d. ——— m. 1832 Catherine E. Thompson. b. ——— d. ———
15. MARY JOHNSTON. b. 1806. d. ———
16. NANCY DOW. b. 1808. d. ———

Children of George Washington (8) and Sarah (Marvin) Trott.

17. ELIHU MARVIN. b. 1805. d. ——— m. 1832 Mary Clark. b. ——— d. ———

Children of George Washington (8) and Lydia (Chapman) Trott.

18. ——— b. ——— d. ——— m. ——— Hon. George W. Woodward of Pennsylvania.

TRUMBULL.

I.

1. JOHN TRUMBLE (or TRUMBULL), b.   d. 1757. m.   Ann Swan, b.   d.   dau. of Richard.
   (From Cumberland, Co. England, to New England.)
   (At Roxbury in 1640.)
   (To Rowley, Essex Co., Mass.)

II.

2. JOSEPH, b.   d.   m.
   (Living in Suffield in 1675.)

III.

3. (Capt.) JOSEPH, b. 1679. d. 1755. m. 1704 Hannah Higley, b. 1683. d. 1768.
   (Removed to Simsbury, Ct., ab. 1703.)   dau. of John and Hannah (Drake) Higley of Windsor and Simsbury, Ct.
   (To Lebanon, Ct., ab. 1704.)

Children of (Capt.) Joseph (3) and Hannah (Higley) Trumbull.

IV.

4. JOSEPH, b. 1705. Lost at sea 1733. m. 1727 Sarah Buckley. b.   d.
5. JOHN, b. 1722. (?) d.
6. (Gov.) JONATHAN, b. 1710. d. 1785. m. 1735 Faith Robinson, b. 1718. d. 1780.
   (Governor of Connecticut 1769–83.)   dau. of Rev. John and Hannah (Wiswall) Robinson of Duxbury, Mass.
   (Lebanon, Ct.)
7. MARY, b. 1713. d.   m.   Joshua Fitch.
8. HANNAH, b. 1715. d. young.
9. HANNAH, b. 1717.
10. ABIGAIL, b. 1719. d. 1744. m. 1741 Ebenezer Backus.
11. DAVID, b. 1723. drowned 1741 in a mill pond when home on a college vacation.

Children of (Gov.) Jonathan (6) and Faith (Robinson) Trumbull.

V.

12. (Com. Gen.) JOSEPH, b. 1737. d. 1778 s. p. m. 1777 Amelia Dyer, b. 1750. d. 1818.
    dau. of Col. Eliphalet and Huldah (Bowen) Dyer of Windham, Ct.
    She m (2) 1785 Col. Hezekiah Wyllys, b. 1747. d. 1827. of Hartford, Ct.
    son of Col. George and Mary (Woodbridge) Wyllys.
13. (Gov.) JONATHAN, b. 1740. d. 1809. m. 1767 Eunice Backus, b. 1749. d.   dau. of Ebenezer and Eunice (Dyer) Backus of Norwich, Ct.
    (Governor of Connecticut 1797–1809.)
    (H. C. 1759.)
    (Lebanon, Ct.)
14. FAITH, b. 1743. d. 1775. m. 1766 Gen. Jedediah Huntington.
15. MARY, b. 1745. d.   m. 1771 William Williams, b. 1731. d. 1811. son of Rev. Solomon and Mary (Porter) Williams of Lebanon, Ct.
    (H. C. 1751)

TRUMBULL.—Continued.

V.

16. DAVID. b. 1751. d. 1822. m. 1778 Sarah Backus. b. 1760. d. 1846. dau. of Ebenezer and Sarah (Clark) Backus.
17. (Col.) JOHN. b. 1756. d. 1843 s. p. m. Sarah b. 1773. d. 1824. dau. of Sir John Hope.

VI.

Children of (Gov.) Jonathan (13) and Eunice (Backus) Trumbull.

18. JONATHAN. b. 1767. d. young.
19. FAITH. b. 1769. d. m. Daniel Wadsworth. b. d. s. p. of Hartford, Ct. son of Col. Jeremiah Wadsworth.
20. MARY. b. 1777. d. young.
21. HARRIET. b. 1783. d. m. 1809 Prof. Benjamin Silliman of Yale College. b. 1779. d. 1794. son of Gen. Gold Selleck Silliman of Fairfield, Ct.
22. MARIA. b. 1775. d. ab. 1808. m. Henry Hudson. b. d. of Hartford, Ct.

Children of David (16) and Sarah (Backus) Trumbull.

23. SARAH. b. 1779. d. m. William T. Williams. b. d.
24. ABIGAIL. b. 1781. d. m. 1801 Peter Lauman, Jun. b. 1769. d. son of Peter and Sarah (Coit) Lauman.
25. JOSEPH. b. 1782. d.
26. JOHN. b. 1784. d.
27. JONATHAN. b. 1786. d. inf.
28. JONATHAN. b. 1789. d. 1853. m. 1815 Jane Eliza Lathrop. b. 1795. d. 1843.

TURNER.

I.

1. HUMPHREY TURNER. b. ab. 1593. d. 1673. m. Lydia Gamer. b. d. bef. 1673.
(Said to have come from Essex, Eng., to Plymouth, ab. 1722–30.)
(To Scituate, Mass., ab. 1633.)
(Was a tanner, prominent citizen, deputy and constable.)

II.

2. "YOUNG" JOHN. b. d. 1687. m. 1649 Ann James. b. d.

III.

3. PHILIP. b. 1673. d. m. Elizabeth Nash. d. ( ) Nash of Weymouth, later of Scituate, Mass.
perh. dau. of Joseph and Elizabeth ( )

IV.

4. (Capt.) PHILIP. b. 1715. d. 1755. m. 1739 Anne (Huntington) Adgate. b. 1715. d. 1759.
widow of Thomas Adgate and dau. of Daniel and Abigail (Bingham) Huntington.
She m. (1) 1731 Thomas Adgate.
m. (3) 1757 Capt. Joshua Abel.

V.

Children of (Capt.) Philip (4) and Anne (Huntington) (Adgate) Turner.

5. (Dr.) PHILIP. b. 1739–40. d. 1815. m. 1763 Lucy Tracy. b. 1744. d.
6. BELA. b. 1742. d. m. (1) 1763 Anne Hyde. b. 1749. d. 1795. dau. of Elisha and Lydia (Tracy) Hyde.
m. (2) 1765 Lydia Frink. b. d.
7. JOHN. b. 1744. d. 1762.
8. ANNA. b. 1746. d.
9. ROGER. b. d. 1754.

VI.

Children of (Dr.) Philip (5) and Lucy (Tracy) Turner.

10. (Dr.) JOHN. b. 1764. d. 1837. m. Hannah Huntington. b. 1765. d. 1845.
11. (Dr.) WILLIAM PITT. b. 1766. d. m. 1813 at New York City Phebe Ferris. b. d.
12. LUCY. b. 1769. d. m. 1791 Dr. Gurdon Lathrop.
13. ANNA. b. 1772. d. 1851. m. 1810 (as third wife) Judge Marvin Waite. b. 1740. d. 1815. of New London.
son of Richard and Elizabeth (Marvin) Waite of Lyme, Ct.
He m. (1) 1779 Patty Jones of New London, Ct. b. d. 1804.
m. (2) 1805 Harriet (Babcock) Saltonstall. b. d. 1805.
widow of Gilbert Saltonstall.
14. ELIZABETH TRACY. b. 1774. d. 1859. m. 1793 Daniel Lathrop.
15. SOPHIA. b. d. s. p. m. Judge Alexander Richards. b. d. of New London, Ct.

TURNER.—Continued.

VI.

Children of Bela (6) and Anne (Hyde) Turner.

16. ANNE, b. 1763. d. 1764.

Children of Bela (6) and Lydia (Frink) Turner.

17. BELA, b. 1767.
18. ANNA, b. d. m. Hopkins.
19. LUCY, b. d. m. Cary.
20. LYDIA, b. d. m. Jones.
21. BELA, b. d. m. Hannerford.

VII.

Children of (Dr.) John (10) and Hannah (Huntington) Turner.

22. MARIONETTE, b. ab. 1789. d. 1829. m. 1817 Rev. George Perkins, b. 1783. d. son of Dr. Elisha and Sarah (Douglas) Perkins of Plainfield, Ct.
23. GEORGE FREDERICK, b. ab. 1792. d. 1813.
24. CHARLES WILLIAMS, b. 1793. d. 1794.
25. BETSEY HUNTINGTON, b. ab. 1794. d. 1835. m. 1829 (as second wife) her brother-in-law, Rev. George Perkins.
26. JULIA FRANCES(?) bapt. 1803. d.

Children of William Pitt (11) and Phebe (Ferris) Turner.

27. GEORGE FREDERICK, b. d.
28. FRANK LATHROP, b. d.
29. MARIONETTE, b. d. m. Ballantyne.
30. MARTIN WARE, b. d.

38

[58]

WATERMAN.

I.

1. ROBERT WATERMAN. b.   d. 1652.   m. 1638 Elizabeth Bourne. b.   d.   ) Bourne of Marshfield, Mass.
   dau. of Dea. Thomas and Martha (
   (At Salem in 1636.)
   (At Plymouth, 1638, and then moved to Marshfield, Mass.)

II.

2. (Sergt.) THOMAS. b. 1644. d. 1708. m. 1668 Miriam Tracy. b. 1649-50. d.
   (To Norwich, Ct., in 1660.)

III.

Children of Thomas (2) and Miriam (Tracy) Waterman.

3. (Ensign) THOMAS. b. 1669-70. d. 1755. m. 1691 Elizabeth Allyn. b. 1665. d. 1755. dau. of John and Elizabeth (Gager) Allyn.
4. JOHN. b. 1672. d.   m. (1) 1701 Elizabeth Lathrop. b. 1679. d. 1708.
                        m. (2) 1709 Judith Woodward. b. 1683. d. 1720.
                        m. (3) 1721 Elizabeth Basset. b.   d.   p-rh. a dau. of David Basset, Boston, Mass.
5. ELIZABETH. b. 1675. d. 1751. m. 1695 John Pitch of Windham. b. 1667. d. 1743.
6. MIRIAM. b. 1678. d. 1760. unm.
7. MARTHA. b. 1680. d. 1755. m. 1708 (as second wife) Capt. Reinold Marvin. b. 1669. d. 1737. of Lyme, Ct.
                                    son of Reinold and Sarah (Clark) Marvin.
                                    (Lyme, Ct.)
8. LYDIA. b. 1683. d.   m. 1708 Eleazer Burnham, Jun. b. 1678. d.   son of Thomas and Lydia (Paigree) Burnham of Ipswich, Mass.
                                    (Norwich, Ct.)
9. JOSEPH. b. 1685. d. 1773. m. 1717 Elizabeth Woodward. b. 1691. d.
10. ANNE. b. 1689. d.   m. 1713 Josiah D-Wolf of Lyme, Ct. b. 1689. d.   son of Simon and Sarah (Lay) DeWolf.
                                    (Lyme, Ct.)

IV.

Children of John (4) and Elizabeth (Lathrop) Waterman.

11. ELIZABETH. b. 1702. d. 1752. m. 1724 Jonathan Avery of Norwich. b. 1683. d.
                                        son of Thomas and Hannah (Miner) Avery of Montville, Ct.
    He m. (2) 1752 Dorothy (Denison) Copp, widow of David Copp of Montville, Ct.
12. ELEAZER. b. 1704. d.   m. 1731 Martha Adgate. b. 1710. d. 1755.
13. JOHN. b. 1706. d. 1730. unm.
14. HANNAH. b. 1708. d. 1759. m. (1) 1730 Capt. Absalom King. b.   d. 1732. of Southold, L. I., and Norwich, Ct.
                              m. (2) 1733 Capt. Benedict Arnold. b.   d.

WATERMAN.—Continued.

IV.

Children of John (4) and Judith (Woodward) Waterman.

15. WILLIAM. b. 1710. d. 1789 m. 1733 Margaret Tracy. b. 1710. d.
16. SAMUEL. b. 1712. d.
17. EBENEZER. b. 1715. d. m. (?) 1748-9 Elizabeth (Chapman) Comstock of New London. b. d.
    dau. of Jeremiah Chapman and widow of
18. PETER. b. 1717. d.

Children of John (4) and Elizabeth (Basset) Waterman.

19. MARY. b. 1722. d.
20. DAVID BASSET. b. 1725. d.
21. ELIZABETH. b. 1730. d. 1795. m. 1751 Nathaniel Backus. b. 1727. d. 1777. son of Nathaniel and Hannah (Baldwin) Backus.
    He m. (2) 1749 Elizabeth Leffingwell.
    She m. (2) 1790 Rev. Levi Hart.

WHEATLEY.

I.

1. LIONEL WHEATLEY. b.   d.   m.   Elinor   b.   d.
   (Boston, Mass.)

II.

Children of Lionel (1) and Elinor (   ) Wheatley.

2. SAMUEL. b. and d. 1654.
3. JANE. b. 1655. d.
4. MARY. b. 1659. d.
5. JOHN. b. 1661. d.
6. ELINOR. b. 1665. d.

IV. (?)

7. (Capt.) JOHN. b.   d.   m. 1743 Submit (Peck) Cook. b. 1722. d.   widow of Aaron Cook.
   (To Norwich, Ct.)

V. (?)

Children of (Capt.) John (7) and Submit (Peck) (Cook) Wheatley.

8. LYDIA. bapt. 1744 at Franklin. d.
9. JOHN. bapt. 1746 at Franklin. d.
10. (Lt.) JOHN. bapt. 1748 at Franklin. Killed in the Revolution, 1776. m.   Jane   b.   d.
11. ANDREW. bapt. 1753 at Bozrah. d.
12. LUCINDA. bapt. 1757 at Bozrah. d.
13. LUTHER. bapt. 1761 at Bozrah. d.
14. SUBMIT. bapt. 1765 at Bozrah. d.

VI.

Children of (Lt.) John (10) and Jane (   ) Wheatley.

15. HARRY. } bapt. 1777 at Norwich. d.
16. JOHN. }   d.

[584]

WHITING.

I.

1. (Maj.) WILLIAM WHITING. b.   d. 1647.   m.   Susannah   b.   d. 1673.
(Between 1631–3, assoc. with Lords Say and Brooke   She m. (2) 1650 Samuel Fitch of Hartford, Ct. b.   d. 1659.
and George Wyllys in the Piscataqua purchase.)   m. (3)   (as second wife) Alexander Bryan of Milford, Ct. b.   d. 1679.
(Early settler of Hartford, Ct.)
(A man of wealth and education, and styled in records, "W. Whiting, Gentleman.")
(Magistrate in 1642.)
(Treasurer of the Colony from 1641 till his death.)

II.

2. (Rev.) JOHN.   b. 1635.   d. 1689.   m. (1) ab. 1654 Sibyl Collins.   b.   d.   dau. of Dea. Edward Collins of Cambridge, Mass.
(H. C. 1653.)   m. (2) 1673 Phebe Gregson.   b. 1643   d. 1730.   dau. of Thomas Gregson of New Haven, Ct.
(Pastor of church at Salem, Mass.)   She m. (2) 1692 Rev. John Russell of Hadley, Mass.   b. ab. 1626.   d. 1692
(Ordained 1660 as pastor of First Church of Hartford, Ct.)

III.

3. (Col.) WILLIAM.   b. 1659.   d.   m. 1689 Mary Allyn.   b. 1657.   d. 1724.   dau. of Col. John and Ann (Smith) Allyn of Hartford, Ct.
(Representative from 1710–15.)
(Speaker in General Court, 1714.)
(1693 Captain of a company in Maine.)
(1695 Major. 1709–10–11 Colonel in French and Indian war.)
(Sheriff of Hartford Co., 1722.)
(Removed later to Newport, R. I.)

IV.

4. CHARLES. b. 1692.   d. 1738 at Montville, Ct.   m. 1716–17 Elizabeth Bradford. b. 1696. d. 1777.
(To Montville, Ct.)   dau. of Samuel and Hannah (Rogers) Bradford of Duxbury, Mass.
                                                          She m. (2) 1739 Dea. John Noyes of Stonington, Ct.

WHITING.—Continued.

V.

Children of Charles (4) and Elizabeth (Bradford) Whiting.

5. MARY. b. 1717. d. m. Gardner. b. d. of Hingham, Mass.
6. (Col.) JOHN. b. 1719. d. 1779 at New London, Ct. m. Philena Cogswell or Coggeshall. b. d.
7. SIBYL. b. 1722. d. 1790. m. William Noyes. b. 1715-16. d. son of Dea. John and Mary (Gallup) Noyes of Stonington, Ct.
8. (Capt.) CHARLES. b. 1725. d. ab. 1765. m. 1749 Honor Goodrich. b. 1732. d. dau. of Hezekiah and Honor (Deming) Goodrich of Wethersfield, Ct. She m. (2) 1774 Rev. Joshua Belden of Newington. (Norwich, Ct.)
9. ELIZABETH. b. 1725. d. m. 1775 Samuel Goodrich of Tolland, Ct. b. 1721. d.
10. GAMALIEL. b. 1727. d. m. 1752 Anna Gilbett. b. 1738. d. of New Canaan.
11. WILLIAM BRADFORD. b. 1731. d. at Canaan, N. Y., 1790. m. (1) 1754 Abigail Carew. b. 1728-9. d. 1759. m. (2) 1757 Amy Lathrop. b. 1735. d. 1815. (Norwich, Ct. and Canaan, N. Y.)
12. EBENEZER. b. 1735. d. 1791 at Westfield, Mass. m. 1767 Ann Fitch. b. 1747. d. 1827. dau. of Col. Eleazer and Amy (Bowen) Fitch of Windham, Ct. (Norwich, Ct.)

VI.

Children of (Col.) John (6) and Philena (Cogswell) (?) Whiting.

13. (Dr.) JAMES WOLF. b. d. s. p.
14. ELIZABETH. b. 1759. d. 1831. m. 1772 Daniel Leffingwell.
15. PHILENA. b. d. m. Houghton of Montville, Ct.
16. POLLY. b. d. m. Root.

Children of Charles (8) and Honor (Goodrich) Whiting.

17. CHARLES. b. 1751. d. at Great Barrington, Mass. unm.
18. HONOR. b. 1753. d. m. 1775 Samuel Goodrich. b. 1748. d. son of Samuel and Elizabeth (Whiting) Goodrich of Tolland, Ct.
19. HEZEKIAH. b. 1755. Lost at sea. unm.
20. MARY. b 1757. d. 1799. m. 1778 Capt. John Ducasse (a French officer.) b. d. 1780. She m. (2) Willis of N. C.
21. ELIZABETH. b. 1760. d. 1848. m. Romans.
22. JEFFREY. b. 1762. d. 1790 at Bath, N. C. unm.

[586]

WHITING.—Continued.

VI.

Children of William Bradford (11) and Abigail (Carew) Whiting.

23. ABIGAIL, b. and d. 1756.

Children of William Bradford (11) and Amy (Lathrop) Whiting.

24. WILLIAM, b. 1758, d. 1759.
25. ABIGAIL, b. 1760, d. 1802, m. 1783 Jason Warren.
26. ANNE, b. 1762, d. 1732, m. 1789 Isaiah Tiffany, b.   d. 1800.
27. JOHN, b. 1764, d.   m. (1) 1793 Lydia Lothrop well, b. 1773, d. bef. 1801.
    m. (2) 1801 Rhoda Ellsworth.
28. WILLIAM BRADFORD, b. 1766, d. 1810, m. 1798 Abby Lothrop, b. 1772, d. 1805.
29. DANIEL, b. 1768, d. 1855 at Philadelphia, m. 1794 Betsey Powers, b.   d.
30. HANNAH, b. 1770, d. 1774.
31. ARTHUR, b. 1772, d. 1848 at New Haven, Ct. m. 1801 Lydia Backus, b.   d. 1832, dau. of Ebenezer and Elizabeth (Fitch) Backus.
    (To New Haven, Ct.)   m. (2) 1838 Mrs. N. B. Williams.
32. SAMUEL, b. 1775, d. 1834, m. (1) 1802 Fanny Lothingwell, b. 1783, d. 1804.
    m. (2) 1806 Mrs. Innuel Kittsley.
33. HARRIET, b. 1777, d. 1804, m.   Ebenezer Fitch Backus, b. 1779, d. 1859, son of Ebenezer and Elizabeth (Fitch) Backus.
    He m. (2) 1807 Elizabeth Chester, b. 1774, d. 1847,
    dau. of Col. John and Elizabeth (Huntington Chester of Wethersfield, Ct.
34. CHARLES, b. and d. 1778.

[587]

WHITON (or WHITING.)

I.

1. JAMES WHITON (or WHITING.) b.   d. 1710. m. 1647 Mary Beal.   dau. of John and Margaret (Hobart) Beal.
   (At Hingham in 1647.)
   (Farmer and wealthy citizen.)

II.

2. JAMES. b. 1651. d. 1724-5. m.   Abigail.   b. ab. 1655. d. 1740.
   (South Hingham.)
   (Farmer.)

III.

3. SAMUEL. b. 1675. d.   m. (1) 1711-2 Margaret Tower. b. 1686-7.   d. 1738. dau. of Samuel and Silence (Danon) Tower.
   (Farmer.)   m. (2) 1739 Mrs. Elizabeth (Garnet) Williams. b. 1693. d. 1747.
   (Commonly known as   widow of Charles Williams and dau. of James and Elizabeth (Ward) Garnet.
   "King" Whiting.)   m. (3) 1747 Mrs. Rebecca Garnet. b.   d. 1767. widow of John Garnet.

IV.

4. DANIEL. b. 1722. d.   m.   Joel Danon. b. ab. 1710. d. 1812. of Scituate, Mass.
   (Constable.)

V.

5. ZENAS. b. 1754. d.   m. (1) 1773 Sarah Loring. b.   d. 1779.
                          m. (2) 1779 Leah Loring. b. 1754. d.   dau. of Thomas and Bethia (Smith) Loring.
                          m. (3)   Phebe (   ) Raymond. b.   d.   widow of Ebenezer (?) Raymond.

VI.

6. SARAH. b. 1779. d.   m.   Peakes Groce. b.   d.

Children of Zenas (5) and Sarah (Loring) Whiting.

7. ZENAS LORING. b. 1780 at Hingham. d. 1801 at Norwich, Ct.
8. HARRIET. b. 1782. d.

Children of Zenas (5) and Leah (Loring) Whiting.

9. SOPHIA. b. 1784. d. 1865 at New Haven, Ct. m.   Capt. Shubael Bronson. b. 1788. Lost at sea 1819.
10. FRANCES. b.   d.
11. LEAH.   } bapt. 1792.
12. DANIEL. }

[588]

WICKWIRE.

I.

1. JOHN WICKWIRE. b.   d. 1712. m. 1676 Mary Tongue. b. 1656. d.   ) Tongue of New London, Ct.
(Settled early at Mohegan or Montville, Ct.)   dau. of George and Margery (
(Col. John Livingston was one of the executors of his will.)

Children of John (1) and Mary (Tongue) Wickwire.

II.

2. GEORGE. b. 1677.
3. CHRISTOPHER. b. 1679–80. d.   m.
4. JOHN. b. 1685. d.   m. 1705 Abigail Houghton. b.   d.
5. ELIZABETH. b. 1688–9.
6. JONATHAN. b. 1691. d.   m. 1717 Elizabeth Haughton. b.   d.
   (To Norwich, Ct.)
7. PETER. b. 1694. d. 1744. m.   Patience Chappell. b.   d.
8. ANN. b. 1697. d.   m. 1712 James Brown of Colchester, Ct.

Children of Jonathan (6) and Elizabeth (Haughton) Wickwire.

III.

9. KATHARINE. bapt. 1722. d.   m. 1746 Mary Barstow. b.   d.
10. ALPHEUS. bapt. 1722. d.
    (To Norwich, Ct.)
11. JONATHAN. b. 1725. d.
12. DELIGHT. b. 1735. d.

Children of Peter (7) and Patience (Chappell) Wickwire.

13. PETER. b. 1724. d.   m.   Rhoda Schofield. b.   d.
    (To Nova Scotia.)
14. SARAH. b. 1725. d. 1750.
15. GEORGE. b. 1727–8. d.   m. 1749–50 Elizabeth Culver. b.   d.   dau. of John (?) Culver.
    (To Norwich, Ct.)
16. JAMES. b. and d. 1729.
17. EUNICE. b. 1730. d. 1732.
18. AMY. b. 1732. d.   m.   McClennahan. b.   d.
19. JOSEPH b. 1734. d.   m.   Story. b.   d.
20. JEREMIAH. b. 1736. d.   m.   Phebe Baker. b.   d.
21. SAMUEL. b. 1738. d.
22. JOHN. b. 1740. d.
23. EZEKIEL. b. 1741. d.

WICKWIRE.—Continued.

IV.

Children of Alpheus (10) and Mary (Barstow) Wickwire.

24. MARY. b. 1747. d.
25. ANNA. b. 1750. d.
26. JEDEDIAH. b. 1753. d. m.
    (Norwich, Ct.)

Children of George (15) and Elisabeth (Culver) Wickwire.

27. BETTY. b. 1750. d. m. 1771 Capt. Alpheus Billings. b.   d.
28. PATIENCE. b. 1753. d.
29. LUCY. b. 1755. d.
30. HANNAH. b. 1757. d.

[59]

WINSHIP.

I.

1. EDWARD WINSHIP. b. ab. 1613. d. 1688. m. (1) Jane Wilkinson. b. d. prob. dau. of widow Isabella Wilkinson. b. ab. 1633. d. 1690.
(Settled in Cambridge, Mass., in 1635.) m. (2) bef. 1652 Elizabeth
(Served as Lieutenant, Selectman and Representative.)

II.

2. JOSEPH. b. 1661. d. 1725. m. (1) 1687 Sarah Harrington. b. 1671. d. 1710.
dau. of Robert and Susanna (George) Harrington of Watertown, Ct.
(Lived at Menot.) m. (2) Sarah b. d.
(Selectman.)

III.

3. JOSEPH. b. 1700-1 d. 1761. m. Anna b. ab. 1705. d. 170..
(Moved from Menot to Charlestown, Mass.)

IV.

Children of Joseph (3) and Anna ( ) Winship.

4. FRANCIS. b. 1723. d. 1752. (?) (A Francis Winship married in Norwich in 1760, Eunice Geer, and had a son Joseph. b. 1760.)
5. SARAH. b. 1725. d. 1744. m. Henry Spring. b. d.
6. (Capt.) JOSEPH. b. 1727. Lost at sea, 1765. m. 1750 Elizabeth Lathrop. b. 1730. d.
(To Norwich, Ct.)
7. ANNA. b. 1728. d. 1792. m. 1749 Samuel Manning of Norwich.
(To Norwich, Ct.)
8. MARY. b. 1730. d. m. 1751 Ebenezer Wyeth. b. d.
9. AMOS. b. 1731. d. young.
10. JOANNA. b. 1733. d. m. 1757 Andrew Wilson. b. d.
11. PHILEMON. b. 1735. d. m. 1762 Mary Stedman. b. 1742. d. dau. of Nathan and Abigail (Hazen) Stedman of Norwich, Ct.
(To Norwich, Ct.)
12. AMOS. b. 1736. d.

[59]

WINSHIP.—Continued.

V.

Children of (Capt.) Joseph (6) and Elizabeth (Lathrop) Winship.

13. JOSEPH. b. 1750-1. d. 1752.
14. JABEZ. b. 1752. d. m. 1771 Hannah Foresides of New London, (prob. Forsyth.) b. d.
15. JOSEPH. b. 1754. Lost at sea, 1765.
16. ELIZABETH. b. 1756. d. m. Green. b. d.
17. NABBY. b. 1758. d.
18. ANNA. b. 1759. d. 1759. m. Irijah Sanger. b. 1759. d. son of Irijah and Lydia (Roath) Sanger.
19. PHILOTHETA. b. 1761. d. m. Simon Bundy. b. d.
20. PHILEMON. b. 1763. d.

Children of (Capt.) Philemon (11) and Mary (Stedman) Winship.

21. ABIGAIL. b. 1765. d.
22. GEORGE. b. 1770. d.
23. MARY. b. 1771. d. m. 1790 Stephen Barker, Jun. b. d.
24. JOHN STEDMAN. b. 1787. d. m. 1807 Patty Smith. b. d.

WOODBRIDGE.

I.

From "The Woodbridge Record" by Louis Mitchell, formerly of Norwich, Ct.:

1. (Rev.) JOHN. b. 1613. d. 1695. m. 1639 Mercy Dudley. b. 1621. d. 1691.) Dudley of Roxbury, Mass. dau. of Gov. Thomas and Dorothy (

   (Son of Rev. John Woodbridge of the parish of Stanton, near Highworth in Wiltshire, and Sarah Parker, dau. of Rev. Robert Parker.)
   (Educated at Oxford.)
   (Came in 1634 in ship Mary and John to Newbury, Mass.)
   (Town Clerk of Newbury from 1634 to 1638.)
   (1643 kept school in Boston.)
   (Ordained minister at Andover 1645.)
   (Returned to England in 1647. Was Chaplain to Parliamentary Commissioners who treated with the King at the Isle of Wight, and afterward minister at Andover, Hants, and Barford St. Martin, Wiltshire, until ejected at the Restoration.)
   (Established a school at Newbury, Eng., from which he was driven by the Bartholomew Act in 1663.)
   (Returned to Newbury, Mass., and became assistant to his uncle, Rev. Thomas Parker, until 1670.)
   (Assistant of Massachusetts Colony 1683-4.)

II.

2. (Rev.) JOHN. b. 1644. d. 1691. m. 1671 Abigail Leete. b.   d. 1710 at Simbury, Ct. dau. of Gov. William Leete of Guilford, Ct.
   (H. C. 1664.)
   (Minister at Killingworth and Wethersfield, Ct.)

III.

3. (Rev.) EPHRAIM. b. 1680. d. 1725. m. 1704 Hannah Morgan. b.   d.   dau. of Capt. John Morgan of Groton, Ct.
   (H. C. 1701.)
   (Minister at Groton, Ct.)

IV.

4. (Dr.) DUDLEY. b. 1705. d. 1791. m.   Sarah Sheldon. b. 1721. d. 1796. dau. of Dea. Isaac and Elizabeth (Pratt) Sheldon of Hartford, Ct.
   (H. C. 1724.)
   (Physician at Stonington, Ct.)

[593]

WOODBRIDGE.—Continued

V.

Children of (Dr.) Dudley (4) and Sarah (Sheldon) Woodbridge.

5. WILLIAM. b. 1745. d. 1825 s. p. m. Zerviah Williams. b. d.
   (Y. C. 1765.)
   (To Norwich, Ct.)
6. (Hon.) DUDLEY. b. 1747. d. 1823. m. 1774 Lucy Backus. b. 1757. d. 1817. dau. of Elijah and Lucy (Griswold) Backus.
   (Y. C. 1766.)
   (To Norwich, Ct, and Marietta, O.)
7. JOSEPH. b. 1749. d. 1809. m. (1) Elizabeth Sheldon. b. ab. 1754. d. 1777. dau. of Capt. Isaac and Anna (Marsh) Shelton of Hartford, Ct.
   (Y. C. 1771.)   m. (2) 1788 Lucy Sheldon. b. d. dau. of Daniel and Lucretia (La Grosse) Sheldon.
   (Groton and Hartford, Ct.)
8. ELIZABETH. b. 1752. d. 1793. m. 1774 Daniel Rodman. b. 1747. d. ab. 1799.
   (Norwich, Ct, and New York.)   son of Samuel and Penelope (Halloway) Rodman of So. Kingston, R. I.
                                   He m. (2) 1794 Mary Story. b. d. dau. of Capt. Zebedee and Dorothy (Chappell) Story.
9. SAMUEL. b. 1757. d. ab. 1828. m. (1) 1778 Elizabeth Rogers. b. 1758. d. 1800. dau. of Col. Zabdiel and Elizabeth (Tracy) Rogers.
                                 m. (2) Abigail M. Walker. b. d. 1814 at Stratford, Ct.
10. BENJAMIN. b. 1758. d. 1770 in Europe. (?)
11. LUCY. b. 1760. d. unm.
12. CHARLOTTE. b. 1761. d. m. (1) 1779 Capt. Giles Mumford. b. 1759. d. 1795.
                                        son of Thomas and Catharine (Havens) Mumford of Groton, Ct.
                              m. (2) Dr. Simon Wolcott of New London. b. 1749. d.
                                        son of Dr. Alexander and Mary (Richards) Wolcott of Windsor, Ct.
13. SARAH. b. 1767. d. 1855. m. 1793 Col. Simon Rhodes. b. 1760. d. 1844. of New York City.

VI.

Children of (Hon.) Dudley (6) and Lucy (Backus) Woodbridge.

14. LUCY. b. 1775 at Norwich. d. 1816 at Marietta, O. m. 1795 Dr. J. G. Petit of Ohio. b. d. 1826.
15. SARAH. b. 1777. d. 1852. m. 1803 John Mathews. (Putnam) Mathews of New Britain, Mass.
    (To Putnam, O. Afterward near Zanesville, O.)
16. DUDLEY. b. 1778. d. 1853. m. (1) 1807 Jane R. Gilman. b. d. dau. of Benjamin Ives Gilman.
    (To Marietta, O.)   m. (2) Maria Morgan. b. d. dau. of Gen. George Morgan of Morganza.

WOODBRIDGE.—Continued.

VI.

17. (Gov.) WILLIAM. b. 1780. d. 1861 at Detroit, Michigan. m. 1806 Juliana Trumbull. b. d. dau. of Judge John Trumbull of Hartford, Ct., author of "McFingal."
    (M. C. 1819. of Michigan.)
    (Gov. 1839. " ".)
    (U. S. Senator 1841-7 " ".)
18. DAVID. b. 1783. d. 1795 at Gallipolis, O.
19. JOHN. b. 1785. d. 1864. m. 1816 Elizabeth Buchanan of Bourbon, Ky.
    (Settled at Chillicothe, O.)

Children of Samuel (9) and Elizabeth (Rogers) Woodbridge.

20. ELIZA. b. 1780. d. m. 1804 James F. Brown of Norwich, Ct.
    (Later to Roxbury, Mass.)
21. CHARLOTTE. b. 1782. d. young.
22. FRANCES ANN. b. 1785. d. 1806. unm.
23. CHARLOTTE SOPHIA. b. 1787. d. 1851 at Rochester, N. Y. m. 1805 Dyar Perkins. b. 1782. d. 1817 at Trinidad, W. I. son of John and Bedlidh (Baker) Perkins.
24. (Rev.) GEORGE ALFRED. b. 1792. d. m. 1844 Maria McConnel. b. d.
    (Settled at Ross Station, Iowa.)
25. HARRIET. b. 1794. d. 1795.
26. HARRIET. b. 1795. d. 1796.
27. CAROLINE MATILDA. b. 1796. d. m. (1) 1819 Theophilus M. Rogers. b. 1791. d. 1825 at Natchez, Miss.
    son of Zebulon and Fanny (Eldridge) Rogers of Stonington, Ct.
    m. (2) Rev. Barber of Byfield, Mass.
28. HARRIET AUGUSTA. b. 1798. d. m. Augustin Humphrey. b. d.
    (To Winfield, Iowa.) son of Jonathan and Rachel (Dewb) Humphrey of East Bloomfield, N. Y.

Children of Samuel (9) and Abigail (Walker) Woodbridge.

29. ROBERT WALKER. b. 1806. d. 1824 at Stonington, Ct.
30. FRANCES. b. d.
31. ABBY MARGARET. b. 1810. d

[595]

WOODWARD.

I.

1. PETER WOODWARD. b.   d. 1685. m.
   (At Dedham in 1642.)

II.

2. PETER. b.   d. 1721. m.   Mehitable   b.   d.
   (Dedham, Mass.)

Children of Peter (2) and Mehitable (   ) Woodward.

III.

3. WILLIAM. b. 1668. d.
4. ANNA. b. 1669. d.
5. (Rev.) JOHN. b. 1671. d. 1746. m. 1703 Sarah Rosewell. b. 1782. d.   dau. of Richard and Lydia (Trowbridge) Rosewell of New Haven, Ct.
   (H. C. 1693.)
   (Settled at Norwich, Ct., in 1699–1700. To New Haven in 1716.)
6. EBENEZER. b. 1675. d. 1743.
7. MEHITABLE. b. 1677. d. ab. 1700.
8. PETER. b. 1679. d.
9. JUDITH. b. 1683. d. 1720. m. 1709 John Waterman.
   (To Norwich, Ct.)
10. SAMUEL. b. 1685. d.
11. ANNA. b. 1688. d.
12. ELIZABETH. b. 1691. d.   m. 1717 Joseph Waterman.
    (To Norwich, Ct.)

Children of (Rev.) John (5) and Sarah (Rosewell) Woodward.

IV.

13. SARAH. b. 1704. d.
14. LYDIA. b. 1706. d.
15. ROSWELL. b. 1708. d.
16. MARY. b. 1710. d.
17. JOHN. b. 1712. d.
18. ELIZABETH. b. 1713. d.
19. RICHARD. b. 1716. d.

[596]

A few records relating to some residents in Part I, whose lineage we have not been able to trace satisfactorily, are given here.

ROSWELL GAYLORD, b.   d.   m. 1791 Clarissa Downer.   PAGE 71.

PAGE 39.

I.

WILLIAM JAY, b.   d. 1779, m.   Elizabeth   b.   d.

II.

WILLIAM JAY, b.   d.   m. 1501 Fanny Rogers, b. 1776, d.   dau. of George and Desire (Springer) Rogers of New London

---

PAGE 70.

THOMAS MORROW, b.   d.   m. 1775 Esther Baldwin, b.   d.

PAGE 207.

1. DAVID ROGERS, b.   d.   m. 1741 at New London, Elizabeth Sawyer, b. ab 1733, d. 1777.

Children of David (1) and Elizabeth (Sawyer) Rogers.

2. AMOS, b. 1743, d.
3. WILLIAM, b. 1760, d. 1797.
4. BETSEY, b. 1765, d.
5. DESIRE, b. 1771, d.
6. DAVID WHEELER, bapt. 1772, d.
7. JEREMIAH, bapt. 1775, d.

PAGE 71.

1. WILLIAM RUSSELL, b.   d.   m.   Mehitable   b.   d.

Children of William (1) and Mehitable (   ) Russell.

2. WILLIAM, bapt. at Christ Church 1773, d.
3. ELIZABETH, bapt. at Christ Church 1775, d.
4. PAMYLIA, bapt. at Christ Church 1778, d.

It is possible that William Russell, 1st, often of Litchfield, m. 1791 Zilpah Grist, b. 1750(?), d. 1841, dau. of Peter and Ann (Bedient) Grist.

[597]

SLAVES.

Baptisms in the First Church.

Children of Scipio and Dinah (slaves of the Rev. Benjamin Lord).

(Dinah admitted to the Church 1743.)

DINAH, bapt. 1744.
CATO, } Twins, bapt. 1745.
ELUS, }
EOLUS, bapt. 1747.
EXETER, bapt. 1751.
PERO, bapt. 1752.
FORTIN (perhaps Fortune), bapt. 1754.
RUBY, bapt. 1756.
DAPHNS, bapt. 1762.
CHLOE, bapt. 1766.
CUMAN, bapt. 1768.
(Recorded as Dinah's twentieth child.)

Children of Primus (slave of Col. Simon Lathrop).

FLORA, } bapt. 1756.
JOB, }

Child of Bess (slave of Col. Simon Lathrop)

(Admitted to the Church 1746.)

LEAH, bapt. 1761.

Children of Cuffee (slave of Thomas Baldwin (?).

(Baptized and admitted to the Church 1742.)

PHILLIS, bapt. 1742.
CAESAR, bapt. 1742.
LOIS, bapt. 1742.
JACK, bapt. 1742.
BEULAH, bapt. 1743.

Children of Qui (slave of Joshua Abel).

JASON, bapt. 1751.
AMOS, bapt. 1753.
JEMINA, bapt. 1755.
ELIAS, bapt. 1745.
NANCY, bapt. 1747.
DINAH, bapt. 1749.
PETER, bapt. 1755.
NECTAR, bapt. 1760.
SYLVIA, bapt. 1763.

Children of Boston (slave of Daniel Tracy).

(Baptized and admitted to the Church 1741.)

JASON, bapt. 1745.
JASON, bapt. 1743.
JOSEPH, bapt. 1747.

SLAVES.—Continued.

Scipio. bapt. 1738.

Children of Rose (slave of Theophilus Rogers).

Tamar. bapt. 1738.

Children of Jack.

Pompey. bapt. 1759.   Sylvia. bapt. 1759.   Kate. bapt. 1759.

Child of Galloway and Zina (slaves of Col. Christopher Leffingwell).
(Father admitted to the Church 1768. Died before 1769.)

Zilpha. bapt. 1768.

Adult Baptisms.

Jennie (adult slave of Joshua Huntington). bapt. 1738.
Boston (adult slave of Daniel Tracy). bapt. and adm. to the Church 1741.
George (Indian slave of Hezekiah Huntington). bapt. and adm. to the Church 1741.
Peter (adult slave of John Leffingwell). bapt. and adm. to the Church 1741.
Quo (adult slave of Hugh Calkins). bapt. and adm. to the Church 1741.
Cook (adult slave of Aaron Fargo). bapt. and adm. to the Church 1742.
Peter (adult slave of Abial Marshall). bapt. and adm. to the Church 1742.
Scipio (adult slave of Joshua Huntington). bapt. and adm. to the Church 1742.
Guy (servant boy of Benajah Bushnell). bapt. 1742.
Dinah (slave of William Waterman). bapt. 1742.
Zelpha (adult slave of Benajah Leffingwell). bapt. and adm. to the Church 1743.
Cuffee (slave of Thomas Baldwin). bapt. and adm. to the Church 1742.
Cuffee (slave of the widow Post). bapt. and adm. to the Church 1749.
Cuffee (adult slave of Daniel Lathrop). bapt. in Christ Church 1788.

Recorded Births.

Violet. b. 1751. (slave of Azariah Lathrop).
Java. b. 1755. (slave of Azariah Lathrop).
Bristow. b. 1758. son of Nancy (slave of Azariah Lathrop).
Rose. b. 1760. dau. of Nancy (slave of Azariah Lathrop).
Jenny. b. 1762. dau. of Zylpha (slave of Rev. Joseph Strong).
Martin. b. 1777. son of Chloe (slave of Desire Dennis).
Jude. b. 1780. dau. of Phillis (slave of Joseph Williams).
Anthony. b. 1757.
Boshar. b. 1761. } (slaves of Thomas Coit.)
James. b. 1769.
Cuffee (negro). m. 1799 Sylvia Freem.
Sylvia. child of Cuffee and Sylvia. b. 1773.

SLAVES.—Continued.

Freed Slaves.

Slave.	Master.	Year of Manumission.
FORTUNE and wife TIME	Samuel Gager	1774
PETER	Samuel Gager	1774
PEGGY	Rufus Lathrop	1777
CATO	Jonathan Brewster	1777
PHARAOH and wife KATE	Capt. William Coit	1778
CATO	Samuel Tracy	1778
ARKELUS and VIOLET	Samuel Tracy	1780
FLORA AMMER (former slave of Ebenezer Lathrop)	Samuel Tracy	1782
PERO	Capt. Joseph Coit	1780
BRISTOL, BARNEY	Capt. Joseph Coit	1775
EXETER	Daniel Lathrop	1783
GUY	Jabez Huntington	1787
SAMUEL	Jabez Huntington	1781
BENA	Col. Joshua Huntington	1781
DAVID (26 years old)	Asa Peabody	1795
BRISTOL (ab. 30 years old)	Heirs of Jonathan Starr of Lisbon	1797
OLINDA and her little child, BERINTE	Albertus Straut Destouches	1791
DAVID, DINAH, and their children, PRINCE, CHRISTINE and FREEMAN	Albertus Straut Destouches	1792
PETER HOVEY (a cooper, resid. in Norwich)	Joseph Hovey of St. Eustatia	1791

Daniel Brewster frees his slave, Lebbeus Quy, in 1777, "in Consideration of his now Ingaging to serve in the Continental Service during the present Warr."

PART II.

ERRATA AND ADDENDA.

PAGE 487, No. 200, Read John Turvill Adams. b. 1805 at Essequibo, S. A. d. 1882 at Norwich.
son of Richard and Mary Rebecca (Turvill) Adams.
of Essequibo, S. A., and Norwich, Ct.
He m. (2) 1839 Elizabeth (Lee) Dwight. b. 1801. d. 1865.
dau. of Benjamin and Elizabeth (Leighton) Lee
of Norwich, Ct.

PAGE 507, No. 36, Read John Bishop. b. 1685 at Ipswich. d. 1755 at Norwich.
son of Samuel and Hester (Cogswell) Bishop of Ipswich, Mass.

PAGE 512, No. 125, Read George Burbank Ripley. b. 1801. d. 1858.
son of Dr. Dwight and Eliza (Coit) Ripley.

As it is difficult to find satisfactory records of many of the early Huguenots, it has been thought best to publish as complete genealogies as possible of two Huguenot families of Connecticut, the Perits (or Peirets) and the Fountains (or Fontaines). The former has been compiled from family papers, grave-stone inscriptions, the Connecticut Colonial Records, and information furnished by THE HUGUENOT SOCIETY of New York and Miss LOUISE TRACY of New Haven; the latter, from Norwich, New London, and Stamford records, that valuable work, "The Huguenot Emigration to America," by the late Charles W. Baird, and from data furnished by WM. A. E. THOMAS of Brooklyn, New York. The latter has spent several years in collecting information about the Fountain family, and, at his request, some of the family lines are here for the first time published, which have no connection with Norwich history, but may, nevertheless, be of interest to other Connecticut residents.

The Kinney family genealogy was compiled by Mrs. FREDERIC L. OSGOOD. Mr. SIDNEY MINER of New London has furnished the record of the Seth Miner family, ANSON TITUS of Tuft's College, Mass., the early records of the Abbots, and Miss CAROLYN STERRY of Norwich the later records of the Sterry family.

APPENDIX TO PART I.

PAGE 53.

Jonathan Pierce, b. 1715-6, was located at Brattleboro, Cumberland Co., N. Y., in 1774.
Cyprian Pierce, b. 1724, was located at Halifax, Cumberland Co., N. Y., in 1774.

PAGE 105.

When changes were being made, some years ago, in a wall on the former site of this old highway, the late Angell Stead rescued from destruction an old mile-stone which is said to have formerly stood there, and this is still owned by his widow.

PAGE 223, Line 6.

In The Norwich Packet of April 8, 1776, appears, in very small type, this notice of Gen. Washington's first visit to Norwich:

"*Norwich, April 8.*
"*Since our last, four or five Regiments of the Continental Troops, under the Command of Brigadier-General SULLIVAN, have passed through this Town in their Way to New York.... His Excellency General WASHINGTON, with four more Regiments, arrived here this day from Cambridge.*"

And in The Packet of April 15:

"*Since our last, sundry Regiments of the Continental Troops, have passed through this Town, from Cambridge, in their way to New York.*"

PAGE 274, Line 18.

Miss Caulkins alludes, in her History of Norwich, to the occupancy of the Wm. Bradford Whiting (now Fitch) house by Thomas Hubbard, and that his three sons, Thomas, Russell and Amos H. Hubbard, were born there.

PAGE 352. CHURCH PLANS.

It has been a difficult matter to give a perfectly accurate plan of the old church, begun in 1753, but not entirely finished until 1770, as there were so many erasures and substitutions in the original plan, of which an imperfect copy is given at page 352. This plan was probably made about 1756-7, as the widow, Anne Turner, who is mentioned as a pew occupant, married Capt. Joshua Abel in 1757. Two other plans of 1756 exist, both differing from this one, and from each other. The first of these, marked "exhibited in Society meeting, March 3rd, 1756, and approved," is much larger than the other plans, and has a seat for the deaf people, and one for the deacons in front of the pulpit, and a double row of pews at that end of the church, also benches in the middle aisle, in the places later occupied by pews No. 36, 37, 69, 38, 35, 36, — and 37, and there are only nine pews, instead of twelve, at the main entrance end of the church. The second plan, "exhibited in Society meeting, March 15th, 1756," resembles in arrangement the plan at page 352, except that the benches still remain in the middle aisle. These benches were probably soon replaced by pews, as in the plan presented in this book. Some of the names of pew owners in the original drawing are very indistinct, either almost obliterated by time, or by being partly blotted out, and one name written over another, so that it is often impossible to decipher them even with a magnifying glass. The pews were not sold yearly, but were a family possession, and two names may not always indicate a joint occupancy, but possibly an inheritance, or a sale from one owner to another.

The names Asa Lord and Asa Lathrop are given in pew No. 2, at the right of the pulpit—only one name, which might read either Asa or Eleazer, is prefixed to the names Lord and Lathrop in the original plan. The first owner in this case was probably Eleazer Lord, succeeded later by his son-in-law, Asa Lathrop. In No. 4, the name of one owner is indecipherable. In No. 11, the name of Aaron Chapman is faintly visible. In No. 13, Simeon Case is crossed out, and Joseph Winship substituted. Two almost obliterated names in No. 15, appear to be Elijah Lathrop and ——— Fitch (possibly Jabez). In No. 23, there is also a Peter ———. In No. 24, one name is crossed out, and Nathaniel Parish substituted. In No. 30, a line is drawn across the names of Lydia and Elizabeth Reynolds, and a barely perceptible Jonathan Goodhue is added.

In the six middle seats of the upper row, some changes have been evidently made, indicated by lines. No names are given for the pews, Nos. 35, 36 and 37 of this row, and in Nos. 38 and 39 names have been blotted out, and a blurred Matthew Adgate is added to No. 39. In No. 68 of the second row, a name resembling Nathaniel Lathrop, and a faint Marsh, can be traced. In No. 52 of the third row, the paper is torn, and though the name resembles Starr, it might read also ———let Hazzen, and we are inclined to believe that the owner was Howlett Hazen, who had married a daughter of Eleazer Lord. It is impossible to decipher the name in No. 67. In No. 38 of this row, the word Thomas appears. The number of Theophilus and Zabdiel Rogers' pew is not easily read, but might be 70. In No. 41, the name is possibly Daniel Burnham instead of Birchard, and the names ——— Allen and ——— Totman (probably Stephen Totman) appear. No. 50 of the fifth row has beside Samuel Starr another occupant, ——— Starr. In No. 47, the name Ebenezer Lathrop seems to be written over the name Leffingwell. In No. 44, is a puzzling name which may be Jabez Lathrop. In No. 43, the name of Joseph Reynolds is blotted out.

In No. 9, in the gallery plan, another indecipherable name appears with Nathaniel Huntington. Beside the other names given in No. 10, are James ——— and B. Leffingwell. In addition to Jonathan Chester in No. 11, appears ——— Abbot. In No. 14, may be seen Simeon ———, and an almost indistinguishable John Case. In No. 20, there is a faint E. Vernum (probably Ephraim Farnham.)

PAGE 353.

When the church of 1756 was built, the old church on the hill was sold to the ancestor of John Post of Wawecus Hill, who still owns the hinges and door-handle of the old church-door, which have been photographed by Charles E. Briggs, and may be seen with the gallery plan.

PAGE 367.

The mourning piece at page 367 was painted and embroidered by Charlotte Peck (later Mrs. Ebenezer Learned of New London), and Harriet Peck (Mrs. Gen. Wm. Williams of Norwich), while they were at the celebrated Moravian boarding school, at Bethlehem, Pa. The taller figure is said to be a likeness of the elder sister, Charlotte, then 15 years old; and the shorter, of Harriet, aged 11.

PAGE 381.

George Bliss taught in the Lathrop school (the brick school-house on the Plain) in 1829. In that year this school was discontinued, and in 1843, by the terms of the will, the property reverted and was paid to the heirs of Dr. Daniel Lathrop's nephew, Thomas Coit.

For additional information about Jonathan and Cyprian Pierce, Gen. Washington's first visit to Norwich, description of Church Plans of 1756, the last relics of the last "Church on the Hill," an account of the Mourning Piece by Charlotte and Harriet Peck, and the discontinuing of the Lathrop School, see Appendix on preceding pages 602 and 603.

INDEX TO PART I.

[*Married Names of Wives, or Daughters, in parentheses.*]
[*Maiden Names of Wives, without parentheses.*]

ABBOT 277.
  Daniel 261, 394. John 248. Samuel 124, 248, 61; 398. Elizabeth Phipps 248. Phebe Edgerton 248. Sarah Reynolds 261.
ABEL.
  Caleb 3, 351. Joshua 82; 137, 71, 7; 309. Samuel 351.
  Abigail (Huntington) 82, 111. Anne Backus 82. Anne Huntington (Adgate) (Turner) 309. Bethiah Gager 137. Elizabeth (Chapman) 313. Eunice (Birchard) 171. Jerusha Frink 171. Jerusha (Williams) 117. Lucy (Lord) 177. Lucy Edgerton 177. Lydia (Lathrop) 137, 60.
ABNER 52, 77.
ADAMS 246.
  Eliphalet 100; 295. (Pres.) John 228; 366. (Judge) 243. William 293, 5, 6.
  Abiel (Metcalf) 295, 6. Alice (Collins) 296. Alice Bradford (Fitch) 266, 93, 4, 5, 6. Elizabeth (Whiting) (Niles) 100, 296.
ADGATE 106, 56, 68, 9, 71, 6, 7, 80.
  Asa 172. Daniel 169. Matthew 168, 72, 5. Thomas 2, 4, 58, 87; 100, 4, 6, 30, 1, 55, 6, 7, 69, 71, 5, 8, 9, 80, 3; 212, 29, 31; 309, 51. William 169, 175.
  Abigail Culverhouse (Waterman) 175. Abigail (Tracy) 231. Anne Huntington (Turner) (Abel) 309. Elizabeth (Bushnell) 4; 157, 74, 75. Elizabeth Morgan (Starr) 175. Eunice Baldwin 172. Eunice Waterman 175. Hannah Hyde 172, 5. Hannah (Lathrop) 131, 74; 340. Jane — (Williams) 172. Lucy (Lord) 175, 7. Lucy Waterman 172. Mary Marvin (Bushnell) 4, 58; 157, 74, 5. Ruth (Edgerton) 248. Ruth Brewster 175. Sarah (Huntington) 179. — — (Norton) 172.

ALDEN.
  John 220. Mary (Gale) 280. Priscilla 220.
ALLEN.
  Fitch 91. James 203. John 4. Robert 3, 4.
  Abigail (Shepherd) 321. Deborah (Gager) 4. Hannah (Rose) 4. Hannah (Needham) 269. Mary (Parke) 4. Mehitable (Case) 147. Rachel (Tracy) 192.
ANDERSON Elizabeth 219.
ANDRE (Maj.) 223.
ANDROS Sir Edmund 295.
ANSWORTH Sarah (Manning) 92.
APEANTCHSUCK 32.
ARMS Hiram P. 270, 358.
ARMSTRONG.
  Henry 281.
  Isabella (Needham) 269. Kesiah (Parish) 168.
ARNOLD 225, 67; 391.
  Benedict 20, 43, 5, 54; 101, 9, 51; 252, 64. John 251, 64, 7; 374. Oliver 185. William 264. Hannah Waterman (King) 101. Mary (Manley) 251.
ATTAWANHOOD 1.
AUSTIN David 153.
AVERILL Polly 35.
AVERY 90, 1; 171, 4, 94; 204, 33. Charles 314. Henry 194, 214. Jabez 45, 88, 9; 125. James 206. John 88, 9; 180, Jonathan 185. Richard 338. Sam 171, 2, 4, 80, 1, 3, 92, 4; 233, 6. Thomas 32. William 270. Candace Charlton 180. Elizabeth (Tracy) 180, 233.
AVERY.
  Hannah (Butler) 270. Harriet (Robinson) 314. Lucy Bushnell 89. Lucy Lord (Perkins) 338. Louisa Coolidge 314. Lydia — (Perkins) 280. Lydia Smith 89. Prudence Miner 180.
AYER.
  Joseph B. 256.
  Sarah (Park) 121.

BABCOCK.
  Harriet (Saltonstall) (Wait) 101. Mary 259, 61.
BACHELER (Mrs.) 232, 3.
BACKUS.
  Ebenezer 185, 235. Elijah 11; 221, 54; 361. George Whitney 192. John 356. Joseph 8, 285, 99; 340. Nathaniel 11, 88, 101. Samuel 283, 5. Simon 88. Stephen 4, 31, 64, 6, 7, 74; 130, 92. Thomas 262. William 2, 4, 5, 6, 24, 66; 156, 89, 94; 231, 351.
  Abigail (Perkins) 235. Abigail Trumbull 235. Ann — (Bingham) 4. Ann (Lathrop) 273, 310. Clorinda (Lathrop) 88. Cynthia 90, 1, 2. Elizabeth (Huntington) 194, 222, 283. Elizabeth Huntington 285, 340. Elizabeth Pratt 4. Elizabeth Tracy 283, 5. Elizabeth Waterman 101. Eunice Edwards 88. Eunice Whitney 92. Lucy Griswold 221, 361. Lucy (Woodbridge) 361. Lucretia Hubbard (Tracy) 254. Mary (Crane) 188. Mary (Rudd) 365. Sarah (Reynolds) 23. Sarah Spencer 67.
BACON.
  James 330. Leonard 81, 82.
  Hannah (Williams) 117. Martha — (Peck) 330.
BAKER Henry M. 35.
BALDWIN 75.
  John 4. Samuel 172. Simeon 129. William 92, 259; 376, 80, 1, 2.
  Alice Huntington 92; 259, 61; 381. Eunice Adgate 172. Hannah 4. Sarah 4.
BARREL.
  Henry 35. Louis 35, 52. Lucretia 35. Mary 35. Mary Beckwith 35.
BARET.
  Christopher 178.
  Margaret (Huntington) (Stoughton) 178.
BARRET James 184.

INDEX TO PART I.

BARROWS Henry 214.
BASSET.
    Abner 248. David 101. Francis 308.
    Elizabeth (Waterman) 100. Marie Madeleine Nuquerque 308. Susanna (Ramé) 308.
BAXTER Howland & 275.
BEACH Nathaniel 107, 175.
BEAMAN Charles 233.
BEARD Nathaniel 118. William 118.
BECKWITH Mary (Barrel) 35.
BEEBE Samuel 308.
BEEBS.
    Isaac 81.
    Sally (Leffingwell) 81.
BELLAMY.
    Jonathan 135; 211, 39. Joseph 135.
BENTLEY.
    Anna (Trapp) (Lancaster) 292.
BERNON Gabriel 184.
BETTS Thaddeus 263.
BILL.
    Ephraim 152, 4. 64; 272, 6, 8.
    Elizabeth (Coit) 154, 64; 384. Hannah (Lathrop) 152. Lydia (Howland) 154. Lydia Huntington 152, 64; 272, 6, 8.
BILLINGS 81.
    Richard Leffingwell 78. Roger 78. William 77, 8; 125.
    Abigail Denison 78. Abigail (Coit) 372. Betsey (Peck) 131, 2. Mary Leffingwell 77, 8, 9, 82.
BINGHAM 320.
    Thomas 4, 40, 66, 188, 231. William 92.
    Abigail (Huntington) 246, 309. Ann — (Backus) 4, 66.
BIRCHARD.
    Elisha 170, 1. Gideon 124, 170. John 2, 4, 170. Samuel 216.
    Ann Calkins 216. Ann (Grist) 216, 52. Christian Andrews 4. Jane Hyde 170.
BIRON Duke de 226.
BISHOP Temperance (Holmes) 167.
BISSELL.
    Nathaniel 98.
    Dorothy Fitch 98.
BLACKMAN Caroline F. 308.
BLAKE Lucy 147.
BLISS 38, 67, 200.
    Charles 34, 8; 192. Curtis 147. Elias 33, 4, 6. George 34, 6; 121. John 32, 3, 6; 124, 5, 6, 73; 335, 54, 96. Samuel 4, 34, 2, 3, 7. 54; 105. Thomas 4, 34, 3, 66, 192, 234. William 34, 6, 46, 9, 106. Zepheniah 33, 4, 6.
    Ann Elderkin 32. Dolinda (or

BLISS.—Continued.
    Deliver) (Perkins) 4. Elizabeth — 4, 31, 2. Elizabeth Smith 4. Elizabeth (White) 32, 3. Lydia 34. Mary (Calkins) 4. Margaret Lawrence 31. Rebecca (Lathrop) 207, 8. Sarah 34. Sarah (Shuman) (Tracy) 4, 234.
BOARDMAN.
    Elijah 372.
    Mary Tyler (Coit) 372.
BORODELL Ann (Denison) 78, 391.
BOSTWICK Jared 376.
BOURNE.
    Thomas 265.
    Martha (Bradford) (Tracy) 265.
BOWEN Huldah (Dyer) 259.
BOWERS.
    Morgan 4.
    Judah 4.
BOYER Jean Pierre 94, 389.
BRADDICK John 162.
BRADFORD 205, 66, 7, 82, 3.
    John 4, 230, 45, 64, 5. Joseph 98, 266, 305. Thomas 265, 6. William 220, 65, 93, 5, 6.
    Alice (Adams) (Fitch) 266, 93, 4, 5, 6. Alice (Richards) 266, 95. Ann Fitch 98, 266. Ann Smith 266. Dorothy May 265. Elizabeth (Whiting) 219, 73. Martha Bourne (Tracy) 4, 230, 65. Melatiah (Steele) 266.
BRANCH.
    Samuel 379.
    Hannah Witter 379. Sally (Kinney) 379.
BRADSTREET Simon 328.
BRECK.
    Edward 189.
    Elinor (Crane) 189.
BREED.
    John McC. 362. Gershom 396. Shubael 164.
    Mary (Coit) 164.
BREWSTER.
    Benjamin 175. Elijah 185. Jonathan 179, 207.
    Ann Dart 175. Elizabeth (Watrous) 180. Judith Stevens (Huntington) 179. Ruth (Adgate) 175.
BROMFIELD Edward 203.
BROMLEY.
    Bethuel 89.
    Arabella Herrick 89. Rebecca (Sterry) 89.
BROOKS Jonathan 273.
BROWN.
    Chad 316. James 253. James Noyes 185, 316, 18. Jesse 362, 3, 4, 5, 6, 7. John 331. Samuel 10. Nicholas 73.

BROWN —Continued.
    Ann Noyes 316, 253. Ann (Vernet) 366. Ann Mason 331. Anna Rudd 365. Lucy Perkins 367. Lucy Rudd 365. Mary Carew (Huntington) 185, 307. 16, 81. Mary (Perkins) 191, 253, 316. Robe Carr 316.
BROWNE.
    Jackson 36. Thomas Sanford 36. Emily 36. Louisa 36. Sophia 36.
BRYAN.
    Samuel Bryan 321.
    Martha Whiting 321. Mary (Perit) 321.
BUCHANAN James 370.
BUCK.
    Daniel 49.
    Elizabeth Perkins 49.
BULL.
    Doxey 325.
    (Lt.) Thomas 327.
BURNHAM.
    Eleazer 170, 208. Jonathan 49.
    Lydia Waterman 208. Mary Norman 170. Mary Chester 49.
BURR Aaron 135, 211, 39.
BUSH Hannah (Rood) 172.
BUSHNELL.
    104, 56, 61, 8, 72, 5.
    Benajah 150, 2, 9, 60; 216, 20. Caleb 64, 157, 8; 235, 351. Chauncey K. 393. Ebenezer 81, 211, 54. Jonathan 59. Joseph 4, 38, 9, 47, 52, 3, 4, 8, 9, 60, 1; 106, 52, 74; 351. Richard 4, 40, 58, 9, 89; 104, 6, 30, 52, 6, 7, 8, 9, 65, 74, 9, 84; 230, 94, 9; 305, 74, 5, 95, 6.
    Abigail (Tracy) 220, 35. Ann (Hyde) 157, 75. Ann Leffingwell 157. Betsey Webster 159. Caroline (Tracy) 220. Elizabeth Adgate 157, 75. Elizabeth (Hyde) 157. Elizabeth (Tracy) 159, 60. Hannah Griswold 159; 220, 1. Hannah — 59. Jerusha (Hutchins) 54. Lucy Perkins 89. Mary Leffingwell 54, 8; 174. Mary (Leffingwell) 4. Mary Marvin (Adgate) 4; 157, 74, 5. Mercy (Rudd) (Cary) 4, 174. Rebecca (Barstow) 59. Susannah Hubbard (Mauwaring) 254. Zerviah Leffingwell 157. Zerviah (Holden) 152, 9, 60.
BULKELEY Gershom 206.
BUTLER 307.
    Benjamin 124; 267, 8, 9, 70; 392. Daniel 269. Richard 269. Thomas 269, 70. Abigail Craft 269. Diadema Hyde 269, 70 (by mistake, Jerusha) 392.

BUTLER.—Continued.
Jerusha (Denison) 270, 392.
Hannah Avery 270. Minerva
270. Rosamond 270. Ruth
Huntington 269, 70. Sarah
Denison 270.

CADY Damaris (Howe) 338.
CALKINS.
Hugh 5. John 5.
Ann — 5. Anna (Birchard) (Rockwell) 216. Lucy 142. Sarah Royce 5.
CAMPBELL.
Mary Bowers (Huntington) 286.
CANFIELD (Col.) 262.
CAPRON C. R. 150.
CARDER (by mistake, Caider).
Richard 32.
CAREW.
Daniel 82, 112. Ebenezer, 84, 5; 135, 51, 91; 278. Eliphalet 93, 125. John 85. Joseph 84, 5; 125, 58, 85; 261, 2, 76, 7; 361, 8, 97. Palmer 84, 5. Richard 84. Simeon 251, 6. Simon 278, 323. Thomas 84, 5.
Abigail Huntington 84, 273. Abigail (Whiting) 273. Anne Tompson 85. Anne 85. Eunice Huntington 84, 5; 278. Eunice (Huntington) 262, 70, 91. Eunice Edgerton 262, 3. Hannah Hill 84. Mary Huntington 84, 5; 262. Mary (Brown) (Huntington) 185, 307, 16, 81. Mehetabel Gardiner 85. Sally Eels 85.
CARPENTER.
Gardner 261, 2, 70; 307, 68, 9, 86. Gerard 369. Joseph 307, 10, 67, 8, 9, 89.
Elizabeth Lathrop (Peck) 307, 10, 68. Eunice Fitch 369. Mary Huntington 307. Rebecca Hunter 369.
CARR Robe (Brown) 316.
CARRIER.
Richard 306, 10.
Hannah (Peck) 310. Remembrance (Cleveland) 306, 7. Thankful — 310.
CARTER 218.
CARY Thomas 261. (Mrs.) 48.
CASE.
Asahel 91, 168, 9, 70. Barnard 146. Benjamin 146. Calvin 168. Ebenezer 168, 70. John 146, 7, 68. Luther 90. Moses 146, 7. Samuel 147, 69. Simeon 146, 7, 68.
Desire Manton 146. Hannah Ormsby 146, 7, 68. Mary Haskins 146. Mary Killgrove

CASE.—Continued.
168. Mehitabel Allen 147. Nancy (Smith) 168. Prudence Cooley 168. Susanna Cowdrey 147.
CAULKINS.
Frances 1, 2, 3, 5, 14, 19, 25, 32, 5, 9, 40, 2, 8, 61, 2, 7, 71, 4, 5, 89; 106, 7, 15, 21, 9, 30, 3, 6, 8, 50, 5, 6, 7, 8; 65, 9, 71, 6, 84; 205, 7, 9, 25, 46, 54, 5, 65, 9, 80, 95, 6; 311, 2, 3, 23, 8, 35, 6, 50, 3, 4, 6, 7, 64, 5, 73, 4, 5, 6, 8, 96, 7, 401.
CHAFFEE Lydia (Spalding) 214.
CHANDLER.
John 32, 294.
Mehetabel (Coit) 42, 160.
CHAPMAN.
Aaron 172. Joseph 50, 172, 313. William 172.
Elizabeth Abel 313. Kesiah Rood 172. Lois (Trott) 313. Lydia (Trott) 313. Mercy Taylor 172. Nancy 88.
CHAPPELL Patience (Wickwire) 315.
CHARLES.
King Charles I. 202. John 66. — 163.
Sarah (Backus) 66.
CHARLTON.
Charles 77, 252, 386. Henri 251. Jesse 252. John 393. Richard 168, 80; 251, 2, 6. Samuel 252, 394.
Anna (Miner) 370. Candace (Avery) 180. Sarah Williams (Williams) 77, 252. Sarah (Grist) 180, 252.
CHASTELLEUX Marquis 236, 40.
CHAUNCEY (Judge) 290.
CHESTER.
John 285. Jonathan 248.
Elizabeth Huntington 15, 285. Freelove (Huntington) 248. Hannah (Talcott) 285. Hannah (Williams) 285. Mary (Burnham) 49. Penelope (Williams) 285. Sarah Noyes 285.
CHILDS.
Timothy 286.
Mary Huntington 286.
CHRISTOPHERS.
Christopher 301. Richard 70. Lucy (Douglas) (Palmes) 162. Mary 304. Sarah Prout 301.
CHOATE.
Francis 134. Jabez 401. Rufus Lathrop 134.
Eunice Culver 401. Hannah (Lathrop) 134.
CHURCH.
Anthony 60. Benjamin 190, 388.
CLAGHORN Samuel 312.

CLARK.
Elisha 116. John 246, 314. Jeremiah 316. McDonald 7, 10; 379. William 105, 270, 307.
Ann 205. Hannah (Leffingwell) 116. Rachel (Jones) 314. Sarah (Huntington) 246.
CLEMENT.
Peabody 48, 166.
Elizabeth Shipman 48. Elizabeth (Bliss) 48. Mary Ann (Huntington) 48.
CLEVELAND.
Aaron 129, 290. Curtis 306, 7. Grover 129, 338. Isaac 109, 12; 306, 14. Moses 306. William 115; 322, 3, 38, 40.
Elizabeth Curtis (Stratford) 306, 14. Kesiah (Jones) 306. Remembrance Carrier 306, 7. Sarah (Dodge) 271. Susan (Fuller) 322.
CLEGG.
William 93, 4.
Mary — 88.
COBB.
Henry 167, 8, 77. Nathan 124, 6, 67, 8, 77.
Katherine Copp 168, 77. Mary (Cobb) 177.
CODDINGTON William 316.
COGSWELL.
James 239, 41; 334. Mason Fitch 81, 2; 211.
Martha Lathrop (Devotion) 238, 9, 40, 1, 2.
COIT 361.
Benjamin 163, 372. Daniel L. 10, 86; 151, 4, 5, 61, 2, 4, 8. Henry 164. John 42, 160, 297. Joseph 43, 8, 79; 109, 28, 51, 60, 1, 2; 210, 97, 8. Joshua 162, 4. Levi 164. Samuel 41, 372. Thomas 129, 61, 254. William 127, 8, 62, 3.
Abigail Billings 372. Elizabeth Bill 19, 151, 61. Elizabeth (Gilman) 164. Elizabeth (Leffingwell) 70. Elizabeth Palmes 162. Harriet Frances (Coit) 164. Lucy (Huntington) 210, 11, 42. Lydia Lathrop 43, 161. Lydia (Kingsley) 164. Lydia Howland 164. Lydia (Hubbard) 153. Maria Perit 164. Mary Breed 164. Mary Hunting 160. Mary Prentice (Gray) 253, 4. Martha (Hubbard) (Greene) 42, 3. Rebecca Parkman (Townsend) 279. Sarah Mosier (Prentice) 109. Sarah Spalding 372.
COLES (or COWLES) Moses 87.
COLLIER Richard 125, 6; 341.

COLLINS.
  Nathaniel 296.
  Alice Adams 296.
CONVERSE.
  Augustus 191. William 191, 244.
COOK.
  Aaron 211.
  Submit Peck (Wheatley) 311.
COOLEDGE.
  Henry J. 314.
  Louisa (Avery) 314. Lucy Jones 314, 5.
COPP.
  Jonathan 177.
  Margaret Stanton 168, 77.
CORNER Sarah (Mandell) 165.
COX.
  William 35, 51, 71, 113. George 35. John 35.
  Anna 35. Elizabeth Thompson 35. Maria Merryfield 35. Mary Abby 35. Mary M. Baker 35. Olive 35. Polly Averill 35. Sarah — 35.
CRAFT Abigail (Butler) 269.
CRANE.
  Benjamin 188, 9. Jonathan 104, 88, 9, 94; 232.
  Deborah Griswold 189. Elinor Breck 189. Mary Backus 188.
CRANK.
  Phebe Harris (Prentis) (Edgerton) 248, 360.
CRUDEN 163.
CULVER.
  John 315.
  Elizabeth (Wickwire) 315. Eunice (Choate) 401.
CURTIS.
  Elizabeth (Cleveland) (Stratford) 306, 14.
CUSHING Mercy (Eels) 149.
CUTLER William 244.

DABOLL Nathan 121.
DAMON Jael (Whiton) 274.
DANFORTH.
  Daniel 202, 4. John 202, 3, 4. Nicholas 202. Samuel 202, 3, 4, 14. Thomas 124; 202, 3, 4. 15, 51, 6; 309, 15.
  Elizabeth Hartshorn 204. Hannah Allen 203. Lucy Hartshorn 204. Lydia (Cogsdall) 204. Mary (Nichols) 204. Sarah — 203.
DARBY.
  William 307.
  Elizabeth (Huntington) 82.
DART Ann (Morgan) 288.
DAVENPORT.
  John 309, 68.
  Nancy 201.
DAVIS 135.

DAWSON Hannah 171.
DAY.
  James 60.
  Hannah Lincoln 60.
DAYNES Abraham 359.
DEAN Mary Rudd (Huntington) 182.
DEANE W. R. 301.
DEMING.
  Honor (Goodrich) 220. (Mrs.) Clarence 274.
DENISON.
  Andrew 160. Edward 331. George 78, 391. Gideon 270, 391. John 331. Joseph 270.
  Abigail (Billings) 78. Ann Borodell 78, 391. Ann Mason 331. Elizabeth (Henley) 392. Elizabeth Weld 331. Hannah Phelps 211. Jerusha Butler 270, 392. Louisa (Wadsworth) 392. Margaret (Mason) 331. Mercy Eels 85. Minerva (Rodgers) 392.
DENNIS.
  Benjamin 397. George 125, 6.
  Desire Bliss 129.
DENTON Gabriel 228.
DESHON.
  Daniel 184.
  Lucretia (Thomas) 192.
DEVEREUX John C. 347.
DEVILLS (Mr.) 303.
DEVOTION.
  Ebenezer, 239, 41, 42. John L. 239.
  Betsey 239. Hannah (Huntington) 241. Martha Lathrop (Cogswell) 238, 39, 40, 1, 2. Martha (Huntington) 238, 9, 40.
DICKEY 105; 250, 2, 3.
DICKINSON Ann (Leffingwell) 40.
DOANE.
  John 207.
  Abigail (Lathrop) 207.
DODGE.
  David Dow 270.
  Julia Stewart (Huntington) 270. Sarah Cleveland 270.
DONAHUE Thomas 106, 47, 67.
DORR Elizabeth (Tracy) 392.
DOUGLASS.
  Nathan 79.
  Deborah (Spooner) 79. Lucy Christophers (Palmes) 162.
DOYLE Richard 277.
DRAKE Samuel Adams 236.
DUDLEY Thomas 360.
DUNLAP Margaretta (Perit) 187.
DURKEE.
  Benjamin 169.
  Mary (Wallbridge) 195.
DWIGHT Theodore 301.

DYER.
  Benjamin 55. Eliphalet 55, 259. John 70.
  Amelia (Trumbull) 258, 9. Huldah Bowen 259. Mary Marsh 55.

EATON (Gov.) 309. (Dr.) 90.
EDGERTON 57, 61, 2, 3, 4, 104, 5, 6, 9.
  George 65, 6. John 31, 248, 62; 360. Richard 4. Sims 388.
  Elizabeth 4. Elizabeth (Peek) 310. Eunice (Carew) 262, 3. Hannah 4. Lucy (Abel) 177. Mary Reynolds (Lathrop) 4, 1, 131. Phebe (Abbot) 248. Phebe Harris (Crank) (Prentis) 248, 62; 360. Ruth Adgate 248. Ruth (Huntington) 248. Sarah (Huntington) 233. Sarah (Reynolds) 25. Temperance (Lord) 280.
EDWARDS.
  Jonathan 88. Timothy 88.
  Eunice (Backus) 88.
EELS.
  Cushing 149, 76. Edward 85. Nathaniel 147, 9.
  Hannah North 149. Mercy Denison 85. Mercy (Lathrop) 147, 8, 9. Sally (Carew) 85.
ELDERKIN 170, 213.
  John 2, 3, 32; 205, 7, 99; 350, 1.
  Ann (Bliss) 32.
ELIOT John 203.
ELLIS Joseph 397.
ELY 26.
  Ezra Stiles 318. Zebulon 317.
  Mary (Lathrop) 317. Mary (Noyes) 372.
EVEREST Cornelius 358.
EYRE Thomas 375.

FAIRFAX Sir Thomas 324.
FANNING Thomas 124, 63.
FAWKES Guy 19.
FENTON Lucius 323.
FISH Aaron 268.
FISHER Alvan 164.
FITCH 88, 90, 103; 307, 14.
  Daniel 98, 100; 372. Eleazer 41, 97, 8; 256. (Gov.) Fitch 284. Jabez 97, 8; 296. James 2, 4, 74, 87, 95, 6, 7, 8; 100, 30, 74, 5; 229, 30, 1, 4, 45, 6, 60, 4, 6, 93, 4, 5, 6, 7, 8; 319, 31, 50, 1, 8, 72. Jeremiah 97, 8. John 55, 98. Joseph 97, 8. Nathaniel 97, 8. Oliver 195. Samuel 4, 40, 95, 8. Stephen 145. Thomas 95. William 205, 19, 22, 28.

FITCH.—Continued.
(Mrs.) William 272, 6. Abigail (Mason) 4, 98; 331. Abigail Whitfield 97, 8; 293; 331. Alice Bradford (Adams) 266, 93, 4, 5, 6. Ann — 95. Ann (Bradford) 98. Alice (Marsh) 55. Dorothy (Bissell) 98. Elizabeth (Taylor) 4, 98. Elizabeth Mason 331. Eunice (Carpenter) 369. Hannah (Mix) 4, 98. Mary (Hillhouse) (Owen) (Dorrance) 372. Priscilla Mason 98, 100, 331.

FONTAINE James 308.

FOOTE.
Admiral 82. Nathaniel 230.
Mary (Stoddard) (Goodrich) (Tracy) 230.

FOSTER Faith (Patten) 387.

FOUNTAIN.
Aaron 308. Edward 308. William 308.
Elizabeth Ramé 308, 9. Hannah — 308. Mary Beebe 308. Susanna Beebe 308.

FRANCIS Mary (Peck) 394.

FRANKLIN Benjamin 9, 11; 301.

FRENCH Phebe (Lathrop) 189.

FRINK.
Hannah (Huntington) 40. Hannah Miner 40. Jerusha (Abel) 171.

FULLER.
Asa 182. George 253, 322, 3. (Mr.) 348.
Susan Cleveland 322.

GAGER 66, 79; 106, 30, 2. John 5, 260. Samuel 4, 128. William 261. Bethiah (Abel) 137. Elizabeth Gore 4. Elizabeth (Allyn) 4. Hannah (Brewster) 4. Lydia (Huntington) 260, 1; Sarah (Forbes) 4.

GAINE Samuel 277.

GALE.
Azor 280. Edmund 280. Joseph 280.
Eunice Lord 280. Mary Alden 280. Polly (Lathrop) 171, 280. Sarah Huntington 280. Sarah Leach (McDonald) 280.

GALLUP.
John 325, 359.
Hannah (Gore) 359. Hannah Lake 359.

GARDINER.
John 85, 147, 325. Lion 327. Samuel 85.
Elizabeth (Greene) 43. Abigail 85. Hannah (Lathrop) 147. Mehetabel (Carew) 85.

GATES Mary (Pierce) 53.

GAYLORD Roswell 71.

GEER Prudence (Punderson) 377.

GEORGE IV, 226.

GIFFORD 360.
James 93. John 354. Stephen 299, 333, 59.
Hannah Gallup 359. Hannah Gore 359. Anna (Manning) 93. Susanna Hubbard 93.

GILDON 276, 8.
Charles 277. Richard 277, 8. Betsey (Leach) 278. Isabella 277, 8, 394.

GILMAN.
Daniel C. 72, 3; 283, 4, 5. William 72, 164.
Eliza (Coit) 115, 64. (Misses) 104, 30, 1, 2, 8, 61, 8, 74, 5, 6, 94.

GILROY Thomas 39, 51.

GOLDSWORTHY (Mrs.) 35.

GOODELL.
Silas 79. William 79.
Lucretia 79, 121. Sally 79; 121.

GOODHUE.
David 320. Jonathan 318, 9. Joseph 320. William 320.
Abigail — 320.

GOODRICH.
Hezekiah 220. John 230. Samuel (?) 376.
Honor (Whiting) 220. Honor Deming 220. Mary Foote (Stoddard) (Tracy) 230.

GOOKIN Edmund 216; 305, 6, 7, 23.

GORE.
John 359.
Hannah (Gallup) 359. Rhoda — 359.

GORDON (Maj.-Gen.) 400.

GOULD (Judge) 263.

GLOVER (Gen.) 227, 324.

GRACE Lucretia 135.

GRANT.
Noah 183. Ulysses S. 183.
Martha Huntington 183.

GRAY.
Ebenezer 253.
Mary (Hubbard) 253. Mary Prentice (Coit) 254.

GREEN.
Francis 248, 9. Timothy 79, 80. Rebecca Spooner 79.

GREENE.
Gardiner 104, 6, 61, 6, 280. Nathaniel 43. Thomas 43.
Ann Gould 43. Elizabeth Gardiner 43. Martha (Coit) Hubbard) 42, 3; 252, 77.

GREENLEAF 49, 71, 7, 8, 9.
Daniel 77. David 76, 7; 134. Stephen 77. William 77.
Mary Johnson 76.

GREENWOOD J. 366.

GRIFFIN.
Edward D. 242.
Frances Huntington 242.

GRIFFING.
Ebenezer 171. James 171. Jeremiah 169, 70, 1.
Betsey Spinck 171. Mary Harris (Hubbell) 171.

GRIFFITHS 312, 7.

GRIGNON.
René 159, 83, 4; 231, 352.

GRINDAL.
Edmund 263.

GRIST 215, 7, 8.
John 187, 216, 7. Thomas 215, 6, 52.
Ann Birchard 216, 52. Anna 216. Delight Lathrop 187. Hannah 216. Mary 217. Sarah (Charlton) 186, 252. Theophila (Huntington) 216. Zillah (Russell) (?) 216.

GRISWOLD 26.
Francis 5, 394. Isaac 397. John 159, 221, 86. Joseph 332. Matthew 28, 221, 361. Roger 361, 2, 4. Samuel 40, 121.
Deborah (Crane) 189. Elizabeth Mary Huntington 286. Hannah (Bushnell) 220, 1. Hannah (Clark) 5. Hannah Lee 159, 221. Lucy (Backus) 221, 361. Lydia (Loudon) 221. Mary (Tracy) 5. Sarah (Chapman) 5. Ursula Wolcott 361, 2.

GROVER Sally (or Molly) 120.

GULLIVER 288.
Daniel 202, 5, 89.
(Mrs.) 111, 289.

HADLEY.
John 236.
Elizabeth Young (Perkins) 236.

HALE.
Herbert 319, 22, 89. Nathan 109.

HALL Hannah (Danforth) 203.

HALLAM 206.

HANCOCK 284.
(Gov.) 77. John 72, 243, 4.
Dorothy Quincy 77.

HARDING Seth 11.

HARLAND 62; 106, 7, 9, 11, 12, 15, 20, 66, 74.
Henry 60, 72, 111, 322. Thomas 59, 60, 76; 113, 4, 5, 6, 26; 389.
Fanny 116. Hannah Clark 116. Mary 116.

HARRIS.
Dyer 121. Edward Doubleday 313. John 70.
Elizabeth (Ledlingwell) 70. Phebe (Crank) (Prentis) (Edgerton) 248.

HART.
　Levi 48, 64.
　Lydia Leffingwell (Backus) 48.
　Sarah (Marsh) 54.
HARTSHORN.
　David 278, 374.
　Abigail Hebard 278. Elizabeth (Danforth) 204. Lucy (Danforth) 204. Zipporah (Hughes) 278.
HASKELL Daniel 384, 5.
HASKINS.
　David Greene 43.
　Hannah (Thomas) 253. Mary (Case) 146.
HAUGHTON Richard 207.
HAVENS Daniel 183.
HAYNES John 337.
HENDY Richard 3.
HENLEY.
　John D. 392.
　Elizabeth Dennison 392.
HILL.
　Charles 331.
　Rachel Mason 331.
HILLHOUSE.
　James 372. William 371.
　Mary Fitch (Owens) (Dorrance) 372.
HINCKLEY Anna (Tracy) 109.
HOBART.
　Peter 331.
　Rebecca (Mason) 331.
HOFFMAN (Mrs.) 324.
HOLDEN.
　Phinehas 152, 9, 60; 216.
　Zerviah Bushnell 152, 9, 60.
HOLLOWAY.
　William 156.
　Hannah (Read) 156. Grace (Read) 156, 7.
HOLMES.
　David 167. Oliver Wendell 166, 7.
　Temperance Bishop 167.
HOLMS Abigail (Sterry) 89.
HOOKER.
　Nathaniel 337. Thomas 95, 7; 246, 337.
　Abigail (Lord) 337. Mary Stanley 337.
HOPKINS (Dr.) 80.
HOTHAM (Admiral) 312.
HOUGH John 374.
HOUSE 63.
HOWARD Thomas 5.
HOWE.
　Joseph 45; 333, 8, 9.
　Perley 338. Damaris Cady 338.
HOWLAND 275, 367.
　Joseph 154, 64.
　Lydia Bill 154. Lydia (Coit) 164.
HUBBARD 43, 4.
　Daniel 42. John 42. Joseph 44.

HUBBARD.—Continued.
　Russell 71; 252, 3, 4, 77. Thomas 71, 81; 254, 77. William 42, 3, 4, 5, 75; 124, 52, 61; 212, 53; 345.
　Joanna Perkins 44. Lucretia (Tracy) (Backus) 44, 254. Lydia Coit 43, 4; 152. Lydia (Lathrop) 152, 383. Mabel Russell (Woodbridge) 42, 311. Martha Coit (Greene) 42, 277. Martha (Wright) 254. Mary Gray 253. Mary (Nevins) 254. Susannah (Bushnell) (Manwaring) 254. Susanna (Gifford) 93.
HUBBELL.
　Ebenezer 171.
　Mary Harris (Griffing) 171.
HUGHES.
　John 170, 276, 8, 9.
　Eunice (Leach) 278. Hannah (Townsend) 279. Zipporah Hartshorn 278, 9.
HUNT 35.
HUNTER Rebecca (Carpenter) 369.
HUNTING.
　Nathaniel 160.
　Mary (Coit) 160.
HUNTLEY.
　Elisha 195. Ezekiel 195, 6, 201.
　Lydia Howard 195. Lydia (Sigourney) (see Sigourney). Mary Wallbridge 195. Zerviah Wentworth 195, 6; 201.
HUTCHINS.
　John 54, 60.
　Jerusha Bushnell 54, 60. Sarah (Prior) 170.
HUNTINGTON 1, 113, 32, 87, 94; 261, 65, 83, 84, 88.
　Andrew 124, 61, 82; 202, 10, 11. 12, 13, 22, 41, 62, 72, 81; 376. Barnabas 185. Benjamin 12, 31; 124, 61, 85, 7; 307, 16. Caleb 174, 80, 1, 2. Charles P. 72; 110, 23; 263; 322, 3, 61, 3, 4. Christopher 4, 38, 40; 104, 5, 6; 169, 74, 8, 9, 80, 3, 4, 5, 8; 194; 210, 25, 6, 9, 31, 3, 46. Daniel 185, 91; 225, 46, 67; 309, 351. Ebenezer 205, 22, 6, 8, 33, 47, 60, 1, 6, 7, 8, 86; 356. Elijah 185. Ezra 181, 2. E. B. 3. Felix 191, 2; 213, 4. George 16. Gilbert 48. Hezekiah 11, 40, 1, 3, 5, 6, 54; 107, 24, 80; 213, 18, 19, 53, 84. Isaac 1, 65, 9, 80, 3, 4, 5, 94; 340. Jabez 11, 15, 124, 9, 80; 209, 10, 18, 21, 2, 4, 8, 35, 6, 62, 3, 7, 72, 6, 8, 9, 80, 1, 2, 3, 4, 5, 6, 8; 90, 2.

HUNTINGTON.—Continued.
　James 82, 182; 207, 46, 7, 51, 66; 389. Jedediah 72, 93; 102, 24; 222, 3, 4, 7, 33, 6, 9, 49, 57, 62, 85; 345, 70, 97. Jesse 111. Jeremiah 181, 2. John 79, 82; 104, 11, 12, 25, 72, 3, 9, 80, 1, 2, 3. Jonathan 85. Joseph Otis 262. Joseph 185; 222, 38, 9, 42, 6, 62, 3, 7, 70, 2, 6, 91; 323, 61, 3, 4. Joshua 109, 17, 29, 69, 91; 269, 10, 15, 17, 18, 19, 21, 5, 47, 51, 66, 7, 8, 72, 82, 3, 4, 8. Levi 262. Lynde 181. Matthew 180. Monroe 56. Nathaniel 238, 9, 47. Nehemiah 185. Oliver 181. Peter 247, 8, 51, 66, 9. Philip 187. Roger 194, 214. Roswell 233. Rufus 135. Samuel 81; 124, 35; 233, 7, 8, 9, 40, 1, 2, 3, 6, 8; 64, 5, 6, 7, 77, 96; 322. Simeon 124; 248, 9, 50, 3, 60, 1, 2, 4, 5, 6, 7, 78, 80; 324. Simon 2, 4, 87, 105, 78, 81; 229, 32, 45, 7, 66, 7, 70, 82, 93, 6; 300, 23, 56. Thomas 182, 94; 225. Thomas Mumford 286. P. Webster 68. William 182. Wolcott 75, 86; 212, 14, 28. Zachariah 166; 210, 11, 21, 62, 3, 72, 5, 6, 7, 81, 3, 4, 5, 6; 356. Zephaniah 217.
　Abigail Abel 82, 111. Abigail Bingham 246, 309, 317. Abigail (Carew) 273. Abigail (Lathrop) 183. Abigail (Lathrop) 40, 1. Abigail (Pierce) 135. Alice (Baldwin) 259, 61. Ann Moore 224, 5. Anna (Huntington) 181. Anne (Adgate) (Turner) (Abel) 309. Civil (Tracy) 182. Dorcas (Lathrop) 194, 5, 6. Dorothy Paine (Williams) 40, 1, 5. Elizabeth Backus 194; 222, 83, 5. Elizabeth (Backus) 285, 341. Elizabeth (Chester) 15, 285. Elizabeth Hyde (Lathrop) 182. Elizabeth (Wolcott) 219. Elizabeth Mary (Griswold) 286, 7. Eliza Waite 102. Eunice Carew 262, 70, 91. Eunice (Carew) 84, 5; 278. Eunice Lathrop 85, 135. Eunice (Strong) 263, 291. Eunice (Williams) 41, 5. Faith Trumbull 223, 4, 57. Frances (Griffin) 242. Freelove Chester 248. Hannah 17. Hannah Devotion 242. Hannah (Huntington) 218, 9, 39, 42. Hannah Lyman 267. Hannah Mum-

HUNTINGTON.—*Continued.*
ford 286. Hannah Perkins (Lynde) (Lathrop) 191; 209, 10, 12, 19, 83. Hannah Phelps 211, 12. Hannah Tracy 232. Hannah Williams 228, 83, 5, 6, 90. Hannah Watrous 180. Judith (Leffingwell) 40. Judith Stevens (Brewster) 179. Julia Stewart Dodge 270. Ladies Huntington 228. Lucy 16. Lucy Coit 211, 12. Lucy (Miner) 267. Lucy (Tracy) 393. Lucy (Williams) 45. Lucretia 135. Lucretia (Porter) 82. Lydia Gager 260, 1. Lydia (Bill) 152, 272, 6, 8. Mary 4. Mary (Carew) (Brown) 185, 307, 16, 81. Mary (Carew) 85, 262. Mary (Carpenter) 307. Mary Bowers Campbell 286. Mary (Childs) 286. Mary Clark 265. Mary Ann Clement 48. Mary Lucretia McClellan 228. Mary Rudd (Dean) 182. Mary Strong 10, 376. Mary Tracy 182. Margaret Baret 178. Margaretta Perit 73. Martha Devotion 238, 41, 2. Maria Perit 322. Patience — (Keeney) 248. Priscilla Miller 246, 7. Rachel (Tracy) 16. Rebecca Lathrop 185, 94; 340. Rebecca (Huntington) 191. Ruth 4. Ruth (Butler) 269, 70. Ruth (Edgerton) 248, 69. Ruth Rockwell 4, 178. Sarah Adgate 179. Sarah Clark 4, 246. Sarah Edgerton 233. Sarah (Gale) 280. Sarah Isham 228. Sarah Lathrop 195, 289. Sarah Read 233. Sarah Reynolds 180. Sarah (Tracy) 4. Sally Ann Huntington 262, 3. Thankful Warner 186. Theophila Grist 187, 213. Zipporah (Huntington) 213.

HYDE.
Bela B. 56. Benjamin 56. Elisha 356. Jabez 157, 351. James 254. Jedediah 124, 269. John 50, 1, 2, 71, 116. Lewis 187. Philip 35. Phinehas 182. Richard 91, 107, 82; 216. Samuel 4, 5, 24, 157. William 3, 4, 24; 157, 74, 5; 319.
Abigail (Harland) 50, 116. Ann Bushnell 157, 75. Ann Rogers 182. Diadema (Butler) 269, 70; 392. Elizabeth Bushnell 157. Elizabeth (Lord) 6, 25. Elizabeth (Tracy) 235. Hannah (Adgate) 172. Jane Lee

HYDE.—*Continued.*
4, 157. Jane (Birchard) 170. Jerusha (Butler) 269. Jerusha Perkins 269. Lucy (Waterman) 172. Martha Nevins 254. Mary Marsh 56. Nancy Maria 18, 200. Lucy (Waterman) 172. Rachel Tracy 50. Sarah Leffingwell 50.

INGERSOLL Jared 82, 396.
ISHAM.
Joseph 228.
Sarah (Huntington) 228.

JACKSON William 194.
JEARSON Jane 184.
JEWETT 190.
JOHNSON Mary (Greenleaf) 76.
JOHONNOT Daniel 32.
JONES.
Benjamin 84. Caleb 314. Ebenezer 88; 314, 5, 6, 92. Parmenas 394. Sylvanus 306, 7, 14.
Elizabeth Rogers 314. Eunice Herrick 394. Kesiah Cleveland 306, 14, 94. Lucy (Cooledge) 314, 5. Lydia 84. Martha (Wait) 101. Rachel (Lathrop) 88, 314. Rachel Clark 314. Rosanna Weeks 394. Thankful 84. Thankful Vergason 84.

KEENEY Patience — (Huntington) 248.
KELLY Mary (Lathrop) 189.
KEMBLE.
Thomas 300.
Elizabeth Trarice 300. Sarah (Knight) 300, 1, 2, 3, 4, 5.
KILLGROVE Mary (Case) 168.
KING.
Absalom 54, 101.
Hannah Waterman Arnold 54, 101.
KINGSLEY.
James L. 164. Junius 244, 8. Lydia Coit 164.
KINNEY.
Joseph 379. Newcomb 259; 312, 77, 8, 9.
Jemima Newcomb 379. Sally Branch 379.
KITTLE Ephraim 56.
KNIGHT.
David 374. Richard 300. Elijah (Livingston) 300, 1, 5.
Sarah Kemble 300, 1, 2, 3, 4, 5.
KNOX Joseph 276.

LADD.
Jacob 56. Russell 56.

LAFAYETTE.
Marquis de 35, 163; 226, 7, 8, 84; 324. George W. 227.
LAKE Hannah (Gallup) 359.
LAMBERT 321.
LANCASTER
John 125, 292. Robert 292. Anna Bentley (Trapp) 292.
LANMAN Peter 317, 8.
LAPIERRE 313.
LARNED Ellen D. 294, 5; 339.
LASTHAUS (Mrs.) 202.
LATHROP 131, 2, 43, 5, 6, 51, 2, 76, 7, 91, 9; 212, 13, 21, 31.
Asa 87, 8; 101, 2; 259, 76. Augustus 171, 280, 341. Azariah 124, 9; 256, 72, 80; 316, 17, 18, 40, 2, 63; 400. Azel 182. Benjamin 208. Charles 79, 83, 341. Daniel 11, 15, 9, 81; 125, 38, 43, 5, 50, 1, 2, 61, 2, 3, 72, 6, 7, 9; 91; 354, 76. Ebenezer 107, 24, 34, 71, 90, 1; 208, 9, 10, 12, 13, 32; 396. Elisha 128. Eleazer 92, 102, 3. Frank Turner 145. Gerard 317, 8. Gurdon 317, 23, 61. Israel 104, 5, 69, 85, 8, 9, 90, 4; 207, 8, 15, 31, 2, 47. Jabez 90, 104, 5, 6, 74, 5, 6, 8, 9, 81; 208, 9, 32. Jedediah 191, 2, 4; 213. John 168, 90; 205, 6, 8. Joseph 207, 8, 15. Joshua 12, 59, 86, 7; 145, 7, 8, 9, 50, 1, 2, 62, 3, 72, 6, 7, 85, 91; 322, 56. Nathaniel 10, 88, 101, 31; 206, 59, 73, 4; 310, 38, 40, 67, 8, 96. Rufus 79, 84; 117, 8, 22, 5, 34. Samuel 100, 4, 6, 31, 7, 8, 46, 57, 83; 205, 6, 7, 8, 15, 29; 310, 50. Simon 11, 74, 81; 112, 17, 22, 5, 31, 2, 3, 4, 7, 47, 71; 238, 54, 47. Thomas 36, 44, 59, 60; 107, 24, 31, 7, 8, 50, 1, 2, 3, 4, 5, 60, 3, 9, 72; 205; 356, 83. William 95, 101, 3, 5, 25, 89, 90, 4; 208. Zebediah 87, 8, 9.

Abigail Doane 207. Abigail Huntington 318, 40, 1. Amy (Whiting) 273, 4. Ann Backus 273; 310, 40, 6, 7, 8. Anna — 206. Anna Eames 191. Anna (Perkins) 280. Civil Perkins 191. Clorinda Backus 88. Cornelia (Willis) 145. Delight (Grist) 187. Delight Otis 208. Dorcas Huntington 194, 5, 6. Elizabeth Burnham 208. Elizabeth (Carpenter) (Peck) 307, 10, 67. Elizabeth Hyde (Huntington) 182. Elizabeth Lord 259. Elizabeth Macalester 145. Elizabeth Scudder

LATHROP.—*Continued.*
 206. Elizabeth Turner 145. Elizabeth (Waterman) 100. Elizabeth (Winship) 90. Hannah Adgate 100, 31; 340. Hannah Choate 134. Hannah Gardiner 147. Hannah Perkins (Huntington) (Lynde) 191, 209. Hannah Bill 36, 152, 4. Jerusha (Perit) 153, 383. Jerusha Talcott 139, 43, 4, 5, 63, 96. Jerusha Thomas 103. Lucy Turner 317. Lydia Abel 137, 60. Lydia (Coit) 160, 1. Lydia Hubbard 44, 152, 383. Lydia (Lathrop) 213. Lydia Leffingwell 190. Lydia — (Wetherell) 208. Margaret Fuller (?)(Baldwin)259. Martha (Devotion) (Cogswell) 238, 9, 40, 1, 2. Martha (Lathrop) 134. Mary Ely 217. Mary Gale 171, 280. Mary Hartshorn 215. Mary Kelly 189, 90. Mary (Nevins) (Bingham) 254. Mary Reynolds (Edgerton) 131. Mary Scudder 207, 15. Mercy Eels 147, 8, 9. Phebe French 189. Rachel Jones 88, 314. Rebecca Bliss 207, 8. Rebecca Huntington 185, 94. Rebecca Perit 322. Sarah Huntington 189, 94. Sibyl (Tracy) 213, 14, 32. Zerviah (Lathrop) 213, 4.

LATOUR Marguerite Grenier (Perit) 321.

LEACH.
 Jeremiah 278. Thomas 278, 379. Betsey Gildon 278. Eunice Hughes 278. Eunice (Story) 278. Sarah Reynolds 278, 379. Sarah (McDonald) (Gale) 279, 280; 379.

LEASKE 32.
LEAVENWORTH Mark 150.
LEDLIE Hugh 124.
LEDYARD John 41.
LEE 218.
 Benjamin 366. (Gen.) Charles 223. George W. 217, 8, 92. Samuel 55.
 Hannah Griswold 159, 221. Hephzibah (Reynolds) 25. Jane (Hyde) 157. Phebe Reynolds 25. Sarah Marsh 55.

LEETE (Gov.) William 361.
LEFFINGWELL 9, 106, 32.
 Andrew 48. Benajah 47, 8, 69, 70, 4, 6, 185. Christopher 34, 5, 45, 56, 62, 70, 2, 3, 5, 6, 8, 9, 81, 3; 112, 3, 4, 21, 61; 277; 345, 56, 82. Elisha 34, 70, 2, 177, 92; 318. Hezekiah

LEFFINGWELL.—*Continued.*
 60, 70, 6. John 69. Jonathan 4, 39. Joseph 4, 39. Martin 48, 125. Nathaniel 4, 39, 169. Richard 70. Samuel 25, 9, 40, 7, 9, 50, 1, 2, 4, 9. Stephen 39. Thomas 2, 4, 23, 24, 38, 9, 40, 6, 7, 8, 9, 52, 3, 4, 5, 6, 7, 8, 60, 1, 2, 3, 4, 5, 7, 8, 9, 76; 106, 7, 9, 11, 17, 19, 25, 57, 8, 60, 61, 90, 2, 4; 232, 5; 306, 51, 95. William 56, 75, 81, 2.
 Abigail (Tracy) 232. Anne (Bushnell) 157. Alice Tracy 192. Caroline Mary (Street) 82. Elizabeth Lord 64. Elizabeth (Tracy) 159, 285. Frances Thomas 192. Hannah Buck 49. Hannah (Clark) 116. Joanna Christopher (Dyer) 69, 70. Joanna (Lathrop) 79, 81. Lydia Tracy 49, 62, 3. Mary Bushnell 58, 68, 9, 70; 174. Mary (Bushnell) 4, 39. Mary (Richards) (Billings) 78. Mary Rudd (Norman) 169. Mary (Tracy) 234, 5. Mary White 439. Rachel (Park) 439. Ruth Webster (Perit) 73, 322. Sally Beers 81. Sarah Russell 116. Zerviah (Bushnell) 157. Zerviah (Lord) 101.

LEONARD.
 Elkanah 235.
 Abiel 45. Dorothy Huntington 45. Dorothy (Huntington) 45 Jemina (Perkins) 235, 53. Rebecca (Perkins) 235, 95, 6.

LESTER Timothy 49, 77, 275.
LEWIS.
 David 194, 201. Russell 248, 77.
L'HOMMEDIEU Giles 26, 8, 30. Abigail Reynolds 26, 30, 46.
LINCOLN.
 James 60, 1, 76; 112, 4.
 Hannah (Day) 60.
LITTLE.
 Deodat 311. Ephraim 311.
 Elizabeth Woodbridge 311.
LIVINGSTON.
 (Col.) John 305.
 Elizabeth Knight 69; 300, 1, 5. Mary Winthrop 304.
LORD.
 Benjamin 2, 3, 33, 64; 101, 25, 9, 55, 89; 207, 80, 9; 323, 33, 4, 5, 6, 7, 8, 9, 40, 3, 5, 58, 9, 60, 9. Ebenezer 168; 280; 338, 45, 60, 1. Eleazer 101, 2, 25; 220, 59; 345. Henry 273. Joseph 175, 6, 7. Nathan 254. Richard 25.
 Abigail Hooker 337. Abigail — (Mumford) 101. Ann Tay-

LORD.—*Continued.*
 lor 337, 69. Caroline 334. Elizabeth (Lathrop) 101, 2. Elizabeth (Leffingwell) 64. Elizabeth (Lord) 101; 338, 45. Elizabeth Pratt 101; Elizabeth — (Tisdale) 337. Eunice (Gale) 280. Lucy Adgate 175, 7. Lucy (Avery) (Perkins) 338. Mary Nevins 254. Nabby (Tracy) 101, 220, 59. Lydia (Reynolds) 25. Temperance (Bliss) 33. Temperance Edgerton 280, 366.

LORING.
 Leah (Whiton) 274. Sarah (Whiton) 274.
LOUDON.
 Samuel 221, 2.
 Lydia Griswold 221.
LOVETT Samuel 105, 91.
LOWREY 36.
LUCY.
 Sir William 229.
 Barbara (Tracy) 229.
LYMAN 192.
 Hannah (Huntington) 267.
LYNDE.
 Samuel 191, 210.
 Hannah Perkins (Huntington) (Lathrop) 191, 209, 10, 12, 19, 83.
LYON Matthew 81.

MABREY 262.
 Louis 256. Orimel 292, 307.
 Anna Trapp 292.
MACALESTER Elizabeth (Lathrop) 145.
MCCLELLAN.
 (Gen.) Samuel 228.
 Grace 87; 245, 70, 93; 307. Lucretia Mary (Huntington) 228.
MCCURDY.
 Lynde 163. Theodore 218, 92.
MCDONALD.
 Alexander 71; 280; 322, 77, 9. Sarah Leach (Gale) 279, 80; 379.
MCGARITY Thomas 88.
MCNELLY Henry 72, 107.
MANDELL 163.
 John 165. Noah 164. Mary 165.
MANDELL Sarah Corner 165.
MANLY 316.
 John 251; 315, 6.
 Mary Arnold 251. Sarah 251.
MANNING 95.
 Asa 93. Diah 93, 4; 249, 341. Fred 91, 3. John 92, Mausur 92. Rockwell 91, 2, 3. Roger 93. Samuel 90, 2. William 92.
 Abigail Winship 92. Anna Gifford 93. Anna Winship 90, 92.

MANNING.—(Continued.)
Eunice (Waterman) 93. Polly (Sturtevant) 83. Sally 92. Sarah Answorth 92.
MANSFIELD Achilles 84.
MANWARING.
Robert 254.
Susanna Hubbard (Bushnell) 254.
MARRIOTT 342.
MARSH 53.
Ebenezer 54. John 54. Jonathan 54, 5, 6, 9, 60. Joseph 56. Phinehas 56.
Abigail (Ripley) 55, 6. Alice Fitch 55, 6. Ann Webster 54. Hannah (Sumner) 95. Mary (Dyer) 55. Mary (Hyde) 56. Mary Parsons 54. Sarah Hart 54. Sarah (Lee) 55.
MARSHALL Abial 172.
MARVIN.
Elihu 313, 400. Matthew 130, 57, 74.
Elizabeth (Olmstead) 130. Elizabeth (Wait) 101. Eunice (Noyes) 372. Mary (Bushnell) (Adgate) 157, 74, 5. Sally (Trott) 313.
MASCARENE.
Jean 44. Jean Paul 44.
Joanna (Perkins) 44.
MASON 132, 58; 333, 8.
Daniel 4, 118; 331, 74. Edward 230. —— (Tracy) 230. John 1, 2, 4, 5; 266, 93, 8, 9; 325, 6, 7, 8, 9, 30, 1, 2, 50, 95. Samuel 4, 331.
Abigail Fitch 98, 331. Anne (Brown) 4, 331. Anne (Denison) 331. Anne (Mason) 332. Anne Peck 96, 329, 30. Anne Sanford (Noyes) 332. Elizabeth (Fitch) 4, 293, 331. Elizabeth Peck 331. Margaret Denison 331. Priscilla (Fitch) 4, 98, 331. Rachel (Hill) 1, 331.
MATHER.
Cotton 85, 96, 203. Samuel 300.
MATHEWSON Luther 393.
MAY Dorothy (Bradford) 265.
MERRYFIELD Maria (Cox) 36.
MEACHAM Esther (Strong) 289.
MEAD.
John 52. Sampson 52.
Charlotte 52.
METCALF.
Joseph 296. Abiel (Adams) 296. Mary (Rudd) 365.
MILLER.
Jacob 72.
Priscilla (Huntington) 246, 7.
MINER 390.
Asher 370. Charles 26; 153, 80; 212, 55; 311, 15, 41, 7, 54,

MINER.—(Continued.)
71, 2, 3, 8, 9. Cyrus 267. Hugh 370. Seth 223; 369, 70, 3, 88, 92. Thomas 206.
Anna (Charlton) 370. Lucy Huntington 267. Hannah (Ponderson) 377. Prudence (Avery) 180.
MITCHELL.
Donald G. 311. Louis 311.
MOODY.
Eleazer 85.
Elinor Thompson (Symmes) 85.
MOORE.
Benjamin 225. Sir Francis 224. John 224, 5. Richard Channing 225. Thomas L. 224, 5. Ann (Huntington) 229, 30.
MORAN Thomas 36.
MORGAN 289, 92, 317.
John 288. Joseph 215. Peter 288. Nathan D. 313. Richard Rose 288. William 315, 6, 9, 20.
Ann Dart 288. Elizabeth (Starr) (Adgate) 175. Elizabeth Whitmore 288. Martha (Perkins) (Lathrop) 215.
MORROW Thomas 76.
MORTON Nathaniel 206.
MOTLEY John Lothrop 190.
MOULTHROP & Street 342.
MUMFORD.
Thomas 101, 286.
Abigail (Lord) 101. Catharine Havens 286. Hannah (Huntington) 286.
MURRAY Solomon & 347.

NASH Elizabeth (Turner) 309.
NEEDHAM 272.
Anthony 268. Daniel 268, 9, 72; 316.
Isabella Armstrong 269. Hannah Allen 269.
NEVINS.
David 71, 112; 250, 2, 4, 5, 77. Henry 219, 53. William 255.
Martha (Hyde) 254. Mary 255. Mary Hubbard 254. Mary Lathrop 254. Mary (Lord) 254.
NEWCOMB Jemina (Kinney) 379.
NEWELL 134.
NILES.
Samuel 296.
Elizabeth Adams (Whiting) 296.
NORMAN.
Caleb 169, 70. James 169. Joshua 169, 70, 71.
Content Fanning 171. Elizabeth (Bartlett) 169. Mary (Burnham) 169, 70. Mary Rudd (Leffingwell) 169.
NORMANDY Jane 184.

NORTH.
Lord North 149.
Hannah (Eels) 149.
NORTON.
Rufus 172. —— (Adgate) 172.
NORTHROP Charles A. 105, 215, 358.
NOYES.
James 316, 22. Moses 372. William 371, 2.
Ann (Brown) 254, 316. Ann Sanford (Mason) 331. Eunice Marvin 372. Mary Ely 372. Sarah (Chester) 285.
NEQUITTENSUE Marie Madeleine (Basset) 308.

OGDEN Matthew 135.
OLMSTEAD 130, 2, 8, 74; 212, 15.
James 130. John 4, 66, 74, 87; 100; 20, 7, 74; 234.
Elizabeth Marvin 4, 130.
ORMSBY.
John 146.
Hannah (Case) 146, 7, 68. Susanna —— 146.
OSBORN William 304.
OSGOOD Hugh H. 164.
OTIS.
Amos 206. Joseph 208.
Dorothy Thomas 208.
OWANECO 1, 158.

PARKER.
John 32.
Sarah (Bliss) 32.
PAINE.
Nathaniel 40.
Dorothy Ransford 40. Dorothy (Williams) (Huntington) 40.
PALMER.
Elisha 225, 39. William S. 105.
PALMES.
Guy 162.
Elizabeth (Coit) 162. Lucy Christophers (Douglas) 162.
PAPINEAU Jean 184.
PARISH.
Nathaniel 168.
Kesiah Armstrong 168.
PARKE.
Robert 39. Silas 121.
Sobra (Storry) 121. Sarah Ayer 121. Rachel Leffingwell 139.
PARKMAN Rebecca (Coit) (Townsend) 279.
PARSONS.
Samuel Holden 164. (Colonel) 280.
PATRICK (Captain) 327.
PATTEN.
Nathaniel 15, 89, 387.
Faith Foster 387.
PEASE John 5.

PECK.
Anthony 318. Bela 243; 307, 12, 13, 15, 18, 41, 64, 7, 73, 79; 389. Benjamin 309. Darius 388, 9, 91. Henry 309. Ira 105; 204, 13, 91. Jonathan 390. Joseph 125; 307, 9, 10, 11, 30, 1, 67, 8, 389. Robert 339, William Billings 367.
Ann (Mason) 329, 30. Anne — 330. Bethiah Bingham 396. Betsey Billings 312. Elizabeth Edgerton 310. Elizabeth Lathrop (Carpenter) 307, 10, 67, 8. Elizabeth (Mason) 331. Hannah Carrier 309, 10. Hannah Warner 390. Hannah (Williams) 364. Lydia Shipman (Spaulding) 243, 367. Mary Francis 2. Martha — (Bacon) 330. Submit (Cook) (Wheatley) 311.

PERCY.
Robert 156.
Ruth (Read) 156.

PERIT 243; 318, 22, 3; 400.
John 70; 124, 87; 320, 1, 2, 63, 82, 3. John Webster 322. Pelatiah 153, 64; 322, 82, 3, 4. Peter 320, 1. Thaddeus 82.
Abigail Shepherd 321. Jerusha Lathrop 153, 383. Margaretta Dunlap 187, 322. Margaretta Huntington 187. Margaret 321. Marguerite Greiner Latour 321. Maria Coit 164, 384. Maria (Huntington) 322. Mary Bryan 321. Rebecca (Lathrop) 322. Ruth Webster (Leffingwell) 70; 321, 82. Sophia Webster 382.

PERKINS.
Andrew 127, 8. Erastus 338, 67. Elisha 275. George 228. Jabez 48; 165, 6, 7; 209, 35, 6, 79, 80. Jacob 124; 235, 52, 3, 77; 397. James 44. John 128, 91. Joseph 235, 400. Joshua 128. Matthew 128. Roger 235.
Abigail Backus 235. Abigail Thomas 253. Anna (Huntington) 191. Anna Lathrop 279, 80. Eliza P., 48, 49. Elizabeth Young (Hadley) 236. Hannah 128. Hannah Lathrop 209. Hannah Huntington (Lynde) (Lathrop) 283. Jemima Leonard 235, 53. Joanna (Hubbard) 44. Joanna Mascarene 44. Lucy (Brown) 367. Lydia — (Avery) 280. Lydia Tracy 191. Martha Morgan (Lathrop) 215. Mary (Brown)

PERKINS.—Continued.
191; 253; 316. Rebecca Leonard 235, 79.

PETTIS Margaret (Tracy) 192.

PHELPS.
Charles 211; 2.
Hannah Denison 211. Hannah (Huntington) 211.

PHILIP King 62, 3, 96; 179.
PHILLIPPS (Dea.) William 45.
PHIPPS Elizabeth (Abbot) 248.

PIERCE.
Cyprian 52. Ebenezer 52. Gilbert 52, 8, 9, 60. Jonathan, 52, 3, 4. Moses 52; 367. Thomas 52.
Abigail Huntington 135. Ann — 52. Hannah Mix 54. Hannah Wilson 52. Rachel Bacon 52. Thankful — 52.

PIERPONT Hezekiah Beers 75
PORTER.
Epaphras 36, 82, 3, 9; 110, 11. Ezekiel 54, 5.

POST.
John 2, 4; 400. Samuel 351. Thomas 4.
Elizabeth 4. Hester Hyde 4. Margaret (Abel) 4. Mary Andrews 4. Ruth Lathrop 185. Sarah (Hough) 4. Sarah (Vincent) 4.

POTTER Henry 81, 3.
POTTS Christopher 83.

PRATT.
Elizabeth (Lord) 101. Sarah (Watrous) 215.

PRENTICE 304.
Phebe Harris (Crank) (Prentis) (Edgerton) 248, 360. Mary (Coit) (Gray) 253, 4. Sarah Mosier (Coit) 259.

PRIOR.
Joshua 125, 69, 70; 315, 6, 9. Sarah Hutchins 170.

PROCTOR.
John 313.
Lydia Richards 313. Lydia (Trott) 392.

PROUT 304.
Sarah Christophers 301, 4.

PUNDERSON.
Ebenezer 377, 8, 87.
Hannah Miner 377. Prudence Geer 377.

PUTNAM 376.
Gen. Israel 93, 280.

QUINCY.
Josiah 45.
Dorothy (Hancock) 77. Sally (Greenleaf) 77.

RAM.
George 308. Simon 308.
Elizabeth (Fountain) 308, 9. Susanne (Bassett) 308.

RAYMOND.
Ebenezer 274. George 105, 45, 92. Joshua 12.
Phebe — (Whiton) 274.

READ 104, 56, 75.
Hezekiah 156. John 156, 7. Joseph 156, 7. Josiah 57, 8; 104, 5, 6, 52, 5, 6, 7, 88, 9. William 157.
Hannah Holloway 156. Grace Holloway 156, 7. Ruth Percy 156. Sarah (Huntington) 233.

REEVES (Judge) 263.

REYNOLDS.
Charles 24, 6. Elisha 26, 261. Henry 26. John 4, 5, 23, 4, 5, 6, 66; 131, 46, 80. Joseph 4, 5, 23, 4, 5, 35; 125, 91. Robert 23. Stephen 23.
Abigail L'Hommedieu 26, 46. Elizabeth (Fowler) (Lyman) 23. Lydia (Miller) 23. Lydia Lord 25. Phebe Lee 25, 6. Mary Edgerton (Lathrop) 131. Sarah Backus 4, 66. Sarah (Post) 4, 23. Sarah (Abbott) 261. Sarah (Huntington) 180. Sarah (Leach) 278; 379. Susanna 4.

RICHARD.
André 314. Hephzibah Grant 268.
Louise 268. Lucie 268. Sarah 268.

RICHARDS.
George 78. Francis 102. James T. 233. John 32, 76, 112, 296, 304. Nathaniel 78. Thomas 266, 295. William 82.
Alice (Bradford) 266, 96. Ann Thomas Tracy 233. Ann Winthrop 296. Harriet Wait 102. Lydia (Proctor) 313. Mary Leffingwell (Billings) 78.

RIPLEY.
Chas. S. 229. Dwight 12, 134, John 55.
Abigail Marsh 55, 9. Hannah 128. (Mrs.) Geo. B. 148, 210, 356.

ROATH Lyman 250, 267.
ROBERT 354.
& Charles 163.

ROBERTSON 80.
Alexander 389, 90. James 389, 90.
Amy 390.

ROBINSON Charles 88.
Faith (Trumbull) 256, 7. Harriet Avery 314.

ROCHAMBEAU Count 257.
ROCKWELL.
    Josiah 24. William 178.
    Ruth (Huntington) 178.
RODGERS.
    John 392.
    Minerva Denison 392.
RODMAN.
    Daniel 361.
    Elizabeth Woodbridge 361.
ROGERS 101, 246.
    Amos 267. David 267. John 297. Nathaniel 95. Samuel 304. Theophilus 44, 345. Wheeler 267. Zabdiel 361.
    Betsey 267. Desire 267. Elizabeth (Jones) 344. Elizabeth Sawyer 267. Elizabeth Tracy 361. Fanny 361.
ROOD.
    George 172. Samuel 47.
    Hannah Bush 172. Kesiah (Chapman) 172.
ROSEWELL.
    Richard 299.
    Sarah (Woodward) 299.
ROYCE.
    Jonathan 4.
    Deborah 4.
RUDD.
    Daniel 365. George 192. Hezekiah 24. Nathaniel 363, 5.
    Lucy (Brown) 364. Mary Backus 365. Mary (Leffingwell) (Norman) 169. Mary Metcalf 364. Mary (Dean) (Huntington) 182. Mary Bushnell (Cary) 174.
RUGGLES Thomas 97.
RUSSELL.
    Joseph 49. William 71.
    Mable (Hubbard) (Woodbridge) 311. Sarah (Leffingwell) 116. Sarah Paine 49.

SAGIS Comfort 82.
SANFORD.
    John 316, 32. Peleg 316, 32.
    Ann (Noyes) (Mason) 331.
SALTMARSH John 89.
SALTONSTALL.
    Gilbert 101. (Gov.) 295, 304. Gurdon 101. Winthrop 101.
    Harriet Babcock (Wait) 101.
SCOFIELD William C. 358.
SCROPE William 118.
SCUDDER.
    John 206.
    Elizabeth (Lathrop) 206, 15. Mary (Lathrop) 207, 15.
SELDEN (Col.) Samuel 344.
SHELDON Sarah (Woodbridge) 360, 1.

SHEPHARD.
    John 321.
    Abigail Allen 321. Abigail (Perit) 321.
SHERMAN 284.
SHIPMAN.
    Nathaniel 41, 111, 66, 259.
    Thomas Leffingwell 64, 8, 111.
SIGOURNEY.
    Charles 200.
    Lydia Huntley 6, 7, 11, 18; 119, 20, 2, 37, 9, 11, 3, 4, 5, 9, 51, 3, 4, 63, 4, 95, 8, 9; 200, 1, 11, 12, 18, 26, 8, 42, 91, 2; 317, 8, 54, 5, 80, 1, 92, 3.
SKINNER Henry 202.
SLOCUM Edward 400.
SLUMAN 179, 93, 4.
    Thomas 193, 234.
    Sarah Bliss (Tracy) 193, 234.
SMALLEY Sarah (Reynolds) 261.
SMITH.
    Alba 277. Asher 121. Jabez 342. John G. 168. Joseph 171. Nehemiah 4, 266. Owen 194, 201. Solomon 151, 62.
    Ann Bourne 4. Ann (Bradford) 4, 266. Hannah 4. Lydia 4. Mary (Raymond) 4. Mehitable (Abel) 4. Mercy 4. Nancy Case 168. Sarah 4.
SOLOMON & Murray 347.
SPAULDING 243.
    Asa 83; 243, 4, 8, 72; 322, 3, 67. Charles 244. Ebenezer 243. Luther 92; 237, 44, 8, 75; 322. Rufus 272, 8.
    Lydia Payne 275. Lydia Shipman (Peck) 243. Sarah (Coit) 372.
SPENCER.
    Jared 67.
    Sarah (Backus) 67.
SPINCK Betsey (Griffin) 171.
SPOONER.
    Judah Paddock 79, 80, 1. Thomas 79.
    Deborah Douglas 79, 81. Rebecca (Greene) 79.
STAEBEHEN Charles 85.
STANDLEY Mary (Hooker) 337.
STANTON Margaret (Copp) 168.
STARR.
    Jonathan 175.
    Elizabeth Morgan (Adgate) 175.
STEAD Angell 34, 6, 106.
STEELE.
    John 266.
    Meletiah Bradford 266.
STEDMAN.
    Charles 244. Ferdinand 233. James 191, 2; 290. Nathan 52, 316.
    Mary (Winship) 52.

STEREY 338.
    Consider 36, 89, 129, 1. Edward 250. John 36, 45, 89, 90, 121; 332, 41. Roger 89.
    Abigail Holms 89. Rebecca Bromley 89. Siora Park 94, 121.
STEVENS Judith Brewster (Huntington) 179.
STEWART Alexander 318.
STILES (Pres.) 1, 129, 252.
STODDARD
    John 239.
    Mary Foote (Goodrich) (Tracy) 239.
STONE (Rev.) 97.
STORY.
    Jedidiah 278.
    Eunice Leach 278.
STOUGHTON.
    Thomas 178, 216.
    Margaret Paret (Huntington) 178.
STRATFORD Earl 195.
STRATFORD
    Clement 306.
    Elizabeth Curtis (Cleveland) 306.
STREET.
    Augustus Russell 82.
    Caroline (Foote) 82. Caroline Mary Leffingwell 82. Moulthrop & 312.
STRONG.
    Henry 71, 111; 263, 89, 90, 1. Joseph 18, 46, 96, 129, 43, 8; 215, 17, 44, 6, 76, 88, 9, 90, 1, 2; 333, 6, 57, 8. Nathan 289.
    Esther Meacham 289. Eunice Huntington 263, 94. Mary (Cleveland) 290. Mary (Gulliver) 289. Mary Huntington 15, 16; 288, 9, 90, 4, 2.
STUART Gilbert 224, 257, 8.
STURTEVANT Rufus 82.
SUMNER.
    Joshua 59.
    Hannah Marsh 55, 9.
SLAVES.
    Anthony 129. Bena 129. Beulah 133, 42. Black Bess 133. Boston Trow-trow 129, 191. Bristo Zibbero 129. Bristol Barney 128. Bristow 129. Chloe 129. Cudge 128. Cuffee 142, 342. Dinah 129. Eunice 128. Fortune 128. Flora 128. Guy 128. Jack 129. James 129. Jean 128. Jude 129. Leah 133. Leb Quy 129. Martin 129. Nancy 129. Peter 128. Pero 128. Pharaoh 127, 8. Phillis 129. Primus 122, 3, 33. Robert 129. Rose 129. Samson Mead

SLAVES —*Continued*.
 52. Scipio 129. Tine 128. Violet 128, 9. Zylpha 129.

TALCOTT.
 Joseph 143.
 Jerusha (Lathrop) 143. Hannah (Chester) 285.
TALLEYRAND 236, 7.
TAYLOR.
 Edward 98, 335.
 Elizabeth Fitch 98. Mercy (Chapman) 172. Ruth Wyllis 337.
TEEL Hannah (Thatcher) 134, 5.
THATCHER Hezekiah 134 Hannah Teel 134, 5.
THOMAS.
 Ebenezer 124, 253. Henry 154. Samuel 115, 6. Simeon 192. W. A. E. 308.
 Caroline L. 184, 6, 152. Dorothy (Otis) 208. Frances (Leffingwell) 192. Jerusha (Lathrop) 103. Hannah Haskins 253. Lucretia (Deshon) 192.
THOMPSON Elizabeth (Cox) 35.
THROOP Cary 79, 83, 118, 21.
THURSTON Gardner 106, 47, 9.
TILDEN Thomas 91.
TISDALE Elizabeth — (Lord) 357.
TOMLSON.
 Benjamin 85. William 85.
 Anne (Carew) 85.
TONGUE.
 George 315.
 Elizabeth (Winthrop) 315. Mary (Wickwire) 315
TOSSET Ira 83.
TOWNSEND.
 Jeremiah 279. John 279, 8; 386. Nathaniel 236, 7, 18, 9; 386.
 Hannah Hughes 279. Rebecca Parkman (Coit) 279. Rebecca 279.
TRACY 345, 49, 79; 109, 10, 11, 32, 94; 204, 32, 45, 361.
 Albert Haller 392. Daniel 183, 92, 4; 203, 15, 16, 20, 30, 1, 2, 3; 217, 54, 94. Edward 109, 392. Elisha 124; 356, 62, 92. Geo. William 109, 10. Isaac 147, 59, 60; 397. John 4, 159, 230, 85, 94; 351, 97. Jonathan 2, 4; 230. Joseph 8, 109, 353. Josiah 192. Moses 255, Mundator 32, 101, 181; 219, 20, 7, 32, 59. Nathaniel 229. Paul 229. Peleg 50. Philemon 118; 302, 94, 2, 3. Phinehas 392. Richard 229. Richard Proctor 393. Samuel 1, 124, 85; 211, 32, 3. Simon

TRACY.—*Continued*.
 107, 24, 82, 94; 202, 20, 32, 4, 5, 8, 82, 92. Solomon 4, 62; 192, 4; 230, 1, 4, 8, 94; 375, 95. Thomas 3, 4, 87; 160, 71, 4, 8, 80, 94; 205, 12, 29, 30, 2, 3, 45, 65, 93. Uriah 109 William Gedney 16.
 Abigail Adgate 231. Abigail Bushnell 220, 35. Abigail (Leffingwell) 232. Abigail (Tracy) 313 Abigail Trott 392. Alice (Leffingwell) 192. Anna Hinckley 109. Ann Thomas (Richards) 233. Caroline Bushnell 220. Elizabeth Avery 182, 233. Elizabeth Backus 283, 5. Elizabeth Bushnell 159, 60. Elizabeth Hyde 235. Elizabeth Leffingwell 159, 285. Elizabeth (Rogers) 361. Hannah Backus (Bingham) 231. Hannah (Huntington) 232. Harriet Frances 392. Lucretia Hubbard (Backus) 254. Lucy 192. Lucy (Tracy) 192. Lucy (Turner) 101, 317. Lydia Hallam 109. Lydia (Leffingwell) 62, 3. Lydia (Perkins) 194. Margaret Pettis 192. Martha Bourne (Bradford) 230, 265. Mary Leffingwell 182; 234, 5. Mary Foote (Stoddard) (Goodrich) 230. — (Mason) 230. Miriam (Waterman) 4, 100. Nabby Lord 92; 101; 220, 59. Nancy 192. Rachel Allen 192. Rachel Huntington 16 Rachel (Hyde) 59. Sarah Bliss (Shuman) 192, 234. Sybyl Lathrop 213, 4, 32.
TRAPP.
 Ephraim 292. Thomas 396.
 Anna Bentley (Lancaster) 292. Ann (Mabrey) 296.
TRARICE.
 Nicholas 300.
 Elizabeth (Kemble) 300.
TROTT.
 George W. 313. John Proctor 313. Jonathan 311, 92.
 Abigail (Tracy) 392. Lois Chapman 313. Lydia Chapman 313. Lydia Proctor 313, 392. Sally Marvin 313.
TROWBRIDGE 304.
TROW-TROW Boston 401.
TRUMBULL 39, 329.
 David 135. John 224, 72, 80; 389. Jonathan 41, 72, 135; 223, 4, 8, 35, 49, 56, 7, 8, 9, 84. Joseph 224, 56, 7, 8, 9, 76; 345, 79.

TRUMBULL.—*Continued*.
 Abigail (Backus) 235. Amelia Dyer 258, 9. Faith (Huntington) 223, 4, 57. Faith Robinson 256, 7.
TURNER.
 John 356 Philip 101, 45, 85; 251, 70; 309, 10, 15, 7, 43, 92, 6. William Pitt 341, 2.
 Anne Huntington (Adgate) (Abel) 309. Elizabeth (Lathrop) 145. Elizabeth Nash 309. Lucy Tracy 317. Nancy (Wait) 101.
TYLER.
 Hopestill 14. John 200, 16.
 Mary (Boardman) (Coit) 372.

UNCAS 1, 39, 96, 332. Betty 399.
UNDERHILL Capt. 326, 7.
URENNE Mary 184.

VASSEUR Mons. de 227.
VERNET.
 John 366.
 Ann Brown 366.

WADE.
 Robert 5.
 Susannah 5.
WADSWORTH.
 Daniel 200. Jeremiah 258. Louisa Denison 392
 & Carter 218.
WAINWRIGHT Bishop 200.
WAIT.
 John T. 90, 1; 102, 11, 18, 21; 337, 40; 402. Marvin 101, 2, 11. Richard 101.
 Eliza (Huntington) 102. Elizabeth Marvin 101. Harriet Babcock (Saltonstall) 101 Harriet Richards 102. Martha Jones 101. Nancy Turner 101, 2, 11.
WALES Prince of (George IV.) 226.
WALBRIDGE.
 Ebenezer 195.
 Mary Durkee 195. Mary (Huntley) 195.
WALLIS Richard 3.
WALWORTH Chancellor 172, 7; 229, 69.
WARD Ichabod 281.
WARNER.
 Hannah (Peck) 390.
 Thankful (Huntington) 183.
WASHINGTON (General) 19, 73, 93, 102; 222, 81; 301.
WATERMAN 74, 5, 87, 8.
 Asa 125, 72. David Basset 92, 101. John 87, 100, 1, 5, 75; 319, 51. Joseph 320. Samuel 319. Thomas 3, 4; 100, 57; 230; 325, 51, 3, 95.

WATERMAN.—*Continued.*
  Abigail Culverhouse (Adgate) 175. Elizabeth (Backus) 101 Elizabeth Basset 92, 101. Elizabeth Lathrop 160. Hannah (King) (Arnold) 101. Judith Woodward 100, 319. Lucy (Adgate) 172. Lucy Hyde 172. Lydia (Burnham) 208. Miriam Tracy 100.
WATROUS
  Isaac 180, 215.
  Elizabeth Brewster 180. Elizabeth (Lathrop) 215. Hannah (Huntington) 180. Sarah Pratt 215
WATTLES Andrew 163.
WEAVER William 55, 259.
WEBB Richard 261.
WEBSTER.
  Pelatiah 70, 89, 322.
  Betsey (Bushnell) 159. Ruth (Perit) (Leffingwell) 70, 322, 82.
WEITZEL Charles T. 267, 358.
WELD Elizabeth (Denison) 331.
WELLS Julia Chester 16.
WENTWORTH.
  James 368. Jared 195.
  Zerviah (Huntington) 195.
WETHERELL Lydia — (Lathrop) 208.
WETMORE Mrs. Ichabod 301.
WHARTON 339.
WHEAT Samuel 124, 397.
WHEATLEY.
  Andrew 311. John 311, 87.
  Jane — 311. Submit Peck (Cook) 311.
WHEELER Joshua 304.
WHITE.
  Charles 370, 7, 8. Daniel 32. Peregrine 301.
  Elizabeth Bliss 32. (Mrs.) John 105, 66; 209. Mary (Leffingwell) 4, 39.
WHITEFIELD (Rev.) 190, 354.
WHITFIELD.
  Henry 97, 8.
  Abigail (Fitch) 97, 8, 331.
WHITING.
  Charles 219, 20, 33, 51, 2, 73. Ebenezer 124; 219, 273. Ed-

WHITING.—*Continued.*
  ward 292. Nathan 296. Samuel 100, 296. William 219, 20. William Bradford 219, 72, 3, 4.
  Abigail Carew 273. Amy Lathrop 273, 4. Elizabeth Adams (Niles) 100, 296. Elizabeth Bradford 291, 73. Eunice Backus 192. Honor Goodrich 219.
WHITON.
  Daniel 274. Zenas 274, 5. Jael Damon 274.
  Phebe — (Raymond) 274. Leah Loring 274. Sarah Loring 274.
WICKWIRE 316, 7.
  George 315, 6. John 315. Jonathan 315, 8. Peter 315.
  Elizabeth Culver 315. Mary Tongue 315. Patience Chappell 315.
WILKES John 310.
WILLES Henry 264.
WILLIS.
  George 145.
  Cornelia Lathrop 145.
WILLIAMS.
  Daniel 71. Ebenezer 117; 228, 83, 5. Elisha 117. Hezekiah 41, 2, 5, 6, 9. Jedediah 77. Jesse 52, 77, 125, 252. John 40, 5, 9; 169. Joseph 128, 9; 400. Roger 328. Samuel 45, 77. Thomas 83, 112, 7, 25. William 36, 364, 7.
  Dorothy Paine (Huntington) 40, 1, 45, 6. Eunice Huntington 41, 5. Hannah Bacon 117. Hannah Dawson 77. Hannah (Huntington) 228, 85, 5, 6. Harriet Peck 358, 64, 7. Mrs. Isabella 219. Jane Adgate 172. Mary — 77. Penelope Chester 255. Sarah (Charlton) 77, 252.
WILCOX (Elder) 90.
WILSON.
  John 203.
  William 203.
WINSHIP.
  Edward 90. Joseph 52, 90, 1, 2. Philemon 52, 77.
  Abigail (Manning) 92. Anna

WINSHIP.—*Continued.*
  (Manning) 90, 2, 3. Elizabeth (Green) 90. Elizabeth Lathrop 90. Mary Stedman 52.
WINTHROP.
  Fitzjohn 294, 315. Wait-still 234, 341. (Gov.) John 296, 61; 304. Ann (Richards) 296. Mary (Livingstone) 304.
WITTER.
  Jacob 396, 7. William 307, 15, 6, 9.
WOOD 27.
WOODBRIDGE 75, 323.
  Dudley 262; 317, 360, 1, 4, 76. Ephraim 360. John 360. Samuel 311, 61. William 361.
  Elizabeth (Little) 311. Elizabeth (Rodman) 361. Lucy 361. Lucy Backus 361. Mabel Russell (Hubbard) 311. Sarah Sheldon 360.
WOODRUFF Hezekiah 379.
WOODWARD 331.
  Ashbel 55, 130, 264. John 100, 5; 297, 8, 9; 302, 23, 40, 58, 9, 60. Peter 100, 298.
WOODWORTH Elias 252.
WOLCOTT.
  Frederick 41, 219.
  Elizabeth Huntington 219. Ursula 361.
WORCESTER (Gen.) 284.
WORTHINGTON Edward 273.
WRIGHT.
  David 254.
  Martha Hubbard 254.
WYLLIS.
  George 259, 337. Hezekiah 259. Amelia Dyer (Trumbull) 259. Ruth (Taylor) 337.

YEOMANS David 35.
YERRINGTON Herbert 104, 5, 83.
YOUNG.
  Charles 237, 8, 44, 5, 8; 324. Henry 236.
  Elizabeth Hadley (Perkins) 236.
ZACHARY 45.
ZUBBERO Bristo 129.

The author feels that there are many errors and omissions in these family genealogies, which she hopes, however, that descendants will correct, when in their power, and also aid in filling in the many unavoidable blanks. More attention has been given to the earlier than to the later generations, as when brought down to the nineteenth century, it is supposed that descendants can supply the missing links, and easily establish their own connection with their ancestral lines.

If any readers wish to carry further the study of family history, they will find much valuable information in Miss Frances M. Caulkins' Histories of Norwich and New London; in that invaluable work, Chancellor Walworth's Genealogy of the Hyde Family; in the Huntington and Lathrop Family Memoirs, prepared by the late Rev. E. B. Huntington; in the forthcoming Leffingwell and Bushnell genealogies; in the various town histories and genealogical magazines, especially in the encyclopedic volumes of the New England Historical and Genealogical Register. To these, and to genealogical literature in general, Durrie's Genealogical Index will serve as a key. Those of Tracy descent may be interested in "The Ancestors of Lt. Thomas Tracy" by Lt. Chas. Stedman Ripley.

INDEX TO PART II.

The genealogies are arranged alphabetically, and will serve as a general index. In the following index will be found only the names of those wives and husbands whose earlier lineage is not given.

Abbot 471, 537.
Abel 468, 15, 20, 1, 31, 52, 5, 61, 80, 9, 98; 506, 7, 15, 19, 25, 62, 70, 2, 8; 575, 80.
Adams 425, 87; 563, 7, 71.
Alden 460.
Allen 469, 28, 37, 48, 93; 538, 40, 64, 72.
Allyn 440; 582, 5.
Amsden 559.
Andrews, 419, 81, 93.
Andrus 513.
Angell 411.
Annable 551.
Answorth 528.
Appleton 452.
Armstrong 509, 40, 4.
Arnold 429, 61, 90; 582.
Atwater 557.
Atwood 424.
Austin 510.
Avery 413, 7, 22, 32; 519, 53, 8, 82.
Ayers 509.

Babcock 580.
Backus 474, 99; 508, 17, 53, 75, 8, 9, 83, 7, 94.
Bacon, 410.
Bailey, 410, 27, 31, 8, 59, 60, 85; 580.
Baker 407, 15, 25, 45; 513, 89.
Baldwin 469, 91, 93; 517.
Ballantyne 589.
Barber 595.
Baret 476, 88.
Barker 407, 20.
Barnard 471.
Barr 460.
Barrett 476, 88.
Barstow 499; 547, 89.
Bartlett 424, 5, 42.
Bassett 490; 506, 64, 82.
Beal 577, 88.
Beckwith 449.
Beebe 437, 57.
Beeks 407.
Beers 518.
Belden 586.
Belding 447.
Bellamy 517.
Bennett 485.
Bentley 504.
Bigelow 432, 54.
Bill 433, 45, 74, 9; 510, 5.
Billings 580.
Bingham 414, 76, 87, 9, 93; 508, 34, 41, 6, 52, 60, 70.
Bishop 507, 16, 52, 5, 61.
Bissell 453, 5; 533.
Blake 421.
Bliss 567.
Blunt 502.
Boalt 469.

Boardman 417.
Bond 415.
Booth 489.
Boradill 451.
Borman 551.
Boutineau 511.
Bourne 424; 570, 82.
Boutell 460.
Bowen 456.
Bowman 537, 65.
Braddick 459.
Bradford 507, 85.
Brainard 534.
Branch 582.
Breck 447.
Breed 446, 554.
Bridges 451.
Bromley 566.
Brooks 425, 89.
Brown 418, 52, 3, 78; 516, 23, 33, 5, 66, 89, 95.
Browne 551.
Brewer 500.
Brewster 408, 88, 9; 519, 32, 44, 59, 67.
Brockway 547.
Bronson 588.
Buchanan 595.
Buck 516, 52.
Buckingham 477.
Buckley 578.
Buell 490, 524.
Bull 478.
Burch 472.
Burnham 507, 16, 42, 51, 3, 72, 82.
Burrell 420.
Busby 418.
Bushnell 413, 31; 501, 7.
Butler 530.
Bryan 549, 85.

Cabot 455.
Cady 472, 563.
Cahoone 502.
Calkins 415, 19, 22, 8, 54, 61, 80, 98; 560, 2.
Calligan 493.
Campbell 487, 575.
Canfield 561.
Carew 426.
Carpenter 424.
Carr 426.
Carrier 441, 546.
Carter 591.
Cary 428, 81; 552, 84.
Caswell 559.
Chadwell 589.
Chaffee 563.
Champlin 513, 36.
Chandler 425, 44.
Chapman 433, 59; 514, 9, 77, 83.
Chappell 489, 589.

Charles 494.
Chase 564.
Cheeney 493.
Cheesebrough 412, 3, 91; 555.
Chester 445, 81, 2; 518, 87.
Choate 453; 518, 24.
Christophers 441, 515.
Claghorn 564.
Clark 415, 39, 59, 6, 7, 85, 8, 95; 504, 2, 9, 15, 47, 71, 6, 7.
Clarke 426.
Cleland (or Kneeland) 569.
Clement 423, 81, 4.
Cleveland 450, 3, 87; 509, 12, 17, 68.
Closen 499.
Cobb 443.
Coffin 464.
Cogsdall 449.
Cogswell 508, 34, 85.
Coit 418, 46, 74; 509, 25, 48, 61, 9, 75.
Colfax 485.
Collins 548, 85.
Comstock 583.
Conant 447, 91.
Congdon 505.
Cook 453; 527, 46.
Cooke 486.
Cooledge 501.
Cooley 420, 37.
Cooper 565.
Copp 443.
Corliss 495.
Cornell 518.
Corning 421, 3; 545.
Cowdrey 437.
Cowles 564.
Craft, 432.
Crane 456, 7, 88.
Crocker 514.
Cross 411.
Crow 596, 31.
Culver 444; 510, 9, 89.
Curtis 441, 80; 589, 10.
Cutler 492.

Damon 588.
Dane 463, 71.
Daniels 489.
Darby 453.
Dart 538.
Davenport 454.
Davis 472, 92; 569.
Davison 571.
Day 521.
Dean 492, 555.
Denning 552.
Denison 443, 7, 8, 32, 54, 84; 513, 34, 4, 5.
Dennis 423.
Denton 485.
Devotion 479, 508.
Dewey 502.

DeWitt 485.
DeWolff 439, 68, 72, 98; 582.
Dibble 457.
Dickinson 484.
Dilaby 459.
Dixey 469.
Doane 505, 76.
Dodge 487.
Dole 464.
Dorr 458.
Dorrance 454.
Dory 466.
Douglas 565.
Dow 484, 552.
Dowe 495.
Ducasse 585.
Dudley 593.
Dunham 549.
Dunlap 559.
Dunton 414.
Durkee 468, 84; 524.
Dwight 487.
Dyer 415, 53, 81; 515, 31, 78.

Eames 549.
Eaton 492, 5.
Edgcomb 567.
Edgerton 407, 8, 44, 21, 33, 78, 82, 9, 90; 545, 23, 46, 7, 60, 72, 4.
Edmunds 495.
Edwards 415, 7, 89.
Eels 434, 79; 576.
Elderkin 422.
Ellsworth 479; 518, 87.
Ely 468; 511, 61.
Ensworth 489.

Eales 433, 95.
Fanning 512, 61, 8, 55.
Farnham 407, 29; 524.
Farwell 563.
Fassett 563.
Fellowes 596.
Ferris 584.
Fillmore 555.
Finney 425.
Fish 509, 13.
Fiske 463, 551.
Fitch 455, 54, 78, 87, 91; 508, 31, 2, 45, 8, 53, 4, 9, 85, 6.
Fobes (or Forbes) 456.
Foote 550, 5.
Ford 531, 68.
Foresyth 465, 592.
Fosdick 441, 573.
Fowler 590.
Frances 547.
Franklin 427.
Frazier 481.
Freeman 492.
French 485, 506.
Frink 489, 91; 543.
Fuller 482, 508.

INDEX TO PART II.

Gager 476, 99; 517.
Gale 453.
Gallup 448, 61; 544.
Gardiner 433, 44, 53; 507.
Gardner 454, 588.
Garner 584.
Garnet 588.
Gates 529.
Gaylord 485.
Geer 558, 91.
Gedding (or Gilden) 514.
Gerrish 454.
Gibbs 455.
Gifford 452, 61; 515, 29.
Gildon 514.
Gillett 585.
Gilman 446, 594.
Glover 554.
Goodrich 484; 570, 86.
Gookin 454, 484.
Gordon 511, 45.
Gore 461.
Gorham 454.
Gorton 484.
Grant 415, 90.
Gray 454, 73, 9.
Greene 444, 73, 4.
Green 415, 94.
Greenslade 412.
Gregory 458.
Gregson 555.
Griffin 483, 582.
Griswold 415, 30, 47, 69, 77, 85, 8; 526, 70.
Groce 588.
Growth 185.
Guppie 555.

Hadley 553.
Hale 439, 565.
Hall 448, 90.
Hallam 415, 74; 554.
Hallet 416.
Halsey 554.
Hamilton 524.
Hammond 484, 515.
Hand 565.
Hanley 524.
Hungerford 554.
Hardy 495.
Harris 444, 66; 514, 6, 24, 67.
Harrington 504.
Hart 515, 7, 31, 9, 83.
Hartshorn 420, 48, 9, 75; 504, 7.
Haskell 453.
Hastings 547.
Hatch 526.
Haughton 441; 514, 89.
Hawke 524.
Hawley 440.
Hays 549.
Hazen 506, 24, 53, 66.
Heldard 439, 47; 508, 54, 74.
Hemans 555.
Henley 454.
Henshaw 440.
Herrick 504.
Hewitt 494, 568.
Higley 575.
Hildreth 441.
Hill 439, 56, 64; 533.
Hillhouse 454.
Hinckley 464, 78, 90; 519, 48, 77.
Hobart 496, 24; 555, 4, 5.
Hodges 554.
Holden 439.
Holloway 559.
Holmes 566.
Holmes 442, 24; 565.
Holton 466, 568.
Hood 539.
Hooker 523.

Hooper 551.
Hopkins 554.
Hough 461, 89; 505, 19.
Houghton (or Holton) 472.
Houlder 540.
Hovey 490.
Howard 494.
Hoyt 458.
Hubbard 424, 33; 564.
Hudson 559.
Huet 565.
Humphrey 521, 95.
Hunn 547.
Hunt 425, 557.
Hunter 485.
Hunting 444.
Huntington 464, 78.
Hurst 445.
Hutchins 428.
Huxley 524.
Hyde 408, 14, 20, 32, 54, 5, 61, 8, 78, 9, 84, 1, 2, 9, 92, 3, 9; 549, 24, 24, 44, 6, 7, 52, 72, 3, 4.

Ingalls 467.
Ingles 564.
Ingraham 524.
Isaacs 549.
Isham 482, 557.

Jackson 474.
James 580.
Jenner 568.
Jenners (or Ganners) 444.
Jennings 543.
Jermain 566.
Johnson 449, 64, 90, 5.
Jones 449, 54, 65, 83; 506, 81.

Kasson 544.
Keeney 457, 84.
Kelly 506, 61.
Keiping 440.
Kennedy 447.
Key 544.
Keyes 444.
Killgrove 485.
Kimball 439, 506.
King 439, 82.
Kingsley 496.
Kinnard 557.
Kinsley 587.
Kirtland 552, 75.
Kneeland (or Cleland) 589.
Knapp 479.
Knight 415, 47, 97; 502.
Knowlton 453.

Ladd 440.
Lamb 502.
Lambert 484.
Lamprey 495.
Landphere 402.
Lane 428, 69.
Lanman 471, 85; 579.
Lansdale 408.
Lathrop 440, 1, 20, 84, 5, 9, 91, 2, 9; 5, 9, 13, 53, 79, 94.
Latimer 434.
Latour 549.
Lawrence 422.
Lay 454, 575.
Leach 460, 6, 7; 565.
Learned 548.
Ledyard 575.
Lee 468, 84, 93, 8; 534, 64.
Leete 593.
Leffingwell 468, 13, 5, 61, 99; 525, 73.
Leonard 469, 89, 84; 554, 2.
Lester 446, 35, 6; 575.
Leverett 473.
Lewis 547.

L'Hommedieu 440, 564.
Lincoln 490, 524.
Lippincott 535.
Livingston 543.
Lloyd 456.
Longbottom 450.
Loomer 422, 8.
Loomis 449, 507, 52.
Lord 440, 98; 508, 64.
Loring 588.
Lovell 554.
Lovett 553.
Luce 429, 32.
Lyman 429, 84; 534, 60.
Lynde 477; 536, 52.

Maculester 512, 4.
Manning 554, 72.
Mansfield 485, 589.
Manton 457.
Manwaring 474, 541.
Marks 429.
Marsh 492.
Marshall 464.
Marvin 428; 577, 82.
Mason 415, 77; 567.
Mather 496.
Matthews 487, 594.
Mawney 485.
May 424.
Maynard 457.
McClellan 482.
McClenahan 589.
McConnell 595.
McDonald 464, 514.
McKee 542.
McKenzie 543.
Meacham 432, 568.
Meech 496.
Merrill 426, 95.
Metcalf 475.
Miller 476; 564, 5.
Mills 457.
Miner 442, 85; 514, 57, 74.
Mix 452.
Moore 489, 2.
Morgan 408, 49, 89; 505, 15, 51, 93, 4.
Morse 483.
Mosier 444, 567.
Moss 565.
Mould 536.
Mumford 482; 523, 4, 594.
Munsell 514.

Nash 584.
Newcomb 425, 502.
Newdigate 569.
Newton 555.
Nichols 449, 64.
Norman 515, 66.
Norris 487.
Norton 409, 41, 77, 83; 575.
Noyes 426, 69; 554, 85, 6.

Olney 596.
Ormsby 487, 9.
Otis 447, 57.
Owen 454.
Owens 484.

Packer 422.
Paddock 565.
Page 495.
Paine 487, 9; 563.
Palmer 438; 536, 66, 71, 6.
Palmes 415, 599.
Parish 571.
Parke 515, 44, 71.
Parker 554.
Parkhurst 416.
Parkison 438.
Parkman 487, 589.

Parks 548.
Parsons 534.
Partridge 455, 555.
Paterson 449.
Payson 577.
Peabody 474; 562, 43.
Peck 533.
Pelton 429.
Pepper 439.
Pembroke 458.
Percy 559.
Perley 471.
Perkins 422, 7, 9, 33, 68, 9, 74, 3, 83, 6; 509, 42, 46, 84.
Perry 454, 3, 8.
Petit 594.
Pettis 499.
Phelps 482.
Philleo 458.
Phipps 407.
Pierce 415, 89; 552.
Pike 540.
Porter 484.
Post 415, 24; 599.
Potter 483, 564.
Poulaine 555.
Powers 490, 587.
Pratt 444, 62, 88; 523, 56, 62, 5.
Prentice 444, 567.
Preston 542.
Prevost 481.
Pride 408, 572.
Proctor 577.
Prythatch 551.

Quimby 564.
Quintard 549.

Rainey 485.
Rame 458.
Ranger 569.
Ranstord 412.
Ray 464.
Raymond 588.
Read 453.
Reynolds 467, 514.
Rhodes 594.
Richards 418, 24, 70, 2, 4, 6, 80, 5; 546.
Richardson 464.
Richmond 554.
Ripley 425, 54, 77; 542, 34, 54, 70.
Rix 550.
Robinson 534, 54, 78.
Rock 447.
Rockwell 419, 22, 3, 40, 76, 7, 88, 90.
Rodgers 454.
Rodman 594.
Rogers 424, 66, 8, 73, 99; 594, 56, 94, 5.
Romans 586.
Root 439, 544.
Roots 460.
Rose 566.
Rosewell 596.
Rouse 433.
Royce 444, 505.
Rudd 427, 8, 79, 92; 515, 24, 42, 7, 74.
Ruggles 552.
Russell 473, 516.
Ryan 481.

Sabin 472.
Safford 571.
Sage 561.
Salisbury 542.
Saltonstall 485, 589.
Sanford 534, 49, 69.
Sanger 592.
Sargeant 444.

INDEX TO PART II.   621

Sayer 599.
Schofield 589.
Scott 455, 519.
Scudder 516.
Sears 531, 9.
Sheldon 593, 4.
Shepherd 434, 2; 551, 9.
Sherburne 495.
Sherman 554.
Sherwood 425, 52, 8.
Shipman 418; 547, 45, 61, 3.
Sigourney 494.
Silliman 539.
Simons 447.
Simpson 511.
Sims 483.
Sisson 530.
Skinner 454, 75.
Slade 492.
Slaves 598, 9; 600.
Sloan 435.
Smith 413, 22, 4, 9, 28, 78, 85; 513, 5, 7, 33, 67, 92.
Snow 483.
Spalding 450.
Sparks 551.
Spencer 414, 45.
Sperry 549.
Spink 466.
Spring 591.
Standish 489, 90; 567.
Stanley 513.
Stanton 555.
Stark 519, 59.
Starr 430, 3; 511, 6, 9.
Stearns 527, 9.
Stedman 434, 591.
Steele 425.
Stevens 488.
Stoddard 570.

Stone 452, 521.
Storrs 554.
Story 502, 14, 89.
Stoughton 456, 88; 505.
Stout 512.
Stratford 441.
Street 549.
Strong 450, 87; 512.
Stuart 458, 84.
Sturtevant 522.
Sumner 531, 61.
Sutherland 549.
Swain 456, 96.
Swan 558.
Symmes 448.

Talcott 547.
Taylor 430, 52; 523.
Tenbrook 541.
Thomas 421, 6, 40; 512, 19, 41, 53, 5.
Thompson, 515, 77.
Throop 477, 8.
Thurston 477.
Tiffany 429, 587.
Tilley 484.
Tillinghast 434.
Tilton 513.
Tisdale 452, 523.
Titus 552.
Todd 516, 52.
Tomlinson 439.
Tompson 433, 54.
Tongue 589.
Tower 583.
Townsend 541.
Tracy 414, 27, 30, 7, 99; 514, 9, 44, 6, 74.
Trarice 513.
Trapp 504.

Treadwell 554.
Truman 464.
Trumbull 555.
Turner 565.
Tuttle 536.

Vermayos 425.
Vermilye 513.
Vernet 425.
Vetch 455.

Wadsworth 451; 579.
Wait 584.
Waldo 445.
Wales 490.
Walker 594.
Wallbridge 494.
Walls 423.
Ward 492, 549.
Waring 484.
Warner 435, 99; 525, 47.
Warren 424, 8; 522, 64, 87.
Waterhouse 437.
Waterman 408, 9, 61, 80, 99; 506, 19, 29, 74, 95.
Watkinson 486.
Watrous 489, 595.
Watson 464.
Wattles 567.
Weare 464.
Webb 439, 63, 79.
Webster 430; 516, 31, 49.
Weeks 504.
Wellman 536.
Wells 551.
Wentworth 491, 572.
West 492; 541, 64.
Wetherell 515, 16.
Wetmore 488, 94; 565.
Wheatley 599.

Wheeler 489.
Wheelock 489.
White 422, 87; 515, 54.
Whitfield 452.
Whiting 452, 5; 512, 35, 9.
Whitmore 454; 558, 61.
Whitney 416.
Whitteridge 539.
Whittlesey 557.
Wibird 455.
Wilcox 530.
Wilkinson 594.
Willes 546.
Willey 536.
Williams 409, 23, 40, 79, 82, 3, 9, 94; 516, 9, 48, 74, 8, 9, 88, 94.
Willis 522, 41, 7, 84.
Willoughby 422.
Wilson 435, 41, 8, 66, 77, 87; 594.
Winn 441.
Winship 525, 9.
Winslow 552, 70.
Wiswall 424.
Witter 571.
Woolbridge 522.
Woodward 557.
Woodworth 413, 55; 509, 24, 45, 52, 76.
Wolcott 468, 76, 84; 594.
Worcester 492.
Worden 541.
Worthington 429; 504, 34.
Wright 440, 71, 7; 547, 27, 9, 36.
Wyeth 594.
Wyllis 452, 578.

Young 528, 48, 53.

Milton Keynes UK
Ingram Content Group UK Ltd.
UKHW052245040324
438787UK00004B/162